Social
Issues
Primary
Sources
Collection

Social Policy

Essential Primary Sources

Social
Issues
Primary
Sources
Collection

Social Policy

Essential Primary Sources

K. Lee Lerner, Brenda Wilmoth Lerner, and Adrienne Wilmoth
Lerner, Editors

THOMSON

GALE

Detroit • New York • San Francisco • New Haven, Conn. • Waterville, Maine • London • Munich

THOMSON

GALE

Social Policy: Essential Primary Sources

K. Lee Lerner, Brenda Wilmoth Lerner, and Adrienne Wilmoth Lerner, Editors

Project Editors
Dwayne D. Hayes and John McCoy

Editorial
Luann Brennan, Grant Eldridge, Anne Marie Hacht, Joshua Kondek, Andy Malonis, Mark Milne, Rebecca Parks, Mark Springer, Jennifer Stock

Permissions
Shalice Shah-Caldwell, Tim Sisler, Andrew Specht

Imaging and Multimedia
Dean Dauphinais, Leitha Etheridge-Sims, Lezlie Light, Michael Logusz, Dan Newell, Christine O'Bryan, Kelly A. Quin, Denay Wilding, Robyn Young

Product Design
Pamela A. Galbreath

Composition and Electronic Capture
Evi Seoud

Manufacturing
Rita Wimberley

Product Manager
Carol Nagel

LIBRARY OF CONGRESS CATALOGING-IN-PUBLICATION DATA

Social policy : essential primary sources / K. Lee Lerner, Brenda Wilmoth Lerner, and Adrienne Wilmoth Lerner, editors.
p. cm. — (Social issues primary sources collection)
Includes bibliographical references and index.
ISBN-13: 978-1-4144-0328-1
ISBN-10: 1-4144-0328-3 (hardcover : alk. paper)
1. United States—Social policy—Sources. I. Lerner, K. Lee. II. Lerner, Brenda Wilmoth.
III. Lerner, Adrienne Wilmoth.

HN57.S6243 2007
320.60973—dc22   2006023437

This title is also available as an e-book.
ISBN-13: 978-1-4144-1264-1
ISBN-10: 1-4144-1264-9
Contact your Thomson Gale sales representative for ordering information.

Printed in the United States of America
10 9 8 7 6 5 4 3 2 1

Table of Contents

1 SHAPING SOCIAL POLICY: GOVERNMENTS, ORGANIZATIONS, THE INTERNATIONAL COMMUNITY AND THE INDIVIDUAL

3 THE GILDED AGE AND THE PROGRESSIVE ERA

6 THE GREAT SOCIETY

7 CURRENT ISSUES IN SOCIAL POLICY: HEALTHCARE, HOUSING, WELFARE, AND SOCIAL SECURITY

Advisors and Contributors

While compiling this volume, the editors relied upon the expertise and contributions of the following scholars, journalists, and researchers who served as advisors and/or contributors for *Social Policy: Essential Primary Sources*:

Steven Archambault, Ph.D. Candidate
University of New Mexico
Albuquerque, New Mexico

Alicia Cafferty
University College
Dublin, Ireland

James Anthony Charles Corbett
Journalist
London, U.K.

Bryan Davies, J.D.
Ontario, Canada

Larry Gilman, Ph.D.
Sharon, Vermont

Amit Gupta, Ph.D.
Ahmedabad, India

Stacey N. Hannem
Journalist
Quebec, Canada

Alexander Ioffe, Ph.D.
Russian Academy of Sciences
Moscow, Russia

S. Layman, M.A.
Abingdon, MD

Adrienne Wilmoth Lerner, J.D. Candidate
University of Tennessee College of Law
Knoxville, Tennessee

Pamela V. Michaels, M.A.
Forensic Psychologist
Santa Fe, New Mexico

Caryn Neumann, Ph.D.
Ohio State University
Columbus, Ohio

Mark Phillips, Ph.D.
Abilene Christian University
Abilene, Texas

Rebecca Rustin, M.A.
Montreal, Quebec, Canada

Nephele Tempest
Los Angeles, California

Jeremy A. Wimpfheimer, M.S.
Beit Shemesh, Israel

Melanie Barton Zoltán, M.S.
Amherst, Massachusetts

Social Policy: Essential Primary Sources is the product of a global group of multi-lingual scholars, researchers, and writers. The editors are grateful to Christine Jeryan, Amy Loerch Strumolo, Kate Kretschmann, Judy Galens, and John Krol for their dedication and skill in copyediting both text and translations. Their efforts added significant accuracy and readability to this book. The editors also wish to acknowledge and thank Adrienne Wilmoth Lerner and Alicia Cafferty for their tenacious research efforts.

The editors gratefully acknowledge and extend thanks to Peter Gareffa, Carol Nagel, and Ellen McGeagh at Thomson Gale for their faith in the project and for their sound content advice. Special thanks go to the Thomson Gale copyright research and imaging teams for their patience, good advice, and skilled research into sometimes vexing copyright issues. The editors offer profound thanks to project managers

Dwayne Hayes and John McCoy. Their clear thoughts, insights and trusted editorial judgment added significantly to the quality of *Social Policy: Essential Primary Sources*.

Acknowledgements

Copyrighted excerpts in *Social Policy: Essential Primary Sources*, were reproduced from the following periodicals:

The Boston Globe, January 21, 2006. Copyright © 2005 New York Times Company. Republished with permission of *The Boston Globe,* conveyed through Copyright Clearance Center, Inc.—*Cato Institute,* January 7, 1998; October 13, 2003. Copyright © 1998, 2003 *Cato Institute.* All rights reserved. Both reproduced by permission.—*The Chronicle of Higher Education,* September 30, 1992; December 7, 2001. Copyright © 1992, 2001 by *The Chronicle of Higher Education.* Both articles may not be published, reposted, or redistributed without express permission from *The Chronicle.*— *Documenting the Justice Gap in America,* September, 2005. Copyright © 2005 LSC. Reproduced by permission.—*The Future of Children,* v. 14, 2004. Copyright 2004 The David and Lucile Packard Foundation. Reproduced by permission.—*Health Affairs,* v. 20, January/February, 2001. Copyright © 2001 Project Hope - The People to People Health Foundation, Inc. Republished with permission of Health Affairs, conveyed through Copyright Clearance Center, Inc.—*The Journal News (New York),* November 8, 2005. Copyright 2005 Newspaper Name, a Gannett Co. Inc. Reproduced by permission.—*Journal of Marriage and the Family,* v. 60, November, 1998. Reproduced by permission.

National Review, February 7, 1994. Copyright © 1994 by National Review, Inc., 215 Lexington Avenue, New York, NY 10016. Reproduced by permission.— *New York Times,* August 15, 1965; August 15, 1994; July 27, 2002; July 13, 2005; November 24, 2005; January 9, 2006; February 12, 2006; February 22, 2006. Copyright © 1965, 1994, 2002, 2005, 2006 by The New York Times Company. All reproduced by permission.—*NYT,* February 3, 2006. Copyright © 2006 by The New York Times Company. Reproduced by permission.—*The Associated Press Newswire,* December 27, 1993. Reproduced by permission.—*Philosophy and Public Affairs,* v. 14, summer, 1985. Copyright © 1985 Basil Blackwell Ltd. Reproduced by permission of Blackwell Publishers. www.blackwell-synergy.com—*Political Science Quarterly,* v. 108, autumn, 1993. Reprinted by permission from *Political Science Quarterly.*—*Time,* October 22, 1990. Copyright © 1990 Time, Inc. All rights reserved. Reproduced by permission.—*Washington Post,* November 1, 1995. Copyright © 1995, *Washington Post.* Reprinted with permission.—*WebMemo # 704,* March 29, 2005. Copyright © 2005 The Heritage Foundation. Reproduced by permission.

Copyrighted excerpts in *Social Policy: Essential Primary Sources,* were reproduced from the following books:

Angelou, Maya. From "Momma Welfare Roll," in *And Still I Rise.* Random House, 1978, Virago Press Ltd, 1986. Copyright © 1978 by Maya Angelou. Used by permission of Random House, Inc. In the United Kingdom by Time Warner Books UK.—Gatto, John Taylor. From *Dumbing Us Down: The Hidden Curriculum of Compulsory Schooling.* New Society Publishers, 1992. Reproduced by permission.—Murray, Charles. From *Losing Ground: American Social Policy 1950-1980.* Basic Books, Inc, 1985. Copyright © 1984 by Charles Murray. Reprinted by permission of Basic Books, Inc., a member of Perseus Books, L.L.C.—Riis, Jacob. From "XVI: Waifs of the City Slums," in *How the*

Other Half Lives. Edited by Sam Bass Warner, Jr. Belknap Press of Harvard University Press, 1970. Copyright © 1970 by the President and Fellows of Harvard College. All rights reserved. Reproduced by permission of Harvard University Press.

Photographs and illustrations appearing in *Social Policy: Essential Primary Sources*, were received from the following sources:

Herb Block cartoon contrasting inner city schools and suburban schools, photograph © Herb Block Foundation.—A billboard in downtown Baltimore displays a message of abstinence towards teen sex, photograph. AP Images.—A British police hand out CCTV (closed circuit television) image shows Southampton and Charlton Athletic soccer fans clashing on April 13, 2002 near Maze Hill train station in south London in 2003, photograph. © Handout/ Reuters/Corbis.—A crowd of about 150 students protest in favor of affirmative action outside the University of California Irvine campus administration building, photograph. AP Images.—A female teacher hands out textbooks at the Ameer Doust Mohammad Khan primary school in Kabul, Afghanistan, photograph. © Reuters/Corbis.—A group of Japanese-American civilians wait to board trucks taking them to internment camps April 1942, photograph. AP Images.—A helicopter lifts sandbags used to repair a broken levee in New Orleans, in the aftermath of Hurricane Katrina, photograph. AP Images.—A large number of people line up outside of a food stamp distribution office in Minneapolis, 1940, photograph. © Minnesota Historical Society/Corbis.—A participant in the New York Work Experience Program (WEP) carries a broom on his shoulder while helping to clean the streets, photograph. © Najlah Feanny/Corbis SABA.—A person on a bicycle rides past a sign that reads "25 days to go before slavery starts Sept 1, stop W2," photograph. AP Images.

A Red Cross volunteer comforting a hurricane victim in the Houston Astrodome, photograph. AP Images.—A young man chops firewood for cooking and heating in a California migrant workers camp, photograph by Horace Bristol. © Horace Bristol/Corbis.—Abortion opponent Nick Schadler from Dubuque, Iowa, left, holds a rosary as pro-choice supporter Ash Roberts from Detroit, Michigan, shouts as pro-choice and pro-life opponents face off in front of the Supreme Court in Washington, photograph. AP Images.—Ad Council Girl Scouts Math and Science for Girls Campaign shows a night sky with updated text for the poem Twinkle, Twinkle, Little Star. Twinkle, Twinkle — The Kaplan Thaler Group.—Addams, Jane, Chicago, Illinois, photograph. AP Images.—

Aerial view of sprawling neighborhood in Corona, California, photograph. AP Images.—African American students get off bus at predominantly white South Boston high school as police stand guard, photograph. © Bettmann/Corbis.—American veterans crowd an office of the veterans administration bureau, waiting to file application forms for their bonus bonds, photograph. © New York Times Co./Getty Images.—An 1844 campaign ribbon for the Know-Nothing Party, also known as the American Party. The Know-Nothings were a nativist party opposed to immigration, photograph. © David J. and Janice L. Frent Collection/Corbis.—An empty wheelchair in the shower of a handicapped-accessible bathroom, photograph. AP Images.

An unidentified man smokes outside a bar on Parnell Street in Dublin. Ireland became the first country in the world to outlaw smoking in all its pubs, restaurants and closed public spaces on March 29, 2004, photograph. © Fran Veale/Getty Images.—Angel, 20, is from Puerto Rico. She ran away from her family, photograph. © Sophie Elbaz/Sygma/Corbis.—Angelou, Maya, photograph. © Mitchell Gerber/Corbis.—Anti-gun protest in San Diego, California during Republican Convention, 1996, photograph. © David Butow/Corbis SABA.—Anti-Newt Gingrich faction of health reform protesters holding signs and demonstrating against Medicaid and Medicare cuts, photograph. © Najlah Feanny/Corbis SABA.—Armenian waifs, street children, dressed in ragged clothes stand in the entryway to Miss Cushman's Orphanage, 1920, photograph. © Bettmann/Corbis.—Barry and Maria Prince read to their children Alex, 4, second left, Monica, 1, center, and Olivia, 3, in home, photograph. AP Images.—Bek, Lidia, left, of North Beach Haven, NJ, and Crystal Amador of Lakehurst, NJ, listen as the Reverend Bruce Davidson speaks about the needs of low-income families and individuals during a news conference, photograph. AP Images.—Black students from the Clarendon County school district carry signs reading "Fulfill the dream for our children!", photograph. AP Images.—Blackmun, Harry, photograph. AP Images.—California Insurance Commissioner John Garamendi, right, tours the Science Center Elementary School before a news conference in Los Angeles, California, photograph. AP Images.—Candidate Safia Siddiqi met with constituents on election day as she arrived to place her own vote in her village of Nazarabad, Afghanistan, photograph.© Stephanie Sinclair/Corbis.—Carter, Jimmy, photograph. The Library of Congress.

Carter, Jimmy, and Rosalynn Carter working on a house for Habitat for Humanity, photograph. ©

Bettmann/Corbis.—Cartoon criticizing President Truman's Fair Deal program, photograph. © MPI/Getty Images.—Cartoon depicting Van Burens Free Soil opposition to Democratic nominee Lewis Cass Van Buren and his supporters. The Library of Congress.—Chairman of the Federal Reserve Alan Greenspan adjusts his microphone while speaking at the President's Advisory Panel on Federal Tax Reform, photograph. © Kevin Lamarque/Reuters-Corbis.—Children eat at a nutritional center in Kinshasa, the Democratic Republic of the Congo, February 26, 2006, photograph. © Lionel Healing/AFP/Getty Images).—Clay, Henry, painting. The Library of Congress.—Close-up of President Truman as he delivers his State of the Union address to a joint session of Congress, January 5, 1949, photograph. © Bettmann/Corbis.—"Colored Drinking Fountain", photograph. The Library of Congress.—Computers displaying the Google Desktop search engine are on display at the Digitallife show at New York's Jacob K. Javitz convention center, photograph. AP Images.—Construction workers make wooden concrete forms during the building of the Pentagon, photograph. AP Images.—Coughlin, Charles E., photograph. AP Images.—December 3, 1949: Jubilee Buildings, owned by a private landlord, virtually the only poor housing left in Wapping, east London, where council replaced most of the slums, photograph. © Bert Hardy/Picture Post/Getty Images.—Delegates to the convention of the Women's Organization for National Prohibition Reform gather in front of the Capitol Building, photograph. AP Images.

Dental patients being treated in large numbers by dentists at Guys Hospital in London, 1949, photograph. © Bettmann/Corbis.—Depression Breadline: Women receiving food from priests of the New Hope Mission in New York, 1930s, photograph. © Bettmann/Corbis.—Detail showing poor figures from The Depression Breadline by George Segal, photograph. © James P. Blair/Corbis.—Disabled demonstrators rally June 13, 2000 in Los Angeles, CA to protest the state of California's challenge to the Americans with Disabilities Act of 1990 in the Supreme Court, photograph. © David McNew/Newsmakers/Getty Images.—Displaced New Orleans residents lining up on the freeway to board military helicopters that will evacuate them to safety, photograph. © Master Sgt. Scott Reed/USAF/epa/Corbis.—Domenech, Christian who has ADHD, with his parents Paula and Steve Johnson, photograph. AP Images.—Elevated view of New Deal, photograph. © Margaret Bourke-White/Time & Life Pictures/Getty Images.—European immigrants wait for the ferry that will transport them to New York City, photograph. © Bettmann/

Corbis.—Family receiving welfare poses for a photo in Friars Point, Mississippi, 1995, photograph. © Shepard Sherbell/Corbis SABA.—Federal troops escorting black students, Little Rock, Arkansas, photograph. © Corbis-Bettmann.—Firefighters bring a patient into a Baltimore trauma center in 1999, photograph. © Marc Asnin/Corbis SABA.—Food distribution to freed slaves, ca. 1865, photograph. © Corbis.—Former President Jimmy Carter, founder of Habitat for Humanity, kneels on scaffolding in Tijuana, Mexico, photograph. AP Images.—Four African American students on their way to attempt to integrate North Little Rock High School on September 10, 1957, photograph. © Bettmann/Corbis.—Fowler, Henry H. former treasury secretary, presided over the "guns and butter" economic policy of the Johnson administration from 1965 to 1968, photograph. AP Images.

Galich, Dave, and Coyne, Kelly members of the University of California College Republicans try to entice fellow students to buy cookies from their affirmative action bake sale where the treats are priced according to the buyer's ethnicity, photograph. AP Images.—Goldstein, Heidi, right, nurses her two and a half-year-old daughter, Katy Thomason while talking with Amy Berry Pogrebin, second from right, about the upcoming breastfeeding record attempt, at a health clinic in Berkeley, California, photograph. AP Images.—Govenor Sonny Perdue is joined by grandson, Jack Ghioto, at a Capitol press conference to promote the Georgia Higher Education Savings Plan, photograph. AP Images.—Governor Bill Clinton during his 1992 campaign for the presidency, photograph. © Reuters/Corbis.—Group of people living in a crowded one-room tenement in New York, photograph. © Hulton-Deutsch Collection/Corbis.—Hayes, George E.C. (left), Thurgood Marshall (center), and James M. Nabrit (right), celebrate the Brown v. Board of Education, Topeka landmark U.S. Supreme Court decision, Washington, D.C., 1954, photograph. The Library of Congress.—Home school student Daniel Pittman, 15, reads from a workbook while he watches a video on writing skills at his home in Petal, Mississippi, photograph. AP Images.—Homestead Act settlers in front of their farmhouse, Nebraska, photograph. © Bettmann/Corbis.—Hoover, Herbert, photograph. The Library of Congress.—Hurricane Katrina refugees reach for clothing on the floor of the Astrodome September 1, 2005, photograph. © Erich Schlegel/Dallas Morning News/Corbis.—Ida M. Fuller, first person receiving increased benefits under new Social Security law, photograph. AP Images.

Image of a table showing the results of the first national census in the United States. US Census Bureau—Immigrant family in new quarters circa 1900, photograph. © Bettmann/Corbis.—Inside cover of book The Jungle, by Upton Sinclair, illustration. © Bettmann/Corbis.—Jacob Coxey's Army of unemployed workers on 36-day march from Masillon, Ohio to Washington, D.C., photograph. © Corbis.—James Madison Middle School student Blair Ellis turns to watch teacher Dana Ball explain the class assignment in this all-girl language arts class, photograph. AP Images.—Japanese Americans in a prison bus, on their way to be processed for internment during World War II, photograph. © Bettmann/Corbis.—Johnson, Andrew (Impeachment), political cartoon. The Library of Congress.—Johnson, Lyndon B., photograph by Arnold Newman. AP Images.—Kuhn, Maggie, photograph. © UPI/Corbis-Bettmann.—LaFollette, Robert Marion, photograph. © Corbis.—Langston, Ronald N. left, national director of the Minority Business Development Agency of the US Deptartment of Commerce, visits with Herman McKinney, right, vice president for urban affairs of the Greater Seattle Chamber of Commerce, photograph. AP Images.—Latinos protest federal discrimination in the city's welfare bureaucracy July 23, 2003 in New York City, photograph. © Mario Tama/Getty Images.—Lawyer Johnny Cochran (front R) sits with lawyer Douglas Wigdor (L) as he speaks at a news conference to discuss a complaint made to the Equal Employment Opportunity Commission (EEOC), photograph. © Reuters/Corbis.—Lease, Mary E., photograph. The Library of Congress.—Lincoln, Abraham, photograph. The Library of Congress.—Lithograph of Flathead Indian men, women, and children crossing a river on rafts and horses Circa 1850, photograph. © Corbis.—Loving, Richard P. and his wife Mildred, challenged Virginia's law against mixed race marriages in court and, in 1967, the Supreme Court ruled Virginia's anti-miscegination laws unconstitutional in Loving v. Virginia, photograph. AP Images.

Maundu, Philip, Kenyan student attending Morehouse College in Atlanta, Georgia, walks past a racially discriminatory real estate sign in Atlanta, 1960, photograph. © Ted Russell/Time Life Pictures/Getty Images.—Mayor Jane Campbell of Cleveland and Mayor Bill Purcell of Nashville visit with Jalon Cambridge, a 4 year-old boy attending the Tom Joy Head Start Center in Nashville, Tennessee, photograph. AP Images.—Members of Coxey's Army stop to listen to a speaker led by populist Jacob Coxey, photograph. © MPI/Getty Images.—Men sleep on the floor of a New York homeless shelter, photograph by Jacob Riis. © Bettmann/Corbis.—Morrill, Justin S., photograph.

The Library of Congress.—National Recovery Administration (NRA) emblem, photograph. AP Images.—Nebraskan farm scene by Marguerite Zorach. Photo by MPI/Getty Images.—New York City - "Doing the Slums" - A scene in the five points. From a sketch by a staff artist, photograph. © Corbis.—New York City Housing Authority poster advocating planned communities over tenement housing Circa 1940, photograph. © Corbis.—Night photo shows lighted construction site at the Fontana Dam on the Little Tennessee River in western North Carolina during the early 1940's. AP Images.—Older, traditional food stamps are displayed June 24, 2004 at an Illinois Department of Human Services office in Skokie, Illinois, photograph. © Tim Boyle/Getty Images.—Painting of artists in a studio, photograph by Moses Soyer. © MPI/Getty Images.—Panarello, Donnie Jr, left, and his father, Donnie Panarello, Sr., evacuate their home in Chalmette, Louisiana days after he and his father survived Hurricane Katrina with their dogs, photograph. © Michael Ainsworth/Dallas Morning News/Corbis.—Part of the multinational force in Iraq, the Mozambican Quick Reaction Demining Force (QRDF) soldiers remove unexploded ordnance in a residential area south of Baghdad, Iraq, photograph. © Reuters/Corbis.—Passman, Erin, center, laughs as Allison Hughes, left, places a see-through picture of a female chimpanzee over her face at the Explore Evolution exhibit at the Natural History Museum and Biodiversity Research Center on the campus of The University of Kansas, photograph. AP Images.

Pharmacist Milton Chapman poses at Dougherty's Pharmacy in Dallas, Texas, photograph. AP Images.—Political cartoon by Thomas Nast, 1866 Andrew Johnson Veto's the Freedmen's Programs. Illustration by Thomas Nast, provided courtesy of HarpWeek—Political cartoon showing a caricature of Teddy Roosevelt, photograph. © MPI/Getty Images.—Poster containing signup information for Social Security, illustration. The Library of Congress.—Poster displaying Social Security information, photograph. © Bettmann/Corbis.—Prada, Claudia, left, teaches Spanish to eighth graders at View Park Prep Charter School in South Los Angeles, photograph. AP Images.—President Bill Clinton shakes hands with 10-year-old Jeremy Kanka as his mother Maureen looks on at ceremonies May 17, 1996 at the White House where Clinton signed legislation called Megan's Law after Jeremy's sister, who was raped and murdered two years prior by a man who had twice previously been convicted of child molestation, photograph. © STR/AFP/Getty Images.—President Bill Clinton speaking on health care reform, photograph. © Cynthia Johnson/Time Life Pictures/Getty Images.—

President Bill Clinton, surrounded by members of Congress and adopted children, signs the Adoption and Safe Families Act of 1997 in the East Room of the White House, photograph. AP Images.—President Bush, center, stands with Casey Harrington, left, and Wade Hobson, right, after speaking to workers at the John Deere-Hitachi Machinery Corporation, photograph. AP Images.—President Franklin D. Roosevelt endorses New Deal candidates during a radio broadcast from his Hyde Park, New York home November 4, 1938, photograph. © Bettmann/Corbis.—President Franklin D. Roosevelt speaking from the observation platform of his train in Montana, 1934, photograph. © Corbis.—President George W. Bush boards Air Force One after participating in an event promoting welfare reform, photograph. © Brooks Kraft/Corbis.

President George W. Bush greets Steven Tingus of California after a ceremony announcing the transmittal of the New Freedom Initiative, photograph. © Paul J. Richards/AFP/Getty Images.—President George W. Bush speaks to an audience at the Union Bethel African Methodist Episcopal Church, photograph. © Brooks Kraft/Corbis.—President Johnson and Mrs. Johnson greeting Tom Fletcher, an unemployed saw mill worker, and his family and friends, April 24, 1964, photograph. © Bettmann/Corbis.—President Johnson signing Medicare Bill as Vice President Humphrey and Harry S. Truman both check the time, photograph. © Bettmann/Corbis.—Racket Court, in the interior of the Fleet Prison, photograph. © Hulton Archive/Getty Images.—Residential neighborhood in Fairfax, Delaware, in the 1950s, photograph. © Bettmann/Corbis.—Rooms for rent at Carries Apartments, photograph. © Margaret Bourke-White/Time & Life Pictures/Getty Images.—Roosevelt, Franklin D. preparing for his first "fireside chat," photograph. AP Images.—Roosevelt, Theodore 1885, photograph. © Mansell Mansell/Time & Life Pictures/Getty Images.—Roosevelt, Theodore delivering another fiery address to a crowd of 50,000 on July 21, 1915, photograph. AP Images.—Roosevelt, Theodore, portrait. © Bettmann/Corbis.—Sagan, Carl, photograph. © Bettmann/Corbis.—San Antonio parents and teachers wishing to warn Texas Legislators of what they believe are failures in the Edgewood School voucher program are shown outside the Capitol, photograph. AP Images.—Senator Huey Long is shown addressing the students of Louisiana State University in New Orleans on Nov 12, 1934, photograph. AP Images.—Senior citizen, Emaline Palumbo of Nutley receives an explanation of information about different Medicare plans, photograph. © Jerry McCrea/Star Ledger/Corbis.—Simons, Jim, a businessman and founder of Math for America, gives an interview at his New York office, photograph. AP Images.—Students and teachers outside a Freedmen's Bureau school in Beaufort, South Carolina. © Corbis.

Students from all over the UK participate in a demonstration February 20, 2002 in London, photograph. © Sion Touhig/Getty Images.—Students raise their hands to answer a teacher's question at the Knowledge is Power Program (KIPP) Academy in the South Bronx, photograph. © Andrew Lichtenstein/Corbis.—TennCare advocates stage a rally in Nashville, Tenn, photograph. AP Images.—The arrival of electricity in rural areas of the 1940's Tennessee Valley brings modern conveniences like washing machines and electric stoves, photograph. AP Images.—The fear of miscegenation, which motivated the Asiatic Exclusion League and other organizations to support anti-Chinese legislation during the 1870s and 1880s, finds sympathetic expression in this 1877 cartoon. © Bettmann/Corbis.—The giant blue eagle float symbolizing the National Recovery Administration (NRA) participates in the firemen's annual Labor Day Parade, photograph. AP Images.—The MÈdecins Sans FrontiÈres (Doctors Without Borders) hospital on the Sudanese border where Sudanese refugees are being treated, photograph. © Patrick Robert/Corbis.—The Peace Corp's first volunteers leaving for duty overseas, photograph. AP Images.—The population of the United States as recorded on the current population clock in the US Census Bureau, photograph. © Bettmann/Corbis.—Three girls at Kamehameha Prep School in 1955, a school that traditionally takes only children of Hawaiian descent, photograph. Photo by Evans/Three Lions/Getty Images.—To help project outdoor speeches during his 1934 US Senate campaign, Harry Truman used this car equipped with loudspeakers, an amplifier and a microphone, photograph. AP Images.—U.S. President Bill Clinton announces a lower student loan default at a White House ceremony in Washington, DC, photograph. © Reuters/Corbis.

U.S. President Franklin D. Roosevelt signs Public Law 346, the Servicemen's Readjustment Act of 1944, also known as the GI Bill of Rights on June 22, 1944, photograph. AP Images.—U.S. President George W. Bush speaks about his No Child left Behind education policy at the CT Kirkpatrick Elementary School, photograph. © Jaon Reed/Reuters/Corbis.—Ukranian poster from 1921 which states in Ukranian and Russian They give Soviet Russia coal Give them machines, clothing, and food. Slavic and Baltic Division, The New York Public Library, Astor, Lenox and Tilden Foundations.—US Army Sgt. Chase Johnson, center, talks with a benefit manager during the annual veterans benefits expo in Savannah, Georgia, photograph. AP Images.—Vietnam Veterans holding an American Flag, photograph. © Leif Skoogfors/Corbis.—Volunteers distribute baskets of food at the Westside Campaign Against Hunger's food pantry on West 86th Street, photograph. © Viviane Moos/Corbis.—Volunteers load relief supplies into a truck in the Van Nuys section of Los Angeles, photograph. AP Images.—Washington consumer advocate Ralph Nader, at a news conference, said a move in Congress to overturn the proposal that all cars be equipped with air bags or automobile seat belts is "doomed to defeat", photograph. © Bettmann/Corbis.—With support from the British Embassy in Macedonia, citizens of Veles have started the Ecological Democracy project with the aim of fighting pollution and organizing help for the affected children, photograph. © Valentin Ogneov/COVER/Corbis.—Wolfstich, Noreen, a nurse at Fletcher Allen Health Care in Burlington, holds letters to lawmakers as she speaks outside the State house in Montpelier, Vt, photograph. AP Images.—Woman walking towards slum housing in Detroit's near East Side, photograph. © Bettmann/Corbis.—Workers at the Bell Aircraft plant wear safety goggles and masks while working in areas where their eyes might be damaged, photograph. © Corbis.—Yoshida, Ken, right, gets a handshake of apology from National Japanese American Citizens League President Floyd Mori during a Recognition and Reconciliation Ceremony, photograph. AP Images.—Young women walk between classes at Spellman College in the largest African American education center in the US, photograph. © Bob Krist/Corbis.

Copyrighted excerpts in *Social Policy: Essential Primary Sources*, were reproduced from the following websites or other sources:

Matt Kempner Andrea Jones, "College is already affordable, likely for most recipients," *ajc.com*, November 11, 2003. Republished with permission of *Atlanta Constitution Journal*, conveyed through Copyright Clearance Center, Inc.—"Law Limits Ritalin Recommendations," *CNN.com*, July 17, 2001. Copyright © 2001 The Associated Press. All rights reserved. Reproduced by permission.—"State Seeks to Block 'No Child Left Behind'", *CNN.com*, February 2, 2006. Copyright © 2006 Reuters. All rights reserved. Reproduced by permission.—United Nations, Office of the United Nations High Commissioner for Human Rights, "United Nations Millennium Declaration," *General Assembly Resolution 55/2*, September 8, 2000. Copyright © 2000 United Nations. Reproduced by permission.—Sheryl Gay Stolberg, "Abstinence-Only Initiative Advancing," *NYTimes.com*, February 28, 2002. Reproduced by permission.—Erik Eckholm, "Once Woeful, Alabama is Model in Child Welfare," *NYT*, August 20, 2005. Copyright © 2005 The New York Times Company. Reproduced by permission.—Brian A. Gallagher, "Katrina: Our System for Fixing Broken Lives is Broken," *Position Statements, United Way of America*, September 12, 2005. Reproduced by permission.—Sheryll D. Cashin, "Race, Class, and Real Estate," *Washingtonpost.com*, August 1, 2004. Copyright © 2004 The Washington Post Company. Reproduced by permission of the author. This article was excerpted from the author's book, *The Failures of Integration: How Race and Class Are Undermining the American Dream* (Public Affairs 2004).—"CWLA Testimony Submitted to The House Subcommittee on Human Resources of the Committee on Ways and Means for the Hearing on the Implementation of the Adoption and Safe Families Act," Child Welfare League of America, April 8, 2003. Reproduced by permission.—"School Vouchers: The Wrong Choice for Public Education," Anti Defamation League, 2005. Copyright © 2005 Anti-Defamation League. All rights reserved. Reproduced by permission.—United Nations, Division for the Advancement of Women Department of Economic and Social Affairs, "Fourth World Conference on Women, Platform for Action," September, 1995. Copyright © United Nations. Reproduced by permission.

About the Set

Essential Primary Source titles are part of a ten-volume set of books in the Social Issues Primary Sources Collection designed to provide primary source documents on leading social issues of the nineteenth, twentieth, and twenty-first centuries. International in scope, each volume is devoted to one topic and will contain approximately 150 to 175 documents that will include and discuss speeches, legislation, magazine and newspaper articles, memoirs, letters, interviews, novels, essays, songs, and works of art essential to understanding the complexity of the topic.

Each entry will include standard subheads: key facts about the author; an introduction placing the piece in context; the full or excerpted document; a discussion of the significance of the document and related events; and a listing of further resources (books, periodicals, Web sites, and audio and visual media).

Each volume will contain a topic-specific introduction, topic-specific chronology of major events, an index especially prepared to coordinate with the volume topic, and approximately 150 images.

Volumes are intended to be sold individually or as a set.

THE ESSENTIAL PRIMARY SOURCE SERIES

- *Terrorism: Essential Primary Sources*
- *Medicine, Health, and Bioethics: Essential Primary Sources*
- *Environmental Issues: Essential Primary Sources*
- *Crime and Punishment: Essential Primary Sources*
- *Gender Issues and Sexuality: Essential Primary Sources*
- *Human and Civil Rights: Essential Primary Sources*
- *Government, Politics, and Protest: Essential Primary Sources*
- *Social Policy: Essential Primary Sources*
- *Immigration and Multiculturalism: Essential Primary Sources*
- *Family in Society: Essential Primary Sources*

Introduction

Social policy decisions shape societies and influence social justice and social change. Accordingly, the resources and readings contained in *Social Policy: Essential Primary Sources* include treatments of traditional social policy issues involving civil rights, children, education, housing, health, and welfare policy. In addition, the selected primarily sources also provide insight into the development and implementation of polices involving language, disabilities, and other emerging social issues. Although placing emphasis on social policy issues as they have evolved in the United States and Europe, *Social Policy: Essential Primary Sources* is broadly international in scope, and contains readings related to an increasingly global society.

Covering the development and implementation of social policy since the nineteenth century, *Social Policy: Essential Primary Sources* is designed to help younger students and readers understand and evaluate the means by which governments and groups shape and implement social policy. In recognition of the fact that there are varying academic perspectives on the definition, nature, and role of social policy (as well as differing approaches to measuring the effectiveness of policy) the editors have chosen primary sources that provide more general overviews of policy issues rather that detailed political or sociological analysis. The guiding selection criteria were aimed toward the inclusion of primary sources that would be empower critical consideration and discussion of both the nature of policy and the ethical dimensions of policy (e.g. equality issues) rather than providing detailed and often highly mathematical analysis of policy efficiency that, in turn, would demand readers apply more advanced mathematical skills to critically evaluate.

As with other volumes in this series, there was insufficient space to fully portray all facets of issues, and such completeness is not implied. In an effort toward balance, the experts and writers contributing to *Social Policy: Essential Primary Sources* reflect a diversity of cultures, backgrounds, and opinions. In addition, the editors specifically encourage readers to frame and understand the significance of the primary sources offered in light of their own social experience. Such exercises sharpen critical thinking and often provide insight into the diversity of analysis and opinion.

Lastly, the editors intend that *Social Policy: Essential Primary Sources* spur interest and further reading toward understanding the root causes of inequalities, especially how economic inequalities impact both the power to shape policy—and the quality of life for citizens living under those policies. Toward this goal, the editors have also attempted to include a number of resources that reflect the marginalization of various groups in the making of social policy.

K. Lee Lerner, Brenda Wilmoth Lerner, & Adrienne Wilmoth Lerner, editors
London, U.K., and Jacksonville, Florida
August, 2006

About the Entry

The primary source is the centerpiece and main focus of each entry in *Social Policy: Essential Primary Sources*. In keeping with the philosophy that much of the benefit from using primary sources derives from the reader's own process of inquiry, the contextual material surrounding each entry provides access and ease of use, as well as giving the reader a springboard for delving into the primary source. Rubrics identify each section and enable the reader to navigate entries with ease.

ENTRY STRUCTURE

* Primary Source/Entry Title, Subtitle, Primary Source Type
* Key Facts—essential information about the primary source, including creator, date, source citation, and notes about the creator.
* Introduction—historical background and contributing factors for the primary source.
* Primary Source—in text, text facsimile, or image format; full or excerpted.
* Significance—importance and impact of the primary source related events.
* Further Resources—books, periodicals, websites, and audio and visual material.

NAVIGATING AN ENTRY

Entry elements are numbered and reproduced here, with an explanation of the data contained in these elements explained immediately thereafter according to the corresponding numeral.

Primary Source/Entry Title, Subtitle, Primary Source Type

---

[1] Katrina

[2] Our System for Fixing Broken Lives is Broken

---

[3] **Position statement**

[1] **Primary Source/Entry Title:** The entry title is usually the primary source title. In some cases where long titles must be shortened, or more generalized topic titles are needed for clarity primary source titles are generally depicted as subtitles. Entry titles appear as catchwords at the top outer margin of each page.

[2] **Subtitle:** Some entries contain subtitles.

[3] **Primary Source Type:** The type of primary source is listed just below the title. When assigning source types, great weight was given to how the author of the primary source categorized the source.

Key Facts

[4] **By:** Brian A. Gallagher

[5] **Date:** September 12, 2005

[6] **Source:** Gallagher, Brian A. "Katrina: Our System for Fixing Broken Lives is Broken." United Way of America, September 12, 2005.

[7] **About the Author:** *About the Author:* Brian A. Gallagher is the President and Chief Executive Officer of the United Way of America. The United Way is one

of the largest charity and assistance-providing organizations in the United States, and includes a national network of volunteers, caregivers, and smaller charity providers.

[4]   Author, Artist, or Organization: The name of the author, artist, or organization responsible for the creation of the primary source begins the Key Facts section.

[5]   Date of Origin: The date of origin of the primary source appears in this field, and may differ from the date of publication in the source citation below it; for example, speeches are often delivered before they are published.

[6]   Source Citation: The source citation is a full bibliographic citation, giving original publication data as well as reprint and/or online availability.

[7]   About the Author: A brief bio of the author or originator of the primary source gives birth and death dates and a quick overview of the person's work.. This rubric has been customized in some cases. If the primary source written document, the term "author" appears; however, if the primary source is a work of art, the term "artist" is used, showing the person's direct relationship to the primary source. For primary sources created by a group, "organization" may have been used instead of "author." Other terms may also be used to describe the creator or originator of the primary source. If an author is anonymous or unknown, a brief "About the Publication" sketch may appear.

Introduction Essay

[8]   INTRODUCTION

When Hurricane Katrina struck the Gulf Coast of the United States in the late summer of 2005, the result was one of the most widespread and costly natural disasters in the history of the country. Most directly affecting the states of Louisiana, Alabama, and Mississippi, the storm and the massive floods that came afterward left many thousands of people homeless and billions of dollars worth of damage. Approximately 1,600 people died directly as a result of the storm or from conditions caused by the storm.

Even while the winds and rain that battered the Gulf Coast area were less powerful than forecasters had initially predicted, the storm itself did cause many homes and large buildings to be destroyed. However, the more costly damages resulting from Katrina came from the flooding of the city of New Orleans. The city, which is uniquely located below sea level, is heavily dependent on a system of pumps and levees that keep water from pouring into the city from the various large bodies of water that sit on both sides. As a result of the massive amount of rain that Katrina dumped on the area in a very small amount of time, the system—which was not designed to handle such large amounts of rain and wind—failed in several places, flooding more than eighty percent of the city of New Orleans and some of the surrounding suburbs.

In the days following the hurricane, many thousands of New Orleans residents who had been unable to evacuate prior to the storm were stranded in the city. Delivery of supplies to the affected areas and transportation of the residents out of the city took a period of several days. During that period, a great deal of unrest and looting took place throughout the New Orleans area and authorities on occasion were forced to retreat from rescue situations because they were being fired upon. In the days, weeks, and months following the hurricane, the alleged slow response of authorities become a focus of much discussion. Critics of the government response, particularly that of the Federal Emergency Management Agency (FEMA), which is charged with coordinating rescue and recovery efforts following large disasters of this type that take place in the United States, claimed that the government was not prepared for this type of disaster and failed to properly respond, resulting in further damage and loss of life.

[8]   Introduction: The introduction is a brief essay on the contributing factors and historical context of the primary source. Intended to promote understanding and equip the reader with essential facts to understand the context of the primary source.

To maintain ease of reference to the primary source, spellings of names and places are used in accord with their use in the primary source. According names and places may have different spellings in different articles. Whenever possible, alternative spellings are provided to provide clarity.

To the greatest extent possible we have attempted to use Arabic names instead of their Latinized versions. Where required for clarity we have included Latinized names in parentheses after the Arabic version. Alas, we could not retain some diacritical marks (e.g. bars over vowels, dots under consonants). Because there is no generally accepted rule or consensus regarding the format of translated Arabic names, we have adopted the straightforward, and we hope sensitive, policy of using names as they are used or cited in their region of origin.

Primary Source

[9]   PRIMARY SOURCE

The unrivaled impact of Hurricane Katrina is measured not only in dollars and cents, but in human lives. Untold thousands are feared dead, and hundreds of thousands have been displaced from their homes or have lost all of their earthly possessions.

Therefore, while contributing to the various relief funds is an essential element of our response to this national tragedy, money alone doesn't fix broken lives. What is needed is a human-based response that outlives the news media's attention to the Gulf States and addresses the less obvious, but no less significant challenges created by the devastation.

If the Oklahoma City bombing and the September 11th terrorist attacks are any indication, two things will surely occur in the aftermath of Hurricane Katrina. First, our emergency response preparedness will be dissected. Second, the American people will respond with characteristic generosity to meet the immediate needs of those affected. Each response is important, but each is ultimately predictable and insufficient.

The assessment of our emergency response capabilities will likely be politicized and polarized, yielding changes only at the margins. And while the immediate response from people shows our immense capacity to care, it will not change the desperate conditions in which hundreds of thousands of people in the Gulf States, and millions of Americans elsewhere, live each day.

What America needs to do now—not only in response to Hurricane Katrina, but in addressing the long-standing challenges facing communities nationwide—is to think and act beyond the traditional stimulus-response formula to serving those in need. Hurricane Katrina has arrested the nation's attention, while leading to a spike in fund raising for numerous charities. Yet, if a similar tragedy were to befall New Orleans in ten years, would the human anguish still fracture along the same racial and socioeconomic lines?

The current delivery system for relief and social services is heroic but clearly inadequate. A new system, based on the principles described below, constitutes America's best course of action for having a long-term, positive impact on those in need.

Adopt a human-based approach. Contrary to the system-or institution-based approach, which often results in bureaucratic gridlock because agencies require clients to conform to their individual intake and service systems, the human-based approach caters to the needs of the affected person. The customer-first principle is a hallmark of successful companies, but remains a stubborn challenge for public and private agencies.

Operate from a master plan. Community leaders need to develop a comprehensive plan to serve all Gulf State evacuees in any community that has accepted them. The elements of this plan will cover a broad scope of services ranging from crisis counseling, housing and daycare to cash assistance, education and job training. This same comprehensive approach is no less valid for communities seeking to eradicate teen pregnancy, drug use or illiteracy.

Integrate the delivery of services. Hurricane Katrina offers a compelling microcosm of the need for a single source of information regarding relief services. 2-1-1, a toll-free phone number that citizens can use to access essential services and volunteer opportunities, exists in Louisiana and now serves as the state's primary clearing house for requests for assistance and has accepted thousands of calls. Conversely, Mississippi, which lacks a 2-1-1 system, doesn't have a coordinated, statewide means of managing such requests. With 2-1-1 operating in less than half of the country, Congress should enact legislation and provide funding to establish an integrated nationwide 2-1-1 network that would allow service providers to seamlessly help those in need—regardless of where they are physically located.

Stay committed to a community's long-term needs. In the last few months, when is the last time you encountered a news article about the rebuilding efforts in those Southeast Asian countries affected by the last year's tsunami, despite the fact that these efforts will take years to complete? We need to resist the temptation to shape programs and deploy resources based on the day's headline and remember that mental health counselors were getting new requests for service seven years after the bombing in Oklahoma City. This points to the need for agencies to set long-term goals and make the necessary commitments to achieve them.

Create a $10 billion Human Development Fund. We will pour billions of dollars into rebuilding the physical infrastructure of New Orleans and the Gulf Coast, but let's also invest billions in rebuilding human lives through the creation of mixed income housing communities and neighborhoods; the creation of jobs that pay enough to sustain a family; and the placement of services like grocery stores in all neighborhoods. Let's create family development accounts for college and home ownership; neighborhood redevelopment accounts that provide incentives to establish small businesses in challenged areas; and quality early education and education support services that includes the building of YMCA's attached to public schools to better serve kids and their families.

While the human cost of Hurricane Katrina is ultimately incalculable, what is acutely apparent is that rebuilding the Gulf States will require a historic concentration of diverse resources spread across many years. Successfully managing an effort of such scale will require a measure of precision, coordination and commitment that our current delivery system simply cannot accommodate. With the wellbeing of hundreds of thousands of people hanging in the balance, isn't it time that America forged a new and better way of serving those in need?

[9] **Primary Source:** The majority of primary sources are reproduced as plain text. The primary source may appear excerpted or in full, and may appear as text, text facsimile (photographic reproduction of the original text), image, or graphic display (such as a table, chart, or graph).

The font and leading of the primary sources are distinct from that of the context—to provide a visual clue to the change, as well as to facilitate ease of reading. As needed, the original formatting of the text is preserved in order to more accurately represent the original (screenplays, for example). In order to respect the integrity of the primary sources, content some readers may consider sensitive (for example, the use of slang, ethnic or racial slurs, etc.) is retained when deemed to be integral to understanding the source and the context of its creation.

Primary source images (whether photographs, text facsimiles, or graphic displays) are bordered with a distinctive double rule. Most images have brief captions.

The term "narrative break" appears where there is a significant amount of elided (omitted) material with the text provided (for example, excerpts from a work's first and fifth chapters, selections from a journal article abstract and summary, or dialogue from two acts of a play).

Significance Essay

[10] **SIGNIFICANCE**

Following the storm, a great deal of public and media attention focused on the many allegations that the response of the government authorities had been inadequate and as a result thousands of people were left without basic supplies, many of whom were in desperate conditions.

The response of many individuals such as Gallagher was to seek ways to ensure that when future disasters struck the United States, the relevant authorities would be far better prepared. Much attention had been placed on questions regarding why the United States, which is one of the world's most wealthy and developed countries, failed to produce a rescue plan and access stranded people in a shorter amount of time. Some critics, as shown in this statement, asserted that the government response was caught up in bureaucracy, slowing down rescue efforts. The suggestion for a more human-based approach would present a big change for government agencies, which are usually built on a bureaucratic model. Also on September 12, 2005, Mike Brown resigned as director of the Federal Emergency Management Agency. He was replaced by R. David Paulison, a career firefighter and head of FEMA's emergency preparedness force

The United Way's statement was designed to show that helping the people of the Gulf Coast most directly affected by Hurricane Katrina would require longer-term solutions beyond just rebuilding the damaged areas. By focusing on the years and decades ahead, the United Way is working to allow residents of one of the nation's poorest regions an opportunity to build a higher quality of life.

[10] **Significance:** The significance discusses the importance and impact of the primary source and the event it describes.

[11] **FURTHER RESOURCES**

[11] **Further Resources:** A brief list of resources categorized as Books, Periodicals, Web sites, and Audio and Visual Media provides a stepping stone to further study.

Books

Brinkley, Douglas. *The Great Deluge: Hurricane Katrina, New Orleans, and the Mississippi Gulf Coast*. New York: William Morrow, 2006.

Childs, John Brown, ed. *Hurricane Katrina: Response and Responsibilities*. Santa Cruz, Calif.: New Pacific Press, 2006.

Periodicals

Horne, Jed. "Help Us, Please." *Times Picayune* (September 2, 2005).

Web sites

The United Way. "A Recap of United Way's Efforts to Assist During 2005." <http://national.unitedway.org/hs06/hs05.cfm> (accessed June 8, 2006).

SECONDARY SOURCE CITATION FORMATS (HOW TO CITE ARTICLES AND SOURCES)

Alternative forms of citations exist and examples of how to cite articles from this book are provided below:

APA Style

Books:

Steinbeck, John. (1870). *The Grapes of Wrath*. New York: Viking. Excerpted in K. Lee Lerner and Brenda Wilmoth Lerner, eds., (2006) *Social Policy: Essential Primary Sources*, Farmington Hills, Mich.: Thomson Gale.

Periodicals:

Green, William. (1926). "The Need for Safety from the Worker's Point of View." *Annals of the American Academy of Political and Social Science* 123, 4–5. Excerpted in K. Lee Lerner and Brenda Wilmoth Lerner, eds., (2006) *Social Policy: Essential Primary Sources*, Farmington Hills, Mich.: Thomson Gale.

Web sites:

United States Department of Labor. "The Family and Medical Leave Act of 1993." Retrieved from http://www.dol.gov/csa/rcgs/statutcs/whd/fmla.htm. Excerpted in K. Lee Lerner and Brenda Wilmoth Lerner, eds., (2006) *Social Policy: Essential Primary Sources*, Farmington Hills, Mich.: Thomson Gale.

Chicago Style

Books:

Steinbeck, John. *The Grapes of Wrath*. New York: Viking, 1939. Excerpted in K. Lee Lerner and Brenda Wilmoth Lerner, eds., *Social Policy: Essential Primary Sources*, Farmington Hills, Mich.: Thomson Gale, 2006.

Periodicals:

Green, William. "The Need for Safety from the Worker's Point of View." *Annals of the American Academy of Political and Social Science* 123 (1926): 4–5. Excerpted in K. Lee Lerner and Brenda Wilmoth Lerner, eds., *Social Policy: Essential Primary Sources*, Farmington Hills, Mich.: Thomson Gale, 2006.

Web sites:

United States Department of Labor. "The Family and Medical Leave Act of 1993." <http://www.dol.gov/esa/regs/statutes/whd/fmla.htm> (accessed May 31, 2006). Excerpted in K. Lee Lerner and Brenda Wilmoth Lerner, eds., *Social Policy: Essential Primary Sources*, Farmington Hills, Mich.: Thomson Gale, 2006.

MLA Style

Books:

Steinbeck, John. *The Grapes of Wrath*, New York: Viking, 1939. Excerpted in K. Lee Lerner and Brenda Wilmoth Lerner, eds., *Social Policy: Essential Primary Sources*, Farmington Hills, Mich.: Thomson Gale, 2006.

Periodicals:

Green, William. "The Need for Safety from the Worker's Point of View." *Annals of the American Academy of Political and Social Science*, 123, 1926: 4–5. Excerpted in K. Lee Lerner and Brenda Wilmoth Lerner, eds., *Social Policy: Essential Primary Sources*, Farmington Hills, Mich.: Thomson Gale, 2006.

Web sites:

"The Family and Medical Leave Act of 1993." *United States Department of Labor*. 31 May, 2006. <http://www.dol.gov/esa/regs/statutes/whd/fmla.htm> Excerpted in K. Lee Lerner and Brenda Wilmoth Lerner, eds., *Social Policy: Essential Primary Sources*, Farmington Hills, Mich.: Thomson Gale, 2006.

Turabian Style

Books:

Steinbeck, John. *The Grapes of Wrath* (New York: Viking, 1939). Excerpted in K. Lee Lerner and Brenda Wilmoth Lerner, eds., *Social Policy: Essential Primary Sources* (Farmington Hills, Mich.: Thomson Gale, 2006).

Periodicals:

Green, William. "The Need for Safety from the Worker's Point of View." *Annals of the American Academy of Political and Social Science* 123 (1926): 4–5. Excerpted in K. Lee Lerner and Brenda Wilmoth Lerner, eds., *Social Policy: Essential Primary Sources* (Farmington Hills, Mich.: Thomson Gale, 2006).

Web sites:

United States Department of Labor. "The Family and Medical Leave Act of 1993." available from http://www.dol.gov/esa/regs/statutes/whd/fmla.htm; accessed 31 May, 2006. Excerpted in K. Lee Lerner and Brenda Wilmoth Lerner, eds., *Social Policy: Essential Primary Sources* (Farmington Hills, Mich.: Thomson Gale, 2006).

Using Primary Sources

The definition of what constitutes a primary source is often the subject of scholarly debate and interpretation. Although primary sources come from a wide spectrum of resources, they are united by the fact that they individually provide insight into the historical *milieu* (context and environment) during which they were produced. Primary sources include materials such as newspaper articles, press dispatches, autobiographies, essays, letters, diaries, speeches, song lyrics, posters, works of art—and in the twenty-first century, web logs—that offer direct, first-hand insight or witness to events of their day.

Categories of primary sources include:

- Documents containing firsthand accounts of historic events by witnesses and participants. This category includes diary or journal entries, letters, email, newspaper articles, interviews, memoirs, and testimony in legal proceedings.
- Documents or works representing the official views of both government leaders and leaders of terrorist organizations. These include primary sources such as policy statements, speeches, interviews, press releases, government reports, and legislation.
- Works of art, including (but certainly not limited to) photographs, poems, and songs, including advertisements and reviews of those works that help establish an understanding of the cultural milieu (the cultural environment with regard to attitudes and perceptions of events).
- Secondary sources. In some cases, secondary sources or tertiary sources may be treated as primary sources. In some cases articles and sources are created many years after an event. Ordinarily,

a historical retrospective published after the initial event is not be considered a primary source. If, however, a resource contains statement or recollections of participants or witnesses to the original event, the source may be considered primary with regard to those statements and recollections.

ANALYSIS OF PRIMARY SOURCES

The material collected in this volume is not intended to provide a comprehensive overview of a topic or event. Rather, the primary sources are intended to generate interest and lay a foundation for further inquiry and study.

In order to properly analyze a primary source, readers should remain skeptical and develop probing questions about the source. As in reading a chemistry or algebra textbook, historical documents require readers to analyze them carefully and extract specific information. However, readers must also read "beyond the text" to garner larger clues about the social impact of the primary source.

In addition to providing information about their topics, primary sources may also supply a wealth of insight into their creator's viewpoint. For example, when reading a news article about an outbreak of disease, consider whether the reporter's words also indicate something about his or her origin, bias (an irrational disposition in favor of someone or something), prejudices (an irrational disposition against someone or something), or intended audience.

Students should remember that primary sources often contain information later proven to be false, or contain viewpoints and terms unacceptable to future generations. It is important to view the primary source within the historical and social context existing at its creation. If for example, a newspaper article is written within hours or days of an event, later developments may reveal some assertions in the original article as false or misleading.

TEST NEW CONCLUSIONS AND IDEAS

Whatever opinion or working hypothesis the reader forms, it is critical that they then test that hypothesis against other facts and sources related to the incident. For example, it might be wrong to conclude that factual mistakes are deliberate unless evidence can be produced of a pattern and practice of such mistakes with an intent to promote a false idea.

The difference between sound reasoning and preposterous conspiracy theories (or the birth of urban legends) lies in the willingness to test new ideas against other sources, rather than rest on one piece of evidence such as a single primary source that may contain errors. Sound reasoning requires that arguments and assertions guard against argument fallacies that utilize the following:

- false dilemmas (only two choices are given when in fact there are three or more options)
- arguments from ignorance (*argumentum ad ignorantiam*; because something is not known to be true, it is assumed to be false)
- possibilist fallacies (a favorite among conspiracy theorists who attempt to demonstrate that a factual statement is true or false by establishing the possibility of its truth or falsity. An argument

where "it could be" is usually followed by an unearned "therefore, it is.")
- slippery slope arguments or fallacies (a series of increasingly dramatic consequences is drawn from an initial fact or idea)
- begging the question (the truth of the conclusion is assumed by the premises)
- straw man arguments (the arguer mischaracterizes an argument or theory and then attacks the merits of their own false representations)
- appeals to pity or force (the argument attempts to persuade people to agree by sympathy or force)
- prejudicial language (values or moral judgments are attached to certain arguments or facts)
- personal attacks (*ad hominem*; an attack on a person's character or circumstances)
- anecdotal or testimonial evidence (stories that are unsupported by impartial or data that is not reproducible)
- *post hoc* (after the fact) fallacies (because one thing follows another, it is held to cause the other)
- the fallacy of the appeal to authority (the argument rests upon the credentials of a person, not the evidence).

Despite the fact that some primary sources can contain false information or lead readers to false conclusions based on the "facts" presented, they remain an invaluable resource regarding past events. Primary sources allow readers and researchers to come as close as possible to understanding the perceptions and context of events and thus, to more fully appreciate how and why misconceptions occur.

Chronology

So that the events in this volume may be placed in a larger historical context, the following is a general chronology of important historical and social events along with specific events related to the subject of this volume.

1675–1799

1679: The *Habeas Corpus* Act is formally passed by English Parliament.

1689: British Bill of Rights is adopted.

1772: England outlaws slavery.

1773: Boston Tea Party.

1774: First Continental Congress meets in Philadelphia.

1775: British and American forces clash at the battles of Lexington and Concord, igniting the American Revolution.

1775: James Watt invents the steam engine. The invention marks the start of the Industrial Revolution.

1776: Declaration of Independence asserts American colonies' independence from the British Empire and proclaims that "all men are created equal."

1781: The thirteenth state ratifies the Articles of Confederation, creating the United States.

1783: American Revolutionary War ends with the signing of the Treaty of Paris.

1785: *The Daily Universal Register*, later known as *The Times* (London), publishes its first issue.

1786: Britain establishes its first colony in Southeast Asia, beginning an age of European colonial expansion in Asia.

1787: The Constitutional Convention in Philadelphia adopts the U.S. Constitution.

1787: The Society for the Abolition of the Slave Trade is established in Britain.

1789: First nationwide election in the United States.

1789: Citizens of Paris storm the Bastille prison. The event ignites the French Revolution.

1789: Declaration of the Rights of Man is issued in France.

1790: First U.S. census is taken.

1791: The states ratify the Bill of Rights, the first ten amendments to the U.S. Constitution.

1793: Louis XVI, king of France, is guillotined by revolutionaries.

1793: "Reign of Terror" begins in France. Almost 40,000 people face execution.

1794: The French Republic abolishes slavery.

1796: Edward Jenner administers the first vaccination for smallpox.

1798: Irish tenant farmers rebel against British landowners in the Irish Rebellion of 1798.

1798: The United States enacts the Alien and Sedition Acts making it a federal crime to "write, publish, or utter false or malicious statements" about the United States government.

1800–1849

1800: World population reaches 1 billion.

1801: Union of Great Britain and Ireland.

1803: Napoleonic Wars begin. Napoleon's army conquers much of Europe before Napoleon is defeated at Waterloo in 1815.

1803: The United States pays France $15 million for the Louisiana Territory extending from the Mississippi River to the Rocky Mountains.

1807: The importation of slaves is outlawed in the United States, but the institution of African slavery continues until 1864.

1812: The North American War of 1812 between the United States and the United Kingdom of Great Britain and Ireland. The war lasted until the beginning of 1815.

1814: The Congress of Vienna redraws the map of Europe after the defeat of Napoleon.

1819: South American colonial revolutions begin when Columbia declares its independence from Spain in 1819.

1820: Temperance movement begins in United States.

1822: American Colonization Society advocates the repatriation of freed African slaves to the Colony of Liberia.

1829: Lambert-Adolphe-Jacques Quetelet (1796–1874), Belgian statistician and astronomer, gives the first statistical breakdown of a national census. He correlates death with age, sex, occupation, and economic status in the Belgian census.

1830: Indian Removal Act forces the removal of Native Americans living in the eastern part of the United States.

1838: More than 15,000 Cherokee Indians are forced to march from Georgia to present-day Oklahoma on the "Trail of Tears."

1838: Samuel Finley Breese Morse (1791–1872) and Alfred Vail (1807–1859) unveil their telegraph system.

1840: John William Draper (1811–1882), American chemist, takes a daguerreotype portrait of his sister, Dorothy. This is the oldest surviving photograph of a person.

1840: Pierre-Charles-Alexandre Louis (1787–1872), French physician, pioneers medical statistics, being the first to compile systematically records of diseases and treatments.

1841: Horace Greeley (1811–1872), American editor and publisher, founds the *New York Tribune* which eventually becomes the *Herald Tribune* after a merger in 1924.

1842: The first shipment of milk by rail in the United States is successfully accomplished.

1845: The potato famine begins in Ireland. Crop failures and high rents on tenant farms cause a three-year famine. Millions of Irish immigrate to flee starvation.

1846: Mexican War begins as the United States attempts to expand its territory in the Southwest.

1847: John Collins Warren (1778–1856), American surgeon, introduces ether anesthesia for general surgery. It is soon taken up worldwide as an essential part of surgery.

1847: Richard March Hoe (1812–1886), American inventor and manufacturer, patents what proves to be the first successful rotary printing press. He discards the old flatbed press and places the type on a revolving cylinder. This revolutionary system is first used by the *Philadelphia Public Ledger* this same year, and it produces 8,000 sheets per hour printed on one side.

1848: Karl Marx publishes *The Communist Manifesto*.

1848: Delegates at the Seneca Falls Convention on Woman Rights advocate equal property and voting rights for women.

1848: Series of political conflicts and violent revolts erupt in several European nations. The conflicts are collectively known as the Revolution of 1848.

1848: A group of six New York newspapers form an association or news agency to share telegraph costs. It is later called the Associated Press.

1848: The first large-scale department store opens in the United States. The Marble Dry Goods Palace in New York occupies an entire city block.

1849: John Snow (1813–1858), English physician, first states the theory that cholera is a water-borne disease and that it is usually contracted by drinking. During a cholera epidemic in London in 1854, Snow breaks the handle of the Broad Street Pump, thereby shutting down what he considered to be the main public source of the epidemic.

1850–1899

1852: Harriet Beecher Stowe's novel, *Uncle Tom's Cabin* is published. It becomes one of the most influential works to stir anti-slavery sentiments.

1854: Crimean War begins between Russia and allied forces of Great Britain, Sardinia, France, and the Ottoman Empire.

1854: Violent conflicts erupt between pro-and anti-slavery settlers in Kansas Territory. The "Bleeding Kansas" violence lasts five years.

1854: Florence Nightingale (1823–1910), English nurse, takes charge of a barracks hospital when the Crimean War breaks out. Through dedication and hard work, she goes on to create a female nursing service and a nursing school at St.

Thomas' Hospital (1860). Her compassion and common sense approach to nursing set new standards and create a new era in the history of the sick and wounded.

1854: Cyrus West Field (1819–1892), American financier, forms the New York, Newfoundland and London telegraph Company and proposes to lay a transatlantic telegraph cable.

1856: *Illustrated London News* becomes the first periodical to include regular color plates.

1857: Supreme Court of the United States decision in *Dred Scott v. Sanford* holds that slaves are not citizens and that Congress cannot prohibit slavery in the individual states.

1857: The Indian Mutiny revolt against British colonial rule in India begins.

1859: Charles Robert Darwin (1809–1882), English naturalist, publishes his landmark work *On the Origin of Species by Means of Natural Selection.* This classic of science establishes the mechanism of natural selection of favorable, inherited traits or variations as the mechanism of his theory of evolution.

1860: The U.S. Congress institutes the U.S. Government Printing Office in Washington, D. C.

1861: The Civil War begins in the United States.

1861: The popular press begins in England with the publication of the *Daily Telegraph.*

1864: U.S. President Abraham Lincoln issues the Emancipation Proclamation, freeing the slaved in Union-occupied lands.

1865: The Civil War ends with the surrender of the secession states. The United States is reunified.

1865: President Lincoln is assassinated by John Wilkes Booth.

1865: The Thirteenth and Fourteenth Amendments to the U.S. Constitution are ratified. The Thirteenth Amendment outlaws slavery; the Fourteenth Amendment establishes all persons born or naturalized in the United States as U.S. citizens and extends equal protection under the law.

1867: Britain grants Canada home rule.

1869: The first transcontinental railroad across the United States is completed.

1870: The Franco-Prussian War (1870–1871) begins.

1871: The era of New Imperialism, or "empire for empire's sake," starts a multinational competition for colonies in Africa, Asia, and the Middle East.

1876: Alexander Bell files for a patent for the telephone.

1876: The American Library Association is founded in Philadelphia, Pennsylvania, by American librarian, Melvil Dewey (1851–1931), the founder of the decimal system of library classification.

1877: Reconstruction, the period of rebuilding and reunification following the U.S. Civil War, ends.

1884: International conference is held at Washington, D.C., at which Greenwich, England, is chosen as the common prime meridian for the entire world.

1885: Karl Benz invents in automobile in Germany.

1885: Louis Pasteur (1822–1895), French chemist, inoculates a boy, Joseph Meister, against rabies. He had been bitten by a mad dog and the treatment saves his life. This is the first case of Pasteur's use of an attenuated germ on a human being.

1886: Richard von Krafft-Ebing (1840–1902), German neurologist, publishes his landmark case history study of sexual abnormalities, *Psychopathia Sexualis*, and helps found the scientific consideration of human sexuality.

1890: The U.S. Census Bureau announces that the American frontier is closed.

1890: Herman Hollerith (1860–1929), American inventor, puts his electric sorting and tabulating machines to work on the U.S. Census. He wins this contract after a trial "run-off" with two other rival systems and his system performs in one year what would have taken eight years of hand tabulating. This marks the beginning of modern data processing.

1892: Ellis Island becomes chief immigration station of the eastern United States.

1893: Panic of 1893 triggers a three-year economic depression in the United States.

1893: Sigmund Freud (1856–1939), Austrian psychiatrist, describes paralysis originating from purely mental conditions and distinguishes it from that of organic origin.

1894: Thomas Alva Edison (1847–1931), American inventor, first displays his peep-show Kinetoscopes in New York. These demonstrations serve to stimulate research on the screen projection of motion pictures as well as entertain.

1896: Landmark Supreme Court of the United States decision, *Plessy v. Ferguson*, upholds racial segregation laws.

1897: Havelock Ellis (1859–1939), English physician, publishes the first of his seven-volume work *Studies in the Psychology of Sex.* This contributes to the more open discussion of human sexuality and supports sex education.

1898: *USS Maine* sinks in harbor in Havana, Cuba; Spanish-American War begins.

1900–1949

1901: Guglielmo Marconi (1874–1937), Italian electrical engineer, successfully sends a radio signal from England to Newfoundland. This is the first transatlantic telegraphic radio transmission and as such, is considered by most as the day radio is invented.

1903: Wright brothers make first successful flight of a controlled, powered airplane that is heavier than air.

1903: *The Great Train Robbery*, the first modern movie, debuts.

1904: Russo-Japanese War (1904–1905): Japan gains territory on the Asian mainland and becomes a world power.

1905: Albert Einstein (1879–1955), German-Swiss-American physicist, submits his first paper on the special theory of relativity titled "Zur Elektrodynamik bewegter Korpen." It states that the speed of light is constant for all conditions and that time is relative or passes at different rates for objects in constant relative motion. This is a fundamentally new and revolutionary way to look at the universe and it soon replaces the old Newtonian system.

1908: A. A. Campbell-Swinton of England first suggests the use of a cathode ray tube as both the transmitter (camera) and receiver. This is the first description of the modern, all-electronic television system.

1914: Assassination of Archduke Franz Ferdinand of Austria-Hungary and his wife, Sophie; World War I begins.

1914: Panama Canal is completed.

1914: The beginning of the massacre of 1.5 million Armenians by the Turkish government, later known as the Armenian Genocide.

1915: German U-boats sink the British passenger steamer *RMS Lusitania*.

1916: Easter Rising in Ireland begins fight for Irish independence.

1917: United States enters World War I, declaring war on Germany.

1917: The Russian Revolution begins as Bolsheviks overthrow the Russian monarchy.

1918: World War I ends.

1918: The Great Flu; nearly 20 million perish during the two-year pandemic.

1918: The Red Terror in Russia: Thousands of political dissidents are tried and imprisoned; 5 million die of famine as Communists collectivize agriculture and transform the Soviet economy.

1919: The ratification of the Nineteenth Amendment to the U.S. constitution gives women the right to vote.

1919: Mahatma Gandhi initiates satyagraha (truth force) campaigns, beginning his nonviolent resistance movement against British rule in India.

1920: Red Scare (1920–1922) in the United States leads to the arrest, trial, and imprisonment of suspected communist, socialist, and anarchist "radicals."

1920: KDKA, a Pittsburgh Westinghouse station, transmits the first commercial radio broadcast.

1922: 26 of Ireland's counties gain independence, the remaining six become Northern Ireland and remain under British rule.

1922: Mussolini forms Fascist government in Italy.

1925: Geneva Protocol, signed by sixteen nations, outlaws the use of poisonous gas as an agent of warfare.

1925: The Scopes Monkey Trial (July 10-25) in Tennessee debate the state's ban on the teaching of evolution.

1927: Charles Lindbergh makes the first solo nonstop transatlantic flight.

1928: Alexander Fleming discovers penicillin.

1929: Black Tuesday. The U.S. stock market crashes, beginning the Great Depression.

1930: Rubber condoms made of a thin latex are introduced.

1932: Hattie Wyatt Caraway of Arkansas is the first woman elected to the U.S. Senate.

1932: The Nazi party capture 230 seats in the German Reichstag during national elections.

1932: RCA (Radio Corporation of America) makes experimental television broadcasts from the Empire State Building in New York.

1933: Adolf Hitler named German chancellor.

1933: President Franklin D. Roosevelt announces the New Deal, a plan to revitalize the U.S. economy and provide relief in during the Great Depression. The U.S. unemployment rate reaches twenty-five percent.

1933: U.S. President Franklin Delano Roosevelt (1882–1945) makes the first of his "fireside chats" to the American people. He is the first national leader to use the radio medium comfortably and regularly to explain his programs and to garner popular support.

1935: Germany's Nuremburg Laws codify discrimination and denaturalization of the nation's Jews.

1938: Anti-Jewish riots across Germany. The destruction and looting of Jewish-owned businesses is know as *Kristalnacht*, "Night of the Broken Glass."

1938: Hitler marches into Austria; political and geographical union of Germany and Austria proclaimed. Munich Pact—Britain, France, and Italy agree to let Germany partition Czechoslovakia.

1939: U.S. declares its neutrality in World War II.

1939: Germany invades Poland. Britain, France, and Russia go to war against Germany.

1939: The Holocaust (Shoah) begins in German-occupied Europe. Jews are removed from their homes and relocated to ghettos or concentration camps. The *Einsatzgruppen*, or mobile killing squads, begin the execution of one million Jews, Poles, Russians, Gypsies, and others.

1939: Television debuts to the public at the World's Fair.

1941: The U.S. Naval base at Pearl Harbor, Hawaii, is bombed by Japanese Air Force. Soon after, the United States enters World War II, declaring war on Germany and Japan.

1941: The first Nazi death camp, Chelmno, opens. Victims, mainly Jews, are executed by carbon monoxide poisoning in specially designed killing vans.

1942: Executive Order 9066 orders the internment of Japanese immigrants and Japanese-American citizens for the duration of World War II.

1942: Enrico Fermi (1901–1954), Italian-American physicist, heads a Manhattan Project team at the University of Chicago that produces the first controlled chain reaction in an atomic pile of uranium and graphite. With this first self-sustaining chain reaction, the atomic age begins.

1943: Penicillin is first used on a large scale by the U.S. Army in the North African campaigns. Data obtained from these studies show that early expectations for the new drug are correct, and the groundwork is laid for the massive introduction

of penicillin into civilian medical practice after the war.

1945: Auschwitz death camp is liberated by allied forces.

1945: World War II and the Holocaust end in Europe.

1945: Atomic bombings of Hiroshima and Nagasaki; Japan surrenders on August 15.

1945: Trials of Nazi War criminals begin in Nuremberg, Germany.

1945: United Nations is established.

1945: Displaced Persons (DP) camps established throughout Europe to aid Holocaust survivors. In the three years following the end of World War II, many DPs immigrate to Israel and the United States.

1945: United States destroys the Japanese city of Hiroshima with a nuclear fission bomb based on uranium-235. Three days later a plutonium-based bomb destroys the city of Nagasaki. Japan surrenders on August 14 and World War II ends. This is the first use of nuclear power as a weapon.

1948: Gandhi assassinated in New Delhi.

1948: Soviets blockade of Berlin. United States and Great Britain begin airlift of fuel, food, and necessities to West Berlin. The event, the first conflict of the Cold War, became known as the Berlin Airlift (June 26-Sept 30, 1949).

1948: United Nations issues the Universal Declaration of Human Rights.

1948: Israel is established as an independent nation.

1948: American zoologist and student of sexual behavior Alfred C. Kinsey (1894–1956) first publishes his *Sexual Behavior in the Human Male*.

1949: South Africa codifies apartheid.

1949: Soviets test their first atomic device.

1950–1999

1950: President Truman commits U.S. troops to aid anti-Communist forces on the Korean Peninsula. The Korean War lasts from 1950 to 1953.

1951: First successful oral contraceptive drug is introduced. Gregory Pincus (1903–1967), American biologist, discovers a synthetic hormone that renders a woman infertile without altering her capacity for sexual pleasure. It soon is marketed in pill form and effects a social revolution with its ability to divorce the sex act from the consequences of impregnation.

1952: First hydrogen bomb is detonated by the U.S. on an atoll in the Marshall Islands.

1954: Sen. Joseph R. McCarthy begins hearings of the House Un-American Activities Committee, publicly accusing military officials, politicians, media, and others of Communist involvement.

1954: Landmark decision of the United States Supreme Court, *Brown v. Board of Education*, end of segregation of schools in the United States.

1955: Emmett Till, age 14, is brutally murdered for allegedly whistling at a white woman. The event galvanizes the civil rights movement.

1955: Rosa Parks refuses to give up her seat on a Montgomery, Alabama, bus to a white passenger, defying segregation.

1955: Warsaw Pact solidifies relationship between the Soviet Union and it communist satellite nations in Eastern Europe.

1957: President Eisenhower sends federal troops to Central High School in Little Rock, Ark., to enforce integration.

1957: Soviet Union launches the first satellite, Sputnik, into space. The Space Race between the USSR and the United States begins.

1958: Explorer I, first American satellite, is launched.

1960: African-American students in North Carolina begin a sit-in at a segregated Woolworth's lunch counter; the sit-in spread throughout the South.

1961: Soviet Cosmonaut Yuri Gagarin becomes first human in space.

1961: Berlin Wall is built.

1961: Bay of Pigs Invasion; the United States sponsors an to overthrow Cuba's socialist government but fails.

1962: *Silent Spring* published; environmental movement begins.

1962: Cuban Missile Crisis.

1963: Rev. Martin Luther King Jr., delivers his "I Have a Dream" speech at a civil rights march on Washington, D.C.

1963: The United States and the Soviet Union establish a direct telephone link called the "hot line" between the White House and the Kremlin. It is intended to permit the leaders of both countries to be able to speak directly and immediately to each other in times of crisis.

1964: U.S. President Lyndon Johnson announces ambitious social reform programs known as the Great Society.

1964: President Johnson signs the Civil Rights Act of 1964.

1965: March to Selma; state troopers and local police fight a crowd of peaceful civil rights demonstrators, including the Rev. Martin Luther King Jr., as the group attempted to cross a bridge into the city of Selma.

1965: First U.S. combat troops arrive in South Vietnam.

1965: Voting Rights Act prohibits discriminatory voting practices in the United States.

1965: Watts Riots: 35 people are killed and 883 injured in six days of riots in Los Angeles.

1966: Betty Friedan and other leaders of the feminist movement found the National Organization for Women (NOW).

1968: Rev. Martin Luther King Jr., is assassinated in Memphis, Tennessee.

1968: Cesar Chavez leads a national boycott of California table grape growers, which becomes known as "La Causa."

1969: Stonewall Riots in New York City spark the gay rights movement.

1969: United States successfully lands a manned mission, Apollo 11, on the moon.

1972: Arab terrorists massacre Israeli athletes at Olympic Games in Munich, Germany.

1973: *Roe v. Wade*; Landmark Supreme Court decision legalizes abortion on demand during the first trimester of pregnancy.

1973: The American Psychiatric Association removes the classification of homosexuality as a mental disorder.

1976: Steve Jobs and Steve Wozniak invent personal computer.

1977: International human rights advocacy group Amnesty International awarded the Noble Peace Prize.

1978: The Camp David Accord ends a three-decade long conflict between Israel and Egypt.

1979: Iran hostage crisis begins when Iranian students storm the U.S. embassy in Teheran. They hold 66 people hostage who are not released until 1981, after 444 days in captivity.

1980: President Carter announces that U.S. athletes will boycott Summer Olympics in Moscow to protest Soviet involvement in Afghanistan (Jan. 20).

1981: Urban riots breakout in several British cities, protesting lack of opportunity for minorities and police brutality.

1981: AIDS identified.

1986: U.S. space shuttle Challenger explodes 73 seconds after liftoff.

1987: U.S. President Ronald Reagan challenges Soviet leader Mikhail Gorbachev to open Eastern Europe and the Soviet Union to political and economic reform.

1989: Fall of the Berlin Wall.

1989: Tiananmen Square protest in Beijing, China.

1989: World Wide Web.

1989: The Internet revolution begins with the invention of the World Wide Web.

1991: Soviet Union dissolves.

1991: Persian Gulf War (January 16 -February 28); United States leads "Operation Desert Storm" to push Iraqi occupying forces out of Kuwait.

1992: U.S. and Russian leaders formally declare an end to the Cold War.

1992: L.A. Riots; The acquittal of four white police officers charged with police brutality in the beating of black motorist Rodney King sparks days of widespread rioting in Los Angeles.

1992: WHO (World Health Organization) predicts that by the year 2000, 30 to 40 million people will be infected with the AIDS-causing HIV. A Harvard University group argues the that the number could reach more than 100 million.

1993: A terrorist bomb explodes in basement parking garage of World Trade Center, killing six.

1994: First all-race elections in South Africa; Nelson Mandela elected president.

1998: Torture and murder of gay college student Matthew Shepherd.

1999: NATO forces in former Yugoslavia attempt to end mass killings of ethnic Albanians by Serbian forces in Kosovo.

2000–

2001: Terrorists attacks on the World Trade Center in New York and the Pentagon in Washington, D.C., killing 2,752.

2001: Controversial Patriot Act passed in the United States.

2001: United States and coalition forces begin War on Terror by invading Afghanistan (Operation Enduring Freedom), overthrowing the nation's Islamist Taliban regime in December 2001.

2002: Slobodan Milosevic begins his war crimes trial at the UN International Criminal Tribunal on charges of genocide and crimes against humanity. He is the first head of state to stand trial in an international war-crimes court, but died before the trial concluded.

2002: After U.S. and coalition forces depose Islamist Taliban regime in Afghanistan, girls are allowed to return to school and women's rights are partially restored in areas controlled by U.S. and coalition forces.

2003: U.S. space shuttle Columbia breaks apart upon re-entry, killing all seven crew members.

2003: United States and coalition forces invade Iraq.

2003: The United States declares an end to major combat operations in Iraq. As of June 2006, U.S. fighting forces remain engaged in Iraq.

2003: November 18, the Massachusetts Supreme Judicial court rules denying same-sex couples marriage rights violates the state constitution, legalizing same-sex marriages.

2004: Islamist terrorist bombing of commuter rail network in Madrid, Spain.

2005: Islamist terrorist bombings in London. Bombs simultaneously detonate in on the Underground and city buses.

Shaping Social Policy: Governments, Organizations, the International Community and the Individual

1

Shaping Social Policy: Governments, Organizations, the International Community and the Individual

Social policy involves more than the development of the welfare state or social programs. It encompasses a larger debate on the responsibilities of citizens and governments to meet basic human needs and promote equality and justice. The study of social policy requires thoughtful consideration of the following fundamental questions: What are basic human needs? How can individuals, organizations, and governments best meet those needs? Who, if anyone, is responsible for the welfare of others? What social ills can be addressed through policy? Who has the most resources, skill, and ability to address social ills? Who is most in need of aid? What kinds of aid should be given to individuals in need? Should aid be given to whole populations or nations in need? Who should give aid? Who should social policy most benefit? These basic questions underscore the elemental principles and tensions of all modern social policy.

Social policy is based on relationships among individuals, organizations, and governments. This chapter introduces the major actors in social policy movements, entities that form our collective response to social problems. Profiled in this chapter are the efforts of international agencies, national governments, nongovernmental organizations (NGOs), and private individuals to respond to social problems. Organizations under the umbrella of the United

Nations often lead cooperative efforts to address broad, global issues such as hunger and access to medical care. Profiles of nongovernmental organizations such as the International Red Cross and Habitat for Humanity demonstrate the commitment of organizations providing basic human needs. Articles such as "How Not to Help Our Poorer Brothers," "The Role of the State in Citizen's Lives," and "Civic Cooperation" frame a still controversial and timely century-old debate over the social policy responsibilities of national governments and individuals. This chapter also provides a brief introduction to some of the social policy issues that arise throughout the volume—hunger, healthcare, pensions and social security, housing, government welfare programs, legal aid, peace and security, property ownership, civil liberties, and discrimination.

Subsequent chapters of this volume are divided by time period, with the last two chapters covering current social policy issues. Implied in each chapter division is a shift—sometimes subtle, sometimes radical—in United States and international social policy. The editors encourage readers to approach material throughout this volume using the fundamental questions and concepts proposed here as a framework for critical analysis of social policy.

How Not to Help Our Poorer Brothers

Magazine article

By: Theodore Roosevelt

Date: 1897

Source: Roosevelt, Theodore, and Stead, W.T., eds. "How Not to Help Our Poorer Brothers." *Review of Reviews.* 15 (1897): 36.

About the Author: Theodore Roosevelt Jr., served as a New York State Assemblyman, the Police Commissioner of New York City, Assistant Secretary of the U.S. Navy, and other public offices before volunteering for military service during the Spanish-American War (1898). He helped lead the Rough Riders unit to fame during the war and was elected governor of New York later that year. In 1900 he was elected vice president of the United States on the Republican ticket, and in 1901 he became the nation's twenty-sixth president after the assassination of President William McKinley. Roosevelt held the office until 1909. As president he supported progressive reforms, such as greater government control over business and the conservation of nature. Dissatisfied with his successor, President Taft, Roosevelt ran for a third term in 1912 under the banner of the Progressive or "Bull Moose" Party. He finished second, ahead of Taft but behind Democrat Woodrow Wilson. Theodore Roosevelt's fifth cousin is Franklin D. Roosevelt, president of the United States from 1933 to 1945.

A portrait of a young, seated Theodore Roosevelt in 1885.
PHOTO BY MANSELL/MANSELL//TIME & LIFE PICTURES/GETTY IMAGES.

INTRODUCTION

Theodore Roosevelt authored many books and essays on a variety of topics, including his views on public policy, his experiences as an outdoorsman, and his take on historical figures and events. His article, "How Not to Help Our Poorer Brothers," was a response to a letter he received from Thomas Watson, a Populist Party candidate for vice-president in 1896. Watson wrote the letter to further explain his political ideals, which he believed Roosevelt had misrepresented in an earlier *Review of Reviews* article.

In that article, entitled, "The Three Vice-Presidential Candidates and What They Represent," Roosevelt had outlined his thoughts on the role of the vice-president in the United States, and gave his opinion about the three vice-presidential candidates. Watson's response explained his position concerning wealthy individuals who were leaders of companies and banks. Using his own family's legacy as an example, Watson explained that he wanted to see the wealthy play a greater role in governance, something he said they are able to do. Roosevelt, who was New York City's Police Commissioner at the time, began his response to the letter by saying he held Watson in high regard, and explained it was not Watson he was criticizing, but those who claimed to hold his views, but in reality had different motivations.

The late nineteenth century was a period in American history in which industrialization and commerce had built mighty corporations and monopolistic trusts, and brought tremendous wealth and power to those who controlled them. As a consequence, they lived lives of privilege, and had great influence over politics and society. The rise of industry had also led to the concentration of millions of people in cities like New York and Chicago to work in the factories. Many of them worked long hours in dangerous, difficult jobs, but earned little pay and lived in crowded slums. By the 1890s, the disparity between the lives of the privileged and the lot of the workingman had given rise to much criticism and demands for reform. Reformers, the Populist Party among them, wanted to use the power of government to control corporations, establish better working conditions, and improve the life of the poor in general. This would necessarily come at the expense of the rich, who many among the reformers felt were deliberately exploiting average Americans so they could live in ever-increasing luxury.

■ PRIMARY SOURCE

There are plenty of ugly things about wealth and its possessors in the present age, and I suppose there have been in all ages. There are many rich people who so utterly lack patriotism, or show such sordid and selfish traits of character, or lead such mean and vacuous lives, that all right-minded men must look upon them with angry contempt; but, on the whole, the thrifty are apt to be better citizens than the thriftless; and the worst capitalist cannot harm laboring men as they are harmed by demagogues.

As the people of a State grow more and more intelligent the State itself may be able to play a larger and larger part in the life of the community, while at the same time individual effort may be given freer and less restricted movement along certain lines; but it is utterly unsafe to give the State more than the minimum of power just so long as it contains masses of men who can be moved by the pleas and denunciations of the average Socialist leader of to-day. There may be better schemes of taxation than these at present employed; it may be wise to devise inheritance taxes, and to impose regulations on the kinds of business which can be carried on only under the especial protection of the State; and where there is a real abuse by wealth it needs to be, and in this country generally has been, promptly done away with; but the first lesson to teach the poor man is that, as a whole, the wealth in the community is distinctly beneficial to him; that he is better off in the long run because other men are well off; and that the surest way to destroy what measure of prosperity he may have is to paralyze industry and the well-being of those men who have achieved success.

I am not an empiricist; I would no more deny that sometimes human affairs can be much bettered by legislation than I would affirm that they can always be so bettered. I would no more make a fetish of unrestricted individualism than I would admit the power of the State offhand and radically to reconstruct society. It may become necessary to interfere even more than we have done with the right of private contract, and to shackle cunning as we have shackled force. All I insist upon is that we must be sure of our ground before trying to get any legislation at all, and that we must not expect too

much from this legislation, nor refuse to better ourselves a little because we cannot accomplish everything at a jump. Above all, it is criminal to excite anger and discontent without proposing a remedy, or only proposing a false remedy. The worst foe of the poor man is the labor leader, whether philanthropist or politician, who tries to teach him that he is a victim of conspiracy and injustice, when in reality he is merely working out his fate with blood and sweat as the immense majority of men who are worthy of the name always have done and always will have to do.

The difference between what can and what cannot be done by law is well exemplified by our experience with the negro problem, an experience of which Mr. Watson must have ample practical knowledge. The negroes were formerly held in slavery. This was a wrong which legislation could remedy, and which could not be remedied except by legislation. Accordingly they were set free by law. This having been done, many of their friends believed that in some way, by additional legislation, we could at once put them on an intellectual, social, and business equality with the whites. The effort has failed completely. In large sections of the country the negroes are not treated as they should be treated, and politically in particular the frauds upon them have been so gross and shameful as to awaken not merely indignation but bitter wrath; yet the best friends of the negro admit that his hope lies, not in legislation, but in the constant working of those often unseen forces of the national life which are greater than all legislation.

It is but rarely that great advances in general social well-being can be made by the adoption of some far-reaching scheme, legislative or otherwise; normally they come only by gradual growth, and by incessant effort to do first one thing, then another, and then another. Quack remedies of the universal cure-all type are generally as noxious to the body politic as to the body corporal.

Often the head-in-the-air social reformers, because people of sane and wholesome minds will not favor their wild schemes, themselves decline to favor schemes for practical reform. For the last two years there has been an honest effort in New York to give the city good government, and to work intelligently for better social conditions, especially in the poorest quarters. We have cleaned the streets; we have broken the power of the ward boss and the saloon-keeper to work injustice; we have destroyed the most hideous of the tenement houses in which poor people are huddled like swine in a sty; we have made parks and playgrounds for the children in the crowded quarters; in every possible way we have striven to make life easier and healthier and to give man and woman a chance to do their best work; while at the same time we have warred steadily against the pauper-producing, maudlin philanthropy of the free soup-kitchen and tramp lodging-house kind. In all this we have had practically no help from either the parlor socialists or the scarcely more noxious beer-room socialists, who are always howling about the selfishness of the rich and their unwillingness to do anything for those who are less well off.

There are certain labor unions, certain bodies of organized labor,—notably those admirable organizations which include the railway conductors, the locomotive engineers and the firemen,—which to my mind embody almost the best hope that there is for healthy national growth in the future; but bitter experience has taught men who work for reform in New York that the average labor leader, the average demagogue who shouts for a depreciated currency, or for the overthrow of the rich, will not do anything to help those who honestly strive to make better our civic conditions. There are immense numbers of workingmen to whom we can appeal with perfect confidence; but too often we find that a large proportion of the men who style themselves leaders of organized labor are influenced only by sullen, short-sighted hatred of what they do not understand, and are deaf to all appeals, whether to their national or to their civic patriotism.

What I most grudge in all this is the fact that sincere and zealous men of high character and honest purpose, men like Mr. Watson, men and women such as those he describes as attending his Populist meetings, or such as are to be found in all strata of our society, from the employer to the hardest-worked day laborer, go astray in their methods, and are thereby prevented from doing the full work for good they ought to. When a man goes on the wrong road himself he can do very little to guide others aright, even though these others are also on the wrong road. There are many wrongs to be righted; there are many measures of relief to be pushed; and it is a pity that when we are fighting what is bad and championing what is good, the men who ought to be our most effective allies should deprive themselves of usefulness by the wrong-headedness of their position. Rich men and poor men both do wrong on occasions, and whenever a specific instance of this can be pointed out all citizens alike should join in punishing the wrong-doer. Honesty and right-mindedness should be the tests; not wealth or poverty.

In our municipal administration here in New York we have acted with an equal band toward wrong-doers of high and low degree. The Board of Health condemns the tenement-house property of the rich landowner, whether this landowner be priest or layman, banker or railroad president, lawyer or manager of a real estate business; and it pays no heed to the intercession of any politician, whether this politician be Catholic or Protestant, Jew or Gentile. At the same time the Police Department promptly suppresses, not only the criminal, but the rioter. In other words, we do strict justice. We feel we are defrauded of help to which we are entitled when men who ought to assist in any work to better the condition of the people decline to aid us because their brains are turned by dreams only worthy of a European revolutionist.

Many workingmen look with distrust upon laws which really would help them; laws for the intelligent restriction of immigration, for instance. I have no sympathy with mere dislike of immigrants; there are classes and even nationalities of them which stand at least on an equality with the citizens of native birth, as the last election showed. But in the interest of our workingmen we must in the end keep out laborers who are ignorant, vicious, and with low standards of life and comfort, just as we have shut out the Chinese.

Often labor leaders and the like denounce the present conditions of society, and especially of our political life, for shortcomings which they themselves have been instrumental in causing. In our cities the misgovernment is due, not to the misdeeds of the rich, but to the low standard of honesty and morality among citizens generally; and nothing helps the corrupt politician more than substituting either wealth or poverty for honesty as the standard by which to try a candidate. A few months ago a socialistic reformer in New York was denouncing the corruption caused by rich men because a certain judge was suspected of giving information in advance as to a decision in a case involving the interests of a great corporation. Now this judge had been elected some years previously, mainly because he was supposed to be a representative of the "poor man"; and the socialistic reformer himself, a year ago, was opposing the election of Mr. Beaman as judge because he was one of the firm of Evarts & Choate, who were friends of various millionaires and were counsel for various corporations. But if Mr. Beaman had been elected judge no human being, rich or poor, would have dared so much as hint at his doing anything improper.

Something can be done by good laws; more can be done by honest administration of the laws; but most of all can be done by frowning resolutely upon the preachers of vague discontent; and by upholding the true doctrine of self-reliance, self-help, and self-mastery. This doctrine sets forth many things. Among them is the fact that though a man can occasionally be helped when he stumbles, yet that it is useless to try to carry him when he will not or cannot walk; and worse than useless to try to bring down the work and reward of the thrifty and intelligent to the level of the capacity of the weak, the shiftless, and the idle. It further shows that the maudlin philanthropist and the maudlin sentimentalist are almost as noxious as the demagogue, and that it is even more necessary to temper mercy with justice than justice with mercy.

The worst lesson that can be taught a man is to rely upon others and to whine over his sufferings.

If an American is to amount to anything he must rely upon himself, and not upon the State; he must take pride in his own work, instead of sitting idle to envy the luck of others; he must face life with resolute courage, win victory if he can and accept defeat if he must, without seeking to place on his fellow-men a responsibility which is not theirs.

Let me say, in conclusion, that I do not write in the least from the standpoint of those whose association is purely with what are called the wealth classes. The men with whom I have worked and associated most closely during the last couple of years here in New York, with whom I have shared what is at least an earnest desire to better social and civic conditions (neither blinking what is evil nor being misled by the apostles of a false remedy), and with whose opinions as to what is right and practical my own in the main agree, are not capitalists, save as all men who by toil earn, and with prudence save, money are capitalists. They include reporters on the daily papers, editors of magazines as well as of newspapers, principals in the public schools, young lawyers, young architects, young doctors, young men of business, who are struggling to rise in their profession by dint of faithful work, but who give some of their time to doing what they can for the city, and a number of priests and clergymen; but as it happens the list does not include any man of great wealth, or any of those men whose names are in the public mind identified with great business corporations. Most of them have at one time or another in their lives faced poverty and know what it is; none of them are more than well-to-do. They include Catholics and Protestants, Jews, and men who would be regarded as heterodox by professors of most recognized creeds; some of them were born on this side, others are of foreign birth; but they are all Americans, heart and soul, who fight out for themselves the battles of their own lives, meeting sometimes defeat and sometimes victory. They neither forget that man does owe a duty to his fellows, and should strive to do what he can to increase the well-being of the community; nor yet do they forget that in the long run the only way to help people is to make them help themselves. They are prepared to try any properly guarded legislative remedy for ills which they believe can be remedied; but they perceive clearly that it is both foolish and wicked to teach the average man who is not well off that some wrong or injustice has been done him, and that he should hope for redress elsewhere than in his own industry honest and intelligence.

SIGNIFICANCE

Roosevelt was himself a reformer, but as demonstrated in this article he did not believe that big business and the wealthy were inherently bad. In fact he thought that their success could help the country as a whole, and the poor as well. While he believed that some reform and control was necessary, he disagreed with those who felt that the system was exploitative by nature.

As president, Roosevelt put many of his political values into practice, persuading Congress to create the Bureau of Corporations to regulate big business. He filed his first antitrust suit against J. P. Morgan's Northern Securities Corporation. Roosevelt brought forty more such suits against big companies and regulated interstate commerce, drawing attention to his theory that equal footing for all American businesses and labor would benefit the common good. Big business was shocked by Roosevelt's efforts to decrease its power, while labor representatives said his reforms did not go far enough. During his presidency Roosevelt worked to provide protection to the working class, including the passage of food and drug safety laws. He also worked to protect natural resources, creating several national parks and wildlife reserves. He passed the National Monuments Act, protecting such places as the Grand Canyon.

Roosevelt and his supporters formed the Progressive Party in 1912, after the Republican Party rejected him as their nominee for presidency, despite his overwhelming success in the primaries. During the campaign, Roosevelt pushed for women's suffrage, an end to child labor, insurance for the unemployed, pensions for the elderly, and increased regulation of business trusts. Roosevelt lost the election, but is credited for initiating reforms that came about in later years, after his death in 1919. He won the Nobel Peace Prize in 1906 for his role in mediating the Russo-Japanese War.

Many of Roosevelt's writings have contributed to American political and social thought. His first book, "Naval War of 1812," which he began while a student at Harvard University, was required reading on naval strategy at the naval academy for many years. "How Not to Help Our Poorer Brother" was included in his 1897 publication "American Ideals," which includes essays about his theory of politics. In many of his works, Roosevelt stressed such virtues as fairness, hard work, and the moral duty to help the poor.

FURTHER RESOURCES
Books
Miller, Nathan. *Theodore Roosevelt: A Life*. New York: William Morrow and Company, 1992.

Roosevelt, Theodore. *American ideals, and other essays, social and political.* New York, London: G.P. Putnam's sons., 1897.

———. *Theodore Roosevelt: An Autobiography.* New York: MacMillan, 1913.

Periodicals

Roosevelt, Theodore. "The Three Vice-Presidential Candidates and What They Represent." *Review of Reviews.* 14 (September 1896): 289–91.

Web sites

Public Broadcasting Service (PBS). The American Experience: The Presidents. ":The Story of Theodore Roosevelt." 2003 <http://www.pbs.org/wgbh/amex/presidents/26_t_roosevelt/t_roosevelt_domestic.html> (accessed May 26, 2006).

Robert Marion LaFollette. © CORBIS.

The Danger Threatening Representative Government

Speech

By: Robert M. La Follette Sr.

Date: 1897

Source: *Wisconsin Historical Society.* "Excerpts from Robert M. LaFollette's speech: 'The Danger Threatening Representative Government.'" <http://www.wisconsinhistory.org/teachers/lessons/lafollette/pdfs/lfspeech.pdf> (accessed May 28, 2006).

About the Author: Robert M. La Follette Sr. (1855–1925) was a nineteenth- and twentieth-century politician from Wisconsin. With his wife, an active feminist, he championed populist causes, founding the Progressive Party in 1924 and running for U.S. president. La Follette served in the U.S. House of Representatives, as governor of Wisconson, and in the U.S. Senate.

INTRODUCTION

Robert M. La Follette Sr. was born in Wisconsin in 1855. He attended the University of Wisconsin and was elected to the U.S. House of Representatives in 1885. Returning to Wisconsin in 1891, he staked out a strongly populist platform and ran for various positions, ultimately reaching the governor's office in 1900. During his term as governor he was instrumental in reforming Wisconsin politics. He also adopted radical new political techniques, such as taking private political disputes to the general public in order to force a compromise.

La Follette was an unabashedly progressive politician best characterized as a populist. Populism is a political movement primarily concerned with the rights of individuals. Populists generally take the perspective that individuals are broadly mistreated by powerful forces within society, including the wealthy, the government, and corporations. Populists advocate the use of government authority to reduce the influence of these elite groups. Populism as a philosophy has enjoyed recurring popularity throughout U.S. history, though the short-lived Populist Party vanished during the nineteenth century.

Following his election to the U.S. Senate in 1906, La Follette retained his seat until his death in 1825. Although a populist, La Follette initially aligned himself with the Republican Party, achieving significant political reforms in his home state of Wisconsin. In 1924, a platform dispute convinced La Follette that his goals would not be achieved with the Republicans, and he left their ranks to launch the League for Progressive Political Action, better known as the Progressive Party. La Follette entered the 1924 presidential race as the Progressive candidate, garnering thirteen electoral votes.

La Follette was a vigorous reformer, tirelessly articulating populist doctrines in numerous speeches. Among his targets, corporations were frequently vilified as stealing the labor of the poor in order to expand the estates of the wealthy.

▋ PRIMARY SOURCE

What is it then that is swelling the ranks of the dissatisfied? Is it not a growing conviction in state after state, that we are fast being dominated by forces that thwart the will of the people and menace representative government?

Since the birth of this Republic, indeed almost within the last generation, a new and powerful factor has taken its place in our business, financial and political world and is there exercising a tremendous influence.

The existence of the corporation, as we have it with us today, was never dreamed of by the fathers. Until the more recent legislation, of which it is the product, the corporation was regarded as a purely public institution. The corporation of today has invaded every department of business and its powerful but invisible hand is felt in almost all the activities of life. From the control of great manufacturing plants to the running of bargain counters, from the operation of railways to the conduct of cheese factories, and from the management of each of these singly to the consolidation of many into one of gigantic proportions,—the corporation has practically acquired dominion over the business world. The effect of this change upon the American people is radical and rapid. The individual is fast disappearing as a business factor and in his stead is this new device, the modern corporation. I repeat, the influence of this change upon character cannot be overestimated. The business man at one time gave his individuality, stamped his mental and moral characteristics upon the business he conducted. He thought as much of bequeathing his business reputation to his son, as he did of bequeathing the business upon which that reputation had been so deeply impressed. This made high moral attributes a positive essential in business life, and marked business character everywhere.

Today the business once transacted by individuals in every community is in the control of corporations, and many of the men who once conducted an independent business are gathered into the organization, and all personal identity, and all individuality lost. Each man has become a mere cog in one of the wheels of a complicated mechanism. It is the business of the corporation to get money. It exacts but one thing of its employees: Obe-

dience to orders. It cares not about their relations to the community, the church, society, or the family. It wants full hours and faithful service, and when they die, wear out or are discharged, it quickly replaces them with new material. The corporation is a machine for making money, but it reduces men to the insignificance of mere numerical figures, as certainly as the private ranks of the regular army....

I do not wish to be misunderstood. The corporation, honestly operated in the function of a public servant and in certain lines as a business instrumentality purely, has an unlimited field of opportunity and usefulness in this country. As a public servant, as a business instrumentality, the corporation is everywhere,—before the courts, in the legislature and at the bar of public opinion, entitled to the same measure of consideration, the same even-handed justice as the individual. I have the same contempt for the demagogue who assails a corporation solely because it is a corporation, that I have for the ready tool, who surrenders his conscience in its dishonest service.

■▬▬

SIGNIFICANCE

In La Follette's account, corporate evolution in America followed a clear progression, beginning with individual workers and progressing through multiple stages before finally reaching the enormous conglomerates he claimed posed a threat to the nation itself. Consistent with this perspective, La Follette consistently supported trade unions as a restraint on unchecked corporate power.

One hundred fifty years after his birth, the legacy of populist Robert La Follette and his movement still remains. Speaking in 2003, journalist Bill Moyers described the populist movement as a tradition dating to the birth of the nation: men and women fighting inequality in general and specifically the preferential treatment frequently afforded the wealthy. He noted that the founders of the United States rejected a property ownership requirement for office holders as inconsistent with the principles on which the Union was formed. Presidents Thomas Jefferson and Andrew Jackson, each in his own time, fought to overcome forces perceived as giving inequitable privilege to a minority of wealthy individuals.

Enormous grants of government-owned land given to the railroads were among the government misdeeds that La Follette and his contemporaries saw and criticized. Also, tariffs kept consumer prices high and helped corporations become entrenched and profitable. Moyers also describes federal monetary policy that rewarded creditors (the wealthy) and destroyed borrowers (the poor).

While the Populist Party itself was short-lived and relatively unsuccessful, many of its ideas outlived it, becoming part of the public consciousness and informing federal legislation. Populism remains a vital force in contemporary American politics. Though the two major parties of La Follette's day remain in power, populist sentiment frequently rears its head in the face of government or corporate excess. In the wake of the Enron scandal, in which employees were paid with ultimately worthless stock options while executives awarded themselves large cash bonuses, populist sentiment has stirred again. The passage of the Sarbanes-Oxley Act of 2002, which specifically requires corporate executives to sign off on financial results rather than claiming ignorance and passing the blame for misdeeds to underlings, represents populism at its best.

Populism has always been fueled by frustration and outrage at the perception that those in authority have taken advantage of their position to benefit themselves and their allies. Yet once the most extreme inequities are addressed, all but the most committed and vocal populists typically lose interest in the cause. As an inherently reactionary movement, populism appears doomed to remain forever an outsider, a referee assessing the behavior of the more central players. Given populism's inherent distrust of government, it appears somewhat better suited to the role of watchdog and critic than of a majority party.

FURTHER RESOURCES
Books

Goodwyn, Lawrence. *The Populist Movement: A Short History of the Agrarian Revolt in America.* New York: Oxford University Press, 1978.

Lukacs, John. *Democracy and Populism: Fear and Hatred.* London: Yale University Press, 2005.

McGerr, Michael. *A Fierce Discontent: The Rise and Fall of the Progressive Movement in America, 1870–1920.* New York: Oxford University Press, 2005.

Unger, Nancy C. *Fighting Bob La Follette: The Righteous Reformer.* Chapel Hill: University of North Carolina Press, 1999.

Periodicals

"The Return of Populism." *Economist* 378 (2006): 39–40.

Baldwin, William. "Bigness and Badness." *Forbes* 177 (2006): 16.

Roberts, Kenneth M. "Populism, Political Conflict, and Grass-Roots Organization in Latin America." *Comparative Politics* 38 (2006): 127–148.

Web sites

Moyers, Bill. "This Is Your Story—The Progressive Story of America. Pass It On." June 10, 2003 <http://www.com-mondreams.org/views03/0610–11.htm> (accessed May 28, 2006).

The Nation. "The Rise of Market Populism: America's New Religion." October 12, 2000 <http://www.then-ation.com/doc/20001030/frank> (accessed May 28, 2006).

Wisconsin Historical Society. "La Follette and the Progressive Era." <http://www.wisconsinhistory.org/teachers/lessons/lafollette/> (accessed May 28, 2006).

Theodore Roosevelt on the Role of the State in Its Citizen's Lives

Speech

By: Theodore Roosevelt

Date: December 30, 1900

Source: Roosevelt, Theodore. *The Strenuous Life.* New York: Review of Reviews, 1904.

About the Author: Theodore Roosevelt (1858–1919) served as president of the United States from 1901 to 1909. A progressive reformer and strong nationalist, he delivered this address before members of the Young Men's Christian Association at Carnegie Hall in New York.

INTRODUCTION

President Theodore Roosevelt lived in an age of enormous political and business corruption. A Progressive reformer, he argued that Christian ethics could cure the ills of the nation. He promoted a nationalist vision that involved preserving order and advancing American culture. He encouraged young men to follow his example.

Roosevelt became president in 1901 upon the assassination of William McKinley (1843–1901). He soon became known as a trust buster because he attacked business monopolies, arguing that every businessman should have the same chance to get ahead. He sought to keep out the crooks and protect the competent, striking a balance between free enterprise and corporate responsibility.

Despite his reform credentials, Roosevelt was a conservative who spoke often about the virtues of government. He viewed public service as the highest call-

Theodore Roosevelt delivers a firey address to a crowd of 50,000 on July 21, 1915. AP IMAGES.

ing, asserting that the United States needed a dynamic federal government to hold together the innovators and opportunists within its borders. Government would serve as a check on evil, a pervasive force throughout the world, according to the president. A devout member of the Dutch Reformed Church, he firmly believed in the existence of sin. He argued that people would use their strength to oppress others unless stopped by good men. Roosevelt believed that such good men needed to be sound in body as well as in mind to contribute to the national well-being.

The Young Men's Christian Association (YMCA) was founded in London in 1844 and brought to the United States in 1851. The middle-class Protestant men who began the organization sought to provide a buffer between young men away from home for the first time and the dangers of the city. Emphasizing the triangle of mind, body, and spirit, they aimed to build a Christian superman who would be sober, moral, and physically fit to face the perils of the modern age.

PRIMARY SOURCE

It is a peculiar pleasure to me to come before you tonight to greet you and to bear testimony to the great good that has been done by these Young Men's and Young Women's Christian Associations throughout the United States. More and more we are getting to recognize the law of combination. This is true of many phases in our industrial life, and it is equally true of the world of philanthropic effort. Nowhere is it, or will it ever be, possible to supplant individual effort, individual initiative; but in addition to this there must be work in combination. More and more this is recognized as true not only in charitable work proper, but in that best form of philanthropic endeavor where we all do good to ourselves by all joining together to do good to one another. This is exactly what is done in your associations.

It seems to me that there are several reasons why you are entitled to especial recognition from all who are interested in the betterment of our American social system. First and foremost, your organization recognizes the vital need of brotherhood, the most vital of all our needs here in this great Republic. The existence of a Young Men's or Young Women's Christian Association is certain proof that some people at least recognize in practical shape the identity of aspiration and interest, both in things material and in things higher, which must be widespread through the masses of our people if our national life is to attain full development. This spirit of brotherhood recognizes of necessity both the need of self-help and also the need of helping others in the only way which ever ultimately does great good, that is, of helping them to help themselves. Every man of us needs such help at some time or another, and each of us should be glad to stretch out his hand to a brother who stumbles. But while every man needs at times to be lifted up when he stumbles, no man can afford to let himself be carried, and it is worth no man's while to try thus to carry some one else. The man who lies down, who will not try to walk, has become a mere cumberer of the earth's surface.

These Associations of yours try to make men self-helpful and to help them when they are self-helpful. They do not try merely to carry them, to benefit them for the moment at the cost of their future undoing. This means that all in any way connected with them not merely retain but increase their self-respect. Any man who takes part in the work of such an organization is benefited to some extent and benefits the community to some extent—of course, always with the proviso that the organization is well managed and is run on a business basis, as well as with a philanthropic purpose.

The feeling of brotherhood is necessarily as remote from a patronizing spirit, on the one hand, as from a spirit of envy and malice, on the other. The best work for our uplifting must be done by ourselves, and yet with brotherly kindness for our neighbor. In such work, and therefore in the kind of work done by the Young Men's Christian Associations, we all stand on the self-respecting basis of mutual benefit and common effort. All of us who take part in any such work, in whatever measure, both receive and confer benefits....

Besides developing this sense of brotherhood, the feeling which breeds respect both for one's self and for others, your Associations have a peculiar value in showing what can be done by acting in combination without aid from the State. While on the one hand it has become evident that under the conditions of modern life we can not allot the unlimited individualism which may work harm to the community, it is no less evident that the sphere of the State's action should be extended very cautiously, and so far as possible only where it will not crush out healthy individual initiative. Voluntary action by individuals in the form of associations of any kind for mutual betterment or mutual advantage often offers a way to avoid alike the dangers of State control and the dangers of excessive individualism. This is particularly true of efforts for that most important of all forms of betterment, moral betterment—the moral betterment which usually brings material betterment in its train.

It is only in this way, by all of us working together in the spirit of brotherhood, by each doing his part for the betterment of himself and of others, that it is possible for us to solve the tremendous problems with which as a nation we are now confronted. Our industrial life has become so complex, its rate of movement so very rapid, and the specialization and differentiation so intense that we find ourselves face to face with conditions that were practically unknown in this nation half a century ago. The power of the forces of evil have been greatly increased, and it is necessary for our self-preservation that we should similarly strengthen the forces for the good. We are all of us bound to work toward this end. No one of us can do everything, but each of us can do something, and if we work together the aggregate of these somethings will be very considerable....

It ought not to be necessary for me to warn you against mere sentimentality, against the philanthropy and charity which are not merely insufficient but harmful. It is eminently desirable that we should none of us be hard-hearted, but it is no less desirable that we should not be soft-headed. I really do not know which quality is most productive of evil to mankind in the long run, hardness of heart or softness of head. Naked charity is not what we permanently want. There are of course certain classes, such as young children, widows with large families, or crippled or very aged people, or even strong men temporarily crushed by stunning misfortune, on whose behalf we may have to make a frank and direct appeal to charity, and who can be the recipients of it without any loss of self-respect. But taking us as a whole, taking the mass of Americans, we do not want charity, we do not want sentimentality; we merely want to learn how to act both individually and together in such fashion as to enable us to hold our own in the world, to do good to others according to the measure of our opportunities, and to receive good from others in ways which will not entail on our part any loss of self-respect....

So far, what I have had to say has dealt mainly with our relations to one another in what may be called the service of the State. But the basis of good citizenship is the home. A man must be a good son, husband, and father, a woman a good daughter, wife, and mother, first and foremost. There must be no shirking of duties in big things or in little things. The man who will not work hard for his wife and his little ones, the woman who shrinks from bearing and rearing many healthy children, these have no place among the men and women who are striving upward and onward. Of course the family is the foundation of all things in the States. Sins against pure and healthy family life are those which of all others are sure in the end to be visited most heavily upon the nation in which they take place. We must beware, moreover, not merely of the great sins, but of the lesser ones which when taken together cause such an appalling aggregate of misery and wrong. The drunkard, the lewd liver, the coward, the liar, the dishonest man, the man who is brutal to or neglectful of parents, wife, or children—of all of these the shrift should be short when we speak of decent citizenship. Every ounce of effort for good in your Associations is part of the ceaseless war against the traits which produce such men. But in addition to condemning the grosser forms of evil we must not forget to condemn also the evils of bad temper, lack of gentleness, nagging and whining fretfulness, lack of consideration for others—the evils of selfishness in all its myriad forms. Each man or woman must remember his or her duty to all around, and especially to those closest and nearest, and such remembrance is the best possible preparation for doing duty for the State as a whole.

We ask that these Associations, and the men and women who take part in them, practice the Christian doctrines which are preached from every true pulpit. The Decalogue and the Golden Rule must stand as the foundation of every successful effort to better either our social or our political life. "Fear the Lord and walk in his ways" and "Love thy neighbor as thyself"—when we practice these two precepts, the reign of social and civic righteousness will be close at hand. Christianity teaches not only that each of us must so live as to save his own soul, but that each must also strive to do his whole duty by his neighbor. We can not live up to these teachings as we should; for in the presence of infinite might and infinite wisdom, the strength of the strongest man is but weakness, and the keenest of mortal eyes see but dimly. But each of us can at least strive, as light and strength are given him, toward the ideal. Effort along any one line will not suffice. We must not only be good, but strong. We must not only be high-minded, but brave-hearted. We must think loftily, and we must also work hard. It is not written in the Holy Book that we must merely be harmless as doves. It is also written that we must be wise as serpents. Craft unaccompanied by conscience makes the crafty man a social wild beast who preys on the community and must be hunted out of it. Gentleness and sweetness unbacked by strength and high resolve are almost impotent for good.

The true Christian is the true citizen, lofty of purpose, resolute in endeavor, ready for a hero's deeds, but never looking down on his task because it is cast in the day of small things; scornful of baseness, awake to his own duties as well as to his rights, following the higher law with reverence, and in this world doing all that in him lies, so that when death comes he may feel that mankind is in some degree better because he has lived.

SIGNIFICANCE

Theodore Roosevelt remains as controversial in the twenty-first century as he was during his lifetime. Some historians continue to view him as a perennial adolescent, proto-fascist, sheer opportunist, or a combination of all three. Others insist that he was a sophisticated conservative or a sincere and enlightened progressive. Virtually everyone agrees that Roosevelt was a fervent nationalist and a remarkable president who set the stage for much of the American foreign and domestic policies of the twentieth century.

A man of surpassing charm, extraordinary charisma, and broad intellectual interests, Roosevelt was a curious combination of realist and idealist, pragmatist and moral absolutist. In practice, his idealism and intellectualism were diluted by his love of power. As a young politician, he had once argued that the United States was engaged in a fateful struggle for markets, prestige, and power. As president, the more mature Roosevelt concluded that the nation's real interests lay in a stable world balance of power. He was the first president to understand and respond constructively to both the domestic and international changes that had been created by the industrial revolution.

FURTHER RESOURCES
Books

Friedenberg, Robert V. *Theodore Roosevelt and the Rhetoric of Militant Decency.* New York: Greenwood Press, 1990.

Harbaugh, William H. *The Life and Times of Theodore Roosevelt.* New York: Oxford University Press, 1975.

Watts, Sarah Lyons. *Rough Rider in the White House: Theodore Roosevelt and the Politics of Desire.* Chicago: University of Chicago Press, 2003.

Theodore Roosevelt on Manhood and Statehood

Speech

By: Theodore Roosevelt

Date: August 2, 1901

Source: Roosevelt, Theodore. "Manhood and Statehood." Address at the Quarter-Centennial Celebration of Statehood in Colorado, Colorado Springs, August 2, 1901.

About the Author: Theodore Roosevelt (1858–1919) served as president of the United States from 1901–1909. A progressive reformer and strong nationalist, he became the model for subsequent presidents by doing everything that was not specifically prohibited to the president by the Constitution.

INTRODUCTION

At the beginning of the twentieth century, many white middle-class Americans feared that a shift in lifestyle from manual labor and frontier expansionism to professional careers and urban living could result in weakening America's next generation of manhood. President Theodore Roosevelt created a new image of masculinity that combined education, physical strength, and rugged individualism. He urged men to live a "strenuous life" by emulating his model.

Roosevelt first discussed the requirements of the strenuous life in a speech in Chicago in 1899. He celebrated body vigor as a method of getting soul vigor. He argued that personal success could be achieved by some natural power or innate gift in an individual. Accomplishments in this category derived from a skill or virtue that no amount of training or willpower could create in an ordinary man. A much more common type of success was that achieved by hard labor. It

President Theodore Roosevelt. © BETTMANN/CORBIS.

required responsible and mature judgment as well as careful planning and the willingness to work long hours. The strenuous life did not necessarily have to involve military triumphs, but could be something as sedate as writing poetry, as long as the poet also took risks and worked hard.

To Roosevelt, the strenuous life involved the actions through which individuals and societies achieve meaning in history, as exemplified by his mention of the pioneers' pressing toward the country's westward boundaries in his speech. Success was the reward for refusing to shrink from the hardships and dangers of life, and Americans should demand of their nation as a whole what they demanded from themselves.

■ PRIMARY SOURCE

MANHOOD AND STATEHOOD

This anniversary, which marks the completion by Colorado of her first quarter-century of Statehood, is of interest not only to her sisters, the States of the Rocky Mountain region, but to our whole country. With the exception of the admission to Statehood of California, no other event emphasized in such dramatic fashion the full

meaning of the growth of our country as did the incoming of Colorado.

It is a law of our intellectual development that the greatest and most important truths, when once we have become thoroughly familiar with them, often because of that very familiarity grow dim in our minds. The westward spread of our people across this continent has been so rapid, and so great has been their success in taming the rugged wilderness, turning the gray desert into green fertility, and filling the waste and lonely places with the eager, thronging, crowded life of our industrial civilization, that we have begun to accept it all as part of the order of Nature. Moreover, it now seems to us equally a matter of course that when a sufficient number of the citizens of our common country have thus entered into and taken possession of some great tract of empty wilderness, they should be permitted to enter the Union as a State on an absolute equality with the older States, having the same right both to manage their own local affairs as they deem best, and to exercise their full share of control over all the affairs of whatever kind or sort in which the nation is interested as a whole. The youngest and the oldest States stand on an exact level in one indissoluble and perpetual Union.

To us nowadays these processes seem so natural that it is only by a mental wrench that we conceive of any other as possible. Yet they are really wholly modern and of purely American development. When, a century before Colorado became a State, the original thirteen States began the great experiment of a free and independent Republic on this continent, the processes which we now accept in such matter-of-course fashion were looked upon as abnormal and revolutionary. It is our own success here in America that has brought about the complete alteration in feeling. The chief factor in producing the Revolution, and later in producing the War of 1812, was the inability of the mother country to understand that the freemen who went forth to conquer a continent should be encouraged in that work, and could not and ought not to be expected to toil only for the profit or glory of others. When the first Continental Congress assembled, the British Government, like every other government of Europe at that time, simply did not know how to look upon the general question of the progress of the colonies save from the standpoint of the people who had stayed at home. The spread of the hardy, venturesome backwoodsmen was to most of the statesmen of London a matter of anxiety rather than of pride, and the famous Quebec Act of 1774 was in part designed with the purpose of keeping the English-speaking settlements as a hunting-ground for savages, a preserve for the great fur-trading companies; and as late as 1812 this project was partially revived.

.... Under any governmental system which was known to Europe, the problem offered by the westward thrust, across a continent, of so masterful and liberty-loving a race as ours would have been insoluble. The great civilized and colonizing races of antiquity, the Greeks and the Romans, had been utterly unable to devise a scheme under which when their race spread it might be possible to preserve both national unity and local and individual freedom. When a Hellenic or Latin city sent off a colony, one of two things happened. Either the colony was kept in political subjection to the city or state of which it was an offshoot, or else it became a wholly independent and alien, and often a hostile, nation. Both systems were fraught with disaster. With the Greeks race unity was sacrificed to local independence, and as a result the Greek world became the easy prey of foreign conquerors. The Romans kept national unity, but only by means of a crushing centralized despotism.

When the modern world entered upon the marvelous era of expansion which began with the discoveries of Columbus, the nations were able to devise no new plan. All the great colonizing powers, England, France, Spain, Portugal, Holland, and Russia, managed their colonies primarily in the interest of the home country. Some did better than others,—England probably best and Spain worst,—but in no case were the colonists treated as citizens of equal rights in a common country. Our ancestors, who were at once the strongest and the most liberty-loving among all the peoples who had been thrust out into new continents, were the first to revolt against this system; and the lesson taught by their success has been thoroughly learned.

In applying the new principles to our conditions we have found the Federal Constitution a nearly perfect instrument. The system of a closely knit and indestructible union of free commonwealths has enabled us to do what neither Greek nor Roman in their greatest days could do. We have preserved the complete unity of an expanding race without impairing in the slightest degree the liberty of the individual. When in a given locality the settlers became sufficiently numerous, they were admitted to Statehood, and thenceforward shared all the rights and all the duties of the citizens of the older States. As with Columbus and the egg, the expedient seems obvious enough nowadays, but then it was so novel that a couple of generations had to pass before we ourselves thoroughly grasped all its features. At last we grew to accept as axiomatic the two facts of national union and local and personal freedom. As whatever is axiomatic seems commonplace, we now tend to accept what has been accomplished as a mere matter-of-course incident, of no great moment. The very completeness with which the vitally

important task has been done almost blinds us to the extraordinary nature of the achievement.

You, the men of Colorado, and, above all, the older among those whom I am now addressing, have been engaged in doing the great typical work of our people. Save only the preservation of the Union itself, no other task has been so important as the conquest and settlement of the West. This conquest and settlement has been the stupendous feat of our race for the century that has just closed. It stands supreme among all such feats. The same kind of thing has been in Australia and Canada, but upon a less important scale, while the Russian advance in Siberia has been incomparably slower. In all the history of mankind there is nothing that quite parallels the way in which our people have filled a vacant continent with self-governing commonwealths, knit into one nation. And of all this marvelous history perhaps the most wonderful portion is that which deals with the way in which the Pacific Coast and the Rocky Mountains were settled.

The men who founded these communities showed practically by their life-work that it is indeed the spirit of adventure which is the maker of commonwealths. Their traits of daring and hardihood and iron endurance are not merely indispensable traits for pioneers; they are also traits which must go to the make-up of every mighty and successful people. You and your fathers who built up the West did more even than you thought; for you shaped thereby the destiny of the whole Republic, and as a necessary corollary profoundly influenced the course of events throughout the world. More and more as the years go by this Republic will find its guidance in the thought and action of the West, because the conditions of development in the West have steadily tended to accentuate the peculiarly American characteristics of its people.

There was scant room for the coward and the weakling in the ranks of the adventurous frontiersmen—the pioneer settlers who first broke up the wild prairie soil, who first hewed their way into the primeval forest, who guided their white-topped wagons across the endless leagues of Indian-haunted desolation, and explored every remote mountain-chain in the restless quest for metal wealth. Behind them came the men who completed the work they had roughly begun: who drove the great railroad systems over plain and desert and mountain pass; who stocked the teeming ranches, and under irrigation saw the bright green of the alfalfa and the yellow of the golden stubble supplant the gray of the sage-brush desert; who have guilt great populous cities—cities in which every art and science of civilization are carried to the highest point—on tracts which, when the nineteenth century had passed its meridian, were still known only to the grim rappers and hunters and the red lords of the wilderness with whom they waged eternal war.

Such is the record of which we are so proud. It is a record of men who greatly dared and greatly did; a record of wanderings wider and more dangerous than those of the Vikings; a record of endless feats of arms, of victory after victory in the ceaseless strife waged against wild man and wild nature. The winning of the West was the great epic feat in the history of our race....

It would be a sad and evil thing for this country if ever the day came when we considered the great deeds of our forefathers as an excuse for our resting slothfully satisfied with what has been already done. On the contrary, they should be an inspiration and appeal, summoning us to show that we too have courage and strength; that we too are ready to dare greatly if the need arises; and, above all, that we are firmly bent upon that steady performance of every-day duty which, in the long run, is of such incredible worth in the formation of national character.

The old iron days have gone, the days when the weakling died as the penalty of inability to hold his own in the rough warfare against his surroundings. We live in softer times. Let us see to it that, while we take advantage of every gentler and more humanizing tendency of the age, we yet preserve the iron quality which made our forefathers and predecessors fit to do the deeds they did. It will of necessity find a different expression now, but the quality itself remains just as necessary as ever. Surely you men of the West, you men who with stout heart, cool head, and ready hand have wrought out your own success and built up these great new commonwealths, surely you need no reminder of the fact that if either man or nation wishes to play a great part in the world there must be no dallying with the life of lazy ease. In the abounding energy and intensity of existence in our mighty democratic Republic there is small space indeed for the idler, for the luxury-loving man who prizes ease more than hard, triumph-crowned effort.

We hold work not as a curse but as a blessing, and we regard the idler with scornful pity. It would be in the highest degree undesirable that we should all work in the same way or at the same things, and for the sake of the real greatness of the nation we should in the fullest and most cordial way recognize the fact that some of the most needed work must, from its very nature, be unremunerative in the material sense. Each man must choose so far as the conditions allow him the path to which he is bidden by his own peculiar powers and inclinations. But if he is a man he must in some way or shape do a man's work. If, after making all the effort that his strength of body and of mind permits, he yet honorably fails, why, he is still entitled to a certain share of respect because he has made the effort. But if he does not make the effort,

or if he makes it half-heartedly and recoils from the labor, the risk, or the irksome monotony of his task, why, he has forfeited all right to our respect, and has shown himself a mere cumberer of the earth. It is not given to us all to succeed, but it is given to us all to strive manfully to deserve success....

To be a good husband or a good wife, a good neighbor and friend, to be hard-working and upright in business and social relations, to bring up many healthy children— to be and to do all this is to lay the foundations of good citizenship as they must be laid. But we can not stop even with this. Each of us has not only his duty to himself, his family, and his neighbors, but his duty to the State and to the nation. We are in honor bound each to strive according to his or her strength to bring ever nearer the day when justice and wisdom shall obtain in public life as in private life. We can not retain the full measure of our self-respect if we can not retain pride in our citizenship. For the sake not only of ourselves but of our children and our children's children we must see that this nation stands for strength and honesty both at home and abroad. In our internal policy we can not afford to rest satisfied until all that the government can do has been done to secure fair dealing and equal justice as between man and man. In the great part which hereafter, whether we will or not, we must play in the world at large, let us see to it what we neither do wrong nor shrink from doing right because the right is difficult; that on the one hand we inflict no injury, and that on the other we have a due regard fro the honor and the interest of our mighty nation; and that we keep unsullied the renown of the flag which beyond all others of the present time or of the ages of the past stands for confident faith in the future welfare and greatness of mankind.

SIGNIFICANCE

Roosevelt lived in an age of imperialism. The struggle for national survival had given way to a larger contest among nations seeking to dominate the global balance of power. As the staunchly imperialist Roosevelt argued in multiple speeches on the strenuous life, the United States could not afford to isolate itself from developments in world politics. In 1901, the United States still remained mired in a controversial war in the Philippines, the islands acquired from Spain in the Spanish-American War of 1898. Roosevelt insisted that Americans had to remain in the islands as part of a responsibility to do a share of the world's work and elevate the quality of life of racial minorities. Additionally, a policy of isolationism would be self-defeating. To keep the thriving domestic economy, Americans needed to hold its own in the competition for naval and trade advantages. This involved building up power outside of U.S. borders, such as in the Philippines.

With his ideas, Roosevelt established the foundation of American foreign policy for much of the twentieth century. As subsequent presidents would argue, American national interests involved much more than making the world safe for capitalism and overseas corporate investments. Commercial prosperity and material well-being were only aspects of being American. As a great country, the United States had the obligation to act upon loftier duties. It had to protect and advance other nations around the globe. In time, Roosevelt would support American entrance into World War I for just these reasons.

FURTHER RESOURCES

Books

Bederman, Gail. *Manliness and Civilization: A Cultural History of Gender and Race in the United States, 1880–1917.* Chicago: University of Chicago Press, 1996.

Friedenberg, Robert V. *Theodore Roosevelt and the Rhetoric of Militant Decency.* New York: Greenwood Press, 1990.

Harbaugh, William H. *The Life and Times of Theodore Roosevelt.* New York: Oxford University Press, 1975.

Watts, Sarah Lyons. *Rough Rider in the White House: Theodore Roosevelt and the Politics of Desire.* Chicago: University of Chicago Press, 2003.

Civic Cooperation

Book excerpt

By: Jane Addams

Date: 1912

Source: Addams, Jane. *Twenty Years at Hull-House with Autobiographical Notes.* New York: The MacMillan Co., 1912.

About the Author: Jane Addams was an active advocate for a variety of social causes. She co-founded Hull-House, a social settlement in Chicago. She helped launch the National Association for the Advancement of Colored People (NAACP), and in 1931 became the first American woman to win the Nobel Peace Prize.

INTRODUCTION

As cities rapidly expanded during the late nineteenth century, a variety of social problems began to flourish within them. Many of these problems particularly afflicted the poor and their children, who often fended for themselves while their parents labored in the newly opened factories. In an era prior to the modern safety net of government aid programs and institutionalized assistance, little help was available for the working poor.

These problems of rapid growth were not limited to the United States; similar situations existed in most of the industrialized nations, and a variety of solutions were proposed and tried. In England, a unique approach was developed during the 1880s when a London vicar invited several university students to live with him and his wife in a poor urban neighborhood. Whereas other approaches to urban improvement centered on the quality and quantity of services offered, this method focused on the value of good citizens within a community. Toynbee Hall was founded in 1884, and its success led to similar settlements in other nations. Five years later, Jane Addams and Ellen Starr rented a large abandoned home on Chicago's West Side, which they named Hull-House after the home's builder.

The neighborhood surrounding Hull-House was fertile soil for the women's urban improvement efforts. Most of the area's residents were recent immigrants from more than a dozen nations in Europe. Richard Lindberg, describing the neighborhood around Hull-House, termed it "the darkest corner of Chicago," a place rife with crime, bribery, and corruption. Brothels and saloons lined the streets and opium was readily available. Criminals unable to make it in other parts of Chicago often drifted to the West Side, and the overcrowded neighborhood was among the most blighted in the country.

Addams was particularly moved by the plight of the children, who faced an uncertain and unsafe future with few opportunities. One of the first programs offered at Hull-House was a kindergarten and nursery school that quickly filled and had a lengthy waiting list. Mothers bringing their children to the school found a side room specifically set aside for them to sit and talk comfortably.

Older children were also cared for. Addams created a club for teenage boys who frequently found their way into crime. She also organized classes in sewing for teenage girls, many of whom would otherwise be recruited to work as prostitutes. Educational programs were offered free of charge, including appearances by such noted speakers as John Dewey,

Jane Addams sitting with a group of children at Hull House. AP/WIDE WORLD PHOTOS. REPRODUCED BY PERMISSION.

Susan B. Anthony, and Frank Lloyd Wright. The hungry were fed, and the homeless found a place to sleep. Hull-House became a model of social work in an area desperately needing assistance.

■ PRIMARY SOURCE

One of the first lessons we learned at Hull-House was that private beneficence is totally inadequate to deal with the vast numbers of the city's disinherited. We also quickly came to realize that there are certain types of wretchedness from which every private philanthropy shrinks and which are cared for only in those wards of the county hospital provided for the wrecks of vicious living or in the city's isolation hospital for smallpox patients.

I have heard a broken-hearted mother exclaim when her erring daughter came home at last too broken and

diseased to be taken into the family she had disgraced, "There is no place for her but the top floor of the County Hospital; they will have to take her there," and this only after every possible expedient had been tried or suggested. This aspect of governmental responsibility was unforgettably borne in upon me during the smallpox epidemic following the World's Fair, when one of the residents, Mrs. Kelley, as State Factory Inspector, was much concerned in discovering and destroying clothing which was being finished in houses containing unreported cases of smallpox. The deputy most successful in locating such cases lived at Hull-House during the epidemic because he did not wish to expose his own family. Another resident, Miss Lathrop, as a member of the State Board of Charities, went back and forth to the crowded pest house which had been hastily constructed on a stretch of prairie west of the city. As Hull-House was already so exposed, it seemed best for the special smallpox inspectors from the Board of Health to take their meals and change their clothing there before they went to their respective homes. All of these officials had accepted without question and as implicit in public office the obligation to carry on the dangerous and difficult undertakings for which private philanthropy is unfitted, as if the commonalty of compassion represented by the State was more comprehending than that of any individual group.

Certainly the need for civic cooperation was obvious in many directions, and in none more strikingly than in that organized effort which must be carried on unceasingly if young people are to be protected from the darker and coarser dangers of the city. The cooperation between Hull-House and the Juvenile Protective Association came about gradually, and it seems now almost inevitably. From our earliest days we saw many boys constantly arrested, and I had a number of most enlightening experiences in the police station with an Irish lad whose mother upon her deathbed had begged me "to look after him." We were distressed by the gangs of very little boys who would sally forth with an enterprising leader in search of old brass and iron, sometimes breaking into empty houses for the sake of the faucets or lead pipe which they would sell for a good price to a junk dealer. With the money thus obtained they would buy cigarettes and beer or even candy, which could be conspicuously consumed in the alleys where they might enjoy the excitement of being seen and suspected by the "coppers." From the third year of Hull-House, one of the residents held a semiofficial position in the nearest police station; at least, the sergeant agreed to give her provisional charge of every boy and girl under arrest for a trivial offense.

Mrs. Stevens, who performed this work for several years, became the first probation officer of the Juvenile Court when it was established in Cook County in 1899. She was the sole probation officer at first, but at the time of her death, which occurred at Hull-House in 1900, she was the senior officer of a corps of six. Her entire experience had fitted her to deal wisely with wayward children. She had gone into a New England cotton mill at the age of thirteen, where she had promptly lost the index finger of her right hand, through "carelessness" she was told, and no one then seemed to understand that freedom from care was the prerogative of childhood. Later she became a typesetter and was one of the first women in America to become a member of the typographical union, retaining her "card" through all the later years of editorial work. As the Juvenile Court developed, the committee of public-spirited citizens who first supplied only Mrs. Stevens' salary later maintained a corps of twenty-two such officers; several of these were Hull-House residents

who brought to the house for many years a sad little procession of children struggling against all sorts of handicaps. When legislation was secured which placed the probation officers upon the payroll of the county, it was a challenge to the efficiency of the civil service method of appointment to obtain by examination men and women fitted for this delicate human task. As one of five people asked by the civil service commission to conduct this first examination for probation officers, I became convinced that we were but at the beginning of the nonpolitical method of selecting public servants, but even stiff and unbending as the examination may be, it is still our hope of political salvation.

In 1907, the Juvenile Court was housed in a model court building of its own, containing a detention home and equipped with a competent staff. The committee of citizens largely responsible for this result thereupon turned their attention to the conditions which the records of the court indicated had led to the alarming amount of juvenile delinquency and crime. They organized the Juvenile Protective Association, whose twenty-two officers meet weekly at Hull-House with their executive committee to report what they have found and to discuss city conditions affecting the lives of children and young people.

The association discovers that there are certain temptations into which children so habitually fall that it is evident that the average child cannot withstand them. An overwhelming mass of data is accumulated showing the need of enforcing existing legislation and of securing new legislation, but it also indicates a hundred other directions in which the young people who so gaily walk our streets, often to their own destruction, need safeguarding and protection.

The effort of the association to treat the youth of the city with consideration and understanding has rallied the most unexpected forces to its standard. Quite as the basic needs of life are supplied solely by those who make money out of the business, so the modern city has assumed that the craving for pleasure must be ministered to only by the sordid. This assumption, however, in a large measure broke down as soon as the Juvenile Protective Association courageously put it to the test. After persistent prosecutions, but also after many friendly interviews, the Druggists' Association itself prosecutes those of its members who sell indecent postal cards; the Saloon Keepers' Protective Association not only declines to protect members who sell liquor to minors, but now takes drastic action to prevent such sales; the Retail Grocers' Association forbids the selling of tobacco to minors; the Association of Department Store Managers not only increased the vigilance in their waiting rooms by supplying more matrons, but as a body they have become regular contributors to the association; the special watchmen in all the railroad yards agree not to arrest trespassing boys but to report them to the association; the firms manufacturing moving picture films not only submit their films to a volunteer inspection committee, but ask for suggestions in regard to new matter; and the Five-Cent Theaters arrange for "stunts" which shall deal with the subject of public health and morals, when the lecturers provided are entertaining as well as instructive.

It is not difficult to arouse the impulse of protection for the young, which would doubtless dictate the daily acts of many a bartender and poolroom keeper if they could only indulge it without giving their rivals an advantage. When this difficulty is removed by an even-handed enforcement of the law, that simple kindliness which the innocent always evoke goes from one to another like a slowly spreading flame of good will. Doubtless the most rewarding experience in any such undertaking as that of the Juvenile Protective Association is the warm and intelligent cooperation coming from unexpected sources— official and commercial as well as philanthropic. Upon the suggestion of the association, social centers have been opened in various parts of the city, disused buildings turned into recreation rooms, vacant lots made into gardens, hiking parties organized for country excursions, bathing beaches established on the lake front, and public schools opened for social purposes. Through the efforts of public-spirited citizens a medical clinic and a Psychopathic Institute have become associated with the Juvenile Court of Chicago, in addition to which an exhaustive study of court-records has been completed. To this carefully collected data concerning the abnormal child, the Juvenile Protective Association hopes in time to add knowledge of the normal child who lives under the most adverse city conditions.

SIGNIFICANCE

Hull-House gradually expanded over the years, eventually encompassing twelve buildings and most of a city block. In addition to direct services such as the kindergarten and other educational programs, it was also home to extensive research efforts. Investigators at the center painstakingly researched and chronicled the demographics of the surrounding neighborhoods. Their work, published as "The Hullhouse Maps and Papers," included extensive statistical analysis, including color-coded maps showing income levels on different blocks.

In addition to helping Hull-House in its local efforts, the research had other important effects; most significantly, it helped redefine poverty as an economic condition rather than a moral failure. This new perspective was instrumental in the birth of Sociology as a field of scientific study. A second important project was conducted by Dr. Bayard Holmes, who spent two years assessing the physical growth of children. Dr. Holmes was able to statistically demonstrate that children employed in factories had slower physical development than children in schools. This finding proved important in efforts to expand child labor laws.

Over time, Jane Addams' experiences at Hull-House brought her recognition as an expert in social work. She was asked to serve on the boards of numerous organizations and she became active in politics. President Theodore Roosevelt proclaimed that her efforts had placed the scandal of the slums before the eyes of the entire nation, and she was awarded the Nobel Peace Prize in 1931. When Jane Addams died in 1935, mourners from around the world mourned her passing, and she was eulogized in the local press as "Saint Jane."

Hull-House remained open until 1963; the original building of the settlement has been preserved as a museum.

FURTHER RESOURCES

Books

Bryan, Mary Lynn McCree. *The Selected Papers of Jane Addams: Volume 1, Preparing to Lead, 1860–81.* Champaign, Ill.: University of Illinois Press, 2003.

Dilberto, Gioia. *A Useful Woman: The Early Life of Jane Adams.* New York: Scribner, 1999.

Elshtain, Jean Bethke. *Jane Addams and the Dream of American Democracy.* New York: Basic Books, 2001.

Periodicals

Grace, Clement. "Embodied Care: Jane Addams, Maurice Merleau-Ponty, and Feminist Ethics." *NWSA Journal* 18 (2006): 224–226.

Hamington, Maurice. "Public Pragmatism: Jane Addams and Ida B. Wells on Lynching." *Journal of Speculative Philosophy* 19 (2005): 167–174.

Ross-Sheriff, Fariyal and Mary E. Swignoski. "Women, War, and Peace Building." *Journal of Women and Social Work* 21 (2006): 129–132.

Web sites

National Association of Social Workers. <http://www.naswdc.org> (accessed June 11, 2006).

Jane Addams Hull House. <http://www.hullhouse.org/about.asp> (accessed June 11, 2006).

U.S. Department of Labor. "Social Workers." <http://www.bls.gov/oco/ocos060.htm> (accessed June 11, 2006).

The Diffusion of Property Ownership

Magazine article

By: Herbert Hoover

Date: April, 1927

Source: Hoover, Herbert. "The Diffusion of Property Ownership." *Proceedings of the Academy of Political Science in the City of New York.* 11 (1925): 137–139.

About the Author: Herbert Hoover was the thirty-first President of the United States, serving from 1929–1933. His presidency was marred by the stock market crash and the early years of the Great Depression. He spent his later years as an advocate for humanitarian and reform causes.

INTRODUCTION

Presidencies are often defined by economic events. This relationship is so commonly observed that political commentators frequently sum up the political importance of a healthy economy with the expression, "It's the economy, stupid." President Jimmy Carter was unable to reduce double-digit inflation and interest rates, contributing to his demise; his successor Ronald Reagan, though responsible for spiraling federal deficits, was reelected in a landslide due largely to the rapidly growing economy. President Bill Clinton's impeachment and removal might have succeeded had he not presided over one of the strongest economies on record.

President Herbert Hoover is frequently contrasted with his replacement, Franklin Roosevelt, who is credited with leading the United States out of the Depression and through World War II. Roosevelt's legacy is as author of the New Deal. Hoover's name was appropriated by individuals hard-hit by the Depression who named the small clusters of shacks they inhabited "Hoovervilles."

Hoover found himself traversing uncharted territory. His belief that the economy would quickly rebound was shared by most economists, thus he was reluctant to interfere in the economy. Hoover declined to take immediate steps to shore up the banking system, possibly failing to curtail the severity of the Depression. By the time Hoover formulated a relief program, the country was deep into decline.

In the years before his presidency, Hoover's extensive efforts in public service clearly demonstrated his

President Herbert Hoover. THE LIBRARY OF CONGRESS.

genuine dedication to humanitarian concerns. Hoover was conducting business in London when the start of World War I stranded more than 100,000 Americans in the city. At the request of the U.S. government, he was instrumental in getting these citizens safely back to the United States. Later that year, the U.S. Ambassador to Belgium asked Hoover to coordinate humanitarian relief efforts to the beleaguered nation. From 1914–1917, Hoover guided an effort that gathered tons of food and thousands of dollars for relief. He later coordinated massive wartime efforts to save food in the United States for distribution to embattled Europe.

Hoover was named Secretary of Commerce in 1921, an office he held under two presidents. While in office, he helped end twelve-hour workdays in steel mills. He also organized numerous conferences to address social issues, such as child labor and sanitary housing.

■ PRIMARY SOURCE

The Diffusion of Property Ownership

I regret my inability to attend the dinner which you are so finely enjoying tonight. It is a little difficult, however, to attend two public dinners at the same moment, especially when they are two hundred miles apart, and I have had to compromise by making my participation with you through a ten-minute message by telephone.

I am deeply interested in your discussion tonight because I am convinced that one of the continuous and underlying problems of sustained democracy is the constant and wider diffusion of property ownership. Indeed I should become fatalistic of ultimate destruction of democracy itself if I believed that the result of all of our invention, all our discovery, all our increasing economic efficiency and all our growing wealth would be toward the further and further concentration of ownership. In the large vision we have a wider diffusion of ownership today than any other nation in the world. It has been so since the beginning of the Republic. In our enormous growth in wealth there have been periods when the tendencies were toward concentration of ownership and other periods when economic forces (and public action) made toward greater diffusion. Certainly the forces of diffusion were dominant during the great migration which occupied the West. And the economic shift of the last war has been still another period of increasing diffusion of ownership of property. Our high real wages during the past three years, with consequent general expansion of savings, have, I believe, also marked another period of wider diffusion of property ownership.

It is appropriate that the evidences and the tendencies in this matter should be earnestly examined. We are all fundamentally interested that our economic forces, our public and private policies, should be so directed that with our increasing wealth the tendencies of diffusion of ownership shall be greater than the tendencies of concentration. And if we would grow in standards of living it is equally important that we shall maintain this dominant tendency without destruction of the moral, spiritual and economic impulses of production.

We are woefully lacking in actual facts upon this most important question. From the vast fund of statistical information in the nation we can only indicate tendencies, and then only with some uncertainty. Aside from our inability to determine more than bare tendencies we are unable from the information we have to make the proper and necessary distinction between distribution of wealth, diffusion of ownership, and diffusion of control of wealth— all equally important in any consideration of social as well as economic questions.

For the purposes of analysis of diffusion of ownership we might divide property ownership into two categories: on the one hand bank deposits, bonds, mortgages, preferred stocks, in other words, the prior lien securities; and on the other hand the equities generally, as represented by common stocks, land holdings, stocks of goods, tools etc. If we were to make such a division I believe we should find

that the high real wages and the vast increase of savings of the past few years have brought about an extraordinary diffusion of what we might call the prior lien ownership. No doubt savings among the people at large first seek the direction of greatest safety by their investment in such prior liens. The vast increase in number of savings banks and other distributed deposits, the great growth of industrial and life insurance, the large expansion of the building and loan associations, and the unprecedented absorption of all sorts of governmental securities in small sales all evidence this. In this direction there appears to be an undoubted increase in diffusion of ownership.

The ownership of common stock, land, homes, current goods and other forms which include the equity are, however, the part of the property which carries the control of management, and which in the long run participates most largely in the growth of national wealth. It is in increasing the diffusion of ownership in this area that we shall secure a contribution to the powerful forces which make for social stability. There are a multitude of problems in it when we come to close range. He who owns in this field must take larger risks. That here are many indications of a movement toward diffusion in this field also is indicated by your discussions. The increase in common stock holdings by employees, by consumers and the public, and in a way also the increase in mutualized banks and insurance companies, the increased volume of operations by farmers' cooperatives, tend toward such a movement.

But there is another field of equity ownership—that of home ownership—where I regret to say that we are going backwards. For twenty years the national ratio of owned homes has fallen slowly and slightly, but steadily. This may be accounted from by special reasons.

In the matter of distribution of wealth as distinguished from diffusion of ownership we have but little fact basis upon which to proceed outside of the income-tax statistics. While they show superficially that a diffusion of wealth is increasing yet the exemptions are such as to destroy much of their statistical usefulness. Again we have little information as to the diffusion or concentration of the control of wealth as distinguished from ownership. My impression is that the establishment of the Federal Reserve System and the effect of the Restraint of Trade laws and the inheritance taxes all tend to make for diffusion in this direction also. But at every turn in the study of distribution of wealth and of ownership of control we are confronted with a woeful lack of accurate data.

One of the first requisites for adequate economic discussion, and thus the development of any economic or social policy, must be the determination of the economic fact. We can adduce economic argument, we can point out economic tendencies, but until we have so searching an examination of these questions that we can evaluate them in actual quantities, whether it is dollars or good, we shall be far afield from the truth. I have seen forty economic arguments in opposition destroyed by one single affirmative argument when quantitative determination was attached to each of them.

I believe your discussions will be a valuable contribution to this subject. The elaboration and development of sound ideas is, of course, the first and fundamental step towards well directed national impulse and national action, and if from your discussion can come the development of method by which we can secure more searching, scientific investigation, more accurate determination of fact, you will have made a great accomplishment.

SIGNIFICANCE

Herbert Hoover was a consistent and vocal advocate of individual home ownership. In numerous speeches, he vividly portrayed the home as the economic and moral building block of America, noting that personal home ownership was a primary goal of virtually every citizen. In 1931, Hoover oversaw the Conference on Home Building and Home Ownership, at which he described home ownership as the key to happier marriages, stronger children, and better citizenship. While idealistic in his tone, Hoover was convinced of the benefits of widespread home ownership and firm in his commitment to make that vision a reality.

After his presidential term ended, Hoover remained active on behalf of numerous important causes. He continued to work for hunger relief in Finland and other nations and served on the boards of several educational and charitable organizations, donating his entire federal pension to benevolent causes.

In the twenty-first century, home ownership remains a top goal for most Americans. A 2002 federal report used language strikingly similar to Hoover's to describe home ownership, labeling it the cornerstone of healthy communities and the foundation of family financial security. Home ownership in 2005 was at an all-time high of seventy percent, up from sixty-five percent just ten years before. Disparities do remain: young families (those under age thirty-five) had ownership rates of less than forty-five percent. The report found that minorities were also less likely to own homes; Hispanic and African-American ownership rates remain below fifty-percent.

Some regions of the United States face particular difficulties related to home ownership. The state of California lags the rest of the nation in home ownership rates, largely because of median home prices that by 2005 were $300,000 above the national average. Residents of some rural regions and inner-city areas still face problems securing safe and sanitary housing. The U.S.-Mexico border region remains home to several thousand colonias, small unincorporated developments filled with substandard homes lacking plumbing and electricity and lying outside the reach of city zoning authorities.

FURTHER RESOURCES
Books

Dexter, Walter Friar. *Herbert Hoover and American Individualism: A Modern Interpretation of a National Ideal*. New York: MacMillan Co., 1932 .

Myers, William Starr (ed). *The State Papers and Other Public Writings of Herbert Hoover, vol. 2*. Garden City, California: Doubleday, Doran and Co., 1934.

Nash, George H. *Life of Herbert Hoover: The Humanitarian, 1914–1917*. New York: W. W. Norton, 1988.

Periodicals

"Analysis of the Changing Influences on Traditional Households' Ownership Patterns." *Journal of Urban Economics*. 39(1996):318-341.

Masnick, George S. "Home Ownership Trends and Racial Inequality in the United States in the 20th Century." *Joint Center for Housing Studies, Harvard University*. 2001.

Nevin, Alan. "Homeownership in California." *A CBIA Economic Treatise*. (2006):1–11.

Web sites

Herbert Hoover Presidential Library and Museum. "Herbert Hoover Presidential Library and Museum." <http://hoover.archives.gov/> (accessed July 5, 2006).

U.S. Department of Housing and Urban Development. "Fair Housing and Equal Opportunity." <http://www.hud.gov/offices/fheo/index.cfm> (accessed June 2,2006).

The White House. "Herbert Hoover." <http://www.whitehouse.gov/history/presidents/hh31.html> (accessed July 5, 2006).

Justice as Fairness: Political not Metaphysical

Journal article

By: John Rawls

Date: 1985

Source: Rawls, John. "Justice as Fairness: Political not Metaphysical." *Philosophy and Public Affairs* 14, 3 (1985): 226–230.

About the Author: John Rawls (1921–2002) was a renowned professor of political philosophy at Harvard University. He obtained his PhD at Princeton University in 1950. Rawls was a prolific writer and made many significant academic contributions over his career, particularly in the area of criminal justice philosophy. Among his best-known works are his books *A Theory of Justice* (1971), *The Law of Peoples* (1999) and *Justice as Fairness* (2001). .

INTRODUCTION

The work of John Rawls has played a significant role in reviving interest in philosophical questions of justice. The publication of his 1971 book *A Theory of Justice* was met with immediate accolades, sold over two hundred thousand copies, and was translated into twelve languages. The primary focus of Rawl's *Theory of Justice* was his conception of justice as fairness, an intuitive moral conception of justice, based in the belief that "each person possesses an inviolability founded on justice that even the welfare of society as a whole cannot override." This theory posits an approach for the creation of just and equal social policy within constitutional democracies. His perspective is discussed in the primary source, excerpted from a 1985 article.

■ PRIMARY SOURCE

There are, of course, many ways in which political philosophy may be understood, and writers at different times, faced with different political and social circumstances, understand their work differently. Justice as fairness I would now understand as a reasonably systematic and practicable conception of justice for a constitutional democracy, a conception that offers an alternative to the dominant utilitarianism of our tradition of political thought. Its first task is to provide a more secure and acceptable basis for constitutional principles and basic rights and liberties than utilitarianism seems to allow. The need for such a political conception arises in the following way.

There are periods, sometimes long periods, in the history of any society during which certain fundamental questions give rise to sharp and divisive political controversy, and it seems difficult, if not impossible, to find any shared basis of political agreement. Indeed, certain questions may prove intractable and may never be fully settled. One task of political philosophy in a democratic society is to focus on such questions and to examine whether some underlying basis of agreement can be uncovered and a mutually acceptable way of resolving these questions publicly established. Or if these questions cannot be fully settled, as may well be the case, perhaps the divergence of opinion can be narrowed sufficiently so that political cooperation on a basis of mutual respect can still be maintained.

The course of democratic thought over the past two centuries or so makes plain that there is no agreement on the way basic institutions of a constitutional democracy should be arranged if they are to specify and secure the basic rights and liberties of citizens and answer to the claims of democratic equality when citizens are conceived as free and equal persons.

A deep disagreement exists as to how the values of liberty and equality are best realized in the basic structure of society.

What must be shown is that a certain arrangement of the basic structure, certain institutional forms, are more appropriate for realizing the values of liberty and equality when citizens are conceived as such persons, that is (very briefly), as having the requisite powers of moral personality that enable them to participate in society viewed as a system of fair cooperation for mutual advantage. So to continue, the two principles of justice (mentioned above) read as follows:

1. Each person has an equal right to a fully adequate scheme of equal basic rights and liberties, which scheme is compatible with a similar scheme for all.

2. Social and economic inequalities are to satisfy two conditions: first, they must be attached to offices and positions open to all under conditions of fair equality of opportunity; and second, they must be to the greatest benefit of the least advantaged members of society.

Each of these principles applies to a different part of the basic structure; and both are concerned not only with basic rights, liberties, and opportunities, but also with the claims of equality; while the second part of the second principle underwrites the worth of these institutional guarantees. The two principles together, when the first is given priority over the second, regulate the basic institutions which realize these values. But these details, although important, are not our concern here.

We must now ask: how might political philosophy find a shared basis for settling such a fundamental question as that of the most appropriate institutional forms for liberty and equality? Of course, it is likely that the most that can be done is to narrow the range of public disagreement. Yet even firmly held convictions gradually change: religious toleration is now accepted, and arguments for persecution are no longer openly professed; similarly, slavery is rejected as inherently unjust, and however much the aftermath of slavery may persist in social practices and unavowed attitudes, no one is willing to defend it. We collect such settled convictions as the belief in religious toleration and the rejection of slavery and try to organize the basic ideas and principles implicit in these convictions into a coherent conception of justice. We can regard these convictions as provisional fixed points which any conception of justice must account for if it is to be reasonable for us. We look, then, to our public political culture itself, including its main institutions and the historical traditions of their interpretation, as the shared fund of implicitly recognized basic ideas and principles. The hope is that these ideas and principles can be formulated clearly enough to be combined into a conception of political justice congenial to our most firmly held convictions. We express this by saying that a political conception of justice, to be acceptable, must be in accordance with our considered convictions, at all levels of generality, on due reflection (or in what I have called "reflective equilibrium").

The public political culture may be of two minds even at a very deep level. Indeed, this must be so with such and enduring controversy as that concerning the most appropriate institutional forms to realize the values of liberty and equality. This suggests that if we are to succeed in finding a basis of public agreement, we must find a new way of organizing familiar ideas and principles into a conception of political justice so that the claims in conflict, as previously understood, are seen in another light. A political conception need not be an original creation but may only articulate familiar intuitive ideas and principles so that they can be recognized as fitting together in a somewhat different way than before. Such a conception may, however, go further than this: it may organize these familiar ideas and principles by means of a more fundamental intuitive idea within the complex structure of which the other familiar intuitive ideas are then systematically connected and related. In justice as fairness, as we shall see in the next section, this more fundamental idea is that of society as a system of fair social cooperation between free and equal persons. The concern of this section is how we might find a public basis of political agreement. The point is that a conception of justice will only be able to achieve this aim if it provides a reasonable way of shaping into one coherent view the deeper bases of agreement embedded in the public political culture of a constitutional regime and acceptable to its most firmly held considered convictions.

SIGNIFICANCE

In his book, Rawls asks the reader to imagine that a group of individuals wish to create a just social con-

tract—the foundation for a just and peaceful society. He suggests that the only means by which they may make truly objective decisions about what is most fair and just is if they operate from behind a "veil of ignorance"—if no one is aware of his or her own social status, race, gender, economic position or religion. Without an awareness of these basic indicators of identity, an individual would not know his or her position in the social hierarchy, whether he or she is near the top or at the bottom. Therefore, assuming with Hobbes that individuals are self-interested and wish to maximize their pleasure and minimize their discomfort, and not knowing how the decisions made will effect one's own situation, the rational choice is to choose policies that are fair. Each person will press for social structures and institutions that are in the best interests of all citizens and that are inherently just, because he or she would not want to risk ending up at the bottom of the social hierarchy in an intolerant and unjust society.

According to Rawls' theory, the decisions made by a rational person from behind the "veil of ignorance" will necessarily conform to two basic principles of justice, which he outlines. First, the "liberty principle": "each person has an equal right to a fully adequate scheme of equal basic liberties which is compatible with a similar scheme of liberties for all." Essentially, Rawls is arguing that the first principle of justice is that each person is given basic freedoms and rights, and as many freedoms and rights as possible, without impeding on the rights of any other individual. This is essentially a libertarian conception of freedom that believes that the rights of one individual end only where the rights of another begin. The types of liberties that Rawls is arguing for are political freedom (the right to vote and to run for public office), freedom of speech, integrity of the person and the right to own personal property, freedom from arbitrary arrest and seizure, and the liberty of consciousness, or freedom of thought, including freedom of religion. These are the types of freedoms that are enshrined in the constitutions of most liberal democracies. The second principle of justice is the "difference principle": "social and economic inequalities are to be arranged so that they are both a) reasonably expected to be to everyone's advantage [including the most disadvantaged persons] and b) attached to positions and offices [that are] open to all." While the liberty principle guarantees moral equality to all people, the difference principle acknowledges that real-world conditions and competition between individuals will lead to social and economic differences—inequalities. The difference principle states that these inequalities are acceptable, providing that those who are in advantaged positions utilize their wealth and power for the betterment of society as a whole and providing that all individuals have an opportunity to attain these positions of power. In the United States and almost every democratic country in the world, for example, a basic education is provided to each child free of charge, paid for by the taxes of citizens. In this sense, all children are given equal opportunity to become educated and to work their way into positions of power. What this theory does not adequately account for are the many sources of inequality and prejudice that may constrain individuals' ability to succeed in a competitive, capitalist society. Equal opportunity does not necessarily mean equal access for all.

Rawls' conception of the "veil of ignorance" is as a philosophical construct—a useful tool for understanding how governments and societies can become more equal and just. While policy makers in our society cannot literally get behind the "veil of ignorance" in order to make decisions, in order for any individual or group of persons to create just policy, they necessarily must attempt to set aside their own interests and position in society and consider only what is fair for all. Unfortunately, because human beings are self-interested, this is a very difficult reality to achieve. However, Rawls' theory is the philosophical basis for policies such as affirmative action and equal opportunity. These approaches acknowledge the reality of racial prejudice and systemic inequality and endeavor to level the playing field by giving some advantage to those who are traditionally disadvantaged. In this sense, a policy like affirmative action that is inherently unequal in its application is justified and fair because it promotes equality of opportunity and equal access to positions of power.

The famous last sentence of Rawls' book states: "Purity of heart, if one could attain it, would be to see clearly and to act with grace and self-command from this point of view." Although this "purity of heart" and "veil of ignorance" is a difficult ideal to achieve in politics, the function of the constitutions and bills of rights of many nations is to act as a social consciousness and a view that is pure of heart in its regard for the moral equality of all persons. The constitutionality of legislation and policy then is not merely a matter of legality, but one of justice and morality, and the constitution is the safeguard that curtails the self-interest of those in positions of power.

FURTHER RESOURCES

Books

Barry, Brian M. *Theories of Justice*. Berkley, Calif.: University of California Press, 1989.

Daniels, Norman. *Reading Rawls: Critical Studies on Rawls' "A Theory of Justice."* New York: Basic Books, 1974.

Martin, R. *Rawls and Rights*. Lawrence, Kans.: University Press of Kansas, 2001.

Rawls, John. *Justice as Fairness: A Restatement*. Boston: Harvard University Press, 2001.

Periodicals

Brighouse, Harry. "Political Equality in Justice as Fairness." *Philosophical Studies* 86 (1997): 155–184.

Nagel, Thomas. "Rawls on Justice." *The Philosophical Review* 82, 2 (1973): 220–234.

Rawls, John. "The Law of Peoples." *Critical Inquiry* 20, 1: 36–68.

Habitat for Humanity

Photograph

By: Lenny Ignelzi

Date: June 19, 1990

Source: AP Images.

About the Photographer: Lenny Ignelzi is a photographer with the Associated Press, which is a worldwide news agency based in New York.

INTRODUCTION

Habitat for Humanity International (HFH or HFHI) is a nonprofit organization that helps provide housing to low-income families. Established in 1976 by millionaire Millard Fuller (1935–) and his wife Linda, HFH offers interest-free home loans to eligible families in exchange for two hundred hours of work (known as "sweat equity"). According to the organization, HFH and its affiliates have provided more than 150,000 homes in more than 3,000 communities worldwide. Mainly funded by philanthropists and charitable organizations, the group describes itself as an ecumenical Christian organization; HFH maintains, however, that homeowners and volunteers are chosen without regard to race, religion, or ethnicity.

Habitat for Humanity's work is accomplished at the community level by affiliates that are independent, locally run, nonprofit organizations. Affiliates are responsible for the house-building efforts while the HFH provides resources like mortgage loans and infrastructure support. All Habitat affiliates are asked to give ten percent of the contributions they receive to fund house-building work in other nations.

On several occasions, HFH has collaborated with U.S. government organizations. On February 13, 2002, the organization signed an agreement with the U.S. Environmental Protection Agency (EPA), pledging to work together on the cleanup and redevelopment of "Brownfields" in distressed communities. Brownfields are abandoned, idled, or under-used industrial and commercial properties where redevelopment is complicated by environmental contamination. A key purpose of the collaboration was to encourage the use of Brownfields for developing affordable housing.

In the past, many prominent personalities have worked with Habitat for Humanity. Former U.S. President and Nobel Peace Prize laureate Jimmy Carter, along with his wife Rosalynn, became actively involved with the Habitat for Humanity community in 1984. Carter's first project for the organization involved restoring a six-story building in New York City. The building eventually accommodated as many as nineteen families in need of shelter. Ever since, Carter has been an influential advocate for the organization, helping to raise money, recruit volunteers, and raise awareness of the importance of affordable housing. Each year Carter and his wife sponsor the Jimmy Carter Work Project, an internationally recognized HFH event.

■ **PRIMARY SOURCE**

HABITAT FOR HUMANITY
See primary source image.

■

SIGNIFICANCE

Habitat for Humanity has provided thousands of affordable houses to low-income families around the world. The Jimmy Carter Work Project (JCWP) alone, through various initiatives, has accommodated more than ten thousand people in the United States, Hungary, the Philippines, Mexico, South Korea, India, and South Africa. The involvement of Carter and his wife has reportedly attracted many volunteers. During the 2005 JCWP, held in Michigan, hundreds of volunteers helped build 238 homes for needy families.

■ **PRIMARY SOURCE**

Habitat for Humanity: Former president Jimmy Carter, one of the most visible supporters of Habitat for Humanity, helps to construct a home in Tijuana, Mexico. AP IMAGES.

However, critics of HFH argue that the organization's efforts to provide low-cost housing do not benefit those living below the poverty line. According to these critics, the fact that people who can afford monthly mortgage payments are eligible for Habitat houses indicates that they are not poor. Moreover, foreclosures on the houses provided to Habitat families occur infrequently, and opponents argue that HFH curbs its risks by partnering only with middle-income families instead of the homeless.

HFH has also been embroiled in other controversies. In 2003, the Sacramento Habitat for Humanity chapter was sued for providing a moldy house. In December 2003, an infestation of prairie dogs on a Habitat building site in Greely, Colorado, ultimately ended with the extermination of these animals after much negotiation with several animal rights groups. In a 2004 action alert titled "Stop Habitat for Humanity's War on Wildlife," published at the website for

Former president Jimmy Carter and his wife Rosalynn help build a new home at a Habitat for Humanity site in Atlanta, Georgia, 1988. © BETTMANN/CORBIS.

People for the Ethical Treatment of Animals (PETA), PETA urged HFH to amend its policies on house selection.

In January 2005, HFH announced the dismissal of founders Millard and Linda Fuller, amid accusations that Millard behaved inappropriately toward a former female employee. Several other former employees accused Fuller of prior sexual misconduct. Some observers suggested the Fullers' departure stemmed from philosophical differences among the organization's leaders. The Fullers went on to form the Fuller Center for Housing, based on principles similar to those of HFH.

HFH has been supported by numerous charitable institutions as well as governmental agencies. Studies have shown that Habitat partner families enjoy better health, children of the family do better in school, and parents often improve their own education after moving into their own home. The government benefits

from an increase in tax revenue as a result of property taxes paid by homeowners of Habitat-sponsored houses. Further, studies involving low-cost houses have also shown that Habitat houses increase property values rather than having an adverse effect on other properties in the neighborhood.

On June 7, 2001, U.S. Secretary of Housing and Urban Development Mel Martinez addressed the United Nations General Assembly, commending the efforts of Habitat for Humanity. He said, "I took hammer in hand and joined the President in Tampa, Florida, to help kick off Habitat for Humanity International's World Leaders Build. We support Habitat for Humanity and its faith-based cousins wholeheartedly—they are helping to instill in our citizens something that government alone cannot: a sense of hope, and a sense of pride."

The 2004 and 2005 natural disasters Hurricane Katrina, Hurricane Rita, and the South Asian tsunami have prompted HFH to provide housing assistance to families left homeless by these calamities. The organization is reportedly involved in building more than 250 homes in areas affected by Katrina and Rita. According to HFH, by the end of 2007, it also plans to build 7,500 permanent homes for families affected by the tsunami. For these and other efforts, Habitat for Humanity has received funds from CitiGroup, Verizon, Bank of America, and the Bush-Clinton Tsunami Aid (founded by former U.S. presidents George Bush and Bill Clinton).

FURTHER RESOURCES
Books

Baggett, Jerome P. *Habitat for Humanity: Building Private Homes, Building Public Religion.* Philadelphia: Temple University Press, 2000.

Web sites

Habitat for Humanity. "Habitat for Humanity Receives Bush-Clinton Tsunami Funding For Indonesia." May 2, 2006. <http://www.washingtonpost.com/wp-dyn/articles/A18460–2005Mar8.html> (accessed May 23, 2006).

Learning to Give. "Carter, James Earl, Jr. (Jimmy Carter)." <http://www.learningtogive.org/papers/index.asp?bpid=82> (accessed May 23, 2006).

U.S. Department of Housing and Urban Development. "Secretary Martinez's Remarks to the United Nations General Assembly." June 7, 2001. <http://www.hud.gov/news/speeches/assembly.cfm> (accessed May 23, 2006).

U.S. Environmental Protection Agency. "EPA Memorandum of Understanding with Habitat for Humanity." February 13, 2002. <http://www.epa.gov/brownfields/pdf/habitat.pdf> (accessed May 23, 2006).

Washington Post. "Harassment Claims Roil Habitat for Humanity." March 9, 2005. <http://www.washingtonpost.com/wp-dyn/articles/A18460–2005Mar8.html> (accessed May 23, 2006).

Reparations: A National Apology

Magazine article

By: Anonymous

Date: October 22, 1990

Source: "Reparations: A National Apology." *Time.* October 22, 1990.

About the Author: The primary source was written by an anonymous staff writer of *Time*, an American newsweekly.

INTRODUCTION

On December 7, 1941, Japanese forces attacked the U.S. Naval base at Pearl Harbor. The following day, the United States declared war on Japan, entering World War II. While the U.S. military prepared to engage the Japanese on the battlefield, concerns arose regarding the loyalty of Japanese immigrants and their descendents residing in the United States. The Federal Bureau of Investigation (FBI) began to detain groups of Japanese residents located on the West coast. Attorney General Francis Biddle proclaimed that the government would not target the entire Japanese-American population, but by December 11th, just days after Pearl Harbor, law enforcement detained approximately 1,200 individuals of Japanese descent. Stripped of citizenship rights, Japanese residents were declared "enemy aliens," even if born in the United States. By the end of 1941, Attorney General Biddle had authorized raids without search warrants on residences of Japanese Americans as long as one occupant was a Japanese alien.

Racist media had long characterized Japanese immigrants and their descendents as racially inferior, disloyal, and unable to assimilate into American society. The attack on Pearl Harbor exacerbated these racist sentiments, influencing government and military policy. The Western Defense Command, led by Lieutenant General John L. Dewitt, was tasked with assessing the alleged threat posed by Japanese-descended residents of the West Coast. Japanese Americans and resident aliens were forced to relinquish their shortwave radios and cameras and a curfew of 7 am to 7 pm was imposed. Those with Japanese ancestry could not congregate or travel in groups larger than five people and a special permit was required for those wanting to travel more than twenty-five miles from their homes.

In January 1942, a report prepared by the Chief Justice of the Supreme Court, Owen Roberts, suggested (without hard evidence) that Japanese Americans living in Hawaii aided the Japanese Navy attack Pearl Harbor. Following a visit to the military base, Navy Secretary Frank Knox proclaimed that "Japanese subversives" residing in Hawaii assisted in planning the attack. FBI Director J. Edgar Hoover reported to President Roosevelt that such allegations were unfounded.

Japanese Americans in a prison bus are on their way to be processed for internment during World War II, Long Beach, California, February 3, 1942. © BETTMANN/CORBIS.

Racism and sensationalist concerns over wartime security fueled public momentum to remove Japanese residents from the West Coast. In February 1942, Secretary of War, Henry Stimson, as well as several members of Congress and General Dewitt, requested that Japanese resident aliens and American citizens of Japanese decent be removed from California, Oregon and Washington, claiming that internment was a legal exercise of the President's war powers

Two and a half months after the Japanese naval attack on Pearl Harbor, President Roosevelt signed Executive Order 9066 authorizing the internment of Japanese immigrants and U.S.-born Japanese-Americans. On March 18, 1942, President Roosevelt signed Executive Order 9102, creating the War Relocation Authority to facilitate the removal of Japanese Americans and aliens from the West coast. The first "relocation" occurred on March 22, 1942. Residents from Los Angeles were sent to Manzanar center in Northern California, a 6,000-acre detainment site sur-

rounded by barbed wire. Official notification to relocate often came in the form of notices posted on telephone poles, on sides of buildings, or on community bulletin boards. Those affected were given as little as four hours to liquidate their possessions and prepare for their indefinite internment.

Eventually, over 120,000 men, women, and children of Japanese descent were sent to the ten internment camps located in California, Idaho, Utah, Arizona, Wyoming, Colorado, and Arkansas. Approximately 77,000 of those interned were American born *Nisei*, meaning "second generation." The remaining 43,000 interned were immigrants, many of whom were *Issei*. These first generation immigrants were prevented by law from gaining U.S. citizenship, the result of a series of so-called Exclusion Acts curtailing Asian immigration and naturalization.

The internment program was challenged at the time, but the 1944 landmark case, *Korematsu v. United*

Ken Yoshida, right, was drafted to fight in the U.S. military while being held in an internment camp for Japanese Americans during World War II. He refused to fight for the government that had interned him, was sent to prison, and was branded a traitor by fellow Japanese Americans who advocated cooperation with the government. On May 11, 2002, the Japanese American Citizens League offered its apologies for this treatment. AP IMAGES.

States ruled that the program was legal. Three justices dissented, noting the inherent racism, unlawful deprivation of personal property, and the abuse of military authority associated with internment. The Japanese surrendered on August 14, 1945, with the official signing ceremony occurring on September 2, 1945. The last internment camp closed in March of 1946. When released from internment, many Japanese Americans had lost their homes and businesses. Racism continued to be a problem as several West Coast communities campaigned to prevent former internees from returning.

■ PRIMARY SOURCE

Stooping before nine elderly Japanese-Americans, several of them more than 100 years old and in wheelchairs, Attorney General Dick Thornburgh last week presented each one a formal Presidential apology, and a reparation check, for an episode that still stands out as one of the nation's worst violations of individual rights. During World War II, supposedly in order to forestall possible attacks by Japanese agents against strategic installations in the U.S., the federal government summarily ordered the "relocation" of 120,000 ordinary citizens and immigrants of Japanese descent to 10 internment camps.

Culminating decades of lobbying by Japanese-Americans to redress the pain and blot caused by the unjustified imprisonments, the bittersweet event commenced a race against time to reimburse, over the next three years, the 65,000 victims who remain alive. The $1.25 billion Civil Liberties Act of 1988, funded by Congress only this year, authorizes a $20,000 payment to every man, woman and child who suffered as a result of the internment policy and was still alive at the time the law was passed.

■ SIGNIFICANCE

In 1981, the Commission on Wartime Relocation and Internment of Civilians (CWRIC) convened public hearings to investigate the internment of Japanese Americans during World War II. Over 750 witnesses recalled their experiences, spurring a campaign for an official government apology and monetary reparations to those interned. By 1983, the CWRIC submitted a formal request to the U.S. Congress to further investigate and provide payments to those who spent time in the camps and were still alive. That same year, Japanese-American Fred Korematsu returned to court seeking to overthrow the conviction that sparked his case against internment. The court dismissed Korematsu's arrest and conviction for evading internment orders, but failed to discuss its general ruling on internment. The case garnered further public support for reparations.

The 1988 Civil Liberties Act provided for an official apology and reparations payment of $20,000 a piece to the living victims of U.S. internment policies. An additional $400 million dollars for reparations was authorized in 1992.

FURTHER RESOURCES

Periodicals

Friedrich, Otto. "Pearl Harbor: A Time of Agony for Japanese Americans Interning 120,000 in Desolate Camps." *Time*. December 2, 1991.

Leo, John. "An Apology to Japanese-Americans; the Senate Says they Were Wrongly Interned During World War II." *Time*. May 2, 1988.

Molotsky, Irvin. "Senate Votes to Compensate Japanese-American Internees." *New York Times*. April 21, 1988.

Web sites

Truman Presidential Museum and Library. "The War Relocation Authority and the Incarceration of Japanese Americans During World War II." <http://www.trumanlibrary.org/whistlestop/study_collections/japanese_internment/background.htm> (accessed May 10, 2006).

Fourth World Conference on Women

Platform for Action

Mission statement

By: United Nations

Date: September 1995

Source: United Nations. Fourth World Conference on Women. "Platform for Action." September 1995.

INTRODUCTION

The United Nations declared 1975 the International Women's Year, and as such began to sponsor a series of conferences on women's issues. The first, which met that year in Mexico City, produced UN resolution 33/185, which proclaimed 1976–1985 the United Nations Decade for Women: Equality, Development, and Peace.

The next conference, held in 1980 in Copenhagen to assess progress made toward the goals originally identified in Mexico City, penned the "Programme of Action for the Second Half of the United Nations Decade for Women: Equality, Development and Peace." The declaration identified additional obstacles in the quest for equality and produced an international agreement focusing on actions needed to address them. The Third World Conference for Women met in July 1985 in Nairobi and produced the "Nairobi Forward-Looking Strategies for the Advancement of Women." This agreement addressed objectives for the advancement of women through the year 2000, identifying concrete objectives for evaluation. These objectives were based on the United Nations Charter and other declarations and covenants addressing international cooperation toward the elimination of gender inequalities.

In 1995, the Fourth World Conference for Women convened in Beijing with representatives from 189 member nations, after meeting in Cairo the year before at the United Nation's International Conference on Population and Development to establish a conference platform. There, delegates determined that advancing the status of women would be instrumental in resolving issues of population, environmental destruction, and sustainable economic development.

The Beijing conference produced a platform for action that concentrated on advancing the aspiration of equality, sustainable development, and peace for all women. It asserts that poverty affects women and children disproportionately and that empowering and advancing women's causes—including the rights to freedom of thought, conscience, religion, and belief; economic independence; freedom from violence; and equal access to medical treatment, education, resources—would contribute to a more peaceful world.

Despite security concerns, candidate Safia Siddiqi meets with constituents on election day as she arrives to place her own vote in her village of Nazarabad, Afghanistan. © STEPHANIE SINCLAIR/CORBIS.

■ PRIMARY SOURCE

United Nations Fourth World Conference on Women

Beijing, China

4–15 September 1995

Chapter I

Mission Statement

1. The Platform for Action is an agenda for women's empowerment. It aims at accelerating the implementation of the Nairobi Forward-looking Strategies for the Advancement of Women and at removing all the obstacles to women's active participation in all spheres of public and private life through a full and equal share in economic, social, cultural, and political decision-making. This means that the principle of shared power and responsibility should be established between women and men at home, in the workplace, and in the wider national and international communities. Equality between women and men is a matter of human rights and a condition for social justice and is also a necessary and fundamental prerequisite for equality, development and peace. A transformed partnership based on equality between women and men is a condition for people-centred sustainable development. A sustained and long-term commitment is essential, so that women and men can work together for themselves, for their children and for society to meet the challenges of the twenty-first century.

2. The Platform for Action reaffirms the fundamental principle set forth in the Vienna Declaration and Programme of Action, adopted by the World Conference on Human Rights, that the human rights of women and of the girl child are an inalienable, integral, and indivisible part of universal human rights. As an agenda for action, the Platform seeks to promote and protect the full enjoyment of all human rights and the fundamental freedoms of all women throughout their life cycle.

3. The Platform for Action emphasizes that women share common concerns that can be addressed only by working together and in partnership with men towards the common goal of gender equality around the world. It respects and values the full diversity of women's situa-

tions and conditions and recognizes that some women face particular barriers to their empowerment.

4. The Platform for Action requires immediate and concerted action by all to create a peaceful, just, and humane world based on human rights and fundamental freedoms, including the principle of equality for all people of all ages and from all walks of life, and to this end, recognizes that broad- based and sustained economic growth in the context of sustainable development is necessary to sustain social development and social justice.

5. The success of the Platform for Action will require a strong commitment on the part of Governments, international organizations, and institutions at all levels. It will also require adequate mobilization of resources at the national and international levels as well as new and additional resources to the developing countries from all available funding mechanisms, including multilateral, bilateral, and private sources for the advancement of women; financial resources to strengthen the capacity of national, subregional, regional, and international institutions; a commitment to equal rights, equal responsibilities and equal opportunities and to the equal participation of women and men in all national, regional and international bodies and policy- making processes; and the establishment or strengthening of mechanisms at all levels for accountability to the world's women....

Chapter III

Critical Areas of Concern

41. The advancement of women and the achievement of equality between women and men are a matter of human rights and a condition for social justice and should not be seen in isolation as a women's issue. They are the only way to build a sustainable, just and developed society. Empowerment of women and equality between women and men are prerequisites for achieving political, social, economic, cultural and environmental security among all peoples.

42. Most of the goals set out in the Nairobi Forward-looking Strategies for the Advancement of Women have not been achieved. Barriers to women's empowerment remain, despite the efforts of Governments, as well as non-governmental organizations and women and men everywhere. Vast political, economic and ecological crises persist in many parts of the world. Among them are wars of aggression, armed conflicts, colonial or other forms of alien domination or foreign occupation, civil wars and terrorism. These situations, combined with systematic or de facto discrimination, violations of and failure to protect all human rights and fundamental freedoms of all women, and their civil, cultural, economic, political, and social rights, including the right to development and ingrained prejudicial attitudes towards women and girls

are but a few of the impediments encountered since the World Conference to Review and Appraise the Achievements of the United Nations Decade for Women: Equality, Development and Peace, in 1985.

43. A review of progress since the Nairobi Conference highlights special concerns - areas of particular urgency that stand out as priorities for action. All actors should focus action and resources on the strategic objectives relating to the critical areas of concern which are, necessarily, interrelated, interdependent and of high priority. There is a need for these actors to develop and implement mechanisms of accountability for all the areas of concern.

44. To this end, Governments, the international community and civil society, including non-governmental organizations and the private sector, are called upon to take strategic action in the following critical areas of concern:

- —The persistent and increasing burden of poverty on women
- —Inequalities and inadequacies in and unequal access to education and training
- —Inequalities and inadequacies in and unequal access to health care and related services
- —Violence against women
- —The effects of armed or other kinds of conflict on women, including those living under foreign occupation
- —Inequality in economic structures and policies, in all forms of productive activities and in access to resources
- —Inequality between men and women in the sharing of power and decision-making at all levels
- —Insufficient mechanisms at all levels to promote the advancement of women
- —Lack of respect for and inadequate promotion and protection of the human rights of women
- —Stereotyping of women and inequality in women's access to and participation in all communication systems, especially in the media
- —Gender inequalities in the management of natural resources and in the safeguarding of the environment
- —Persistent discrimination against and violation of the rights of the girl child

Chapter IV

Strategic Objectives and Actions

45. In each critical area of concern, the problem is diagnosed and strategic objectives are proposed with concrete actions to be taken by various actors in order to achieve those objectives. The strategic objectives are derived from the critical areas of concern and specific actions to be taken to achieve them cut across the

boundaries of equality, development and peace—the goals of the Nairobi Forward-looking Strategies for the Advancement of Women—and reflect their interdependence. The objectives and actions are interlinked, of high priority and mutually reinforcing. The Platform for Action is intended to improve the situation of all women, without exception, who often face similar barriers, while special attention should be given to groups that are the most disadvantaged.

46. The Platform for Action recognizes that women face barriers to full equality and advancement because of such factors as their race, age, language, ethnicity, culture, religion, or disability, because they are indigenous women or because of other status. Many women encounter specific obstacles related to their family status, particularly as single parents; and to their socio- economic status, including their living conditions in rural, isolated or impoverished areas. Additional barriers also exist for refugee women, other displaced women, including internally displaced women as well as for immigrant women and migrant women, including women migrant workers. Many women are also particularly affected by environmental disasters, serious and infectious diseases and various forms of violence against women.

SIGNIFICANCE

The United Nations twenty-third special session, "Women 2000: Gender Equality, Development, and Peace for the Twenty-First Century" met at Hunter College in New York. The agreement that emerged from the conference was called "Further Actions and Initiatives to Implement the Beijing Declaration and Platform for Action." The declaration examined the effectiveness of programs created at the Beijing Conference and identified achievements and obstacles to reaching the goals set there.

In the area of women's health, the declaration acknowledged an increased life expectancy for women and girls and improved concentration on sexual and reproductive health issues, which includes reproductive rights. In addition, the platform cited achievements in contraception education and family planning, HIV/AIDS education, and increased awareness toward nutrition and breastfeeding.

The document also acknowledged obstacles. In developing nations, for example, women's health is hindered by a lack of clean water, adequate nutrition, and safe sanitation. In addition, a lack of gender-specific health research in some countries created an impediment. The conference called for additional investment into obstetric care and a holistic approach toward women's health care. At the UN Millennium

Summit held in New York in 2001, over 150 member nations signed the Millennium Declaration and agreed to work toward the Millennium Development Goals, which include empowering of women and moving toward gender equality.

FURTHER RESOURCES
Periodicals

Johnson, Jeanette, and Wendy Turnbull. "The Women's Conference: Where Aspirations and Realities Met." *International Family Planning Perspectives* 21, no. 4 (December 1, 1995) 155–159.

Web sites

United Nations. "Third World Conference on Women, Nairobi." <http://www.earthsummit2002.org/toolkits/Women/un-doku/un-conf/narirobi.htm> (accessed May 10, 2006).

United Nations. "Further Actions and Initiatives to Implement the Beijing Declaration and Platform for Action." <http://www.un.org/womenwatch/daw/followup/ress233e.pdf> (accessed May 10, 2006).

United Nations Millennium Declaration

Declaration

By: United Nations

Date: September 8, 2000

Source: "United Nations Millennium Declaration." United Nations, September 8, 2000.

About the Author: The United Nations was first conceptualized by U.S. President Franklin D. Roosevelt soon after World War II. To promote democracy and fight against various problems of the world, representatives from fifty-one countries officially established the United Nations on October 24, 1945. Headquartered in New York, the United Nations is committed to preserving world peace through international cooperation and collective security. The organization has six main entities—the General Assembly, the Security Council, the Economic and Social Council, the Trusteeship Council, the Secretariat, and the International Court of Justice.

INTRODUCTION

Since the 1980s, many countries of the world have chosen to adopt globalization, an integration of economic, cultural, political, and social systems across all geographical regions. Global integration gives rise to new rules of trade that bind national policies. In the era of globalization, government decisions have significant impact on not just the local community but also on the international community.

According to the 1999 Human Development Report, global opportunities are unevenly distributed between countries and people. Incomes and lifestyles of people vary drastically throughout the world. Between 1990 and 1997, nearly 1.3 billion people lived on less than a dollar a day, and close to one billion were unable to meet their basic daily requirements—a majority of these in underdeveloped or developing countries. Moreover, about 840 million people were reported to be undernourished or starving. In the same period, more than 260 million children were out of school at the primary and secondary levels.

Health and pollution standards also require significant improvement, especially in underdeveloped countries. Every year, nearly three million people die from air pollution—more than eighty percent of them from indoor air pollution—and more than five million from gastro-intestinal diseases caused by water contamination. On the health front as well, an alarming trend has been observed. In 1998, more than thirty-three million people had HIV/AIDS, with almost six million new infections in that year. In this case, as many as ninety-five percent of the 16,000 people infected with this disease each day were living in developing countries.

Gender equality is another key concern. In the twentieth century, little change was observed in the status of women, especially in southern and western Asia and northern Africa. In these regions, women occupied only twenty percent of paying jobs (outside the agricultural sector). Other cases of gender inequality are seen throughout the world. On an administrative level, though representation of women in governments increased since the early 1990s, they held only sixteen percent of parliamentary seats worldwide.

With the aim of addressing such global concerns and strengthening the role of the world body in meeting the challenges of the twenty-first century, the United Nations General Assembly decided to designate its fifty-fifth session (starting on September 5, 2000) as the Millennium Assembly of the Millennium Summit. During the Millennium Summit, 147 heads of state and governments representing 189 member states of the United Nations (UN) adopted the Millennium Declaration with the purpose of combating poverty, hunger, disease, illiteracy, environmental degradation, and discrimination against women across the world. In order to achieve these goals, eight Millennium Development Goals (MDGs) were drawn that address a variety of issues. These goals were set for the year 2015 with reference to the global situation prevalent in 1990. The text of the Millennium Declaration is excerpted here.

■ PRIMARY SOURCE

UNITED NATIONS MILLENNIUM DECLARATION

The General Assembly

Adopts the following Declaration:

United Nations Millennium Declaration

I. Values and principles

1. We, heads of State and Government, have gathered at United Nations Headquarters in New York from 6 to 8 September 2000, at the dawn of a new millennium, to reaffirm our faith in the Organization and its Charter as indispensable foundations of a more peaceful, prosperous and just world.

2. We recognize that, in addition to our separate responsibilities to our individual societies, we have a collective responsibility to uphold the principles of human dignity, equality and equity at the global level. As leaders we have a duty therefore to all the world's people, especially the most vulnerable and, in particular, the children of the world, to whom the future belongs.

3. We reaffirm our commitment to the purposes and principles of the Charter of the United Nations, which have proved timeless and universal. Indeed, their relevance and capacity to inspire have increased, as nations and peoples have become increasingly interconnected and interdependent.

4. We are determined to establish a just and lasting peace all over the world in accordance with the purposes and principles of the Charter. We rededicate ourselves to support all efforts to uphold the sovereign equality of all States, respect for their territorial integrity and political independence, resolution of disputes by peaceful means and in conformity with the principles of justice and international law, the right to self-determination of peoples which remain under colonial domination and foreign occupation, non-interference in the internal affairs of States, respect for human rights and fundamental freedoms, respect for the equal rights of all without distinction as to race, sex, language or religion and international coopera-

tion in solving international problems of an economic, social, cultural or humanitarian character.

5. We believe that the central challenge we face today is to ensure that globalization becomes a positive force for all the world's people. For while globalization offers great opportunities, at present its benefits are very unevenly shared, while its costs are unevenly distributed. We recognize that developing countries and countries with economies in transition face special difficulties in responding to this central challenge. Thus, only through broad and sustained efforts to create a shared future, based upon our common humanity in all its diversity, can globalization be made fully inclusive and equitable. These efforts must include policies and measures, at the global level, which correspond to the needs of developing countries and economies in transition and are formulated and implemented with their effective participation.

6. We consider certain fundamental values to be essential to international relations in the twenty-first century. These include:

- Freedom. Men and women have the right to live their lives and raise their children in dignity, free from hunger and from the fear of violence, oppression or injustice. Democratic and participatory governance based on the will of the people best assures these rights.
- Equality. No individual and no nation must be denied the opportunity to benefit from development. The equal rights and opportunities of women and men must be assured.
- Solidarity. Global challenges must be managed in a way that distributes the costs and burdens fairly in accordance with basic principles of equity and social justice. Those who suffer or who benefit least deserve help from those who benefit most.
- Tolerance. Human beings must respect one other, in all their diversity of belief, culture and language. Differences within and between societies should be neither feared nor repressed, but cherished as a precious asset of humanity. A culture of peace and dialogue among all civilizations should be actively promoted.
- Respect for nature. Prudence must be shown in the management of all living species and natural resources, in accordance with the precepts of sustainable development. Only in this way can the immeasurable riches provided to us by nature be preserved and passed on to our descendants. The current unsustainable patterns of production and consumption must be changed in the interest of our future welfare and that of our descendants.
- Shared responsibility. Responsibility for managing worldwide economic and social development, as

well as threats to international peace and security, must be shared among the nations of the world and should be exercised multilaterally. As the most universal and most representative organization in the world, the United Nations must play the central role.

7. In order to translate these shared values into actions, we have identified key objectives to which we assign special significance.

II. Peace, security and disarmament

8. We will spare no effort to free our peoples from the scourge of war, whether within or between States, which has claimed more than 5 million lives in the past decade. We will also seek to eliminate the dangers posed by weapons of mass destruction.

9. We resolve therefore:

- To strengthen respect for the rule of law in international as in national affairs and, in particular, to ensure compliance by Member States with the decisions of the International Court of Justice, in compliance with the Charter of the United Nations, in cases to which they are parties.
- To make the United Nations more effective in maintaining peace and security by giving it the resources and tools it needs for conflict prevention, peaceful resolution of disputes, peacekeeping, post-conflict peace-building and reconstruction. In this context, we take note of the report of the Panel on United Nations Peace Operations and request the General Assembly to consider its recommendations expeditiously.
- To strengthen cooperation between the United Nations and regional organizations, in accordance with the provisions of Chapter VIII of the Charter.
- To ensure the implementation, by States Parties, of treaties in areas such as arms control and disarmament and of international humanitarian law and human rights law, and call upon all States to consider signing and ratifying the Rome Statute of the International Criminal Court.
- To take concerted action against international terrorism, and to accede as soon as possible to all the relevant international conventions.
- To redouble our efforts to implement our commitment to counter the world drug problem.
- To intensify our efforts to fight transnational crime in all its dimensions, including trafficking as well as smuggling in human beings and money laundering.
- To minimize the adverse effects of United Nations economic sanctions on innocent populations, to subject such sanctions regimes to regular reviews and to eliminate the adverse effects of sanctions on third parties.

• To strive for the elimination of weapons of mass destruction, particularly nuclear weapons, and to keep all options open for achieving this aim, including the possibility of convening an international conference to identify ways of eliminating nuclear dangers.

• To take concerted action to end illicit traffic in small arms and light weapons, especially by making arms transfers more transparent and supporting regional disarmament measures, taking account of all the recommendations of the forthcoming United Nations Conference on Illicit Trade in Small Arms and Light Weapons.

• To call on all States to consider acceding to the Convention on the Prohibition of the Use, Stockpiling, Production and Transfer of Anti-personnel Mines and on Their Destruction, as well as the amended mines protocol to the Convention on conventional weapons.

10. We urge Member States to observe the Olympic Truce, individually and collectively, now and in the future, and to support the International Olympic Committee in its efforts to promote peace and human understanding through sport and the Olympic Ideal.

SIGNIFICANCE

Endorsement of the Millennium Declaration is considered a significant event in world history as it was signed by world leaders and not ambassadors of countries (which is usually the case). The Millennium Declaration gave an impetus to the United Nations to pursue various goals and policies in addressing serious concerns. In implementing one of the most comprehensive declarations in the history of the UN, several changes had to be made to existing policies. The Declaration assumes great significance as it addresses numerous issues faced by the entire world.

The eight MDGs based on the Declaration are to eradicate extreme poverty and hunger, achieve universal primary education, promote gender equality and empower women, reduce child mortality, improve maternal health, combat HIV and AIDS, malaria and other diseases, ensure environmental sustainability, and to devise a global partnership for development of countries. Experts state that the MDGs are significant because they are people-centric, achievable, measurable, and time-bound. Moreover, they provide an appropriate medium for channeling global development efforts.

World leaders claim that a global initiative such as the Millennium Declaration is essential to effectively address discrepancies in growth in different regions of the world. For instance, in 1990, the proportion of extremely poor people in developing countries was twenty-eight percent, compared to twenty-one percent in 2001. However, these positive gains were observed in certain developing regions, such as Asia, only. In sub-Saharan Africa, a reverse trend was observed as millions experienced abject poverty.

Though the Millennium Declaration is acknowledged as a step in the right direction, slow and uneven progress has been achieved since it was implemented. The UN is also confronted with several complex challenges. One of the goals of the Declaration is to reduce child mortality by two-thirds in 2015. The UN states that progress in this case has been hampered due to several reasons such as political unrest, increase in population, diseases, lack of medical care, and malnutrition. Similarly, owing to diverse country-specific impediments, there has not been much improvement in maternal health and widespread diseases, such as AIDS and malaria.

Some of the other challenges faced by the global community are establishing mobility of financial resources and political will, motivating governments to re-engage and re-orient their development policies, and garnering adequate support from the private sector. Concerns about improper data collection have also been raised. According to the UN, inconsistent data on poverty, unemployment, and illiteracy in developing and underdeveloped countries affects implementation of MDGs in these countries. Nevertheless, the Millennium Declaration has led to slow, but positive, gains.

FURTHER RESOURCES

Books

United Nations Development Programme. *Human Development Report 1999: Tenth Anniversary Edition*. New York: Oxford University Press, 1999.

Web sites

Choike.org. "In Depth: Millennium Development Goals—MDGs." <http://www.choike.org/nuevo_eng/informes/302.html> (accessed June 8, 2006).

Global Policy Forum. "The Millennium Summit and Its Follow-Up." <http://www.globalpolicy.org/msummit/millenni/index.htm> (accessed June 8, 2006).

United Nations. "Road Map Towards the Implementation of the United Nations Millennium Declaration: Report of the Secretary-General." September 6, 2001. <http://www.un.org/documents/ga/docs/56/a56326.pdf> (accessed June 8, 2006).

United Nations Statistics Division. "Progress towards the Millennium Development Goals, 1990–2005." June 13, 2005. <http://unstats.un.org/unsd/mi/mi_coverfinal.htm> (accessed June 8, 2006).

Establishment of White House Office of Faith-Based and Community Initiatives

Executive Order

By: George W. Bush

Date: January 29, 2001

Source: *White House Office of Faith-Base and Community Initiatives.* "Executive Order 13199: Establishment of White House Office of Faith-Based and Community Initiatives." January 29, 2001. <http://www.white-house.gov/news/releases/2001/01/20010129-2.html> (accessed May 27, 2006).

About the Author: George W. Bush is the forty-third President of the United States. An Executive Order is a regulation or declaration issued by the president that has the force of law.

INTRODUCTION

In 2001, President George W. Bush created the Office of Faith-Based and Community Initiatives primarily to support social initiatives run by faith-based and community organizations and to help them benefit from federal funding opportunities. Historically these organizations had been limited in their ability to receive federal support because of regulations and laws that prohibit U.S. governmental support of religious institutions. The president believes that these organizations often are involved with critical social activities that benefit the poor, and that they require the support of the federal government. As a result, he established the Office of Faith-Based and Community Initiatives by Executive Order 13199.

The Office of Faith-Based and Community Initiatives is an official office of the executive branch of the federal government, and it operates within the White House. With the creation of the office, an infrastructure was set up to draft appropriate legislation, facilitate necessary regulatory changes, and promote the federal government's involvement with these organizations. The office also regularly disseminates

President George W. Bush speaks at the Union Bethel African Methodist Episcopal Church. Bush sought to increase support among African American voters for his plan to let religious charities in on more federal spending. © BROOKS KRAFT/CORBIS.

information about available federal funding opportunities to the relevant organizations, hosts conferences, and produces written materials to educate the public about the role that the federal government has come to play with faith-based and community organizations.

The Office of Faith-Based and Community Initiatives is committed to equality and offers all relevant organizations an equal opportunity to benefit from federal support. The Office also promotes non-governmental support of these initiatives by encouraging corporate and private philanthropic donations toward these efforts. Because of the office's role as a federal agency that interacts with religious groups, its legal legitimacy has been questioned on several occasions by groups who believe it violates the constitutional prohibition of federal governmental support of religion. The office maintains that its activities are constitutional because it supports no specific religion or religious organizations, but rather supports a wide variety of programs that benefit the society at large.

PRIMARY SOURCE

By the authority vested in me as President of the United States by the Constitution and the laws of the United States of America, and in order to help the Federal Government coordinate a national effort to expand opportunities for faith-based and other community organizations and to strengthen their capacity to better meet social needs in America's communities, it is hereby ordered as follows:

Section 1. Policy. Faith-based and other community organizations are indispensable in meeting the needs of poor Americans and distressed neighborhoods. Government cannot be replaced by such organizations, but it can and should welcome them as partners. The paramount goal is compassionate results, and private and charitable community groups, including religious ones, should have the fullest opportunity permitted by law to compete on a level playing field, so long as they achieve valid public purposes, such as curbing crime, conquering addiction, strengthening families and neighborhoods, and overcoming poverty. This delivery of social services must be results oriented and should value the bedrock principles of pluralism, nondiscrimination, evenhandedness, and neutrality.

Sec. 2. Establishment. There is established a White House Office of Faith-Based and Community Initiatives (White House OFBCI) within the Executive Office of the President that will have lead responsibility in the executive branch to establish policies, priorities, and objectives for the Federal Government's comprehensive effort to enlist, equip, enable, empower, and expand the work of faith-based and other community organizations to the extent permitted by law.

Sec. 3. Functions. The principal functions of the White House OFBCI are, to the extent permitted by law:

(a) to develop, lead, and coordinate the Administration's policy agenda affecting faith-based and other community programs and initiatives, expand the role of such efforts in communities, and increase their capacity through executive action, legislation, Federal and private funding, and regulatory relief;

(b) to ensure that Administration and Federal Government policy decisions and programs are consistent with the President's stated goals with respect to faith-based and other community initiatives;

(c) to help integrate the President's policy agenda affecting faith-based and other community organizations across the Federal Government;

(d) to coordinate public education activities designed to mobilize public support for faith-based and community nonprofit initiatives through volunteerism, special projects, demonstration pilots, and public-private partnerships;

(e) to encourage private charitable giving to support faith-based and community initiatives;

(f) to bring concerns, ideas, and policy options to the President for assisting, strengthening, and replicating successful faith-based and other community programs;

(g) to provide policy and legal education to State, local, and community policymakers and public officials seeking ways to empower faith-based and other community organizations and to improve the opportunities, capacity, and expertise of such groups;

(h) to develop and implement strategic initiatives under the President's agenda to strengthen the institutions of civil society and America's families and communities;

(i) to showcase and herald innovative grassroots nonprofit organizations and civic initiatives;

(j) to eliminate unnecessary legislative, regulatory, and other bureaucratic barriers that impede effective faith-based and other community efforts to solve social problems;

(k) to monitor implementation of the President's agenda affecting faith-based and other community organizations; and

(l) to ensure that the efforts of faith-based and other community organizations meet high standards of excellence and accountability.

Sec. 4. Administration.

(a) The White House OFBCI may function through established or ad hoc committees, task forces, or interagency groups.

(b) The White House OFBCI shall have a staff to be headed by the Assistant to the President for Faith-Based and Community Initiatives. The White House OFBCI shall have such staff and other assistance, to the extent permitted by law, as may be necessary to carry out the provisions of this order. The White House OFBCI operations shall begin no later than 30 days from the date of this order.

(c) The White House OFBCI shall coordinate with the liaison and point of contact designated by each executive department and agency with respect to this initiative.

(d) All executive departments and agencies (agencies) shall cooperate with the White House OFBCI and provide such information, support, and assistance to the White House OFBCI as it may request, to the extent permitted by law.

(e) The agencies' actions directed by this Executive Order shall be carried out subject to the availability of appropriations and to the extent permitted by law.

Sec. 5. Judicial Review. This order does not create any right or benefit, substantive or procedural, enforceable at law or equity by a party against the United States, its agencies or instrumentalities, its officers or employees, or any other person.

GEORGE W. BUSH
THE WHITE HOUSE,
January 29, 2001.

SIGNIFICANCE

The U.S. government has long been committed to a policy of separation of church and state. This policy has historically prohibited federal government support of any specific religion. As a result of this principle, established by the First Amendment to the U.S. Constitution, the creation of the Office of Faith-Based and Community Initiatives has been viewed as historic and significant. President George W. Bush, who created the office through this Executive Order, believed that federal government support is an important way to maximize the ability of these organizations to institute social and charitable programs. With the rationale that these organizations operate activities that are not specifically religious, but rather ones that benefit the U.S. population at large, this Office was created to better help them carry out their programs.

Critics of the office contend that the use of taxpayer dollars to fund programs of religious organizations, whether or not the activities are explicitly of a religious nature, is unconstitutional. By introducing new opportunities for faith-based organizations and changing the relationship between the federal government and the religious community, the creation of the Office of Faith-Based and Community Initiatives has been viewed as one of the more significant and historic policy decisions of the Bush Administration.

FURTHER RESOURCES
Books

Black, Amy M., Douglas M. Koopman, and David K. Ryden. *Of Little Faith: The Politics of George W. Bush's Faith-Based Initiative*. Washington, D.C.: Georgetown University Press, 2004.

Web sites

The White House. "White House Office of Faith-Based and Community Initiatives." <http://www.whitehouse.gov/government/fbci/index.html> (accessed May 27, 2006).

UNICEF

Photograph

By: Jim Hollander

Date: March 25, 2002

Source: © Reuters/Corbis.

About the Photographer: Jim Hollander is a chief photographer for Reuters, a worldwide news agency based in London. Hollander has operated primarily out of Israel since 1983.

INTRODUCTION

On December 11, 1946, the United Nations General Assembly created the United Nations International Children's Emergency Fund (UNICEF). The fund was created with the mandate to swiftly meet the emergency food, clothing, and health needs of children in Europe and China. From 1946 to 1950, as Europe reconstructed following World War II, UNICEF provided approximately $112 million in aid to children in twelve countries. The organization delivered five million in clothing, vaccinated eight million against tuberculosis, provided supplementary meals to children, and rebuilt milk factories.

As Europe emerged from rebuilding after the war, UNICEF adopted a new mandate. In 1950, the organization broadened its directive to include meeting the long-term needs of mothers and children in developing countries. To aid in reaching this goal, the United Nations made UNICEF part of its permanent system in 1953. To meet the long-range needs of children in developing nations, UNICEF worked against diseases such as leprosy, malaria, and tuberculosis. The organization worked with countries to develop clean sanitation and programs to develop and distribute food. In

PRIMARY SOURCE

UNICEF: A female teacher hands out textbooks produced by UNICEF to eager school girls at the Ameer Doust Moham-mad Khan primary school, on March 25, 2002, the day before classes begin. Girls in Afghanistan have not attended schools for the past six years during the Taliban rule. © REUTERS/CORBIS.

addition, education became part of the UNICEF mandate, as healthcare education programs for mothers and children were developed, in addition to training for mothers, daycare, and neighborhood centers.

After winning the Nobel Prize in 1965, UNICEF once again broadened its scope of concern as it developed programs to become advocates for children in developing nations. This approach works with the nations' governments to address the physical, intellectual, psychological, and vocational needs of children. The United Nations marked 1979 as the International Year of the Child and encouraged the governments and organizations to reaffirm their focus as articulated in the 1965 adoption of the Declaration of the Rights of the Child. To meet this goal, in 1983, UNICEF launched a health-care campaign which focused on

immunizations, oral rehydration therapy, and support for breastfeeding and good nutrition.

In 1996, UNICEF began to address the issue of violence and its impact on children. The group funded "A Report of the Expert of the Secretary-General, Ms. Graça Machel: The Impact of Armed Conflict on Children," which discussed the effects of war on children. In 1998, the United Nations Security Council opened its first debate on the impact of wars on children.

PRIMARY SOURCE

UNICEF

See primary source image.

On February 26, 2006, children eat at a nutritional centre in Kinshasa, the Democratic Republic of the Congo. Executive Director of the World Food Programme (WFP) James Morris, UNICEF Executive director Ann Veneman, and the High Commissioner of the UN Refugee Agency (UNHCR) Antonio Guterres are visiting the facility. LIONEL HEALING/AFP/GETTY IMAGES.

SIGNIFICANCE

In 1992, the Soviet-backed government in Afghanistan dissolved, which led to rival warlords struggling for power. As civil war broke out across the nation, the Taliban was the only group successful in establishing peace. The Taliban, a group of mullahs, or Islamic scholars, were led by Mullah Mohammad Omar and began to seize power throughout Afghanistan through policies of aggressively attacking opponents. In 1996, the Taliban captured Kabul, the capital, and then created the Islamic Emirate of Afghanistan. The Taliban instituted *Sharia* (Islamic law) as the foundation for the government. One of the first policies implemented by the Taliban was the closing of girls' schools. Women were forced to stop working. Policies dictating social behavior were enforced by the Ministry for the Enforcement of Virtue and Suppression of Vice, or the *Amr bil-Maroof wa Nahi An il-Munkir*. Those girls who attended clandestine schools held in the home risked being punished by beatings.

In addition to the closing of girls' schools, the Taliban's ban on working women left other schools without teachers—as many as seventy percent of teachers were women. As a result, nationwide illiteracy rates began to climb.

Since the overthrow of the Taliban in 2001, international organizations have worked to recreate the educational system in Afghanistan. As of 2006, enrollment in primary and secondary schools in the rebuilding country rose from nine hundred thousand to over five million. Many of these new students are girls who were not allowed to attend school under the Taliban. By 2003, over two hundred schools were rebuilt and approximately forty percent of school-aged girls were attending. Programs directed and funded by the U.S. Agency for International Development have sought to quickly retrain and develop a base of teachers.

However, the fundamentalist forces have launched campaigns against these girls' schools. In 2006, schools that educate girls were the targets of arson. Those opposing the education of girls have left letters of intimidation at teachers' homes or even killed teachers and headmasters to dissuade parents from sending their children to school.

FURTHER RESOURCES

Periodicals

Barker, Kim. "Extremists Target Schools in Afghanistan." *Chicago Tribune* (April 12, 2006).

Kugler, R. Anthony. "Educating Afghanistan's Girls." *Faces* (September 1, 2003).

Powell, Sian. "Afghan Girls Fight to Learn." *The Australian* (May 22, 2006).

Web sites

UNICEF. <http://www.unicef.org.uk> (accessed June 11, 2006).

To Walk the Earth in Safety

The United States Commitment to Humanitarian Demining

Government report (excerpt)

By: U.S. Department of State; Bureau of Political-Military Affairs

Date: September 2002

Source: *U.S. Department of State.* "To Walk the Earth in Safety: The United States Commitment to Humanitarian Demining, 4 ed." <http://www.state.gov/t/pm/rls/rpt/walkearth/2002/14868.htm> (accessed March 1, 2006).

About the Author: The U.S. State Department has responsibility for U.S. relations with foreign governments. The department is headed by the Secretary of State, who serves as the President's primary envoy.

INTRODUCTION

Land mines are simultaneously one of the least expensive and one of the deadliest weapons in use today. Their name originated with an early method that involved digging a tunnel, or mine, under an enemy position, filling the mine with explosives, and detonating the charges. Common in the Civil War and World War I, this technique became less useful as armies became increasingly mobile.

Landmines came into common use during World War II and are used throughout the world today. These portable explosive devices, costing as little as $3.00 apiece, can be quickly spread across roadways and other strategic territory to either contain or repel enemy forces. Landmines function by lying silent until triggered, then exploding. Most are relatively small antipersonnel mines, intended to kill or maim one or more troops; larger versions are designed to disable tanks or other armored equipment. Unlike troops and most weapon systems, landmines remain behind after formal hostilities end, creating further hazards for civilians and particularly children. Mines can remain active for decades. Adults stepping on a mind typically lose one or more limbs and may lose their sight due to shrapnel. Children are typically injured more seriously or killed due to their small size.

The United Nations Children's Fund (UNICEF) estimates that 110 million undetonated land mines remain hidden throughout the world. Africa alone is believed to contain thirty-seven million mines scattered across nineteen different nations. The nation of Angola is thought to have ten million mines and is currently home to 70,000 amputees. Because of their natural curiosity, children frequently pick up unexploded mines or attempt to use them as toys.

The presence of unexploded mines slows reconstruction efforts following a war. Combatants frequently mine fields, preventing their use for food production. Mined roads impede efforts to return refugees and obstruct delivery of humanitarian aid. Aid agencies and governments throughout the world began to recognize the danger posed by unexploded mines during the 1980s, and widespread mine removal efforts were soon underway throughout the world. As of 2002, the United States had spent more than $600 million assisting mine removal and mine safety education efforts throughout the world.

▮ PRIMARY SOURCE

Humanitarian Mine Action

Humanitarian mine action is comprised of four major components: mine awareness, mine detection, mine clearance, and survivor assistance. Depending on the needs of a given country, the United States may assist with one, some, or all four of these mine-action activities. In most instances, the affected nation will establish a MAC or a national demining office (NDO) to coordinate demining priorities and mine-action activities.

Part of the multinational force in Iraq, Mozambican Quick Reaction Demining Force (QRDF) soldiers remove unexploded ordnance in a residential area south of Baghdad, Iraq, May 12, 2003. © REUTERS/CORBIS.

Mine Awareness (or Mine-Risk Education)

Teaching people how to recognize, avoid, and inform demining authorities of the presence of landmines helps to reduce the number of casualties significantly. Mine awareness utilizes a variety of materials and media to convey important messages. The materials, and the manner in which mine awareness is presented, must be sensitive to the cultural mores of the local population. For example, in Afghanistan, women, not men, teach mine awareness to other women.

Mine awareness attempts to educate whole populations, allowing them to incorporate safety procedures into their daily lives, not just during a single event. Often, young children are a target audience for mine awareness. Mine-awareness teachers must discourage children from picking up and playing with mines and unexploded ordnance (UXO). Educating children to the dangers of landmines and UXO is often difficult, because they are fascinated with these toy-like metal and plastic objects. Still, the majority of mine casualties are young men. Informing adolescents and adults about the types of mines they may encounter and the injuries they inflict, and teaching them the proper procedures to follow if a mine is found can save lives.

U.S. military personnel provide mine-awareness training. These personnel are fluent in the languages of mine-affected countries, and they undergo country-specific cultural training prior to engagement in this activity.

Mine Detection

A Landmine Impact Survey helps to determine the nature and extent of the landmine problem in a specific country. The conduct of this survey entails identifying the broad areas within a country where mines exist and roughly estimating the extent of the problem. Areas where mines do not exist are also recorded in the survey. Next, a Technical Survey is conducted to obtain more specific detail on the landmine problem. Mined areas are demarcated and the number and types of mines found within the area are noted.

There is no single technology to employ in all circumstances, in all terrain and weather conditions, and against all types of mines. Metal detectors and hand-held probes remain the primary means to find many individual mines. The technology of these two devices is essentially 60 years old. Increasingly, however, deminers are recognizing the value of mine-detection dogs (MDDs), and the integration of man, dogs, and machines. Dogs are able to detect the chemical explosives in mines and are becoming increasingly important as their success rate increases and their reputation for safe and efficient mine detection spreads. Various mechanical technologies have greatly assisted overall mine-clearance efforts, significantly reducing areas that ultimately require manual mine clearance.

Even with advanced mine-detection methods, the locations of the majority of landmines in the ground today are unknown. International law requires that persons laying mines identify the type of landmines emplaced and make maps of their locations so that they may be removed at the conclusion of hostilities. Whether they are combatants in a war between nation-states or factions in a civil war, hostile parties are increasingly ignoring international law, placing mines indiscriminately without marking or recording their use or emplacement. Even when maps and other records are available, natural events may, over time, make them useless. To complicate matters, mines migrate from their original location as a result of shifting sands, as in the desert of the Middle East, or when heavy rains wash away the topsoil in tropical areas, as in Central America or Africa.

Mine Clearance

Clearing mines is slow, laborious, tedious, and highly dangerous. U.S. law states that "as a matter of policy, U.S. Forces shall not engage in physically detecting, lifting, or destroying landmines, unless it does so for the concurrent purpose of supporting a U.S. military operation; or provides such assistance as part of a military operation that does not involve the armed forces." Therefore, U.S. military personnel use a train-the-trainer approach to assist a country in clearing landmines. These personnel train an initial team of host-nation personnel in mine-clearance techniques, including medical evacuation procedures in the event of a demining accident. This indigenous cadre, in turn, trains another group, and so forth, until a large number of the country's nationals are sufficiently competent to clear mines safely and efficiently.

Once found, mines will not be removed from their location. Rather, the landmines will be left in place, marked, and then destroyed. If the terrain is suitable, specially equipped vehicles are maneuvered through the minefield in order to destroy multiple mines. The United Nations (UN) standard for a successful mine-clearance operation is that landmines and UXO down to twenty centimeters be destroyed. A process much like mine detection, called quality assurance, is generally used to assess mine-clearance operations. MDDs are very efficient for this process.

Survivor Assistance

The last mine-action component is survivor assistance that requires a long-term commitment to both the landmine survivor and to his or her family members. Although important, it is not enough simply to treat the initial injuries. Many children are landmine survivors. As a child grows, new prosthetic limbs are required, and a lifetime of additional operations and expenses is necessary. Over time, the psychological injury to landmine survivors also becomes a factor in their recovery and for their family members as well. For these reasons, mine-action programs encourage a holistic approach to providing assistance to the survivors of landmine injuries.

As a general rule, neither PM/HDP nor the DoD uses humanitarian demining funds for survivor assistance. PM/HDP does fund some survivors' assistance initiatives from a special fund appropriated to support the Republic of Slovenia's International Trust Fund (ITF) for Demining and Victims Assistance. However, the major PM/HDP-managed demining fund does not support such initiatives. The DoD, using Overseas Humanitarian, Disaster, and Civic Aid (OHDACA) and other operations and maintenance funds, pays for Blast Resuscitation and Victims Assistance. Additionally, USAID and the State Department's Bureau of Population, Refugees and Migration (PRM) fund programs to alleviate the suffering of landmine accident survivors and their families. USAID uses money from the LWVF to provide long-term treatment and prosthetics to these survivors. PRM's programs assist with the resettlement of refugees and internally displaced persons, many of whom are endangered by landmines in the course of flight from their homes and subsequent return.

SIGNIFICANCE

Many potential solutions to the ongoing problem of landmine deaths have been proposed. Research continues on a self-defeat feature, which would render mines inert after a set period of time. The United States' efforts include four separate objectives encompassing not just removal, but also education and rehabilitation. The International Campaign to Ban Landmines has actively campaigned for an international ban on the use of landmines, along with initiatives to destroy existing stocks of the weapons. In 1996, President Bill Clinton committed the United States to signing a treaty banning the use of mines, and in 1999, the International Mine Ban Treaty was ratified by numerous nations, although the United States was not a signatory.

Mines combine low deployment costs with high removal costs. Costing just a few dollars apiece, mines can be spread by air at rates of several thousand per hour; in some cases, mine removal can cost up to $1,000 per mine. Demining by hand is a tedious process, requiring a skilled technician to crawl along the ground and requiring most of a day to demine a fifty square yard area. Specialized equipment has also been developed for demining, including massive earth-battering machines which shred or explode buried mines in a controlled manner. More than 600 Mine Detection Dogs are also deployed throughout

the world, providing mine detection in areas unreachable by mechanized mine removal techniques.

The United States remains one of only a few nations that have not ratified the anti-mine treaty, with U.S. leaders expressing reluctance to give up any potentially useful weapon in their arsenal. Although U.S. funding for mine removal activities has climbed substantially, additional mines continue to be laid in war-torn regions throughout the world.

FURTHER RESOURCES

Books

Landau, Elaine. *Land Mines: 100 Million Hidden Killers*. Berkeley Heights, New Jersey: Enslow, 2000.

Winslow, Philip C. *Sowing the Dragon's Teeth: Landmines and the Global Legacy of War*. New York: Beacon Press, 1998.

Periodicals

Brinkert, Kerry. "The convention banning anti-personnel mines: applying the lessons of Ottawa's past in order to meet the challenges of Ottawa's future." *Third World Quarterly*. 24(2003):781–793.

Deane, Alexander. "Landmines—The Best Hope for Peace." *Contemporary Review*. 268(2005):14–16.

Obhodas, Jasmina et al. "Dynamics of soil parameters relevant for humanitarian demining." *Nuclear Instruments and Methods in Physics Research*. 241(2005):759–764.

Web sites

Humanitarian Demining. "Landmine Threats." <http://www.humanitarian-demining.org/demining/threats/proliferation.asp> (accessed May 28,2006).

International Committee to Ban Landmines. "What does the treaty cover?" <http://www.icbl.org/tools/faq/treaty/cover> (accessed June 2,2006).

United Nations Childrens Fund (UNICEF). "The legacy of land-mines." <http://www.unicef.org/sowc96/91dmines.htm> (accessed June 2,2006).

The Millennium Declaration to End Hunger in America

Declaration

By: Brandeis University, The Heller Center for Social Policy and Management: Institute on Assets and Social Policy—Center on Hunger and Poverty

Date: June 2003

Source: *Center on Hunger and Poverty.* " The Millennium Declaration to End Hunger in America" <http://www.centeronhunger.org/pdf/millenniumdeclaration.pdf> (accessed June 24, 2006).

About the Author: The Center on Hunger and Poverty, a division of the Institute on Assets and Social Policy (IASP), is a nonprofit organization associated with several projects on hunger and poverty across the United States. Its key activities include policy analysis, public education initiatives, and assistance enforcing legislation.

INTRODUCTION

Hunger and poverty issues in the United States are quite distinct from those in developing and under-developed countries. Many developing nations experience frequent famines and other natural calamities, which lead to acute malnutrition. Hunger in a developed country such as the United States is usually a consequence of poverty, unemployment, high costs, and low financial resources. The U.S. Census bureau reported that in 2001, thirty million people experienced hunger or food insecurity (inability to meet basic nutritional needs). These included families below the official poverty line, and those headed by single women, Hispanics, or African-Americans.

High rates of adult and childhood obesity are also related to hunger and low-income status. Even though hunger would seem not to be associated with obesity, research indicates a direct correlation between the two. For those with limited resources, low-nutrition, high-calorie junk food is cheap and easily available. The Center on Hunger and Poverty has found that a significant number of low-income individuals are obese or overweight, and the Interagency Board for Nutrition Monitoring and Related Research reported that poor adults are more likely to be obese than those with adequate means. Other reasons include the need to maximize caloric intake and overeating when food is available. Consequently, many poor people who are obese may actually be malnourished.

In a comprehensive national survey of emergency feeding programs, America's Second Harvest, a non-profit hunger relief organization, found that an increase in the number of households seeking 'emergency' food at feeding programs, food pantries, and soup kitchens in the late 1990s. Although the United States is the wealthiest nation in the world, in 2003 more than thirty-six million people, including thirteen million children, experienced hunger, an increase of six million in two years.

A volunteer carries a basket of food at the Westside Campaign Against Hunger's food pantry. The non-profit organization was founded as part of the New York City Coalition Against Hunger (NYCCAH). © VIVIANE MOOS/CORBIS.

According to the Food Research and Action Center (FRAC), in the school year ending in 2003 an average of 8.2 million children participated in the school breakfast program each day—6.8 million of them belonged to low-income households. Sixteen million low-income children participated in the national school lunch program the same year. Further, a FRAC national survey of nutritional risk determined that elderly people living in low-income households had lower nutrient intakes than those in higher-income households.

Following the 1996 World Food Summit, the U.S. government initiated the 'Healthy People 2010' campaign aimed at cutting the nation's food insecurity in half by 2010. On an international level, in September 2000, 147 leaders and heads of United Nations members (including the United States) affirmed a set of international development goals known as the 'Millennium Development Goals' (MDGs), part of the U.N. Millennium Declaration. Among other issues, the declaration urged member nations to address issues of hunger, poverty, and health.

In December 2003, the National Anti-Hunger Organizations (NAHO), an association of hunger relief organizations in the United States, issued the Millennium Declaration to End Hunger in America, calling upon leaders and citizens to end hunger in America. The declaration, excerpted in the primary source, outlines the causes and costs of hunger in the United States. It also recommends solutions to end hunger in the nation by 2015.

PRIMARY SOURCE

The Millennium Declaration to End Hunger in America

We call upon our nation's leaders and all people to join together to end hunger in America.

America carries the wound of more than 30 million people—more than 12 million of them children—whose households cannot afford an adequate and balanced diet. Hunger should have no place at our table. It is inconsistent with our commitment to human rights and objectionable to the American values of fairness, opportunity, family, and community.

Our nation is committed to leaving no child behind. But children who are hungry cannot keep up. They cannot develop and thrive; they cannot learn or play with energy and enthusiasm. Hunger stunts the physical, mental and emotional growth of many of our children, and stains the soul of America.

Many different points of view unite us in this declaration. Some of us work to end hunger because of deeply held religious beliefs. Others are motivated by hunger's impact on health and cognitive development. Still others are driven by the long-term economic, human and ethical costs of hunger. But all of us are moved by the recognition that America's moral authority in the world is undermined by so much hunger in our midst. Regardless of our religious beliefs or political commitments, we share the conviction that we as a nation must act to end hunger—now.

Ending hunger is a two-step process. We can make rapid progress by expanding and improving effective initiatives like public nutrition programs. This, combined with strengthened community-based efforts, has the capacity to feed all in need. But we need to go even further, to attack the root causes of hunger.

Our nation's own past experience, and the successes of other countries, demonstrate that this two-pronged strategy can work.

Ending hunger

America made great progress in reducing hunger during the 1960s and 1970s, as the economy grew and the nation built strong public nutrition programs—food stamps, school lunches and breakfasts, summer food, WIC, and elderly nutrition programs. These vital programs provide the fuel for children to develop and learn, and for adults to succeed at work and as parents.

As a country we did not sustain that momentum. One response has been the emergence of a strong private anti-hunger sector: food banks, pantries, soup kitchens, food rescue and other emergency feeding programs have become a key bulwark against hunger for many Americans. Volunteers, businesses, non-profits and religious organizations now help millions of needy Americans put food on their table.

But emergency feeding programs alone cannot end hunger. They cannot reach the scale essential to address the desperate need many people face, nor can they provide long-term security for the families they serve. Our country's experience over the past 20 years shows that charity can fill gaps and ameliorate urgent needs. But charity cannot match the capacity of government to protect against hunger, nor the capacity of the private sector to foster economic growth and provide living wages.

Ending hunger requires a sustained public commitment to improve federal nutrition programs, and to reduce red tape to reach every household and every individual in need:

- We can begin with the millions of at-risk children who start their school days without food, or who miss meals during the summer months, when they lose access to regular year school meal programs. Expanding programs for school lunch, breakfast, summer food, after-school meals for school age children, and child care food and WIC for pre-schoolers, is essential, cost-effective and a moral imperative.
- The food stamp program, the cornerstone of the nation's hunger programs, has the capacity to wipe out hunger for millions of families. We should reduce the red tape that often keeps working families and others from getting essential food stamp help. And the help families get should be enough so they do not run out of food toward the end of each month.
- We also must better protect elderly citizens whose frail bodies and meager incomes make them susceptible to hunger and nutrition-related diseases. Improving food stamps, home delivered meals, congregate feeding programs, and commodity donations will ensure that increasing age does not also mean an empty cupboard.

These and related nutrition programs can become readily available through the support of innovative community efforts across our country. And all programs can be re-woven to deliver healthy, nutritious meals to insure an end to hunger in America.

Ending the cause of hunger

The root cause of hunger is a lack of adequate purchasing power in millions of households. When individuals and families do not have the resources to buy enough food, hunger results. As a nation we must encourage work and also ensure all who work that the results of their labor will be sufficient to provide for the basic needs of their families. For those unemployed or disabled, or too old or young to support themselves, other means can ensure sufficient income to protect them from hunger.

Many steps can be taken to help families achieve independence and security: a strong economy; an adequate minimum wage that, like the one a generation ago, lifts a small family out of poverty; private and public sector provision of jobs and job training; strategies to create and increase assets among working families; social insurance protection for the unemployed and retired; and child care, refundable tax credits, food stamps, and health insurance that reward work efforts of families trying to make ends meet.

A sustained and comprehensive investment in the efforts of all American families will ensure that inadequate income never again results in lack of needed nutrition for the children and adults of our country.

Taking these steps to reward work and effort, along with the ready availability of nutritious food programs, will ensure that residents of the United States are not hungry tomorrow or any time in the future. Ending hunger in America will reduce dramatically the deprivation that currently saps the lives of so many of our children and families. Ending hunger will make us a stronger nation.

This goal is achievable. The time is now. We call upon the President, Congress, and other elected leaders in states and cities to provide decisive leadership to end hunger in America. Let us all work together, private and public leaders, community, religious and charitable groups, to achieve an America where hunger is but a distant memory and we live true to the values of a great nation.

SIGNIFICANCE

In the twentieth century, core programs managed by United States Department of Agriculture (USDA) such as the food stamp program, Child Nutrition Commodity Programs, the school meals programs, the Special Supplemental Nutrition Program for Women, Infants, and Children (WIC), and commodity distribution programs, have helped reduce vulnerability to food insecurity.

In the past, however, many families in need have not been able to participate in these programs. The millennium declaration unified several prominent antihunger organizations to eradicate hunger in the United States by ensuring higher participation in government programs. Although little has changed in the short time since the declaration, experts indicate that it is a step in the right direction.

NAHO members helped enact several programs after the declaration was issued. On June 3, 2004, the group released a "Blueprint to End Hunger" that mapped a targeted strategy to address hunger throughout the United States: "The fastest, most direct way to reduce hunger is to improve and expand the national nutrition programs so that they can provide people at risk of hunger with the resources they need." NAHO groups have sought bipartisan support for these recommendations.

In May 2005, the Hunger Free Communities Act was introduced in the U.S. Senate, reaffirming the commitment set forth by the blueprint. The act empowers authorities to gather more information on domestic hunger and strengthen local efforts through competitive grants to organizations such as food banks. The act also authorizes aid up to 50 million dollars a year for five years to assist hunger-relief organizations with infrastructure improvements, training and technical assistance, and expanding access to more nutritious food, including protein and produce.

According to NAHO members, eradicating hunger in the United States is possible through the joint effort of the government and various public health organizations, local dietetic associations, and community organizations. As outlined in the millennium declaration, such collaboration should not only provide food, but also develop educational programs that raise general awareness on food insecurity and undernourishment.

FURTHER RESOURCES

Books

Schwartz-Nobel, Laura. *Growing Up Empty: The Hunger Epidemic in America*. New York: HarperCollins, 2002.

Web sites

Center on Hunger and Poverty. "Understanding Food Security: Data and Methodology." March 2004. <http://www.centeronhunger.org/pdf/understanding.pdf> (accessed May 26, 2006).

Economic Research Service/USDA. "Improving Food Security in the United States." February 2003. <http://www.ers.usda.gov/publications/GFA14/GFA14-h.pdf> (accessed May 26, 2006).

Food and Agriculture Organization of the United Nations. "Committee on World Food Security : International Alliance against Hunger." September 2004. <http://www.fao.org/docrep/meeting/008/J2789e.htm> (accessed May 26, 2006).

Food Research and Action Center (FRAC). "Hunger in America, and its Solutions : Basic Facts." July 2005. <http://www.frac.org/pdf/HungerFacts.pdf> (accessed May 26, 2006).

———. "Hunger in the U.S." . <http://www.frac.org/html/hunger_in_the_us/hunger_index.html> (accessed May 26, 2006).

Heritage Foundation. Rector, Robert E., and Kirk A. Johnson. "Understanding Poverty in America." Backgrounder no. 1713. January 5, 2004. <http://www.heritage.org/Research/Welfare/bg1713.cfm> (accessed May 26, 2006).

United States Senate. Lugar, Richard G. "Lugar Introduces Hunger Free Communities Act." May 25, 2005. <http://lugar.senate.gov/pressapp/record.cfm?id=238197> (accessed May 26, 2006).

Model Colonia

Creative Solutions for Tough Problems

Report excerpt

By: U.S. Department of Housing and Urban Development

Date: 2004

Source: U.S. Department of Housing and Urban Development. "Model Colonia: Creative Solutions for Tough Problems." *Delivering Results to Colonias and Farmworker Communities* (February 2004).

About the Author: The U.S. Department of Housing and Urban Development (HUD) is the primary government agency responsible for ensuring equal access to housing and for improving the quality of affordable housing in the United States.

INTRODUCTION

The border between the United States and Mexico stretches through some of the most inhospitable land in North America, an arid semi-desert stretching from California to Texas. Scattered through this vast wasteland lie approximately 3,000 small settlements known as *colonias.* In Texas alone, more than 400,000 residents live in these impoverished villages, where housing is generally substandard. Inadequate or non-existent sewage and water systems contribute to high rates of diseases more commonly seen in undeveloped nations. Unemployment rates in the colonias are as much as nine times the overall rate for the region.

Colonias first appeared in the border region in the 1950s, when developers bought otherwise worthless land and began creating small housing developments. Because these neighborhoods lay outside incorporated towns, few regulations governed their design and construction. Targeting poor buyers, the developers frequently packed the homes tightly together, skimping on basic amenities such as paving, water, and electricity. The poorly built homes would never have passed inspection in an incorporated area.

Given the poor quality of the homes, colonias appealed only to the poorest buyers; a recent study found that Texas counties along the Mexican border have average incomes less than half that of the rest of the state and that colonia residents in particular earn an average of just $5,000 per year. Colonia buyers were frequently enticed by a financing technique known as a contract for deed. Under this arrangement, the seller accepts a low down payment and low monthly payments but retains title to the property until it is fully paid off. Similar to a rent-to-own arrangement, these contracts often include high interest rates and provide the buyer little chance of ever taking ownership of the property.

Efforts to improve living conditions in the colonias have faced numerous obstacles. In a few colonias, water mains are in place but residents whose houses will not pass inspection are not allowed to connect before making extensive repairs and improvements. In many cases, residents are forced to purchase water in buckets or rely on uninspected wells. In addition, poverty, illiteracy, and language barriers make it difficult for many of the residents to navigate the complicated system of regulations involved in taking legal action against dishonest developers. For these reasons, modern colonias are often little more than disease-ridden rural ghettos with dirt roads running between cardboard and wood shacks.

Responding to the deplorable conditions in the colonias, the U.S. Department of Housing and Urban Development (HUD) in 1996 began studying the situation along the border. Among the goals of the HUD effort was improved coordination among the numerous state, federal, and local agencies attempting to alleviate the problem. The result was an initial effort to redevelop a single model colonia, in the hope that this project would serve as both a learning laboratory and a model for future efforts throughout the region.

▌ PRIMARY SOURCE

The Model Colonia is representative of HUD's efforts to involve local residents and key partners in the process of making real change happen.

Dona Ana County, the largest of the eleven New Mexico border counties, has the highest number of colonias in the state of New Mexico. And of those 37 Dona Ana colonias, Vado/Del Cerro residents live in some of the poorest conditions. Vado began as a farming settlement in 1886, and Del Cerro was established as an extension by farmworkers thereafter. According to 1999 figures, 33 percent of the families in Vado/Del Cerro live below the poverty level. In addition, 77 percent of the population over 25 are not high school graduates, so families tend to survive on low-wage employment at nearby dairies or truck stops. But Vado/Del Cerro also has a very active and involved group of partners committed to community improvement.

To show what county, state, federal, and nonprofit partners can do together to improve the lives of colonia residents, HUD has funded a comprehensive, community-based planning process in Vado/Del Cerro.

HUD funding is leveraging other federal and private sector investors to demonstrate how a colonia can be transformed into an economically and socially viable community.

Anticipated outcomes of the Model Colonia are:

A comprehensive plan that paves the way for public and private investment, leading to substantial improvement in living conditions.
Elimination of unplanned, colonias-style growth. All new homes in the community will be required to meet basic housing and infrasructure standards.
Enhanced coordination among federal, state, and local agencies.
A model that can be replicated in other colonias or farmworker communities.

The Model Colonia reflects HUD's broadest goals. It will help ensure equal opportunity in housing, increase homeownership opportunities, and promote decent, affordable housing. It promotes the participation of faith-based and community organizations, and will strengthen communities by improving economic conditions.

Model Colonia Partners: Investing in Change

Many organizations are helping HUD transform Vado/Del Cerro:

Community Leaders. Vado/Del Cerro residents have taken ownership of the project and are guiding priorities for action. Centro Fuerza y Unidad, a grassroots organization, has been the driving force behind progress in Del Cerro for over 10 years. It currently receives HUD technical assistance so it can obtain a nonprofit designation, which will open new opportunities for funding.

Dona Ana County Board of Commissioners. The county has designated the Vado/Del Cerro Community as the initial model colonia for the U.S. Department of Housing and Urban Development Model Colonia Initiative and has prioritized infrastructure needs in the county's other 36 colonias. The county has also created a new Community Outreach Division within the Department of Health and Human Services and a special coordinator to work specifically on colonias.

New Mexico State Legislature. Southern New Mexico legislators have pledged to assist with the Model Colonia. In the 2004 legislative session, legislators introduced multiple model colonia bills, and $285,000 was secured.

Vado Water Mutual Domestic Association. This nonprofit organization has advocated for infrastructure improvements in the community of Vado since the 1960's.

Las Cruces-Dona Ana Housing Authority. This public housing authority has committed to use proceeds from the sales of existing housing authority units to purchase land for an 18-unit affordable housing pilot using self-help/alternative materials. Model Colonia land has been purchased, and the development process has begun.

Gadsden Independent School District. GISD will be locating a new elementary school in the Model Colonia. Construction is slated to begin soon, and the school will open in fall 2005.

Additional Partners such as Las Cruces Affordable Housing Inc. (a Community Housing Development Organization), New Mexico Mortgage Finance Authority, the Enterprise Foundation, U.S. Department of Agriculture Rural Development, and the Housing Assistance Council are contributing as well.

Colonia/Farmworker Initiatives...

HUD began its coordinated focus on the Southwest Border, colonias, and migrant/farmworker communities in 1996. In 2001, a Department-wide Southwest Border, Colonias, and Migrant/Farmworker Task Force developed a unified plan with specific actions assigned to HUD's different program offices. Implementation managers from these program offices have been turning the plan into action.

A small team is dedicated full-time to coordination of this effort. This Southwest Border, Colonias, and Migrant/Farmworker Initiatives (SWBR) work group—with staff assigned in HUD headquarters and field offices in states with colonias and high farmworker populations—is part of an office that reports directly to HUD's Deputy Secretary.

HUD has also begun developing partnerships with other federal agencies to address the complex needs along the border and among migrant farmworkers.

SIGNIFICANCE

The widespread poverty and public health problems in the colonias are symptomatic of a variety of underlying problems. By locating outside of established towns, unscrupulous developers are able to flourish with little or no oversight. The narrow, unpaved roads they build are difficult for school buses to navigate, reducing resident access to education, while the inadequate sewage systems they install lead to higher levels of disease. HUD's current project includes efforts to close the regulatory loopholes through which these developers are able to slide.

HUD is also focusing its efforts on coordination among local, state, and federal agencies. The GNMA (Ginnie Mae) Targeted Lending Initiative has provided $12 million to assist in the Model Colonia experiment, and faith-based and community improvement organizations are being encouraged to participate, adding their resources to the $46 million HUD has invested in the project. As a result, participating development groups can receive assistance with lot purchase and development, while qualified homeowners are eligible for down-payment assistance. Homeowners can also receive loan forgiveness on a portion of their mortgage, provided they meet payment obligations.

HUD and other involved organizations are optimistic that the Model Colonia experiment will provide the first practical solutions in addressing the persistent, pervasive poverty along the Texas-Mexico border.

FURTHER RESOURCES
Books

Riis, Jacob A. and Luc Sante. *How the Other Half Lives: Studies among the Tenements of New York*. New York: Penguin Group, 1997.

Sanchez Korrol, Virginia E. *From Colonia to Community: The History of Puerto Ricans in New York City*. Los Angeles: University of California Press, 1994.

Ward, Peter M. *Colonias and Public Policy in Texas and Mexico: Urbanization by Stealth*. Austin: University of Texas Press, 1999.

Periodicals

Myers, Dowell and Cathy Yang Liu. "The Emerging Dominance of Immigrants in the US Housing Market: 1970–2000." *Urban Policy & Research* 23 (2005): 347–365.

Saegert, Susan and Gary Evans. "Poverty, Housing Niches, and Health in the United States." *Journal of Social Issues* 59 (2003): 569–589.

Shroder, Mark. "Does Housing Assistance Perversely Affect Self-sufficiency? A Review Essay." *Journal of Housing Economics* 11 (2002): 381–417.

Web sites

Housing Assistance Council. "Model Loan Program Provides Assistance to Colonia Residents." <http://www.hud.gov/local/nm/groups/goodstory01.cfm> (accessed June 1, 2006).

Texas Secretary of State Roger Williams. "Colonia Legislation in Texas." <http://www.sos.state.tx.us/border/colonias/legislation.shtml> (accessed June 1, 2006).

U.S. Department of Housing and Urban Development. "The Model Colonias Project: A New Mexico Success Story." <http://www.hud.gov/local/nm/groups/goodstory01.cfm> (accessed June 1, 2006).

International Red Cross

Photograph

By: Andrea Booher

Date: September 2, 2005

Source: Booher, Andrea. "Hurricane Katrina Refugees." AP Images, September 2, 2005.

About the Photographer: This photograph was taken by Andrea Booher, a contributor to the Associated Press. Based in New York, the Associated Press (AP) is the world's largest and oldest news organization.

INTRODUCTION

In October 1863, The International Red Cross and Red Crescent Movement was initiated in Geneva, Switzerland. With the aim of providing nonpartisan

PRIMARY SOURCE

International Red Cross: A Red Cross volunteer comforting a hurricane Katrina victim in the Houston Astrodome on September 2, 2005. AP IMAGES.

care to the wounded and sick in times of war, the Movement adopted the Red Cross emblem as a symbol of neutrality. Ever since, the Red Cross and Red Crescent have been universally accepted symbols of relief operations. As of the twenty-first century, the International Red Cross and Red Crescent Movement, boasting more than one hundred million members and volunteers, is active in almost every country of the world.

The seven basic tenets that govern the Movement are humanity, impartiality, neutrality, independence, voluntary service, unity, and universality. The Movement comprises the International Committee of the Red Cross (ICRC), National Red Cross and Red Crescent Societies (National Societies) in about 180 countries, and the International Federation of Red Cross and Red Crescent Societies (The International Federation). Each of these organizations is independ-

ent with unique status and rights and has no authority over the other.

The ICRC, based in Geneva, Switzerland, was established in 1863. It is an independent organization with a mission to help victims of war and internal violence. It directs and coordinates international relief activities conducted by the Movement in situations of conflict.

Established in 1919, the International Federation acts as an official representative of the Movement's member societies in the international community and coordinates relief operations during natural and man-made disasters. One of the main objectives of the Federation is to promote cooperation between National Societies—which work at national levels to co-ordinate disaster relief, health, and socio-economic programs—and strengthen their disaster-relief capacity.

To plan their humanitarian agenda, representatives from member associations meet at the International Conference of the Red Cross and Red Crescent, held every four years. Over the years, the International Red Cross and Red Crescent Movement, along with associated organizations, has undertaken numerous disaster-relief operations across the world, including the 2005 disasters caused by hurricane Katrina (in New Orleans) and the Asian tsunami (in southern Asia). Most of these disaster-relief programs are organized by the local National Societies. The American Red Cross (ARC) is a National Society operating in the United States. The American Red Cross, in addition to donations, also receives reimbursement for its programs from the Federal Emergency Management Agency (FEMA).

PRIMARY SOURCE

INTERNATIONAL RED CROSS

See primary source image.

SIGNIFICANCE

The International Red Cross and Red Crescent Movement, through its National Societies, has helped millions of disaster victims around the world. These societies assist in various ways, raising funds, acting as government liaisons, providing health and family services, organizing volunteers and temporary shelters, and imparting training for disaster preparedness and management to local authorities. In the aftermath of hurricane Katrina and hurricane Rita, more than 225,000 volunteers of the American Red Cross assisted in providing food, water, and shelter to the storm survivors—making it one of the biggest disaster relief operations in the history of the United States. Thousands of victims were provided temporary shelter in 1,200 shelters across twenty-seven states. In addition, Red Cross Emergency Response Vehicles (ERVs) delivered more than sixty-five million meals to affected communities.

The cost of such massive operations to societies like the ARC, which depends on donations and federal funding, is extensive. Considered the most expensive disaster in the United States, the World Trade Center terrorist attacks of September 11, 2001, reportedly cost the organization more than $997 million in disaster aid. According to the Red Cross and Red Crescent Movement, the key to providing timely relief during such disasters is partnership with local associations and authorities. The American Red Cross,

On September 1, 2005, nearly 5,000 Hurricane Katrina refugees fill the Astrodome in Houston for relief and goods. © ERICH SCHLEGEL/DALLAS MORNING NEWS/CORBIS.

for instance, has numerous partners such as the Air Transport Association of America (ATA), American Hospital Association (AHUA), American School Food Service Association (ASFSA), Central United States Earthquake Consortium (CUSEC), National Association of Social Workers, U.S. Geological Survey, and others. During the relief operations for hurricanes Katrina and Rita, the ARC partnered with several schools, churches, and recreation centers to provide 3.4 million overnight stays between August and December of 2005.

However, both the International Red Cross and Red Crescent Movement and the American Red Cross have been embroiled in controversies for several years. Reportedly, allegations exist against the two organizations relating to mismanagement of funds and maltreatment. After the devastating San Francisco earthquake of 1989, the Red Cross, news reports stated, used only $10 million of the $50 million raised for disaster relief operations. After the World Trade Center bombings, the ARC, under the Liberty Fund, is said to have collected $564 million in donations. Out of this, only $154 million were reported to have been distributed to the affected families. Following hearings instituted by the House Energy and Commerce Committee, American Red Cross President Dr. Bernadine Healy quit the organization.

The policies of ICRC have also been criticized in the United States. In June 2005, Jon Kyl, Chairman of the United States Republican Policy Party, mentioned that the ICRC is "disserving American interests." He accused the international agency of trying to "reinterpret and expand international law so as to afford terrorists and insurgents the same rights and privileges as military personnel of states party to the Geneva Conventions" and also attempting to "lobby for arms control issues that are not within the organization's mandate, e.g. the reinterpretation of the Chemical Weapons Convention and banning land mines."

Over the years, the functioning of the International Red Cross and Red Crescent Movement has drawn flak from legislators, media, and the public. Even so, thousands of relief operations have been undertaken by the movement, with the ARC alone responding to nearly 73,000 domestic disasters each year.

FURTHER RESOURCES

Books

Haug, Hans. *Humanity for All: The International Red Cross and Red Crescent Movement.* Bern, Switzerland: Paul Haupt Publishers, 1993.

International Committee of the Red Cross. *Handbook of the International Red Cross and Red Crescent Movement.* International Federation of Red Cross and Red Crescent Societies, 1994.

Web sites

American Red Cross. "Challenged by the Storms." <http://www.redcross.org/sponsors/drf/stewardship/HurrStewRep06.asp> (accessed June 11, 2006).

International Federation of Red Cross and Red Crescent Societies. <http://www.ifrc.org> (accessed June 11, 2006).

The U.S. Senate Republican Policy Committee. "Are American Interests Being Disserved by the International Committee of the Red Cross?" June 13, 2005. <http://rpc.senate.gov/_files/Jun1305ICRCDF.pdf> (accessed June 11, 2006).

Katrina: Our System for Fixing Broken Lives is Broken

Editorial

By: Brian A. Gallagher

Date: September 12, 2005

Source: Gallagher, Brian A. "Katrina: Our System for Fixing Broken Lives is Broken." United Way of America, September 12, 2005.

About the Author: Brian A. Gallagher is the President and CEO of the United Way of America. The United Way is one of the largest charity and assistance-providing organizations in the United States and is a national network of volunteers, caregivers and smaller charity providers.

INTRODUCTION

When Hurricane Katrina struck the Gulf Coast of the United States in the late summer of 2005, the result was one of the most widespread and costly natural disasters in the history of the country. Most directly affecting the states of Louisiana, Alabama, and Mississippi, the storm and the massive floods which came afterward left many thousands of people homeless and billions of dollars worth of damage. Approximately 1,600 people died directly as a result of the storm or from conditions caused by the storm.

Even while the winds and rain that battered the Gulf Coast area were less powerful than forecasters had initially predicted, the storm itself did cause many homes and large buildings to be destroyed. However, the more costly damages resulting from Katrina came from the flooding of the city of New Orleans. Much of the city is located below sea level. It is heavily dependent on a system of pumps and levees that keep water from pouring into the city from the various large bodies of water that sit on both sides. The system proved incapable of standing up to Katrina's combination of winds, rain, and storm surges. It failed in several locations, allowing water to pour in and flood over eighty percent of the city. While Katrina's impact on New Orleans was particularly spectacular and widely reported on, damage to the rest of the region was also severe.

In the days following the hurricane, many thousands of New Orleans residents who had been unable to evacuate prior to the storm were stranded in the city. Delivery of supplies to the affected areas and

Hurricane survivors evacuate their home in Chalmette, Louisiana, September 3, 2005, days after surviving Hurricane Katrina. © MICHAEL AINSWORTH/DALLAS MORNING NEWS/ CORBIS.

PRIMARY SOURCE

The unrivaled impact of Hurricane Katrina is measured not only in dollars and cents, but in human lives. Untold thousands are feared dead, and hundreds of thousands have been displaced from their homes or have lost all of their earthly possessions.

Therefore, while contributing to the various relief funds is an essential element of our response to this national tragedy, money alone doesn't fix broken lives. What is needed is a human-based response that outlives the news media's attention to the Gulf States and addresses the less obvious, but no less significant challenges created by the devastation.

If the Oklahoma City bombing and the September 11th terrorist attacks are any indication, two things will surely occur in the aftermath of Hurricane Katrina. First, our emergency response preparedness will be dissected. Second, the American people will respond with characteristic generosity to meet the immediate needs of those affected. Each response is important, but each is ultimately predictable and insufficient.

The assessment of our emergency response capabilities will likely be politicized and polarized, yielding changes only at the margins. And while the immediate response from people shows our immense capacity to care, it will not change the desperate conditions in which hundreds of thousands of people in the Gulf States, and millions of Americans elsewhere, live each day.

What America needs to do now—not only in response to Hurricane Katrina, but in addressing the long-standing challenges facing communities nationwide—is to think and act beyond the traditional stimulus-response formula to serving those in need. Hurricane Katrina has arrested the nation's attention, while leading to a spike in fund raising for numerous charities. Yet, if a similar tragedy were to befall New Orleans in ten years, would the human anguish still fracture along the same racial and socioeconomic lines?

The current delivery system for relief and social services is heroic but clearly inadequate. A new system, based on the principles described below, constitutes America's best course of action for having a long-term, positive impact on those in need.

Adopt a human-based approach. Contrary to the system-or institution-based approach, which often results in bureaucratic gridlock because agencies require clients to conform to their individual intake and service systems, the human-based approach caters to the needs of the affected person. The customer-first principle is a hallmark of successful companies, but remains a stubborn challenge for public and private agencies.

transportation of the residents out of the city took a period of several days. During that period, a great deal of unrest and looting took place throughout the New Orleans area. There are reports that authorities on occasion were forced to retreat from rescue situations because they were being fired upon. In the days, weeks, and months following the hurricane, the alleged slow response of authorities become a focus of much discussion. Critics saw the government's response as ineffective and poorly coordinated. They claimed that the government had shown that it was not prepared for this type of disaster and had failed to properly respond, resulting in further damage and loss of life. Criticism of the Federal Emergency Management Agency (FEMA), which is charged with coordinating rescue and recovery efforts following large disasters, was particularly strong.

Volunteers load relief supplies bound for Hurricane Katrina victims into a truck in the Van Nuys section of Los Angeles, September 7, 2005. AP IMAGES.

Operate from a master plan. Community leaders need to develop a comprehensive plan to serve all Gulf State evacuees in any community that has accepted them. The elements of this plan will cover a broad scope of services ranging from crisis counseling, housing and daycare to cash assistance, education and job training. This same comprehensive approach is no less valid for communities seeking to eradicate teen pregnancy, drug use or illiteracy.

Integrate the delivery of services. Hurricane Katrina offers a compelling microcosm of the need for a single source of information regarding relief services. 2-1-1,

a toll-free phone number that citizens can use to access essential services and volunteer opportunities, exists in Louisiana and now serves as the state's primary clearing house for requests for assistance and has accepted thousands of calls. Conversely, Mississippi, which lacks a 2-1-1 system, doesn't have a coordinated, statewide means of managing such requests. With 2-1-1 operating in less than half of the country, Congress should enact legislation and provide funding to establish an integrated nationwide 2-1-1 network that would allow service providers to seamlessly help those in need—regardless of where they are physically located.

Stay committed to a community's long-term needs. In the last few months, when is the last time you encountered a news article about the rebuilding efforts in those Southeast Asian countries affected by the last year's tsunami, despite the fact that these efforts will take years to complete? We need to resist the temptation to shape programs and deploy resources based on the day's headline and remember that mental health counselors were getting new requests for service seven years after the bombing in Oklahoma City. This points to the need for agencies to set long-term goals and make the necessary commitments to achieve them.

Create a $10 billion Human Development Fund. We will pour billions of dollars into rebuilding the physical infrastructure of New Orleans and the Gulf Coast, but let's also invest billions in rebuilding human lives through the creation of mixed income housing communities and neighborhoods; the creation of jobs that pay enough to sustain a family; and the placement of services like grocery stores in all neighborhoods. Let's create family development accounts for college and home ownership; neighborhood redevelopment accounts that provide incentives to establish small businesses in challenged areas; and quality early education and education support services that includes the building of YMCA's attached to public schools to better serve kids and their families.

While the human cost of Hurricane Katrina is ultimately incalculable, what is acutely apparent is that rebuilding the Gulf States will require a historic concentration of diverse resources spread across many years. Successfully managing an effort of such scale will require a measure of precision, coordination and commitment that our current delivery system simply cannot accommodate. With the wellbeing of hundreds of thousands of people hanging in the balance, isn't it time that America forged a new and better way of serving those in need?

SIGNIFICANCE

Following the storm, a great deal of public and media attention focused on the many allegations that the response of the government authorities had been inadequate and as a result thousands of people were left without basic supplies, many of whom were in desperate conditions.

The response of many individuals such as Gallagher was to seek ways to ensure that when future disasters struck the United States, the relevant authorities would be far better prepared. Much attention had been placed on questions regarding why the United States—one of the world's most wealthy and developed countries—failed to produce a rescue plan and access stranded people in a shorter amount of time. Some critics, as shown in this statement, asserted that the government response was caught up in bureaucracy, slowing down rescue efforts. The suggestion for a more human-based approach would present a big change for government agencies, which are usually built on a bureaucratic model.

The United Way's statement was designed to show that helping the people of the Gulf Coast most directly affected by Hurricane Katrina would require longer-term solutions beyond just rebuilding the damaged areas. By focusing on the years and decades ahead, the United Way is working to allow residents of one of the nation's poorest regions an opportunity to build a higher quality of life.

FURTHER RESOURCES
Books

Brinkley, Douglas. *The Great Deluge: Hurricane Katrina, New Orleans, and the Mississippi Gulf Coast*. New York: William Morrow, 2006.

Hurricane Katrina: Response and Responsibilities, edited by John Brown Childs. Santa Cruz, Calif.: New Pacific Press, 2006.

Web sites

The United Way. <http://www.unitedway.org> (accessed June 8, 2006).

Google Subpoena Roils the Web

Newspaper article

By: Hiawatha Bray

Date: January 21, 2006

Source: Bray, Hiawatha. "Google Subpoena Roils the Web." *Boston Globe* (January 21, 2006).

About the Author: Hiawatha Bray is a staff reporter for the *Boston Globe*, a nationally distributed newspaper based in Boston.

INTRODUCTION

In 1998, the U.S. Congress passed the Child Online Protection Act, one of whose provisions would have required commercial distributors of online sexual materials to block access by minors to that material. The law was challenged as an infringement on free

Computers display the Google Desktop search engine at a convention in New York's Jacob K. Javitz convention center, October 14, 2004. AP IMAGES.

speech. Enforcement of the act was blocked starting in 1998 by a ruling of a Federal district court, and the block was upheld in 2004 by the U.S. Supreme Court in *Ashcroft v. American Civil Liberties Union*. However, the Court returned the case to a lower Federal court for further consideration instead of overturning the Act altogether. The case was still being considered as of early 2006.

In August 2005, in order to bolster its case for the Child Online Protection Act, the U.S. Justice Department issued a subpoena to the Google corporation for data on Internet searches. It sought information that would show that sexual information is easily accessible on the Internet (therefore presumably a threat to children). A subpoena is a court order that requires a party to testify to the court; disobedience may entail criminal penalties.

The Justice Department sought access to records for all of the billions of search queries performed by U.S. computer users over a one-week period, along with a random sample of one million Internet addresses searchable by Google. The Justice Department did not request information that would have

allowed it to identify which computer users had searched which sites, although Google does record this information. It is collected using cookies, which are small files that are sent from a Web site, such as Google.com, to the Web browser software on a user's computer, then re-sent from that computer to the same Web site every time it is accessed. User logs can show that a particular user accessed a specific site on a certain date.

Three other Internet search companies received similar subpoenas, but only Google said that it would not comply. Although its refusal was widely reported as an effort to protect its customers' privacy, Google denied that it was refusing the request on privacy-protection grounds. At the same time, it refused to explain what its reasons for withholding the information actually were. Some Internet experts speculated that Google was afraid that trade secrets could be deduced from the information.

In January, 2006 the Justice Department asked a Federal court to force Google to comply with the subpoena. In March, after the Justice Department agreed to shrink its request, the judge said that he would order Google to supply the information. Google complied with the reduced request, which was for 50,000 searchable Internet addresses and no search queries.

■ PRIMARY SOURCE

The US government's demand for millions of Internet search records from Google Inc. and other prominent search firms has raised new questions about the vast amounts of personal information collected by companies.

While federal investigators said they weren't seeking any data that could be traced to individuals, Internet privacy activists and some lawmakers said the action underscored concerns about what the search engines know about computer users and what could become of that information.

"Internet search engines provide an extraordinary service," said Representative Edward Markey, a Malden Democrat, "but the preservation of that service [should] not rely on a bottomless, timeless database that can do great damage despite good intentions."

Markey said yesterday that he will propose legislation as early as next month that would force search companies to destroy records containing personal information after "a reasonable period of time." Markey said that he'd been working on the legislation since last year, modeling it on a law that requires cable television firms to destroy personal data about customers' viewing habits.

Google is vowing to resist efforts by the U.S. Justice Department to obtain information about the searches run by millions of its users, even though investigators are seeking aggregate data about Internet use, not individual users' records. The Justice Department wants the information as part of its effort to defend the Child Online Protection Act, a 1998 federal law that seeks to ban Internet sites from displaying content that the government deems "harmful to minors." The Supreme Court has ruled that the law can't be enforced unless the government shows less intrusive measures such as Internet filtering are inadequate. The government hopes to use search results from Google and other companies to show that Internet pornography is so pervasive that only a federal law can protect children from it.

Yahoo Inc., Microsoft Corp.'s MSN search service, and Time Warner Inc.'s AOL service have all agreed to provide the information, according to a Justice Department spokesman. But Google has refused, saying that releasing the data would compromise its users' privacy and the company's trade secrets. "Google is not a party to this lawsuit and their demand for information overreaches," said Nicole Wong, Google's associate general counsel. "We intend to resist their motion vigorously."

Meanwhile, shares of Google had their biggest decline ever yesterday as the company continued to resist the Justice Department's demand. Google dropped nearly 8.5 percent, to close at $399.46.

During each visit to Google or any other Internet site, a visitor's computer reveals a numerical address assigned by the user's Internet provider. The site can store that information, along with the date and time of the visit. This information can be used by researchers, marketers, or investigators to trace the visitor's identity.

In papers filed yesterday at a federal court in San Jose, Calif., government attorneys said that they are not seeking information about individuals. They want the search companies to provide a sample of a million websites from the billions they currently index, as well as all the search terms typed into the services during a one-week period. All information that could identify individuals is to be removed before the data is given to the government. The government could use the data to estimate how pervasive pornography is on the Internet and how often pornographic sites come up in random Internet searches.

The federal subpoenas have dismayed Internet privacy activists. "There's something disturbing about the notion that when you search for something the government is going to be looking over your shoulder," said Kurt Opsahl, staff attorney for the Electronic Frontier Foundation, an Internet civil liberties group.

The subpoenas also drew attention to how the major search services have become repositories of their users' personal data. "They have lots of information," said Danny Sullivan, editor of Search Engine Watch, an industry trade publication. "They know what people are clicking on. They know what people are searching for." By analyzing their vast databases of past searches, the companies can improve their software to help users find data more quickly. The companies can also upgrade the lucrative software that places paid advertisements on the search results pages. Currently, Google retains information about Web users' online activity for as long as it deems the data useful, according to a company spokesman.

Some privacy activists have long feared that companies like Google could abuse the data, by providing it to government officials or by using it themselves to track individual Internet usage. One public interest group, Public Information Research Inc. of San Antonio, runs scroogle.org, an Internet service that disguises the Internet address of searchers who want to run Google and Yahoo searches anonymously.

Opsahl suggested that Internet users concerned about privacy should do their Internet searches through

Scroogle or other Internet "proxies" that hide the address of the searcher. But he also urged Google and other search companies to regularly erase their database of saved searches. "Perhaps they should consider whether it's worthwhile to keep all this information indefinitely," he said.

SIGNIFICANCE

The Google subpoena controversy reveals a source of increasing tension in modern society: the ability of computers to track the behaviors of millions of individuals over time in a highly specific way, whether they are suspected of any crime or not. Computer records from credit-card transactions, cell-phone and land-line calls, Internet searches, Web site visits, online purchases and downloads, automatic toll-booths, built-in automotive navigation systems, Global Positioning System devices, hospitals, police and military organizations, and other sources can all be compiled with relative ease and, potentially, delivered to government authorities. When compiled, such records can give a remarkably complete picture of a person's movements, habits, and contacts. Some experts argue that the possession of so much information by intelligence agencies, police, and the like could be used to monitor personal behavior in ways that infringe on basic liberties. They point to countries that not only censor Internet usage but use it to track down and punish political dissidents. One such is China, where dozens of political dissidents have been jailed in recent years using data gleaned from Internet usage records—including data supplied voluntarily by Yahoo!, a rival of Google.

In May, 2006, in an affair reminiscent of the Google subpoena case, it was reported by the newspaper *USA Today* that the National Security Agency had been secretly collecting records from the telecommunications companies AT&T, Verizon, and BellSouth. The records allegedly collected showed the source and destination of all telephone calls made in the United States since just after September 11, 2001. Actual conversations were not recorded. (However, debate was also occurring over 2005 revelations that the National Security Agency had for several years been recording the telephone conversations of some U.S. citizens and others without obtaining search warrants). The stated purpose of the en masse call monitoring was to look for calling patterns that might signify terrorist planning, but critics of the program expressed outrage that the phone records of tens of millions of U.S. citizens had been obtained without warrant or reason to suspect criminal activity. In a press conference the same

day, President George W. Bush defended the program, saying, "Al-Qaeda is our enemy, and we want to know their plans. We are not mining or trolling through the personal lives of innocent Americans." According to *USA Today*, the President "didn't address specifics of the program and walked away without responding to reporters' questions."

Computer network technologies, by their very nature, can make their users highly visible and traceable. Debate will continue over the distinction between legitimate tracking of security threats and uses of computerized information that violate basic liberties.

FURTHER RESOURCES

Books

Vise, David A. *The Google Story*. New York: Delacorte Press, 2005.

Periodicals

Hafner, Katie. "After Subpoenas, Internet Searches Give Some Pause." The *New York Times* (January 25, 2006).

Hafner, Katie and Matt Richtel. "Google Resists U.S. Subpoena of Search Data." The *New York Times* (January 19, 2006).

Shenk, David. "A Growing Web of Watchers Builds a Surveillance Society." The *New York Times* (January 25, 2006).

Web sites

American Civil Liberties Union. "Plaintiff's Response to Motion to Compel Google." February 17, 2006. <http://www.aclu.org/images/asset_upload_file415_24 211.pdf> (accessed May 29, 2006).

More Companies Ending Promises for Retirement

Newspaper article

By: Mary Williams Walsh

Date: January 9, 2006

Source: New York Times

About the Author: Mary Walsh has been a financial reporter with the *New York Times* since 2000. She has also written for the *Los Angeles Times* and the *Wall Street Journal*. She is the recipient of the Overseas Press Club of America citation for excellence in 1995.

President Bush speaks with workers at the John Deere-Hitachi Machinery Corporation in Kernersville, North Carolina, December 5, 2005. President Bush called on American businesses to live up to their pension promises, saying too many companies are not putting away enough money to protect the retirement benefits of their workers. AP IMAGES.

INTRODUCTION

For most Americans during the first half of the twentieth century, an ideal career followed a fairly predictable path. Following high school, a person would take a job with a large corporation. He would work there for the next forty years, gradually moving to positions of greater authority and higher pay. At retirement, he would enjoy a festive party at which his coworkers would celebrate his success and present him with an expensive gold wristwatch as a retirement gift. And for the remainder of his life, his former employer would pay him a comfortable monthly wage, along with medical care and other benefits.

The promise of a lifetime pension and a comfortable retirement provided some consolation for work-ers laboring at repetitive jobs in hot, noisy factories. As the American economy expanded, a rapidly growing marketplace led to soaring profits for large manufacturers, and their rapid growth enabled them to pay their pension obligations to former employees easily. By the 1960s, a majority of American workers were covered by a retirement plan of some sort in which benefits were guaranteed for life.

During this same time span, however, several factors were converging to bring about the death of the traditional pension. First, economic growth slowed, meaning that large industrial companies could no longer depend on reliable earnings growth from which to pay retirees. Second, increasing life spans meant that retired workers lived longer, and consequently received their pensions for far longer than their employers had planned. Finally, as medical science advanced, retiree health-care costs also soared, making each one more expensive to support. In many companies, projections suggested that the traditional pension model was no longer viable, and that runaway retiree costs posed a threat to the business's survival. In response, corporate managers began making wholesale changes to the way in which retirement benefits are paid.

The primary danger of the traditional pension plan lies in its dependence on a series of educated guesses, including how long retirees will live, how much the pension funds can earn in investments, and what future benefits will cost. When these guesses are wrong, as when employees predicted to live to age seventy-five actually reach eighty years old, the company must pay the difference, in this case an additional five years of pension income. Traditional plans are called defined benefit plans, meaning the company promises to pay a defined or set amount of money for as long as the retiree lives. They guarantee benefits while placing the risk of the plan and its predictions entirely on the company.

As corporations began to stagger under their enormous retiree costs, however, they had to limit their risk to avoid the cost overruns of traditional systems. To achieve this goal, most companies began phasing out their defined benefit systems in favor of defined contribution plans. These new plans, including plans such as the 401(k), commit the company to contribute a set amount to an employee retirement account each year and also allow employees to add additional funds from their paychecks. However the company's obligation is limited to the contributions made while the employee is working, meaning that the retiree's actual income from this plan may be higher or lower than expected. More importantly to the company, the firm's liability after the employee retires is zero, thus moving most of the risk for these plans from the company to the employee.

■ PRIMARY SOURCE

The death knell for the traditional company pension has been tolling for some time now. Companies in ailing industries like steel, airlines and auto parts have thrown themselves into bankruptcy and turned over their ruined pension plans to the federal government.

Now, with the recent announcements of pension freezes by some of the cream of corporate America—Verizon, Lockheed Martin, Motorola and, just last week,

IBM—the bell is tolling even louder. Even strong, stable companies with the means to operate a pension plan are facing longer worker lifespans, looming regulatory and accounting changes and, most important, heightened global competition. Some are deciding they either cannot, or will not, keep making the decades-long promises that a pension plan involves.

IBM was once a standard-bearer for corporate America's compact with its workers, paying for medical expenses, country clubs and lavish Christmas parties for the children. It also rewarded long-serving employees with a guaranteed monthly stipend from retirement until death.

Most of those perks have long since been scaled back at IBM and elsewhere, but the pension freeze is the latest sign that today's workers are, to a much greater extent, on their own. Companies now emphasize 401(k) plans, which leave workers responsible for ensuring that they have adequate funds for retirement and expose them to the vagaries of the financial markets.

"IBM has, over the last couple of generations, defined an employer's responsibility to its employees," said Peter Capelli, a professor of management at the Wharton School of Business at the University of Pennsylvania. "It paved the way for this kind of swap of loyalty for security."

Mr. Capelli called the switch from a pension plan to a 401(k) program "the most visible manifestation of the shifting of risk onto employees." He added: "People just have to deal with a lot more risk in their lives, because all these things that used to be more or less assured—a job, health care, a pension—are now variable."

IBM said it is discontinuing its pension plan for competitive reasons, and that it plans to set up an unusually rich 401(k) plan as a replacement. The company is also trying to protect its own financial health and avoid the fate of companies like General Motors that have been burdened by pension costs. Freezing the pension plan can reduce the impact of external forces like interest-rate changes, which have made the plan cost much more than expected.

"It's the prudent, responsible thing to do right now," said J. Randall MacDonald, IBM's senior vice president for human resources. He said the new plan would "far exceed any average benchmark" in its attractiveness.

Pension advocates said they were dismayed that rich and powerful companies like IBM and Verizon would abandon traditional pensions.

"With Verizon, we're talking about a company at the top of its game," said Karen Friedman, director of policy studies for the Pension Rights Center, an advocacy group in Washington. "They have a huge profit. Their CEO has given himself a huge compensation package. And then they're saying, 'In order to compete, sorry, we have to freeze the pensions.' If companies freeze the pensions, what are employees left with?"

Verizon's chief executive, Ivan Seidenberg, said in December that his company's decision to freeze its pension plan for about 50,000 management employees would make the company more competitive, and also "provide employees a transition to a retirement plan more in line with current trends, allowing employees to have greater accountability in managing their own finances and for companies to offer greater portability through personal savings accounts."

In a pension freeze, the company stops the growth of its employees' retirement benefits, which normally build up with each additional year of service. When they retire, the employees will still receive the benefits they earned before the freeze.

Like IBM, Verizon said it would replace its frozen pension plan with a 401(k) plan, also known as a defined-contribution plan. This means the sponsoring employer creates individual savings accounts for workers, withholds money from their paychecks for them to contribute, and sometimes matches some portion of the contributions. But the participating employees are responsible for choosing an investment strategy. Traditional pensions are backed by a government guarantee; defined-contribution plans are not.

Precisely how many companies have frozen their pension plans is not known. Data collected by the government are old and imperfect, and companies do not always publicize the freezes. But the trend appears to be accelerating.

As recently as 2003, most of the plans that had been frozen were small ones, with less than 100 participants, according to the Pension Benefit Guaranty Corporation, which insures traditional pensions. The freezes happened most often in troubled industries like steel and textiles, the guarantor found.

Only a year ago, when IBM decided to close its pension plan to new employees, it said it was "still committed to defined-benefit pensions."

But now the company has given its imprimatur to the exodus from traditional pensions. Its pension fund, the third largest behind General Motors and General Electric, is a pace-setter. Industry surveys suggest that more big, healthy companies will do what IBM did this year and next.

"There's a little bit of a herd mentality," said Syl Schieber, director of research for Watson Wyatt Worldwide, a large consulting firm that surveyed the nation's 1,000 largest companies and reported a sharp increase in

the number of pension freezes in 2004 and 2005. The thinking grows out of boardroom relationships, he said, where leaders of large companies compare notes and discuss strategy.

Another factor appears to be impatience with long-running efforts by Congress to tighten the pension rules, Mr. Schieber said. Congress has been struggling for three years with the problem of how to make sure companies measure their pension promises accurately—a key to making sure they set aside enough money to make good. But it is likely to be costly for some companies to reserve enough money to meet the new rules, and they—and some unions—have lobbied hard to keep the existing rules intact, or even to weaken them. So far, consensus has eluded the lawmakers.

"If Congress will not do its job and clarify the regulatory environment, then I think more and more companies will come to the conclusion that, given everything else that they've got to face, this just isn't the way to go," Mr. Schieber said of the traditional pension route.

Defined-benefit pensions proliferated after World War II and reached their peak in the late 1970's, when about 62 percent of all active workers were covered solely by such plans, according to the Employee Benefit Research Institute, a Washington organization financed by companies and unions. A slow, steady erosion then began, and by 1997, only 13 percent of workers had a pension plan as their sole retirement benefit. The percentage has held steady in the years since then. The growth of defined-contribution plans has mirrored the disappearance of pension plans. In 1979, 16 percent of active workers had a defined contribution plan and no pension, but by 2004 the number had grown to 62 percent.

For many workers, the movement away from traditional pensions is going to be difficult. Already there are signs that people are retiring later, or taking other jobs to support themselves in old age. Participation in a pension plan is involuntary, but most 401(k) plans let employees decide whether to contribute any money—or none at all. Research shows that many people fail to put money into their retirement accounts, or invest it poorly once it is there.

Even skillful 401(k) investors can be badly tripped up if the markets tumble just at the time they were planning to retire. Mr. Schieber of Watson Wyatt ran scenarios of what would happen to a hypothetical man who went to work at 25, put 6 percent of his pay into a 401(k) account every year for 40 years, retired at 65, then withdrew his account balance and used it to buy an annuity, a financial product that, like a pension, pays a lifelong monthly stipend.

He found that if the man turned 65 in 2000 he would have enough 401(k) savings to buy an annuity that paid

134 percent of his pre-retirement income. But if he turned 65 in 2003, his 401(k) savings would only buy an annuity rich enough to replace 57 percent of his pre-retirement income.

When a company switches from a pension plan to a 401(k) plan, the transition is hardest on the older workers. That is because they lose their final years in the pension plan—often the years when they would have built up the biggest part of their benefit. They then start from zero in the new retirement plan.

Jack VanDerhei, an actuary who is a fellow at the Employee Benefit Research Institute, offered a hypothetical example. If a man joins a firm at 40, works 15 years, and is making $80,000 a year by age 55, he might expect to have built up a pension worth $16,305 a year by that time, Mr. VanDerhei said. If he keeps on working under the same pension plan, that benefit will have increased to $27,175 a year when he retires at 65.

But if instead when the man turns 55 his company freezes the pension plan and sets up a 401(k) plan, the man will get just the $16,305 a year, plus whatever he is able to amass in the 401(k). It will take both discipline and investment skill to reach the equivalent of the old pension payments in just ten years, Mr. VanDerhei said.

For women, the challenge is even tougher. They have longer life expectancies, so they have to pay more than men if they buy annuities in the open market. It turns out the traditional, pooled pension offered them a perk they did not even know they had.

SIGNIFICANCE

Despite its security and simplicity, the traditional pension might actually be less practical for many workers today. By 2006, the median length of time in a single job had fallen to only four years, while the traditional forty-year stint at a single employer had virtually vanished. Consequently, many of today's increasingly mobile workers are better served by defined-contribution plans, in which they receive their promised benefits regardless of whether they remain with the same firm or move on. An employee beginning a career today should expect a retirement nest egg consisting of several company retirement plans, as well as an individual retirement account and other instruments. Today's workers confront a dizzying array of choices, including determining how much to save and how to invest those funds. As the employer-funded pension fades into history, a comfortable retirement will increasingly depend on workers' individual choices, particularly their willingness to save, throughout their careers.

FURTHER RESOURCES

Books

Krass, Stephen J. *The 2006 Pension Answer Book*. Aspen Publishers, 2005.

Mitchell, Olivia, and Sylvester Schieber, eds. *Living with Defined Contribution Pensions: Remaking Responsibility for Retirement*. Philadelphia: University of Pennsylvania Press, 1998.

Skyrms, Brian. *Evolution of the Social Contract*. Cambridge, UK; New York: Cambridge University Press, 1996.

Periodicals

Cauchon, Dennis. "Huge Bill for Public Retirees Hits Soon." *USA Today*. May 18, 2006:1a.

Henry, David. "Shortfall at Exxon." *Business Week*. (May 29, 2006): 35–36.

Web sites

Cornell University Law School. Legal Information Institute. "Pension Law: An Overview." <http://www.law.cornell.edu/wex/index.php/Pension> (accessed May 23, 2006).

Pension Benefit Guarantee Corporation. "PBGC Assumes Pension Plan of Pittsburgh Brewing Co." May 23, 2006 <http://www.pbgc.gov/media/news-archive/2006/pr06-48.html> (accessed May 23, 2006).

Social Policy before 1878

Social policies were not primary concerns of the U.S. federal or state governments in the early nineteenth century. Private relief organizations were primarily located in cities; many addressed only the most needy. With little government investment in social policy, many lived on a thin line between solvency and destitution. Insurance, credit, and loans were rarities; there were no fail-safes in the event of unemployment. There were no subsidies for the aged, save for pensions provided from employers or community associations.

Government was not wholly absent from social policy. From the time of the ratification of the Bill of Rights, the Eighth Amendment (barring cruel and unusual punishment) guided the criminal justice and prison systems. Prison reform advocates ensured that conditions improved. Debtor's prisons, such as Fleet Prison profiled in this chapter, were outlawed in both England and the United States in the nineteenth century. State and local governments invested in public education. In the United States, the first state made elementary education compulsory in 1852. Ten years later, the federal government created the land-grant universities through the Morrill Act.

During the Civil War and Reconstruction, the federal government took a more active role in social policy. The enactment of the Thirteenth and Fourteenth Amendments fundamentally changed the social system of the nation and laid the groundwork for other changes to come. With the creation of the Freedman's Bureau, the government aided the establishment of schools, clinics, and other immediate aid programs for former slaves. The Homestead Act opened the American west to settlement, promising families plots of land to farm and develop.

Rapid population growth and the rise of the cities were also significant in the early nineteenth century. By 1842, New York and London shared many of the same problems—poor public health, tenement slums, and crime. English author and journalist Charles Dickens recorded his impressions of New York's tenements, most especially its notorious Five Points neighborhood. Private relief organizations became more common and pushed for reforms.

A few years later, immigration to the United States dramatically increased. The influx of immigrants fleeing famine in Ireland changed the character of both American cities and social reform movements. As poor neighborhoods became ethnic enclaves, many associated the problems of the slums with ethnic stereotypes. Anti-immigrant sentiment drove the formation of a political party, the Know-Nothings. By 1870, U.S. anti-immigrant sentiment had shifted its target from the Irish in the East to Chinese laborers in the West. The increasing Asian immigrant population was viewed as a social concern. Many Americans held deep prejudices and regarded Asian immigrants as worthless and a threat to American society, as evidenced by the cartoon in this chapter.

Amendment XIII to the United States Constitution

Legislation

By: Lyman Trumbull

Date: 1865

Source: *The National Archives Experience*. "The Charters of Freedom. The Constitution: Amendments 11–27 <http://www.archives.gov/national-archives-experience/charters/constitution_amendments_11-27.html>

About the Author: Lyman Trumbull represented the state of Illinois in the United States Senate from 1855 to 1873. A former schoolteacher who studied law and became a lawyer before entering the Senate, Trumbull switched from Democrat to the Republican as a result of the slavery issue, though he returned to the Democratic party during an unsuccessful bid to become the Governor of Illinois.

INTRODUCTION

Slavery had been a part of United States society for more than three centuries when tension over the issue peaked in the mid-nineteenth century. As new states readied for admittance as "slave" or "free" under the terms of the Missouri Compromise, the question of slavery continued to spark fierce debate, as evidenced in the 1846 Wilmot Proviso. Violence erupted in "Bleeding Kansas" during the 1850s, an illustration of the growing divide between the North and the South that led, finally, to Civil War in 1861.

Each side in the debate used religion, politics, economics, and physiological studies to make its case. Abolitionists called for an end to the slave system on moral and religious grounds. Slavery supporters argued that the South's power as a cotton source stemmed from slave labor; they also cited Bible verses to support their cause. Proslavery religious leaders such as Samuel Blanchard How wrote:

> Does the Apostle then teach the slaves that they ought to be free? That their Christian masters sin in holding them in bondage? And does he, with apostolic authority and in the name of Jesus Christ, command the masters to give them their freedom? He does nothing of the kind. He not only does not require these Christian masters to set their slaves at liberty, but he speaks of them as "faithful and beloved" brethren, "partakers of the benefit," and for this very reason he exhorts Christian slaves not to despise them, but rather to do them service. It

seems impossible for the question before us to be more fully and directly settled.

By the middle of the Civil War President Abraham Lincoln, elected in 1860, came to realize that nothing short of a constitutional amendment would end the slavery question, and thus help end the war. During his bid for the presidency, Lincoln had campaigned on a platform that would bring no new slave states into the union, but permit slavery to continue in existing slave states. His attempt to appease both sides did nothing to prevent the first battle of the Civil War just six weeks into his term.

In 1863 and 1864 Lincoln spoke with Republican Illinois Senator Lyman Trumbull about the prospects of a constitutional amendment to ban slavery. While southerners were concerned that the 4 million slaves might revolt, steal, or cause complete chaos if freed, Lincoln worried that his Emancipation Proclamation of 1863, which freed slaves in all territories not controlled by the Union, would be invalidated if the Constitution was not amended to end slavery.

Trumbull, chair of the Senate Judiciary Committee, wrote the first draft of what would become the Thirteenth Amendment; it passed the Senate by a 38–6 vote on April 8, 1864, but failed to get through the House of Representatives. Lincoln, preparing for the amendment's eventual ratification, looked ahead to the three-fourths of states that needed to be ready to ratify the abolition of slavery. On October 31, 1864, Nevada was admitted into the union as a free state, even though it did not meet the minimum population required for statehood. The Thirteenth Amendment made its way through the House of Representatives and was ratified on December 18, 1865.

▮ PRIMARY SOURCE

AMENDMENT XIII

Section 1

Neither slavery nor involuntary servitude, except as a punishment for crime whereof the party shall have been duly convicted, shall exist within the United States, or any place subject to their jurisdiction.

Section 2

Congress shall have power to enforce this article by appropriate legislation.

SIGNIFICANCE

By invalidating all state laws permitting slavery, as well as local, state, and federal court decisions, including *Dred Scott v. Sanford*, which declared slaves and former slaves ineligible for citizenship, the Thirteenth Amendment, ratified after Lincoln's assassination, accomplished what Lincoln had hoped to achieve with the Emancipation Proclamation. It removed a contentious issue from politics, shored up Republican support, gave Reconstruction a core concept around which to build, and fulfilled a campaign promise.

By granting 4 million former slaves the basic right of freedom from forced servitude, the Thirteenth Amendment changed race relations in the former slave states. While attitudes did not change overnight, laws did, and the federal government used a variety of tactics to enforce the new amendment. By creating the Bureau of Refugees, Freedmen, and Abandoned Lands, also known as the Freedmen's Bureau, the federal government provided former slaves with needed supplies, food, and land. This action angered poor whites who experienced the devastation of the Civil War and Reconstruction, reinforcing resentment toward former slaves who now flooded into low-wage positions and crowded out poorer white workers.

Southern states, however, found ways to work around the new amendment, passing state laws that limited labor options for former slaves, removed parental rights for former slaves whose children entered into apprenticeship, and created extremely broad vagrancy laws that jailed anyone those charged with vagrancy and forced them to perform unpaid labor as the criminal sentence. These "black codes" reinforced the separation of the races in the South, along with later laws that banned interracial marriage and mandated separate schools and public facilities for separate races. The Thirteenth Amendment shaped social and civil life for former slaves, their families, and white Americans alike after the Civil War, as the nation rebuilt itself with new legal principles while balancing old prejudices.

FURTHER RESOURCES
Books

Jeffrey, Julie Roy. *Great Silent Army of Abolitionism: Ordinary Women in the Antislavery Movement.* Chapel Hill, NC: University of North Carolina Press, 1998.

How, Samuel Blanchard. *Slaveholding Not Sinful.* New Brunswick, NJ: J. Terhune's Press, 1856.

Lerner, Gerda. *The Grimké Sisters from South Carolina: Pioneers for Women's Rights and Abolition.* Chapel Hill, NC: University of North Carolina Press, 2004.

Mayer, Henry. *All on Fire: William Lloyd Garrison and the Abolition of Slavery.* New York: St. Martin's Griffin, 2000.

Tsesis, Alexander. *The Thirteenth Amendment and American Freedom: A Legal History.* New York: New York University Press, 2004.

XIV Amendment

Legislation

By: Thaddeus Stevens

Date: 1868

Source: Stevens, Thaddeus. "United States Constitutional Amendment XIV." United States Congress, 1868.

About the Author: Thaddeus Stevens (1792–1868), a Whig and later a Republican who served for the state of Pennsylvania in the House of Representatives for both parties, crafted the Fourteenth Amendment and the Reconstruction Act of 1867. A lifelong opponent of slavery, Stevens was known as the leader of the Radical Republicans; he died in 1868.

INTRODUCTION

The Fourteenth Amendment to the United States Constitution followed the Thirteenth Amendment, which abolished slavery in the aftermath of the Civil War. Designed to guarantee citizenship for all former slaves and their descendants, the five provisions in the amendment shaped reconstruction efforts after the war.

Reconstruction led to the passage by the Republican-dominated Congress of an 1867 act that stripped Confederate supporters of voting rights and the right to hold office. Thaddeus Stevens, chairman of the House Reconstruction Committee, had led the passage of the first Reconstruction Act of 1867; Congress had passed the Fourteenth Amendment in 1867 but the requisite twenty-eight states had not ratified it.

Under the terms of the Reconstruction Act, which President Andrew Johnson had vetoed and Congress voted to override, the South was divided into military zones and occupied by the Union army. Under duress, many states that rejected the Fourteenth Amendment initially later ratified it as a condition for readmittance into the Union. The Fourteenth Amendment's first section made all slaves full citizens of the United

Associate Justice Harry Blackmun of the U.S. Supreme Court. ARCHIVE PHOTOS, INC. REPRODUCED BY PERMISSION.

States, overturning the 1856 Supreme Court decision *Scott v. Sandford,* known as the Dred Scott decision, which had determined that slaves and former slaves were not and never had been citizens, and therefore did not possess the legal rights afforded to citizens by the Constitution. By requiring southern states to ratify the Fourteenth Amendment, the first Reconstruction Act set the stage for contentious debate in later years concerning the amendment's legitimacy.

■ PRIMARY SOURCE

XIV AMENDMENT

Section 1.

All persons born or naturalized in the United States, and subject to the jurisdiction thereof, are citizens of the United States and of the State wherein they reside. No State shall make or enforce any law which shall abridge the privileges or immunities of citizens of the United States; nor shall any State deprive any person of life, liberty, or property, without due process of law; nor deny to any person within its jurisdiction the equal protection of the laws.

Section 2.

Representatives shall be apportioned among the several States according to their respective numbers, counting the whole number of persons in each State, excluding Indians not taxed. But when the right to vote at any election for the choice of electors for President and Vice-President of the United States, Representatives in Congress, the Executive and Judicial officers of a State, or the members of the Legislature thereof, is denied to any of the male inhabitants of such State, being twenty-one years of age,* and citizens of the United States, or in any way abridged, except for participation in rebellion, or other crime, the basis of representation therein shall be reduced in the proportion which the number of such male citizens shall bear to the whole number of male citizens twenty-one years of age in such State.

Section 3.

No person shall be a Senator or Representative in Congress, or elector of President and Vice-President, or hold any office, civil or military, under the United States, or under any State, who, having previously taken an oath, as a member of Congress, or as an officer of the United States, or as a member of any State legislature, or as an executive or judicial officer of any State, to support the Constitution of the United States, shall have engaged in insurrection or rebellion against the same, or given aid or comfort to the enemies thereof. But Congress may by a vote of two-thirds of each House, remove such disability.

Section 4.

The validity of the public debt of the United States, authorized by law, including debts incurred for payment of pensions and bounties for services in suppressing insurrection or rebellion, shall not be questioned. But neither the United States nor any State shall assume or pay any debt or obligation incurred in aid of insurrection or rebellion against the United States, or any claim for the loss or emancipation of any slave; but all such debts, obligations and claims shall be held illegal and void.

Section 5.

The Congress shall have the power to enforce, by appropriate legislation, the provisions of this article.

■

SIGNIFICANCE

In the American court system, the "equal protection" clause in Section 1 of the Fourteenth Amendment has received extensive study and interpretation over the nearly 140 years since it was added to the Constitution. From cases such as the 1879 *Ex Parte Virginia,* which held that states, officers, and law enforcement personnel cannot deny equal protection to a person within its borders, to the 1973 *Roe v. Wade* decision, which used the Fourteenth Amendment as part of a grouping of amendments in which the majority found a right to privacy for women seeking abortions, the Fourteenth Amendment has had a history of broad application.

The equal protection clause has shaped social conditions in the United States not only in the case of *Roe v. Wade* but also in fighting racial discrimination, gender discrimination, and age discrimination of older workers, as well as working for equal educational opportunity for children with special needs. Until the Fourteenth Amendment, the Constitution defended breaches of individual rights from federal government encroachment; the Fourteenth Amendment specifically cites protection from state governments, part of the Radical Republican agenda in protecting the rights of former slaves from southern states wishing to strip African Americans of rights.

One of the most famous pairs of Supreme Court decisions, the 1896 *Plessy v. Ferguson* and the 1954 *Brown v. Board of Education*, used the Fourteenth Amendment in distinctly different ways. In the Plessy case, the majority decision stated that the equal protection clause applied only to legal rights—not to social equality. Fifty-eight years later, in the Brown decision, the majority made the opposite statement, argued carefully by Thurgood Marshall and fellow lawyers from the NAACP: the social stigma of unequal protection under the law bred a society in which irreparable harm came to those who were treated as "separate" from the majority white society in segregated schooling situations.

In 2000, the Supreme Court used the equal protection clause in the *Bush v. Gore* case, which determined the outcome of the contested presidential election between Republican George W. Bush and Democrat Al Gore. The court decided in a 7–2 decision that the recount of voting ballots in the state of Florida violated the equal protection clause; no single recount procedure applied statewide, possibly leading to voting irregularities. This application of the Fourteenth Amendment found that irregularities existed, but the court ultimately stopped recounts for other reasons, leading to George W. Bush's presidency. The equal protection clause has shaped not only issues related to gender, housing, employment, and education, but also a contested presidential election; its far-ranging application in American law makes the Fourteenth Amendment one of the central components of law and society in the United States.

FURTHER RESOURCES

Books

Breyer, Stephen. *Active Liberty: Interpreting Our Democratic Constitution.* New York: Knopf, 2005.

Jeffrey, Julie Roy. *Great Silent Army of Abolitionism: Ordinary Women in the Antislavery Movement.* Chapel Hill, N.C.: University of North Carolina Press, 1998.

Perry, Michael J. *We the People: The Fourteenth Amendment and the Supreme Court.* New York: Oxford University Press, 2001.

First Census

Table

By: Anonymous

Date: 1791

Source: *United States Census Bureau.* "First Census." <http://www2.census.gov/prod2/decennial/documents/1790a-02.pdf> (accessed June 18, 2006).

About the Photographer: This document is part of the public domain of the United States Government.

INTRODUCTION

In 1790, the United States undertook the first national census in keeping with the constitutional requirement that every person in the country be accounted for once every ten years. The primary purpose of the census was to keep accurate records of the population and its distribution between the states so that the House of Representatives could adjust the number of representatives per district as necessary. In later years, the Federal government used the census records to determine how best to distribute funds for various programs, taking into consideration not just population but income and employment records that were included in the census.

■ PRIMARY SOURCE

FIRST CENSUS

See primary source image.

[3]

SCHEDULE *of the whole number of* PERSONS *within the several Districts of the* UNITED STATES, *taken according to* " An Act providing for the Enumeration of the Inhabitants of the United States;" *passed March the 1st, 1790.*

DISTRICTS.	Free white Males of sixteen years and upwards, including heads of families.	Free white Males under sixteen years.	Free white Females, including heads of families.	All other free persons.	Slaves.	Total.
* Vermont	22435	22328	40505	255	16	85539
New Hampshire	36086	34851	70160	630	158	141885
{ Maine	24384	24748	46870	538	NONE	96540 }
{ Massachussetts	95453	87289	190582	5463	NONE	378787 }
Rhode Island	16019	15799	32652	3407	948	68825
Connecticut	60523	54403	117448	2808	2764	237946
New York	83700	78122	152320	4654	21324	340120
New Jersey	45251	41416	83287	2762	11423	184139
Pennsylvania	110788	106948	206363	6537	3737	434373
Delaware	11783	12143	22384	3899	8887	59094
Maryland	55915	51339	101395	8043	103036	319728
{ Virginia	110936	116135	215046	12866	292627	747610 }
{ Kentucky	15154	17057	28922	114	12430	73677 }
North Carolina	69988	77506	140710	4975	100572	393751
South Carolina	—					
Georgia	13103	14044	25739	398	29264	82548

	Free white Males of twenty-one years and upwards, including heads of families.	Free Males under twenty one years of age.	Free white Females, including heads of families.	All other Persons	Slaves.	Total.
S. Western territory	6271	10277	15365	361	3417	35691
N. Ditto	—					

Truly stated from the original Returns deposited in the Office of the Secretary of State.

TH. JEFFERSON.

October 24, 1791.

* This return was not signed by the Marshal, but was enclosed and referred to in a letter written and signed by him.

PRIMARY SOURCE

First Census: A table dating from 1791 showing the results of the first national census in the United States. The first census was taken after the passage of the Census Act in 1790. U.S. CENSUS BUREAU.

SIGNIFICANCE

Even before the United States became an independent nation, census-taking was a fairly regular, if unregulated, activity. In the early 1600s, a census was taken in the then-colony of Virginia, and all colonies experienced a census at some point prior to their joining as the United States. The first national census was initiated by Thomas Jefferson, who was at that time Secretary of State. Marshals from the various U.S. judicial districts were assigned the duty of collecting the information in their region and covered the original thirteen states as well as the districts of Kentucky, Maine, and Vermont, and the territory that later became Tennessee. There was no formal questionnaire for the original census. The census takers were responsible for visiting every household, chronicling the name of the head of the house, and categorizing the inhabitants under one of the following descriptions: free, white males sixteen years or older; free, white males under the age of sixteen; free white females; all other free people (including sex and color); and slaves. The marshals traveled on horseback and collected the information on their own paper, as no materials had been provided by the government. Once completed, copies of the census records for each district were required by law to be posted in two of the most frequented public locations in the area, and the totals by category were sent to the President. The census took a total of eighteen months to complete, cost $45,000, and the marshals counted a total of 3.9 million people. The results provided the nation not only with information regarding population distribution for the purpose of maintaining an accurate number in Congress, but also showed the number of men in each district who were of employment age or old enough to participate in military actions in time of war.

The 1791 census provided a basis for all future records. Over the next few decades, the information recorded by the census takers remained very much the same, with the occasional addition of a new age bracket to be counted as a category. The states began providing forms for the marshals to use after the first census, and in 1830, the government printed the first official forms to be used nationwide. Additional questions began to appear in greater numbers, including inquiries as to regional agriculture, fishing, mining, and industries. In 1850, the census began to include all free individuals by name, occupation, and place of birth, instead of just the heads of households. Social issues also became a part of the census, with questions asked regarding taxation, church attendance, poverty, and crime rates, providing the government with a much clearer image of the types of people living in each district and the relative wealth of each area of the

The estimated population of the United States is recorded on the "population clock" at the U.S. Census Bureau, April 11, 1972. © BETTMANN/CORBIS.

nation. U.S. marshals continued to operate as census takers until 1880, when an official census office was established as part of the Department of the Interior, and professionals were hired for this duty.

Changes in the nation, both physical and social, can be tracked through the development of the census. The most obvious physical change is the growth of the country, accounted for both by the addition of territories and states over the decades, and by the increase in population due to birth rates and improved living conditions and medical care. In addition, regions of the nation altered as new cities grew and demographics were altered by shifts in populations. People moved west as the nation expanded, and immigrants coming to the United States from Europe and beyond gravitated toward cities and other areas with job opportunities. All of these shifts were reflected in the census results. Social and political trends were also reflected in the questions asked by the census and by the ways in which the population was recorded. In 1868, the United States ratified the Fourteenth Amendment, and African Americans were no longer counted by the three-fifths rule as a result. As of 1870, American Indians began to be included in census numbers, assuming they were not living on a reservation or in one of the territories, and members of the Chinese population also began to be counted. It was not until 1970 when census takers began to indicate whether a person was of Hispanic descent. The definition of the head of household changed in 1980, allowing that a woman might be the head of her household. Over the history of the census, the numbers reflect not only how many people live in the United States, and where, but how the United States categorizes and considers its citizens.

FURTHER RESOURCES

Books

Holt, William S. *The Bureau of the Census: Its History, Activities, and Organization*. New York: AMS Press, 1929.

Scott, Anna H. *Census, USA: Fact Finding for the American People*. Boston: Houghton Mifflin Co., 1968.

Web sites

U.S. Census Bureau. "History." May 29, 2003. <http://www.census.gov/acsd/www/history.html> (accessed June 18, 2006).

U.S. Census Bureau. "Measuring America: The Decennial Census from 1790 to 2000." February 6, 2006. <http://www.census.gov/prod/www/abs/ma.html> (accessed June 18, 2006).

Yale University Library Government Documents and Information Center. "Guide to Decennial Censuses." 2002. <http://www.library.yale.edu/govdocs/cengdc.html> (accessed June 18, 2006).

On Indian Removal

President Andrew Jackson's Message to Congress

Speech

By: Andrew Jackson

Date: December 6, 1830

Source: Our Documents. Transcript of President Andrew Jackson's Message to Congress "On Indian Removal" (1830) <http://www.ourdocuments.gov/> (accessed June 18, 2006).

About the Author: Andrew Jackson (1767–1845) served as the seventh president of the United States from 1829 to 1837. One of the most influential men in American history, Jackson is best known for leading the victory over the British at New Orleans during the War of 1812 and for his Indian policies as president.

INTRODUCTION

Upon taking office in 1829, President Andrew Jackson addressed the so-called "Indian problem." Many thousands of Native Americans lived in the South and the old Northwest on land desired by whites. Jackson declared in his first annual message to Congress that removing the Indians to territory west of the Mississippi was the only way to save them. If the Indians remained in their ancestral lands, white civilization would doom them by destroying their resources. Jackson never wavered from this theme, returning to it in his next seven annual messages.

Previous government leaders had tried different Indian policies. Starting in 1819, Congress granted $10,000 a year to various missionary associations eager to promote their version of civilization to the Indians by converting them to Christianity. The missionaries also encouraged assimilation by teaching the Indians literacy in English, encouraging them to dress according to white fashions, and pushing them to follow white agricultural practices. Many Indians, notably the Cherokee, did assimilate to the point of acquiring plantations and slaves. The federal government also pursued treaties with many tribes, dealing with the Indians as if they were foreign nations.

Jackson believed that these policies did nothing to remedy the Indian problem. He shared the ethnocentric views of his contemporaries, seeing the Indians as savages who would benefit from becoming replicas of civilized whites. He said that the Indians had only three choices: They could adapt to white ways and thereby become culturally extinct, move away from whites, or stay and be killed. He thought that it was absurd to address the Indians as if they were foreigners. In his view, they were subjects of the United States. He stated that he wished to protect them. Congress backed Jackson and passed the Indian Removal Act of 1830, appropriating $500,000 to relocate eastern tribes to land west of the Mississippi River.

A lithograph of Flathead Indian men, women, and children crossing a river on rafts and horses, circa 1850. © CORBIS.

PRIMARY SOURCE

President Andrew Jackson's Message to Congress "On Indian Removal" (1830)

It gives me pleasure to announce to Congress that the benevolent policy of the Government, steadily pursued for nearly thirty years, in relation to the removal of the Indians beyond the white settlements is approaching to a happy consummation. Two important tribes have accepted the provision made for their removal at the last session of Congress, and it is believed that their example will induce the remaining tribes also to seek the same obvious advantages.

The consequences of a speedy removal will be important to the United States, to individual States, and to the Indians themselves. The pecuniary advantages which it promises to the Government are the least of its recommendations. It puts an end to all possible danger of collision between the authorities of the General and State Governments on account of the Indians. It will place a dense and civilized population in large tracts of country now occupied by a few savage hunters. By opening the whole territory between Tennessee on the north and Louisiana on the south to the settlement of the whites it will incalculably strengthen the southwestern frontier and render the adjacent States strong enough to repel future invasions without remote aid. It will relieve the whole

State of Mississippi and the western part of Alabama of Indian occupancy, and enable those States to advance rapidly in population, wealth, and power. It will separate the Indians from immediate contact with settlements of whites; free them from the power of the States; enable them to pursue happiness in their own way and under their own rude institutions; will retard the progress of decay, which is lessening their numbers, and perhaps cause them gradually, under the protection of the Government and through the influence of good counsels, to cast off their savage habits and become an interesting, civilized, and Christian community.

What good man would prefer a country covered with forests and ranged by a few thousand savages to our extensive Republic, studded with cities, towns, and prosperous farms embellished with all the improvements which art can devise or industry execute, occupied by more than 12,000,000 happy people, and filled with all the blessings of liberty, civilization and religion?

The present policy of the Government is but a continuation of the same progressive change by a milder process. The tribes which occupied the countries now constituting the Eastern States were annihilated or have melted away to make room for the whites. The waves of population and civilization are rolling to the westward, and we now propose to acquire the countries occupied by the red men of the South and West by a fair exchange, and, at the expense of the United States, to send them to land where their existence may be prolonged and perhaps made perpetual. Doubtless it will be painful to leave the graves of their fathers; but what do they more than our ancestors did or than our children are now doing? To better their condition in an unknown land our forefathers left all that was dear in earthly objects. Our children by thousands yearly leave the land of their birth to seek new homes in distant regions. Does Humanity weep at these painful separations from everything, animate and inanimate, with which the young heart has become entwined? Far from it. It is rather a source of joy that our country affords scope where our young population may range unconstrained in body or in mind, developing the power and facilities of man in their highest perfection. These remove hundreds and almost thousands of miles at their own expense, purchase the lands they occupy, and support themselves at their new homes from the moment of their arrival. Can it be cruel in this Government when, by events which it can not control, the Indian is made discontented in his ancient home to purchase his lands, to give him a new and extensive territory, to pay the expense of his removal, and support him a year in his new abode? How many thousands of our own people would gladly embrace the opportunity of removing to the West on such conditions! If the offers made to the Indians were extended to them, they would be hailed with gratitude and joy.

And is it supposed that the wandering savage has a stronger attachment to his home than the settled, civilized Christian? Is it more afflicting to him to leave the graves of his fathers than it is to our brothers and children? Rightly considered, the policy of the General Government toward the red man is not only liberal, but generous. He is unwilling to submit to the laws of the States and mingle with their population. To save him from this alternative, or perhaps utter annihilation, the General Government kindly offers him a new home, and proposes to pay the whole expense of his removal and settlement.

SIGNIFICANCE

During Jackson's presidency the United States acquired about 100 million acres of eastern Indian land. Nearly 46,000 Native Americans immigrated to the West. Only about 9,000 Indians—mostly in New York and the Great Lakes—were not covered by treaties calling for their removal. These Indians were fortunate, since removal did not proceed as smoothly as Congress and Jackson had expected.

Not all Indians abandoned their ancestral lands quietly to venture into the unknown West. In 1832, in western Illinois, Black Hawk, a leader of the Sauk and Fox Indians, led a revolt. Militias attacked and chased the Indians into southern Wisconsin. After a deadly battle, Black Hawk was captured and about 400 of his people were massacred. In the South, the powerful Creek, Chickasaw, Choctaw, and Cherokee tribes refused to relocate. The Cherokee responded with a unique legal challenge: They appealed to the Supreme Court and won. In 1832, the Court under John Marshall ruled that the Cherokee were a distinct political community that occupied its own territory. An angry Jackson ignored the Court's decision and pushed for the removal of his "red children." Under armed guard, in 1838 the Cherokees embarked on a 1,200-mile journey now known as the Trail of Tears. Nearly a quarter of the Cherokee died on the journey. Survivors joined 15,000 Creek, 12,000 Choctaw, 5,000 Chickasaw, and several thousand Seminoles who had already been forcibly removed to Indian Territory (present-day Oklahoma). Meanwhile, a second Seminole War broke out in 1836 as Indians in Florida took up arms against relocation.

When he left the presidency in 1837, Jackson used his farewell address to profess his belief in the benefits of Indian removal. Jackson sincerely believed that exile to the West was necessary to save Indian culture. But the costs of forced relocation were very high. To this day, Indians condemn Jackson for actions that killed their ancestors.

FURTHER RESOURCES
Books

Akers, Donna L. *Living in the Land of Death: The Choctaw Nation, 1830–1860*. East Lansing: Michigan State University Press, 2004.

Remini, Robert. *Andrew Jackson and His Indian Wars*. New York: Viking, 2001.

Rozema, Vicki, ed. *Vocies from the Trail of Tears*. Winston-Salem, NC: J.F. Blair, 2003.

Satz, Ronald N. *American Indian Policy in the Jacksonian Era*. Norman: University of Oklahoma Press, 1975.

American Notes

Book excerpt

By: Charles Dickens

Date: 1842

An illustration shows tourists "doing the slums" in nineteenth century New York City. © CORBIS.

Source: Dickens, Charles. *American Notes*. Islington, U.K.: Granville Publishing, 1985.

About the Author: Charles Dickens was one of the most popular English novelists of the nineteenth century.

INTRODUCTION

In 1842, English novelist Charles Dickens (1812–1870) made a trip to the United States. He was already famous on both sides of the Atlantic as a writer of tales that were vivid, humorous, and yet passionately concerned with the injustices of the day.

Dickens ended up being highly critical of American society, but he did not set out to be. Before making the trip he read several recent books critical of the United States and was convinced that he, with his sympathy for the non-aristocratic classes of England, was better equipped than earlier writers to understand a democratic society that had been liberated from the chains of class rule.

But instead of a classless Utopia of free-thinking individualists, Dickens found a real-world society with some virtues and glaring faults. Foremost among the faults, as he portrayed them in *American Notes* (1842), were slavery, poverty, and an almost obsessive need to declare the unique superiority of American society and to demand that Dickens acknowledge it too—which he refused to do.

Dickens traveled widely in America, visiting the South, New England, New York City, and the Midwest. His greatest condemnation was reserved for slavery; he cut short his time in the South because he could not bear to stay at hotels where he knew his meals had been cooked by slaves, and devoted a whole chapter of his book to denouncing slavery. However, he was also greatly concerned about poverty and sanitation. In New York, escorted by two policemen (the other part of the "we" in the excerpt given here), he visited the Five Points neighborhood in Manhattan, America's most notorious slum. Here Irish immigrants and black Americans were crowded together in conditions of extreme filth and poverty. Dickens, however, unlike many American writers of his time, did not denounce immigrants and blacks; his writing is notably free from the newspaper stereotypes of the day, which portrayed the Irish as stupid, drunk, and violent and blacks as stupid, laughable, and ape-like. Rather, he denounced the degrading conditions in which he found these persons surviving.

■ PRIMARY SOURCE

Let us go forth again, into the cheerful streets.

Once more in Broadway! Here are the same ladies in bright colours, walking to and fro, in pairs and singly; yonder the very same light blue parasol which passed and repassed the hotel window twenty times while we were sitting there. We are going to cross here. Take care of the pigs. Two portly sows are trotting up behind this carriage, and a select party of half-a-dozen gentlemen hogs have just now turned the corner.

We have seen no beggars in the streets by night or day; but of other kinds of strollers plenty. Poverty, wretchedness, and vice are rife enough where we are going now.

This is the place, these narrow ways, diverging to the right and left, and reeking everywhere with dirt and filth. Such lives as are led here, bear the same fruits here as elsewhere. The coarse and bloated faces at the doors have counterparts at home, and all the wide world over. Debauchery has made the very houses prematurely old. See how the rotten beams are tumbling down, and how the patched and broken windows seem to scowl dimly, like eyes that have been hurt in drunken frays. Many of those pigs live here. Do they ever wonder why their masters walk upright in lieu of going on all-fours? And why they talk instead of grunting?

So far, nearly every house is a low tavern; and on the bar-room walls are coloured prints of Washington, and Queen Victoria of England, and the American Eagle. Among the pigeon-holes that hold the bottles are pieces of plate glass and coloured paper, for there is, in some sort, a taste for decoration even here. And, as seamen frequent these haunts, there are maritime pictures by the dozen: of partings between sailors and their lady loves, portraits of William of the ballad, and his Black-Eyed Susan; of Will Watch, the Bold Smuggler; of Paul Jones the Pirate, and the like: on which the painted eyes of Queen Victoria, and of Washington to boot, rest in as

strange companionship as on most of the scenes that are enacted in their wondering presence.

What place is this, to which the squalid street conducts us? A kind of square of leprous houses, some of which are attainable only by crazy wooden stairs without. What lies beyond this tottering flight of steps, that creak beneath our tread—A miserable room, lighted by one dime candle, and destitute of all comfort, save that which may be hidden in a wretched bed. Beside it sits a man: his elbows on his knees: his forehead hidden in his hands. "What ails this man?" asks the foremost officer. "Fever," he sullenly replies, without looking up. Conceive the fancies of a fevered brain in such a place as this!

Ascend these pitch-dark stairs, heedful of a false footing on the trembling boards, and grope your way with me into this wolfish den, where neither ray of light nor breath of air appears to come. A negro lad, startled from his sleep by the officer's voice—he knows it well—but comforted by his assurance that he has not come on business, officiously bestirs himself to light a candle. The match flickers for a moment, and shows great mounds of dusky rags upon the ground; then dies away and leaves a denser darkness than before, if there can be degrees in such extremes. He stumbles down the stairs, and presently comes back, shading a flaring taper with his hand. Then the mounds of rags are seen to be astir, and rise slowly up, and the floor is covered with heaps of negro women, waking from their sleep; their white teeth chattering, and their bright eyes glistening and winking on all sides with surprise and fear, like the countless repetition of one astonished African face in some strange mirror.

Mount up these other stairs with no less caution (there are traps and pitfalls here for those who are not so well escorted as ourselves) into the housetop; where the bare beams and rafters meet overhead, and calm night looks down through the crevices in the roof. Open the door of one of these cramped hutches full of sleeping negroes. Pah! They have a charcoal fire within; there is a smell of singeing clothes, or flesh, so close they gather round the brazier; and vapours issue forth that blind and suffocate. From every corner, as you glance about you in these dark retreats, some figure crawls half awakened, as if the judgment hour were near at hand, and every obscene grave were giving up its dead. Where dogs would howl to lie, women, and men, and boys slink off to sleep, forcing the dislodged rats to move away in quest of better lodgings.

Here too, are lanes and alleys, paved with mud knee deep; underground chambers, where they dance and game; the walls bedecked with rough designs of ships, and forts, and flags, and American Eagles out of number: ruined houses, open to the street, whence, through wide gaps in the walls, other ruins loom upon the eye, as though the world of vice and misery had nothing else to show: hideous tenements which take their name from robbery and murder; all that is loathsome, dropping, and decayed is here.

SIGNIFICANCE

Dickens was appalled by sanitary conditions throughout America, and not only in the slums. He also believed that personal dirtiness and the near-universal (among men) habit of tobacco chewing and spitting on the floors contributed to disease. "Above all," he wrote in the last chapter of *American Notes*, "in public institutions, and throughout the whole of every town and city, the system of ventilation, and drainage, and removal of impurities, requires to be thoroughly revised. There is no local Legislature in America which may not study Mr. Chadwick's excellent report upon the Sanitary Condition of our Labouring Classes, with immense advantage."

The Mr. Chadwick that Dickens referred to was Edwin Chadwick (1800–1890), a political economist who served in the British government and founded the sanitary reform movement in England. Chadwick's report, "The Sanitary Condition of the Labouring Population of Great Britain" (1841), sold tens of thousands of copies in England. The report detailed the defective sewage and water systems of urban Britain at the time. A supporter of Chadwick described typical sources of pollution of drinking water supplies as follows: "soaking straw and cabbage leaves in some miserable cellar, or the garbage of a slaughter house, or an overflowing cesspool, or dead dogs floated at high water into the mouth of a sewer, or stinking fish thrown overboard at Billingsgate dock, or the remains of human corpses undergoing their last chemical changes in consecrated earth." Many deaths were caused every year by contaminated water, with epidemics of cholera an ever-present threat.

Chadwick, knowing Dickens's power to sway the emotions of the public, sought out his acquaintance so the two could talk about sanitation. He had previously sent Dickens his paper on sanitary conditions, in time for Dickens to mention it in *American Notes*. The two met in 1844, and Dickens was completely won over to Chadwick's water-and-sewage-centered view of public health and away from his earlier, pre-scientific belief that rotting vegetation releases unhealthful particles into the air. Over the next few decades, Dickens wrote frequently in newspapers about the need to support improved water and sewage systems. His influence was primarily in England, although he identified similar problems first-hand in New York City.

Slowly, over the next three quarters of a century, and thanks to thousands of reformers such as Dickens and Chadwick, the improved drainage and "removal of impurities" (sewage processing) that Dickens called for in 1842 did arrive in both London and New York. Even the poorest slums in cities in industrialized nations now have better water supplies and sanitation than did those cities in the mid-nineteenth century. Globally, however, even more people live in such unsafe conditions today than ever before, due to the rapid growth of cities in the third (i.e., undeveloped) world; approximately 1.4 billion people have no safe drinking water and 2.4 billion have no access to sewage disposal. At least a million people a year die from water/sewage-related diseases other than malaria.

FURTHER RESOURCES

Books

Moss, Sidney Phil. *Charles Dickens' Quarrel with America*. Troy, N.Y.: Whitson Publishing, 1984.

Periodicals

Litsios, Socrates. "Charles Dickens and the Movement for Sanitary Reform." *Perspectives in Biology and Medicine* 46, 2 (Spring 2003): 183–200.

Web sites

Christiano, Gregory. *Urbanography.com*. "The Five Points." 2003 <http://www.urbanography.com/5_points/index.html> (accessed June 11, 2006).

The Fleet Prison

Illustration

By: Anonymous

Date: 1774

Source: Getty Images.

About the Artist: This advertisement is part of the collection at Getty Images, a worldwide provider of visual content materials to such communications groups as advertisers, broadcasters, designers, magazines, news media organizations, newspapers, and producers.

INTRODUCTION

Fleet Prison was built in London, England, in 1197 and was used primarily to house debtors and their families and those sentenced for contempt of

PRIMARY SOURCE

The Fleet Prison: A 1774 illustration shows Racket Court, the central courtyard at the heart of Fleet Prison, London's infamous debtor's prison. GETTY IMAGES.

court. The prison was not segregated, and both men and women were housed at Fleet Prison, often with their children. During the Middle Ages and well into the eighteenth century, prisons were operated for profit and the prisoners were required to pay for their lodging, food, and other services, such as the locking and unlocking of shackles and cells. At Fleet Prison, which charged some of the highest fees in England, there was a grille built into the prison walls to enable the prisoners to beg from within the prison. The donations of passers-by enabled prisoners to pay their keep to the warden of the prison. Some prisoners were able to live outside of the prison and take employment, as long as they paid fees for lost revenue to the prison warden.

Prisoners at Fleet Prison were often subjected to maltreatment, including extortion, physical abuse, and torture. The most infamous of its wardens was Thomas Bambridge, who became warden in 1728; he was eventually imprisoned himself in Newgate Prison for his barbarous treatment of the prisoners. Bambridge's abuses of power were discovered by a House

of Commons committee that was convened to investigate and report on the state of Britain's jails.

In February 1773, John Howard (1726–1790), a devout Christian, was appointed high sheriff of Bedford, England. As part of his appointment, Howard was required to inspect the local prison, and he was appalled at the conditions that he found. He believed that the for-profit aspect of the prison was in large part responsible for the poor conditions and suggested to Bedford officials that the wardens be paid a salary. The officials did not want to pay more for maintenance of the prison, pointing out that the whole country used the same system. Howard decided to visit Britain's other prisons, including Fleet Prison, and he found the circumstances elsewhere to be as bad or worse. In March 1774, he presented his findings to the House of Commons, suggesting that the for-profit nature of the prisons exacerbated the poor conditions. On the basis of John Howard's testimony, the House of Commons passed the 1774 Gaol Act, abolishing jailer's fees and giving recommendations for the improvement of sanitary conditions and the health of prisoners.

Howard began a tour of foreign prisons in 1775. Upon his return, he made a second tour of Britain's prisons to find out if the 1774 Gaol Act had been implemented. Although Howard had sent copies of the act to every prison in Britain, he discovered that the wardens and justices failed to adhere to the act for the most part. In 1777, Howard published the results of his prison investigations in *The State of Prisons in England and Wales, with an Account of Some Foreign Prisons,* and his revelations shocked the British public. Howard continued to tour and write accounts of prisons until his death in 1790. He is commonly acknowledged as a pioneer in prison reform.

PRIMARY SOURCE

THE FLEET PRISON
See primary source image.

SIGNIFICANCE

Fleet Prison and others like it were the precursors to the modern penitentiary. Prison reformers like John Howard, Elizabeth Fry, Jeremy Bentham, and Cesare Beccaria were instrumental in exposing the abuses and cruel treatment that were perpetrated in the name of justice. With the elimination of for-profit prisons in Europe came the genesis of the Pennsylvania penitentiary system. Under the Pennsylvania system, prisoners were kept in solitary confinement in individual cells where they were given handiwork to perform and Bibles to read. This combination of punishment through segregation, industry, and penitence was felt to be effective in reforming inmates and turning them into good citizens. The Pennsylvania system was very expensive to maintain, however, and it resulted in high rates of inmate suicide and insanity. It was replaced with the Auburn system in the mid-nineteenth century.

In the Auburn system, prisoners were forced to participate in hard labor and everyday routine as a group, working and eating in complete silence. Prisoners were allowed to read scriptures and exercise for an hour a day. Silence was enforced to keep prisoners from influencing one another and to provide opportunity for reflection and penance. Harsh corporal discipline was used to maintain order and silence in the institution. The Auburn system also marked a return to prison-for-profit as the institutions housed large factories to manufacture goods with prison labor. The profit from the prisoners' labor covered the costs of prison operations and often resulted in a profit.

Although prisoners are now allowed to speak and corporal punishment is no longer the norm, modern prisons have their roots in the Auburn system and continue to maintain the practice of assigning prisoners to jobs or placing them in treatment programs.

The evolution of prison policy in western society is reflective of changes in moral and political ideals, and yet the approach to imprisonment has actually changed little since the days of jailers collecting rent at Fleet Prison. With the increasing trend to privatize prisons in the United States, the for-profit prison has returned. Ignoring John Howard's warning about the effect of profit motive on the conditions of imprisonment, modern prison corporations turn a profit by reducing the costs of housing and feeding prisoners, cutting rehabilitative programs, and using fewer guards and more locks to maintain order.

FURTHER RESOURCES

Books

Ignatieff, M. *A Just Measure of Pain: The Penitentiary in the Industrial Revolution, 1750–1850.* New York: Pantheon Books, 1978.

Morris, N. and D. J. Rothman, eds. *The Oxford History of the Prison: The Practice of Punishment in Western Society.* New York: Oxford University Press, 1995.

Periodicals

Basett, Margery. "The Fleet Prison in the Middle Ages." *The University of Toronto Law Journal* 5 (2) (1944): 383–402.

Sellin, Thorsten. "Penal Servitude: Origin and Survival." *Proceedings of the American Philosophical Society* 109 (5): 277–281.

Smoking Him Out

Editorial cartoon

By: Nathaniel Currier

Date: 1848

Source: Nathaniel Currier. "Smoking Him Out." 1848. Courtesy of the Library of Congress.

About the Photographer: Nathaniel Currier was one of the earliest early lithographers trained in the United States. He began his career by producing lithographic plates and prints for books and journals and rapidly expanded to the production of a variety of items, ranging from sheet music to architectural prints. He discovered that public interest was piqued when he began to create prints of news events, as newspapers of that era (1830s) did not publish photographs or illustrations. He created progressively more original art lithographs, based on current events, public interest, and his own creativity. He developed a business partnership with James Merritt Ives, which led to a large scale lithographic art printing business, which employed an early variant of the production assembly line, in order to mass produce colored prints. During the course of their career, Currier and Ives produced more than one million prints.

INTRODUCTION

The primary subjects in the featured editorial cartoon are Martin Van Buren (1782–1862) along with his son John, and Lewis Cass. At the time that this piece was created, Van Buren and Cass were political opponents, both attempting to run for the American Presidency. Van Buren, the former president from 1837–1841, was active in both the Barnburner segment of the Democratic political party, and the Free Soil movement. Cass was a member of the traditional Democratic party and was their candidate for President of the United States in 1848.

The term barnburner was a reference to the farmer notion that the only way to get rid of a rodent (in this case, rat) infestation in a barn would be by burning the structure to the ground. In the case of the political party, the barnburners assumed that the way to eliminate corruption was to get rid of the institutions fostering it. The Barnburners considered big businesses and corporate structures as inherently corrupt, and that the best way to eradicate the corruption would be by doing away with the entire corporate structure. The central tenets of the Barnburner faction of the Democratic party were the abolition of slavery, the limitation of the system of public debt by preventing the expansion of the banking system across America, and the elimination of the corporate structure in the country.

The Barnburners collaborated with another political and philosophical splinter group called the Free Soil party, the primary goal of which was the abolition of slavery and the prevention of the practice of slavery from expansion into newly acquired territories of the country. The Free Soil Party was active for less than twenty years. One of its organizing principles concerned a document called the Wilmot Proviso, sponsored by David (Davy) Wilmot, which stipulated that none of the territory acquired as a result of the Mexican War could employ the use of slavery. The Proviso was extremely controversial and ultimately unsuccessful. Its abolitionist tone served to further polarize a country that was already deeply divided and philosophically unsettled over the issue of slavery in America. The new territories, which later became New Mexico and Utah, invoked the concept of popular sovereignty, which allowed them to make independent choices about whether they would join the Union as free or slave states.

PRIMARY SOURCE

SMOKING HIM OUT

See primary source image.

SIGNIFICANCE

The business of American politics was at the forefront of society much of the time during the nineteenth century. The country was attempting to establish itself as an independent political entity, truly created 'by the people and for the people,' with the voice of the average voting citizen genuinely heard. During this period, the population of eligible voters was sufficiently small so as to have a small block of ballots potentially make the difference between victory and loss for a candidate.

At the start of the nineteenth century, the country was still early in the development of its current two-(major) Party system, with the main blocks being Federalists and Democratic-Republicans. Federalists were those who generally agreed with a sort of corporate political structure: centralization of government, development of big banking systems, and the growth of corporations. Democratic-Republicans held essentially opposite views. By the middle of the century, the Federalist Party had more or less vanished, and the Whig Party had come to the fore. In essence, the largest philosophical difference between the Whigs and the Democratic-Republicans lay in their beliefs about the appropriate location for the seat of political power in the country. The Democrats favored placing the power in the executive (Presidential) branch of the government, while the Whigs felt that the voice of the people was best reflected by the (relative) diversity of Congress. The Whigs based their party politics on the English Whig Party, which believed that political power should be removed from Royalty (monarchy) and returned to the people. The Whigs were relatively short lived, and their party was inactive within three decades. Many of the Whigs joined with members of the dissolving Free Soil Party members and a group of abolitionist Democrats and formed the Republican

SMOKING HIM OUT.

Smoking Him Out: A political cartoon depicting Van Buren's Free Soil opposition to Democratic nominee Lewis Cass.
THE LIBRARY OF CONGRESS.

Party, during the middle decades of the nineteenth century.

Another major issue during what was called the era of Jacksonian politics had to do with political patronage. Patronage was a common practice during that time (in many places, similar activities still occur), in which supporters of a political candidate were openly rewarded with government jobs and other benefits if their candidate was elected. Many members of the nascent Republican Party opposed this and felt that the vast majority of official positions should result from elections by the citizen voters.

Rapidly evolving party political systems, as well as the growing unrest between those who favored slavery and the abolitionists, helped to pave the way for growing discord among the states of the American Union, ultimately aiding to set the stage for the Civil War (1861–1865). The country was rapidly expanding to

the west, with large new territories being opened up to settlers. There was much division over the question of slavery in the new areas, with the Whigs/Republicans believing that slavery should be abolished, and the Democrats espousing a belief in the concept of popular sovereignty, in which the pioneers moving into the territories would be free to make their own decisions on slavery, as they created newly settled areas and joined the Union (this was especially significant in the Kansas, Nebraska, Utah, and New Mexico territories).

The discord between the barnburner and free soil Democrats, represented by Martin Van Buren, and the regular Democrats, represented by Lewis Cass, is exemplified by the political editorial cartoon above. Ultimately, such in-fighting by candidates aligned with factions of the same party led to dilution of political power. Neither candidate won the election of 1848. The party was divided, with insufficient votes going to either candidate—resulting in a rare win for the Whigs, who successfully elected Zachary Taylor (1784–1850) to the Presidency.

FURTHER RESOURCES

Books

Dippie, Brian W. *Catlin and His Contemporaries: The Politics of Patronage*. Lincoln, Nebraska: University of Nebraska Press, 1990.

Foner, Eric. *Free Soil, Free Labor, Free Men: The Ideology of the Republican Party Before the Civil War*. New York: Oxford University Press, 1995.

Holt, Michael F. *The Rise and Fall of the American Whig Party: Jacksonian Politics and the Onset of the Civil War*. New York: Oxford University Press, 1999.

Klunder, Carl. *Lewis Cass and the Politics of Moderation*. Kent, Ohio: The Kent State University Press, 1996.

Leonard, Gerald. *The Invention of Party Politics: Federalism, Popular Sovereignty, and Constitutional Development in Jacksonian Illinois*. Chapel Hill, North Carolina: University of North Carolina Press, 2002.

Periodicals

Altschuler, Glenn C., and Stuart M. Blumin. "Limits of Political Engagement in Antebellum America: A New Look at the Golden Age of Participatory Democracy." *Journal of American History*. 84 (December 1997): 878–879.

Web sites

The American Civil War Homepage. "General resources." May 05, 2006. <http://sunsite.utk.edu/civil-war/warweb.html#general> (accessed May 10, 2006).

Henry Clay. THE LIBRARY OF CONGRESS.

Clay's Resolutions

The Compromise of 1850

Legislation

By: Henry Clay

Date: January 29, 1850

Source: *Library of Congress. Primary Documents in American History*. "Compromise of 1850" <http://www.ourdocuments.gov/> (accessed June 18, 2006).

About the Author: Henry Clay (1777–1852), a Kentucky lawyer, served three terms in the House of Representatives, often serving as speaker of the House, and four terms as a senator. A titan of nineteenth-century politics and a famous orator, Clay supported the War of 1812, opposed the Mexican War, and declared that he would side with the Union against his home state in the event of Civil War.

INTRODUCTION

Henry Clay's last hurrah as a political leader came when, as senator from Kentucky, he promoted the Compromise of 1850. The compromise admitted California into the Union as a free state, divided the rest of the land acquired from Mexico into the territories of New Mexico and Utah, ended the slave trade in the District of Columbia and, most controversially, created a strong Fugitive Slave Law. It also helped set the United States on the road to the Civil War, an outcome that Clay did not expect.

During the 1840s, the national debate over slavery focused on its expansion into the newly acquired western territories rather than its outright abolition. Southerners believed that it was their constitutional right to take slaves into the territories with them and that Congress lacked the authority to stop them. Militant Southerners threatened secession if slavery was banned in the new lands. Northerners opposed the expansion of slavery, some on moral grounds and some because they feared competing with slave labor.

After several heated debates in Congress, Clay proposed a compromise bill. He hoped that the legislation would satisfy politicians on both sides of the issue. Instead, it aroused fierce opposition. In one pivotal moment during the debate, Senator John Calhoun of South Carolina argued that the South had been reduced to a subordinate position and that disunion would follow unless the North made concessions to restore the political balance. Congress approved Clay's resolutions, including the seventh resolution that led to the Fugitive Slave Act of 1850.

PRIMARY SOURCE

CLAY'S RESOLUTIONS

January 29, 1850

It being desirable, for the peace, concord, and harmony of the Union of these States, to settle and adjust amicably all existing questions of controversy between them arising out of the institution of slavery upon a fair, equitable and just basis: therefore,

1. Resolved, That California, with suitable boundaries, ought, upon her application to be admitted as one of the States of this Union, without the imposition by Congress of any restriction in respect to the exclusion or introduction of slavery within those boundaries.

2. Resolved, That as slavery does not exist by law, and is not likely to be introduced into any of the territory acquired by the United States from the republic of Mexico, it is inexpedient for Congress to provide by law either for its introduction into, or exclusion from, any part of the said territory; and that appropriate territorial governments ought to be established by Congress in all of the said territory, not assigned as the boundaries of the proposed State of California, without the adoption of any restriction or condition on the subject of slavery.

3. Resolved, That the western boundary of the State of Texas ought to be fixed on the Rio del Norte, commencing one marine league from its mouth, and running up that river to the southern line of New Mexico; thence with that line eastwardly, and so continuing in the same direction to the line as established between the United States and Spain, excluding any portion of New Mexico, whether lying on the east or west of that river.

4. Resolved, That it be proposed to the State of Texas, that the United States will provide for the payment of all that portion of the legitimate and bona fide public

debt of that State contracted prior to its annexation to the United States, and for which the duties on foreign imports were pledged by the said State to its creditors, not exceeding the sum of ——dollars, in consideration of the said duties so pledged having been no longer applicable to that object after the said annexation, but having thenceforward become payable to the United States; and upon the condition, also, that the said State of Texas shall, by some solemn and authentic act of her legislature or of a convention, relinquish to the United States any claim which it has to any part of New Mexico.

5. Resolved, That it is inexpedient to abolish slavery in the District of Columbia whilst that institution continues to exist in the State of Maryland, without the consent of that State, without the consent of the people of the District, and without just compensation to the owners of slaves within the District.

6. But, resolved, That it is expedient to prohibit, within the District, the slave trade in slaves brought into it from States or places beyond the limits of the District, either to be sold therein as merchandise, or to be transported to other markets without the District of Columbia.

7. Resolved, That more effectual provision ought to be made by law, according to the requirement of the constitution, for the restitution and delivery of persons bound to service or labor in any State, who may escape into any other State or Territory in the Union. And,

8. Resolved, That Congress has no power to promote or obstruct the trade in slaves between the slaveholding States; but that the admission or exclusion of slaves brought from one into another of them, depends exclusively upon their own particular laws.

SIGNIFICANCE

Widely regarded as the chief concession to the South, the Fugitive Slave Law caused widespread outrage among people in the North by putting teeth in the 1793 Fugitive Slave Act. Slaves who escaped from their masters could now be pursued by federal marshals who had the power to assist anyone trying to recapture a slave and to punish anyone who aided a runaway. Abolitionists were furious at the legislation and several celebrated cases, particularly the Anthony Burns episode, helped their cause.

Burns, a Virginia slave, escaped in 1854 and went to Boston. When a fugitive slave commissioner ordered him returned to slavery, the people of Boston rioted and killed a jailer. Hundreds of state militia and federal soldiers then ushered Burns at enormous cost to the ship that returned him to captivity. In reality, strong Northern opposition meant that few escaped slaves were ever returned to slavery and few rescuers were actually prosecuted. But the law struck fear in the hearts of blacks, both slave and free. Any person of color could be kidnapped, identified as a former slave, and sent into slavery. To avoid Burns's fate, many blacks immigrated to Canada.

Additonally, it soon became obvious that the compromise only offered a temporary solution to the problem. By allowing the residents of New Mexico and Utah to choose whether or not to permit slavery, Congress placed its imprimatur on the idea of popular sovereignty. In 1854, Congress passed the Kansas–Nebraska Act, which decreed that popular sovereignty should settle the issue of slavery in the two territories. Conflict erupted as soon as the bill became law. Proslavery forces clashed with antislavery settlers in years of violence that came to be known as "Bleeding Kansas"; the era is often regarded as a prelude to the Civil War.

FURTHER RESOURCES
Books

Baxter, Maurice G. *Henry Clay and the American System*. Lexington: University Press of Kentucky, 1995.

Remini, Robert. *Henry Clay: Statesman for the Union*. New York: W. W. Norton, 1991.

Waugh, John C. *On the Brink of Civil War: The Compromise of 1850 and How it Changed the Course of American History*. Wilmington, DE: Scholarly Resources, 2003.

An Act Concerning the Attendance of Children at School

Legislation

By: General Court of Massachusetts

Date: 1852

Source: An Act Concerning the Attendance of Children at School (1852).

About the Author: The General Court of Massachusetts is the name of the Massachusetts legislature. Founded in 1630 when the Massachusetts Bay Colony received its charter from England, the General Court created legis-

lation and sat in judgment of certain cases as well. The General Court is composed of the Massachusetts Senate and the Massachusetts House of Representatives.

INTRODUCTION

Massachusetts created the first education law in the North American colonies. Enacted in 1642, it required parents and apprenticeship masters to teach children religious principles and the laws of the commonwealth. The law said nothing of schools or schooling in formal institutions; educating children was placed in the hands of parents and masters as a legal duty and requirement. Five years later Massachusetts passed the "Old Deluder Satan" law of 1647 mandating that all towns of more than fifty families appoint a teacher to teach reading and writing to the children. The 1647 law also required all towns of more than 100 families to establish a grammar school to prepare students for university.

For the next 200 years education in the colonies and later the United States was a combination of teaching by parents, self-directed learning, private and public school attendance, overseas school attendance, and private tutoring. Literacy rates for all white men and women in the United States hovered around eighty percent in 1870, just as compulsory attendance laws began to pass throughout northern states. Literacy rates in the north were over ninety percent, but in the south the rates were only about fifty-five percent. Only five to eight percent of slaves and former slaves were literate.

Although the 1647 law did not make school attendance compulsory, it did establish the basis for later compulsory attendance laws. In 1852, Massachusetts was the first state to pass a law that required school attendance. New York enacted a similar compulsory attendance law in 1854.

■ PRIMARY SOURCE

Be it enacted by the Senate and the House of Representatives

Section 1. Every person who shall have any child under his control between the ages of eight and fourteen years, shall send such child to some public school within the town or city in which he resides, during at least twelve weeks, if the public schools within such town or city shall be so long kept, in each and every year during which such child shall be under his control, six weeks of which shall be consecutive.

Section 2. [Describes fine of $20 for truancy]

Students raise their hands to answer a teacher's question at the Knowledge is Power Progam (KIPP) Academy in the South Bronx, New York. The program requires parents and students to sign a contract committing to long hours, extra homework, summer school, and excellent attendance records, and is considered a model for educating poor children. © ANDREW LICHTENSTEIN/CORBIS.

Section 3. It shall be the duty of the school committee in the several towns or cities to inquire into all cases of violation of the first section of this act, and to ascertain of the persons violating the same, the reasons, if any, for such violation and they shall report such cases, together with such reasons, if any, to the town or city in their annual report; but they shall not report any cases such as are provided for by the fourth section of this act.

Section 4. If, upon inquiry by the school committee, it shall appear, or if upon the trial of any complaint or indictment under this act it shall appear, that such child has attended some school, not in the town or city in which he resides, for the time required by this act, or has been otherwise furnished with the means of education for a like period of time, or has already acquired those branches of learning which are taught in common schools, [also describes physical incapacity or poverty as being valid excuses for absence from school] shall not be held to have violated the provisions of this act.

Section 5. It shall be the duty of the treasurer of the town or city to prosecute all violations of this act.

SIGNIFICANCE

By the mid–1900s all states had passed some form of compulsory attendance law for children, with some exceptions for minority children. The Massachusetts law required twelve weeks of schooling per year, six of which needed to be consecutive, for children ages eight to fourteen; the twelve week requirement has evolved, over time, to a thirty-six week requirement, and in Massachusetts in 2006 all children between the ages of six and sixteen were required to attend school.

Compulsory attendance laws, paired with child labor laws in the first three decades of the twentieth century, reduced the participation of children in the labor force while increasing literacy rates in the United States. Proponents of compulsory attendance laws pointed to the school's role as a social agent, taking the children of immigrants and poor children and promoting civic development and literacy. Social workers and Progressive Era reformers viewed the schools as agents for change. Education was considered the primary vehicle for lifting people out of poverty, and school officials and teachers could act as front-line monitors for children at risk.

Most states in the United States, as of 2005, require children ages six to sixteen to attend school. The age requirement begins at four-and-two-thirds years old in the District of Columbia, while in Pennsylvania and Washington state all children age eight and older must attend school. All other states fall between the two extremes. More than ninety-seven percent of all children ages six to sixteen attend school in the United States, with slightly less than two percent of all children homeschooled by parents.

When the current homeschooling trend began in the U.S. in the 1970s, compulsory attendance laws caused legal problems for parents who chose to homeschool. In Massachusetts, the 1987 Supreme Judicial Court case *Care and Protection of Charles* sets the standard for homeschooling for all districts, with a balance between parent choice and district demands required in each student's case. As of 2006, homeschooling is legal in all fifty states, and various court decisions and exceptions give homeschoolers a means to fulfill compulsory attendance laws—homeschooling is considered a form of school "attendance."

In most states, students can leave school at the age of sixteen, approximately two years before formal secondary education ends with graduation from the twelfth grade. In 1972, the dropout rate in the U.S. was fifteen percent, and it hit a historic low in 2003 at ten percent. Some states, such as Kansas, have seen dropout rates decline since raising the minimum dropout age to eighteen. Michigan was considering a similar increase in the compulsory attendance age as of 2006. Literacy rates in the United States are an estimated at eighty-six to ninety-five percent—one of the lowest rates among developed countries. Compulsory attendance, an important tool for social change in the nineteenth and early twentieth centuries, continues to play an important social and cultural role in the early twenty-first century.

FURTHER RESOURCES
Books

Gatto, John Taylor. *Dumbing Us Down: The Hidden Curriculum of Compulsory Schooling*. Gabriola Island, BC: New Society Publishers, 2005.

Mondale, Sarah. *School: The Story of American Public Education*. Boston: Beacon Press, 2002.

Pulliam, John D., and James J. Van Patten. *History of Education in America*. Upper Saddle River, N.J.: Prentice Hall, 2002.

The Know-Nothing Party

Photograph

By: Anonymous

Date: 1844

Source: © David J. & Janice L. Frent Collection/ Corbis.

About the Photographer: This photograph is part of the collection of the Corbis Corporation, headquartered in Seattle. Corbis maintains a worldwide archive of more than seventy million images.

INTRODUCTION

Reflecting a long American tradition of anti-Catholicism, the Know Nothings began in New York City in the 1840s to oppose "Romanism" and immigration. Members of the secretive organization had to prove that they were born in the United States and pledged to oppose Catholics by removing them from public office whenever possible. By 1854, the Know Nothing Party held several seats in Congress and seemed on the verge of becoming a dominant force in American politics.

Resentment and hostility toward Roman Catholics predated the establishment of the American colonies. Following the Protestant Reformation, European nations frequently waged war, pitting Catholics against Protestants for political and economic control. British settlers brought their anti-Catholic prejudices to American shores; however, the numbers of Catholics in the colonies remained fairly small. In the early nineteenth century, significant numbers of immigrants from Ireland and Germany sparked conflict between native-born Protestants and the Catholic newcomers. In the 1830s, vigilantes attacked convents, burning a few to the ground. In 1844, a request by Philadelphia Catholics to permit Catholic students to read from Catholic translations of the Bible rather than the Protestant King James version prompted several months of rioting by nativists that destroyed Catholic schools, churches, and homes.

Partly as a result of the support given to anti-Catholicism, nativists in New York City organized a secretive group known as "The Order of the Star Spangled Banner." During these early days the groups members claimed to "know nothing" about the secretive organization, giving rise to its nickname. By the 1850s, the order had grown substantially in popularity and its members organized into a substantial political presence. Its official name was the American Party. Its political candidates proposed long waiting periods before immigrants could receive American citizenship, restricting officeholding and voting rights to the native born, and strict limitations on immigration.

PRIMARY SOURCE

See primary source image.

SIGNIFICANCE

While the Know Nothings enjoyed political success, the organization's time in the spotlight was short. The American Party disintegrated over the issue of slavery, which seemed to many citizens to be more pressing than immigration. The nativist movement lost considerable ground to the Democratic and Republican parties by the elections of 1858. By 1860, the Know Nothings had effectively ceased to exist.

Anti-Catholicism and nativistic thinking proved remarkably long-lived in American history. The Civil War provided a brief hiatus from anti-Catholicism and many Catholics hoped that their wartime service would illustrate their patriotism. Yet, shortly after Reconstruction, anti-Catholic sentiment rebounded. The American Protective Association, among the more notable of the new nativist groups, followed the same rhetoric and tone of its Know Nothing forebears. Anti-Catholic sentiment in American society remained an issue until John F. Kennedy was elected President in 1960, demonstrating that a Catholic could be elected president. While some voters feared that Kennedy was part of a papal plot aimed at subjecting Americans to Roman Catholic rule from Vatican City, such views no longer formed the mainstream.

FURTHER RESOURCES
Books

Anbinder, Tyler. *Nativism and Slavery: The Northern Know Nothings and the Politics of the 1850s.* New York: Oxford University Press, 1992.

PRIMARY SOURCE

The Know-Nothing Party: An 1844 capaign ribbon for the Know-Nothing Party, also known as the American Party.
© DAVID J. & JANICE L. FRENT COLLECTION/CORBIS.

An immigrant family in new quarters, circa 1900. © BETTMANN/CORBIS.

Mulkern, John R. *The Know-Nothing Party in Massachusetts: The Rise and Fall of the People's Movement.* Boston: Northeastern University Press, 1990.

Voss-Hubbard, Mark. *Beyond Party: Cultures of Antipartisanship in Northern Politics before the Civil War.* Baltimore: Johns Hopkins University Press, 2002.

On the Know-Nothing Party

Letter

By: Abraham Lincoln

Date: August 24, 1855

Source: Lincoln, Abraham. "On the Know-Nothing Party." Public Domain, August 24, 1855.

About the Author: Abraham Lincoln (1809–1865) served as the sixteenth president of the United States. He helped organize the Republican Party in Illinois in 1856 to oppose the spread of slavery. As president, he issued the Emancipation Proclamation to free the slaves in the states in rebellion against the Union during the Civil War.

INTRODUCTION

The Know Nothing or American Party formed in 1853 and soon became the second largest political party in the United States behind the Democratic Party. By 1857, the party was dead. It was a victim of the growing controversy over slavery.

A nativist group, the Know Nothings emerged in response to the influx of millions of Catholics from Ireland and Germany in the 1840s and 1850s. Nativism and anti-Catholicism had long been traditions in American politics, but the waves of immi-

President Abraham Lincoln, 1865. THE LIBRARY OF CONGRESS

grants reignited these sentiments. Prejudice against Catholics among middle-class and working-class Protestants was legitimized by the Protestant intelligentsia. Anti-Catholicism then became associated with the reform program of Protestant social activists campaigning for the abolition of slavery and the prohibition of liquor. Fear and hatred of Catholics created a need for secrecy among the nativists. When asked about their organization, they were instructed to say, "I know nothing."

Using the name American Party, the Know Nothings swept to political victory in Massachusetts, Delaware, Pennsylvania, Connecticut, Rhode Island, New Hampshire, Maryland, and Kentucky. American party tickets also ran strong races in Virginia, Tennessee, Georgia, Alabama, Mississippi, Louisiana, and Texas. By 1855, nativism seemed on the verge of carrying the entire country.

In that year, Joshua F. Speed (1814–1882) of Kentucky, a longtime close friend of Abraham Lincoln, asked the future president about his views on the Know Nothings. Speed, the brother of Lincoln's future attorney general James Speed, was a farmer and one-time state legislator who publicly supported slavery but who came from a family long opposed to it. During the

Civil War, he would remain loyal to the Union and helped coordinate Union activities in Kentucky.

PRIMARY SOURCE

I am not a Know-Nothing. That is certain. How could I be? How can any one who abhors the oppression of negroes, be in favor of degrading classes of white people? Our progress in degeneracy appears to me to be pretty rapid. As a nation, we begin by declaring that "all men are created equal." We now practically read it "all men are created equal, except negroes." When the Know-Nothings get control, it will read "all men are created equal, except negroes, and foreigners, and catholics." When it comes to this I should prefer emigrating to some country where they make no pretence of loving liberty—to Russia, for instance, where despotism can be taken pure, and without the base alloy of hypocracy.

SIGNIFICANCE

Slavery destroyed the Know Nothings. Despite its political success in 1854 and 1855, the national Know Nothing Party could not survive the anti-slavery controversy. As the party gathered in Philadelphia in June 1855, a pro-slavery resolution led to a wild debate and a massive defection led by Massachusetts nativists but including Know Nothings from many states. Further divisions in the party created more problems.

Nativism failed to inspire and unite the nation. It was clear what the Know Nothings opposed, but they had no positive message and a notorious habit for secrecy. They inspired ridicule and laughter. Newspapers gleefully published the secret rituals of the Know Nothings and jokesters set up Owe Nothing, Say Nothing, and Do Nothing societies.

In 1856, the Know Nothings persuaded former President Millard Fillmore to run as their American Party candidate. Fillmore, who happened to be visiting Pope Pius IX at the Vatican at the time of his nomination, disavowed anti-Catholicism. Although Fillmore received twenty percent of the national popular vote, he carried only one state, Maryland. Soon after, the Know Nothings ceased to exist. They became one of the minor parties in American political history.

FURTHER RESOURCES
Books
Anbinder, Tyler. *Nativism and Slavery: The Northern Know Nothings and the Politics of the 1850s.* New York: Oxford University Press, 1992.

Mulkern, John R. *The Know-Nothing Party in Massachusetts: The Rise and Fall of the People's Movement.* Boston: Northeastern University Press, 1990.

Voss-Hubbard, Mark. *Beyond Party: Cultures of Antipartisanship in Northern Politics Before the Civil War.* Baltimore, Md.: Johns Hopkins University Press, 2002.

Homestead Act of 1862

Legislation

By: Galusha A. Grow

Date: May 20, 1862

Source: *National Parks Service.* Homestead National Monument. "The Homestead Act of 1862." <http://www.nps.gov/home/Homestead%20Act%20of%201862.htm> (accessed June 17, 2006).

About the Author: Galusha A. Grow (1822–1907), a Republican from Pennsylvania, served as the Speaker of the U.S. House of Representatives from 1861 to 1863.

INTRODUCTION

The Homestead Act of 1862 helped settle the West by encouraging the westward migration of whites. Under the legislation, the government offered 160 acres of public land to settlers who would live and labor on it. Many people took the offer and settled in the Great Plains.

Since the day that whites first landed in the New World, land ownership had been the key to a prosperous future. Pioneers had a tendency to settle past areas that had been surveyed and announced for sale. As the West became more settled, this tendency to pick a tract in an unopened area increased. Squatters were pioneers who found and claimed choice land before it was marked for sale.

The roots of the Homestead Act date to the 1820s when the U.S. Congress began to give relief to squatters by giving them preemption rights in certain areas. In 1841, a general Preemption Act granted anyone settling on publicly owned land that was surveyed but not yet available for sale the right to buy 160 acres at the minimum price when it was auctioned. The nation's land policy was as liberal as could be consistent with the demand that the public domain be a continuing source of revenue.

In the 1850s, as agitation for land continued, it became apparent that the passage of a homestead law was inevitable. Southerners, who had at one time favored grants to actual settlers, became violently opposed to this as time went on. The typical 160-acre farm proposed by homestead supporters was not large enough to make slave labor economical. To Southerners, it seemed obvious that homesteading would fill the West with antislavery people. Northern congressmen joined forces with westerners because they knew that free land meant free states.

In 1860, a homestead act was passed, but President James Buchanan, fearing that the South would use it as an excuse to secede, vetoed the bill. Two years later, with the Civil War raging and Southerners out of Congress, the Homestead Act of 1862 became law.

PRIMARY SOURCE

The Homestead Act of 1862

37th Congress Session II 1862

Chapter LXXV—An Act to secure Homesteads to actual Settlers on the Public Domain.

Be it enacted by the Senate and House of Representatives of the United States of America in Congress assembled, That any person who is the head of a family, or who has arrived at the age of twenty-one years, and is a citizen of the United States, or who shall have filed his declaration of intention to become such, as required by the naturalization laws of the United States, and who has never borne arms against the United States Government or given aid and comfort to its enemies, shall, from and after the first January, eighteen hundred and sixty-three, be entitled to enter one quarter section or a less quantity of unappropriated public lands, upon which said person may have filed a preemption claim, or which may, at the time the application is made, be subject to preemption at one dollar and twenty-five cents, or less, per acre; or eighty acres or less of such unappropriated lands, at two dollars and fifty cents per acre, to be located in a body, in conformity to the legal subdivisions of the public lands, and after the same shall have been surveyed: *Provided,* That any person owning and residing on land may, under the provisions of this act, enter other land lying contiguous to his or her said land, which shall not, with the land so already owned and occupied, exceed in the aggregate one hundred and sixty acres.

SEC. 2. *And be it further enacted,* That the person applying for the benefit of this act shall, upon application to the register of the land office in which he or she is about to make such entry, make affidavit before the said register or receiver that he or she is the head of a family, or is

Nebraska farmers stand in front of the farm they established under the provisions of the Homestead Act, late nine-teenth century. © BETTMANN/CORBIS.

twenty-one years or more of age, or shall have performed service in the army or navy of the United States, and that he has never borne arms against the Government of the United States or given aid and comfort to its enemies, and that such application is made for his or her exclusive use and benefit, and that said entry is made for the purpose of actual settlement and cultivation, and not either directly or indirectly for the use or benefit of any other person or persons whomsoever; and upon filing the said affidavit with the register or receiver, and on payment of ten dollars, he or she shall thereupon be permitted to enter the quantity of land specified: *Provided, however*, That no certificate shall be given or patent issued therefor until the expiration of five years from the date of such entry; and if, at the expiration of such time, or at any time within two years thereafter, the person making such entry; or, if he be dead, his widow; or in case of her death, his heirs or devisee; or in case of a widow making such entry, her heirs or devisee, in case of her death; shall

prove by two credible witnesses that he, she, or they have resided upon or cultivated the same for the term of five years immediately succeeding the time of filing the affidavit aforesaid, and shall make affidavit that no part of said land has been alienated, and that he has borne true allegiance to the Government of the United States; then, in such case, he, she, or they, if at that time a citizen of the United States, shall be entitled to a patent, as in other cases provided for by law: *And provided, further*, That in case of the death of both father and mother, leaving an Infant child, or children, under twenty-one years of age, the right and fee shall ensure to the benefit of said infant child or children; and the executor, administrator, or guardian may, at any time within two years after the death of the surviving parent, and in accordance with the laws of the State in which such children for the time being have their domicile, sell said land for the benefit of said infants, but for no other purpose; and the purchaser shall acquire the absolute title by the purchase, and be en-titled to a patent from the United States, on payment of the office fees and sum of money herein specified.

SEC. 3. *And be it further enacted*, That the register of the land office shall note all such applications on the tract books and plats of, his office, and keep a register of all such entries, and make return thereof to the General Land Office, together with the proof upon which they have been founded.

SEC. 4. *And be it further enacted*, That no lands acquired under the provisions of this act shall in any event become liable to the satisfaction of any debt or debts contracted prior to the issuing of the patent therefore.

SEC. 5. *And be it further enacted*, That if, at any time after the filing of the affidavit, as required in the second section of this act, and before the expiration of the five years aforesaid, it shall be proven, after due notice to the settler, to the satisfaction of the register of the land office, that the person having filed such affidavit shall have actually changed his or her residence, or abandoned the said land for more than six months at any time, then and in that event the land so entered shall revert to the government.

SEC. 6. *And be it further enacted*, That no individual shall be permitted to acquire title to more than one quarter section under the provisions of this act; and that the Commissioner of the General Land Office is hereby required to prepare and issue such rules and regulations, consistent with this act, as shall be necessary and proper to carry its provisions into effect; and that the registers and receivers of the several land offices shall be entitled to receive the same compensation for any lands entered under the provisions of this act that they are now entitled to receive when the same quantity of land is entered with money, one half to be paid by the person making the application at the time of so doing, and the other half on the issue of the certificate by the person to whom it may be issued; but this shall not be construed to enlarge the maximum of compensation now prescribed by law for any register or receiver: *Provided*, That nothing contained in this act shall be so construed as to im-pair or interfere in any manner whatever with existing preemption rights: *And provided, further*, That all persons who may have filed their applications for a preemption right prior to the passage of this act, shall be entitled to all privileges of this act: *Provided, further*, That no person who has served, or may hereafter serve, for a period of not less than fourteen days in the army or navy of the United States, either regular or volunteer, under the laws thereof, during the existence of an actual war, domestic or foreign, shall be deprived of the benefits of this act on account of not having attained the age of twenty-one years.

SEC. 7. *And be it further enacted*, That the fifth section of the act entitled "An act in addition to an act more effectually to provide for the punishment of certain crimes against the United States, and for other purposes," approved the third of March, in the year eighteen hundred and fifty-seven, shall extend to all oaths, affirmations, and affidavits, required or authorized by this act.

SEC. 7. That nothing in this act shall be so construed as to prevent any person who has availed him or herself of the benefits of the first section of this act, from paying the minimum price, or the price to which the same may have graduated, for the quantity of land so entered at any time before the expiration of the five years, and obtaining a patent therefore from the government, as in other cases provided by law, on making proof of settlement and cultivation as provided by existing laws granting preemption rights.

APPROVED, May 20, 1862.

SIGNIFICANCE

The Homestead Act bolstered western loyalty to the United States but it did not turn out to be the bonanza that many had expected. At the time that the legislation passed, prime fertile lands remained unclaimed only in western Iowa, western Minnesota, eastern Kansas, eastern Nebraska, and the Dakotas. Most of the first-class land was soon taken, however, leaving little except the unclaimed lands west of the hundredth meridian in the Great Plains. Little rain fell in this area. In most of the plains and mountain regions, a 160-acre homestead was impractical because the land was suitable only for grazing livestock. Farms required much more acreage.

It was so easy to circumvent the provisions of the law that land grabbers used it, along with the legislation that still provided for outright purchase, to amass great holdings. Between 1870 and 1900, less than one acre in five that were added to farming rolls belonged to homesteaders. Most were held by big businesses.

FURTHER RESOURCES
Books

Gates, Paul Wallace. *Agriculture and the Civil War*. New York: Knopf, 1965.

Gould, Florence C., and Patrician N. Pando. *Claiming Their Land: Women Homesteaders in Texas* El Paso: Texas Western Press, 1991.

Merrill, Karen R. *Public Lands and Political Meaning: Ranchers, the Government, and the Property btween Them*. Berkeley: University of California Press, 2002.

Morrill Act of 1862

Legislation

By: Justin Smith Morrill

Date: July 2, 1862

Source: Morrill, Justin Smith. "Morrill Act of 1862." United States Congress, July 2, 1862.

About the Author: Justin Smith Morrill (1810–1898) served in the U.S. House of Representatives as a Republican from Vermont in the years from 1855 to 1867. As a member of the House Ways and Means Committee, he sponsored the Land-Grant College Act of 1862. He served in the Senate from 1867 to 1898, guaranteeing funds for the survival of land grant colleges with the Second Morrill Act of 1880.

INTRODUCTION

The Morrill Land Grant provided public lands for colleges with a focus on agricultural and mechanical education. It reflected the intent of the federal government to establish a policy of providing opportunities for higher education to the agricultural and working classes.

Until the Morrill Act, the vast majority of institutions of higher learning were religious or private. By 1862, several state governments, notably Iowa and Illinois, had begun to assume responsibility for higher education because the existing colleges and universities were not including the lower-income people from the agricultural and industrial classes. Illinois had been the first state to propose land grant universities when the state legislature in 1853 sent the U.S. Congress a request that each state receive $500,000 of public land for the express purpose of creating universities to serve the industrial classes.

Justin Smith Morrill used the Illinois resolution to craft the first Morrill Bill for land grant colleges in 1857. He argued that a curriculum focused on practical sciences, rather than Latin and English, would do the greatest good for the greatest number of people. The 1857 bill faced heavy opposition because of complaints from southern and western legislators that it was constitutionally improper to give the federal government a role in education. It narrowly passed Congress only to be vetoed by President James Buchanan on the grounds that it was a financial drain on the Treasury, a threat to existing colleges, and unconstitutional.

Congressman Justin S. Morrill. THE LIBRARY OF CONGRESS.

Abraham Lincoln expressed support for the Morrill Act during the presidential campaign of 1860. Upon his election and the secession of southern states, Morrill made another effort to get the bill into law. It passed the Senate by a vote of 32–7 and the House by a vote of 90–25. On July 2, 1862, Lincoln signed the measure.

PRIMARY SOURCE

MORRILL ACT OF 1862

Chap. CXXX.—AN ACT Donating Public Lands to the several States and Territories which may provide Colleges for the Benefit of Agriculture and Mechanic Arts.

Be it enacted by, the Senate and House of Representatives of the United States of America, in Congress assembled, That there be granted to the several States, for the purposes hereinafter mentioned, an amount of public land, to be apportioned to each State a quantity equal to thirty thousand acres for each Senator and Representative in Congress to which the States are respectively entitled by the apportionment under the census of eighteen hundred and sixty; *Provided*, That no mineral lands shall be selected or purchased under the provisions of this act.

SEC. 2.

And be it further enacted, That the land aforesaid, after being surveyed, shall be apportioned to the several States in sections or subdivisions of sections, not less than one-quarter of a section; and wherever there are public lands in a State, subject to sale at private entry at one dollar and twenty-five cents per acre, the quantity to which said State shall be entitled shall be selected from such lands, within the limits of such State; and the Secretary of the Interior is hereby directed to issue to each of the States, in which there is not the quantity of public lands subject to sale at private entry, at one dollar and twenty-five cents per acre, to which said State may be entitled under the provisions of this act, land scrip to the amount in acres for the deficiency of its distributive share; said scrip to be sold by said States, and the proceeds thereof applied to the uses and purposes prescribed in this act, and for no other purpose whatsoever: *Provided*, That in no case shall any State to which land scrip may thus be issued be allowed to locate the same within the limits of any other State or of any territory of the United States; but their assignees may thus locate said land scrip upon any of the unappropriated lands of the United States subject to sale at private entry, at one dollar and twenty-five cents. or less, an acre: *And provided further*, That not more than one million acres shall be located by such assignees in any one of the States: *And provided further*, That no such location shall be made before one year from the passage of this act.

SEC. 3.

And be it further enacted, That all the expenses of management, superintendence, and taxes from date of selection of said lands, previous to their sales, and all expenses incurred in the management and disbursement of moneys which may be received therefrom, shall be paid by the States to which they may belong, out of the treasury of said States, so that the entire proceeds of the sale of said lands shall be applied, without any diminution whatever, to the purposes hereinafter mentioned.

SEC. 4.

And be it further enacted, That all moneys derived from the sale of the lands aforesaid by the States to which the lands are apportioned, and from the sales of land scrip hereinbefore provided for, shall be invested in stocks of the United States, or of the States, or some other safe stocks, yielding not less than five per centum upon the par value of said stocks; and that the moneys so invested shall constitute a perpetual fund, the capital of which shall remain forever undiminished, (except so far as may be provided in section fifth of this act,) and the interest of which shall be inviolably appropriated, by each State which may take and claim the benefit of this act, to the endowment, support, and maintenance of at least one college where the leading object shall be, without excluding other scientific and classical studies, and including military tactics, to teach such branches of learning as are related to agriculture and the mechanic arts, in such manner as the legislatures of the States may respectively prescribe, in order to promote the liberal and practical education of the industrial classes in the several pursuits and professions in life.

SEC. 5.

And be it further enacted, That the grant of land and land scrip hereby authorized shall be made on the following conditions, to which, as well as to the provisions hereinbefore contained, the previous assent of the several States shall be signified by legislative acts:

First. If any portion of the fund invested, as provided by the foregoing section, or any portion of the interest thereon, shall, by any action or contingency, be diminished or lost, it shall be replaced by the State to which it belongs, so that the capital of the fund shall remain forever undiminished; and the annual interest shall be regularly applied without diminution to the purposes mentioned in the fourth section of this act, except that a sum, not exceeding ten per centum upon the amount received by any State under the provisions of this act, may be expended for the purchase of lands for sites for experimental farms, whenever authorized by the respective legislatures of said States;

Second. No portion of said fund, nor the interest thereon, shall be applied, directly or indirectly, under any pretense whatever, to the purchase, erection, preservation, or repair of any building or buildings;

Third. Any State which may take and claim the benefit of the provisions of this act shall provide, within five years, at least not less than one college, as prescribed in the fourth section of this act, or the grant to such State shall cease; and said State shall be bound to pay the United States the amount received of any lands previously sold, and that the title to purchasers under the State shall be valid;

Fourth. An annual report shall be made regarding the progress of each college, recording any improvements and experiments made, with their costs and results, and such other matters, including State industrial and economical statistics, as may be supposed useful; one copy of which shall be transmitted by mail free, by each, to all the other colleges which may be endowed under the provisions of this act, and also one copy to the Secretary of the Interior;

Fifth. When lands shall be selected from those which have been raised to double the minimum price in consequence of railroad grants, they shall be computed to the States at the maximum price, and the number of acres proportionally diminished,

Sixth. No State, while in a condition of rebellion or insurrection against the Government of the United States, shall be entitled to the benefit of this act;

Seventh. No state shall be entitled to the benefits of this act unless it shall express its acceptance thereof by its legislature within two years from the date of its approval by the President.

Provided, That when any Territory shall become a State and be admitted into the Union, such new State shall be entitled to the benefits of the said act of July two, eighteen hundred and sixty-two, by expressing the acceptance therein required within three years from the date of its admission into the Union, and providing the college or colleges within five years after such acceptance, as prescribed in this act.

SEC. 6.

And be it further enacted, That land scrip issued under the provisions of this act shall not be subject to location until after the first day of January, one thousand eight hundred and sixty-three.

SEC. 7.

And be it further enacted, That land officers shall receive the same fees for locating land scrip issued under the provisions of this act as is now allowed for the location of military bounty land warrants under existing laws: *Provided*, That maximum compensation shall not be thereby increased.

SEC. 8.

And be it further enacted, That the governors of the several States to which scrip shall be issued under this act shall be required to report annually to Congress all sales made of such scrip until the whole shall be disposed of, the amount received for the same, and what appropriation has been made of the proceeds.

Approved, July 2, 1862. (12 Stat. 503.)

SIGNIFICANCE

States used their Morrill Act funds in a variety of ways to establish land grant colleges. While some created the first state universities, others established separate Agricultural and Mechanical (A&M) universities. A few of these A&M schools, such as the University of Kentucky and the University of Maryland, later evolved into state universities. Ultimately, nearly all of the institutions chose a liberal rather than a technical and narrow approach to higher education. This decision upset many agricultural leaders, who viewed the schools as potential training grounds for future farmers and engineers. However, enrollment and graduation rates for land grant universities show that agricultural and industrial workers were not initially attracted to the schools.

Nevertheless, in response to considerable discontent within the farming community, Congress passed the Hatch Act and the Smith-Lever Act. The Hatch Act of 1887 created agricultural experiment stations by authorizing direct payment of federal funds to each state to serve agricultural interests. The Smith-Lever Act created a Cooperative Extension Service associated with each land grant institution.

The 106 land grant colleges and universities established as a result of the Morrill Act include some of the best known and most respected schools in the United States, including the University of Illinois, the University of Tennessee, Pennsylvania State University, The Ohio State University, Louisiana State University, Massachusetts Institute of Technology, and Auburn University.

FURTHER RESOURCES

Books

Christy, Ralph D. and Lionel Williamson. *A Century of Service: Land-Grant Colleges and Universities, 1890–1990.* New Brunswick, N.J.: Transaction Publishers, 1991.

Cross, Coy F. *Justin Smith Morrill: Father of Land-Grant Universities.* East Lansing, Mich.: Michigan State University, 1999.

Edmond, J. B. *The Magnificent Charter: The Origin and Role of the Morrill Land-Grant Colleges and Universities.* Hicksville, N.Y.: Exposition Press, 1978.

An Act to Establish a Bureau for the Relief of Freedmen and Refugees

Legislation

By: U.S. Congress

Date: March 3, 1865

Source: *Freedmen's Bureau Act*. Statutes at Large of the United States of America 13 (1866): 507–509.

About the Author: The thirty-eighth Congress met in two sessions from March 4, 1963 to March 3, 1965. This legislation was passed on the final day of the Congress's second session.

INTRODUCTION

The legislation required to establish the Bureau for the Relief of Freedmen and Refugees was enacted in March 1865. The objectives of what came to be known as the Freedmen's Bureau were to enforce the civil and legal rights of black Americans and of pro-Union southerners, to assist freed slaves in becoming educated, and to aid them in gaining a means of economic survival. One of the major efforts of the Freedmen's Bureau was the creation of schools at every level, from primary and secondary through vocational and industrial schools, to colleges, and universities for black Americans. The Freedmen's Bureau was also instrumental in the creation and implementation of the public school system in the United States, in encouraging legislation mandating compulsory education, and in promoting the funding and development of colleges and universities across America.

Food being distributed to freed slaves in Beaufort, South Carolina, circa 1865. © CORBIS.

In 1866, General Oliver Otis Howard was nominated by General Ulysses S. Grant to head up the Freedmen's Bureau. Howard had a deep belief in the value and power of education and was committed to the construction, development, implementation, and nationwide expansion of a multi-level school system for African Americans. Howard believed that it was only through advanced education that the black population could truly become free, and he set about creating a college, university, and professional education system with which to achieve that goal. In part, his opinions regarding the structure of the educational framework were based on successful European systems. It was also based upon a growing belief among educators that a public program for education was essential to the development of an advanced society, as well as to true equality among all citizens.

For the first couple of years after it was created, there was no governmental funding with which to carry out the programs of the Freedmen's Bureau. Howard put together contributions from aid organizations, relief societies, and philanthropists with available funds from abandoned cotton revenues—taxes on cotton crops, monies generated by harvesting cotton from former plantations, and the like—to pay for the creation of the necessary infrastructure. Howard was able to generate sufficient revenue to keep the Bureau's programs entirely funded until it was subsidized by the War Department.

PRIMARY SOURCE

CHAP. XC.—*AN ACT TO ESTABLISH A BUREAU FOR THE RELIEF OF FREEDMEN AND REFUGEES.*

Be it enacted by the Senate and House of Representatives of the United States of America in Congress assembled, That there is hereby established in the War Department, to continue during the present war of rebellion, and for one year thereafter, a bureau of refugees, freedmen, and abandoned lands, to which shall be committed, as hereinafter provided, the supervision and management of all abandoned lands, and the control of all subjects relating to refugees and freedmen from rebel states, or from any district of country within the territory embraced in the operations of the army, under such rules and regulations as may be prescribed by the head of the bureau and approved by the President. The said bureau shall be under the management and control of a commissioner to be appointed by the President, by and with the advice and consent of the Senate, whose compensation shall be three thousand dollars per annum, and such number of clerks as may be assigned to him by the Secretary of War, not exceeding one chief clerk, two of the fourth class, two of the third class, and five of the first class. And the commissioner and all persons appointed under this act, shall, before entering upon their duties, take the oath of office prescribed in an act entitled "An act to prescribe an oath of office, and for other purposes," approved July second, eighteen hundred and sixty-two, and the commissioner and the chief clerk shall, before entering upon their duties, give bonds to the treasurer of the United States, the former in the sum of fifty thousand dollars, and the latter in the sum of ten thousand dollars, conditioned for the faithful discharge of their duties respectively, with securities to be approved as sufficient by the Attorney-General, which bonds shall be filed in the office of the first comptroller of the treasury, to be by him put in suit for the benefit of any injured party upon any breach of the conditions thereof.

SEC. 2. *And be it further enacted*, That the Secretary of War may direct such issues of provisions, clothing, and fuel, as he may deem needful for the immediate and temporary shelter and supply of destitute and suffering refugees and freedmen and their wives and children, under such rules and regulations as he may direct.

SEC. 3. *And be it further enacted*, That the President may, by and with the advice and consent of the Senate, appoint an assistant commissioner for each of the states declared to be in insurrection, not exceeding ten in number, who shall, under the direction of the commissioner, aid in the execution of the provisions of this act; and he shall give a bond to the Treasurer of the United States, in the sum of twenty thousand dollars, in the form and manner prescribed in the first section of this act. Each of said commissioners shall receive an annual salary of two thousand five hundred dollars in full compensation for all his services. And any military officer may be detailed and assigned to duty under this act without increase of pay or allowances. The commissioner shall, before the commencement of each regular session of congress, make full report of his proceedings with exhibits of the state of his accounts to the President, who shall communicate the same to congress, and shall also make special reports whenever required to do so by the President or either house of congress; and the assistant commissioners shall make quarterly reports of their proceedings to the commissioner, and also such other special reports as from time to time may be required.

SEC. 4. *And be it further enacted*, That the commissioner, under the direction of the President, shall have authority to set apart, for the use of loyal refugees and freedmen, such tracts of land within the insurrectionary states as shall have been abandoned, or to which the United States shall have acquired title by confiscation or sale, or otherwise, and to every male citizen, whether refugee or freedman, as aforesaid, there shall be assigned not more than forty acres of such land, and the person to whom it was so assigned shall be protected in the use and enjoyment of the land for the term of three years at an annual rent not exceeding six per centum upon the value of such land, as it was appraised by the state authorities in the year eighteen hundred and sixty, for the purpose of taxation, and in case no such appraisal can be found, then the rental shall be based upon the estimated value of the land in said year, to be ascertained in such manner as the commissioner may by regulation prescribe. At the end of said term, or at any time during said term, the occupants of any parcels so assigned may purchase the land and receive such title thereto as the United States can convey, upon paying therefor the value of the land, as ascertained and fixed for the purpose of determining the annual rent aforesaid.

SEC. 5. *And be it further enacted*, That all acts and parts of acts inconsistent with the provisions of this act, are hereby repealed.

APPROVED, March 3, 1865.

SIGNIFICANCE

In addition to its educational and job training activities, the Freedmen's Bureau was first responsible for ensuring that the newly freed, and largely disenfranchised, former slaves and refugees—non-slaves who had sympathized with the Union cause during the Civil War—had adequate food, clothing, supplies, and shelter, and that as many as possible of their medical needs were properly met. The bureau was not funded by the government, but was able to generate revenues through a variety of ingenious means, among which was the management of lands and properties confiscated from the former Confederacy. Eventually, it received a small subsidy from the War Department as well.

The bureau was originally intended as a transitional program and was approved for only one year when it was established on March 3, 1865. On July 16, 1866, the bureau was reauthorized and the former slave states were organized into ten regions, each of which had an Assistant Commissioner. Oliver Otis Howard served as the overall Bureau Commissioner, and the bureau functioned under the aegis of the War Department.

Among the statutory responsibilities of the Freedmen's Bureau was the provision of food and other necessary rations; the dispensation of medical care, supplies and medications; procurement of shelter and oversight of resettlement efforts; adjudication of disputes and management of legal and criminal justice issues; job oversight and regulation of labor and workforce issues; utilization and management oversight of abandoned and confiscated properties, businesses, and lands; and creation of a means of education by establishing schools and other trainings and learning institutions. Although the bureau worked conscientiously to fulfill all of its myriad responsibilities, its most notable success was in the area of education. Statistics published in the Semiannual Reports on Schools for Freedmen indicated that more than 4,000 schools were eventually built, which were staffed by nearly 10,000 teachers. By 1870, more than 250,000 students were in the educational system created by the Freedmen's Bureau.

Another significant area of bureau activity involved the negotiation of labor contracts. For the first time, many former slaves were to be paid by employers—some of whom were their former owners. The freedmen lacked both education and the ability to engage in meaningful discourse about labor-related issues, an area that was completely foreign to both the freedmen and the former owners. As a result, the bureau provided training in contract negotiation. It also acted as a sort of employment agency, serving as a conduit between white employers who were in need of workers and freedmen in need of work. The successes achieved in the development and implementation of educational systems for black Americans, as well as the creation of a culture in which African Americans, for the first time, could exercise personal choice regarding where they would work and what they would do, had an enormous, and long-lasting, positive impact for the freedmen and refugees.

One of the most serious social issues embedded in the American slavery system was the dissolution of families and the severing of affectional ties. Slaves were not permitted to marry legally. Family members could be separated and sold to different owners, making it nearly impossible to keep track of one another's whereabouts. In addition, the same slave was often repeatedly sold. In the case of children, time and changing circumstances made it very difficult for babies and children sold as slaves to be reunited with their families after emancipation. One of the many tasks of the Freedmen's Bureau was to assist family members with their attempts at locating and reuniting with relatives, as well as to assist the former slaves with grasping and adopting the concepts of family structure, as conceptualized by white Americans.

The Freedman's Bureau dealt with the problems of the freedmen and refugees on a grassroots, daily basis for three years, and on a more limited basis for another four. In addition to its successes in education and employment, it was able to provide medical care and assistance to more than one million people over the course of its existence. It also helped African Americans secure the funds and facilities to establish churches and other places of worship, which had not been permitted during slavery. Although the Freedman's Bureau had many significant accomplishments, it remains best known for its role in implementing, promoting, and providing for a system of education for black Americans.

FURTHER RESOURCES

Books

Anderson, James D. *The Education of Blacks in the South, 1860–1935*. Chapel Hill: University of North Carolina Press, 1988.

Bently, George R. *A History of the Freedmen's Bureau*. Philadelphia: University of Pennsylvania Press, 1955.

Berlin, Ira. *Slaves No More*. New York: Cambridge University Press, 1992.

Butchart, Ronald V. *Northern Schools, Southern Blacks, and Reconstruction: Freedmen's Education, 1862–1875*. Westport, Conn.: Greenwood Press, 1980.

Finley, Randy. *From Slavery to Freedom*. Fayetteville: University of Arkansas Press, 1996.

Foner, Eric. *A Short History of Reconstruction*. New York: Harper & Row, 1990.

Lawson, Bill E., and Howard McGary. *Between Slavery and Freedom*. Bloomington: Indiana University Press, 1992.

Litwack, Leon F. *Been in the Storm So Long: The Aftermath of Slavery*. New York: Vintage Books, 1980.

Periodicals

Cimbala, Paul. "On the Front Line of Freedom: Freedmen's Bureau Officers and Agents in Reconstruction Georgia, 1865–1868." *Georgia Historical Quarterly* 76 (1992): 577–1611.

Crouch, Barry A. "The 'Chords of Love:' Legalizing Black Marital and Family Rights in Postwar Texas." *Journal of Negro History* 79 (1994): 334–345.

DuBois, W. E. Burghardt. "The Freedmen's Bureau." *Atlantic Monthly* 87 (1901): 354–365.

Lieberman, Robert C. "The Freedmen's Bureau and the Politics of Institutional Structure." *Social Science History* 18 (1994): 405–437.

Special Field Orders No. 15

Document

By: William Tecumseh Sherman

Date: January 16, 1865

Source: Sherman, William Tecumseh. "Special Field Orders No. 15." January 16, 1865.

About the Author: William Tecumseh Sherman, a West Point graduate and a former instructor and banker, volunteered his services at the outset of the Civil War and rose to become Supreme Commander of the western forces during the Civil War. Known for the burning of Atlanta and his march to the sea during that war, Sherman played an important role in Reconstruction efforts.

INTRODUCTION

The emancipation of slaves and the end of legal slavery involved three major turning points: the Emancipation Proclamation of 1863, Special Field Orders No. 15 of 1865, and the Thirteenth Amendment to the United States Constitution in 1865. Each of these actions were important to the abolition of slavery; General William T. Sherman's Special Field Orders No. 15 helped bring an end to slavery while using federal control to enact social and economic change.

One of the pro-slavery arguments posited by southern slave owners was, "What would we do with all the slaves if they were free? Where would they live? What jobs would they take?" This question weighed on President Abraham Lincoln's mind as he considered the slavery issue. By 1863, Lincoln penned the Emancipation Proclamation, freeing slaves in rebel-controlled areas, and offering slaves a place in the Union army. This gradualist approach was followed by the January 1865 Special Field Orders No. 15 issued by Sherman, and then the Thirteenth Amendment to the Constitution later that year.

Sherman's field order, approved by Lincoln, seized portions of the south to redistribute to current and former slaves. In addition, it offered military service opportunities for current and former slaves, encouraging slaves to flock to Union territory to receive commissions and land.

PRIMARY SOURCE

In the Field, Savannah, Georgia, January 16th, 1865.

Special Field Orders, No. 15.

I. The islands from Charleston, south, the abandoned rice fields along the rivers for thirty miles back from the sea, and the country bordering the St. Johns river, Florida, are reserved and set apart for the settlement of the negroes now made free by the acts of war and the proclamation of the President of the United States.

II. At Beaufort, Hilton Head, Savannah, Fernandina, St. Augustine and Jacksonville, the blacks may remain in their chosen or accustomed vocations—but on the islands, and in the settlements hereafter to be established, no white person whatever, unless military officers and soldiers detailed for duty, will be permitted to reside; and the sole and exclusive management of affairs will be left to the freed people themselves, subject only to the United States military authority and the acts of Congress. By the laws of war, and orders of the President of the United States, the negro is free and must be dealt with as such. He cannot be subjected to conscription or forced military service, save by the written orders of the highest military authority of the Department, under such regulations as the President or Congress may prescribe. Domestic servants, blacksmiths, carpenters and other mechanics, will be free to select their own work and residence, but the young and able-bodied negroes must be encouraged to enlist as soldiers in the service of the United States, to contribute their share towards maintaining their own freedom, and securing their rights as citizens of the United States.

Negroes so enlisted will be organized into companies, battalions and regiments, under the orders of the United States military authorities, and will be paid, fed and clothed according to law. The bounties paid on enlistment may, with the consent of the recruit, go to assist his family and settlement in procuring agricultural implements, seed, tools, boots, clothing, and other articles necessary for their livelihood.

III. Whenever three respectable negroes, heads of families, shall desire to settle on land, and shall have selected for that purpose an island or a locality clearly defined, within the limits above designated, the Inspector of Settlements and Plantations will himself, or by such subordinate officer as he may appoint, give them a license to settle such island or district, and afford them such assistance as he can to enable them to establish a peaceable agricultural settlement. The three parties named will subdivide the land, under the supervision of the Inspector, among themselves and such others as may choose to settle near them, so that each family shall have a plot of not more than (40) forty acres of tillable ground, and when it borders on some water channel, with not more than 800 feet water front, in the possession of which land the military authorities will afford them protection, until such time as they can protect themselves, or until Congress shall regulate their title. The Quartermaster may, on the requisition of the Inspector of Settlements and Plantations, place at the disposal of the Inspector, one or more of the captured steamers, to ply between the settlements and one or more of the commercial points heretofore named in orders, to afford the settlers the opportunity to supply their necessary wants, and to sell the products of their land and labor.

IV. Whenever a negro has enlisted in the military service of the United States, he may locate his family in any one of the settlements at pleasure, and acquire a homestead, and all other rights and privileges of a settler, as though present in person. In like manner, negroes may settle their families and engage on board the gunboats, or in fishing, or in the navigation of the inland waters, without losing any claim to land or other advantages derived from this system. But no one, unless an actual settler as above defined, or unless absent on Government service, will be entitled to claim any right to land or property in any settlement by virtue of these orders.

V. In order to carry out this system of settlement, a general officer will be detailed as Inspector of Settlements and Plantations, whose duty it shall be to visit the settlements, to regulate their police and general management, and who will furnish personally to each head of a family, subject to the approval of the President of the United States, a possessory title in writing, giving as near as possible the description of boundaries; and who shall adjust all claims or conflicts that may arise under the same, subject to the like approval, treating such titles altogether as possessory. The same general officer will also be charged with the enlistment and organization of the negro recruits, and protecting their interests while absent from their settlements; and will be governed by the rules and regulations prescribed by the War Department for such purposes.

VI. Brigadier General R. Saxton is hereby appointed Inspector of Settlements and Plantations, and will at once enter on the performance of his duties. No change is intended or desired in the settlement now on Beaufort [Port Royal] Island, nor will any rights to property heretofore acquired be affected thereby.

By Order of Major General W. T. Sherman

SIGNIFICANCE

Special Field Orders No. 15 provided a framework for post-Civil War living conditions and resettlement for former slaves. By offering young, able-bodied black males a position in the Union army, Sherman and Lincoln created encouraging conditions for slaves to abandon their work on plantations and with smaller southern farmers, doubly assisting the Union cause by weakening the south and strengthening Union forces.

The 400,000 acres (162,000 hectares), which stretched from South Carolina to Florida, were taken from Confederate States of America supporters. During Sherman's campaign, thousands of slaves had followed his army; Sherman met with black leaders in Savannah to brainstorm and find a way to help these refugees. Six weeks after Sherman and Lincoln issued Special Field Orders No. 15, Lincoln established the Bureau of Refugees, Freedmen, and Abandoned Lands, known as the Freedman's Bureau, to create a federal agency designed to coordinate assistance for freed slaves to adjust to their new lives. The Freedman's Bureau helped former slaves in finding food, shelter, jobs, and land. However, after Vice President Andrew Johnson assumed the presidency after Lincoln's assassination, he overturned Sherman's order in the fall of 1865. In 1867, Republican Thaddeus Stevens attempted to pass a bill distributing land to former slaves, but the bill failed.

Although very few former slaves received the benefits of Sherman's field order, and President Andrew Johnson returned the seized lands to the planters who had owned the lands before the order, the short-lived program provides an example to modern slave reparations groups who call for payments from the U.S. government to the descendents of former slaves. Representative John Conyers, a Democrat from Michigan, introduced The Commission to Study Reparations Proposals for African Americans Act, or Congressional Bill H.R. 40, in 1989; the bill has not yet passed, but groups such as Black Thought for Justice and Change and the National Coalition of Blacks for Reparations in America have argued that slave reparations would be on par with the 1988 reparations made to Japanese-Americans and their descendents, who were placed in internment camps during World War II. Critics of reparations, such as public policy specialist and cultural analyst Wendy Kaminer, argue that reparations 160 years after the end of slavery apply a form of "inherited guilt" to slavery, and that reparations are not the best way to address inequities and social problems caused by slavery.

The 40 acres (16 hectares) noted by Sherman became part of the "forty acres and a mule" promise cited by historians as one of the great unfulfilled promises made by the U.S. government to former slaves (a later order issued by Sherman called for the loaning of mules to former slaves). While Sherman's field order was short-lived, it provides an example of Lincoln's approach to Reconstruction and also gives modern-day reparations activists a precedent to cite when looking at ongoing social, economic, and racial issues in the United States.

FURTHER RESOURCES

Books

Foner, Eric. *Reconstruction: America's Unfinished Revolution, 1863–1877*. New York: Harper, 2002.

Guelzo, Allen C. *Lincoln's Emancipation Proclamation: The End of Slavery in America*. New York: Simon & Schuster, 2004.

Tsesis, Alexander. *The Thirteenth Amendment and American Freedom: A Legal History*. New York: New York University Press, 2004.

Web sites

Religion & Ethics Newsweekly. "Slave Reparations." January 5, 2001. <http://www.pbs.org/wnet/religionandethics/week419/feature.html> (accessed June 18, 2006).

Andrew Johnson Kicking out the Freedmen's Bureau

Editorial cartoon

By: Thomas Nast

Date: April 14, 1866

Source: Illustration by Thomas Nast, provided courtesy of HarpWeek.

Source: Thomas Nast (1840–1902) is the most famous political cartoonist in nineteenth-century American history. He worked for *Harper's Weekly*, one of the most-read magazines of the era, from 1861 to 1866.

INTRODUCTION

When President Abraham Lincoln issued the Emancipation Proclamation to free slaves in the Confederacy, he did not provide a way for them to

Andrew Johnson Kicking out the Freedmen's Bureau: A political cartoon caricatures President Andrew Johnson's veto of the Freedman's Bureau bill. ILLUSTRATION BY THOMAS NAST, PROVIDED COURTESY OF HARPWEEK.

make a living as free citizens. To ease the transition from slavery to freedom, Congress created the Bureau of Refugees, Freedmen, and Abandoned Lands, popularly known as the Freedmen's Bureau, on March 3, 1865.

The bureau had its roots in an 1865 proposal by Representative George Julian of Indiana and Senator Charles Sumner of Massachusetts to give freed slaves forty-acre homesteads carved out of Confederate

lands taken under the Confiscation Act of 1862. More Southern lands were subsequently seized as abandoned under an 1864 law and for default on taxes levied by Congress early in the war. It made sense to many Radical Republicans [those who favored freedom, equality, and voting rights for blacks] to distribute these lands to former slaves to enable them to take care of themselves. Congress, however, refused to sanction any type of land redistribution, and Johnson, a former slave owner, pardoned a large number of Southern landowners and restored their property to them. As a result, the blacks were given land to rent, not own, in what became the sharecropping system.

The Freedmen's Bureau provided food, clothing, and transportation to freed blacks as well as to whites displaced by the war. It also set up schools, distributed lands, and attempted to monitor labor contracts (something new for both blacks and planters). The bureau had its own courts to deal with labor disputes and land titles, and its agents were further authorized to supervise trials involving blacks in other courts. Andrew Johnson, a former slave owner who became president upon Lincoln's assassination, opposed the Freedmen's Bureau throughout his brief term in office.

ANDREW JOHNSON KICKING OUT THE FREEDMEN'S BUREAU
See primary source image.

SIGNIFICANCE

The Freedmen's Bureau suffered from poor leadership that drastically hampered its effectiveness. Oliver Otis Howard, the bureau's commissioner, was well meaning and sympathetic, as were a number of field agents. However, many regional and local officers were more concerned with gaining the approval of the white communities in which they worked than fulfilling the bureau's mission. They viewed their main responsibility as persuading former slaves to accept contracts with their former masters and preventing the blacks from drifting into towns. Additionally, some of the more dedicated officers who genuinely sought to help the African Americans were removed from office by Johnson.

The president's resistance to the Freedmen's Bureau and Reconstruction killed the agency. Johnson

An illustration of the 1868 impeachment trial of President Andrew Johnson, in the Senate Chambers. THE LIBRARY OF CONGRESS

challenged Congress by vetoing a bill in 1866 that would have extended its life, arguing that it violated the Constitution because it made the federal government responsible for indigents, was passed by a Congress that denied seats to the eleven states of the Confederacy, and was vague in its definition of civil rights. At that time, Johnson still had sufficient clout to persuade the Senate to uphold his veto. After he attacked congressional leaders in a fiery speech, however, moderate Republicans began to abandon him. When Johnson vetoed a Civil Rights Act on the grounds that giving citizenship to native-born blacks went beyond the scope of federal power, Congress overrode his veto and enacted a revised Freedmen's Bureau bill on April 9, 1866. Relations between Johnson and Congress eventually become so poor that Johnson was nearly thrown out of office.

The battle over the bureau and lack of presidential support, however, left the agency severely weak-ened. In the four years of its existence, it fed about 4,000 people and educated many Southerners, but achieved little more. The Freedmen's Bureau was a temporary relief measure, yet it helped earn constitutional and legal rights for African Americans.

FURTHER RESOURCES

Books

Benedict, Michael Les. *The Impeachment and Trial of Andrew Johnson*. New York: W.W. Norton, 1973.

Keller, Morton. *The Art and Politics of Thomas Nast*. New York: Oxford University Press, 1968.

Nieman, Donald G., ed. *The Freedmen's Bureau and Black Freedom*. New York: Garland, 1994.

Oubre, Claude F. *Forty Acres and a Mule: The Freedmen's Bureau and Black Land Ownership*. Baton Rouge: Louisiana State University Press, 1978.

Education of the Freedmen

Newspaper editorial

By: Anonymous

Date: February 10, 1866

Source: Editorial staff. "Education of the Freedmen." *Harper's Weekly*. (February 10, 1866): 53.

About the Author: *Harper's Weekly* was first published on January 3, 1857, and ran for almost six decades. It is considered to have great historical importance in the present day, as it provides an accurate snapshot of events, mores, culture, and political opinions of its time. During its publication run it was a politically, and therefore historically, influential periodical. It provides a quite detailed chronology of American events and culture during the Civil War and Reconstruction periods, as well as a general picture of life and times during that era.

INTRODUCTION

Prior to the abolition of slavery, there was no system of formal education for African American slaves, nor for free blacks. In many areas of the country, particularly in rural or frontier regions, there was no public school system at all. By the mid–1800s public schools, known as common schools, were just beginning to take hold in the Northeast; where no public schools existed, private schools offered education for the wealthier citizens and, through charitable donations, for some poor white children. Overall, the options for the less privileged, whether black or white, were few or nonexistent.

Throughout the South, slaves were not permitted to learn to read or write, to possess paper or writing instruments, or to own books of any kind, regardless of ability to read them. Any form of education for slaves, beyond what was specifically necessary in order to perform their duties, was expressly forbidden and punishable by law. A few white people, primarily those associated with schools or churches, ran underground night schools for slaves, but they did so at great per-

Students and teachers pose outside a Freedmen's Bureau school in Beaufort, South Carolina. © CORBIS. REPRODUCED BY PERMISSION.

sonal risk and were forced to abandon their efforts if discovered.

The north, where slavery had been abolished by the early 1800s, was considerably more liberal in its educational efforts, but racial segregation in education was the norm. In 1787, a facility called the African Free School was opened in New York City. By the early 1820s, seven schools for African Americans were operating in Manhattan, and all were receiving public educational funding.

Before the Civil War ended, a large cadre of teachers from the North had been selected by various aid societies and professional educators' associations to travel to the South and create schools for both African American and white children, albeit in separate school systems, as there was to be complete segregation in education and in all other areas of public life.

After the end of the Civil War, and throughout the Reconstruction period, these northern teachers traveled deep into the South to educate the freedmen (and women and children). At the time, it was the norm in the South for teachers to be marginally educated, and they often had minimal (if any) secondary education. The same was not true in the North. Many of the teachers had completed high school, and quite a few had college degrees. During Reconstruction, the largest percentage of the teachers were white and female, although a significant number were free female African Americans from the North.

PRIMARY SOURCE

"The Freedmen," said our martyr President, "are the Wards of the Nation." "Yes," replied Mr. Stanton, "Ward in Chancery." What is our duty to them as their guardians? Clearly, to clothe them if they are naked; to teach them if they are ignorant; to nurse them if they are sick, and to adopt them if they are homeless and motherless. They have been slaves, war made them freedmen, and peace must make them freemen. They must be shielded from unjust laws and unkindly prejudices; they must be instructed in the true principles of social order and democratic government; they must be prepared to take their place by-and-by in the great army of voters as lately they filled up the ranks in the great army of fighters. The superstitions, the vices, the unthriftiness, the loitering and indolent habits which slavery foisted on the whites and blacks alike, who were cursed by its presence in their midst, must be dispelled and supplanted by all the traits and virtues of a truly Christian civilization.

The North, that liberated the slave, has not been remiss in its duty to the freedman. The common school

has kept step to the music of the advancing army. Willson's Readers have followed Grant's soldiers everywhere. Many of the colored troops on the march had primers in their boxes and primers in their pockets. They were namesakes, but not of the same family. Charleston had not been captured more than a week before the schools for freedmen and poor whites were opened there. It is proposed now to educate all the negroes and poor whites in the South—as a political necessity; in order that henceforth there may be no other insurrections, the result of ignorance, either on the part of the late slave or that late slaveholder. Ignorance has cost us too much to be suffered to disturb us again. In free countries it is not the intelligent but the ignorant who rebel. Ambitious men could never induce an enlightened people to overthrow a free Government. It was because there were over 600,000 white adults in the slave States, and 4,000,000 of slaves who could neither read nor write, that Davis and Toombs and Slidell had power to raise armies against the nation. Let us prevent all social upheavals in the future by educating all men now.

The National Freedmen's Relief Association of New York—of which Francis George Shaw is President and Joseph B. Collins Treasurer—has been the most active of the agencies in relieving the wants and dispelling the ignorance of the freedman. It has expended during the last four years three quarters of a million of dollars in clothing the naked; in establishing the freedmen on farms; in supplying them with tools; in founding orphan homes; in distributing school-books and establishing schools. They have over two hundred teachers in the South at this time. They support orphan homes in Florida and South Carolina. They teach ten thousand children, and large numbers of adults. They have instituted industrial schools to educate the negro women to be thrifty housewives. They are continually laboring, in brief, to make the negroes self-reliant and self-supporting. They appeal for additional aid. There are but a thousand teachers for freedmen in all the Southern States; whereas twenty thousand could find immediate employment. The National Relief Association could find pupils for 5000. It has but 200. As the work is a good and great one, and as the officers of this Society are eminent citizens of New York, we heartily commend their appeal to the generosity of our readers.

SIGNIFICANCE

As teachers from the North began to move into the South, a variety of educational systems began to be created, both for newly freed slaves and for the itinerant and lower socioeconomic classes of whites. The teachers set up an entire educational system, spanning the range from early and elementary education through secondary schools and colleges. They provided not only rudimentary training but also schools for theology, literature, and classical studies. The goal was to provide as broad a base of opportunities as possible. In addition to the more traditional forms of didactic and classroom-based education, educators established centers for technical and vocational training and for a variety of useful skills, such as sewing, cooking, woodworking, and the like.

When the Freedmen's Bureau was established in 1866, it was led by General Oliver Otis Howard (1830–1909), who was deeply committed to seeing that all newly freed slaves were afforded abundant educational opportunities. It was his core belief that true freedom could only be attained by those who had the means to live independently in society—and that the basis for achieving freedom was found in a thorough education. Because of his beliefs, dedication, and the perseverance that he and others associated with him brought to the task, a matrix of colleges and universities designed to prepare African Americans to succeed in the scientific, medical, business, teaching, and other respected professions was created. Although many considered the Freedmen's Bureau to have fallen short of its overall mission, the academic infrastructure created by Howard and his colleagues had a profound impact on the evolution of education, and educational institutions, for southern African Americans.

Howard and his colleagues recognized that there were growing needs in the African American community for many types of professionals. It was their belief that blacks should be given the opportunity to become educated in every possible area in order to meet those needs, rather than having such positions filled by whites, creating yet another social imbalance of power. It was Howard's belief that a strong college and university system was necessary in order to more fully meet the needs of the growing free black population. During the post-Civil War Reconstruction era, two educational models predominated: vocational and industrial training schools, and classical colleges and universities, which typically offered programs of study in theology, education, and medicine. In the classical model, all students were required to study classical languages such as Latin and Greek, physics, and mathematics. Howard believed that the post-secondary systems also needed a school for the study of law, and it was his conviction that schools should be well funded, whether they were public or private institutions, in order to provide the greatest possible educational opportunities for all who sought them. Howard University, the first black-centered college in America, was named in honor of General Howard.

Howard, when put in charge of the Freedmen's Bureau, was given economic support to set up school systems on a large scale. Prior to the creation of the bureau, education of freedmen was largely overseen by the American Missionary Association and other aid and relief societies, who operated with a much more limited budget derived primarily from charitable donations. In 1865, according to Semiannual Reports on Schools for Freedman, there were reported to be more than fifteen hundred teachers working with more than ninety thousand children. By the Tenth Semiannual Report on Schools for Freedmen, published in 1870, there were 4,239 schools employing 9,307 teachers for 247,333 students. The superintendent of schools under the Freedmen's Bureau reported that the total educational budget in 1870 was about one million dollars.

The creation of the educational system for freedmen, and the rapid rise in educational institutions of all kinds, set the stage for developing the philosophy that education ought to be freely available and publicly supported. Although some public school systems had been established in Massachusetts and elsewhere prior to the Civil War, there was, in additioin, a groundswell movement aimed at making primary and secondary education compulsory for all people, regardless of race.

FURTHER RESOURCES

Books

Anderson, James D. *The Education of Blacks in the South, 1860–1935.* Chapel Hill: University of North Carolina Press, 1988.

Butchart, Ronald V. *Northern Schools, Southern Blacks, and Reconstruction: Freedmen's Education, 1862–1875.* Westport, Conn.: Greenwood Press, 1980.

Knight, Edgar W. *A Documentary History of Education in the South before 1860.* Chapel Hill: University of North Carolina Press, 1953.

Swint, Henry L. *The Northern Teacher in the South, 1862–1870.* Nashville, Tenn.: Vanderbilt University Press, 1941.

Willie, Charles V., Antoine M. Garibaldi, and Wornie L. Reed, eds. *The Education of African-Americans.* New York: Auburn House, 1991.

Web sites

Harper's Weekly. "About Harper's Weekly." 2006 <http://www.harpersweekly.com/> (accessed May 23, 2006).

Anti-Chinese Political Cartoon

Editorial cartoon

By: Anonymous

Date: 1877

Source: "Anti-Chinese Political Cartoon." © Bettmann/ Corbis.

Source: This cartoon is a part of the Bettmann Archives of the Corbis Corporation, an international provider of visual content materials to a wide range of consumers in the communications industries. The artist is unknown.

INTRODUCTION

The discrimination practiced against Asian peoples in North America as reflected in this 1877 political cartoon had its impetus from the completion of the American transcontinental railway in 1869. Although there was a significant Chinese labor force in California after 1850, the easier rail access to the West Coast across the American continent had created a movement of Caucasian labor to California after 1870; there quickly arose a feeling in the white population that Chinese and later Japanese laborers, often referred to as "coolies," had driven down the available wages and therefore contributed to greater unemployment in the region. The Asian workers were stereotyped from the earliest days of their immigration to California as fanatical in their desire to work for the lowest possible wage.

The cartoon reflects contemporary societal views of its Asian immigrants on two distinct levels. Miscegenation is a technical term that describes the inter-marriage—or more broadly, the inter-breeding—of two separate races. It is a word that was invented for use in 1863 by D.G. Croly, a New York Democrat who published a pseudo-scientific paper about the inter-marriage of American black and white races to undermine the Lincoln administration and its campaign to emancipate the slaves in the Southern states. Miscegenation became an unintended term of art that was used by the forces opposed to Asian immigration for the next eighty years.

On a broader level, the image of the young Chinese male taking the arm of the young Caucasian female was intended to symbolize the perceived incursion by the Chinese into American society at large.

Anti-Chinese sentiments were not restricted to the United States at the time the cartoon was published. The Canadian province of British Columbia had also experienced a significant increase of Chinese immigration in the late 1870s; as the successful construction of Canada's transcontinental railway hinged on the completion of the dangerous blasting operations that were necessary to build the passes through the Rocky Mountains that were undertaken in the early 1880s. Thousands of Chinese laborers were engaged in the work. It was estimated that in some of the most perilous blasting operations, where liquid nitroglycerine was employed, a Chinese coolie died for every 10 feet (3 meters) of rail line laid.

The Chinese were the most prominent Asian immigrants to North America in the late 1870s. The hostility directed toward their presence in the workforce was later broadened to include the Japanese, who began to arrive in greater numbers on the West Coast of North America and Hawaii after the Japanese government abolished its death penalty in 1888 for those who sought to emigrate from Japan. The feelings against Asian immigration were heightened across North America when Korean and Indian laborers arrived in significant numbers after 1900.

PRIMARY SOURCE

ANTI-CHINESE POLITICAL CARTOON
See primary source image.

SIGNIFICANCE

The primary significance of the 1877 Anti-Chinese cartoon is that the cartoon represents a North American public sentiment that was then just beginning to find its political expression. Policies directed against Asian immigration would be a component of both American and Canadian government policy for the next seventy years.

In the United States, the passage of the Chinese Exclusion Act in 1882 was the first of seven significant Congressional acts directed at Asian peoples in America. The Chinese Exclusion Act prohibited Chinese immigration for ten years and it was subsequently extended. After its transcontinental railway was completed in 1885, Canada determined that it had no need to further encourage Chinese immigration; Canada imposed a "head tax" of $50 on every Chinese person seeking to enter Canada, a figure that approximated the annual net wages of an unskilled laborer. The head tax was increased to $500 per prospective Chinese immigrant

PRIMARY SOURCE

Anti-Chinese Political Cartoon: The fear of miscegenation, which motivated the Asiatic Exclusion League and other organizations to support anti-Chinese legislation during the 1870s and 1880s, finds sympathetic expression in this 1877 cartoon. © BETTMANN/CORBIS.

gration of all Asian people to the United States. The American ban on Asian immigration was not lifted until 1952.

The most visible example of overt public discrimination against Asian persons in North America occurred with the formation of the Asiatic Exclusion League (AEL) in San Francisco in 1905. The AEL was the creation of the local trade unions to combat the effect of Asian labor in the California economy. An AEL was also formed for a brief period in Vancouver, an act that precipitated riots in that city's Chinatown in September, 1907. The participation of numerous trade unions in the AEL was consistent with the forceful campaign waged against Asian immigration by Samuel Gompers (1850–1924), the founder and president of the American Federation of Labor. Gompers wrote a series of political pamphlets directed at Chinese and Japanese labor after 1900, including "Meat versus Rice" and "American Manhood versus Asiatic Coolieism—Which Shall Survive?"

The determined position of Gompers and the San Francisco unions is significant as it stands in contrast to the later prominent role taken by the American labor movement in liberal causes such as women's rights in the workplace, a shorter work week, and various efforts to improve working conditions generally in the United States.

In many respects, the internment of Japanese-American and Japanese-Canadian citizens and naturalized persons in both Canada and the United States after 1941 was a natural extension of the sentiments reflected in the 1877 cartoon. In both countries, persons of Japanese ancestry were either forcibly relocated to places removed from the Pacific coast and the presumed prospect of a Japanese attack on North America or interned in government camps, often with a resulting loss of their property. The impact of internment was felt by a significant population. In the United States, 126,000 persons of Japanese ancestry were subject to internment in 1941, with over sixty percent of these persons being American citizens. In British Columbia, 22,000 such persons were interned or subject to relocation; seventy-five percent of these persons were either naturalized Canadians or were born in Canada.

The ultimate official acknowledgement of the anti-Asian practices common in North America after 1877 took separate but similar turns in Canada and the United States. In 1948, limited compensation was made available to American Japanese internees. In 1988, President Reagan issued an official apology to the Japanese-American community for the policy of internment.

by 1923. Canadian policies through this period toward the Chinese are contrasted with the free land made available through its homestead policy to thousands of eastern European farmers who were encouraged to settle on the Canadian Prairies in the early 1900s.

North American efforts to legislate restrictions against Chinese labor were replicated in Mexico, the countries of modern Central America, and Peru by 1900. The collective anti-Chinese prohibitions have been termed the "Great Wall Against China" in the modern scholarly reviews of this question. Attacks on coolie labor and elements of fear-mongering, seen in expressions such as "Yellow Peril," were common editorial themes in the West Coast newspapers throughout this period. American legislative actions included the exclusion of Asian children from San Francisco schools in 1905, two specific anti-Japanese statutes in California in 1909, and the Johnson Act of 1924, a Federal law that imposed racial quotas on the immi-

In Canada, the federal government issued a formal apology to the Chinese people who had paid its head tax in the period between 1885 and 1923. In 1988, the government had issued a formal apology and compensation package to the Japanese-Canadian survivors of wartime detention.

FURTHER RESOURCES
Books

Daniels, Roger. *Politics of Prejudice: The Anti-Japanese Movement in California and the Struggle for Japanese Exclusion.* Berkeley, Calif.: University of California Press, 1999.

Lee, Erika. *At America's Gates: Chinese Immigration During the Exclusion Era, 1882–1943.* Chapel Hill, N.C.: University of North Carolina Press, 2003.

Miki, Roy. *Redress: Inside the Japanese Canadian Call for Justice.* Vancouver, Canada: Raincoast Books, 2005.

Web sites

City of San Francisco. "Virtual Museum of the City of San Francisco." 2005 <http://www.sfmuseum.org/1906.2/invasion.html> (accessed June 11, 2006).

City of Vancouver. "1906–1908." May 29, 2006 <http://www.vancouverhistory.ca/chronology5.htm> (accessed June 11, 2006).

3 The Gilded Age and the Progressive Era

The Gilded Age and the Progressive Era

The Gilded Age and the Progressive Era in the United States spanned the years from the end of Reconstruction through the 1920s. Many historians overlap the end of the Gilded Age (1870–1900) with the beginning of the Progressive Era (1890–1929).

The Gilded Age was an age of movement. Populations changed, people moved, and trade increased. Migration to the American west, a dramatic increase in immigration to the United States from foreign shores, and the peak of European colonialism in Asia and Africa were aided by the proliferation of railroads, steamers, telegraphs, and the telephone. The Gilded Age was the era of the corporation, the heyday of the "Robber Barons" and "Captains of Industry."

While the Gilded Age brought outstanding prosperity to some, it was also deeply tarnished beneath its gold veneer. The poor became poorer, the tenement slums grew, and new immigrants endured increasing economic and social hardships. Some of the most successful corporate endeavors became monopolies. Consumer prices rose; corruption and industrial labor abuses increased.

The Progressives sought to solve many of the social injustices of the Gilded Age. Where the Gilded Age was highly individualistic, progressive reformers thought that governments had a responsibility to promote socially beneficial programs. Progressives who advocated the government regulation of industry asserted that economic and social policy could not easily be separated. The Progressive movement sought answers to social problems through scientific and methological study. The professions of medicine, social work, and law flourished. Progressive professionals sought to use their disciplines to increase public health and safety, reform prisons and tenement housing, and outlaw child labor.

This chapter includes some of the greatest progressive victories of the era. Temperance supporters championed prohibition as the means to reduce public and domestic violence, strengthen families, and increase worker productivity. The ratification of the 18th Amendment in 1920 began prohibition in the United States, though whether it fulfilled the promises of its progressive champions is debatable.

The Progressive era was the zenith of the muckrakers—journalists, photographers, writers, and film makers whose work exposed social problems. Muckrakers exposed corruption in political parties, governments, labor unions, and corporations (especially oil and railroads). They advanced Progressive causes of public health and worker safety, campaigned against child labor, and pushed for reforms in prisons and slums. Included in this chapter are the famous muckraker works of Upton Sinclair and Jacob Riis. Sinclair's novel *The Jungle* exposed unsanitary conditions in the American meatpacking industry; Riis, a photographer and social reformer, captured the conditions of New York tenement life in *How the Other Half Lives*.

Finally, not all social policy during the Progressive era advanced human rights. Even the progressive and populist movements debated the role of women and minorities in politics and society, though both were more likely to advocate equality. Women won the right to vote in all elections in 1919, but the political and social opportunities of minorities were circumscribed by segregation. This chapter would be incomplete without an excerpt from the 1896 Supreme Court decision *Plessy v. Ferguson*, which upheld segregation laws.

How the Other Half Lives

Photograph

By: Jacob A. Riis

Date: c. 1885

Source: © Hulton-Deutsch Collection/Corbis.

About the Photographer: Jacob Riis (1849–1914) immigrated to the United States from Denmark in 1870 at the age of twenty-one. He began his writing career as a police reporter with the *New York Tribune*, reporting on tenement life in New York City slums. He became known nationally through his books and photography describing the living conditions of the urban poor.

INTRODUCTION

The need for housing sky-rocketed in New York City during the nineteenth century, as immigration accelerated rapidly after the 1820s and 1830s. Tenement houses were considered an economically viable solution to this shortage of living space. These simple dormitories could be constructed quickly, and landlords could maximize profits by packing families of immigrants into small living spaces, sometimes fifteen people to a room. Poorly ventilated tenement houses were notorious for their lack of cleanliness and foul smells. As a pioneer in the field of photojournalism in

PRIMARY SOURCE

How the Other Half Lives: An 1886 Jacob A. Riis photograph shows men sleeping on the floor of a New York homeless shelter. © BETTMANN/CORBIS.

This photo depicts a group of people living in a crowded one-room tenement in New York. It was taken by photographer Jacob A. Riis in the mid 1880s and featured in *How the Other Half Lives*. © HULTON-DEUTSCH COLLECTION/CORBIS.

the late 1800s, Jacob Riis began to describe the substandard living conditions of the poor immigrants to the wealthier segments of society.

Jacob Riis experienced extreme poverty firsthand when he arrived in the United States. In search of meaningful work, Riis traveled to places such as New York City, Buffalo, Philadelphia, Pittsburgh, and Chicago, only to find casual labor jobs making candles, chopping wood, and harvesting ice. For a short time, he worked on a farm, tried hunting and trapping, and even peddled mirrors and irons in exchange for clothing. Desperate and without money, Riis began to write about his own life struggles and those of other immigrants he lived among. In 1877, he landed a job as reporter with the *New York Tribune*.

In the 1880s, Riis began working for reforms to help the poor, collaborating with others who were advocating for better living conditions for the thousands of immigrants arriving yearly in New York. Riis gained popularity through his book, *How the Other Half Lives*, in which he described the ills of urban living. He discussed the connection between poor living conditions and the high crime rates seen in New York City. Riis outlined what measures had already been taken by the government to rectify the situation, calling them important efforts. However, he also suggested additional measures that the government needed to take to address the problem of urban poverty, and he challenged those who benefited economically from the tenement buildings, suggesting they had forgotten their moral duty as Christians to improve living conditions for the poor.

When *How the Other Half Lives* was published, there were 1,250,000 people living in the New York tenement houses. The houses were located in the growing slums of New York City, and lacked running water and proper drainage systems. Sewage and garbage accumulated outside of tenements on roads that were badly in need of repair. These areas had few regulations, and in some areas cattle and other animals were moved through the streets in large numbers. The growth of the slums brought increased death rates. Tuberculosis, measles, mumps, and other infectious diseases were known to spread through the slums very quickly. Physicians began to connect the prevalence of disease with the filth of tenement housing.

PRIMARY SOURCE

HOW THE OTHER HALF LIVES
See primary source image.

SIGNIFICANCE

Riis's work raised awareness about the millions of people living in poor slums throughout the United States. His writings led to growing concern for the poor among the general public and policy makers alike. Many who read his works found Riis's message to be stark, yet optimistic about improving the abysmal living conditions of the poor. By the end of the nineteenth century, purification of city water was underway, the incidence of diseases was decreasing, and efforts to create child labor laws were beginning. The Tenement House Department for the City of New York was created by the New York State legislature in 1900. This new department helped pass the Tenement House Act of 1901, which addressed the need for ventilation and light in helping to reduce the mortality of the tenement house districts. In 1894, Amos G. Warner's, *American Charities*, was the first book on social welfare in the United States. The New York School of Philanthropy was established in 1898 as the first school for social workers. It later became the Columbia University School of Social Work. Social workers began to address the plight of the poor, helping individuals find ways to better lives.

Theodore Roosevelt (1858–1919), who as President of the United States urged the passing of labor protection acts and other legislation to protect poor laborers, recognized Riis as a catalyst for welfare reform. Roosevelt, who was New York's Commissioner of Police while Riis worked as a police reporter, offered Riis powerful positions in his presidential administration. Riis turned down the jobs in Washington D.C., to continue writing on the plight

of poor children and immigrants. His other significant books include *The Battle with the Slum* and *The Children of the Poor.*

FURTHER RESOURCES
Books

Cordasco, Francesco. *Jaccob Riis Revisited: Poverty and the Slum in Another Era.* Garden City, N.Y.: Doubleday, 1968.

Garvin, Alexander. *The American City: What Works, What Doesn't.* Second edition. New York: McGraw-Hill, 2002.

Riis, Jacob, A. *The Battle with the Slum.* New York: MacMillan, 1902.

Riis, Jacob, A. *The Children of the Poor.* New York: Charles Scribner's Sons, 1892.

Riis, Jacob, A. *How the Other Half Lives: Studies Among the Tenements of New York.* New York: Charles Scribner's Sons, 1890.

Waifs of the City Slums

Book excerpt

By: Jacob A. Riis

Date: 1890

Source: Riis, Jacob A. "Waifs of the City Slums." In *How the Other Half Lives.* New York: Belknap, 1890.

About the Author: Jacob A. Riis (1849–1914), born in Denmark, worked in the heart of New York City's immigrant district as a police reporter for a newspaper. With the publication of *How the Other Half Lives,* he became recognized as an authority on urban poverty.

INTRODUCTION

Historically, family and child welfare policy in the United States was defined by a balance between private and public responsibility. Poor relief officials possessed the power to remove children whose parents could not or would not support them. By the 1870s, organized philanthropists and child welfare reformers had begun a national child-saving movement. Part of the Progressive Era, the child-saving movement reflected growing concerns about rising urban poverty, urbanization, immigration, and crime.

Armenian orphans stand in the entryway to Miss Cushman's Orphanage, June 8, 1920. © BETTMANN/CORBIS.

In 1874, the discovery of a young girl who had apparently been abused by her foster mother led to the formation of the Society for the Prevention of Cruelty to Children (SPCC) in New York City. This organization was authorized by city and state statutes to investigate reports of child cruelty and neglect and, if necessary, to remove children from their parents or guardians. Removing children from parents or guardians posed the problem of how to care for them. Until the twentieth century, the SPCC typically placed children in asylums.

Jacob Riis, a crusading newspaper reporter, helped publicize the conditions faced by poor immigrant children. Riis's experience with poverty as a young man made him generally sympathetic toward the lot of the poor. Yet his sympathy had its limits and

was influenced by his success in rising to the top. In general, Riis accepted the environmental cause of poverty, a theory just beginning to win acceptance in 1890, and rejected the notion that the poor owed their condition to sinfulness, laziness, or general unfitness. However, in discussing certain ethnic groups, Riis displayed stereotypical views. He believed that Germans were most able to advance, that Italians and Jews rose only when forced to do so, and that the Chinese were unsuited for advancement. Riis's 1890 report on child welfare in New York City reflected his biases.

■ PRIMARY SOURCE

First among these barriers is the Foundling Asylum. It stands at the very outset of the waste of life that goes on in a population of nearly two millions of people; powerless to prevent it, though it gather in the outcasts by night and by day. In a score of years an army of twenty-five thousand of these forlorn little waifs have cried out from the streets of New York in arraignment of a Christian civilization under the blessings of which the instinct of motherhood even was smothered by poverty and want. Only the poor abandon their children. The stories of richly dressed foundlings that are dished up in the newspapers at intervals are pure fiction. Not one instance of even a well-dressed infant having been picked up in the streets is on record. They come in rags, a newspaper often the only wrap, semioccasionally one in a clean slip with some evidence of loving care; a little slip of paper pinned on, perhaps, with some such message as this I once read, in a woman's trembling hand: "Take care of Johnny, for God's sake. I cannot." But even that is the rarest of all happenings.

The city divides with the Sisters of Charity the task of gathering them in. The real foundlings, the children of the gutter that are picked up by the police, are the city's wards. In midwinter, when the poor shiver in their homes, and in the dog days when the fierce heat and foul air of the tenements smother their babies by thousands, they are found, sometimes three and four in a night, in hallways, in areas and on doorsteps of the rich, with whose comfort in luxurious homes the wretched mother somehow connects her own misery. Perhaps, as the drowning man clutches at a straw, she hopes that these happier hearts may have love to spare even for her little one. In this she is mistaken. Unauthorized babies especially are not popular in the abodes of the wealthy. It never happens outside of the storybooks that a baby so deserted finds home and friends at once. Its career, though rather more official, is less romantic, and generally brief. After a night spent at Police Headquarters it travels up to the Infant's Hospital on Randall's Island in the morning, fitted out with a number and a bottle, that seldom see much wear before they are laid aside for a fresh recruit. Few outcast babies survive their desertion long. Murder is the true name of the mother's crime in eight cases out of ten. Of 508 babies received at the Randall's Hospital last year 333 died, 65.55 percent. But of the 508 only 170 were picked up in the streets, and among these the mortality was much greater, probably nearer ninety percent, if the truth were told. The rest were born in the hospitals. The high mortality among the foundlings is not to be marveled at. The wonder is, rather, that any survive. The stormier the night, the more certain is the police nursery to echo with the feeble cries of abandoned babes. Often they come half dead from exposure. One live baby came in a little pine coffin which a policeman found an inhuman wretch trying to bury in an uptown lot. But many do not live to be officially registered as a charge upon the county. Seventy-two dead babies were picked up in the streets last year. Some of them were doubtless put out by very poor parents to save funeral expenses. In hard times the number of dead and live foundlings always increases very noticeably. But whether traveling by way of the Morgue or the Infants' Hospital, the little army of waifs meets, reunited soon, in the trench in the Potter's Field, where, if no medical student is in need of a subject, they are laid in squads of a dozen.

Most of the foundlings come from the East Side, where they are left by young mothers without wedding rings or other name than their own to bestow upon the baby, returning from the island hospital to face an unpitying world with the evidence of their shame. Not infrequently they wear the bedtick regimentals of the Public Charities, and thus their origin is easily enough traced. Oftener no ray of light penetrates the gloom, and no effort is made to probe the mystery of sin and sorrow. This also is the policy pursued in the great Foundling Asylum of the Sisters of Charity in Sixty-eighth Street, known all over the world as Sister Irene's Asylum. Years ago the crib that now stands just inside the street door, under the great main portal, was placed outside at night; but it filled up too rapidly. The babies took to coming in little squads instead of in single file, and in self-defense the sisters were forced to take the cradle in. Now the mother must bring her child inside and put it in the crib where she is seen by the sister on guard. No effort is made to question her, or discover the child's antecedents, but she is asked to stay and nurse her own and another baby. If she refuses, she is allowed to depart unhindered. If willing, she enters at once into the great family of the good Sister who in twenty-one years has gathered as many thousand homeless babies into her fold. One was brought in when I was last in the asylum, in the middle of July, that received in its crib the number 20715. The death rate is

of course lowered a good deal when exposure of the child is prevented. Among the eleven hundred infants in the asylum it was something over nineteen percent last year; but among those actually received in the twelve-month nearer twice that figure. Even the nineteen percent, remarkably low for a Foundling Asylum, was equal to the startling death rate of Gotham Court in the cholera scourge.

Four hundred and sixty mothers, who could not or would not keep their own babies, did voluntary penance for their sin in the asylum last year by nursing a strange waif besides their own until both should be strong enough to take their chances in life's battle. An even larger number than the eleven hundred were "pay babies," put out to be nursed by "mothers" outside the asylum. The money thus earned payed the rent of hundreds of poor families. It is no trifle, quite half of the quarter of a million dollars contributed annually by the city for the support of the asylum. The procession of these nursemothers, when they come to the asylum on the first Wednesday of each month to receive their pay and have the babies inspected by the sisters, is one of the sights of the city. The nurses, who are under strict supervision, grow to love their little charges and part from them with tears when, at the age of four or five, they are sent to western homes to be adopted. The sisters carefully encourage the home feeding in the child as their strongest ally in seeing its mental and moral elevation, and the toddlers depart happy to join their "papas and mammas" in the faraway, unknown home.

An infinitely more fiendish, if to surface appearances less deliberate, plan of child murder than desertion has flourished in New York for years under the title of baby farming. The name, put into plain English, means starving babies to death. The law has fought this most heinous of crimes by compelling the registry of all baby farms. As well might it require all persons intending murder to register their purpose with time and place of the deed under the penalty of exemplary fines. Murderers do not hang out a shingle. "Baby farms," said once Mr. Elbridge T. Gerry, the President of the Society charged with the execution of the law that was passed through his efforts, "are concerns by means of which persons, usually of disreputable character, eke out a living by taking two, or three, or four babies to board. They are the charges of outcasts or illegitimate children. They feed them on sour milk, and give the paregoric to keep them quiet, until they die, when they get some young medical man without experience to sign a certificate to the Board of Health that the child died of inanition, and so the matter ends. The baby is dead, and there is no one to complain." (1) A handful of baby farms have been registered and licensed by the Board of Health with the approval of the Society for the Prevention of Cruelty to children in the last five years, but none of this kind. The devil keeps the only complete register to be found anywhere. Their trace is found oftenest by the coroner or the police; sometimes they may be discovered hiding in the advertising columns of certain newspapers, under the guise of the scarcely less heartless traffic in helpless children that is dignified with the pretense of adoption—for cash. An idea of how this scheme works was obtained through the disclosures in a celebrated divorce case, a year or two ago. The society has among its records a very recent case of a baby a week old (Baby "blue Eyes") that was offered for sale—adoption, the dealer called it—in a newspaper. The agent bought it after some haggling for a dollar, and arrested the woman slave trader; but the law was powerless to punish her for her crime. Twelve unfortunate women awaiting dishonored motherhood were found in her house.

One gets a glimpse of the frightful depths to which human nature, perverted by avarice bred of ignorance and rasping poverty, can descend, in the mere suggestion of systematic insurance *for profit* of children's lives. A woman was put on trial in this city last year for incredible cruelty in her treatment of a stepchild. The evidence aroused a strong suspicion that a pitifully small amount of insurance on the child's life was one of the motives for the woman's savagery. A little investigation brought out the fact that three companies that were in the business of insuring children's lives, for sums varying from $17 up, had issued not less than a million such policies! The premiums ranged from five to twenty-five cents a week. What untold horrors this business may conceal was suggested by a formal agreement entered into by some of the companies, "for the purpose of preventing speculation in the insurance of children's lives." By the terms of this compact, "no higher premium than ten cents could be accepted on children under six years old." Barbarism forsooth! Did ever heathen cruelty invent a more fiendish plot than the one written down between the lines of this legal paper?

It is with a sense of glad relief that one turns from this misery to the brighter page of the helping hands stretched forth on every side to save the young and the helpless. New York is, I firmly believe, the most charitable city in the world. Nowhere is there so eager a readiness to help, when it is known that help is worthily wanted; nowhere are such armies of devoted workers, nowhere such abundance of means ready to the hand of those who know the need and how rightly to supply it. Its poverty, its slums, and its suffering are the result of unprecedented growth with the consequent disorder and crowding, and the common penalty of metropolitan greatness. If the structure shows signs of being top heavy, evidences are not wanting—they are multiplying day by

day—that patient toilers are at work among the underpinnings. The Day Nurseries, the numberless Kindergartens and charitable schools in the poor quarters, the Fresh Air Funds, the thousand and one charities that in one way or another reach the homes and the lives of the poor with sweetening touch, are proof that if much is yet to be done, if the need only grows with the effort, hearts and hands will be found to do it in ever increasing measure. Black as the cloud is it has a silver lining, bright with promise. New York is today a hundredfold cleaner, better, purer, city than it was even ten years ago.

Two powerful agents that were among the pioneers in this work of moral and physical regeneration stand in Paradise Park today as milestones on the rocky, uphill road. The handful of noble women, who braved the foul depravity of the Old Brewery to rescue its child victims, rolled away the first and heaviest boulder, which legislatures and city councils have tackled in vain. The Five Points Mission (2) and they Five Points House of Industry (3) have accomplished what no machinery of government availed to do. Sixty thousand children have been rescued by them from the streets and had their little feet set in the better way. Their work still goes on, increasing and gathering in the waifs, instructing and feeding them, and helping their parents with advice and more substantial aid. Their charity knows not creed or nationality. The House of Industry is an enormous nursery school with an average of more than four hundred day scholars and constant boarders—"outsiders" and "insiders." Its influence is felt for many blocks around in that crowded part of the city. It is one of the most touching sights in the world to see a score of babies, rescued from homes of brutality and desolation, where no other blessing than a drunken curse was ever heard, saying their prayers in the nursery at bedtime. Too often their white nightgowns hide tortured little bodies and limbs cruelly bruised by inhuman hands. In the shelter of this fold they are safe, and a happier little group one may seek long and far in vain.

(1) Society for the Prevention of Cruelty to Children, New York, Tenth Annual Report (New York, 1885), p. 10.

(2) In 1850 the New York Ladies' Methodist (Episcopal) Home Missionary Society established a mission at 61 Park Street at the Five Points under the management of Rev. Lewis M. Pease. Three years later the group purchased a farm in East Chester to be run as a school. The Guide to the Charities of New York and Brooklyn (New York, 1886), p. 85, reported that the society "educates and maintains missionaries to labor among the poor, and poor children receive education, clothes and food. Families accommodated last year seventeen. Three hundred and fifty children attended mission school during some time."

(3) In 1854 Rev. Lewis M. Pease and a group of gentlemen associated with the Five Points Mission established the House of Industry; the building was completed at 155–159 Worth Street in the spring of 1856. The House contained a dormitory for the destitute, a common dining room, a chapel, and a school for children. The farm at East Chester supplied milk and vegetables, and the House sent its invalids to the farm. In the early years the House made a specialty of seeking country jobs for its residents. Five Points House of Industry, Second Annual Report (New York 1856), pp. 1–9. According to The Guide to the Charities (1886) p. 85, the House "protects, instructs and provides for destitute people; supports neglected and abandoned children, and others incapable of self-support. 721 cases cared for last year." The institution is still alive and now manages a group of schools for homeless and for retarded children in Rockland County, New York.

SIGNIFICANCE

Riis offered no overall plan for helping the poor achieve better lives. His greatest contribution lay in exposing and publicizing the intolerable conditions that existed in the tenements of New York City. With his writing and his photographs, he educated a generation of Americans about the dangers of life in the poor part of the city. Riis's belief in environmental causes of poverty led him to pursue environmental changes. He joined settlement workers, journalists, and other public-spirited citizens in efforts to improve the schools and to build neighborhood parks and playgrounds. His legacy is making life more pleasant for those who live in the city.

By the first decade of the twentieth century, public policy had begun to reflect the growing conviction that families, not institutions, were the best place for children. Moreover, reformers and policymakers had begun to worry that overzealous child savers removed children from their parents too quickly. As a result, both paid foster care and adoption placement increased. However, institutions, rather than private homes, continued to play a dominant role in the care of dependent children until the 1920s. Subsequently, orphanages became increasingly rare. They vanished from the landscape by the 1970s. At that time, welfare programs such as Medicaid and the Special Supplemental Nutrition Program for Women, Infants, and Children were regarded as the best means of aiding poor children. The Child Abuse Prevention and Treatment Act of 1974 provided states with financial incentives for child abuse prevention programs. The act was renewed in 1978 to include newly recognized offenses against children, such as abduction and sexual exploitation.

FURTHER RESOURCES
Books

Ashby, LeRoy. *Saving the Waif: Reformers and Dependent Children, 1890–1917*. Philadelphia, Penn.: Temple University Press, 1984.

Ladd-Taylor, Molly. *Mother-Work: Women, Child Welfare, and the State, 1890–1930*. Urbana, Ill.: University of Illinois Press, 1994.

Lane, James B. *Jacob A. Riis and the American City*. Port Washington, N.Y.: Kennikat Press, 1974.

Coxey's Army

Photograph

By: Anonymous

Date: 1894

Source: Photo by MPI/Getty Images.

About the Photographer: This photograph is part of the collection at Getty Images, a worldwide provider of visual content materials to such communications groups as advertisers, broadcasters, designers, magazines, news media organizations, newspapers, and producers. The identity of the photographer is not known.

INTRODUCTION

Jacob S. Coxey (1854–1951), a wealthy stone quarry owner from Massillon, Ohio, led the first organized protest of the unemployed. The protest culminated in a march of about 500 unemployed workers, known as Coxey's Army, through the streets of Washington, D.C., in May 1894.

In the 1890s, the United States experienced one of the most devastating economic depressions in its history. By 1894, many Americans had reached rock bottom with millions unemployed. A number of workers, notably laid off railroad construction workers, talked of marching on Washington, D.C., but few made it to the capital. One group that did was the Army of the Commonweal of Christ, led by Coxey.

A Populist with a son that he named Legal Tender in honor of monetary reform, Coxey had a long-

PRIMARY SOURCE

Coxey's Army: Led by populist Jacob Coxey, this army of unemployed men marched from Massillon, Ohio to Washington, D.C., in the spring of 1894 to demand a government program of public works to relieve the economic depression.
PHOTO BY MPI/GETTY IMAGES.

standing interest in reform. By the early 1890s, his interest in providing good roads merged with his concerns over unemployment. In 1892, he proposed that Congress hire the unemployed to work on building better roads and he created the Good Roads Association to promote this legislation. In 1894, Coxey again sought to address the unemployment problem by combining his good roads program with a financing proposal that would fund the building of a variety of public buildings. With support from several people, Coxey initiated a protest march from Massillon to Washington, D.C., in March 1894. Coxey and his followers took six weeks to march 400 miles to the capital, where others sympathetic to the cause joined them. The national press followed the march and other "Coxey's Army" groups formed across the nation.

PRIMARY SOURCE

COXEY'S ARMY

See primary source image.

SIGNIFICANCE

Coxey's Army collapsed quickly when Washington police arrested Coxey for walking on the grass in violation of the Capitol Grounds Act and jailed him. He received a twenty-day jail sentence and returned to Massillon when released. However, Coxey's Army and the growing political strength of Populism struck fear into the hearts of many Americans. Critics portrayed Populists like Coxey as Socialists whose election would endanger property rights.

Men from Coxey's Army en route from Masillon, Ohio, to Washington, D.C., in April 1894. © CORBIS. REPRODUCED BY PERMISSION.

For a generation, Coxey's march remained vivid in the public memory. In countless homes, boys and girls grimy from play were warned to clean up or they would look like someone from Coxey's Army. Children also reenacted a version of cops and robbers in which youthful Coxeyites stole wagons and were pursued by federal marshals. These parents and children were perpetuating a widespread, but incorrect, notion that Coxey's Army was merely a collection of dirty thieves.

In reality, Coxey continued as a well-respected political leader. Although the march did not lead to passage of the proposed public works legislation, Coxey continued in the public limelight for years due to his orchestration of the event. In 1896, he unsuccessfully ran for the U.S. Congress on the Populist ticket. He continued to be involved in politics and

finally was elected mayor of Massillon in 1931. He had more success at business and died a wealthy man. In time, the march of Coxey's Army faded from public memory, although its call for public works jobs anticipated a crucial element of the New Deal programs of the 1930s.

FURTHER RESOURCES
Books

Howson, Embrey Bernard. *Jacob Sechler Coxey: A Biography of a Monetary Reformer*. New York: Arno, 1982.

McMurry, Donald L. *Coxey's Army: A Study of the Industrial Army Movement of 1894*. Seattle: University of Washington Press, 1968.

Schwantes, Carlos A. *Coxey's Army: An American Odyssey*. Lincoln: University of Nebraska Press, 1985.

The Greatest Issue of the Day

Speech

By: Lizzie Black Kander

Date: January 1, 1900

Source: Kander, Lizzie Black. "The Greatest Issue of the Day" Milwaukee January 1, 1900. Lizzie Black Kander Papers, State Historical Society of Wisconsin.

About the Author: Born in Wisconsin in 1858 to Jewish immigrants, Leslie Black Kander was involved from an early age in efforts to reform the conditions of American immigrants and help them better acclimate into society. She became a champion of the movement to educate young girls and women on how to manage a home. Kander authored a popular cookbook that was designed to help immigrants adjust American ingredients. The book has been reprinted multiple times and sold more than two million copies.

INTRODUCTION

The nineteenth century was a period in the history of the United States filled with reform movements aimed at raising the profile of certain groups in society. Some of the most prominent reform movements targeted the status of women's and immigrants' rights. As a nation that welcomed hundreds of thousands of immigrants each year, U.S. society faced a challenge as to how to best acclimate these people into the population.

The United States throughout much of its history was viewed as a safe haven and a land of opportunity by peoples throughout the globe. Particularly for people living under harsh conditions in European nations where persecution of particular ethnic groups had become rampant, the shores of the United States offered the chance to escape and build a new life.

Yet, upon arrival in the United States, many immigrants realized that life was no less challenging. Immigrants, often regardless of their social status in their native countries, arrived at or near the bottom

European immigrants at Ellis Island wait for a ferry to transport them to New York City. © BETTMANN/CORBIS.

of the social ladder and were often forced to accept low-paying jobs and live in difficult conditions. In a culture and economy of the late 1800s that was becoming increasingly reliant on large industry and factories, immigrants filled these labor roles in the greatest numbers. These often low-paying positions often led immigrant families into poverty, which made it difficult to become fully acclimated into the greater society.

Recognizing these difficulties, and that the path toward increased socio-economic status for immigrants began with education, efforts were proposed to advance the rights of immigrants. Through these efforts over a period of decades, the status of immigrants would become slowly enhanced and while immigrants would always be forced to face social and economic challenges, the reform movements aided their acclimation process and helped many achieve respect and great success in the United States.

▉ PRIMARY SOURCE

Elizabeth Cady Stanton, Susan B. Anthony, and Mrs. Minona Phipps—scared me most to death by saying I would not be doing my duty to my country, to my children, if I advanced any other cause but that of Woman's Suffrage. And so we came to a mutual understanding and we decided that the greatest issue of the day was The New Woman.

You'd do me the greatest kind of a favor if you'd tell them that I had her almost ready for presentation to the society, this evening. But an incident occurred which changed the whole current of my thoughts.

It was downtown in one of our large furniture stores. The massive front door was gently opened and a small lad of about twelve years, with dark complexion, and bright but rather dirty face, with unmistakable Hebrew features, carrying on his arm a great long basket, timidly approached the proprietor with a genuine business air, offered his matches for sale cheap! He attracted the attention of everyone within hearing and the merchant, more pleased with good salesmanship of the little fellow, than the quality of his wares immediately bought 25 c[en]ts worth.

I followed the lad, asked him his name and address and why he did not go to school. He explained the necessity of his having to help support the family. His father was sick, a sister fourteen years old, had never gone to school was doing the housework and taking care of the children, while his mother was occupied all day, tending a fruit stand at the market.

Having had my attention drawn to numerous similar cases of late, my mind became so absorbed in them, that all other thoughts sank into oblivion, and I resolved then and there that I would submit to you the welfare and happiness of the Little Russian Refugees, knowing that their education and enlightenment is to us the most vital and the Greatest issue of the Day....

We must try and uplift our downtrodden and unfortunate brethren, not alone for their own sakes and for that of humanity, but for the protection and reputation of our own nationality.

Their misdeeds reflect directly on us and every one of us individually ought to do all in his power to help lay the foundation of good citizenship in them.

What wonderful strength of character have these people displayed, when in spite of the hardships heaped upon them, in spite of the oppressions—many of them have surmounted all obstacles are getting along nicely.

The wonderful transition which often takes place in a comparatively short time, is enough to arouse the admiration and wonder of the whole enlightened world; often creating jealousy and hatred in such narrow minded and bigoted relics of the middle ages as are now trying to engender prejudice against the whole Hebrew Race.

Tradition has painted us as proverbial for our skill in money making. I consider this a proud distinction. Who can afford to belittle money. Money is power is necessary for the advancement of civilization, art and science. I do not doubt that through energy and industry, all of those bright little Russians, who have sought refuge in our midst, will in time—be well-to-do.

What I fear most is their ignorance! If we allow things to go on as they are, their education will not keep face with their worldly advancement. And here is where the mischief lies. The fact of it is, they are anxious to learn; but the opportunities are denied them. Can't we help them out of this difficulty? Can't we open up an evening school here where the foundation of their education can be made, the English language taught?

A school of this description was conducted here several years ago, with elegant results, why did we allow it to discontinue?

Let us arouse ourselves and our citizens to the seriousness of the situation; to the necessity of immediate action. Let us all join hands and promise that we will encourage and help this and all other movements towards their educational advancement and you can rest assured, we will gain the respect of the community, and be more than repaid for our time and trouble and the coming generation will be only to glad (proud) to acknowledge their relationship to "the Little Russian Refugee."

▉

SIGNIFICANCE

As a child of Jewish immigrants, Leslie Black Kander saw herself as well positioned to champion the cause of this segment of the population that she considered ignored by society. Throughout the history of the United States, considerable attention has been placed upon the assimilation and contribution of immigrants. With the understanding that the majority of the population today is made up of immigrants or descendents of immigrants who arrived after the nation declared its independence, the rights and opportunities granted to this segment of society has been directly linked to the growth of the nation.

While this speech centers around the story of one young Jewish refugee from Russia, Kander makes it clear that there were many thousands of other immigrants from all over the world facing similar challenges. The greatest obstacle faced by immigrants during Kander's period was their lack of education. Many young children who arrived in the United States were forced by economic conditions immediately into the labor market, and lacked the ability to go to school. While many had a desire to learn and discover their new surroundings and culture, the environment in which they were placed prevented them from doing so.

Kander specifically makes reference to the potential of Jewish immigrants to become financially successful, the message of her statements could be applied to any ethnic or national group. Kander's efforts were aimed at allowing other people to realize the importance of helping immigrants acclimate so that they could better contribute to the overall development of the United States.

Immigration has continued to be a major contributing factor to the rapid population growth of the United States. While the areas of the world from where immigrants have originated have changed over the decades, many undereducated immigrants continue to face similar challenges with low wage jobs and difficult socioeconomic conditions. On the other hand, highly educated immigrants also today migrate to the United States to pursue opportunities in the scientific, academic, and business community. One 1995 study found that on average, the proportion of immigrants to the United States with post-graduate degrees is greater than the proportion of people with post-graduate degrees in the native U.S. population. In the United States today, immigrants continue to be recognized as an important part of the economy and culture of the country.

Educational opportunities for immigrants have been enhanced with federal funding for language instruction for immigrants and their school-age children with limited proficiency in English. Many state programs also provide opportunities for educating immigrant children, with the goal of providing enough specialized instruction that will enable immigrant students to pass the same standardized tests necessary for promotion and graduation as native-born students. University-level immigrant students face continuing barriers to higher education, as limited space in public universities, rising tuition costs in both public and private universities, and lack of official residency status can all deter immigrant students from pursuing a college degree in the U.S. In 2005, a bipartisan group of senators proposed the revised legislation commonly known as the DREAM Act of 2006, that would provide temporary documented status for eligible undocumented immigrant students pursuing higher education, along with access to less expensive in-state college tuition rates.

FURTHER RESOURCES

Books

Daniels, Roger. *Guarding the Golden Door; American Immigration Policy and Immigrants since 1882.* New York, N.Y: Hill and Wang, 2004.

Gabaccia, Donna. *Immigration and American Diversity; A Social and Cultural History.* Malden, Mass.: Blackwell, 2002.

Web sites

National Immigration Forum. <http://www.immigrationforum.org> (accessed May 21, 2006).

Platform of the Populists

Declaration

By: The Populist Party

Date: July 25, 1896

Source: The Populist Party

About the Author: The Populist Party formed in 1891 in the United States to create a more egalitarian world. Reflecting policies unusual for the era, the party counted women and black men among its leadership.

INTRODUCTION

The Populist Party, also known as the People's Party, formed in Cincinnati, Ohio, in May 1891. The

Mary Lease, a writer and lecturer for the Populist movement. THE LIBRARY OF CONGRESS.

party arose in response to anger among farmers about falling commodity prices, high railroad rates, and heavy mortgage debt. It was part of the agrarian reform movement that swept through the South and Midwest in the years after the Civil War.

The Panic of 1873 struck especially hard at farmers and industrial workers. While the overall economic climate soon improved, hard times remained in agriculture. In response, farmers in the Midwest and South organized a wide variety of reform movements. The best known of these efforts was the Patrons of Husbandry, popularly called the Grange. Begun in 1867 as a group intent on improving educational and social opportunities for farm men and women, the Grange expanded in the 1870s to promote such economic and political initiatives as the cooperative movement. The inability of the Grange to influence politics led some members to form the Farmers' Alliance in the 1880s.

In the 1890 elections, supporters of the Alliance movement took control of the state governments in South Carolina, Georgia, and Texas. With this success, Alliance members gathered in Ocala, Florida, to plan the future of the movement. The gathering

included representatives from the Colored Farmers' Alliance, reflecting the populist idea that race should not be allowed to divide people. Alliance members from Kansas proposed the formation of a third political party to compete with the Democrats and Republicans. In 1891, the People's Party began. A reporter for a Columbus, Ohio, newspaper termed the group the Populists and the label stuck. The Populist Party platform, based on the Southern Alliance model, included government ownership of railroads, monetary reforms beneficial to small farmers and a subtreasury (a system by which farmers could turn over a staple crop to a government warehouse and receive a loan for 80 percent of its value at 2 percent interest per month).

▮ PRIMARY SOURCE

The People's Party, assembled in National Convention, reaffirms its allegiances to the principles declared by the founders of the Republic and also to the fundamental principles of just government as enunciated in the platform of the party in 1892.

We recognize that through the connivance of the present and preceding Administrations, the country has reached a crisis in its National life, as predicted in our declaration four years ago, and that prompt and patriotic action is the supreme duty of the hour.

We realize that, while we have political independence, our financial and industrial independence is yet to be attained by restoring to our country the Constitutional control and exercise of the functions necessary to a people's government, which functions have been basely surrendered by our public servants to corporate monopolies. The influence of European moneychangers has been more potent in shaping legislation than the voice of the American people. Executive power and patronage have been used to corrupt our Legislatures and defeat the will of the people, and plutocracy has thereby been enthroned upon the ruins of democracy. To restore the Government intended by the fathers, and for the welfare and prosperity of this and future generations, we demand the establishment of an economic and financial system which shall make us masters of our own affairs and independent of European control, by the adoption of the following declaration of principles:

The Money Plank.—

1. We demand a National money, safe and sound, issued by the General Government only, without the intervention of banks of issue, to be a full legal tender for all debts, public and private; a just, equitable, and efficient means of

distribution, direct to the people, and through the lawful disbursements of the Government.

2. We demand the free and unrestricted coinage of silver and gold at the present legal ratio of sixteen to one, without waiting for the consent of foreign nations.

3. We demand that the volume of circulating medium be speedily increased to an amount sufficient to meet the demands of the business and population, and to restore the just level of prices of labor and production.

4. We denounce the sale of bonds and the increase of the public interest-bearing debt made by the present Administration as unnecessary and without authority of law, and demand that no more bonds be issued, except by specific act of Congress.

5. We demand such legislation as will prevent the demonetization of the lawful money of the United States by private contract.

6. We demand that the Government, in payment of its obligations, shall use its option as to the kind of lawful money in which they are to be paid, and we denounce the present and preceding Administrations for surrendering this option to the holders of Government obligations.

7. We demand a graduated income tax, to the end that aggregated wealth shall bear its just proportion of taxation, and we regard the recent decision of the Supreme Court relative to the income-tax law as a misinterpretation of the Constitution and an invasion of the rightful powers of Congress over the subject of taxation.

8. We demand that postal savings banks be established by the Government for the safe deposit of the savings of the people and to facilitate exchange.

Railroads and Telegraphs.—

1. Transportation being a means of exchange and a public necessity, the Government should own and operate the railroads in the interest of the people and on a non-partisan basis, to the end that all may be accorded the same treatment in transportation, and that the tyranny and political power now exercised by the great railroad corporations, which result in the impairment, if not the destruction of the political rights and personal liberties of the citizen, may be destroyed. Such ownership is to be accomplished gradually, in a manner consistent with sound public policy.

2. The interest of the United States in the public highways built with public moneys, and the proceeds of grants of land to the Pacific railroads, should never be alienated, mortgaged, or sold, but guarded and protected for the general welfare, as provided by the laws organizing such railroads. The foreclosure of existing liens of the United States on those roads should at once follow default in the payment thereof by the debtor companies; and at a reasonable price; and the Government should operate said railroads as public highways for the benefit of the whole people, and not in the interest of the few, under suitable provisions for protection of life and property, giving to all transportation interests equal privileges and equal rates for fares and freights.

3. We denounce the present infamous schemes for refunding these debts, and demand that the laws now applicable thereto be executed and administered according to their intent and spirit.

4. The telegraph, like the Post Office system, being a necessity for the transmission of news, should be owned and operated by the Government in the interest of the people.

The Public Lands.—

1. True policy demands that the National and State legislation shall be such as will ultimately enable every prudent and industrious citizen to secure a home; and therefore, the land should not be monopolized for speculative purposes. All lands now held by railroads and other corporations in excess of their actual needs should, by lawful means, be reclaimed by the Government and held for actual settlers only, and private land monopoly, as well as alien ownership, should be prohibited.

2. We condemn the frauds by which the land-grant Pacific railroad companies have, through the connivance of the Interior Department, robbed multitudes of actual, bona-fide settlers of their homes, and miners of the claims, and we demand legislation by Congress which will enforce the exemption of mineral land from such grants after, as well as before, the patent.

3. We demand that bona-fide settlers on all public lands be granted free homes, as provided in the National homestead law, and that no exception be made in the case of Indian reservations when opened for settlement, and that all lands now patented come under this demand.

Direct Legislations.—We favor a system of direct legislation through the initiative and referendum, under proper Constitutional safeguards.

Elections by the People.—We demand the election of President, Vice President, and United States Senators by a direct vote of the people.

Sympathy for Cuba.—We tender to the patriotic people of the country our deepest sympathy in their heroic struggle for political freedom and independence, and we believe the time has come when the Untied States, the great Republic of the world, should recognize that Cuba is, and of right ought to be, a free and independent State.

Miscellaneous Declarations.—

1. We favor home rule in the Territories and the District of Columbia, and the early admission of the Territories as States.
2. All public salaries should be made to correspond to the price of labor and its products.
3. In times of great industrial depression idle labor should be employed on public works as far as practicable.
4. The arbitrary course of the courts in assuming to imprison citizens for indirect contempt and ruling them by injunction should be prevented by proper legislation.
5. We favor just pensions for our disabled Union soldiers.
6. Believing that the elective franchise and an untrammeled ballot are essential to government of, for, and by the people, the People's Party condemns the wholesale system of disfranchisement adopted in some of the States as unrepublican and undemocratic, and we declare it to be the duty of the several State Legislatures to take such action as will secure a full, free, and fair ballot and an honest count.
7. While the foregoing propositions constitute the platform upon which our party stands, and for the vindication of which its organization will be maintained, we recognize that the great and pressing issue of the pending campaign, upon which the present election will turn, is the financial question, and upon this great and specific issue between the parties we cordially invite the aid and co-operation of all organizations and citizens agreeing with us upon this vital question.

SIGNIFICANCE

The Populist Party found most of its support from cotton farmers in the South and wheat farmers in the North. Although the party tried to attract industrial workers, it remained chiefly an agrarian party. While African Americans were welcomed into the

movement, most members were white. In 1892, the party nominated James B. Weaver of Iowa as its presidential candidate. Weaver carried only four states, all in the West. The Populists had better luck with the elections of 1894, but remained a weak third behind the Republicans and the Democrats.

In 1896, the Populists attempted to increase their strength, employing a tactic that ultimately destroyed the party. The Populists joined with the Democrats to support a fusion candidate for president, William Jennings Bryan (1860–1925). He lost to William McKinley (1843–1901). However, the biggest losers in the election turned out to be the Populists. On the national level, they polled less than 300,000 votes, over a million less than in the 1894 elections. Most Populists gradually drifted back into the Democratic Party. The People's Party remained active until 1908 but never again achieved the gains of the early 1890s. However, populist ideas such as the income tax and antitrust regulations were eventually adopted by the Republicans and the Democrats and became codified as laws in the twentieth century.

FURTHER RESOURCES
Books

Kazin, Michael. *The Populist Persuasion: An American History*. New York: Basic Books, 1995.

McMath, Robert. *American Populism: A Social History, 1877–1898*. New York: Hill and Wang, 1993.

Palmer, Bruce. *The Southern Populist Critique of American Capitalism*. Chapel Hill: University of North Carolina Press, 1980.

Plessy v. Ferguson

Legal decision

By: Henry Billings Brown

Date: May 18, 1896

Source: *Homer A. Plessy v. John H. Ferguson*. 163 U.S. 537. Supreme Court of the United States, May 18, 1896.

About the Author: Supreme Court Justice Henry Billings Brown was appointed to the United States Supreme Court in 1890 by President Benjamin Harrison. Brown wrote the majority opinion for *Plessy v. Fergu-*

An African American girl gets a drink from a segregated public drinking fountain. THE LIBRARY OF CONGRESS.

son, his most famous case, in 1896, ten years before he retired from the Supreme Court at the age of seventy.

INTRODUCTION

Post-Civil War southern society faced daunting social, economic, and political struggles as more than four million slaves, recently freed, looked for acceptance, homes, jobs, and a way to build new lives outside of the slave system. While the Thirteenth Amendment ended slavery and the Fourteenth Amendment granted the newly freed slaves citizenship, the legal rights given to former slaves were sorely tested in the coming decades.

Southern whites used a wide range of laws to restrict the rights of African American citizens. "Black codes" limited the jobs at which they could work, removed parental rights from African-American parents who sent their children to work as apprentices, targeted African American persons with tight vagrancy laws, and created an atmosphere of increased division between the races. African Americans earned less, had fewer educational opportunities, faced higher

rates of violence—including organized violence from groups such as the Ku Klux Klan—and experienced racism in social and civil life through the segregation of public venues such as restrooms, public transportation, motels, and restaurants. Northern discrimination against African Americans was also not uncommon, although it tended to be less systematic and pervasive.

Louisiana passed a law segregating train coaches by race in 1890. When an African-American passenger named Homer Plessy, who was one-eighth black, purchased a ticket on the East Louisiana Railway on June 7, 1892, he represented a group called the Citizens' Committee of African Americans and Creoles. The group had been trying to challenge the 1890 law and prepared to provide Plessy with legal representation in the event of his arrest. After informing a conductor that he was one-eighth black, Plessy sat in the "whites only" section of the railcar and refused to leave or to sit elsewhere. Plessy was arrested and later sued with the contention that the Separate Car Act of 1890 was unconstitutional. The state court determined that the railroad company had the right to discriminate on all traffic within the state of Louisiana, and found for the defendant. The case made its way to the United States Supreme Court in 1896 and the resulting decision established the "separate but equal" doctrine.

PRIMARY SOURCE

So, too, in the Civil Rights Cases it was said that the act of a mere individual, the owner of an inn, a public conveyance or place of amusement, refusing accommodations to colored people, cannot be justly regarded as imposing any badge of slavery or servitude upon the applicant, but only as involving an ordinary civil injury, properly cognizable by the laws of the state, and presumably subject to redress by those laws until the contrary appears. 'It would be running the slavery question into the ground,' said Mr. Justice Bradley, 'to make it apply to every act of discrimination which a person may see fit to make as to the guests he will entertain, or as to the people he will take into his coach or cab or car, or admit to his concert or theater, or deal with in other matters of intercourse or business.'

A statute which implies merely a legal distinction between the white and colored races—a distinction which is founded in the color of the two races, and which must always exist so long as white men are distinguished from the other race by color—has no tendency to destroy the legal equality of the two races, or re-establish a state of involuntary servitude. Indeed, we do not understand that the thirteenth amendment is strenuously relied upon by the plaintiff in error in this connection.

2. By the fourteenth amendment, all persons born or naturalized in the United States, and subject to the jurisdiction thereof, are made citizens of the United States and of the state wherein they reside; and the states are forbidden from making or enforcing any law which shall abridge the privileges or immunities of citizens of the United States, or shall deprive any person of life, liberty, or property without due process of law, or deny to any person within their jurisdiction the equal protection of the laws.

The proper construction of this amendment was first called to the attention of this court in the Slaughter-House Cases, 16 Wall. 36, which involved, however, not a question of race, but one of exclusive privileges. The case did not call for any expression of opinion as to the exact rights it was intended to secure to the colored race, but it was said generally that its main purpose was to establish the citizenship of the negro, to give definitions of citizenship of the United States and of the states, and to protect from the hostile legislation of the states the privileges and immunities of citizens of the United States, as distinguished from those of citizens of the states. The object of the amendment was undoubtedly to enforce the absolute equality of the two races before the law, but, in the nature of things, it could not have been intended to abolish distinctions based upon color, or to enforce social, as distinguished from political, equality, or a commingling of the two races upon terms unsatisfactory to either. Laws permitting, and even requiring, their separation, in places where they are liable to be brought into contact, do not necessarily imply the inferiority of either race to the other, and have been generally, if not universally, recognized as within the competency of the state legislatures in the exercise of their police power. The most common instance of this is connected with the establishment of separate schools for white and colored children, which have been held to be a valid exercise of the legislative power even by courts of states where the political rights of the colored race have been longest and most earnestly enforced.

One of the earliest of these cases is that of Roberts v. City of Boston, 5 Cush. 198, in which the supreme judicial court of Massachusetts held that the general school committee of Boston had power to make provision for the instruction of colored children in separate schools established exclusively for them, and to prohibit their attendance upon the other schools. 'The great principle,' said Chief Justice Shaw, 'advanced by the learned and eloquent advocate for the plaintiff [Mr. Charles Sumner], is that, by the constitution and laws of Massachusetts, all persons, without distinction of age or sex, birth or color, origin or condition, are equal before the law... But, when this great principle comes to be applied to the actual and various conditions of persons in society, it will not warrant the assertion that men and women are legally clothed with the same civil and political powers, and that children and adults are legally to have the same functions and be subject to the same treatment; but only that the rights of all, as they are settled and regulated by law, are equally entitled to the paternal consideration and protection of the law for their maintenance and security.' It was held that the powers of the committee extended to the establish-ment of separate schools for children of different ages, sexes and colors, and that they might also establish special schools for poor and neglected children, who have become too old to attend the primary school, and yet have not acquired the rudiments of learning, to enable them to enter the ordinary schools. Similar laws have been enacted by congress under its general power of legislation over the District of Columbia (sections 281–283, 310, 319, Rev. St. D. C.), as well as by the legislatures of many of the states, and have been generally, if not uniformly, sustained by the courts. State v. McCann, 21 Ohio St. 210; Lehew v. Brummell (Mo. Sup.) 15 S. W. 765; Ward v. Flood, 48 Cal. 36; Bertonneau v. Directors of City Schools, 3 Woods, 177, Fed. Cas. No.

1,361; People v. Gallagher, 93 N. Y. 438; Cory v. Carter, 48 Ind. 337; Dawson v. Lee, 83 Ky. 49.

Laws forbidding the intermarriage of the two races may be said in a technical sense to interfere with the freedom of contract, and yet have been universally recognized as within the police power of the state. State v. Gibson, 36 Ind. 389.

We consider the underlying fallacy of the plaintiff's argument to consist in the assumption that the enforced separation of the two races stamps the colored race with a badge of inferiority. If this be so, it is not by reason of anything found in the act, but solely because the colored race chooses to put that construction upon it. The argument necessarily assumes that if, as has been more than once the case, and is not unlikely to be so again, the colored race should become the dominant power in the state legislature, and should enact a law in precisely similar terms, it would thereby relegate the white race to an inferior position. We imagine that the white race, at least, would not acquiesce in this assumption. The argument also assumes that social prejudices may be overcome by legislation, and that equal rights cannot be secured to the negro except by an enforced commingling of the two races. We cannot accept this proposition. If the two races are to meet upon terms of social equality, it must be the result of natural affinities, a mutual appreciation of each other's merits, and a voluntary consent of individuals. As was said by the court of appeals of New York in People v. Gallagher, 93 N. Y. 438, 448: 'this end can neither be accomplished nor promoted by laws which conflict with the general sentiment of the community upon whom they are designed to operate. When the government, therefore, has secured to each of its citizens equal rights before the law, and equal opportunities for improvement and progress, it has accomplished the end for which it was organized, and performed all of the functions respecting social advantages with which it is endowed.' Legislation is powerless to eradicate racial instincts, or to abolish distinctions based upon physical differences, and the attempt to do so can only result in accentuating the difficulties of the present situation. If the civil and political rights of both races be equal, one cannot be inferior to the other civilly or politically. If one race be inferior to the other socially, the constitution of the United States cannot put them upon the same plane.

SIGNIFICANCE

While Plessy's lawyer, New York attorney Albion Tourgée, and the Citizens' Committee of African Americans and Creoles had been successful in previous railroad rights cases, Tourgée's use of the Thirteenth Amendment troubled the justices; they stated that the Separate Car Act did not enforce servitude, or reduce black people to slave status, regardless of issues of perceived inferiority in society. Tourgée argued that Plessy's right to "equal protection" in the Fourteenth Amendment had been violated by the segregation itself; denying Plessy the right to sit in "whites only" sections contradicted the Fourteenth Amendment.

In his majority decision, Justice Henry Billings Brown addressed the Fourteenth Amendment in both legal and social terms; legal rights are qualitatively different from social policy, and the *Plessy v. Ferguson* decision could not change the fact that, in Justice Brown's words, "When the government, therefore, has secured to each of its citizens equal rights before the law, and equal opportunities for improvement and progress, it has accomplished the end for which it was organized, and performed all of the functions respecting social advantages with which it is endowed. Legislation is powerless to eradicate racial instincts, or to abolish distinctions based upon physical differences, and the attempt to do so can only result in accentuating the difficulties of the present situation." In other words, the "separate but equal" decision hinged on the legal equality of all races; separate facilities were a matter of social discourse, not court decisions, according to the court. In the end the U.S. Supreme Court ruling declared the Louisiana Separate Car Law constitutional.

Not only did Homer Plessy lose the Supreme Court case, he also paid a $25 fine for violating Louisiana law. For the next fifty-eight years, *Plessy* was used to reinforce racial segregation both legally and socially. The case was used to support miscegenation laws, segregated school and public facilities, segregated healthcare systems, zoning laws prohibiting African American citizens from renting or purchasing homes in certain areas, and more. The overall result was a system that strictly separated the races in many areas in the United States. And while the doctrine was nominally "separate but equal," in reality it meant that African Americans were singled out for poor treatment, and their rights were routinely suppressed.

Civil rights activists struggled for years against the results of the *Plessy v. Fergusson* decision. Gradually, they achieved results. The armed forces were integrated in 1948. In 1954, *Brown v. Board of Education* declared that, in fact, "separate but equal" violated the equal protection clause of the Fourteenth Amendment, forcing the integration of schools and paving the way for further gains. The struggle for integrated public transportation would be sparked by another African American who chose to sit in a "whites only" seat on December 1, 1955: Rosa Parks.

Until the 1964 Civil Rights Act, public transportation laws restricting African American riders were legal in many states; *Plessy* was finally overturned, in full, after sixty-eight years.

FURTHER RESOURCES

Books

Fireside, Harvey. *Separate and Unequal: Homer Plessy and the Supreme Court Decision that Legalized Racism*. New York: Carroll & Graf, 2004.

Klarman, Michael. *From Jim Crow to Civil Rights: The Supreme Court and the Struggle for Racial Equality*. New York: Oxford University Press, 2004.

Medley, Keith Weldon. *We As Freemen: Plessy v. Ferguson*. Gretna, La.: Pelican Publishing Company, 2003.

The Jungle

Book excerpt

By: Upton Sinclair

Date: 1906

Source: Sinclair, Upton. *The Jungle*. New York: Doubleday, 1906.

About the Author: Upton Sinclair (1878–1968) was born in Baltimore, Maryland, and raised in New York City. An avid student, he entered New York City College at the age of fourteen, and financed his education by writing newspaper and magazine stories. He was sufficiently successful that, by age seventeen, he had his own apartment and was still able to help support his parents. Sinclair published several novels starting in 1901, but none were successful until he allowed his Socialist beliefs to influence his subject matter. He first wrote *The Jungle* at the behest of *Appeal to Reason* editor, Fred Warren, who had requested a work focused on the immigrant workers in Chicago's meatpacking houses. The work first appeared in serial form, and later, after a number of rejections, was published in book form by Doubleday, to worldwide acclaim. Sinclair published more than ninety books in his lifetime, winning the Pulitzer Prize for his 1942 novel, *Dragon's Teeth*. He also ran unsuccessfully as the Socialist candidate for governor of California, in 1934, capturing more than one-third of the votes.

The inside cover of Upton Sinclar's *The Jungle*. © BETTMANN/CORBIS. REPRODUCED BY PERMISSION.

INTRODUCTION

The Jungle, Upton Sinclair's best-known novel, revealed the truth about the unsanitary, dangerous conditions in the meatpacking industry. The book was an offshoot of the muckraking journalistic style that Sinclair had introduced during the early 1900s in his work for various newspapers and magazines, and used the appalling situation in the meatpacking factories as a propagandist platform to preach the need for reform in the United States and to endorse the tenets of the Socialist Party.

The Jungle is set in Chicago, particularly the Packingtown district that was at the center of Chicago's huge meatpacking industry. Sinclair focused heavily on the conditions that led to the meatpackers strike of 1904, during which time more than 20,000 workers, including both skilled and unskilled butchers and meatpackers, walked out of their jobs to protest against low wages and poor working conditions. Sinclair spent seven weeks researching daily life in the meatpacking plants so that he would be able to highlight every aspect of the corruption and filth that was rampant in the industry.

■ PRIMARY SOURCE

After the elections Jurgis stayed on in Packingtown and kept his job. The agitation to break up the police protection of criminals was continuing, and it seemed to him best to "lay low" for the present. He had nearly three hundred dollars in the bank, and might have considered himself entitled to a vacation, but he had an easy job, and force of habit kept him at it. Besides, Mike Scully, whom he consulted, advised him that something might "turn up" before long.

Jurgis got himself a place in a boardinghouse with some congenial friends. He had already inquired of Aniele, and learned that Elzbieta and her family had gone downtown, and so he gave no further thought to them. He went with a new set, now, young unmarried fellows who were "sporty." Jurgis had long ago cast off his fertilizer clothing, and since going into politics he had donned a linen collar and a greasy red necktie. He had some reason for thinking of his dress, for he was making about eleven dollars a week, and two-thirds of it he might spend upon his pleasures without ever touching his savings.

Sometimes he would ride downtown with a party of friends to the cheap theaters and the music halls and other haunts with which they were familiar. Many of the saloons in Packingtown had pool tables, and some of them bowling alleys, by means of which he could spend his evenings in petty gambling. Also, there were cards and dice. One time Jurgis got into a game on a Saturday night and won prodigiously, and because he was a man of spirit he stayed in with the rest and the game continued until late Sunday afternoon, and by that time he was "out" over twenty dollars. On Saturday nights, also, a number of balls were generally given in Packingtown; each man would bring his "girl" with him, paying half a dollar for a ticket, and several dollars additional for drinks in the course of the festivities, which continued until three or four o'clock in the morning, unless broken up by fighting. During all this time the same man and woman would dance together, half-stupefied with sensuality and drink.

Before long Jurgis discovered what Scully had meant by something "turning up." In May the agreement between the packers and the unions expired, and a new agreement had to be signed. Negotiations were going on, and the yards were full of talk of a strike. The old scale had dealt with the wages of the skilled men only; and of the members of the Meat Workers' Union about two-thirds were unskilled men. In Chicago these latter were receiving, for the most part, eighteen and a half cents an hour, and the unions wished to make this the general wage for the next year. It was not nearly so large a wage as it seemed—in the course of the negotiations the union officers examined time checks to the amount of ten thousand dollars, and they found that the highest wages paid had been fourteen dollars a week, the lowest two dollars and five cents, and the average of the whole, six dollars and sixty-five cents. And six dollars and sixty-five cents was hardly too much for a man to keep a family on. Considering the fact that the price of dressed meat had increased nearly fifty per cent in the last five years, while the price of "beef on the hoof" had decreased as much, it would have seemed that the packers ought to be able to pay it; but the packers were unwilling to pay it—they rejected the union demand, and to show what their purpose was, a week or two after the agreement expired they put down the wages of about a thousand men to sixteen and a half cents, and it was said that old man Jones had vowed he would put them to fifteen before he got through. There were a million and a half of men in the country looking for work, a hundred thousand of them right in Chicago; and were the packers to let the union stewards march into their places and bind them to a contract that would lose them several thousand dollars a day for a year? Not much!

All this was in June; and before long the question was submitted to a referendum in the unions, and the decision was for a strike. It was the same in all the packing house cities; and suddenly the newspapers and public woke up to face the gruesome spectacle of a meat famine. All sorts of pleas for a reconsideration were made, but the packers were obdurate; and all the while they were reducing wages, and heading off shipments of cattle, and rushing in wagonloads of mattresses and cots. So the men boiled over, and one night telegrams went out from the union headquarters to all the big packing centers—to St. Paul, South Omaha, Sioux City, St. Joseph, Kansas City, East St. Louis, and New York—and the next day at noon between fifty and sixty thousand men drew off their working clothes and marched out of the factories, and the great "Beef Strike" was on.

Jurgis went to his dinner, and afterward he walked over to see Mike Scully, who lived in a fine house, upon a street which had been decently paved and lighted for his especial benefit. Scully had gone into semiretirement, and looked nervous and worried. "What do you want?" he demanded, when he saw Jurgis.

"I came to see if maybe you could get me a place during the strike," the other replied.

And Scully knit his brows and eyed him narrowly. In that morning's papers Jurgis had read a fierce denunciation of the packers by Scully, who had declared that if they did not treat their people better the city authorities would end the matter by tearing down their plants. Now, therefore, Jurgis was not a little taken aback when the other demanded suddenly, "See here, Rudkus, why don't you stick by your job?"

Jurgis started, "Work as a scab?" he cried.

"Why not?" demanded Scully. "What's that to you?"

"But—but—" stammered Jurgis. He had somehow taken it for granted that he should go out with his union.

"The packers need good men, and need them bad," continued the other, "and they'll treat a man right that stands by them. Why don't you take your chance and fix yourself?"

"But," said Jurgis, "how could I ever be of any use to you—in politics?"

"You couldn't be it anyhow," said Scully, abruptly.

"Why not?" asked Jurgis.

"Hell man!" cried the other. "Don't you know you're a Republican. And do you think I'm always going to elect Republicans? My brewer has found out already how we served him, and there is the deuce to pay."

Jurgis looked dumfounded. He had never thought of that aspect of it before. "I could be a Democrat," he said.

"Yes," responded the other, "but not right away; a man can't change his politics every day. And besides, I don't need you—there'd be nothing for you to do. And it's a long time to election day, anyhow; and what are you going to do meantime?"

"I thought I could count on you," began Jurgis.

"Yes," responded Scully, "so you could—I never yet went back on a friend. But is it fair to leave the job I got you and come to me for another? I have had a hundred fellows after me today, and what can I do? I've put seventeen men on the city payroll to clean streets this one week, and do you think I can keep that up forever? It wouldn't do for me to tell other men what I tell you, but you've been on the inside, and you ought to have sense enough to see for yourself. What have you to gain by a strike?"

"I hadn't thought," said Jurgis.

"Exactly," said Scully, "but you'd better. Take my word for it, the strike will be over in a few days, and the men will be beaten; and meantime what you get out of it will belong to you. Do you see?"

And Jurgis saw. He went back to the yards, and into the workroom. The men had left a long line of hogs in various stages of preparation, and the foreman was directing the feeble efforts of a score or two of clerks and stenographers and office-boys to finish up the job and get them into the chilling rooms. Jurgis went straight up to him and announced, "I have come back to work, Mr. Murphy."

The boss's face lighted up. "Good man!" he cried. "Come ahead!"

"Just a moment," said Jurgis, checking his enthusiasm. "I think I ought to get a little more wages."

"Yes," replied the other, "of course. What do you want?"

Jurgis had debated on the way. His nerve almost failed him now, but he clenched his hands. "I think I ought to have three dollars a day," he said.

"All right," said the other, promptly; and before the day was out our friend discovered that the clerks and stenographers and office boys were getting five dollars a day, and then he could have kicked himself!

So Jurgis became one of the new "American heroes," a man whose virtues merited comparison with those of the martyrs of Lexington and Valley Forge. The resemblance was not complete, of course, for Jurgis was generously paid and comfortably clad, and was provided with a spring cot and a mattress and three substantial meals a day; also he was perfectly at ease, and safe from all peril of life and limb, save only in the case that a desire for beer should lead him to venture outside of the stockyards gates. And even in the exercise of this privilege he was not left unprotected; a good part of the inadequate police force of Chicago was suddenly diverted from its work of hunting criminals, and rushed out to serve him.

The police, and the strikers also, were determined that there should be no violence; but there was another party interested which was minded to the contrary—and that was the press. On the first day of his life as a strikebreaker Jurgis quit work early, and in a spirit of bravado he challenged three men of his acquaintance to go outside and get a drink. They accepted, and went through the big Halsted Street gate, where several policemen were watching, and also some union pickets, scanning sharply those who passed in and out. Jurgis and his companions went south on Halsted Street, past the hotel, and then suddenly half a dozen men started across the street toward them and proceeded to argue with them concerning the error of their ways. As the arguments were not taken in the proper spirit, they went on to threats; and suddenly one of them jerked off the hat of one of the four and flung it over the fence. The man started after it, and then, as a cry of "Scab!" was raised and a dozen people came running out of saloons and doorways, a second man's heart failed him and he followed. Jurgis and the fourth stayed long enough to give themselves the satisfaction of a quick exchange of blows, and then they, too, took to their heels and fled back of the hotel and into the yards again. Meantime, of course, policemen were coming on a run, and as a crowd gathered other police got excited and sent in a riot call. Jurgis knew nothing of this, but went back to "Packers' Avenue," and in front of the "Central Time Station" he saw one of his companions, breathless and wild with excitement, narrating to an ever growing throng how the four had been attacked and surrounded by a howling mob, and had been nearly torn to pieces. While he stood listening, smiling cynically, several dapper young men stood by with notebooks in their hands, and it was not more than two hours later that Jurgis saw newsboys running about with armfuls of newspapers, printed in red and black letters six inches high:

VIOLENCE IN THE YARDS! STRIKEBREAKERS SURROUNDED BY FRENZIED MOB!

If he had been able to buy all of the newspapers of the United States the next morning, he might have discovered that his beer-hunting exploit was being perused by some two score millions of people, and had served as a text for editorials in half the staid and solemn businessmen's newspapers in the land.

Jurgis was to see more of this as time passed. For the present, his work being over, he was free to ride into the city, by a railroad direct from the yards, or else to spend the night in a room where cots had been laid in rows. He chose the latter, but to his regret, for all night long gangs of strikebreakers kept arriving. As very few of the better class or workingmen could be got for such work, these specimens of the new American hero contained an assortment of the criminals and thugs of the city, besides Negroes and the lowest foreigners—Greeks, Roumanians, Sicilians, and Slovaks. They had been attracted more by the prospect of disorder than by the big wages; and they made the night hideous with singing and carousing, and only went to sleep when the time came for them to get up to work.

In the morning before Jurgis had finished his breakfast, "Pat" Murphy ordered him to one of the superintendents, who questioned him as to his experience in the work of the killing room. His heart began to thump with excitement, for he divined instantly that his hour had come—that he was to be a boss!

Some of the foremen were union members, and many who were not had gone out with the men. It was in the killing department that the packers had been left most in the lurch, and precisely here that they could least afford it; the smoking and canning and salting of meat might wait, and all the by-products might be wasted—but fresh meats must be had, or the restaurants and hotels and brownstone houses would feel the pinch, and then "public opinion" would take a startling turn.

An opportunity such as this would not come twice to a man; and Jurgis seized it. Yes, he knew the work, the whole of it, and he could teach it to others. But if he took the job and gave satisfaction he would expect to keep it—they would not turn him off at the end of the strike? To which the superintendent replied that he might safely trust Durham's for that—they proposed to teach these unions a lesson, and most of all those foremen who had gone back on them. Jurgis would receive five dollars a day during the strike, and twenty-five a week after it was settled.

So our friend got a pair of "slaughter pen" boots and "jeans," and flung himself at his task. It was a weird sight, there on the killing beds—a throng of stupid black Negroes, and foreigners who could not understand a word that was said to them, mixed with pale-faced hollow-chested bookkeepers and clerks, half-fainting for the tropical heat and the sickening stench of fresh blood—and all struggling to dress a dozen or two of cattle in the same place, where twenty-four hours ago, the old killing gang had been speeding, with their marvelous precision, turning out four hundred carcasses every hour!

The Negroes and the "toughs" from the Levee did not want to work, and every few minutes some of them would feel obliged to retire and recuperate. In a couple of days Durham and Company had electric fans up to cool off the room for them, and even couches for them to rest on; and meantime they could go out and find a shady corner and take a "snooze," and as there was no place for any one in particular, and no system, it might be hours before their boss discovered them. As for the poor office employees, they did their best, moved to it by terror; thirty of them had been "fired" in a bunch that first morning for refusing to serve, besides a number of women clerks and typewrites who had declined to act as waitresses.

It was such a force as this that Jurgis had to organize. He did his best, flying here and there, placing them in rows and showing them the tricks; he had never given an order in his life before, but he had taken enough of them to know, and he soon fell into the spirit of it, and roared and stormed like any old stager. He had not the most tractable pupils, however. "See hyar, boss," a big black "buck" would begin, "ef you doan' like de way Ah does dis job, you kin git somebody else to do it." Then a crowd would gather and listen, muttering threats. After the first meal nearly all the steel knives had been missing, and now every Negro had one, ground to a fine point, hidden in his boots.

There was no bringing order out of such a chaos, Jurgis soon discovered; and he fell in with the spirit of the thing—there was no reason why he should wear himself out with shouting. If hides and guts were slashed and rendered useless there was no way of tracing it to any one; and if a man lay off and forgot to come back there was nothing to be gained by seeking him, for all the rest would quit in the meantime. Everything went, during the strike, and the packers paid. Before long Jurgis found that the custom of resting that suggested to some alert minds the possibility of registering at more than one place and earning more than one five dollars a day. When he caught a man at this he "fired" him, but it chanced to be in a quiet corner, and the man tendered him a ten-dollar bill and a wink, and he took them. Of course, before long this custom spread, and Jurgis was soon making quite a good income from it.

In the face of handicaps such as these the packers counted themselves lucky if they could kill off the cattle that had been crippled in transit and the hogs that had developed disease. Frequently, in the course of a two or three day's trip, in hot weather and without water, some hog would develop cholera, and die; and the rest would attack him before he had ceased kicking, and when the car was opened there would be nothing of him left but the bones. If all the hogs in this carload were not killed at once, they would soon be down with the dread disease, and there would be nothing to do but make them into lard. It was the same with cattle that were gored and dying, or were limping with broken bones stuck through their flesh—they must be killed, even if brokers and buyers and superintendents had to take off their coats and help drive and cut and skin them. And meantime, agents of the packers were gathering gangs of Negroes in the country districts of the far South, promising them five dollars a day and board, and being careful not to mention there was a strike; already carloads of them were on the way, with special rates from the railroads, and all traffic ordered out of the way. Many towns and cities were taking advantage of the chance to clear out their jails and workhouses—in Detroit the magistrates would release every man who agreed to leave town within twenty-four hours, and agents of the packers were in the courtrooms to ship them right. And meantime trainloads of supplies were coming in for their accommodations, including beer and whisky, so that they might not be tempted to go outside. They hired thirty young girls in Cincinnati to "pack fruit," and when they arrived put them at work canning corned beef, and put cots for them to sleep in a public hallway, through which the men passed. As the gangs came in day and night, under the escort of squads of police, they stowed them away in unused workrooms and storerooms, and in the car sheds, crowded so closely together that the cots touched. In some places they would use the same room for eating and sleeping, and at night the men would put their cots upon the tables, to keep away from the swarms of rats.

But with all their best efforts, the packers were demoralized. Ninety per cent of the men had walked out; and they faced the task of completely remaking their labor force—and with the price of meat up thirty per cent, and the public clamoring for a settlement. They made an offer to submit the whole question at issue to arbitration; and at the end of ten days the unions accepted it, and the strike was called off. It was agreed that all the men were to be re-employed within forty-five days, and that there was to be "no discrimination against union men."

SIGNIFICANCE

Sinclair's novel follows the lives of Lithuanian immigrants Jurgis Rudkus and Ona Lukoszaite, who live in the Packingtown area of Chicago. The couple, newly married, is facing financial hardship, as work is hard to come by and the meatpacking industry is difficult, dangerous, and unsanitary. Jurgis's father is forced to pay another man one-third of his salary in recompense for his assistance in finding a job, and despite that, soon dies from the backbreaking labor. Jurgis works in the slaughterhouse, unheated during the winter, and frustrated with the poor conditions and his family's hardships, joins a union. He soon learns, however, that corruption touches every aspect of the meatpacking industry, whether or not one is unionized. When he injures himself on the job and is unable to work for three months, the factory stops paying him, despite their responsibility for his condition. Jurgis's wife, Ona, is no better off. She is forced to return to work a mere seven days after giving birth to their first child, and while pregnant with their second, she succumbs to her boss's sexual advances for fear of losing her position. When Jurgis attacks the man as a result, he is arrested and jailed for a month. The family continues in this way, unable to get ahead. Ultimately, at the end of his resources and desperate, Jurgis happens upon a Socialist political rally, where he is inspired by the speaker. He joins the party, agreeing with their philosophy that businesses should be owned by the workers who run them and not by a few wealthy individuals. His newfound attitude and allegiances help Jurgis to begin to turn his life around.

At first, *The Jungle* was thought too shocking to publish, but when it eventually reached the public, it was an immediate success. As a result of the book's revelations, the public called for legislation to improve on the unhealthy, unsanitary conditions in the meatpacking industry. Sinclair, however, had intended the novel to make people more aware of the plight of the workers, with the intention of rallying people behind the Socialist Party. He was disappointed that the public seemed more concerned about the state of the food supply.

This account of the working conditions in Packingtown and the corrupt business practices associated with the meatpacking industry provides a lasting chronicle of early American capitalism at work. Without regulation, there were no standards governing cleanliness or safety in the plants, and wages varied greatly from worker to worker, with many of them earning barely enough to support a family. Because jobs were scarce and workers plentiful, particularly with the steady influx of immigrants, the factories were able to threaten anyone with the loss of their position, secure in the knowledge that there were more workers available to fill the job. Forcing long hours and sustained high rates of production meant that workers were often injured on the job or simply collapsed from the strain, but no one was indispensable.

When the meatpackers ultimately decided to strike, in 1904, they walked off the job for nearly two months, severely crippling the meatpacking industry and causing shortages across the country, despite the presence of strike breakers brought in to keep the businesses running. Both skilled and non-skilled workers participated in the strike, maintaining a united front in the face of management's refusal to negotiate. The press sided with the workers and provided steady front-page reporting on the progress of the strike. Beyond simply walking away from their jobs, the strikers organized protests, parades, and rallies, and gained the support of local churches, the Socialist Party, the Chicago Federation of Labor, and the Stock Yards Aid Society. In retaliation, the packers issued statements to the press as well, hoping to sway public opinion to their side. Ultimately, very little was accomplished, with conditions in the packing plants remaining deplorable. However, the strike laid the groundwork for future protests and provided the fodder for Sinclair's novel and the eventual regulation of the meatpacking industry by the federal government. The Pure Food and Drug Act of 1906 was enacted in no small part due to the public outcry caused by *The Jungle*.

FURTHER RESOURCES
Books
Herms, Dieter, ed. *Upton Sinclair: Literature and Social Reform.* New York: Peter Lang, 1990.

Web sites
Illinois State University High School. "The 1904 Chicago Meatpacker's Strike." <http://www.uhigh.ilstu.edu/soc/labor/meatpackers_strike.htm> (accessed May 27, 2006).

Social Security Online. "Upton Sinclair." <http://www.ssa.gov/history/sinclair.html> (accessed May 27, 2006).

What Roosevelt Stands For

Magazine article

By: Anonymous

Date: August 7, 1912

Source: *The New York Times*

About the Author: *The New York Times* is the major daily newspaper for the city of New York. It is read throughout the United States and has been published since 1851.

INTRODUCTION

The late nineteenth century was an era of rapid industrialization, urbanization, growth, and corruption in the United States and is often called the Gilded Age. Mass immigration from Europe had swelled America's cities, and provided a ready supply of labor for industry. Big business was booming, making fortunes for the magnates and financiers who owned them. Monopolies and trusts had come to control entire industries, stifling competition. Meanwhile, many Americans struggled in dire poverty. They earned meager wages despite working long hours in dangerous factories, and lived in crowded, unsanitary slums. The politics of the time were marked by the heavy influence of rich special interests, and dominated by political bosses and machines that often used their power to reward their supporters and punish their opponents, thereby maintaining themselves in office.

It was in this atmosphere that Theodore Roosevelt entered politics, at the age of 23, when he was elected as a Republican to the New York state assembly in 1881. He was one of many Americans who were unhappy with the state of the nation. They felt that government should regulate the economy and the workplace to the benefit of consumers and workers, that the influence of special interests and political machines needed to be reduced, and that in general changes needed to be made that would make the government more responsive to the general public. These reformers were generally known as progressives or populists.

Roosevelt quickly established a reputation as an intelligent and effective reformer. He was also extremely newsworthy and popular with the general public, known for his energy, his adventurous spirit, and his striking appearance. Thanks to this popularity he was able to rise quickly in the Republican party, to the dismay of conservative politicians opposed to progressive reforms. In 1900, the conservative-dominated Republican leadership asked Roosevelt to run for vice president of the United States, along with President William McKinley. They did so hoping that his presence on the ticket would draw support from progressives, but that as vice president he would have little actual power to make changes. McKinley and Roosevelt won the election handily, and Roosevelt was inaugurated as vice president on March 4, 1901. Barely six months later, McKinley was assassinated. Roosevelt became president of the United States on September 14, 1901.

As president, Roosevelt embarked on a wide-ranging program of reforms, especially after he was elected to a second term in 1904. He used his stature and popularity like few presidents before him had done, speaking out publicly and frequently on the major issues of the day to draw attention to worthy causes and put pressure on Congress to enact his reforms. Under Roosevelt, the Justice Department began to vigorously enforce anti-trust laws, breaking up monopolies in many industries. Roosevelt advocated laws to regulate industry to the benefit of consumers—most notably the Pure Food and Drug Act of 1906—as well as currency and banking reform. Roosevelt's love of the outdoors led him to champion the cause of conservationism, establishing the first national parks and national monuments. He also supported federal dam and irrigation projects. Roosevelt believed that the United States was a great nation that should dominate the western hemisphere and be actively involved in world affairs. He expanded the navy and aided a revolution in Panama in order to gain a right-of-way to build what became the Panama Canal.

By 1908, Roosevelt had led the progressive movement to greater strength and accomplishments than any before him. Roosevelt did not run for reelection in 1908, having sworn not to seek a third term. He left office with every expectation that his successor, William Howard Taft, would continue with his agenda. Taft had served in Roosevelt's cabinet and won election easily with Roosevelt's backing. Taft was not as skillful a politician as Roosevelt, however. Nor was he as aggressive a reformer at heart as Roosevelt. Under Taft's presidency the conservatives gained in power and stalled many progressive initiatives.

Roosevelt grew disillusioned with Taft, and by 1912 decided to break with him entirely. That year, Roosevelt challenged Taft for the Republican presidential nomination, sparking a bitter struggle between the conservative and progressive wings of the Republican party. Taft and the conservatives were victorious, defeating Roosevelt in the party's conven-

tion. Roosevelt's response was to form a new party, the Progressive Party. It gained the nickname the "Bull Moose" Party when Roosevelt responded to critics that he was "fit as a bull moose" to run for office. The newspaper excerpt presented here summarizes the major points of the Progressive Party's political platform, as outlined by Roosevelt at his nominating convention.

■ PRIMARY SOURCE

Preferential primaries in Presidential years.

Election of United States Senators by popular vote.

The short ballot, limiting the number of officials to be voted for.

A stringent and efficient Corrupt Practices act applying to primaries as well as elections.

Publicity of campaign contributions.

Initiative, referendum, and recall.

Recall of judicial decisions.

Simplifying the process for amendment of the Constitution.

Strengthening of the pure food law.

Establishment of a National Health Department.

Social and industrial justice to wage workers including a minimum wage.

Insurance and old-age pensions for employees.

Regulation of conditions of labor, hours of work for women, prohibition of child labor.

Federal control of trusts.

A National Industrial Commission, controlling all inter-State industry.

Revision of the tariff in the interest of employee and consumer.

A permanent tariff commission, non-partisan.

Land monopoly tax.

Suffrage for women.

Regulation of hearing in contempt cases.

Internal waterway improvements.

Reform of the currency to give greater elasticity.

Conservation of forests, mines, water power.

Development and control of the Mississippi River.

Government ownership of Alaska railroads.

Leasing system for Alaska coal fields.

A larger navy.

Fortification of the Panama Canal and strict observance of the canal treaty.

■

SIGNIFICANCE

The campaign of 1912 was a three-way race between Roosevelt, Taft, and the Democratic nomi-

This cartoon caricatures Theodore Roosevelt's supporters as they wait for the opening of Roosevelt's Progressive "Bull Moose" Party convention. PHOTO BY MPI/GETTY IMAGES.

nee: Woodrow Wilson. Roosevelt hoped to win by drawing off progressive members of both the Republican and Democratic parties to join the Progressive Party. Accordingly he called for not just a continuation, but a major expansion, of his previous policies, including the vote for women, insurance and old-age pensions, and direct election of U.S. Senators (at the time, Senators were elected by state legislatures).

Roosevelt's positions gained him the support of many reform-minded Americans, but in the end it was not enough. Some Republicans supported him, but many refused to abandon the party. And with Woodrow Wilson also running on a reform platform, few reformers in that party wanted to switch sides. Wilson ultimately won the election, with 42 percent of the popular vote. Roosevelt came in second, with 27 percent, compared to Taft's 23 percent.

President Wilson went on to enact many reforms, including direct election of Senators, women's suffrage, and the establishment of the Federal Reserve and the Federal Trade Commission. Thus, while Roo-

sevelt's campaign failed to win him the presidency, it did further the progressive cause by drawing away potential supporters from the conservative Republicans and helping to put a reform-minded president in office. With Wilson doing an effective job of leading the reform movement, however, support for an independent Progressive Party rapidly dwindled, and by 1916 it was no longer a major political force. Theodore Roosevelt's legacy lives on, however, in the reforms he enacted and inspired.

FURTHER RESOURCES
Books

Hofstadter, Richard. *The Age of Reform.* New York: Random House, 1955.

Delegates to the convention of the Women's Organization for National Prohibition Reform gather in front of the Capitol Building for a group photo in Washington, D.C., April 13, 1932. The W.O.N.P.R. delegation is on hand to call on their representatives and senators to repeal the dry law. AP IMAGES.

Morris, Edmund. *The Rise of Theodore Roosevelt*. New York: Coward, McCann & Geoghegan, 1979.

Pringle, Henry F. *Theodore Roosevelt*. New York: Harcourt Brace and World, 1956.

Roosevelt, Theodore. *An Autobiography*. New York: Macmillan Co., 1913.

Web sites

American President. "Theodore Roosevelt." <http://www.americanpresident.org/history/theodoreroosevelt/> (accessed July 31, 2006).

The White House. "Theodore Roosevelt." <http://www.whitehouse.gov/history/presidents/tr26.html> (accessed July 31, 2006).

Eighteenth Amendment to the U.S. Constitution

Prohibition of Intoxicating Liquors

Legislation

By: Anonymous

Date: January 16, 1919

Source: U.S. Constitution

About the Author: The text of the Eighteenth Amendment was drafted by activists in the anti-alcohol movement of the early twentieth century.

INTRODUCTION

Starting in the late eighteenth and early nineteenth century, anti-alcohol or, as they were called, "temperance" movements developed in many European countries and in the United States. Early on, these movements tended to advocate moderation rather than abstinence, but by the mid-nineteenth century the word "temperance" had come to mean, usually, advocacy of complete prohibition. The American Temperance Society was founded in 1826, and within a few years this society and others like it boasted hundreds of thousands of members. Fueled partly by fear of relatively hard-drinking immigrant populations in urban areas, especially during the second half of the nineteenth century, the temperance movement achieved notable legislative successes in the United States, persuading many state legislatures to ban the sale of alcohol. Between 1900 and 1916, twenty-six states passed prohibition measures. A few

states had already experimented with prohibition years before; Oregon, for example, had prohibited "ardent spirits," as alcoholic beverages were called, in 1844, but repealed the ban in 1849.

The temperance movement was part of a large and not always internally consistent movement for various kinds of reform or change that is known today as the Progressive Movement. Its goals included votes for women, reduced political corruption, eugenics, racial equality, anti-pollution measures, better urban housing, more humane treatment of prisoners, government regulation of food purity, and other reforms. The temperance movement was dominated by women. The powerful Women's Christian Temperance Union was formed in 1873. (The organization is still in operation today.) Although suffragists (i.e., advocates of votes for women) and temperance activists were allied for some decades, the suffrage movement came to see the fierce resistance to prohibition by many voters as a liability, and, by 1910 or so, the movements had effectively split. Ironically, however, the suffrage movement was not to achieve its goal (votes for women, granted by the Nineteenth Amendment in 1920) until one year after the prohibition movement had achieved its goal (the Eighteenth Amendment, 1919).

To enforce the Eighteenth Amendment, Congress passed the National Prohibition Act of 1919, also known as the Volstead Act after its sponsor, Rep. Andrew Volstead (R-MN). The Volstead Act defined the "intoxicating liquors" mentioned in the Amendment as fluids containing 0.5 percent or more alcohol by volume.

The Eighteenth Amendment was repealed by the passage of the Twenty-first Amendment on December 5, 1933. The Eighteenth is the only Amendment to the U.S. Constitution ever to have been repealed. The Twenty-first is the only Amendment that exists solely to repeal another amendment, and the Twenty-first is also the only Amendment to have been ratified by state conventions rather than by state legislatures (as provided for in Article V of the U.S. Constitution). Whether or not to criminalize the sale of alcohol immediately became a state prerogative with the repeal of the Eighteenth Amendment, and many states immediately legalized alcohol. A few, however, did not. Mississippi, for example, remained a dry state until 1966. Many individual cities, counties, and towns still enforce prohibition locally, especially in the South.

Prohibition was not unique to the United States. Finland, Iceland, Norway, and Russia also instituted alcohol prohibition in the mid–1910s and repealed it in the late 1920s or early 1930s.

PRIMARY SOURCE

Section 1. After one year from the ratification of this article the manufacture, sale, or transportation of intoxicating liquors within, the importation thereof into, or the exportation thereof from the United States and all territory subject to the jurisdiction thereof for beverage purposes is hereby prohibited.

Section 2. The Congress and the several States shall have concurrent power to enforce this article by appropriate legislation.

Section 3. This article shall be inoperative unless it shall have been ratified as an amendment to the Constitution by the legislatures of the several States, as provided in the Constitution, within seven years from the date of the submission hereof to the States by the Congress.

SIGNIFICANCE

Prohibition is viewed by most modern historians as a misstep with many negative consequences for American society, although some present-day anti-alcohol activists disagree. First, Prohibition did not stop alcohol consumption. After a sharp dip in 1921, consumption of alcohol returned quickly to its pre-Prohibition level of about 1.2 gallons of pure alcohol equivalent per person per year. Second, more people took to drinking hard liquor, rather than beer, because virtually all alcohol had to be smuggled into the country and it was more profitable to smuggle a concentrated product than a dilute one. As a percentage of alcohol spending, spending on hard liquor went from forty percent just before Prohibition to between seventy percent and ninety percent during Prohibition and back down to forty percent immediately after its end. Third, tens of thousands of people were blinded or partially paralyzed by drinking adulterated or brewed alcoholic beverages. Fourth, organized crime flourished on the alcohol trade, with gangsters such as Al Capone (1899–1947) specializing in alcohol. Along with increased organized crime came official corruption, as gangsters bribed police to overlook their illegal activities. Sixth, although reformers expected Prohibition to empty the prisons—"We will turn our prisons into factories and our jails into storehouses and corncribs," said the anti-alcohol preacher Billy Sunday (1863–1935) when Prohibition was enacted—the jails soon filled to capacity with persons convicted of alcohol-related crimes.

Some commentators urge that today's laws prohibiting marijuana, cocaine, and other drugs are repeating the failures of Prohibition. They point to the high profitability (under drug prohibition) of developing and smuggling ever-more-concentrated drug substances, the monopoly of organized crime on the illegal drug trade, high rates of illegal drug use despite prohibition, and the strain on the nation's jail system, with persons convicted of drug offenses constituting fifty-five percent of the federal prison population as of 2003. (Over 700,000 people were arrested for marijuana offenses in the U.S. in 2001 alone.) Defenders of the present drug laws argue that drug-use rates would be higher without anti-drug laws, that drug use can be greatly reduced through a combination of education, imprisonment for drug offenses, and military operations, and that recreational drugs other than alcohol are inherently immoral.

Regardless of whether present-day drug prohibition increases the societal cost of drugs or prevents that cost from being higher, it is unlikely that U.S. federal laws prohibiting marijuana and other recreational drugs (besides alcohol) will be repealed any time soon. Several European nations, however, have recently decriminalized the possession of small quantities of marijuana. In the Netherlands, marijuana was decriminalized in 1976, with sales permitted in licensed cafes. Whether or not this has had measurable negative consequences for Dutch society has been much disputed among medical researchers, sociologists, and pro-and anti-drug-prohibition activists. A study of marijuana decriminalization in San Francisco and the Netherlands published in the *American Journal of Public Health* in 2004 found "no evidence to support claims that criminalization reduces use or that decriminalization increases use." Other researchers claim that the effect of marijuana decriminalization on Dutch society has been negative.

FURTHER RESOURCES

Books

Thornton, Mark. *The Economics of Prohibition*. Salt Lake City: University of Utah Press, 1991.

Huggins, Laura E., ed. *Drug War Deadlock: The Policy Battle Continues*. Stanford, Calif.: Hoover Institution Press, Stanford University, 2005.

Web sites

Thornton, Mark. "Alcohol Prohibition Was a Failure." *Cato Institute*, July 17, 1991. <www.cato.org/pubs/pas/pa–157.html> (accessed May 11, 2006).

The Need for Safety from the Worker's Point of View

Journal article

By: William Green

Date: January 1926

Source: Green, William. "The Need for Safety from the Worker's Point of View." *Annals of the American Academy of Political and Social Science* 123 (1926): 4–5

About the Author: William Green, an influential labor leader and reformer, was President of the American Federation of Labor from 1924 to 1952. He was instrumental in bringing about legal protections for workers.

INTRODUCTION

William Green was born in Ohio in 1870. Following in his father's footsteps, he left school at age sixteen to become a coal miner, where he experienced the daily hazards inherent in sub-surface mining. In 1891, he was elected Secretary of the local mining union. After the local union merged with the United Mine Workers of America (UMWA), Green was elected to several offices, including President of the Ohio District.

Green also used political channels to advance the cause of labor. In 1910, after he was elected to the Ohio State Senate, Green sponsored and passed legislation to provide compensation to injured workers. Building on his success in politics, Green held increasingly powerful positions in the UMWA, and in 1916 became the Secretary-Treasurer of the American Federation of Labor (AFL), the nation's largest multiunion umbrella organization.

The AFL was instrumental in improving working conditions and guaranteeing worker rights. Among the union's accomplishments were laws against child labor, shorter hours, higher wages, and workman's compensation protection. Union progress was often accompanied by violence, as union president Samuel Gompers took an openly confrontational approach to securing worker rights. Following his death in 1924, William Green was named the union's new president.

Green's twenty-eight years as AFL president were marked with turbulence. However, his approach was far less confrontational than that of Gompers, and Green's numerous speeches frequently focused on the mutual benefits of employer-employee cooperation. Green's perspective on worker rights was clearly

Workers at the Bell Aircraft plant wear safety goggles and masks while working in areas where their eyes might be damaged. Buffalo, New York, May 1943. © CORBIS.

shaped by his years in the coal mines, and he frequently referred to the hazards of that profession in his speeches and writing.

PRIMARY SOURCE

THE NEED FOR SAFETY FROM THE WORKER'S POINT OF VIEW

Progress seldom comes with the simultaneous forward movement of a whole group or an undertaking. Usually some part is in advance of the others, and there is maladjustment until all can move forward in equitable co-operation. So in industry the material side of technical progress has been speeded up without adequate consideration of the human instrumentalities necessary to direct high technical organization. The machines of industry were first built and installed without a thought of hazards to those in charge of them.

Men, women and even children spent their working hours around unguarded machinery and when rush periods came or the day's work had passed the peak of high production and fatigue made the workers less wary, many an unnecessary accident brought individual suffering and loss as well as loss to the industry.

Control over machine guarding, work processes and other working conditions rests primarily with management. While the worker may express his views he does not have power of decision. The responsibility for compensating industrial accidents rests, therefore, upon the industry. This has become an accepted social policy expressed in our compensation legislation. The enactment of this legislation brought industrial accidents forcefully to management's attention through expense items in accounts. When accidents became expensive, industry began to consider accident prevention devices and methods.

The technical side of accident prevention is primarily a field for experts and technicians, but the problem of carrying any plan into effect makes necessary the co-operation of wage earners. This co-operation can come only through an organized group. Here the union is the logical agency, for it only can offer the worker unwavering support. Putting a safety program into effect is not so simple as it sounds.

Often the rules prescribed for safety first mean doing things other than the speediest way. When management makes high quantity production paramount, the worker who follows safe practices finds himself penalized if not dismissed. Obviously then, co-operation must rest upon confidence and equality.

Human Waste in Industry

An illustration of effective safety work organized on a democratic basis with the co-operation of trade unions, is the safety work of the safety committees of the United Mine Workers. These committees serve as an educational agency as well as an administrative agency for mine safety.

The miner's work is ultra-hazardous. In 1923 there were 28,172 men injured in the anthracite mines. In 1924 there were 30,241 injured, nearly one-fifth of the total number employed in the anthracite industry in one year victims of accident and death. The loss of four million labor days a year by one hundred and fifty-eight thousand men in the anthracite industry through injuries and deaths alone is the loss to the industry. In the whole mining industry there were two thousand four hundred and fifty-two fatal accidents in the year 1923 and two thousand three hundred and eighty-one in 1925.

For the year 1921 in all industries the fatal accidents reported were eight thousand seven hundred and sixty-four and the non-fatal one million, two hundred nine thousand, one hundred fifty-one. This, of course, does not include many unreported accidents, non-fatal accidents or data on those suffering from industrial diseases.

The picture of what industrial hazards mean in the terms of industrial waste is given in the following estimates from the *Waste in Industry Report* of the American Engineering Council:

In 1919 there occurred in all the industries of the United States about 23,000 fatal accidents; about 575,000 non-fatal accidents causing four weeks or more disability; about 3,000,000 accidents in all causing at least one day's disability.

The same report estimates the net waste due to negligence of health supervision in industry at one billion dollars. In addition, preventive measures bring social dividends of high value to the nation.

These figures of course do not disclose the full extent of industrial hazards for miners, for an industrial hazard comprehends disability by disease as well as by sudden injury. We cannot consistently urge one policy for accidents and another for industrial disease. Both are due to work environment. Both result in disability, differing only in rapidity of development.

Preventive measures and programs as well as compensation should therefore apply to both occupational disease and accidents.

To management the problem of industrial safety and hygiene is a problem of efficiency. Whatever interferes with stability of working force is industrial waste—an expense that adds to production costs.

The wage earner has more at stake in the industrial safety movement than any other group. His own physical and mental well-being is involved. The consequences to him are personal or irreparable. Naturally, therefore, the first protest against conspicuous industrial hazards came from wage earners and our protests found effect in compensation legislation and constructive efforts to reduce preventable injuries.

Preventive Measures

The principal methods through which safety work is carried on are safety codes, safe practices and technical advice on desirable working condition standards. For the fully rounded development of these methods, wage earners can make the invaluable contribution of the experience of the workman on the job. This contribution is necessary to assure practicability of recommendations. In serving in this capacity, wage earners should be representatives of the unions, which are the repositories of the work experiences of the craft for many years.

On the health side, the same inadequate consideration of the health of the workers in connection with changes in production processes exists. Chemical research has been making radical and comprehensive changes in manufacturing methods. Some of these changes have been put into effect without thought of the exposure of workers to industrial poisons. The new industrial hazards were discovered only through increasing sickness, and even in some cases through an undermining of the nervous system. Such carelessness on the part of management is bad industrial economy and constitutes a revolting social waste. Labor is seeking better and more accessible sources of information on industrial hygiene, as present agencies are inadequate.

In the fields of industrial accident and disease prevention, wage earners through their only representative agency, the trade union movement, have an immediate and vital interest and stand ready to help in every possible capacity.

SIGNIFICANCE

William Green's tenure as head of the AFL saw division within the group's ranks. The AFL had historically organized workers on the basis of craft or skill, meaning that large industries included multiple unions organized by the type of work involved. But by the mid 1930s, a growing faction within the AFL was advocating a new approach to organizing, in which all workers within an industry would form a single union. In 1935, John Lewis of the UMWA led the formation of the Committee of Industrial Organizations, or CIO, which quickly gained ground in the auto and steel industries and challenged the AFL's national leadership. Renamed the Congress of Industrial Organizations in 1938, the CIO broke away from the AFL and vigorously competed with it before the two eventually remerged in 1955.

William Green's efforts produced significant improvements in the lives of U.S. workers, who formerly enjoyed few legal protections and were frequently abused by employers. Green's support helped pass the Norris-La Guardia Act, which prohibited "yellow dog contracts" forbidding new employees from joining labor unions. Green was also instrumental in passing the National Labor Relations Act, which protected workers' rights to form unions and collectively bargain with management. In 1938, he helped pass legislation creating a minimum wage and the forty-hour work week for all employees.

Because of Green's extensive experience in both labor relations and government, both Presidents Franklin Roosevelt and Harry Truman appointed him to advisory positions on federal boards. His political efforts within his own union, however, were less successful. During his tenure as AFL President, Green worked tirelessly to reunite the craft unionists and the industrial unionists, arguing that the two groups wielded greater power as a single organization. When

several unions ultimately left the AFL to form the CIO, Green openly criticized their choice, claiming that their actions violated the fundamental principle of union solidarity.

William Green led the AFL during what is now viewed as the golden age of labor. In 1945, more than thirty percent of U.S. workers were represented by labor unions, giving them tremendous clout. In the years that followed, unions achieved sweeping improvements in working conditions and compensation. Organized labor also became a powerful political force, able to marshal enormous manpower and channel millions of dollars to favored candidates.

Changes in the makeup of the U.S. economy, combined with abuses by union officials and unrealistic demands by union members soon began to stifle union growth. Ironically, previous union successes, by improving the working conditions of most Americans, actually made new union recruiting more difficult, and by 2005 only 12.5 percent of the U.S. workforce was unionized. Among non-government employees, the rate is even lower, at 7.8 percent.

While the American workplace is demonstrably safer in the twenty-first century than it was in William Green's day, mining remains a hazardous occupation. In May 2006, industry regulators began investigating a rash of fatal mining accidents in which thirty-three miners died in the first five months of the year. Union officials blamed longer work weeks and fatigue due to a rapid increase in demand for coal.

FURTHER RESOURCES

Books

Baldwin, Robert E. *The Decline of U.S. Labor Unions and the Role of Trade*. Washington, D.C.: The Institute for International Economics, 2003.

Jacobs, James B. *Mobsters, Unions, and the Feds: The Mafia and the American Labor Movement*. Albany, N.Y.: New York University Press, 2006.

Zieger, Robert H. and Gilbert J. Gall. *American Workers, American Unions: The Twentieth Century*. Baltimore, Md.: Johns Hopkins University Press, 2002.

Periodicals

Abramsky, Sasha. "Reversing 'Right to Work.'" *Nation*. 282 (2006): 16–21.

Baldwin, William. "Bigness and Badness." *Forbes*. 177 (2006): 16.

Miller, Matt. "Blowing up the Union to Save the Union." *Wall Street Journal—Eastern Edition*. 152 (2005): 36.

4

The Great Depression and the New Deal

The Great Depression and the New Deal

On October 24, 1929, the U.S. stock market crashed. Black Thursday, as the day became known, marked the beginning of the Great Depression. By 1932, many Americans battled job insecurity, decreased wages, unemployment, bank failures, property foreclosure, or loss of personal savings. In 1933, the United States unemployment rate reached twenty-five percent. A series of natural disasters, including a severe drought, exacerbated the economic crisis. The Depression was not limited to the United States; many nations experienced a prolonged period of economic stagnation.

For the first years of the Great Depression, the U.S. federal government did not intervene to provide relief to most effected individuals. Private aid societies and religious organizations staffed soup kitchens, shelters, and other relief operations. However, relief organizations—themselves affected by the Depression—could not keep up with the demand for their services. Some activists pushed for federal and state government intervention. After his inauguration in 1933, President Franklin D. Roosevelt introduced a comprehensive relief and reform program, sponsored and implemented by the federal government. Roosevelt called his plan to provide "relief, reform, and recovery" the New Deal.

The Works Progress Administration (WPA) and Civilian Conservation Corps (CCC) provided jobs on federal projects such as the building of roads, dams, and parks. Many people moved hundreds of miles to find work, living in temporary housing in WPA and CCC camps. Some farmers bankrupted by Dust Bowl crop failures and foreclosures in the American heartland moved west to work as migrant agricultural laborers. Some moved north seeking factory work, aiding the growth of the union labor movement. The WPA mural "A Nebraska Farm Scene"—a striking contrast from the bleakness of the Dust Bowl—reflects the hopes and progress of recovery for Depression-era farmers.

This chapter highlights many key New Deal programs, from the creation of the Tennessee Valley Authority (TVA) to the advent of Social Security. "On the First Hundred Days" is Roosevelt's famous radio address detailing the first wave of New Deal reforms. Though sometimes controversial, the New Deal-era's increase in the size and role of the federal government cemented its ability to direct and implement national social policy. The legacy of the New Deal is discussed further in future chapters.

At a time when the United States government was rapidly expanding its social policy role, the British government was less inclined to intercede in its economic troubles. The era's economic stagnation prompted Italy's turn to fascism and aided the rise of the Nazi party in Germany. The Soviet Union seemed to avoid many of the economic and unemployment problems of the 1930s, but only because the nation was recovering from the devastation of the 1920's brutal collectivization programs. Lingering tensions from the end of World War I and political change heightened by economic downturn fueled the build-up to World War II in Europe in 1939.

On the First Hundred Days

Speech

By: Franklin D. Roosevelt

Date: July 24, 1933

Source: Roosevelt, Franklin D. "On the First Hundred Days," Fireside Chat 3. http://millercenter.virginia.edu/scripps/diglibrary/prezspeeches/roosevelt/fdr_1933_0724.html

About the Author: Franklin D. Roosevelt (1882–1945) served as the thirty-second president of the United States. He tackled the Great Depression of the 1930s by offering the New Deal and became the only president to be reelected three times.

INTRODUCTION

When Franklin D. Roosevelt began his campaign for the presidency in 1932, he promised vigorous federal intervention to end the Great Depression. Roosevelt frankly admitted that he had no clear, consistent economic philosophy or program to end the financial crisis because the nation had never experienced anything that bad before. Upon taking office in March 1933, Roosevelt then enacted the New Deal, a series of government programs and reforms designed to end the Depression. He defended his plan in a radio fireside chat on July 24, 1933.

President Franklin D. Roosevelt at a desk in the White House, preparing for the first of his "Fireside Chat" radio broadcasts on March 12, 1933. AP/WIDE WORLD PHOTOS. REPRODUCED BY PERMISSION.

During his campaign for the presidency, Roosevelt had evoked the idea of the Depression as war-like emergency that required a fundamental change in government's role in domestic affairs. The public did not so much support his plan as seek to get rid of President Herbert Hoover. Blamed for the Depression's misery, Hoover had never been able to form an effective response to the emergency. Diagnosing a crisis of confidence that drove down wages and purchasing power, he tried to restore faith in the spiritual and economic strength of the country. However, lacking expertise in political persuasion, he failed to inspire the public.

Roosevelt, an enormously charismatic man, never had difficulty selling his ideas. During his first hundred days in office, he emphasized federally enforced controls on prices, wages, trading practices, and production. He promoted the New Deal in radio speeches known as fireside chats. The talks were relatively brief and informal reports to the American people, delivered in a conversational tone and in simple, unadorned language. Roosevelt had a clear, bell-like voice and displayed a good-humored style that endeared him to the country. No president had ever before communicated with the public in such a manner. The fireside chats gave his popularity an enormous boost and helped him sell the New Deal.

■ PRIMARY SOURCE

On the First Hundred Days

After the adjournment of the historical special session of the Congress five weeks ago I purposely refrained from addressing you for two very good reasons.

First, I think that we all wanted the opportunity of a little quiet thought to examine and assimilate in a mental picture the crowding events of the hundred days which had been devoted to the starting of the wheels of the New Deal.

Secondly, I wanted a few weeks in which to set up the new administrative organization and to see the first fruits of our careful planning.

I think it will interest you if I set forth the fundamentals of this planning for national recovery; and this I am very certain will make it abundantly clear to you that all of the proposals and all of the legislation since the fourth day of March [Inauguration Day in 1933] have not been just a collection of haphazard schemes but rather the orderly component parts of a connected and logical whole.

Long before Inauguration Day I became convinced that individual effort and local effort and even disjointed Federal effort had failed and of necessity would fail and, therefore, that a rounded leadership by the Federal Government had become a necessity both of theory and of fact. Such leadership, however, had its beginning in preserving and strengthening the credit of the United States Government, because without that no leadership was a possibility. For years the Government had not lived within its income. The immediate task was to bring our regular expenses within our revenues. That has been done.

It may seem inconsistent for a government to cut down its regular expenses and at the same time to borrow and to spend billions for an emergency. But it is not inconsistent because a large portion of the emergency money has been paid out in the form of sound loans which will be repaid to the Treasury over a period of years; and to cover the rest of the emergency money we have imposed taxes to pay the interest and the installments on that part of the debt.

So you will see that we have kept our credit good. We have built a granite foundation in a period of confusion. That foundation of the Federal credit stands there broad and sure. It is the base of the whole recovery plan.

Then came the part of the problem that concerned the credit of the individual citizens themselves. You and I know of the banking crisis and of the great danger to the savings of our people. On March sixth every national bank was closed. One month later 90 per cent of the deposits in the national banks had been made available to the depositors. Today only about 5 per cent of the deposits in national banks are still tied up. The condition relating to state banks, while not quite so good on a percentage basis, is showing a steady reduction in the total of frozen deposits—a result much better than we had expected three months ago.

The problem of the credit of the individual was made more difficult because of another fact. The dollar was a different dollar from the one with which the average debt had been incurred. For this reason large numbers of people were actually losing possession of and title to their farms and homes. All of you know the financial steps which have been taken to correct this inequality. In addition to the Home Loan Act, the Farm Loan Act and the Bankruptcy Act were passed.

It was a vital necessity to restore purchasing power by reducing the debt and interest charges upon our people, but while we were helping people to save their credit it was at the same time absolutely essential to do something about the physical needs of hundreds of thousands who were in dire straits at that very moment. Municipal and State aid were being stretched to the limit. We appropriated half a billion dollars to supplement their efforts and in addition, as you know, we have put 300,000 young men into practical and useful work in our forests and to prevent flood and soil erosion. The wages they earn are going in greater part to the support of the nearly one million people who constitute their families.

In this same classification we can properly place the great public works program running to a total of over Three Billion Dollars—to be used for highways and ships and flood prevention and inland navigation and thousands of self-sustaining state and municipal improvements. Two points should be made clear in the allotting and administration of these projects—first, we are using the utmost care to choose labor creating quick-acting, useful projects, avoiding the smell of the pork barrel; and secondly, we are hoping that at least half of the money will come back to the government from projects which will pay for themselves over a period of years.

Thus far I have spoken primarily of the foundation stones—the measures that were necessary to re-establish credit and to head people in the opposite direction by preventing distress and providing as much work as possible through governmental agencies. Now I come to the links which will build us a more lasting prosperity. I have said that we cannot attain that in a nation half boom and half broke. If all of our people have work and fair wages and fair profits, they can buy the products of their neighbors and business is good. But if you take away the wages and the profits of half of them, business is only half as good. It doesn't help much if the fortunate half is very prosperous—the best way is for everybody to be reasonably prosperous.

For many years the two great barriers to a normal prosperity have been low farm prices and the creeping paralysis of unemployment. These factors have cut the purchasing power of the country in half. I promised action. Congress did its part when it passed the farm and the industrial recovery acts. Today we are putting these two acts to work and they will work if people understand their plain objectives.

First, the Farm Act: It is based on the fact that the purchasing power of nearly half our population depends on adequate prices for farm products. We have been producing more of some crops than we consume or can sell in a depressed world market. The cure is not to produce so much. Without our help the farmers cannot get together and cut production, and the Farm Bill gives them a method of bringing their production down to a reasonable level and of obtaining reasonable prices for their crops. I have clearly stated that this method is in a sense experimental, but so far as we have gone we have reason to believe that it will produce good results.

It is obvious that if we can greatly increase the purchasing power of the tens of millions of our people who make a living from farming and the distribution of farm crops, we will greatly increase the consumption of those goods which are turned out by industry.

That brings me to the final step—bringing back industry along sound lines.

Last Autumn, on several occasions, I expressed my faith that we can make possible by democratic self-discipline in industry general increases in wages and shortening of hours sufficient to enable industry to pay its own workers enough to let those workers buy and use the things that their labor produces. This can be done only if we permit and encourage cooperative action in industry because it is obvious that without united action a few selfish men in each competitive group will pay starvation wages and insist on long hours of work. Others in that group must either follow suit or close up shop. We have seen the result of action of that kind in the continuing descent into the economic Hell of the past four years.

There is a clear way to reverse that process: If all employers in each competitive group agree to pay their workers the same wages—reasonable wages—and require the same hours—reasonable hours—then higher wages and shorter hours will hurt no employer. Moreover, such action is better for the employer than unemployment and low wages, because it makes more buyers for his product. That is the simple idea which is the very heart of the Industrial Recovery Act.

On the basis of this simple principle of everybody doing things together, we are starting out on this nationwide attack on unemployment. It will succeed if our people understand it—in the big industries, in the little shops, in the great cities and in the small villages. There is nothing complicated about it and there is nothing particularly new in the principle. It goes back to the basic idea of society and of the nation itself that people acting in a group can accomplish things which no individual acting alone could even hope to bring about....

We are not going through another Winter like the last. I doubt if ever any people so bravely and cheerfully endured a season half so bitter. We cannot ask America to continue to face such needless hardships. It is time for courageous action, and the Recovery Bill gives us the means to conquer unemployment with exactly the same weapon that we have used to strike down Child Labor.

The proposition is simply this:

If all employers will act together to shorten hours and raise wages we can put people back to work. No employer will suffer, because the relative level of competitive cost will advance by the same amount for all. But if any considerable group should lag or shirk, this great opportunity will pass us by and we will go into another desperate Winter. This must not happen.

We have sent out to all employers an agreement which is the result of weeks of consultation. ... It is a plan—deliberate, reasonable and just—intended to put into effect at once the most important of the broad principles which are being established, industry by industry, through codes. Naturally, it takes a good deal of organizing and a great many hearings and many months, to get these codes perfected and signed, and we cannot wait for all of them to go through. The blanket agreements, however, which I am sending to every employer will start the wheels turning now, and not six months from now....

In war, in the gloom of night attack, soldiers wear a bright badge on their shoulders to be sure that comrades do not fire on comrades. On that principle, those who cooperate in this program must know each other at a glance. That is why we have provided a badge of honor for this purpose, a simple design with a legend. "We do our part," and I ask that all those who join with me shall display that badge prominently. It is essential to our purpose....

To the men and women whose lives have been darkened by the fact or the fear of unemployment, I am justified in saying a word of encouragement because the codes and the agreements already approved, or about to be passed upon, prove that the plan does raise wages, and that it does put people back to work. You can look on every employer who adopts the plan as one who is doing his part, and those employers deserve well of everyone who works for a living. It will be clear to you, as it is to me, that while the shirking employer may undersell his competitor, the saving he thus makes is made at the expense of his country's welfare.

While we are making this great common effort there should be no discord and dispute. This is no time to cavil or to question the standard set by this universal agreement. It is time for patience and understanding and cooperation. The workers of this country have rights under this law which cannot be taken from them, and nobody will be permitted to whittle them away, but, on the other hand, no aggression is now necessary to attain those rights. The whole country will be united to get them for you. The principle that applies to the employers applies to the workers as well, and I ask you workers to cooperate in the same spirit....

The essence of the plan is a universal limitation of hours of work per week for any individual by common consent, and a universal payment of wages above a minimum, also by common consent. I cannot guarantee the success of this nationwide plan, but the people of this country can guarantee its success. I have no faith in "cure-alls" but I believe that we can greatly influence economic forces. ...

That is why I am describing to you the simple purposes and the solid foundations upon which our program of recovery is built. That is why I am asking the employers of the Nation to sign this common covenant with me—to sign it in the name of patriotism and humanity. That is why I am asking the workers to go along with us in a spirit of understanding and of helpfulness.

SIGNIFICANCE

More than any other decade that preceded it, the 1930s witnessed the greatest peacetime expansion in the size and the scope of the federal government in American history. Unlike Hoover, Roosevelt created regulatory agencies to prevent the speculative excesses of Wall Street, eliminate overproduction in agriculture, and shore up a shaky banking system. All of these situations had helped to create the economic crisis and, as Roosevelt realized, all had to be immediately addressed to help halt the Great Depression.

The programs that Roosevelt offered during his first weeks in office did not last long. In 1935 and 1936, the Republican-dominated Supreme Court struck down the major elements of the First New Deal as unconstitutional. Ultimately, many of the agencies created by Roosevelt during the Great Depression were dismantled. Conservative justices and members of Congress terminated some plans on ideological grounds, while other programs ended because they were viewed as irrelevant during the economic boom of the World War II years. However, Social Security has remained intact into the twenty-first century. Part of the Second New Deal that Roosevelt instituted after the First New Deal had collapsed in 1935, it is still the most popular government program in American history and it is one of the major legacies of the New Deal that Roosevelt began in 1933.

FURTHER RESOURCES
Books

Alter, Jonathan. *The Defining Moment: FDR's Hundred Days and the Triumph of Hope.* New York: Simon & Schuster, 2006.

Buhite, Russel D., and David W. Levy, eds. *FDR's Fireside Chats.* New York: Penguin, 1993.

Levine, Lawrence W., and Cornelia R. Levine. *The People and the President: America's Conversation with FDR.* Boston: Beacon Press, 2002.

National Recovery Administration

Photograph

By: The Associated Press

Date: 1933

Source: AP/Wide World Photos.

About the Photographer: The Associated Press is a world-wide news agency based in New York.

INTRODUCTION

The National Recovery Administration (NRA), created when President Franklin D. Roosevelt (1882–1945) signed the National Industrial Recovery Act on June 16, 1933, proved to be one of the most controversial parts of the New Deal. Headed by General Hugh S. Johnson (1882–1942), the NRA aimed to stabilize businesses by reducing competition through the implementation of codes that set wages and prices. It also set out to generate more purchasing power by providing jobs, defining labor standards, and raising wages.

The NRA initially concentrated on those industries that were either strong supporters of industrial self-government or sufficiently organized through trade associations to permit quick codification. The code for the cotton textile industry was the first to be completed and approved in July 1933. It was typical of other industry codes in that it provided for collective bargaining, reduced working days, established minimum wages, and set strong production controls. Business owners possessed a wealth of information about their industries and they generally dominated government forces in the code-making process.

Johnson mobilized the nation behind the NRA with a campaign reminiscent of the war rallies of World War I. Radio speakers, motorcades, torchlight parades, mass rallies, and a nationwide speaking tour by Johnson all trumpeted the benefits of the program. Business owners and the public quickly enlisted in the NRA's army of Depression fighters. The NRA Blue Eagle appeared on posters, billboards, flags, movie screens, magazines, newspapers, and numerous products. Beauty contestants had the Blue Eagle stamped on their thighs and, in Philadelphia, fans cheered a new professional football team dubbed the Eagles after the NRA's icon. This national fervor helped quicken the pace of NRA code drafting. Consumers

PRIMARY SOURCE

National Recovery Administration: The Blue Eagle, the symbol of the National Recovery Administration (NRA), and the organization's motto. AP/WIDE WORLD PHOTOS.

PRIMARY SOURCE

NATIONAL RECOVERY ADMINISTRATION
See primary source image.

SIGNIFICANCE

The NRA only enjoyed popularity for a short period of time. By 1934, signs of economic recovery and a new confidence about the imminent end of the Depression inspired hostility toward the mass of NRA regulations. Since spokespeople for consumers had been largely shut out during the creation of NRA codes and workers received comparatively little in the way of wages and better working hours, complaints were common that the NRA only benefited businesses.

The NRA had other problems as well. Charges mounted that the largest companies dominated the code authorities and that price-fixing robbed small

were asked to patronize only those businesses displaying the Blue Eagle.

A giant blue eagle float symbolizing the National Recovery Administration (NRA) participates in the firemen's annual Labor Day Parade along Pennsylvania Avenue in Washington, D.C. on September 4, 1933. AP IMAGES.

producers of the chance to compete. A congressional investigating committee substantiated some of these charges. Limiting production had discouraged investment, and not all workers were covered by NRA wage codes. The NRA excluded agricultural and domestic workers, thereby excluding three out of every four African Americans from the direct benefits of the program. Lastly, some of the provisions of the NRA appeared bizarre, such as the regulation restricting the number of times that a stripper could remove her clothes each day. When the Supreme Court unanimously struck down the NRA on May 27, 1935, declaring it unconstitutional for delegating legislative power to the president and for interfering with intrastate commerce, few mourned its passing.

The NRA experiment was generally a failure, but it left an enduring legacy. Workers had been seeking a forty-hour work week since the 1870s, and child labor had been under attack for an equally long period of time. The NRA set a forty-hour work week and stan-dardized minimum weekly wages. It also outlawed child labor practices, ending a practice that had kept children out of school and mired in poverty as adults. Additionally, the NRA's endorsement of collective bargaining spurred the growth of unions, turning organized labor into one of the major political and economic forces of the twentieth century.

FURTHER RESOURCES

Books

Bellush, Bernard. *The Failure of the NRA*. New York: W. W. Norton, 1975.

Brand, Donald R. *Corporatism and the Rule of Law*. Ithaca, N.Y.: Cornell University Press, 1988.

Himmelberg, Robert F. *The Origins of the National Recovery Administration: Business, Government, and the Trade Association Issue, 1921–33*. New York: Fordham University Press, 1976.

Social Security Advertisement

Advertisement

By: Anonymous

Date: 1935

Source: The Library of Congress.

About the Author: This advertisement is part of the collection at the Library of Congress.

INTRODUCTION

The single most important feature of the New Deal's emerging welfare state was Social Security. An ambitious, far-reaching, and permanent reform, Social Security was signed into law by President Franklin D. Roosevelt on August 14, 1935 to provide a modest income to relieve the poverty of elderly Americans. By promoting the law, Roosevelt became the first president to advocate protection for the elderly.

Roosevelt acted in response to a critic, Dr. Francis Townsend, who argued that the New Deal should include more far-reaching programs to end the Great Depression. After watching three elderly women rummaging through garbage cans for scraps of food, Townsend called for the government to offer old-age assistance. The Townsend Plan proposed that the federal government pay every American sixty years and older a monthly stipend of $200 on the condition that they leave the work force and spend the money within thirty days. A married couple, both sixty years old, would receive $4,800 annually at a time when eighty-seven percent of American families earned $2,500 or less. However, younger workers would benefit because they would no longer compete with the elderly for jobs and the elderly would rejuvenate the economy through spending.

Roosevelt had an interest in social security legislation. As governor of New York in 1928, he had proposed unemployment insurance for the elderly. Facing a tough reelection battle in 1936, Roosevelt decided to adopt a modified version of Townsend's plan. With the Social Security Act, Americans aged sixty-five or older would receive a monthly payment, starting on January 1, 1942, that initially ranged from $10 to $85. A payroll tax would provide the funding and determine the amount received by each recipient. In 1937, the new tax, the Federal Insurance Contribution Act (FICA), first appeared on workers' paychecks. Funding Social Security through payroll deductions removed the stigma of accepting government funds because the

■ PRIMARY SOURCE

Social Security Advertisement: A 1935 poster explains the new Social Security program and urges eligible Americans to enroll. THE LIBRARY OF CONGRESS.

workers themselves had contributed to their payment. To claim social security, workers needed a Social Security number. To persuade Americans to sign up, the government advertised the benefits of Social Security.

■ PRIMARY SOURCE

SOCIAL SECURITY ADVERTISEMENT

See primary source image.

■

SIGNIFICANCE

With Social Security, millions of ordinary American citizens were numbered, registered, and identified

A 1936 poster explains the newly created Social Security program. © BETTMANN/CORBIS. REPRODUCED BY PERMISSION.

by a government bureaucracy for the first time in U.S. history. The Social Security program created a personal, individualized connection between people and the federal government. It provided the bedrock for the emerging welfare state. The legislation ensured Americans that the government would provide a safety net, a measure of financial aid and support in time of economic and personal crisis.

Since its inception, Social Security has paid approximately $8.4 trillion in benefits to nearly two hundred million people. However, in 1935, no one expected vast numbers of Americans to live well past age sixty-five. In 1935, only 7.5 million people were sixty-five or older. In 2006, thirty-six million Americans (or one in eight) are sixty-five or older. By the mid-twenty-first century, this number is expected to rise to one in five. The ability of Social Security to continue payments to so many people is greatly in

doubt. The Social Security program is largely a pay-as-you-go system with current workers paying for current beneficiaries. This system has worked well over the years because a relatively large number of workers supported each individual receiving benefits. It is not apparent whether a comparatively small number of workers will be able to support a comparatively much larger number of retirees.

FURTHER RESOURCES

Books

Social Security at the Dawn of the Twenty-First Century, edited by Dalmer Hoskins, Donate Dubbernack, and Christiane Kuptsch. New Brunswick, N.J.: Transaction, 2001.

Lubove, Roy. The Struggle for Social Security, 1900–1935. Cambridge, Mass.: Harvard University Press, 1968.

Myles, John. Old Age in the Welfare State: The Political Economy of Public Pensions. Boston: Little Brown, 1984.

Web sites

Social Security Administration. "Social Security History." May 1, 2006. <http://www.ssa.gov/history> (accessed June 5, 2006).

The National Union for Social Justice

Speech

By: Coughlin, Charles

Date: November 11, 1934

Source: Social Security Online. "Father Coughlin and the Search for "Social Justice."" <http://www.ssa.gov/history/fcspeech.html> (accessed May 28, 2006).

About the Author: Charles Coughlin was born in 1891 and was ordained as a Catholic priest in 1916. He was one of the first religious broadcasters and became a well-known advocate for social justice, whose writings became increasingly anti-Semitic in his later years.

INTRODUCTION

Charles Coughlin was born in Toronto in 1891. At twenty-five, he was ordained as a Catholic priest, and in 1927 began the first radio broadcasts of Catholic services. Coughlin's sermons received a warm reception; writers of the time noted that he had

Father Charles E. Coughlin, 1936. AP/WIDE WORLD PHOTOS. REPRODUCED BY PERMISSION.

both a keen understanding of what religious radio listeners wanted and a rich vocal quality that made him pleasant to hear. Coughlin's success led CBS radio to begin airing his show in 1930, and the priest was soon receiving mail from 80,000 listeners weekly. At the height of his popularity, his radio program drew one-third of the nation's listeners.

As his influence grew, he broadened his rhetoric to include politics. Favorite themes included a topic he called "social justice." In the years during and following the Great Depression, numerous thinkers began to examine the American economy and its capitalistic underpinnings; Coughlin was one of many who believed that the U.S. economic system offered far greater opportunities to the wealthy than to those of the working class. He frequently urged listeners to seek radical reform in the nation's economic system.

Coughlin was a vocal and unapologetic supporter of Franklin Roosevelt, whom he considered a fellow political and economic reformer. Coughlin frequently told his listeners that America had only two options in the 1932 election: "Roosevelt or ruin." As Roosevelt rolled toward victory, Coughlin was invited to speak at the Democratic National Convention, an invitation he gladly accepted.

Religion and politics historically make unhappy bedfellows, and Coughlin's story is no exception. Following his election, President Roosevelt quickly instituted reforms aimed at restarting the moribund U.S. economy. While FDR's early policies fit Coughlin's vision of monetary reform, he soon embraced policies that were far less radical than Coughlin desired. FDR also began to distance himself from Coughlin and his radical rhetoric, further alienating the once-ardent supporter.

As Roosevelt struggled to implement the New Deal, he faced opposition from numerous business and political interests. Soon, Charles Coughlin was among them, clearly aligned against the man he had previously claimed was the nation's only hope for survival. On November 11, 1934, Coughlin delivered a speech in which he announced the formation of his own reform organization, the National Union for Social Justice.

■ PRIMARY SOURCE

The National Union for Social Justice

Sunday, November 11, 1934

Today the American people are the judge and jury who will support this Administration and accord it a sportman's chance to make good. It has already subscribed to the principle that human rights must take precedence over financial rights. It recognizes that these rights far outweigh in the scales of justice either political rights or so-called constitutional rights. It appears to be an Administration determined to read into the Constitution the definition of social justice which is already expressed within its very preamble. There we are taught that the object of this Government is to establish justice, to insure domestic tranquility, to promote the general welfare and to provide the blessings of liberty for ourselves and for our posterity.

The task confronting this government consists first, in recognizing and utilizing this constitutional truth; and second, in eliminating and destroying, once and for all, the well known and well established unconstitutional causes of this depression....

I realize that I am more or less a voice crying in the wilderness. I realize that the doctrine which I preach is disliked and condemned by the princes of wealth. What care I for that! And, more than all else, I deeply appreciate how limited are my qualifications to launch this organization which shall be known as the NATIONAL UNION FOR SOCIAL JUSTICE.

But the die is cast! The word has been spoken! And by it I am prepared either to stand or to fall; to fall, if needs be, and thus, to be remembered as an arrant upstart who succeeded in doing nothing more than stirring up the people.

How shall we organize? To what principles of social justice shall we pledge ourselves? What action shall we take? These are practical questions which I ask myself as I recognize the fact that this NATIONAL UNION FOR SOCIAL JUSTICE must be established in every county and city and town in these United States of America.

It is for the youth of the nation. It is for the brains of the nation. It is for the farmers of the nation. It is for everyone in the nation.

Establishing my principles upon this preamble, namely, that we are creatures of a beneficent God, made to love and to serve Him in this world and to enjoy Him forever in the next; that all this world's wealth of field, of forest, of mine and of river has been bestowed upon us by a kind Father, therefore I believe that wealth, as we know it, originates from natural resources and from the labor which the children of God expend upon these resources. It is all ours except for the harsh, cruel, and grasping ways of wicked men who first concentrated wealth into the hands of a few, then dominated states, and finally commenced to pit state against state in the frightful catastrophes of commercial warfare.

Following this preamble, these shall be the principles of social justice towards the realization of which we must strive:

1. I believe in liberty of conscience and liberty of education, not permitting the state to dictate either my worship to my God or my chosen avocation in life.
2. I believe that every citizen willing to work and capable of working shall receive a just, living, annual wage which will enable him both to maintain and educate his family according to the standards of American decency.
3. I believe in nationalizing those public resources which by their very nature are too important to be held in the control of private individuals.
4. I believe in private ownership of all other property.
5. I believe in upholding the right to private property but in controlling it for the public good.
6. I believe in the abolition of the privately owned Federal Reserve Banking system and in the establishment of a Government owned Central Bank.
7. I believe in rescuing from the hands of private owners the right to coin and regulate the value of money,

which right must be restored to Congress where it belongs.
8. I believe that one of the chief duties of this Government-owned Central Bank is to maintain the cost of living on an even keel and arrange for the repayment of dollar debts with equal value dollars.
9. I believe in the cost of production plus a fair profit for the farmer.
10. I believe not only in the right of the laboring man to organize in unions but also in the duty of the Government, which that laboring man supports, to protect these organizations against the vested interests of wealth and of intellect.
11. I believe in the recall of all non-productive bonds and therefore in the alleviation of taxation.
12. I believe in the abolition of tax-exempt bonds.
13. I believe in broadening the base of taxation according to the principles of ownership and the capacity to pay.
14. I believe in the simplification of government and the further lifting of crushing taxation from the slender revenues of the laboring class.
15. I believe that, in the event of a war for the defense of our nation and its liberties, there shall be a conscription of wealth as well as a conscription of men.
16. I believe in preferring the sanctity of human rights to the sanctity of property rights; for the chief concern of government shall be for the poor because, as it is witnessed, the rich have ample means of their own to care for themselves.

These are my beliefs. These are the fundamentals of the organization which I present to you under the name of the NATIONAL UNION FOR SOCIAL JUSTICE. It is your privilege to reject or to accept my beliefs; to follow me or to repudiate me.

SIGNIFICANCE

In summary, Coughlin's organization called for a broad populist rebellion against the existing financial system. Like many reformers before and after him, Coughlin's platform rested on the assertion that the present system was fundamentally inequitable and that only a radical restructuring could correct the injustices. In 1936, Coughlin followed up this announcement by launching a publication called *Social Justice Weekly* in which he wrote at length about his organization's goals. That same year, he publicly labeled Franklin Roosevelt a "betrayer and liar," claiming that Roosevelt was not a true Democrat. Coughlin also used his influence to support a third-party candidate in the 1936 presidential contest and began to forge ties with far-right wing groups.

By the late 1930s, Coughlin's rhetoric became increasingly anti-Semitic, and his writings focused increasingly on alleged Jewish atrocities. In 1938 following *Kristallnacht* ("the night of broken glass"), which was a brutal Nazi attack on German Jews, Coughlin claimed that Jews themselves were responsible for the violence. As Coughlin's comments drew praise in Germany, they sparked sharp criticism in the United States, and some radio stations refused to air his programs.

Coughlin's influence effectively ended in 1942, when the U.S. attorney general convened a grand jury to determine whether *Social Justice Weekly* was publishing antigovernment propaganda. Weeks later the Postal Service revoked Coughlin's second-class mailing status, and after years of effort, the archbishop of Detroit banned Coughlin from publishing his views in any form. Returned to the role of parish priest, Coughlin continued to preach at his original parish for many years.

Charles Coughlin was the first religious leader to fully exploit the power of broadcasting, preaching a message more political than theological. He has been succeeded by hundreds of other religious broadcasters, many of whom have risen to prominence and fallen from grace with equal speed. Countless politicians have also used broadcasting to reach voters, beginning with Coughlin's former hero, Franklin Roosevelt, whose folksy fireside chats became a hallmark of his administration's leadership.

FURTHER RESOURCES

Books

Carpenter, Ronald H. *Father Charles E. Coughlin : Surrogate Spokesman for the Disaffected*. Westwood, CT: Greenwood Press, 1998.

Coughlin, Charles E. *"Am I an Anti-Semite?": 9 addresses on various "isms," answering the question*. Arno Press, 1977.

Warren, David I. *Radio Priest: Charles Coughlin, the Father of Hate Radio*. New York: Free Press, 1996.

Periodicals

Bennett, Stephen Earl. "Americans' Exposure to Political Talk Radio and Their Knowledge of Public Afrairs." *Journal of Broadcasting and Electronic Media*. 46, no. 1 (March 2002): 72–86.

Besser, James D. "Antihumanism on the Air." *New Republic*. 185 (1981): 22–23.

Hatch, David. "Group Hails Religious TV Ruling." *Electronic Media*. 19 (2000): 2–3.

Web sites

Missouri State University. "Documents on the Populist Party." <http://history.missouristate.edu/wrmiller/Pop-ulism/texts/Documents/Documents_on_Pops.htm> (accessed May 28, 2006).

Social Security Online. "Father Charles E. Coughlin." <http://www.ssa.gov/history/coughlinradio.html> (accessed May 28, 2006).

A Nebraska Farm Scene

Painting

By: Marguerite Zorach

Date: 1935

Source: Photo by MPI/Getty Images.

About the Artist: Marguerite Zorach (1887–1968) is one of the founders of the modern art movement in the United States. Primarily an oil painter, she is also known for her fine-art embroidered tapestries.

INTRODUCTION

The Works Progress Administration (WPA) was the centerpiece of President Franklin D. Roosevelt's (1882–1945) New Deal plan to help the United States overcome the Great Depression. During its brief existence, from 1935 to 1943, the WPA spent almost $11 billion and employed about one-third of all unemployed workers. While the majority of its funds were spent on public works construction, the WPA devoted about a quarter of its budget to humanities and arts projects.

The establishment of the WPA by Executive Order 7034 on May 6, 1935, grew out of Roosevelt's strategy for fighting the Great Depression. While President Herbert Hoover (1874–1964) viewed public employment that competed with private enterprise as un-American, Roosevelt was willing to try anything that might get people off soup lines and back to work. Accordingly, he incorporated public works into his relief programs. By 1935, Roosevelt had decided to emphasize public works over direct relief. The WPA, approved by Congress through the Emergency Relief Appropriation Act, constituted the most successful effort at public works ever conducted by the federal government.

The WPA supported the arts and humanities through Federal One, the arts program that included the Federal Art Project, the Federal Music Project, the Federal Theatre Project, and the Federal Writers'

A Nebraska Farm Scene: A painting of a Nebraskan farm scene by Marguerite Zorach, commissioned by the Works Progress Administration, 1935. PHOTO BY MPI/GETTY IMAGES.

Project. Federal One reflected Roosevelt's more radical turn in the Second New Deal as well as his willingness to try anything that might help the American people. The controversial plays and paintings produced by WPA artists prompted criticism from Roosevelt's political opponents, especially since many of the works glorified the New Deal.

A NEBRASKA FARM SCENE

See primary source image.

■

SIGNIFICANCE

While the WPA's cultural activities attracted considerable attention, the vast majority of the agency's efforts were devoted to public works projects. The WPA completed a range of projects, including airports, public buildings, highways, conservation projects, and engineering surveys. WPA workers built 24,000 miles of sidewalks, improved 7,000 miles of paths, constructed 28,000 miles of curb, created or improved 500 water treatment plants, built 1,800 pumping stations, and created over 350 airport landing fields. The WPA is also credited with constructing more than 100,000 new public buildings, such as schools, hospitals, dormitories, and government office buildings.

Despite its productivity, the WPA was a controversial program. In a 1939 public opinion poll, the WPA was simultaneously ranked as Roosevelt's greatest accomplishment and the worst thing that he had done. The WPA did make important contributions to the American economy and culture. Many of the buildings constructed by the WPA still stand and millions of Americans received an education from WPA

A painting of Depression-era artists working in a studio sponsored by the Works Progress Administration. PHOTO BY MPI/GETTY IMAGES.

teachers. Perhaps most important, the billions of dollars spent by the WPA subsidized families of the unemployed and relieved their misery. The agency succeeded in enabling millions of desperate Americans to survive the Great Depression.

In the years after the Great Depression ended, other politicians spoke of creating agencies similar to the WPA. As part of his Great Society in the 1960s, President Lyndon B. Johnson (1908–1973) secured the passage of several laws providing job training, federal employment, highway construction, and education. Such continuing programs as the National Endowment for the Humanities and the National Endowment for the Arts reflect the legacy of government support for the arts.

FURTHER RESOURCES
Books

McDonald, William F. *Federal Relief Administration and the Arts*. Columbus: Ohio State University Press, 1969.

Meltzer, Milton. *Violins and Shovels: The WPA Arts Projects*. New York: Delacorte Press, 1976.

Zorach, Marguerite. *Marguerite and William Zorach: Harmonies and Contrasts*. Portland, Maine: Portland Museum of Art, 2001.

Share Our Wealth

Speech

By: Huey P. Long

Date: March 7, 1935

Source: Huey P. Long. "Share Our Wealth." Washington, D.C., March 7, 1935. Available from *American Rhetoric*. <http://www.americanrhetoric.com/speeches/hueyplongshare.htm> (accessed June 20, 2006).

About the Author: Huey P. Long (1893–1935) served as the Governor of Louisiana (1928–1931) and the U.S. Senator from Louisiana (1930–1935). A flamboyant Democrat with a dictatorial governing style, he was assassinated in 1935 by a Louisiana political opponent just as he was planning to challenge Franklin D. Roosevelt for the presidency.

INTRODUCTION

Louisiana politician Huey P. Long became a national figure in the 1930s by blaming the Great Depression on only one cause, the maldistribution of wealth. In February 1934, Long went on the radio to announce the formation of the Share Our Wealth Society. Although he did not publicly say so, Long planned to use the Society to propel himself into the White House.

Share Our Wealth was based on Long's notion that wealth was finite. He believed that the only way to raise the fortunes of the poor was to take from the

Senator Huey Long addresses the students of Louisiana State University in New Orleans on November 12, 1934. AP IMAGES.

rich. Accordingly, the centerpiece of the plan was a call to appropriate all accumulated wealth above $5 million and all annual earnings over $1 million. The money raised from this tax would be used to provide every American family with a homestead, which included a house, a car, and a radio. Additionally, every family would receive an annual income of between $2000 and $2500 at a time when 18.3 families earned less than $1000 per year. Besides this confiscatory tax, which was the only constant element of Share Our Wealth, Long proposed a number of sweeping reforms. At various times, he added old-age pensions, free college education for students who passed entrance exams, and bonuses for veterans. With realism rare in a southern politician in the Jim Crow era, Long included blacks as recipients of his benefits.

All one had to do to join the Share Our Wealth Society was to write to Long. There were no dues, but Long accepted donations. Members received Long's autobiography, speeches, buttons, and instructions on how to create local chapters. The Society gained 200,000 members within a month. By the time of Long's death, it had 7.5 million members. By the start of 1935, Society officials claimed that 27,000 chapters were in existence. Although many of the members came from Long's traditional power base in the South, the movement was a national one. It particularly attracted African Americans, historically the most downtrodden on the economic ladder. The movement was primarily a lower middle class one, but small business owners and professionals also joined out of fear that the Depression would push them into the ranks of the poverty-stricken.

PRIMARY SOURCE

President Roosevelt was elected on November 8, 1932. People look upon an elected President as the President. This is January 1935. We are in our third year of the Roosevelt depression, with the conditions growing worse...

We must now become awakened! We must know the truth and speak the truth. There is no use to wait three more years. It is not Roosevelt or ruin; it is Roosevelt's ruin.

Now, my friends, it makes no difference who is President or who is senator. America is for 125 million people and the unborn to come. We ran Mr. Roosevelt for the president of the United States because he promised to us by word of mouth and in writing:

1. That the size of the big man's fortune would be reduced so as to give the masses at the bottom enough to wipe out all poverty;

2. That the hours of labor would be so reduced that all would share in the work to be done and in consuming the abundance mankind produced.

Hundreds of words were used by Mr. Roosevelt to make these promises to the people, but they were made over and over again. He reiterated these pledges even after he took his oath as President. Summed up, what these promises meant was: "Share our wealth."

When I saw him spending all his time of ease and recreation with the business partners of Mr. John D. Rockefeller, Jr., with such men as the Astors, etc., maybe I ought to have had better sense than to have believed he would ever break down their big fortunes to give enough to the masses to end poverty—maybe some will think me weak for ever believing it all, but millions of other people were fooled the same as myself. I was like a drowning man grabbing at a straw, I guess. The face and eyes, the hungry forms of mothers and children, the aching hearts of students denied education were before our eyes, and when Roosevelt promised, we jumped for that ray of hope.

So therefore I call upon the men and women of America to immediately join in our work and movement to share our wealth.

There are thousands of share-our-wealth societies organized in the United States now. We want a hundred thousand such societies formed for every nook and corner of this country—societies that will meet, talk, and work, all for the purpose that the great wealth and abundance of this great land that belongs to us may be shared and enjoyed by all of us.

We have nothing more for which we should ask the Lord. He has allowed this land to have too much of everything that humanity needs.

So in this land of God's abundance we propose laws, viz.:

1. The fortunes of the multimillionaires and billionaires shall be reduced so that no one person shall own more than a few million dollars to the person. We would do this by a capital levy tax. On the first million that a man was worth, we would not impose any tax. We would say, "All right for your first million dollars, but after you get that rich you will have to start helping the balance of us." So we would not levy and capital levy tax on the first million one owned. But on the second million a man owns, we would tax that 1 percent, so that every year the man owned the second million dollars he would be taxed $10,000. On the third million we would impose a tax of 2 percent. On the fourth million we would impose a tax of 4 percent. On the fifth million we would impose a tax of 16 percent. On the seventh million we would impose a tax of 32 percent. On the eighth million we would impose

a tax of 64 percent; and on all over the eight million we would impose a tax of 100 percent.

What this would mean is that the annual tax would bring the biggest fortune down to $3 or $4 million to the person because no one could pay taxes very long in the higher brackets. But $3 or $4 million is enough for any one person and his children and his children's children. We cannot allow one to have more than that because it would not leave enough for the balance to have something.

2. We propose to limit the amount any one man can earn in one year or inherit to $1 million to the person.

3. Now, by limiting the size of the fortunes and incomes of the big men, we will throw into the government Treasury the money and property from which we will care for the millions of people who have nothing; and with this money we will provide a home and the comforts of home, with such common conveniences as radio and automobile, for every family in America, free of debt.

4. We guarantee food and clothing and employment for everyone who should work by shortening the hours of labor to thirty hours per week, maybe less, and to eleven months per year, maybe less. We would have the hours shortened just so much as would give work to everybody to produce enough for everybody; and if we get them down to where they were too short, then we would lengthen them again. As long as all the people working can produce enough of automobiles, radios, homes, schools, and theatres for everyone to have that kind of comfort and convenience, then let us all have work to do and have that much of heaven on earth.

5. We would provide education at the expense of the states and the United States for every child, not only through grammar school and high school but through to a college and vocational education. We would simply extend the Louisiana plan to apply to colleges and all people. Yes, we would have to build thousands of more colleges and employ 100,000 more teachers; but we have materials, men, and women who are ready and available for the work. Why have the right to a college education depend upon whether the father or mother is so well-to-do as to send a boy or girl to college? We would give every child the right to education and a living at birth.

6. We would give a pension to all persons above sixty years of age in an amount sufficient to support them in comfortable circumstances, expecting those who earn $1,000 per year or who are worth $10,000.

7. Until we could straighten things out—and we can straighten things out in two months under our program—we would grant a moratorium on all debts which people owe that they cannot pay.

And now you have our program, none too big, none too little, but every man a king.

We owe debts in America today, public and private, amounting to $252 billion. That means that every child is born with a $2,000 debt tied around his neck to hold him down before he gets started. Then, on top of that, the wealth is locked in a vise owned by a few people. We propose that children shall be born in a land of opportunity, guaranteed a home, food, clothes, and the other things that make for living, including the right to education.

Our plan would injure no one. It would not stop us from having millionaires—it would increase them tenfold, because so many more people could make $1 million if they had the chance our plan gives them. Our plan would not break up big concerns. The only difference would be that maybe 10,000 people would own a concern instead of 10 people owning it.

But, my friends, unless we do share our wealth, unless we limit the size of the big man so as to give something to the little man, we can never have a happy or free people. God said so! He ordered it.

We have everything our people need. Too much of food, clothes, and houses—why not let all have their fill and lie down in the ease and comfort God has given us? Why not? Because a few own everything—the masses own nothing.

I wonder if any of you people who are listening to me were ever at a barbecue! We used to go there—sometimes 1,000 people or more. If there were 1,000 people, we would put enough meat and bread and everything else on the table for 1,000 people. Then everybody would be called and everyone would eat all they wanted. But suppose at one of these barbecues for 1,000 people that one man took 90 percent of the food and ran off with it and ate until he got sick and let the balance rot. Then 999 people would have only enough for 100 to eat and there would be many to starve because of the greed of just one person for something he couldn't eat himself.

Well, ladies and gentlemen, America all the people of America, have been invited to a barbecue. God invited us all to come and eat and drink all we wanted. He smiled on our land we grew crops of plenty to eat and wear. He showed us in the earth the iron and other things to make everything we wanted. He unfolded to us the secrets of science so that our work might be easy. God called: "Come to my feast."

Then what happened? Rockefeller, Morgan, and their crowd stepped up and took enough for 120 million people and left only enough for 5 million for all the other 125 million to eat. And so many million must go hungry and without these good things God gave us unless we call on them to put some of it back.

SIGNIFICANCE

The swelling membership of Share Our Wealth masked fundamental problems with the movement. Economists ridiculed the plan. Noting that only forty-three Americans made more than $1 million per year in 1934, they calculated that families would receive only $400 under Long's plan. Further critics contended that, because Share Our Wealth would kill all incentive to make more than $1 million, there would be nothing to confiscate after the first year. In addition, Long failed to explain how he would address non-liquid assets, such as real estate, stocks, and bonds, that could not be easily transferred to the poor.

As he stated privately to friends, Long was more interested in the power that he would derive from his own national organization than in pressing for reforms. The Share Our Wealth Society disintegrated after Long's murder by Dr. Carl A. Weiss at the Louisiana state capitol in September 1935. Long's closest supporters, none of whom had any particular attachment to the plan, were eager to mend their fences with Roosevelt. The president had been withholding federal funds from Louisiana as punishment for Long's disloyalty. Gerald L.K. Smith, who had been responsible for much of the publicity that led to the Society's rapid growth, tried to take it over but Long's men denied him access to the mailing list. Roosevelt's 1935 Wealth Tax bill and the passage of the Social Security Act co-opted some of Long's thunder and hastened the demise of the Society.

FURTHER RESOURCES

Books

Brinkley, Alan. *Voices of Protest: Huey Long, Father Coughlin, and the Great Depression.* New York: Knopf, 1982.

Hair, William Ivy. *The Kingfish and His Realm: The Life and Times of Huey P. Long.* Baton Rouge: Louisiana State University, 1991.

Jeansonne, Glen. *Messiah of the Masses: Huey P. Long and the Great Depression.* New York: HarperCollins, 1993.

Ida M. Fuller was the first person to receive a Social Security payment, in 1940. She posed for this photo in 1950, and is displaying a new Social Security check with an increased benefit amount. AP/WIDE WORLD PHOTOS. REPRODUCED BY PERMISSION.

Source: Roosevelt, Franklin. "Speech upon Signing the Social Security Act." *American Rhetoric.* <http://www.americanrhetoric.com/speeches/fdrsocialsecurityact.htm> (accessed May 30, 2006).

About the Author: Franklin D. Roosevelt (1882–1945) served as the thirty-second president of the United States. He tackled the Great Depression of the 1930s by offering the New Deal and became the only president to be re-elected three times. He also led the United States through World War II.

Speech upon Signing the Social Security Act

Speech

By: Franklin D. Roosevelt

Date: August 14, 1935

INTRODUCTION

Responding to growing pressures to modify the New Deal, President Franklin D. Roosevelt made a major announcement in his 1935 State of the Union address. Roosevelt declared that the government would now focus more on people than on business. The New Deal would target underconsumption rather than low production and low profits. Accordingly, he proposed an old-age program to put money in the pockets of the elderly. It became the Social Security Act.

Social Security reflected the financial conservatism of Roosevelt. It was the only social security system ever established that was self-funding. It was paid for not from general tax revenues, but from a trust fund paid into by workers and their employers. Furthermore, Social Security protected the economy from the inflation that had badly damaged European economies. It was a deflationary measure that took money out of the still-depressed economy and did not return any of it for five years.

Many aspects of Social Security drew the rage of critics. While most Americans supported the bill, many economists predicted that the payroll tax would deepen the Depression by taking money from the marketplace at a time when increased consumer spending was seen as the primary factor needed to stimulate the economy. Another problem with Social Security involved its regressive nature. A uniform payroll tax resulted in lower-income workers paying a higher percentage of their wages in taxes than those who received higher salaries. Lastly, conservative critics objected to the expansion of government and the creation of a government safety net that seemed like the first step toward Socialism. Roosevelt ignored these critics and signed the bill into law.

PRIMARY SOURCE

Today, a hope of many years' standing is in large part fulfilled.

The civilization of the past hundred years, with its startling industrial changes, had tended more and more to make life insecure.

Young people have come to wonder what will be their lot when they came to old age.

The man with a job has wondered how long the job would last.

This social security measure gives at least some protection to 50 millions of our citizens who will reap direct benefits through unemployment compensation, through old-age pensions, and through increased services for the protection of children and the prevention of ill health.

We can never insure 100 percent of the population against 100 percent of the hazards and vicissitudes of life, but we have tried to frame a law which will give some measure of protection to the average citizen and to his family against the loss of a job and against poverty-stricken old age.

This law, too, represents a cornerstone in a structure which is being built but is by no means complete. It is a structure intended to lessen the force of possible future depressions. It will act as a protection to future administrations against the necessity of going deeply into debt to furnish relief to the needy. The law will flatten out the peaks and valleys of deflation and of inflation. It is, in short, a law that will take care of human needs and at the same time provide the United States an economic structure of vastly greater soundness.

I congratulate all of you ladies and gentlemen, all of you in the Congress, in the executive departments and all of you who come from private life, and I thank you for your splendid efforts in behalf of this sound, needed and patriotic legislation.

It seems to me that if the Senate and the House of Representatives, in this long and arduous session, had done nothing more than pass this security Bill, Social Security Act, the session would be regarded as historic for all time.

SIGNIFICANCE

Compared to social insurance programs put into effect by European nations that were not as wealthy as the United States, the American plan seemed skimpy. Initially, it excluded millions of workers employed in agriculture, in domestic service, and in many categories of industrial employment. These restrictions especially hurt women and African Americans, the majority of domestic and agricultural workers. The self-employed also were locked out of the system.

Gradually, Social Security expanded to cover all Americans. Beginning in the 1950s, amendments extended Social Security coverage to previously excluded workers. The addition of disability insurance in 1954, along with a more progressive benefit formula, proved especially helpful to non-white and lower-income workers. Major court decisions in the 1970s overruled the gender biases in survivors' and spousal benefits. Especially important to Social Security's anti-poverty objectives, the 1972 adoption of automatic cost of living allowances has provided crucial protection against inflation.

However, since the 1980s, the future of Social Security has been hotly debated in the halls of government, in newspapers, and on main streets across the nation. There are serious concerns about the program's ability to meet future benefit obligations in the wake of the retirement of the massive baby boom population. Ideological opponents of big government have also attacked the program as being outside of the proper duties of government. A number of plans have been proposed to address the looming financial crisis in the Social Security system. Most include either tax increases, benefit cuts, the implementation of personal retirement savings accounts, or a combination of these measures.

FURTHER RESOURCES

Books

Hoskins, Dalmer, Donate Dubbernack, and Christiane Kuptsch, eds. *Social Security at the Dawn of the Twenty-First Century.* New Brunswick, N.J.: Transaction, 2001.

Lubove, Roy. *The Struggle for Social Security, 1900–1935.* Cambridge, Mass.: Harvard University Press, 1968.

Myles, John. *Old Age in the Welfare State: The Political Economy of Public Pensions.* Boston: Little Brown, 1984.

Web sites

Social Security Administration. "Social Security Online History Pages." May 1, 2006. <http://www.ssa.gov/history/> (accessed May 17, 2006).

Radio Address Roosevelt's Defense of the New Deal

Speech

By: Franklin D. Roosevelt

Date: October 31, 1936

Source: *Miller Center of Public Affairs.* Scripps Library and Multimedia Archive. Franklin D. Roosevelt Speeches. Madison Square Garden (October 31, 1936). <http://www.millercenter.virginia.edu/scripps/diglibrary/prezspeeches/roosevelt/fdr_1936_1031.html>

About the Author: Franklin D. Roosevelt (1882–1945) served as the thirty-second president of the United States. He tackled the Great Depression by enacting the New Deal and became the only president to be reelected three times.

INTRODUCTION

As the Great Depression continued, President Franklin D. Roosevelt faced an increasing number of critics. He responded with the Second New Deal, a series of federal reforms more radical than any that he had tried in the past. Such laws as Social Security dra-

matically expanded the role of government in citizens' lives. However, the New Deal suffered a major blow when the Supreme Court ruled in 1935 that the National Recovery Administration was unconstitutional. Roosevelt interpreted the decision as an effort by conservative forces to end his efforts to restore the American economy. His took his case to the American people and won a landslide victory in 1936.

Upon starting his second term in office, Roosevelt immediately decided to do something about the conservative Supreme Court. In March 1937, Roosevelt announced that he would reorganize the Court. The centerpiece of the program was Roosevelt's decision to add one justice to the Court for every sitting justice over the age of seventy, ostensibly to help the elderly justices with their heavy work load. Critics immediately attacked the measure as a dictatorial attempt to pack the Court to make it more supportive of New Deal legislation. The public largely agreed and Roosevelt retreated.

By 1936, however, Roosevelt had decided that he needed to slow the pace of reform to protect the legislation already passed. The major piece of legislation proposed by the Roosevelt administration in 1937 was the Farm Security Administration (FSA), an agency built on the earlier Agricultural Adjustment Act, part of which had been declared unconstitutional. The FSA provided federal aid to small and tenant farmers. The last major New Deal was the 1938 Fair Labor Standards Act. This law set a minimum wage of forty cents per hour and a forty-hour work week for employees of any company engaged in interstate commerce. By the end of 1938, the nation had shifted its attention from the weak economy to the rising war clouds over Europe.

PRIMARY SOURCE

Campaign Address at Madison Square Garden, New York City

"We Have Only Just Begun to Fight."

October 31, 1936

Senator Wagner, Governor Lehman, ladies and gentlemen:

ON THE eve of a national election, it is well for us to stop for a moment and analyze calmly and without prejudice the effect on our Nation of a victory by either of the major political parties.

The problem of the electorate is far deeper, far more vital than the continuance in the Presidency of any individual. For the greater issue goes beyond units of humanity—it goes to humanity itself.

President Franklin D. Roosevelt endorses New Deal candidates during a radio broadcast from his Hyde Park, New York home on November 4, 1938. © BETTMANN/CORBIS.

In 1932 the issue was the restoration of American democracy; and the American people were in a mood to win. They did win. In 1936 the issue is the preservation of their victory. Again they are in a mood to win. Again they will win.

More than four years ago in accepting the Democratic nomination in Chicago, I said: "Give me your help not to win votes alone, but to win in this crusade to restore America to its own people."

The banners of that crusade still fly in the van of a Nation that is on the march.

It is needless to repeat the details of the program which this Administration has been hammering out on the anvils of experience. No amount of misrepresentation or statistical contortion can conceal or blur or smear that record. Neither the attacks of unscrupulous enemies nor the exaggerations of over-zealous friends will serve to mislead the American people.

What was our hope in 1932? Above all other things the American people wanted peace. They wanted peace of mind instead of gnawing fear.

First, they sought escape from the personal terror which had stalked them for three years. They wanted the peace that comes from security in their homes: safety for their savings, permanence in their jobs, a fair profit from their enterprise.

Next, they wanted peace in the community, the peace that springs from the ability to meet the needs of community life: schools, playgrounds, parks, sanitation, highways—those things which are expected of solvent local government. They sought escape from disintegration and bankruptcy in local and state affairs.

They also sought peace within the Nation: protection of their currency, fairer wages, the ending of long hours of toil, the abolition of child labor, the elimination of wildcat speculation, the safety of their children from kidnappers.

And, finally, they sought peace with other Nations—peace in a world of unrest. The Nation knows that I hate war, and I know that the Nation hates war.

I submit to you a record of peace; and on that record a well-founded expectation for future peace—peace for the individual, peace for the community, peace for the Nation, and peace with the world.

Tonight I call the roll—the roll of honor of those who stood with us in 1932 and still stand with us today.

Written on it are the names of millions who never had a chance—men at starvation wages, women in sweatshops, children at looms.

Written on it are the names of those who despaired, young men and young women for whom opportunity had become a will-o'-the-wisp.

Written on it are the names of farmers whose acres yielded only bitterness, business men whose books were portents of disaster, home owners who were faced with eviction, frugal citizens whose savings were insecure.

Written there in large letters are the names of countless other Americans of all parties and all faiths, Americans who had eyes to see and hearts to understand, whose consciences were burdened because too many of their fellows were burdened, who looked on these things four years ago and said, "This can be changed. We will change it."

We still lead that army in 1936. They stood with us then because in 1932 they believed. They stand with us today because in 1936 they know. And with them stand millions of new recruits who have come to know.

Their hopes have become our record.

We have not come this far without a struggle and I assure you we cannot go further without a struggle.

For twelve years this Nation was afflicted with hear-nothing, see-nothing, do-nothing Government. The Nation looked to Government but the Government looked away. Nine mocking years with the golden calf and three long years of the scourge! Nine crazy years at the ticker and three long years in the breadlines! Nine mad years of mirage and three long years of despair! Powerful influences strive today to restore that kind of government with its doctrine that that Government is best which is most indifferent.

For nearly four years you have had an Administration which instead of twirling its thumbs has rolled up its sleeves. We will keep our sleeves rolled up.

We had to struggle with the old enemies of peace—business and financial monopoly, speculation, reckless banking, class antagonism, sectionalism, war profiteering.

They had begun to consider the Government of the United States as a mere appendage to their own affairs.

We know now that Government by organized money is just as dangerous as Government by organized mob.

Never before in all our history have these forces been so united against one candidate as they stand today. They are unanimous in their hate for me—and I welcome their hatred. I should like to have it said of my first Administration that in it the forces of selfishness and of lust for power met their match. I should like to have it said of my second Administration that in it these forces met their master.

The American people know from a four-year record that today there is only one entrance to the White House—by the front door. Since March 4, 1933, there has been only one pass-key to the White House. I have carried that key in my pocket. It is there tonight. So long as I am President, it will remain in my pocket.

Those who used to have pass-keys are not happy. Some of them are desperate. Only desperate men with their backs to the wall would descend so far below the level of decent citizenship as to foster the current pay-envelope campaign against America's working people. Only reckless men, heedless of consequences, would risk the disruption of the hope for a new peace between worker and employer by returning to the tactics of the labor spy.

Here is an amazing paradox! The very employers and politicians and publishers who talk most loudly of class antagonism and the destruction of the American system now undermine that system by this attempt to coerce the votes of the wage earners of this country. It is the 1936 version of the old threat to close down the factory or the office if a particular candidate does not win. It is an old strategy of tyrants to delude their victims into fighting their battles for them. Every message in a pay envelope, even if it is the truth, is a command to vote according to the will of the employer. But this propaganda is worse—it is deceit.

They tell the worker his wage will be reduced by a contribution to some vague form of old-age insurance. They carefully conceal from him the fact that for every dollar of premium he pays for that insurance, the employer pays another dollar. That omission is deceit.

They carefully conceal from him the fact that under the federal law, he receives another insurance policy to help him if he loses his job, and that the premium of that policy is paid 100 percent by the employer and not one cent by the worker. They do not tell him that the insurance policy that is bought for him is far more favorable to him than any policy that any private insurance company could afford to issue. That omission is deceit.

They imply to him that he pays all the cost of both forms of insurance. They carefully conceal from him the fact that for every dollar put up by him his employer puts up three dollars—three for one. And that omission is deceit.

But they are guilty of more than deceit. When they imply that the reserves thus created against both these policies will be stolen by some future Congress, diverted to some wholly foreign purpose, they attack the integrity and honor of American Government itself. Those who suggest that, are already aliens to the spirit of American democracy. Let them emigrate and try their lot under some foreign flag in which they have more confidence.

The fraudulent nature of this attempt is well shown by the record of votes on the passage of the Social Security Act. In addition to an overwhelming majority of Democrats in both Houses, seventy-seven Republican Representatives voted for it and only eighteen against it and fifteen Republican Senators voted for it and only five against it. Where does this last-minute drive of the Republican leadership leave these Republican Representatives and Senators who helped enact this law?

I am sure the vast majority of law-abiding businessmen who are not parties to this propaganda fully appreciate the extent of the threat to honest business contained in this coercion. I have expressed indignation at this form of campaigning and I am confident that the overwhelming majority of employers, workers and the general public share that indignation and will show it at the polls on Tuesday next.

Aside from this phase of it, I prefer to remember this campaign not as bitter but only as hard-fought. There should be no bitterness or hate where the sole thought is the welfare of the United States of America. No man can occupy the office of President without realizing that he is President of all the people.

It is because I have sought to think in terms of the whole Nation that I am confident that today, just as four years ago, the people want more than promises.

Our vision for the future contains more than promises.

This is our answer to those who, silent about their own plans, ask us to state our objectives.

Of course we will continue to seek to improve working conditions for the workers of America—to reduce hours over-long, to increase wages that spell starvation, to end the labor of children, to wipe out sweatshops. Of course we will continue every effort to end monopoly in business, to support collective bargaining, to stop unfair competition, to abolish dishonorable trade practices. For all these we have only just begun to fight.

Of course we will continue to work for cheaper electricity in the homes and on the farms of America, for better and cheaper transportation, for low interest rates, for

sounder home financing, for better banking, for the regulation of security issues, for reciprocal trade among nations, for the wiping out of slums. For all these we have only just begun to fight.

Of course we will continue our efforts in behalf of the farmers of America. With their continued cooperation we will do all in our power to end the piling up of huge surpluses which spelled ruinous prices for their crops. We will persist in successful action for better land use, for reforestation, for the conservation of water all the way from its source to the sea, for drought and flood control, for better marketing facilities for farm commodities, for a definite reduction of farm tenancy, for encouragement of farmer cooperatives, for crop insurance and a stable food supply.

For all these we have only just begun to fight.

Of course we will provide useful work for the needy unemployed; we prefer useful work to the pauperism of a dole.

Here and now I want to make myself clear about those who disparage their fellow citizens on the relief rolls. They say that those on relief are not merely jobless—that they are worthless. Their solution for the relief problem is to end relief—to purge the rolls by starvation. To use the language of the stock broker, our needy unemployed would be cared for when, as, and if some fairy godmother should happen on the scene.

You and I will continue to refuse to accept that estimate of our unemployed fellow Americans. Your Government is still on the same side of the street with the Good Samaritan and not with those who pass by on the other side.

Again—what of our objectives?

Of course we will continue our efforts for young men and women so that they may obtain an education and an opportunity to put it to use. Of course we will continue our help for the crippled, for the blind, for the mothers, our insurance for the unemployed, our security for the aged. Of course we will continue to protect the consumer against unnecessary price spreads, against the costs that are added by monopoly and speculation. We will continue our successful efforts to increase his purchasing power and to keep it constant.

For these things, too, and for a multitude of others like them, we have only just begun to fight.

All this—all these objectives—spell peace at home. All our actions, all our ideals, spell also peace with other nations.

Today there is war and rumor of war. We want none of it. But while we guard our shores against threats of war, we will continue to remove the causes of unrest and antagonism at home which might make our people easier victims to those for whom foreign war is profitable. You know well that those who stand to profit by war are not on our side in this campaign.

"Peace on earth, good will toward men"—democracy must cling to that message. For it is my deep conviction that democracy cannot live without that true religion which gives a nation a sense of justice and of moral purpose. Above our political forums, above our market places stand the altars of our faith—altars on which burn the fires of devotion that maintain all that is best in us and all that is best in our Nation.

We have need of that devotion today. It is that which makes it possible for government to persuade those who are mentally prepared to fight each other to go on instead, to work for and to sacrifice for each other. That is why we need to say with the Prophet: "What doth the Lord require of thee—but to do justly, to love mercy and to walk humbly with thy God." That is why the recovery we seek, the recovery we are winning, is more than economic. In it are included justice and love and humility, not for ourselves as individuals alone, but for our Nation. That is the road to peace.

SIGNIFICANCE

The term "Second New Deal" only entered the language after the publication of Basil Rauch's *History of the New Deal* in 1944. The nature of the shift between the First and the Second New Deal has been the subject of considerable controversy. Regardless, the national agencies created during this period set in place a new form of national government and created new expectations in the citizenry of what government could and should do.

The New Deal is not considered a success in economic terms, not because of what was done but because critics claim the programs did not go far enough. Roosevelt acted in a conservative manner when, they believe, much higher federal spending was needed to stimulate consumption to end the Great Depression. The economic crisis finally ended because of high demand for military spending during World War II. The New Deal did succeed, however, in setting basic standards for living in the United States and making the federal government a guarantor of those standards. Although many New Deal programs were abolished over time, programs such as Social Security continue to influence American life in the twenty-first century.

FURTHER RESOURCES

Books

Davis, Kenneth. *FDR: The New Deal Years, 1933–1937.* New York: Random House, 1986.

Louchheim, Katie. *The Making of the New Deal: The Insiders Speak.* Cambridge, MA: Harvard University Press, 1983.

McElvaine, Robert S. *The Great Depression: America, 1929–1941.* New York: Random House, 1986.

Romasco, Albert U. *The Politics of Recovery: Roosevelt's New Deal.* New York: Oxford University Press, 1983.

View of New Deal, a Work Relief Shack Town

Photograph

By: Margaret Bourke-White

Date: January 1, 1936

Source: Photo by Margaret Bourke-White/Time & Life Pictures/Getty Images.

About the Photographer: Margaret Bourke-White opened a studio in Cleveland in the late 1920s after graduating from Columbia University and joined *Fortune* as a staff photographer in 1929. She was recruited in 1936 by *Life* magazine and did much of her most notable work as a war correspondent during World War II and the Korean conflict. Bourke-White died from Parkinson's disease in August 1971.

INTRODUCTION

On "Black Tuesday," October 29, 1929, the U.S. stock market crashed, triggering the Great Depression—the worst economic collapse in modern history. Banks failed and many companies all over the country went out of business, causing more than fifteen million workers to lose their jobs.

Franklin Delano Roosevelt (1882–1945) was elected president of the United States in 1932, following a campaign centered around his pledge to restore the confidence of the American people and bring the United States out of the Depression. Soon after he assumed office in 1933—considered by many the worst year of the Great Depression—FDR formulated several economic and relief policies. During the first hundred days of his administration, Congress passed fifteen major pieces of legislation. These initiatives,

PRIMARY SOURCE

View of New Deal, a Work Relief Shack Town: An elevated view of New Deal, one of six towns around the federal work relief project at Fort Peck. Montana, in 1936. PHOTO BY MARGARET BOURKE-WHITE/TIME & LIFE PICTURES/GETTY IMAGES.

known collectively as the "New Deal," had three fundamental goals: relief for the deprived, economic recovery, and financial reform.

New Deal financial recovery programs included the Emergency Banking Relief Act, the Federal Deposit Insurance Corporation, the Home Owners Loan Corporation, and Farm Credit Administration. Prominent initiatives to provide relief for the millions of unemployed were the Federal Emergency Relief Administration (FERA), the Civilian Conservation Corps (CCC), and the Tennessee Valley Authority (TVA). The New Deal also developed highly controversial industrial programs such as the National Recovery Administration (NRA), and farm production control programs, such as the Agricultural Adjustment Administration (AAA). These were, however, invalidated after being declared unconstitutional.

The New Deal also spawned several economic programs, including the Securities and Exchange Commission (SEC) and the Federal Housing Administration (FHA). The Public Works Administration (PWA) was part of the National Industrial Recovery Act of 1933; its purpose was to provide employment in various public works projects. Although the PWA did not significantly improve the economy or lessen unemployment, between July 1933 and March 1939 it funded more than $6 billion to build more than 34,000 projects, including airports, electricity-generating dams, aircraft carriers, seventy percent of new schools and one-third of the hospitals built during that time, tunnels, and highways—the Lincoln Tunnel between New York City and New Jersey, and the Key West Highway in Florida being the most prominent.

Carrie's Apartments, a typical example of the ramshackle housing available in the shack towns around the Fort Peck relief project in 1936. PHOTO BY MARGARET BOURKE-WHITE/TIME & LIFE PICTURES.

Workers from all over the country who came to work on PWA projects stayed in makeshift communities popularly known as shack towns or boomtowns. The primary source is a photograph of one such shack town in Fort Peck, Montana, where the Fort Peck Dam project was undertaken by the PWA.

■ PRIMARY SOURCE

VIEW OF NEW DEAL, A WORK RELIEF SHACK TOWN

See primary source image.

SIGNIFICANCE

Franklin Roosevelt's very first directive as president was to declare a four-day bank holiday, during which congress drafted the Emergency Banking Bill of 1933, giving the federal government authority over banks. This move stabilized the banking system and restored the public's faith in the industry.

Other New Deal initiatives, such as those mentioned above, helped improve the economy. Although most programs yielded immediate results, a few were criticized and subsequently discontinued. One such program was the National Recovery Administration (NRA), of which the PWA was a part. Established on June 16, 1933, the NRA set a minimum wages and work hours for nonunion workers and allowed trade associations to engage in collective bargaining. The NRA was declared unconstitutional by the Supreme Court in 1935. For its part, the PWA was criticized because its workers were housed in low-quality shack towns.

Critics state that New Deal programs did not strengthen the American economy. They point out that the country's 1928 gross national product (in simple terms, total output of the economy) was $100 billion; it had recovered only to $85 billion by 1939, toward the end of the New Deal programs. Similarly, the number of unemployed in 1929 was 2.6 million; by 1940 it was to 8 million. However, the economy was at its peak in 1928 and 1929. New Deal proponents maintain that comparison should begin with the New Deal in 1933, when the GNP was $55 billion and 15 million were unemployed.

Moreover, advocates of the New Deal highlight significant gains made by some of the programs. For instance, between 1935 and 1943 the PWA provided nearly 8 million jobs at a cost of more than $11 billion. In addition, it sponsored the New Deal Cultural Programs, including the Federal Theater Project, Federal Art Project, and Federal Writers' Project. The Social Security Act provided a pension system for senior citizens. The Tennessee Valley Authority (TVA) and the Bonneville Power Authority brought electricity and flood control to the Tennessee and Columbia River Valleys—some of the worst affected regions during the Depression. These also established a permanent federal presence in the generation of electrical power and offered subsidized electricity to farmers in the region.

Nevertheless, criticism of New Deal programs continued, especially after a second wave of legislative reforms in 1935. In 1937, Roosevelt introduced a plan that would have granted him the right to appoint additional justices to the Supreme Court. Opponents argued that such policies were intended to pack the court with friendly judges and overturn previous decisions that had declared New Deal programs unconstitutional. The bill did not get through Congress.

The Great Depression was followed by a recession in 1937, and unemployment rose again. By late 1938, the New Deal had lost momentum both politically and economically. Before the U.S. economy fully recovered from the recession, the country entered World War II, when increased wartime spending and production made most programs unnecessary.

Experts assert that although the New Deal did not fundamentally turn around the U.S. economy, it addressed key issues such as unemployment, the banking system, and the stock market. Many New Deal programs, like Social Security, have become an accepted part of American life.

FURTHER RESOURCES

Books

Badger, Anthony J. *The New Deal: The Depression Years, 1933–1940*. Chicago: Ivan R. Dee, 2002.

Web sites

American Heritage Center, Inc. "About FDR." <http://www.fdrheritage.org/fdrbio.htm> (accessed May 20, 2006).

Busch, Andrew E. *Ashbrook Center for Public Affairs at Ashland University*. "The New Deal Comes to a Screeching Halt in 1938." <http://www.ashbrook.org/publicat/oped/busch/06/1938.html> (accessed May 20, 2006).

Eleanor Roosevelt National Historic Site. "Public Works Administration." <http://www.nps.gov/elro/glossary/pwa.htm> (accessed May 20, 2006).

Library of Congress. "Great Depression and World War II, 1929–1945." February 2, 2004 <http://memory.loc.gov/learn/features/timeline/depwwii/newdeal/newdeal.html> (accessed May 20, 2006).

Maryland Center for Civic Education. "The Stock Market Crash and the Great Depression, 1929–1941." <http://www.marylandciviceducation.org/lessons/depression.htm> (accessed May 20, 2006).

Executive Order 8099— Administration of Benefits Provided by Act of Congress

Government Record

By: United States Congress

Date: April 3, 1939

Source:

About the Author: Executive orders are directives with the force of law, usually written by the president of the United States. On some occasions they are mandated by an act of Congress. This form of governing has been used since 1789 and the first American presidency.

INTRODUCTION

Throughout much of its history, the United States military has been providing for its soldiers' welfare even after they retire from service. The Veterans Affairs Administration administers pensions, medical benefits, and other entitlements for military veterans.

There are more than twenty-five million veterans living in the United States. While special provisions are offered to soldiers injured in battle or to relatives of those killed in action, all veterans, whether or not they have entered into combat can benefit from enti-

U.S. Army Sergeant Chase Johnson, center, talks with a benefit manager on December 7, 2005 during the annual veterans benefits expo in Savannah, Georgia. AP IMAGES.

tlements offered by the Veterans Affairs Administration—including a national network of hospitals, commonly referred to as VA hospitals, that cater to veterans and their families. Veterans are also entitled to burial in military cemeteries. The military code of ethics is committed to the ideal that even after servicemen or -women return home after fulfilling their military service, they will not be forgotten.

Military veterans can also socialize in communities and organizations that are open exclusively to them. Most common is the Veterans of Foreign Wars (VFW), a prominent civic presence in many American cities known for its social activism and memorial efforts on behalf of fallen soldiers.

Veterans' programs have been criticized by those who believe that other, poorer segments of society should be funded instead and supported by those who believe that soldiers' sacrifice entitles them to these benefits. Congress has traditionally granted heavy financial support to veterans, and annual government

spending on the various veteran-related programs has come to exceed $60 billion.

■ PRIMARY SOURCE

Executive Order 8099—Administration of benefits provided by act of Congress approved April 3, 1939

WHEREAS section 1 of the act of August 30, 1935, c. 830, 49 Stat. 1028, as amended by section 5 of the act entitled "An Act to provide more effectively for the national defense by carrying out the recommendations of the President in his message of January 12, 1939, to the Congress," approved April 3, 1939 (Pub., No. 18, 76th Congress), provides, in part, as follows:

"* * * That all officers, warrant officers, and enlisted men of the Army of the United States, other than the officers and enlisted men of the Regular Army, if called or ordered into the active military service by the Federal Government for extended military service in excess of thirty days, and who suffer disability or death in line of duty from disease or injury while so employed shall be deemed to have been in the active military service during such period and shall be in all respects entitled to receive the same pensions, compensation, retirement pay, and hospital benefits as are now or may hereafter be provided by law or regulation for officers and enlisted men of corresponding grades and length of service of the Regular Army."

WHEREAS the said act is silent as to what agency shall administer the benefits provided thereby; and

WHEREAS it is deemed appropriate and desirable that such administration be placed in the Veterans' Administration:

NOW, THEREFORE, by virtue of the authority vested in me as President of the United States, and by the act of July 3, 1930, c. 863, 46 Stat. 1016, the duties, powers, and functions incident to the administration and payment of the benefits provided by the statute as above set out are hereby vested in the Veterans' Administration:

Provided, That in the administration of the retirement-pay provisions of the said statute, the determination of all questions of eligibility for the benefits thereof, including all questions of law and fact relating to such eligibility, shall be made by the Secretary of War, or by someone designated by him in the War Department, in the manner, and in accordance with the standards, provided by law, or regulations for Regular Army personnel:

Provided further, That the administration of the provisions of the act of December 17, 1919 (40 Stat. 367, as amended) as to persons to whom such provisions are extended by the act of December 10, 1941, entitled 'An act to extend the six months' death gratuity benefits, now paid only to dependents of officers and enlisted men of the Regular Army, to dependents of all officers, warrant officers, and enlisted men of the Army of the United States who die in line of duty while in active military service of the United States' (Public Law 329, 77th Congress), shall be vested in the Secretary of War or in such person or persons as may be designated by him in the War Department.

SIGNIFICANCE

This executive order was passed during one of the longest peacetime periods in United States history, yet it was enacted only months before the outbreak of World War II. While American military involvement would not occur for nearly two years, this document, signed by President Franklin Roosevelt, seems to foreshadow the massive callup of soldiers required after December 1941.

Prior to this order, the law limited the availability of many veterans' benefits to officers and enlisted men of the regular army—the military force that exists in peace time—and excluded those drafted into wartime service. By expanding the provision of benefits to all soldiers, the reach and significance of the Veterans Administrations was expanded greatly.

In subsequent decades, as a result of other congressional allocations to increase benefits, many veterans have come to depend on the VA and its many services. Large numbers of soldiers went home after military services to new challenges and economic hardship. The emotional and physical traumas they experienced during wartime often lingered after their discharge from the service. The Veterans Administration helped reacclimatize them into society.

This order reflects the federal governments' recognition of the need to assist military veterans more heavily than other citizens by supporting those who served in the armed forces—whether by choice or through the draft—even after their service is completed. Today the federal government invests billions of dollars in veterans benefits.

FURTHER RESOURCES

Web sites

Veterans of Foreign Wars (VFW). <http://www.vfw.org/> (accessed May 21, 2006).

United States Department of Veterans Affairs. May 12, 2006. <http://www.va.gov> (accessed May 21, 2006).

Tennessee Valley Authority

Photograph

By: Anonymous

Date: c. 1940

Source: AP Images.

About the Photographer: This photograph was taken by a contributor to the Associated Press, a worldwide news agency based in New York.

INTRODUCTION

The Tennessee Valley Authority (TVA) became one of the most successful New Deal programs proposed by President Franklin D. Roosevelt. Created in 1933, it transformed the Tennessee River so that the people in the area could reap social and economic benefits. It is best known for providing universal electrification to the least electrified region of the country.

Unlike most New Deal legislation, the TVA had originated decades earlier. In 1916, Congress gave President Woodrow Wilson authority to select a site for a factory to produce nitrates for explosives. Wilson decided to build a dam at Muscle Shoals, Alabama to provide electricity for the factory. In 1919, Senator George W. Norris of Nebraska called for more dams to provide cheap electric power to develop the entire Tennessee Valley. Eight times between 1921 and 1933, Norris introduced legislation to create a public corporation at Muscle Shoals but Republican Presidents Calvin Coolidge and Herbert Hoover vetoed the bills. In January 1933, the newly-elected Roosevelt endorsed Norris's proposal as a means to recover from the Great Depression. He signed the TVA into law on May 18, 1933.

The authority given to the TVA expanded far beyond the provision of electricity. The agency received a mandate to improve river navigation, control floods, stop soil erosion, protect forests, eliminate marginal lands from agricultural use, bring industries into the region, and improve the public welfare. To do all of this, the TVA had unprecedented power to alter the valley's environment.

PRIMARY SOURCE

TENNESSEE VALLEY AUTHORITY

See primary source image.

Tennessee Valley Authority: In this undated photo, electric appliances are delivered to a home in the rural Tennessee Valley after electricty was brought to the area in the 1940s. When Tennessee Valley Authority (TVA) was created in 1933, only three in ten residents of the region had electricity. AP IMAGES.

SIGNIFICANCE

A unique creation, the TVA harnessed human and natural resources to produce social and economic development. It bears much responsibility for the prosperity enjoyed by residents of the Tennessee Valley for the remainder of the twentieth century. In 1933, only ten percent of valley farms had electricity. By 1943, seventy-five percent of valley farms had power. The electricity led to the growth of manufacturing plants in the area, eventually making the Tennessee Valley one of the most industrialized parts of the South.

Despite its success, the TVA model never reached other economically depressed sections of the nation. Efforts to establish authorities in the Arkansas and Missouri river basins were thwarted by Roosevelt's

waning support, private utility resistance, and state fears of increased federal power. However, the TVA did serve as a model for the creation in 1935 of the Rural Electrification Administration. It was also important in inspiring the creation of smaller authorities, such as the Colorado River Authority, which provides power, flood control, and agricultural support to the citizens of central Texas.

In the 1970s, the huge costs of the TVA led the agency to raise its rates. By the 1980s, the TVA's wholesale rates were little different from those of other southern utilities. Many critics also charged that the TVA had abandoned its traditional role of protecting the welfare of the people in the valley. In its determination to provide power, the TVA also ran afoul of state and federal environmental regulations. Many of

Construction at the site of the Fontana Dam on the Little Tennessee River in western North Carolina, during the early 1940s. The dam is a Tennessee Valley Authority project. AP IMAGES.

its contractual obligations led to relationships with southern coal companies that were despoiling the environment. It also had a poor safety record in the operation of its nuclear power generating facilities. By the millennium, the TVA no longer seemed so marvelous.

FURTHER RESOURCES
Books

Chandler, William U. *The Myth of the TVA: Conservation and Development in the Tennessee Valley, 1933–83.* Cambridge, Mass.: Bellinger Publishing, 1984.

Colignon, Richard. *Power Plays: Critical Events in the Institutionalization of the TVA.* Albany, N.Y.: State University of New York Press, 1997.

TVA: Fifty Years of Grassroots Bureaucracy, edited by Erwin Hargrove and Paul Conklin. Urbana, Ill.: University of Illinois Press, 1983.

Better Housing

The Solution to Infant Mortality in the Slums

Photograph

By: Anthony Velonis

Date: 1940

Source: © Corbis.

About the Artist: Anthony Velonis (1911–1997) was a master silkscreen printer and painter who created a number of posters for the Federal Art Project branch of the WPA during the Depression. This photograph is part of the collection of the Corbis Corporation, headquartered in Seattle, with a worldwide archive of over seventy million images.

PRIMARY SOURCE

Better Housing: The Solution to Infant Mortality in the Slums: A New York City Housing Authority poster advocating planned communities over tenement housing, from 1940. © CORBIS.

INTRODUCTION

The Works Projects Administration (WPA) was a Depression-era government program created by President Franklin Delano Roosevelt in 1935 and headed up by Harry L. Hopkins. The WPA incorporated a broad extension of Herbert Hoover's Emergency Relief and Construction Act of 1932 and Roosevelt's 1933 Federal Emergency Relief Act programs. The project was designed to create work and income for the unemployed—particularly unskilled blue collar workers and artists, musicians, and writers. Most projects were in construction, building, or repairing necessary structures across the country, such as highways, airports, sewers, public libraries, and recreational areas. Projects in the arts included theater productions, concerts, the painting of murals, and the Federal Writers Project. WPA employment was designed to provide relief until the economy recovered, and at its highest level, in November 1938, employed 3.3 million workers. In families with more than one person of working age, only one of them could work for the WPA, the idea being to provide some relief to as many

households as possible. Workers' pay was based on their skills, region of the country, and how urban the area was, making anywhere from nineteen to ninety-four dollars per month for up to thirty hours of work per week. Although the president initiated the program, Congress financed it. Once World War II began, and unemployment dropped significantly due to wartime projects, the WPA was no longer necessary, and Congress ended it in 1943.

■ PRIMARY SOURCE

BETTER HOUSING: THE SOLUTION TO INFANT MORTALITY IN THE SLUMS

See primary source image.

SIGNIFICANCE

A significant part of the WPA was the design and creation of a series of posters that had the twofold purpose of providing work for artists during the Depres-

A woman walks towards a slum housing community in Detroit's near East Side in 1969. At the time, infant mortality in the area was 69 out of 1000 births, more than three times the national average. © BETTMANN/CORBIS.

sion and of advertising the many different government-sponsored programs and projects available at the time, ranging from theatrical productions to educational programs to community activities and health and safety programs. The posters were first done by hand, then created as silk screens, woodcuts, or lithographs, and sometimes were signed by the artist. Anthony Velonis perfected the mass production of the posters in 1936. Predating the WPA by a year, the New York Mayor's Poster Project was part of the Civil Works Administration and served as an inspiration for the national version of the program.

The Depression era and the height of the WPA's productivity coincided with a movement to change the state of housing in the United States, particularly in large cities such as New York. It began with the movement to cease groundless evictions, which became particularly important as unemployment numbers rose and people despaired of making ends meet. After that, there were protests in favor of public housing and wartime rent control and for better conditions in what was essentially slum housing. The first public housing projects were built, advertised by the WPA as a safer, cleaner, healthier option that would, among other things, help lessen the high infant mortality rate of the day. Tenant organizations also began to grow in number and power. Under left-wing guidance, particularly that of the Communist party, tenants drifted away from mass protests and toward organizations of professional advocates. Additionally, the building of new public housing provided much-needed employment for both skilled and unskilled workers.

New Deal relief programs contributed to the overall decline in infant mortality during the latter part of the Depression. At the start of the 1930s, unemployment was over twenty percent and, even after the WPA and other programs were implemented, never dipped below ten percent until the economy began to recover. Logically, a decline in income leads to increases in poverty, and food, medical care, and housing become scarcer, leading to a greater risk of disease and even death, particularly for the very young and the elderly. Poor nutrition during pregnancy also leads to an increased number of miscarriages, stillbirths, and infants born prematurely or without the strength to survive. As social welfare programs were expanded and new ones introduced, the infant mortality rate improved. While the number of deaths still varied widely depending on the geographical region of the country, infant mortality lessened noticeably between the early 1930s and the implementation of the New Deal programs, such as the WPA. It is possible that, since the infant mortality rate was already dropping prior to the Depression, the New Deal programs merely assisted it in resuming its downward trend in the wake of the most serious Depression years, but it is equally possible that the New Deal programs unto themselves were useful in fighting back the effects of poor housing and nutrition.

FURTHER RESOURCES
Books

Denoon, Christopher. *Posters of the WPA*. University of Washington Press, 1987.

Kirst, Sean. *Popular Relief: The WPA Years*. City Newspaper, 1985.

Macmahon, Arthur Whittier, Millett, John David, and Ogden, Gladys. *The Administration of Federal Work Relief (FDR and the Era of the New Deal)*. Da Capo Press, 1971.

Web sites

Environmental Protection Agency. "Indicator: Infant Mortality." <http://www.epa.gov/ncea/ROEIndicators/pdfs/INFANTMORTALITY_FINAL.pdf> (accessed May 27, 2006).

Fishback, Price V., Michael R. Haines, and Shawn Kantor "Births, Deaths, and New Deal Relief During the Great Depression." *Princeton University*. September 2005. <https://www.wws.princeton.edu/chw/papers/haines_citypanel29.pdf> (accessed May 27, 2006).

Naison, Mark. "From Eviction Resistance to Rent Control Tenant Activism in the Great Depression." *Tenant Net: The Tenant Movement in New York City, 1904–984*. <http://www.tenant.net/Community/history/hist03a.html> (accessed May 27, 2006).

The Depression Breadline

Photograph

By: James P. Blair

Date: May 3, 1997

Source: © James P. Blair/Corbis.

About the Photographer: James P. Blair was born in Philadelphia in 1931. He has worked for Time-Life and was a staff photographer for *National Geographic* from 1962 to 1994. This photograph is part of the collection of the Corbis Corporation's worldwide archive of over seventy million images.

PRIMARY SOURCE

The Great Depression Breadline: A detail from George Segal's piece "The Depression Breadline." © JAMES P. BLAIR/COR-BIS.

INTRODUCTION

On October 29, 1929, after a month of dramatic decline, the United States stock exchange crashed. The market plummeted to nearly half of its earlier market value, shattering business confidence, stagnating U.S. investment abroad, halting the flow of trade, and plunging many nations into a global economic depression. In the United States, the era became known as the Great Depression, and the crisis affected almost every citizen's life.

During the next three years, stock prices in the United States continued to fall. By late 1932, they had dropped to a mere twenty percent of their 1929 pre-crash value. Apart from ruining hundreds of thousands of individual investors, the crash broke the backs of many financial institutions. By 1933, 11,000 of the United States' 25,000 banks had failed. Industry plummeted and unemployment rose dramatically. Unemployment rose to nearly fifteen million workers, a staggering twenty-five to thirty percent of the U.S.

work force. Breadlines became a common sight in many cities. Hundreds of thousands roamed the country as migrant workers in search of food, work and shelter. The 1920s had been dubbed the "roaring"decade, but after the jazz age, came the era of the blues, best typified by the refrain of a popular Depression-era song, "Brother, can you spare a dime?"

Each economic depression that hit the United States from the early nineteenth century to the 1930s was worse than the one that preceded it. As America urbanized and industrialized, more of its population became susceptible to the ever-changing market economy. People became dependent on their factory jobs and their employers, rather than the land they had once tilled.

The 1893 panic had marked America's worst economic crisis of the nineteenth century. Between 1892 and 1894, real income dropped shaprly, but the financial crisis was relatively short lived. The Great

Depression was more sustained. America was still feeling the Great Depression's effects at the decade's end.

PRIMARY SOURCE

THE DEPRESSION BREADLINE

See primary source image.

SIGNIFICANCE

President Herbert Hoover was widely criticized for the Great Depression, largely because of his disastrous response to the crisis that enveloped America. The economic catastrophe was dubbed by some contemporaries as the Hoover Depression. His problem was that he was non-interventionist by conviction, even when the prevailing conditions demanded results without concern for method. Hoover was not opposed to helping Depression victims, but what he sought was a vast voluntary effort as opposed to a government-led relief program. He called for a vast charitable effort from those who still had money; a plea that met a sub-

stantial response. In 1932, private giving reached a record level.

However, this response was not enough to correct America's ills. Hoover was obdurately and ideologically opposed to federal intervention, believing unemployment benefit would "Lower wages toward the bare subsistence level and endow the slackers." He persistently rejected federal relief responses, even when poverty increased, believing that it would destroy people's self-reliance and "spiritual responses."

The breadlines and soup kitchens that have come to symbolize the Depression era, particularly the early and most desperate years, were largely funded by private individuals rather than government agencies. Hoover's initiatives, such as the President's Organization for Unemployment Relief (POUR), centered on advertisement campaigns to encourage private giving and create a sense of public optimism. His public outpourings betrayed a man who had not come to grips with the situation his country was facing. "What this country needs is a good big laugh," he said in early 1931. "There seems to be a condition of hysteria. If

Women receiving food from priests of the New Hope Mission in New York during the 1930s. © BETTMANN/CORBIS.

someone could get a good joke every ten days, I think our troubles would be over."

Hoover was defeated in the 1932 Presidential election by Franklin D Roosevelt, who promised a non-ideological and pragmatic approach to the problems facing America. This would manifest itself as a radical economic program to revitalize the American economy and pull its people out of the depression mire. This so-called 'New Deal'—which took on several guises—was around what he termed the "three r's": relief, recovery and reform.

The relief tenet of the New Deal is a misnomer, implying that it was primarily concerned with the provision soup kitchens and dole money. This part of the New Deal was still based around principles of self-help, but by directly intervening in the market economy it provided openings for the destitute to work and so feed themselves and their families. Large public works schemes provided employment and injected money into the wider economy; a Resettlement Administration relocated people from the most des-perate areas to parts of the country where they could find work.

Whether the New Deal or the onset of World War II pulled America out of the Great Depression is still a matter of historical debate. However, the New Deal left a lasting impression on the American political landscape, not so much for the social policy aspects of it—which have largely been overstated—but because it showed that America's historic aversion to government intervention was not as deep-lying as previously thought. The New Deal's great significance for American social policy came not with the establishment of a limited social security program in 1935, but in investing the confidence in government welfare and relief programs.

FURTHER RESOURCES
Books
Galbraith, J.K. *The Great Crash*. Boston: Houghton Mifflin, 1955.

McElvaine, Robert S. *The Great Depression: America 1929–1941*. New York: Times Books, 1993.

World War II and Post-war Social Policy

Depression-era social policies ended with the entry of the United States into World War II in 1941. Unemployment dropped sharply as able men entered military service. War industry—from the making of uniforms to the building of bombers—provided increased employment opportunities for people on the homefront.

Wartime social policy on the homefront encouraged both work and personal sacrifice to the war effort. Many women, who had been largely left out of New Deal policies, left the home to fill factory and defense jobs. Executive Order 8022 prohibited employers in key industries from discriminating against African Americans when hiring workers. Despite the increased opportunity for employment, women and minorities received less pay than their white male peers. Workers in war and defense industries were barred from striking. In the home, conservation efforts and rationing were part of everyday life.

While social policy made some strides to recognize the rights of women and minorities, one particular group faced increasing discrimination during the war years. Executive Order 9066 ordered the relocation of Japanese immigrants and Japanese American citizens to internment camps. Many Japanese Americans lost their personal property, including homes and businesses. The policy led to widespread discrimination of Japanese Americans even after the war and internment ended, and internees received no apology or compensation for the material losses for decades.

When the war ended, social policy shifted its focus from supplying the war effort to caring for soldiers returning home. The U.S. federal government pro-vided returning soldiers with social and economic benefits. Returning soldiers were offered preference in employment, displacing many of the women and minorities who had worked during the war. To meet a rapidly increasing demand for housing, the government sponsored low-priced suburban housing developments and backed low-interest loans for home-buying veterans. The G.I. Bill provided veterans with funding for college education or vocational training. In his 1949 State of the Union Address, President Harry S. Truman offered his "Fair Deal," a new plan for post-war economic and social policy.

War era policies provided the catalyst for two of the greatest movements in the twentieth century, modern feminist and civil rights movements. Many women who lost their jobs to men returning from war returned to working in the home. However, some corporate jobs—such as secretarial and retail work—became largely staffed by women in the post-war years. This chapter ends with the passage of the Equal Pay Act of 1963, an important victory for women's rights in the workplace.

The battle to end segregation fueled the civil rights movement in the 1950s and early 1960s. Though the Supreme Court of the United States declared segregation of schools unconstitutional in 1954 (see, *Brown v. Board of Education*) desegregation cases were still heard by the court a decade later. While some of the most famous acts of the civil rights movement occurred during this period, federal social policy did not fully recognize the cause of civil rights until President Lyndon B. Johnson unveiled the Great Society in 1964.

Executive Order 8802

Prohibiting Employment Discrimination in the Defense Industry

Executive order

By: President Franklin D. Roosevelt

Date: June 25, 1941

Source: *Equal Employment Opportunity Commission.* "Executive Order 8802—Reaffirming Policy of Full Participation in the Defense Program by All Persons, Regardless of Race, Creed, Color, or National Origin, and Directing Certain Action in Furtherance of Said Policy." <http://www.eeoc.gov/abouteeoc/35th/thelaw/eo-8802.html> (accessed May 31, 2006).

About the Author: Franklin Roosevelt (1882–1945) was the thirty-second president of the United States, serving from 1933–1945. Elected during the Great Depression, he led the United States until just prior to the conclusion of World War II.

INTRODUCTION

As the United States' entry into World War II began to appear inevitable, President Franklin Roosevelt faced a looming political crisis in the United States. With the American workplace still segregated by race, African Americans found themselves unable to secure many of the jobs in the rapidly expanding defense industry. Recognizing the pressure President Roosevelt faced to keep peace at home in the face of unrest abroad, civil rights activists crafted a plan to take advantage of the president's precarious position.

Philip Randolph, president of a large minority labor union, met with other activists to develop a strategy. The result was simple but ultimately effective: Randolph would ask President Roosevelt to address the problems of workplace equity in the defense industry. If there was no response, Randolph

On November 5, 1941, construction workers make wooden concrete forms during the construction of the Pentagon in Arlington, Virgnia. AP IMAGES.

and his colleagues would organize a massive protest march in Washington, D.C. The threat of 250,000 African American protestors in the streets of the capital succeeded in bringing Roosevelt to the bargaining table, and after several rounds of discussion between Randolph and Roosevelt's representatives, a deal was reached.

On June 25, 1941, President Roosevelt signed Executive Order 8802, banning racial discrimination in any facility with federal defense contracts and directing government agencies to include non-discrimination clauses in all future contracts. The order also specified that any defense-related training programs administered by the federal government were to be conducted without regard to race. Finally, the act created the Fair Employment Practices Committee (FEPC), which was responsible for investigating alleged violations and specifying penalties for firms found to be in violation.

■ PRIMARY SOURCE

Whereas it is the policy of the United States to encourage full participation in the national defense program by all citizens of the United States, regardless of race, creed, color, or national origin, in the firm belief that the democratic way of life within the Nation can be defended successfully only with the help and support of all groups within its borders; and

Whereas there is evidence that available and needed workers have been barred from employment in industries engaged in defense production solely because of considerations of race, creed, color, or national origin, to the detriment of workers' morale and of national unity:

Now, therefore, by virtue of the authority vested in me by the Constitution and the statutes, and as a prerequisite to the successful conduct of our national defense production effort, I do hereby reaffirm the policy of the United States that there shall be no discrimination in the employment of workers in defense industries or government because of race, creed, color, or national origin, and I do hereby declare that it is the duty of employers and of labor organizations, in furtherance of said policy and of this order, to provide for the full and equitable participation of all workers in defense industries, without discrimination because of race, creed, color, or national origin;

And it is hereby ordered as follows:

1. All departments and agencies of the Government of the United States concerned with vocational and training programs for defense production shall take special measures appropriate to assure that such programs are administered without discrimination because of race, creed, color, or national origin;

2. All contracting agencies of the Government of the United States shall include in all defense contracts hereafter negotiated by them a provision obligating the contractor not to discriminate against any worker because of race, creed, color, or national origin;

3. There is established in the Office of Production Management a Committee on Fair Employment Practice, which shall consist of a chairman and four other members to be appointed by the President. The Chairman and members of the Committee shall serve as such without compensation but shall be entitled to actual and necessary transportation, subsistence and other expenses incidental to performance of their duties. The Committee shall receive and investigate complaints of discrimination in violation of the provisions of this order and shall take appropriate steps to redress grievances which it finds to be valid. The Committee shall also recommend to the several departments and agencies of the Government of the United States and to the President all measures which may be deemed by it necessary or proper to effectuate the provisions of this order.

■ SIGNIFICANCE

Executive Order 8802 was brief and to the point: defense contractors could no longer use race as a criterion for hiring and promotion, and those who did would face potential sanctions and loss of federal contracts. In response, the march on the capital was called off, and African American workers anticipated fuller employment options in the future.

Although the passage of Executive Order 8802 was expected to rapidly open the defense industry to minority applicants, the passage of the legislation had little immediate effect. Some contractors simply ignored the new rule, preferring to take their chances with the lightly staffed enforcement agency, the part-time staff of which was located entirely in Washington, D.C. Other firms responded by interviewing and hiring African Americans, but only for custodial positions and other menial jobs. In the short term, the new law had little impact.

Despite Roosevelt's initial reluctance to issue Executive Order 8802, he was unwilling for defense contractors to simply ignore it. In response to their foot-dragging, Roosevelt strengthened the FEPC in 1943 by significantly raising its enforcement budget and replacing its part-time Washington staff with a full-time force spread throughout the nation. The results remained mixed. By the end of World War II, African American employment in the defense industry had more than doubled, from three percent to eight percent; however, these numbers belied the fact that many of the new jobs were still entry-level and unskilled positions.

Because of its status as an executive order, Roosevelt's nondiscrimination policy had a limited lifespan, and after the end of World War II, the act's future was unclear. Congress and the Truman administration discussed how to proceed with the law, but no agreement was reached on extending the act or making it permanent. Without action, the FEPC expired in 1946.

President Truman would later propose a civil rights package that included a permanent FEPC; this plan, however, was blocked by conservatives in Congress. A permanent FEPC was approved by the House in 1950, but it was filibustered by southern senators and died. Despite these setbacks, workplace discrimination continued to diminish, albeit slowly. In 1948, President Truman issued Executive Order 9981, ordering the elimination of racial discrimination in the military; a companion order prescribed the same step for other federal employees. Six years later, in 1954, the last all-black military unit was disbanded.

When viewed alone, Executive Order 8802 had little immediate impact on discrimination in America. But when viewed as one of hundreds of laws that gradually dismantled a culture steeped in discrimination, the policy was a significant step in a long national journey from discrimination toward equality.

FURTHER RESOURCES

Books

Homan, Lynn M. and Thomas Reilly. *Black Knights: The Story of the Tuskegee Airmen*. Gretna, La.: Pelican Publishing, 2001.

Kennedy, David M. *Freedom from Fear: The American People in Depression and War*. New York: Oxford University Press, 1999.

Mayer, Kenneth. *With the Stroke of a Pen: Executive Orders and Presidential Power*. Princeton, N.J.: Princeton University Press, 2002.

Periodicals

Newby, John L., II. "The Fight for the Right to Fight and the Forgotten Negro Protest Movement: The History of Executive Order 9981 and Its Effect upon Brown v. Board of Education and Beyond." *Texas Journal on Civil Liberties & Civil Rights* 10 (2004): 83–110.

Percy, William Alexander. "Jim Crow and Uncle Sam: The Tuskegee Flying Units and the U.S. Army Air Forces in Europe during World War II." *Journal of Military History* 67 (2003): 773–810.

Web sites

Eleanor Roosevelt National Historic Site. "Fair Employment Practices Committee." <http://www.nps.gov/elro/glossary/fepc.htm> (accessed May 26, 2006).

PBS Online NewsHour. "Divisions in the Divisions." November 29, 1999 <http://www.pbs.org/newshour/bb/military/july-dec99/race_military_11-29.html> (accessed May 31, 2006).

U.S. Army: Redstone Arsenal, AL. "History of Black Military Service." <http://www.redstone.army.mil/history/integrate/history.htm> (accessed May 27, 2006).

On the Home Front

Speech

By: Franklin D. Roosevelt

Date: October 12, 1942

Source: Roosevelt, Franklin D. "On the Home Front." Fireside chat delivered on October 12, 1942. *Miller Center of Public Affairs*. <http://millercenter.virginia.edu/scripps/diglibrary/prezspeeches/roosevelt/fdr_1942_1012.html> (accessed May 30, 2006).

About the Author: Franklin D. Roosevelt (1882–1945) served as the thirty-second president of the United States. He tackled the Great Depression of the 1930s and led the nation through World War II. He was the only U.S. president to be re-elected three times.

INTRODUCTION

On December 7, 1941, the Japanese attacked the U.S. Pacific fleet at Pearl Harbor in Hawaii. The surprise assault was a great tactical victory. Most of the fleet was sunk or disabled. Unfortunately for the Japanese, Pearl Harbor also ended the long debate between American isolationists and interventionists. Furious Americans immediately began mobilizing all of the might of one of the world's greatest industrial powers to defeat Japan and its allies, Germany and Italy. Overnight, Franklin D. Roosevelt shifted from fighting the Great Depression to trying to win World War II.

Homefront sacrifices ultimately made American victory possible. People at home had a range of sponsored activities that linked them to those on the battlefields and to one another in a common cause. An American too young, too old, or too frail to fight

by fifty percent over the course of the war, with the numbers of women in manufacturing rising by 110 percent. As Roosevelt noted, the American people were united as never before and willing to do whatever was required to achieve victory and save the world for democracy.

President Franklin D. Roosevelt speaking from the observation platform of his train in Montana, 1934. © CORBIS.

could still help beat Hitler of Germany, Mussolini of Italy, and Tojo of Japan. Rationing programs that began with rubber and gasoline soon spread to greatly desired foods, including meats, coffee, and butter. Scrap drives, waste fat collections, blackouts, and numerous Red Cross activities were also part of day-to-day wartime life, serving as constant reminders of the war. The new American motto became "Use it up, wear it out, make do, or do without."

One of the most dramatic changes in wartime society involved changes in the labor force. Men aged eighteen to forty-five were subject to the draft, with very few exceptions. As a result, most healthy young men found themselves in the military. Over the course of the conflict, 15 million men and more than 200,000 women served in the armed forces. Roosevelt had begun his administration in 1933 with the problem of finding jobs for people. During WWII, he had to find people for jobs. African Americans left the South in droves for abundant jobs at high wages in urban areas of the West, Midwest, and North. For the first time, women were encouraged to enter the work force and take jobs that had previously been reserved only for men. The number of women in the workforce jumped

PRIMARY SOURCE

My fellow Americans:

As you know, I have recently come back from a trip of inspection of camps and training stations and war factories.

The main thing that I observed on this trip is not exactly news. It is the plain fact that the American people are united as never before in their determination to do a job and to do it well.

This whole nation of one hundred and thirty million free men, women and children is becoming one great fighting force. Some of us are soldiers or sailors, some of us are civilians. Some of us are fighting the war in airplanes five miles above the continent of Europe or the islands of the Pacific—and some of us are fighting it in mines deep down in the earth of Pennsylvania or Montana. A few of us are decorated with medals for heroic achievement, but all of us can have that deep and permanent inner satisfaction that comes from doing the best we know how—each of us playing an honorable part in the great struggle to save our democratic civilization.

Whatever our individual circumstances or opportunities—we are all in it, and our spirit is good, and we Americans and our allies are going to win—and do not let anyone tell you anything different.

…

With every passing week the war increases in scope and intensity. That is true in Europe, in Africa, in Asia, and on all the seas.

…

There are now millions of Americans in army camps, in naval stations, in factories and in shipyards.

Who are these millions upon whom the life of our country depends? What are they thinking? What are their doubts? (and) What are their hopes? And how is the work progressing?

The Commander-in-Chief cannot learn all of the answers to these questions in Washington. And that is why I made the trip I did.

…

In one sense my recent trip was a hurried one, out through the Middle West, to the Northwest, down the length of the Pacific Coast and back through the Southwest and the South. In another sense, however, it was a leisurely trip, because I had the opportunity to talk to the people who are actually doing the work—management and labor alike—on their own home grounds. And it gave me a fine chance to do some thinking about the major problems of our war effort on the basis of first things first.

As I told the three press association representatives who accompanied me, I was impressed by the large proportion of women employed—doing skilled manual (work) labor running machines. As time goes on, and many more of our men enter the armed forces, this proportion of women will increase. Within less than a year from now, I think, there will probably be as many women as men working in our war production plants.

I had some enlightening experiences relating to the old saying of us men that curiosity—inquisitiveness—is stronger among woman. I noticed (that), frequently, that when we drove unannounced down the middle aisle of a great plant full of workers and machines, the first people to look up from their work were the men—and not the women. It was chiefly the men who were arguing as to whether that fellow in the straw hat was really the President or not.

So having seen the quality of the work and of the workers on our production lines—and coupling these firsthand observations with the reports of actual performance of our weapons on the fighting fronts—I can say to you that we are getting ahead of our enemies in the battle of production.

And of great importance to our future production was the effective and rapid manner in which the Congress met the serious problem of the rising cost of living. It was a splendid example of the operation of democratic processes in wartime.

The machinery to carry out this act of the Congress was put into effect within twelve hours after the bill was signed. The legislation will help the cost-of-living problems of every worker in every factory and on every farm in the land.

In order to keep stepping up our production, we have had to add millions of workers to the total labor force of the Nation. And as new factories come into operation, we must find additional millions of workers.

This presents a formidable problem in the mobilization of manpower.

It is not that we do not have enough people in this country to do the job. The problem is to have the right numbers of the right people in the right places at the right time.

We are learning to ration materials, and we must now learn to ration manpower.

The major objectives of a sound manpower policy are:

First, to select and train men of the highest fighting efficiency needed for our armed forces in the achievement of victory over our enemies in combat.

Second, to man our war industries and farms with the workers needed to produce the arms and munitions and food required by ourselves and by our fighting allies to win this war.

In order to do this, we shall be compelled to stop workers from moving from one war job to another as a matter of personal preference; to stop employers from stealing labor from each other; to use older men, and handicapped people, and more women, and even grown boys and girls, wherever possible and reasonable, to replace men of military age and fitness; to train new personnel for essential war work; and to stop the wastage of labor in all non-essential activities.

There are many other things that we can do, and do immediately, to help meet (the) this manpower problem.

The school authorities in all the states should work out plans to enable our high school students to take some time from their school year, (and) to use their summer vacations, to help farmers raise and harvest their crops, or to work somewhere in the war industries. This does not mean closing schools and stopping education. It does mean giving older students a better opportunity to contribute their bit to the war effort. Such work will do no harm to the students.

People should do their work as near their homes as possible. We cannot afford to transport a single worker into an area where there is already a worker available to do the job.

In some communities, employers dislike to employ women. In others they are reluctant to hire Negroes. In still others, older men are not wanted. We can no longer afford to indulge such prejudices or practices.

Every citizen wants to know what essential war work he can do the best. He can get the answer by applying to the nearest United States Employment Service office. There are four thousand five hundred of these offices throughout the Nation. They (are) form the corner grocery stores of our manpower system. This network of employment offices is prepared to advise every citizen where his skills and labors are needed most, and to refer him to an employer who can utilize them to best advantage in the war effort.

Perhaps the most difficult phase of the manpower problem is the scarcity of farm labor in many places. I have seen evidences of the fact, however, that the people are trying to meet it as well as possible.

In one community that I visited a perishable crop was harvested by turning out the whole of the high school for three or four days.

And in another community of fruit growers the usual Japanese labor was not available; but when the fruit ripened, the banker, the butcher, the lawyer, the garage man, the druggist, the local editor, and in fact every able-bodied man and woman in the town, left their occupations, (and) went out gathering(ed) the fruit, and sent it to market.

Every farmer in the land must realize fully that his production is part of war production, and that he is regarded by the Nation as essential to victory. The American people expect him to keep his production up, and even to increase it. We will use every effort to help him to get labor; but, at the same time, he and the people of his community must use ingenuity and cooperative effort to produce crops, and livestock and dairy products.

It may be that all of our volunteer effort—however well intentioned and well administered—will not suffice wholly to solve (the) this problem. In that case, we shall have to adopt new legislation. And if this is necessary, I do not believe that the American people will shrink from it.

SIGNIFICANCE

Franklin Roosevelt did not live to see the end of World War II. Weakened by advanced age and years of difficult public service, he died on April 12, 1945. He did survive long enough to see the nation emerge from the darkness of the Great Depression when war spending boosted the economy.

Some of the other changes brought by the war were not so clearly evident in 1945. While women had been encouraged to work in factories and on farms, men remained in supervisory positions. Returning servicemen forced women out of the workplace, but women had gained a sense of independence that did not disappear so quickly. Years later, many of these women would become involved in political movements, including the women's rights movement. African Americans who had fought Nazis in Europe were no longer willing to tolerate storm trooper tactics at home. The African American civil rights movement is another legacy of World War II.

World War II was the most destructive global war ever fought. Much of Europe and Asia lay in ruins after the fighting stopped in 1945. Warfare, concentration camps, starvation, and atom bombs killed over fifty million human beings, the majority of whom were civilians. Only one percent of the dead were Americans, however. The United States, alone among the major belligerents, emerged from the war with almost no physical damage to its cities and towns. This helped America to become a superpower and the leader of the free world for the remainder of the twentieth century.

FURTHER RESOURCES

Books

Adams, Michael C.C. *The Best War Ever: America and World War II*. Baltimore, Md.: Johns Hopkins University Press, 1994.

Cashman, Sean Dennis. *America, Roosevelt, and World War II*. New York: New York University Press, 1989.

O'Brien, Kenneth Paul, and Lynn Hudson Parsons. *The Home-Front War: World War II and American Society*. Westport, Conn.: Greenwood, 1995.

Executive Order 9066

Authorizing the Secretary of War to Prescribe Military Areas

Executive order

By: Franklin D. Roosevelt

Date: February 19, 1942

Source: Executive Order 9066. February 19, 1942. General Records of the United States Government; Record Group 11; National Archives.

About the Author: Franklin D. Roosevelt was the thirty-second president of the United States, serving from 1933 to 1945.

INTRODUCTION

On December 7, 1941, the Japanese launched an attack on the U.S. Naval base at Pearl Harbor, Hawaii, as well as on military facilities in Guam, the Philippines, and Midway Islands. The next day, the United States declared war on Japan and entered World War II. In addition to the declaration of war, on December 8 the Federal Bureau of Investigation (FBI) began to detain a select group of Japanese residents located on the West Coast. Although Attorney General Francis Biddle proclaimed that the government would not be targeting all Japanese immigrants in the United States, by December 11 approximately 1,200 such individuals had been detained. The 1924 Oriental Exclusion Act prevented immigrants from Asian nations from obtaining citizenship. As such, the Japanese individu-

A group of Japanese-American civilians, baggage piled up, wait to board trucks taking them to internment camps in April, 1942. AP IMAGES.

als detained in 1941 were classified as enemy aliens and were not protected by the U.S. Constitution. Also by December 8, the U.S. borders became closed to anyone of Japanese ancestry. By the end of 1941, Biddle had authorized raids without search warrants on residences of Japanese Americans as long as one occupant was a Japanese alien.

At the beginning of U.S. involvement in World War II, many believed that the Japanese would target the Pacific Coast. The U.S. Army established the Western Defense Command and tasked the newly formed command with defending the Pacific Coast. The Western Defense Command came under the authority of Lieutenant General John L. Dewitt. Dewitt sought to address the concern that the Japanese residents on the West Coast were a security risk. A number of policies were instituted to curb the perceived threat of these residents: short-wave radios and cameras were confiscated; a curfew was imposed; those of Japanese ancestry could not congregate or travel in groups larger than five people; and a special permit was required for those wanting to travel more than twenty-five miles from their homes.

The movement to relocate Japanese Americans and resident aliens of Japanese descent began in early 1942. In January, the chief justice of the Supreme Court, Owen Roberts, prepared a report alleging without documentation that Japanese Americans living in Hawaii helped the Japanese military attack Pearl Harbor. This assertion was seconded by Secretary of the Navy Frank Knox after he visited the island, though the allegations were quickly rebutted by FBI director J. Edgar Hoover. Shortly after Robert's report, Biddle was advised that removing the Japanese from the West Coast would be a legal exercise of the president's war powers. In February, Secretary of War Henry Stimson, as well as several members of Congress and General Dewitt, recommended that Japanese resident aliens and those of Japanese descent be removed from California, Oregon, and Washington.

Two and a half months after the attack on Pearl Harbor, on February 19, 1942, President Roosevelt signed Executive Order 9066, which authorized the relocation of individuals of Japanese descent from the West Coast. On March 2, the Western Defense Command labeled Oregon, Washington, Arizona, and parts of California as a military area and ordered Japanese Americans and resident aliens to relocate. Approximately 8,000 people were forced to move outside the military area at that time. By mid-March, the Roosevelt administration had created the War Relocation Authority to facilitate the removal of Japanese Americans and resident aliens from the West Coast. On March 22, 1942, the first relocation occurred: residents from Los Angeles were sent to the Manzanar Relocation Center, a 6,000-acre site surrounded by barbed wire in Northern California.

■ PRIMARY SOURCE

WHEREAS the successful prosecution of the war requires every possible protection against espionage and against sabotage to national-defense material, national-defense premises, and national-defense utilities as defined in Section 4, Act of April 20, 1918, 40 Stat. 533, as amended by the Act of November 30, 1940, 54 Stat. 1220, and the Act of August 21, 1941, 55 Stat. 655 (U.S.C., Title 50, Sec. 104);

NOW THEREFORE, by virtue of the authority vested in me as President of the United States, and Commander in Chief of the Army and Navy, I hereby authorize and direct the Secretary of War, and the Military Commanders whom he may from time to time designate, whenever he or any designated Commander deems such action necessary or desirable, to prescribe military areas in such places and of such extent as he or the appropriate Military Commander may determine, from which any or all persons may be excluded, and with respect to which, the right of any person to enter, remain in, or leave shall be subject to whatever restrictions the Secretary of War or the appropriate Military Commander may impose in his discretion. The Secretary of War is hereby authorized to provide for residents of any such area who are excluded therefrom, such transportation, food, shelter, and other accommodations as may be necessary, in the judgment of the Secretary of War or the said Military Commander, and until other arrangements are made, to accomplish the purpose of this order. The designation of military areas in any region or locality shall supersede designations of prohibited and restricted areas by the Attorney General under the Proclamations of December 7 and 8, 1941, and shall supersede the responsibility and authority of the Attorney General under the said Proclamations in respect of such prohibited and restricted areas.

I hereby further authorize and direct the Secretary of War and the said Military Commanders to take such other steps as he or the appropriate Military Commander may deem advisable to enforce compliance with the restrictions applicable to each Military area hereinabove authorized to be designated, including the use of Federal troops and other Federal Agencies, with authority to accept assistance of state and local agencies. I hereby further authorize and direct all Executive Departments, independent establishments and other Federal Agencies, to assist the Secretary of War or the said Military Commanders in carrying out this Executive Order, including the furnishing of medical aid, hospitalization, food, clothing, transportation, use of land, shelter, and other supplies, equipment, utilities, facilities, and services.

This order shall not be construed as modifying or limiting in any way the authority heretofore granted under Executive Order No. 8972, dated December 12, 1941, nor shall it be construed as limiting or modifying the duty and responsibility of the Federal Bureau of Investigation, with respect to the investigation of alleged acts of sabotage or the duty and responsibility of the Attorney General and the Department of Justice under the Proclamations of December 7 and 8, 1941, prescribing regulations for the conduct and control of alien enemies, except as such duty and responsibility is superseded by the designation of military areas hereunder.

Franklin D. Roosevelt
The White House
February 19, 1942

SIGNIFICANCE

The U.S. president, as the head of the executive branch of the government, has the authority to initiate directives known as executive orders. On some occasions, executive orders are mandated by an act of the U.S. Congress, but the president often presents executive orders without any specific congressional request. This form of governing has been in use since 1789.

Under Executive Order 9066, over 120,000 people were sent to the ten internment camps located in California, Idaho, Utah, Arizona, Wyoming, Colorado, and Arkansas. Approximately 77,000 of those interned were American citizens, known as Nisei, or second-generation Japanese. The remaining 43,000 interned were legal and illegal immigrants, many of whom were Issei, or first-generation immigrants. Some of those interned had as little as one-eighth Japanese ancestry. Those relocated were often informed of their impending internment by notices posted on telephone poles, on sides of buildings, or on community bulletin boards. Those affected were sometimes given as little as four hours to liquidate their possessions and prepare for their relocation for an indefinite period.

On August 14, 1945, Japan surrendered. It took until late 1946, however, for the last internment camp to close and its residents to be freed. In 1988, the U.S. Congress passed the Civil Liberties Act with bi-partisan support. The act provided an official apology to those interned and awarded the surviving Japanese American internees a tax-free payment of $20,000.

FURTHER RESOURCES

Periodicals

Friedrich, Otto. "A Time of Agony for Japanese Americans." *Time* (December 2, 1991).

Leo, John. "An Apology to Japanese-Americans: The Senate Says They Were Wrongly Interned during World War II." *Time* (May 2, 1988).

Molotsky, Irvin. "Senate Votes to Compensate Japanese-American Internees." *New York Times* (April 21, 1988).

Web sites

Truman Presidential Museum and Library. "The War Relocation Authority and the Incarceration of Japanese Americans During World War II." <http://www.trumanlibrary.org/whistlestop/study_collections/japanese_internment/background.htm> (accessed May 10, 2006).

Servicemen's Readjustment Act

G.I. Bill

Legislation

By: United States Congress

Date: June 22, 1944

Source: "Servicemen's Readjustment Act." U.S. Congress, June 22, 1944.

About the Author: The Congress of the United States was established by Article 1 of the United States Constitution of 1787. It is the legislative arm of the U.S. Federal Government.

INTRODUCTION

The 1944 Servicemen's Readjustment Act, popularly known as the G.I. Bill, provided assistance to veterans returning to civilian life after military service during World War II. One of the most successful bills ever enacted by Congress, it dramatically expanded the ranks of the middle class.

President Franklin D. Roosevelt signed the G.I. Bill into law on June 22, 1944. It provided five benefits to veterans: education and training; guaranteed loans for a home, farm, or business; unemployment pay of $20 per week for up to one year; job placement assistance; and review of dishonorable discharges. The act also called for the building of additional Veteran's Administration hospitals. To be eligible for G.I. Bill benefits, a World War II veteran had to have served ninety days or more after September 1940 and had to have been honorably discharged. A veteran received one year of full-time education plus a period equal to his or her time in service up to a maximum of forty-eight months. Educational institutions received up to a maximum of $500 per year for each veteran admitted for tuition, books, fees, and other costs. The Veterans Administration paid an unmarried veteran an allowance of up to $50 a month while veterans with dependents received additional money.

The legislation emerged from Congress after months of intense debate and parliamentary maneuvering. Opposition came from those concerned about the possible effects that the bill might have on admissions standards at colleges and universities. The eventual success of the legislation is attributed to the American Legion, which publicized the G.I. Bill from its introduction in January 1944 until its passage.

PRIMARY SOURCE

SERVICEMEN'S READJUSTMENT ACT

AN ACT

To provide Federal Government aid for the readjustment in civilian life of returning World War II veterans.

Be it enacted by the Senate and House of Representatives of the United States of America in Congress assembled, That this Act may be cited as the "Servicemen's Readjustment Act of 1944."

TITLE I

CHAPTER I—HOSPITALIZATION, CLAIMS, AND PROCEDURES

SEC. 100. The Veterans' Administration is hereby declared to be an essential war agency and entitled, second only to the War and Navy Departments, to priorities in personnel, equipment, supplies, and material under any laws, Executive orders, and regulations pertaining to priorities, and in appointments of personnel from civil-service registers the Administrator of Veterans' Affairs is hereby granted the same authority and discretion as the War and Navy Departments and the United States Public Health Service: Provided, That the provisions of this section as to priorities for materials shall apply to any State institution to be built for the care or hospitalization of veterans.

SEC. 101. The Administrator of Veterans' Affairs and the Federal Board of Hospitalization are hereby authorized and directed to expedite and complete the construction of additional hospital facilities for war veterans, and to enter into agreements and contracts for the use by or transfer to the Veterans' Administration of suitable Army and Navy hospitals after termination of hostilities in the present war or after such institutions are no longer needed by the armed services; and the Administrator of Veterans Affairs is hereby authorized and directed to establish necessary regional offices, sub-offices, branch offices, contact units, or other subordinate offices in centers of population where there is no Veterans' Administration facility, or where such a facility is not readily available or accessible: Provided, That there is hereby authorized to be appropriated the sum of $500,000,000 for the construction of additional hospital facilities.

SEC. 102. The Administrator of Veterans' Affairs and the Secretary of War and Secretary of the Navy are hereby granted authority to enter into agreements and contracts for the mutual use or exchange of use of hospital and domiciliary facilities, and such supplies, equipment, and material as may be needed to operate properly such facilities, or for the transfer, without reimbursement of appropriations, of facilities, supplies, equipment, or material necessary and proper for authorized care for veterans, except that at no time shall the Administrator of Veterans'

President Franklin D. Roosevelt signs Public Law 346, the Servicemen's Readjustment Act of 1944, also known as the GI Bill of Rights, in Washington, D.C., June 22, 1944. AP IMAGES.

Affairs enter into any agreement which will result in a permanent reduction of Veterans' Administration hospital and domiciliary beds below the number now established or approved, plus the estimated number required to meet the load of eligibles under laws administered by the Veterans' Administration, or in any way subordinate or transfer the operation of the Veterans' Administration to any other agency of the Government.

Nothing in the Selective Training and Service Act of 1940, as amended, or any other Act, shall be construed to prevent the transfer or detail of any commissioned, appointed or enlisted personnel from the armed forces to the Veterans Administration subject to agreements between the Secretary of War or the Secretary of the Navy and the Administrator of Veterans' Affairs: Provided, That no such detail shall be made or extend beyond six months after the termination of the war.

SEC.103. The Administrator of Veterans' Affairs shall have authority to place officials and employees designated by him in such Army and Navy installations as may be deemed advisable for the purpose of adjudicating disability claims of, and giving aid and advice to, members of the Army and Navy who are about to be discharged or released from active service.

SEC. 104. No person shall be discharged or released from active duty in the armed forces until his certificate of discharge or release from active duty and final pay, or a substantial portion thereof, are ready for delivery to him or to his next of kin or legal representative; and no person shall be discharged or released from active service on account of disability until and unless he has executed a claim for compensation, pension, or hospitalization, to be filed with the Veterans' Administration or has signed a statement that he has had explained to him the right to file such claim: Provided, That this section shall not preclude immediate transfer to a veterans' facility for necessary hospital care, nor preclude the discharge of any person who refuses to sign such claim or statement: And provided further, That refusal or failure to file a claim shall be without prejudice to any right the veteran may subsequently assert.

Any person entitled to a prosthetic appliance shall be entitled, in addition, to necessary fitting and training, including institutional training, in the use of such appliance, whether in a Service or a Veterans' Administration hospital, or by out-patient treatment, including such service under contract.

SEC. 105. No person in the armed forces shall be required to sign a statement of any nature relating to the origin, incurrence, or aggravation of any disease or injury he may have, and any such statement against his own interest signed at any time, shall be null and void and of no force and effect.

SIGNIFICANCE

The G.I. Bill ended in July 1956. The program had a dramatic impact upon American higher education by increasing the number of students. In the peak year of 1947, veterans accounted for forty-nine percent of all college enrollments. Almost eight million veterans received training at a total cost to the government of $14.5 billion. Additionally, the program helped control the unemployment rate after demobilization and allowed veterans to enter the labor market with additional skills.

Although the G.I. Bill technically applied equally to both men and women, comparatively few women took advantage of its benefits. While the virtues of the G.I. Bill were extolled to male veterans, the same effort at spreading the information was not made for women. Upwards of a third of female veterans did not even know they were eligible for the G.I. Bill. There were also several provisions of the bill that discriminated against women, specifically the portions that dealt with the reception of benefits by widowers. While WACs (women in the Army after 1943), SPARs (women in the Coast Guard), Women Marines, and WAVES (women in the Navy) were included from the beginning in the G.I. Bill, it was not until the end of the 1970s and the beginning of the 1980s that WAACs (women in the Army from 1941 to 1943) and WASPs (women in the Air Service) were awarded benefits, most of which had expired. The discrimination against male dependents and survivors of female veterans lasted until 1972.

FURTHER RESOURCES
Books

Bennett, Michael J. *When Dreams Came True: The G.I. Bill and the Making of Modern America*. Washington, D.C.: Brassey's, 1996.

Gelber, Sidney. *Politics and Public Higher Education in New York State: Stony Brook*. New York: P. Lang, 2001.

Greenberg, Milton. *The G.I. Bill: The Law That Changed America*. New York: Lickle, 1997.

Statement by the President Upon Signing the National School Lunch Act

Speech

By: Harry S. Truman

Date: June 4, 1946

Source: Truman, Harry. "Statement by the President Upon Signing the National School Lunch Act." June 4, 1946. Truman Library Archives.

About the Author: Harry S. Truman (1884–1972) was the thirty-third president of the United States. He was born at Lamar, Missouri, on May 8, 1884. A leader of the Democrats, Truman served as president from April 12, 1945, to January 20, 1953. During his tenure, he took several steps for the welfare of people, including programs designated for children. One of them was the contentious National School Lunch Program (NSLP), a federally financed meal program for students in public schools, nonprofit private schools, and residential child-care institutions. Truman died in Missouri on December 26, 1972.

INTRODUCTION

Many European countries are known to have initiated school food programs as early as the 1700s. Aiming to feed needy children, the first known school food program in the United States commenced in 1853. Undertaken by the Children's Aid Society of New York, the program served meals to children attending vocational schools in New York. Several other cities, including Boston and Philadelphia, followed suit. However, most of these programs were sporadic and were supported by charitable organizations.

In the early 1900s, research studies indicated a correlation between poor quality of work at school and malnutrition among students. By the 1930s, as many as fifteen states authorized local schools to operate food programs. While the cost of lunches under these programs was low, students did have to pay for their food. During the Great Depression of the 1930s and during World War II, the Works Progress Administration (WPA) and National Youth Administration (NYA) organized various school lunch programs across all states. Mainly aided by donations, these programs covered 92,916 schools (feeding six million children daily) in 1942. However, the worsening economy and lack of funds affected school lunch programs. Advocates realized that legislation providing consistent federal aid to support the programs was required. Subsequently, the National School Lunch Program (NSLP) was launched under the National School Lunch Act, signed by President Harry Truman in 1946.

Over the years, the National School Lunch Act has been amended. To strengthen the program and expand its reach, the Child Nutrition Act of 1966 was implemented. In the same year, the scope of the NSLP was extended—breakfast was offered to students up to eighteen years of age who participated in after-school educational and enrichment programs.

The Food and Nutrition Service of the U.S. Department of Agriculture (USDA) administers NSLP at the federal level and education agencies at the state level. Students of public and nonprofit private schools, as well as those in residential child-care institutions, are provided free lunch on school working days under this program.

The schools listed under NSLP get cash subsidies and receive donated commodities from the USDA for providing free food items as per the administration's guidelines. The guidelines make it mandatory for these schools to ensure that a maximum of thirty percent of a student's calories come from fat, with less than ten percent coming from saturated fat. The schools have also been instructed to provide one-third of the USDA's Recommended Dietary Allowances of protein, Vitamin A, Vitamin C, iron, calcium, and calories.

Ever since the program began, more than 187 billion lunches have been served. The USDA indicates that about 7.1 million children benefited from NSLP in its very first year. The figures rose to twenty-two million children in 1970. A decade later it was close to twenty-seven million, and for the fiscal year 2003, the number of beneficiary students touched 28.4 million in more than 98,000 schools. However, with its reach, costs to the government have also increased. According to USDA, the program's total cost in 1947 was seventy million dollars. In 1950, it rose to 119.7 million dollars. Ten years later, the spending on free food items was 225.8 million dollars.

In 1946, when NSLP was launched, President Harry Truman delivered a speech to mark the occasion. In his speech, Truman termed the NSLP a landmark program that would provide much-needed assistance to poor children at school.

PRIMARY SOURCE

Today, as I sign the National School Lunch Act, I feel that the Congress has acted with great wisdom in providing the basis for strengthening the nation through better nutrition for our school children. In my message to Congress last January, I pointed out that we have the technical knowledge to provide plenty of good food for every man, woman, and child in this country, but that despite our capacity to produce food we have often failed to distribute it as well as we should. This action by the Congress represents a basic forward step toward correcting that failure.

In the long view, no nation is any healthier than its children or more prosperous than its farmers; and in the National School Lunch Act, the Congress has contributed immeasurably both to the welfare of our farmers and the health of our children.

Under previous school lunch programs made possible by year-to-year authorizations we have been able to provide as many as six million children with nutritious lunches at noon. This has laid a good foundation for the permanent program. In the future, increasing numbers will benefit—and on a permanent basis.

I hope that all State and local authorities will cooperate fully with the United States Department of Agriculture in establishing the cooperative school lunch in every possible community.

SIGNIFICANCE

Although deemed a successful program, the NSLP has generated intense debate in the early twentieth century. There has been "food fighting" among two factions—school authorities, including teachers, children, and parents; and the massive food and beverage industry. School authorities, teachers, and parents have often criticized the NSLP, especially the quality of food provided.

More than half of the population in the United States, especially children, is either overweight or obese. According to the National Survey Data, the number of overweight children has quadrupled since 1960. Research indicates that overweight students tend to have lower grades and hardly participate in sporting events. The obesity factor is more worrisome as children face the risk of diseases and ailments such as diabetes, hypertension, kidney failure, arthritis, and cancer. The U.S. surgeon general put the cost of obesity in 2000 at 117 billion dollars. The increase in obese or overweight children is attributed in part to the high fat content of meals served under the NSLP. Critics maintain that these meals do not follow nutrition guidelines and typically include food items such as hot dogs, cheeseburgers, and pork chops—all high in fat content and sodium.

Another controversy that has embroiled the NSLP is the introduction of irradiated beef in school lunches. Irradiated beef, according to researchers, in addition to having low nutritional value, exposes children to radiation. Despite extensive protests from parents and school authorities, the USDA introduced irradiated beef in 2003—allegedly due to mounting pressure from the food irradiation industry.

In the past few years, while the flaws in NSLP have been highlighted by critics, the Bush administration has not, according to reports, taken strong enough steps on the health front. In the 1980s, the Reagan administration was blasted for declaring ketchup a vegetable for NSLP. In the 1990s, the USDA announced that salsa (another low-nutrition food item) was an acceptable part of the school menu.

In 1998, Michele Simon, a public-health lawyer and director of the Center for Informed Food Choices (CIFC), pointed out in an article published in *The Animal's Agenda* that the schools have become a dumping ground for high-fat and high-cholesterol meat and dairy products to salvage industry profits. The program has digressed from its goal of promoting good nutrition to children and opening more business opportunities for farmers. In fact, according to a 1993 survey, the USDA itself found the nutritional quality of most school lunches mediocre.

Moreover, the USDA reimburses schools only for the cost of food. Infrastructure, staff, and other costs associated with managing the NSLP are not included. Subsequently, many schools are facing a financial crunch and sometimes reduce their financial burden by relying on inexpensive foods.

FURTHER RESOURCES
Books

Hiatt, Liisa and Jacob Alex Klerman. *State Monitoring of National School Lunch Program Nutritional Content.* Santa Monica, Calif: Rand, 2002.

Web sites

The Animal's Agenda. "Misery on the Menu: The National School Lunch Program." October 1998 <http://www.informedeating.org/docs/misery_on_the_menu.html> (accessed May 22, 2006).

Food Research and Action Center. "National School Lunch Program." March 2006 <http://www.frac.org/html/federal_food_programs/programs/nslp.html> (accessed May 22, 2006).

Massachusetts Department of Education. "Child Nutrition Programs." <http://www.doe.mass.edu/cnp/programs/nslp.html> (accessed May 22, 2006).

U.S. Department of Agriculture. "The National School Lunch Program Background and Development." <http://www.fns.usda.gov/cnd/Lunch/AboutLunch/NSLP-Program%20History.pdf> (accessed May 22, 2006).

U.S. Department of Agriculture. "USDA Releases Specifications for the Purchase of Irradiated Ground Beef in the National School Lunch Program." May 30, 2003 <http://www.fns.usda.gov/cga/PressReleases/2003/PR-0172.htm> (accessed May 22, 2006).

United States General Accounting Service. "School Lunch Program." May 2003 <http://www.gao.gov/new.items/d03506.pdf> (accessed May 22, 2006).

The Weston A. Price Foundation. "Irradiated Meat: A Sneak Attack on School Lunches." December 6, 2003 <http://www.westonaprice.org/modernfood/irradiated-meat.html> (accessed May 22, 2006).

A Fair Deal

President Truman's January 5, 1949 State of the Union Address

Speech

By: Harry S. Truman

Date: January 5, 1949

Source: *Truman Presidential Museum and Library.* "Annual Message to the Congress on the State of the Union, January 5, 1949." <http://www.trumanlibrary.org/whistlestop/tap/1549.htm> (accessed May 21, 2006).

About the Author: Harry S. Truman (1884–1972) was the thirty-third President of the United States. Truman was president during a seminal period in American history. Although the war in Europe was over in May 1945, the war with Japan continued and Japan refused to surrender. As a result, Truman made the decision to drop atomic bombs on Hiroshima and Nagasaki—Japanese cities that were very actively engaged in war industry. Following the end of World War II, Truman also was a witness to the founding of the United Nations, among the world's foremost organizations dedicated to achieving and preserving peace. He also argued for equality and instituted programs to facilitate desegregation in the U.S. Armed Forces. Truman created a detailed plan, dubbed the "Fair Deal," for economic prosperity and equality for the inhabitants of the United States. The plan, outlined in his 1949

President Truman delivers his State of the Union address to a joint session of Congress on January 5, 1949. He asked the new Democratic congress to increase federal taxes by $4 billion and to authorize limited price and wage ceilings. © BETTMANN/CORBIS.

State of the Union address, paid homage to Roosevelt's "New Deal."

INTRODUCTION

During the years of Harry S. Truman's presidency, the United States was undergoing very rapid and dramatic changes. World War II was ending, thousands of soldiers were returning home, industry was rapidly expanding, the field of medicine was advancing exponentially, and technology was beginning to boom. At the same time, there were significant political upheavals elsewhere in the world, and Communism was spreading in Russia and parts of Europe and Asia. America was active in a rebuilding and peace-keeping role, but was also becoming progressively more wary of the perceived threats to national security and stability posed by Communist Russia, setting the stage for the beginning of the Cold War in the 1950s.

Racial and economic segregation were well entrenched in American society by the 1930s and 1940s. Truman strongly opposed this status quo and was very active in the effort to promote full civil rights for African Americans and an end to segregation in all of its forms. In early 1948, he announced a plan to end segregation in the U.S. Armed Forces, as well as in all civil service occupations. In mid–1948, he enacted legislation that ended segregation and racist activities within all branches of the U.S. military.

Shortly after he assumed the presidency, following President Franklin Roosevelt's death, Truman began proposing an extensive plan to create prosperity, equality and civil rights, and nationwide access to health care throughout the country. In deference to President Roosevelt's "New Deal" program of economic growth and expansion, Truman referred to his wide-ranging program as the "Fair Deal" for all Americans.

Truman developed a twenty-one point program concerned with social and economic development and presented it to the nation during his January 5, 1949 State of the Union address. In the plan, he called for raising the minimum wage for all workers, for nationwide, guaranteed, affordable health insurance and health care, and for abolishing segregation and affording equal rights to all Americans. He proposed federal aid for education, broadening access to higher education for all qualified students, and improving the quality of the public school system. He favored agricultural subsidies, empowering farmers to maintain and expand farm production, with the goal of making America able to grow all its own food. He was a liberal politician who believed that labor unions were good for the protection of workers and that all people should be able to achieve economic stability if given the appropriate tools.

▮ PRIMARY SOURCE

...

During the last 16 years, our people have been creating a society which offers new opportunities for every man to enjoy his share of the good things of life.

In this society, we are conservative about the values and principles which we cherish; but we are forward-looking in protecting those values and principles and in extending their benefits. We have rejected the discredited theory that the fortunes of the Nation should be in the hands of a privileged few. We have abandoned the "trickle-down" concept of national prosperity. Instead, we believe that our economic system should rest on a democratic foundation and that wealth should be created for the benefit of all.

The recent election shows that the people of the United States are in favor of this kind of society and want to go on improving it.

The American people have decided that poverty is just as wasteful and just as unnecessary as preventable disease. We have pledged our common resources to help one another in the hazards and struggles of individual life. We believe that no unfair prejudice or artificial distinction should bar any citizen of the United States of America from an education, or from good health, or from a job that he is capable of performing.

The attainment of this kind of society demands the best efforts of every citizen in every walk of life, and it imposes increasing responsibilities on the Government.

The Government must work with industry, labor, and the farmers in keeping our economy running at full speed. The Government must see that every American has a chance to obtain his fair share of our increasing abundance. These responsibilities go hand in hand.

We cannot maintain prosperity unless we have a fair distribution of opportunity and a widespread consumption of the products of our factories and farms.

Our Government has undertaken to meet these responsibilities.

We have made tremendous public investments in highways, hydroelectric power projects, soil conservation, and reclamation. We have established a system of social security. We have enacted laws protecting the rights and the welfare of our working people and the income of our farmers. These Federal policies have paid for themselves many times over. They have strengthened the material foundations of our democratic ideals. Without them, our present prosperity would be impossible.

...

But, great as our progress has been, we still have a long way to go.

As we look around the country, many of our shortcomings stand out in bold relief.

We are suffering from excessively high prices.

Our production is still not large enough to satisfy our demands.

Our minimum wages are far too low.

Small business is losing ground to growing monopoly.

Our farmers still face an uncertain future. And too many of them lack the benefits of our modern civilization.

Some of our natural resources are still being wasted.

We are acutely short of electric power, although the means for developing such power are abundant.

Five million families are still living in slums and firetraps. Three million families share their homes with others.

Our health is far behind the progress of medical science. Proper medical care is so expensive that it is out of the reach of the great majority of our citizens.

Our schools, in many localities, are utterly inadequate.

Our democratic ideals are often thwarted by prejudice and intolerance.

Each of these shortcomings is also an opportunity—an opportunity for the Congress and the President to work for the good of the people.

Our first great opportunity is to protect our economy against the evils of "boom and bust."

This objective cannot be attained by government alone. Indeed, the greater part of the task must be performed by individual efforts under our system of free enterprise. We can keep our present prosperity, and increase it, only if free enterprise and free government work together to that end.

We cannot afford to float along ceaselessly on a postwar boom until it collapses. It is not enough merely to prepare to weather a recession if it comes. Instead, government and business must work together constantly to achieve more and more jobs and more and more production—which mean more and more prosperity for all the people.

...

The Employment Act of 1946 pledges the Government to use all its resources to promote maximum employment, production, and purchasing power. This means that the Government is firmly committed to protect business and the people against the dangers of recession and against the evils of inflation. This means that the Government must adapt its plans and policies to meet changing circumstances.

At the present time, our prosperity is threatened by inflationary pressures at a number of critical points in our economy. And the Government must be in a position to take effective action at these danger spots. To that end, I recommend that the Congress enact legislation for the following purposes:

1. First, to continue the power to control consumer credit and enlarge the power to control bank credit.
2. Second, to grant authority to regulate speculation on the commodity exchanges.
3. Third, to continue export control authority and to provide adequate machinery for its enforcement.
4. Fourth, to continue the priorities and allocation authority in the field of transportation.
5. Fifth, to authorize priorities and allocations for key materials in short supply.
6. Sixth, to extend and strengthen rent control.
7. Seventh, to provide standby authority to impose price ceilings for scarce commodities which basically

affect essential industrial production or the cost of living, and to limit unjustified wage adjustments which would force a break in an established price ceiling.

8. Eighth, to authorize an immediate study of the adequacy of production facilities for materials in critically short supply, such as steel; and, if found necessary, to authorize Government loans for the expansion of production facilities to relieve such shortages, and to authorize the construction of such facilities directly, if action by private industry fails to meet our needs.

...

One of the most important factors in maintaining prosperity is the Government's fiscal policy. At this time, it is essential not only that the Federal budget be balanced, but also that there be a substantial surplus to reduce inflationary pressures, and to permit a sizable reduction in the national debt, which now stands at $252 billion. I recommend, therefore, that the Congress enact new tax legislation to bring in an additional $4 billion of Government revenue. This should come principally from additional corporate taxes. A portion should come from revised estate and gift taxes. Consideration should be given to raising personal income rates in the middle and upper brackets.

If we want to keep our economy running in high gear, we must be sure that every group has the incentive to make its full contribution to the national welfare. At present, the working men and women of the Nation are unfairly discriminated against by a statute that abridges their rights, curtails their constructive efforts, and hampers our system of free collective bargaining. That statute is the Labor-Management Relations Act of 1947, sometimes called the Taft-Hartley Act.

That act should be repealed!

The Wagner Act should be reenacted. ... The use of economic force to decide issues arising out of the interpretation of existing contracts should be prevented. Without endangering our democratic freedoms, means should be provided for setting up machinery for preventing strikes in vital industries which affect the public interest.

The Department of Labor should be rebuilt and strengthened and those units properly belonging within that department should be placed in it.

The health of our economy and its maintenance at high levels further require that the minimum wage fixed by law should be raised to at least 75 cents an hour.

...

Our national farm program should be improved-not only in the interest of the farmers, but for the lasting prosperity of the whole Nation. Our goals should be abundant farm production and parity income for agriculture. Standards of living on the farm should be just as good as anywhere else in the country.

Farm price supports are an essential part of our program to achieve these ends. Price supports should be used to prevent farm price declines which are out of line with general price levels, to facilitate adjustments in production to consumer demands, and to promote good land use. Our price support legislation must be adapted to these objectives. The authority of the Commodity Credit Corporation to provide adequate storage space for crops should be restored.

Our program for farm prosperity should also seek to expand the domestic market for agricultural products, particularly among low-income groups, and to increase and stabilize foreign markets.

We should give special attention to extending modern conveniences and services to our farms. Rural electrification should be pushed forward. And in considering legislation relating to housing, education, health, and social security, special attention should be given to rural problems.

Our growing population and the expansion of our economy depend upon the wise management of our land, water, forest, and mineral wealth. In our present dynamic economy, the task of conservation is not to lockup our resources but to develop and improve them. Failure, today, to make the investments which are necessary to support our progress in the future would be false economy.

We must push forward the development of our rivers for power, irrigation, navigation, and flood control. We should apply the lessons of our Tennessee Valley experience to our other great river basins. ...

...

In all this we must make sure that the benefits of these public undertakings are directly available to the people. Public power should be earned to consuming areas by public transmission lines where necessary to provide electricity at the lowest possible rates. Irrigation waters should serve family farms and not land speculators.

The Government has still other opportunities-to help raise the standard of living of our citizens. These opportunities lie in the fields of social security, health, education, housing, and civil rights.

The present coverage of the social security laws is altogether inadequate; the benefit payments are too low. One-third of our workers are not covered. Those who receive old-age and survivors insurance benefits receive an average payment of only $25 a month. Many others who cannot work because they are physically disabled are left to the mercy of charity. We should expand our social security program, both as to the size of the benefits and the extent of coverage, against the economic hazards due to unemployment, old age, sickness, and disability.

We must spare no effort to raise the general level of health in this country. In a nation as rich as ours, it is a shocking fact that tens of millions lack adequate medical care. We are short of doctors, hospitals, nurses. We must remedy these shortages. Moreover, we need—and we must have without further delay—a system of prepaid medical insurance which will enable every American to afford good medical care.

It is equally shocking that millions of our children are not receiving a good education. Millions of them are in overcrowded, obsolete buildings. We are short of teachers, because teachers' salaries are too low to attract new teachers, or to hold the ones we have. All these school problems will become much more acute as a result of the tremendous increase in the enrollment in our elementary schools in the next few years. I cannot repeat too strongly my desire for prompt Federal financial aid to the States to help them operate and maintain their school systems.

The governmental agency which now administers the programs of health, education, and social security should be given full departmental status.

The housing shortage continues to be acute. As an immediate step, the Congress should enact the provisions for low-rent public housing, slum clearance, farm housing, and housing research which I have repeatedly recommended. The number of low-rent public housing units provided for in the legislation should be increased to 1 million units in the next 7 years. Even this number of units will not begin to meet our need for new housing.

Most of the houses we need will have to be built by private enterprise, without public subsidy. By producing too few rental units and too large a proportion of high-priced houses, the building industry is rapidly pricing itself out of the market. Building costs must be lowered.

…

The authority which I have requested, to allocate materials in short supply and to impose price ceilings on such materials, could be used, if found necessary, to channel more materials into homes large enough for family life at prices which wage earners can afford.

The driving force behind our progress is our faith in our democratic institutions. That faith is embodied in the promise of equal rights and equal opportunities which the founders of our Republic proclaimed to their countrymen and to the whole world.

The fulfillment of this promise is among the highest purposes of government. The civil rights proposals I made to the 80th Congress, I now repeat to the 81st Congress. They should be enacted in order that the Federal Govern-

ment may assume the leadership and discharge the obligations clearly placed upon it by the Constitution.

…

It should be clear by now to all citizens that we are not seeking to freeze the status quo. We have no intention of preserving the injustices of the past. We welcome the constructive efforts being made by many nations to achieve a better life for their citizens. In the European recovery program, in our good-neighbor policy and in the United Nations, we have begun to batter down those national walls which block the economic growth and the social advancement of the peoples of the world.

…

We stand at the opening of an era which can mean either great achievement or terrible catastrophe for ourselves and for all mankind.

The strength of our Nation must continue to be used in the interest of all our people rather than a privileged few. It must continue to be used unselfishly in the struggle for world peace and the betterment of mankind the world over.

This is the task before us.

It is not an easy one. It has many complications, and there will be strong opposition from selfish interests.

I hope for cooperation from farmers, from labor, and from business. Every segment of our population and every individual has a right to expect from our Government a fair deal.

SIGNIFICANCE

Harry S. Truman had a long history of liberalism and civil rights efforts. He began speaking about the initiatives later to be outlined in his Fair Deal plan shortly after he first assumed the presidency in 1945. Just after the end of World War II, Truman brought a proposal to Congress that included legislation for public housing initiatives, strengthening and broadening the social security program, and a bill that would raise the minimum wage and provide for full employment of the American workforce. In addition, he sought to enact legislation to ensure fair employment practices, in an effort to end racial and ethnic discrimination in the workplace. Nearly all of his proposed legislation was ignored. In response to President Truman's proposal for what he referred to as the Fair Employment Practices Act, Congress did pass legislation called the Employment Act, which made the government responsible for ensuring that the workforce was able to achieve full employment status. The Employment Act also provided for the establishment of the Council of Economic

Advisors, a three-member group charged with maintaining a healthy and stable economy in the United States. After Congress's almost total inaction on his overall program, Truman did not reintroduce his proposals until after he was re-elected in 1948.

After the end of World War II, the political climate in America became progressively more conservative. There was considerable reaction against the remaining vestiges of President Roosevelt's New Deal policies, leading to an almost complete lack of political or popular support for Truman's New Deal-like Fair Deal plan. Overall, the four initiatives that Truman most wished to see enacted were the national health insurance plan, the public housing program designed to end slums and ghettos and raise the quality of life for (working) poor populations, the re-tooling and expansion of the Social Security program for elders, and a sixty-two percent increase in the federal minimum wage (from 40 to 65 cents per hour). None of these proposals was enacted. Truman's liberal views concerning civil rights and his platform for ending segregation and abolishing racism were very poorly received by the socially and fiscally conservative Congress. It was Truman's strongly held belief that the best way to ensure economic stability, and to promote the growth of the economy would be to rectify institutionalized injustices, to create a climate in which full employment would flourish, to support the poorest citizens in order to enable them to be gainfully employed and to secure safe and affordable housing, and to shift the economic power away from the wealthiest citizens, permitting a more equitable distribution of resources.

In the end, the conservative political powers held sway. There was no new national health care system created. The only real educational reform was the creation of the G.I. bill supporting veterans returning from wartime service and attempting to reintegrate into the educational and labor markets. Unemployment benefits were improved, but only marginally. The fight for civil rights gained momentum over the next decade until a variety of federal laws were enacted to address this issue in the 1960s. Eventually, a major public housing reform was enacted, with the intent of supporting a move away from slums and ghettos to safe and affordable housing. Ultimately, Truman moved away from his Fair Deal proposals and began to concentrate his efforts on the emerging Cold War and concerns over perceived threats posed by the rise of Communism. By the end of his term, he had ended segregation in the U.S. Armed Forces and in the federal hiring programs, achieved a higher minimum wage, and enacted wider-ranging social security programs and the beginnings of public housing.

FURTHER RESOURCES

Books

Burnes, Brian. *Harry S. Truman: His Life and Times*. Kansas City, Mo.: Kansas City Star Books, 2003.

Gardner, Michael R. *Harry Truman and Civil Rights: Moral Courage and Political Risks*. Carbondale: Southern Illinois University Press, 2002.

Hillman, William, and Harry Truman. *Mr. President: The First Publication from the Personal Diaries, Private Letters, Papers, and Revealing Interviews of Harry S. Truman*. New York: Farrar, Straus, and Young, 1952.

McCullough, David C. *Truman*. New York: Touchstone, 1992.

Ryan, Halford R. *Harry S. Truman: Presidential Rhetoric*. Westport, Conn.: Greenwood Press, 1993.

Not a Fair Deal

Editorial cartoon

By: Anonymous

Date: January 1, 1952

Source: Photo by MPI/Getty Images.

About the Artist: This photograph is part of the collection at Getty Images, a worldwide provider of visual content materials to such communications groups as advertisers, broadcasters, designers, magazines, news media organizations, newspapers, and producers.

INTRODUCTION

Although President Franklin Roosevelt's health had been declining, many Americans were stunned when the wartime leader died in 1945. Perhaps most surprised was the nation's vice president, Harry S. Truman (1884–1972). Chosen to replace Roosevelt's previous second-in-command, Henry A. Wallace, Truman had been in office barely three months when he was suddenly thrust into the Oval Office. The following day, Truman candidly likened the news of Roosevelt's death to having the moon, stars, and planets dropped on his head.

President Truman inherited an America quite different from the country led by his predecessor. Whereas President Roosevelt had enjoyed strong support as a wartime leader, Truman found both the U.S. Congress and the nation far less malleable. Where Roosevelt had enjoyed broad wartime powers, Tru-

PRIMARY SOURCE

Not a Fair Deal: A cartoon criticizing President Truman's Fair Deal program as a facade propped up by war spending and inflation. PHOTO BY MPI/GETTY IMAGES.

man found himself fighting for approval of his initiatives. In particular, the experiences of the Depression and the trauma of World War II had led to significant shifts in U.S. political thought, and it was now far more conservative than it had previously been. Roosevelt's massive expansion of government programs, while instrumental in restarting the U.S. economy, had also raised the ire of conservatives who opposed expansions of government power.

This resistance to government expansion produced an unlikely alliance in Congress. Southern Democrats, generally more conservative than their northern counterparts and against Democratic initiatives to expand rights for blacks, found themselves uniting with Congressional Republicans to limit Truman's initiatives. Facing this implausible coalition, Truman quickly found himself stymied in most of his major efforts.

Following in the footsteps of the popular Roosevelt, Truman presented the nation with a new set of programs designed to expand the New Deal. In the spirit of Roosevelt's reforms, Truman advocated raising the minimum wage, broadening Social Security coverage, launching housing initiatives, and creating national health insurance. Truman's efforts were largely unsuccessful, and Congress rejected every major element of his plan. Making matters worse, liberal Democrats also attacked Truman as being untrue to the spirit of FDR. With Truman's popularity at an all-time low, the Republicans managed to gain control of Congress for the first time since the 1920s.

PRIMARY SOURCE

NOT A FAIR DEAL

See primary source image.

SIGNIFICANCE

With his own party divided, Congress in the hands of his adversaries, and his legislative initiatives in shambles, Truman appeared dead in the water. As the election of 1948 approached, the Democratic Party splintered further, with two separate groups breaking off to nominate their own candidates. Although Truman's defeat appeared a foregone conclusion, he refused to give up, launching a 200-stop nationwide tour during which he rallied support and criticized Congress for doing nothing to improve the country. Despite his efforts, most reputable newspapers predicted Truman would lose by as much as fifteen percent. To the shock of most pundits, Truman

led the election from start to finish, defeating Republican Thomas Dewey by 4.4 percent. Following the victory, a jovial Truman held aloft a copy of the *Chicago Tribune*, whose premature headline proclaimed Dewey the winner.

Energized by his surprise victory, Truman sought to harness this momentum to launch new social initiatives. Calling his efforts the Fair Deal, he proposed six major initiatives, including expanded civil rights laws, federal funding for housing and education, unemployment insurance, tax cuts for the poor, and a national health care system. While these proposals sat well with liberal Democrats and were true to the spirit of Roosevelt's New Deal, the mood of the country and of Congress had shifted decisively to the right. With the exception of a housing initiative passed in 1949, Truman's Fair Deal went nowhere, stymied by the new conservative coalition in Congress.

Like many other wartime leaders, Truman found himself struggling to govern in peacetime. The economic transition from war to peace was difficult for America; pent-up demand for consumer goods and a slow transition from wartime to peacetime factory production led to rapid inflation and numerous shortages. The nation also struggled to absorb the influx of war veterans, and labor unrest led to numerous strikes, further disrupting the already strained economy. The failure of Truman's Fair Deal marked the beginning of a slow decline for liberal policies in the United States. In the next presidential election, Republican Dwight Eisenhower (1890–1969) won the first of his two terms as the nation sought reassurance in the face of the Cold War.

The unusual coalition of northern Republicans and southern Democrats that blocked Truman's expansion of U.S. government reemerged in the 1980s following the election of Ronald Reagan (1911–2004). With Congress securely in the hands of Democrats, Reagan's conservative agenda faced an uphill battle. But Reagan's program of tax cuts and increased military spending passed Congress due to the support of conservative southern Democrats known as Boll Weevil Democrats. As many as sixty fiscally and socially conservative Democrats joined Reagan's Republicans to pass the major initiatives of the president's plan.

FURTHER RESOURCES

Books

Burnes, Brian. *Harry S. Truman: His Life and Times*. Kansas City, Mo.: Kansas City Star Books, 2003.

Spalding, Elizabeth Edwards. *The First Cold Warrior: Harry Truman, Containment, and the Remaking of Liberal Inter-

To help project outdoor speeches during his 1934 U.S. Senate campaign, Harry Truman used this car equipped with loudspeakers, an amplifier and a microphone. AP IMAGES.

nationalism. Lexington: University Press of Kentucky, 2006.

Truman, Margaret. *Where the Buck Stops: Personal and Private Writings of Harry S. Truman.* New York: Warner Books, 1989.

Periodicals

Dean, Virgil W. "Charles F. Brannan and the Rise and Fall of Truman's 'Fair Deal' for Farmers." *Agricultural History* 69 (1995): 28–53.

McGrath, J. Howard. "Reactions to the Administration's Legislative and Fiscal Program." *Congressional Digest* 28 (1949): 52–56.

"Reviving the American Left." *U.S. News & World Report* 140 (2006): 20.

Shelton, Willard. "The 'Do-less' 82d." *Nation* 172 (1951):5–6.

Web sites

Rutgers University. Eagleton Institute of Politics. "1948 Truman-Dewey Election." <http://www.eagleton.rutgers.edu/e-gov/e-politicalarchive–1948election.htm> (accessed June 6, 2006).

Truman Presidential Museum and Library. <http://www.trumanlibrary.org/> (accessed June 6, 2006).

The Avalon Project at Yale Law School. "Truman Doctrine: President Harry S. Truman's Address Before a Joint Session of Congress, March 12, 1947." <http://www.yale.edu/lawweb/avalon/trudoc.htm> (accessed June 5, 2006).

Executive Order 10521

Administration of Scientific Research by Agencies of the Federal Government

Government record

By: Dwight D. Eisenhower

Date: March 17, 1954

Source: National Archives

At a NASA press conference, astronomer Carl Sagan speaks about photos from Voyager 1 showing the solar system from the outside. © BETTMANN/CORBIS.

About the Author: President Dwight D. Eisenhower served as the thirty-fourth president of the United States from 1953–1961. Before becoming president, Eisenhower was a General in the U.S. Army and held the position of Supreme Allied Commander of forces in Europe during World War II.

INTRODUCTION

Many of the successes of Allied forces during World War II (1938–1945) were the result of scientific advances. The director of the Office of Scientific Research and Development, Vannevar Bush, submitted a report to Franklin Roosevelt in 1945. Bush's report, entitled *Science—The Endless Frontier*, asserted that during the wartime period, scientists had used operations research to create technological advances to help the war such as radar and nuclear weapons. He advocated continued research funded by the government with the caveat that researchers be allowed to be independent. He proposed to fund the work of scientific research through a national research foundation which would empower researchers without govern-

ment interference. He suggested that the military services continue to do policy-directed research, or research driven by policy outlined objectives, for the Department of Defense; however, he asserted that the Defense Department needed more inventive research programs like those at universities. Thus began the debate over the influence U.S. government should have on the research that it funds.

In 1946, President Truman signed an Executive Order to create the President's Scientific Research Board (PSRB) to manage the government's own research, as well as coordinate research with academics. The PSRB was to report to the president reviews of scientific research, both current and proposed, that was occurring within the government structure and outside of the federal government. John Steelman, the director of Office of War Mobilization and Reconversion (OWMR), was appointed the chair of the board. Under Steelman's direction, the PSRB embarked on a ten month study to create a detailed account and analysis of the U.S. research system. The four volumes of the report were published under the name *Science and Public Policy*. The two works, *Science—The Endless Frontier* and *Science and Public Policy* represented the two varying thoughts on government direction of research and development in the U.S. scientific community. *Science—The Endless Frontier* presented a laissez-faire role for government. Its author, Vannevar Bush, acknowledged that private sector funding of research was no longer adequate to support academic research and development. Bush proposed a system for bestowing universities with research support that was designed to operate outside the government bureaucracy and be apolitical. Under Steelman's report, research and development would be funded and organized under the direction of the government.

The National Science Foundation Act of 1947 was submitted to President Truman; this act would create a National Science Foundation who would be directed by the National Science Board, which was appointed by the president. President Truman vetoed the bill, asserting that the Act would force him to delegate his authority to oversee the disbursement of public funds to the National Science Board. However, government agencies continued to fund research and development. The Office of Naval Research, Atomic Energy Commission, and the National Institutes of Health supported university research for several years and with the rise of the Cold War brought a continued need to fund research. As such, President Truman signed the National Science Foundation Act of 1950. The act bridged a compromise in presidential influence that was not present in the legislation proposed in 1947. Leadership in the foundation would be shared between the National Science Board, which was appointed by the president, and a director appointed by the president and approved by the senate. As such, the National Science Foundation was created in 1950 with the expressed purpose to fund basic research and develop a relationship between science and government.

PRIMARY SOURCE

WHEREAS the security and welfare of the United States depend increasingly upon the advancement of knowledge in the sciences; and

WHEREAS useful applications of science to defense, humanitarian, and other purposes in the Nation require a strong foundation in basic scientific knowledge and trained scientific manpower; and

WHEREAS the administration of Federal scientific research programs affecting institutions of learning must be consistent with the preservation of the strength, vital-

ity, and independence of higher education in the United States; and

WHEREAS, in order to conserve fiscal and manpower resources, it is necessary that Federal scientific research programs be administered with all practicable efficiency and economy; and

WHEREAS the National Science Foundation has been established by law for the purpose, among others, of developing and encouraging the pursuit of an appropriate and effective national policy for the promotion of basic research and education in the sciences:

NOW, THEREFORE, by virtue of the authority vested in me as President of the United States, it is hereby ordered as follows:

Section 1. The National Science Foundation (hereinafter referred to as the Foundation) shall from time to time recommend to the President policies for the promotion and support of basic research and education in the sciences, including policies with respect to furnishing guidance toward defining the responsibilities of the Federal Government in the conduct and support of basic scientific research.

[Sec. 1 amended by EO 10807 of Mar. 13, 1959, 24 FR 1897, 3 CFR, 1959–1963 Comp., p. 329]

Sec. 2. The Foundation shall continue to make comprehensive studies and recommendations regarding the Nation's scientific research effort and its resources for scientific activities, including facilities and scientific personnel, and its foreseeable scientific needs, with particular attention to the extent of the Federal Government's activities and the resulting effects upon trained scientific personnel. In making such studies, the Foundation shall make full use of existing sources of information and research facilities within the Federal Government.

Sec. 3. The Foundation, in concert with each Federal agency concerned, shall review the basic scientific research programs and activities of the Federal Government in order, among other purposes, to formulate methods for strengthening the administration of such programs and activities by the responsible agencies, and to study areas of basic research where gaps or undesirable overlapping of support may exist, and shall recommend to the heads of agencies concerning the support given to basic research.

[Sec. 3 amended by EO 10807 of Mar. 13, 1959, 24 FR 1897, 3 CFR, 1959–1963 Comp., p. 329]

Sec. 4. As now or hereafter authorized or permitted by law, the Foundation shall be increasingly responsible for providing support by the Federal Government for general-purpose basic research through contracts and grants. The conduct and support by other Federal agencies of basic research in areas which are closely related to their missions is recognized as important and desirable, especially in response to current national needs, and shall continue.

Sec. 5. The Foundation, in consultation with educational institutions, the heads of Federal agencies, and the Commissioner of Education of the Department of Health, Education, and Welfare,1 shall study the effects upon educational institutions of Federal policies and administration of contracts and grants for scientific research and development, and shall recommend policies and procedures which will promote the attainment of general national research objectives and realization of the research needs of Federal agencies while safeguarding the strength and independence of the Nation's institutions of learning.

Sec. 6. The head of each Federal agency engaged in scientific research shall make certain that effective executive, organizational, and fiscal practices exist to ensure (a) that the Foundation is consulted on policies concerning the support of basic research, (b) that approved scientific research programs conducted by the agency are reviewed continuously in order to preserve priorities in research efforts and to adjust programs to meet changing conditions without imposing unnecessary added burdens on budgetary and other resources, (c) that applied research and development shall be undertaken with sufficient consideration of the underlying basic research and such other factors as relative urgency, project costs, and availability of manpower and facilities, and (d) that, subject to considerations of security and applicable law, adequate dissemination shall be made within the Federal Government of reports on the nature and progress of research projects as an aid to the efficiency and economy of the overall Federal scientific research program.

Sec. 7. Federal agencies supporting or engaging in scientific research shall, with the assistance of the Foundation, cooperate in an effort to improve the methods of classification and reporting of scientific research projects and activities, subject to the requirements of security of information.

Sec. 8. To facilitate the efficient use of scientific research equipment and facilities held by Federal agencies:

(a) the head of each such agency engaged in scientific research shall, to the extent practicable, encourage and facilitate the sharing with other Federal agencies of major equipment and facilities; and

(b) a Federal agency shall procure new major equipment or facilities for scientific research purposes only after taking suitable steps to ascertain that the need cannot be met adequately from existing inventories or facilities of its own or of other agencies.

[Sec. 8 amended by EO 10807 of Mar. 13, 1959, 24 FR 1897, 3 CFR, 1959–1963 Comp., p. 329]

Sec. 9. The heads of the respective Federal agencies shall make such reports concerning activities within the purview of this order as may be required by the President.

Sec. 10. The National Science Foundation shall provide leadership in the effective coordination of the scientific information activities of the Federal Government with a view to improving the availability and dissemination of scientific information. Federal agencies shall cooperate with and assist the National Science Foundation in the performance of this function, to the extent permitted by law.

[Sec. 10 added by EO 10807 of Mar. 13, 1959, 24 FR 1897, 3 CFR, 1959–1963 Comp., p. 329]

SIGNIFICANCE

The National Science Foundation (NSF) was created in 1950. President Eisenhower signed Executive Order 10521 to support continued use of the NSF. In the shadow of the Cold War, the NSF emerged as the funding source for research that was conducted at U.S. colleges and universities. The NSF has become the major source of funding for social sciences, mathematics, and the computer sciences. The NSF has served as the clearinghouse of data in the United States and provides that data to governmental agencies. As such, the foundation monitors scientific progress within the United States and keeps with its mission to keep the United States at the forefront of research and development. In addition to providing a link between government and scientific research, the NSF has created education programs for all levels of education and has sought to foster international cooperation within the scientific community.

FURTHER RESOURCES

Web sites

American Association for the Advancement of Science. "Science and Public Policy." <http://www.aaas.org/spp/yearbook/chap29.htm> (accessed May 17, 2006).

Issues in Science and Technology. "Rethinking what research government should fund." <http://www.issues.org/16.1/branscomb.htm> (accessed May 15, 2006).

National Science Foundation. "About the National Science Foundation." <http://www.nsf.gov/about/history/overview-50.jsp> (accessed May 17, 2006).

Brown v. Board of Education

Court decision

By: U.S. Supreme Court

Date: May 17, 1954

Source: *Brown v. Board of Education*. United States Supreme Court, 347 U.S. 483, May 17, 1954.

About the Author: The U.S. Supreme Court is the highest judicial body in the United States, consisting of eight justices and one chief justice; in this 1954 case, Thurgood Marshall, representing Brown before the court, later became the U.S. Solicitor General and a Supreme Court Justice, serving on the court from 1967 to 1991.

INTRODUCTION

The 1954 United States Supreme Court case *Oliver Brown et al v. The Board of Education of Topeka, Kansas*, known as *Brown v. Board of Education*, overturned the controversial 1896 Supreme Court case *Plessy v. Ferguson*. In *Plessy v. Ferguson*, the court determined that "separate but equal" facilities for different races were legally acceptable as long as the "equal" principle was upheld. This decision applied to social and civil life as well as education; separate schools for black and white children persisted in many states, and in some states, such as California, Asian and Hispanic children went to racially segregated schools as well. Public schools for non-white children had higher rates of teachers who were not licensed or certified, buildings in disrepair, shorter school days or school years, supply shortages, and lack of textbooks; in other words, while such schools were separate, they were often not equal.

While court cases addressing segregation in education included the 1850 Massachusetts case *Roberts v. The City of Boston* and the 1885 California case *Tape v. Hurley*, in both state court cases the court upheld the principle of racially segregated education. In *Tape v. Hurley* children of Chinese descent were denied enrollment in public schools; in response to the court's decision that all children must be permitted to enroll, the school district created a separate school for children of Mongolian or Chinese descent. This move honored the letter of the law and was standard practice until the 1931 California case *Roberto Alvarez vs. the Board of Trustees of the Lemon Grove School District* held that Hispanics could not be segregated into separate facilities. Seventeen states required racial segre-

Attorneys for the NAACP celebrate their victory in *Brown v. Board of Education* on the steps of the U.S. Supreme Court. From left to right: George Hayes, Thurgood Marshall, and James M. Nabrit. THE LIBRARY OF CONGRESS.

gation in education, while sixteen prohibited the practice; by the early 1950s, the United States was a patchwork of varying laws for racially segregated or desegregated schools, and the *Brown v. Board of Education* case created uniformity while engineering monumental social change.

The National Association for the Advancement of Colored People (NAACP) had waited for some time for a strong case to push desegregation in schools. By 1951, NAACP leaders believed that the Kansas city schools were one possible venue for such a court case. Oliver Brown and Charles Scott, two African American parents living in Topeka, attempted to enroll their daughters at local, white-only public schools. Denied the opportunity, Brown contacted a local attorney who then referred Brown to the NAACP; Thurgood Marshall, a young attorney with the organization, was part of the legal team. While the *Brown v. Board of Education* case addressed education facilities, the NAACP aimed for desegregation in public transportation, accommodations, government, employment, and housing.

The district court that heard the Brown case found for the Topeka schools, citing the *Plessy v. Ferguson* case. Thurgood Marshall and the NAACP took the case to the U.S. Supreme Court, which then blended five separate cases from Delaware, Kansas, South Carolina, Virginia, and the District of Columbia to create what would become *Brown v. Board of Education*.

■ PRIMARY SOURCE

MR. CHIEF JUSTICE WARREN delivered the opinion of the Court.

These cases come to us from the States of Kansas, South Carolina, Virginia, and Delaware. They are premised on different facts and different local conditions, but a common legal question justifies their consideration together in this consolidated opinion.

In each of the cases, minors of the Negro race, through their legal representatives, seek the aid of the courts in obtaining admission to the public schools of their community on a nonsegregated basis. In each instance, they had been denied admission to schools attended by white children under laws requiring or permitting segregation according to race. This segregation was alleged to deprive the plaintiffs of the equal protection of the laws under the Fourteenth Amendment. In each of the cases other than the Delaware case, a three-judge federal district court denied relief to the plaintiffs on the so-called "separate but equal" doctrine announced by this Court in *Plessy v. Ferguson*, 163 U.S. 537. Under that doctrine, equality of treatment is accorded when the races are provided substantially equal facilities, even though these facilities be separate. In the Delaware case, the Supreme Court of Delaware adhered to that doctrine, but ordered that the plaintiffs be admitted to the white schools because of their superiority to the Negro schools.

The plaintiffs contend that segregated public schools are not "equal" and cannot be made "equal," and that hence they are deprived of the equal protection of the laws. Because of the obvious importance of the question presented, the Court took jurisdiction. Argument was heard in the 1952 Term, and reargument was heard this Term on certain questions propounded by the Court.

Reargument was largely devoted to the circumstances surrounding the adoption of the Fourteenth Amendment in 1868. It covered exhaustively consideration of the Amendment in Congress, ratification by the states, then-existing practices in racial segregation, and the views of proponents and opponents of the Amendment. This discussion and our own investigation convince us that, although these sources cast some light, it is not enough to resolve the problem with which we are faced. At best, they are inconclusive. The most avid proponents of the post-War Amendments undoubtedly intended them to remove all legal distinctions among "all persons born or naturalized in the United States." Their opponents, just as certainly, were antagonistic to both the letter and the spirit of the Amendments and wished them to have the most limited effect. What others in Congress and the state legislatures had in mind cannot be determined with any degree of certainty.

An additional reason for the inconclusive nature of the Amendment's history with respect to segregated schools is the status of public education at that time. In the South, the movement toward free common schools, supported by general taxation, had not yet taken hold. Education of white children was largely in the hands of private groups. Education of Negroes was almost nonexistent, and practically all of the race were illiterate. In fact, any education of Negroes was forbidden by law in some states. Today, in contrast, many Negroes have achieved outstanding success in the arts and sciences, as well as in the business and professional world. It is true that public school education at the time of the Amendment had advanced further in the North, but the effect of the Amendment on Northern States was generally ignored in the congressional debates. Even in the North, the conditions of public education did not approximate those existing today. The curriculum was usually rudimentary; ungraded schools were common in rural areas; the school term was but three months a year in many states, and compulsory school attendance was virtually unknown. As a consequence, it is not surprising that there should be so little in the history of the Fourteenth Amendment relating to its intended effect on public education.

In the first cases in this Court construing the Fourteenth Amendment, decided shortly after its adoption, the Court interpreted it as proscribing all state-imposed discriminations against the Negro race. The doctrine of "separate but equal" did not make its appearance in this Court until 1896 in the case of *Plessy v. Ferguson*, supra, involving not education but transportation. American courts have since labored with the doctrine for over half a century. In this Court, there have been six cases involving the "separate but equal" doctrine in the field of public education. In *Cumming v. County Board of Education*, 175 U.S. 528, and *Gong Lum v. Rice*, 275 U.S. 78, the validity of the doctrine itself was not challenged. In more recent cases, all on the graduate school level, inequality was found in that specific benefits enjoyed by white students were denied to Negro students of the same educational qualifications. *Missouri ex rel. Gaines v. Canada*, 305 U.S. 337; *Sipuel v. Oklahoma*, 332 U.S. 631; *Sweatt v. Painter*, 339 U.S. 629; *McLaurin v. Oklahoma State Regents*, 339 U.S.

637. In none of these cases was it necessary to reexamine the doctrine to grant relief to the Negro plaintiff. And in *Sweatt v. Painter*, supra, the Court expressly reserved decision on the question whether *Plessy v. Ferguson* should be held inapplicable to public education.

In the instant cases, that question is directly presented. Here, unlike *Sweatt v. Painter*, there are findings below that the Negro and white schools involved have been equalized, or are being equalized, with respect to buildings, curricula, qualifications and salaries of teachers, and other "tangible" factors. Our decision, therefore, cannot turn on merely a comparison of these tangible factors in the Negro and white schools involved in each of the cases. We must look instead to the effect of segregation itself on public education.

In approaching this problem, we cannot turn the clock back to 1868, when the Amendment was adopted, or even to 1896, when *Plessy v. Ferguson* was written. We must consider public education in the light of its full development and its present place in American life throughout the Nation. Only in this way can it be determined if segregation in public schools deprives these plaintiffs of the equal protection of the laws.

Today, education is perhaps the most important function of state and local governments. Compulsory school attendance laws and the great expenditures for education both demonstrate our recognition of the importance of education to our democratic society. It is required in the performance of our most basic public responsibilities, even service in the armed forces. It is the very foundation of good citizenship. Today it is a principal instrument in awakening the child to cultural values, in preparing him for later professional training, and in helping him to adjust normally to his environment. In these days, it is doubtful that any child may reasonably be expected to succeed in life if he is denied the opportunity of an education. Such an opportunity, where the state has undertaken to provide it, is a right which must be made available to all on equal terms.

We come then to the question presented: Does segregation of children in public schools solely on the basis of race, even though the physical facilities and other "tangible" factors may be equal, deprive the children of the minority group of equal educational opportunities? We believe that it does.

In *Sweatt v. Painter*, supra, in finding that a segregated law school for Negroes could not provide them equal educational opportunities, this Court relied in large part on "those qualities which are incapable of objective measurement but which make for greatness in a law school." In *McLaurin v. Oklahoma State Regents*, supra, the Court, in requiring that a Negro admitted to a white graduate school be treated like all other students, again resorted to intangible considerations: "…his ability to study, to engage in discussions and exchange views with other students, and, in general, to learn his profession." Such considerations apply with added force to children in grade and high schools. To separate them from others of similar age and qualifications solely because of their race generates a feeling of inferiority as to their status in the community that may affect their hearts and minds in a way unlikely ever to be undone. The effect of this separation on their educational opportunities was well stated by a finding in the Kansas case by a court which nevertheless felt compelled to rule against the Negro plaintiffs:

Segregation of white and colored children in public schools has a detrimental effect upon the colored children. The impact is greater when it has the sanction of the law, for the policy of separating the races is usually interpreted as denoting the inferiority of the negro group. A sense of inferiority affects the motivation of a child to learn. Segregation with the sanction of law, therefore, has a tendency to [retard] the educational and mental development of negro children and to deprive them of some of the benefits they would receive in a racial[ly] integrated school system.

Whatever may have been the extent of psychological knowledge at the time of *Plessy v. Ferguson*, this finding is amply supported by modern authority. Any language in *Plessy v. Ferguson* contrary to this finding is rejected.

We conclude that, in the field of public education, the doctrine of "separate but equal" has no place. Separate educational facilities are inherently unequal. Therefore, we hold that the plaintiffs and others similarly situated for whom the actions have been brought are, by reason of the segregation complained of, deprived of the equal protection of the laws guaranteed by the Fourteenth Amendment. This disposition makes unnecessary any discussion whether such segregation also violates the Due Process Clause of the Fourteenth Amendment.

Because these are class actions, because of the wide applicability of this decision, and because of the great variety of local conditions, the formulation of decrees in these cases presents problems of considerable complexity. On reargument, the consideration of appropriate relief was necessarily subordinated to the primary question—the constitutionality of segregation in public education. We have now announced that such segregation is a denial of the equal protection of the laws. In order that we may have the full assistance of the parties in formulating decrees, the cases will be restored to the docket, and the parties are requested to present further argument on Questions 4 and 5 previously propounded by the Court for the reargument this Term The Attorney

General of the United States is again invited to participate. The Attorneys General of the states requiring or permitting segregation in public education will also be permitted to appear as amici curiae upon request to do so by September 15, 1954, and submission of briefs by October 1, 1954.

It is so ordered.

SIGNIFICANCE

Thurgood Marshall had been the head of the NAACP Legal Defense Fund since 1939; Marshall had honed his skills in preparing for the Brown case with such previous Supreme Court cases as *Sweatt v. Painter* and *McLaurin v. Oklahoma State Regents*, in which the court found that separate black law schools and separate library and lecture hall seats for African American students could not provide equal educational opportunities for black students and violated the Fourteenth Amendment's equal protection clause.

In arguing for Brown in *Brown v. Board of Education*, Marshall reiterated the previous arguments that segregated schooling did not provide equal opportunities for students and violated the Fourteenth Amendment, but this time he also addressed *Plessy v. Ferguson* head-on. The Plessy case dealt with segregated public transportation for intrastate lines; the "separate but equal" doctrine applied to one of the arenas the NAACP hoped to desegregate.

Marshall also posited a social nuance; by denying black students the opportunity to attend school side-by-side with white students, who represented ninety percent of American society, segregated schooling policy reinforced a pervasive system of inferiority for black students and stripped white students of the opportunity to study and work with black students on an even playing ground. The court's decision centered on the Fourteenth Amendment and also discussed the change in the status of public education in the United States from 1896 to 1954, citing its larger role in society.

Southern reaction to the decision was immediate fury. The Jackson, Mississippi *Daily News* stated that "White and Negro children in the same schools will lead to miscegenation. Miscegenation leads to mixed marriages and mixed marriages lead to mongrelization of the human race." Meanwhile the Atlanta, Georgia *Constitution* called for cooler heads to prevail: "It is no time for hasty or ill-considered actions. It is no time to indulge demagogues on either side nor to listen to those who always are ready to incite violence and hate." Violence broke out throughout the south; nine

years after Brown, on June 11, 1963, Alabama Governor George Wallace physically blocked the entrance to the Foster Auditorium at the University of Alabama at Tuscaloosa after a court required the integration of the university. Wallace's famous inaugural speech, in which he intoned "segregation now, segregation tomorrow, and segregation forever" reflected the feelings of many southerners. Private school enrollments in white-only schools surged; new private schools were created as a parallel system to the integrated public schools in many areas of the deep south.

A 1955 decision known as "Brown II" required all school districts to move "with all deliberate speed" in desegregating. The Supreme Court gave the responsibility for implementing the desegregation to local school officials, and while the court did not give specific timetables, when many southern schools refused to desegregate or intentionally dragged out the process, the Supreme Court or lower courts intervened at times to enforce the "deliberate speed" requirement, and in 1964 Supreme Court Justice Hugo Black stated that the time for "deliberate speed" had run out. In some cases, desegregation had not been completed by the 1970s, and the cross-town busing crises in inner cities in the north, especially Boston, revealed a level of racism in the north that led to social turmoil and violence.

While Brown and Brown II addressed the issue of public educational facilities only, the case set a precedent for desegregation in other areas of social and civic life. The Civil Rights movement gained momentum as a result of Brown, and the 1964 Civil Rights Act, with protections for minorities and women in the areas of employment housing, education, and law, passed ten years after Brown, incorporated the integration the NAACP and civil rights leaders had envisioned in 1952 while working on the initial stages of Brown.

FURTHER RESOURCES

Books

Clotfelter, Charles T. *After "Brown": The Rise and Retreat of School Desegregation*. Princeton, N.J.: Princeton University Press, 2004.

Klarman, Michael J. *From Jim Crow to Civil Rights: The Supreme Court and the Struggle for Racial Equality*. New York: Oxford University Press, 2004.

Patterson, James T. *Brown v. Board of Education: A Civil Rights Milestone and Its Troubled Legacy*. New York: Oxford University Press, 2001.

Executive Order 10730

Desegregation of Central High School

By: Dwight D. Eisenhower

Date: September 23, 1957

Source: Eisenhower, Dwight D. "Executive Order 10730: Desegregation of Central High School." National Archives, September 23, 1957.

About the Author: Dwight David Eisenhower (1890–1969) was a decorated United States Army General who led the Allied Forces in North Africa during World War II and acted as Supreme Commander of forces on D-Day during the same war. He was the 34th President of the United States, serving from 1953–1961; during his tenure in office, the 1954 *Brown v. Board of Education* decision triggered a new era in civil rights in the United States.

INTRODUCTION

The 1954 United States Supreme Court decision *Brown v. Board of Education* overturned the "separate but equal" doctrine of the 1896 Supreme Court decision *Plessy v. Ferguson*; in the 1955 court decision known as Brown II, the Supreme Court required all school districts throughout the United States to desegregate all public schools "with all deliberate speed." While the court did not give a specific time table, the Brown decision was clear: desegregation was now the law of the land.

Seventeen U.S. states required segregated public schools, while sixteen prohibited segregation; throughout the southern United States, governors and citizens reacted to the Brown decision with derision, anger, and fear. The Sons of the American Revolution declared the decision a "communist plot," while the New York Times declared that "The folkways in southern communities will have to be adapted to new conditions if white and Negro children, together with white and Negro teachers, are to enjoy not only equal facilities but the same facilities in the same schools." Many

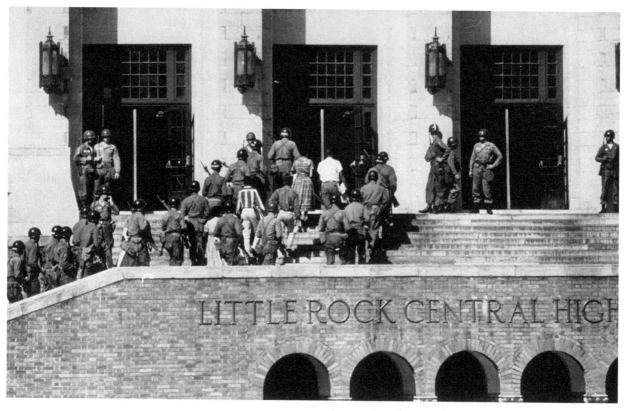

Nine African American students enter Central High School in Little Rock, Arkansas, as the school is desegregated on September 25, 1957. They are being escorted by soldiers from the 101st Airborne Division. © CORBIS-BETTMANN. REPRODUCED BY PERMISSION.

southerners expressed fears of miscegenation and interracial relationships should desegregation occur; white enrollment in private schools increased dramatically in parts of the south, and new, whites-only private schools formed in some areas as a direct response to the Brown decision.

By 1956, the Topeka city schools were completely integrated, though many southern districts blocked integration by filing lawsuits, filling the courts with challenges to Brown. In 1956, riots broke out at the University of Alabama when Autherine Lucy attempted to attend classes; university officials asked her to withdraw. While violence in the south erupted, desegregation continued quietly in such states as Arizona, Delaware, Maryland, and in Washington D.C.

Three years after *Brown v. Board of Education*, in Little Rock, Arkansas, nine black children were selected to attend the all-white Central High School. A federal court ordered the school district to comply with the desegregation. Arkansas Governor Orval Faubus refused, and ordered the Arkansas National Guard to Central High School to prevent the "Little Rock Nine" from attending classes on September 3, 1957. On September 4, Daisy Bates, the president of the local NAACP, organized eight of the nine students at her home to arrive at the school together. The ninth student, Elizabeth Eckford, did not have a phone and did not learn of the gathering; when she attempted to enter the school through the front entrance she was met by angry protestors and the National Guard, all blocking her. A white woman in the crowd, Grace Lorch, helped Eckford to safety.

Governor Faubus met with President Dwight D. Eisenhower on September 14, and as a result of that meeting agreed instead to use the National Guard to protect the African-American students. Upon his return to Little Rock, however, Faubus dismissed the troops, leaving the nine students, Thelma Mothershed, Elizabeth Eckford, Melba Pattillo, Jefferson Thomas, Ernest Green, Minniejean Brown, Carlotta Walls, Terrence Roberts, and Gloria Ray, exposed to an angry mob of white citizens. Local police officers helped the students to leave the building as rioters attacked reporters, threw bricks through windows, and destroyed school property.

For the next week large crowds of white citizens physically blocked the school entrances, parents withdrew white students from the school, and the "Little Rock Nine" were unable to attend classes. On September 20, NAACP lawyers Thurgood Marshall and Wiley Branton received a court injunction prohibiting Governor Faubus from using the National Guard to block the students from attending classes; Faubus complied, but warned the black students to stay at home.

On September 23, 1957, President Eisenhower issued the following Executive Order, sending in federal troops and placing the Arkansas National Guard under federal command to enforce the desegregation order.

PRIMARY SOURCE

EXECUTIVE ORDER 10730

PROVIDING ASSISTANCE FOR THE REMOVAL OF AN OBSTRUCTION OF JUSTICE WITHIN THE STATE OF ARKANSAS

WHEREAS on September 23, 1957, I issued Proclamation No.3204 reading in part as follows:

"WHEREAS certain persons in the state of Arkansas, individually and in unlawful assemblages, combinations, and conspiracies, have wifully obstructed the enforcement of orders of the United States District Court for the Eastern District of Arkansas with respect to matters relating to enrollment and attendance at public schools, particularly at Central High School, located in Little Rock School District, Little Rock, Arkansas; and

"WHEREAS such willful obstruction of justice hinders the execution of the laws of that State and of the United States, and makes it impracticable to enforce such laws by the ordinary course of judicial proceedings; and

"WHEREAS such obstruction of justice constitutes a denial of the equal protection of the laws secured by the Constitution of the United States and impedes the course of justice under those laws:

"NOW, THEREFORE, I, DWIGHT D. EISENHOWER, President of the United States, under and by virtue of the authority vested in me by the Constitution and Statutes of the United States, including Chapter 15 of Title 10 of the United States Code, particularly sections 332, 333 and 334 thereof, do command all persons engaged in such obstruction of justice to cease and desist therefrom, and to disperse forthwith;" and

WHEREAS the command contained in that Proclamation has not been obeyed and willful obstruction of enforcement of said court orders still exists and threatens to continue:

NOW, THEREFORE, by virtue of the authority vested in me by the Constitution and Statutes of the United States, including Chapter 15 of Title 10, particularly sections 332, 333 and 334 thereof, and section 301 of Title 3 of the United States Code, It is hereby ordered as follows:

SECTION 1. I hereby authorize and direct the Secretary of Defense to order into the active military service of the

United States as he may deem appropriate to carry out the purposes of this Order, any or all of the units of the National Guard of the United States and of the Air National Guard of the United States within the State of Arkansas to serve in the active military service of the United States for an indefinite period and until relieved by appropriate orders.

SEC. 2. The Secretary of Defense is authorized and directed to take all appropriate steps to enforce any orders of the United States District Court for the Eastern District of Arkansas for the removal of obstruction of justice in the State of Arkansas with respect to matters relating to enrollment and attendance at public schools in the Little Rock School District, Little Rock, Arkansas. In carrying out the provisions of this section, the Secretary of Defense is authorized to use the units, and members thereof, ordered into the active military service of the United States pursuant to Section 1 of this Order.

SEC. 3. In furtherance of the enforcement of the aforementioned orders of the United States District Court for the Eastern District of Arkansas, the Secretary of Defense is authorized to use such of the armed forces of the United States as he may deem necessary.

SEC. 4. The Secretary of Defense is authorized to delegate to the Secretary of the Army or the Secretary of the Air Force, or both, any of the authority conferred upon him by this Order.

DWIGHT D. EISENHOWER

THE WHITE HOUSE,

September 24, 1957.

SIGNIFICANCE

President Eisenhower ordered the 101st Airborne Division to Little Rock at the request of Little Rock Mayor Woodrow Mann to protect the nine black students; each student had a guard assigned to them for personal protection. Many southerners resented the federal intrusion into a states' rights issue. The shadow of Reconstruction and federal occupation after the Civil War to enforce black civil rights loomed over Eisenhower's Executive Order.

The students remained at Central High School, with protection, through the end of the school year. One of the students, Minniejean Brown, was suspended for pouring a bowl of chili on a white student who was harassing her. Ernest Green graduated in 1958, the first black student to graduate from the school.

In an address to the public in 1958, President Eisenhower countered criticism and accusations of communism or heavy-handed federal intervention with his explanation that "Our enemies are gloating over this incident and using it everywhere to misrepresent our whole nation. We are portrayed as a violator of those standards of conduct which the peoples of the world united to proclaim in the Charter of the United Nations. There they affirmed 'faith in fundamental human rights' and 'in the dignity and worth of the human person' and they did so 'without distinction as to race, sex, language or religion.'" By acknowledging the worldwide attention the Little Rock incident brought to racial affairs in the United States, and connecting it to human rights in general, President Eisenhower brought a global perspective to the civil rights issue.

Governor Faubus received a court injunction allowing him to delay school integration until 1961, but in 1958 the U.S. Supreme Court upheld the earlier ruling and enforced the desegregation. In response, Faubus closed all public schools in Little Rock for the 1958–1959 school year. White students flooded private schools, which blocked black student enrollment, and for that year black students in Little Rock created informal study groups and tutoring sessions to fill in the gap in their education; some students enrolled in correspondence courses at the University of Arkansas. In 1959, Faubus was forced to reopen the schools, with two of the original "Little Rock Nine" enrolling and graduating by the end of the year. The standoff over integration at Central High School was the first major test of the *Brown v. Board of Education* decision and changed the racial balance of public schools and private schools for decades to come, foreshadowing integration issues related to forced busing, housing, employment, and voting in coming years.

The experience at Central High School also motivated nascent civil rights leaders to push for integrated public transportation, public facilities, and to use physical protest as an effective medium for changing public opinion and bringing attention to their cause; the nine teenagers who braved the social conditions of the 1957–1958 school year at central High School provided an example to civil rights protestors of peaceful progress.

FURTHER RESOURCES

Books

Clotfelter, Charles T. *After "Brown": The Rise and Retreat of School Desegregation*. Princeton, N.J.: Princeton University Press, 2004.

Klarman, Michael J. *From Jim Crow to Civil Rights: The Supreme Court and the Struggle for Racial Equality.* New York: Oxford University Press USA, 2004.

Patterson, James T. *Brown v. Board of Education: A Civil Rights Milestone and Its Troubled Legacy.* New York: Oxford University Press USA, 2001.

Establishment of Peace Corps

Government memorandum

By: John F. Kennedy

Date: March 1, 1961

Source: Kennedy, John F. "Executive Order 10924: Establishment of Peace Corps." National Archives, March 1, 1961.

About the Author: John F. Kennedy served as the thirty-fifth president of the United States from 1961–1963. Kennedy won a Pulitzer Prize in 1957 for his work, *Profiles in Courage*, which outlines eight historical figures who displayed bravery in the face of great opposition.

INTRODUCTION

Long before Senator John F. Kennedy took to the campaign trail, two proposals were sent to Congress to create an organization that would send American citizens to aid those in the developing world. Representative Henry S. Reuss of Wisconsin first proposed a government study of the idea and Senator Hubert Humphrey first submitted legislation for the creation of the Peace Corps. However, at the time these bills were introduced, the idea of a corps of volunteers sent abroad lacked popular support. On October 14, 1960, Senator Kennedy arrived at the University of Michigan at Ann Arbor. After a long day of campaigning, Kennedy had stopped at the school to rest. However, ten thousand students were still congregated at 2 A.M. to hear him speak when he arrived at the school. Kennedy asked the students if they were willing to serve their country and work toward the goal of peace by working in Asia, Africa, and Latin America. Weeks later, a petition of over one thousand signatures had been gathered in support of the idea.

Kennedy tasked Sargent Shriver, his brother-in-law, to do a study of the feasibility of such a volunteer force. Shriver completed his study between Kennedy's election in November 1960 and his inauguration the next year. As a result, less than two months after taking office, Kennedy signed Executive Order 10924 to establish the Peace Corps within the State Department. Sargent Shriver was made the first director of the organization. In his address at the signing of the executive order, Kennedy set the goal to have five hundred volunteers in the field by the year's end. He asserted that the program was not designed for diplomacy or propaganda, but that it permits U.S. citizens to assist in world development and to bring a decent way of life to the developing world as a way to promote freedom. In his speech, he determined that with no salary or allowances, the volunteers would be expected to live and work alongside those they would serve. In doing so, volunteers would be encouraging peace and understanding.

■ PRIMARY SOURCE

TRANSCRIPT OF EXECUTIVE ORDER 10924: ESTABLISHMENT OF THE PEACE CORPS. (1961)

Executive Order 10924

ESTABLISHMENT AND ADMINISTRATION OF THE PEACE CORPS IN THE DEPARTMENT OF STATE

By virtue of the authority vested in me by the Mutual Security Act of 1954, 68 Stat. 832, as amended (22 U.S.C. 1750 et seq.), and as President of the United States, it is hereby ordered as follows:

SECTION 1. Establishment of the Peace Corps. The Secretary of State shall establish an agency in the Department of State which shall be known as the Peace Corps. The Peace Corps shall be headed by a Director.

SEC. 2. Functions of the Peace Corps. (a) The Peace Corps shall be responsible for the training and service abroad of men and women of the United States in new programs of assistance to nations and areas of the world, and in conjunction with or in support of existing economic assistance programs of the United States and of the United Nations and other international organizations.

(b) The Secretary of State shall delegate, or cause to be delegated, to the Director of the Peace Corps such of the functions under the Mutual Security Act of 1954, as amended, vested in the President and delegated to the Secretary, or vested in the Secretary, as the Secretary shall deem necessary for the accomplishment of the purposes of the Peace Corps.

The first members of the Peace Corps board a plane in Washington, D.C., on the way to their to Ghana for their first assignments, August 29, 1961. AP/WIDE WORLD PHOTOS. REPRODUCED BY PERMISSION.

SEC. 3. Financing of the Peace Corps. The Secretary of State shall provide for the financing of the Peace Corps with funds available to the Secretary for the performance of functions under the Mutual Security Act of 1954, as amended.

SEC. 4. Relation to Executive Order No. 10893. This order shall not be deemed to supersede or derogate from any provision of Executive Order No. 10893 of November 8, 1960, as amended, and any delegation made by or pursuant to this order shall, unless otherwise specifically provided therein, be deemed to be in addition to any delegation made by or pursuant to that order.

JOHN F. KENNEDY

THE WHITE HOUSE,

March 1, 1961.

SIGNIFICANCE

In 1961, Kennedy began to implement his plan to fight poverty, help cities develop, and expand government programs for citizens. This program was called the "New Frontier" and was based on President Roosevelt's New Deal. On the foreign policy front, Kennedy was concerned with the growth and spread of communism, particularly in third-world nations. As such, he sought alternatives to military activities. The Peace Corps was one such alternative. With its mission determined to spread friendship and peace, Kennedy sought to stem the expansion of communism in the developing world through the use of the idealistic volunteers. As a result, on March 1, 1961, the executive order to establish the Peace Corps was signed. Five months later, in July 1961, assignments had been created in Ghana, Tanzania, Colombia, the Philippines, Chile, and St. Lucia, and over five thousand applicants took the first exam to enter the Peace Corps. On August 28, 1961, President Kennedy hosted the inaugural group of volunteers at the White House Rose Garden. These volunteers were about to depart to serve in Ghana and Tanzania. The next month, congress approved legislation in Public Law 87-293 to mandate the goals of the Peace Corps to promote friendship and peace and to establish the track for the Peace Corps' permanence and autonomy. In 1963, merely two years after its inception, over 7,300 volunteers were in the field, operating in forty-four countries and working in education, community development, agriculture, health care, and public works. In 1966, fifteen thousand volunteers were active in field work.

In the decades that followed, the Peace Corps continued to develop. In 1979, President Carter signed an executive order granting the Peace Corps autonomy. In 1981, Congress passed legislation that created the Corps as an independent federal agency. In addition, the Peace Corps developed a Fellows Program in conjunction with Teachers College/Colombia University. The Fellows Program recruits and trains returning volunteers to become New York schoolteachers. Other programs include the World Wise Program, unveiled in 1989, which allows students to correspond with volunteers in the field.

Since its inception, the Peace Corps has had over 182,000 volunteers work in 138 host nations. In keeping with a changing world, these volunteers work in the areas of HIV/AIDS education, business development, environmental preservation, and information technology.

FURTHER RESOURCES

Web sites

John F. Kennedy Library and Museum. "Statement Upon Signing Order Establishing the Peace Corps." <http://www.jfklibrary.org/Historical+Resources/Archives/Reference+Desk/Speeches/JFK/003POF03PeaceCorp03011961.htm> (accessed June 15, 2006).

Peace Corps. "About the Peace Corps." <http://www.peacecorps.gov/index.cfm?shell=learn> (accessed June 15, 2006).

U.S. News and World Report. "The People's Vote: 100 Documents that shaped America." <http://www.usnews.com/usnews/documents/docpages/document_page92.htm> (accessed June 15, 2006).

Equal Pay Act of 1963

Legislation

By: Edith Green and Edith Rogers

Date: 1963

Source: "Equal Pay Act of 1963." *Pub. L.88–38* (10 June 1963).

About the Author: Representative Edith Green, a Democrat from Oregon, and Representative Edith Rogers, a Republican from Massachusetts, wrote the first draft of the Equal Pay Act in 1955. Green served in the House of Representatives for the state of Oregon for twenty years, while Rogers served thirty-five years for Massachusetts, the longest tenure of any female representative in Congress.

INTRODUCTION

Wisconsin passed the first piece of protective legislation for female workers in the United States; the 1867 law and others that followed assumed that women were less able to handle certain work because of physical differences between women and men and that women's health, pregnancy, and motherhood could be compromised by long work hours in poor settings. In the early 1900s as industrialization gained steam and families—including women and children—worked in factory settings, Progressive Era reformers sought to protect women and children from the worst abuses of the factory system. By 1912 twenty percent of women in the United States were in the labor force, a substantial labor shift that spurred states to pass protective laws for women and children that restricted work hours, shift lengths, and abuses.

Such legislation led to lower wages for women; employers argued that the legal restrictions on women's work made their work less valuable, and argued that as the "weaker" sex women's work was inherently less important than that of men, who were expected to support families. Protective legislation often created unequal labor conditions for men and women, in spite of reformers and legislators who worked to pass minimum wage laws for women.

World War I and World War II gave women an opportunity to fill jobs in traditionally male fields such as factory work, engineering, and auto mechanics; the United States government engaged in public relations campaigns such as "Rosie the Riveter" with the goal of changing public perception of factory jobs as men's work. The National War Labor Board recommended in 1942 that women receive equal pay for equal work in war industry jobs; the measure was voluntary and few employers followed through, but the suggestion helped to change attitudes concerning women's wages.

In 1955 Edith Rogers and Edith Green cowrote the first version of the Equal Pay Act, but struggled to find support for such a bill. President John F. Kennedy's President's Commission on the Status of Women, formed in 1961 to investigate issues such as employment, health, education, and law, opened discussion on the social and economic implications of women's work. Former First Lady Eleanor Roosevelt chaired the commission, and in 1963 issued a report detailing the need for improvements in antidiscrimination legislation, paid pregnancy and family leave, and the need for high-quality, affordable childcare. At the same time, Congress passed the Equal Pay Act, which included provisions for minimum wage laws that applied equally to men and women.

◼ PRIMARY SOURCE

U. S. Code

Title 29

Chapter 8

Section 206. Minimum Wage

[Section 5]

(d) Prohibition of sex discrimination

(1) No employer having employees subject to any provisions of this section shall discriminate, within any establishment in which such employees are employed, between employees on the basis of sex by paying wages to employees in such establishment at a rate less than the rate at which he pays wages to employees of the opposite sex in such establishment for equal work on jobs the performance of which requires equal skill, effort, and responsibility, and which are performed under similar working conditions, except where such payment is made pursuant to

(i) a seniority system;

(ii) a merit system;

(iii) a system which measures earnings by quantity or quality of production; or

(iv) a differential based on any other factor other than sex: Provided, That an employer who is paying a wage rate differential in violation of this subsection shall not, in order to comply with the

provisions of this subsection, reduce the wage rate of any employee.

(2) No labor organization, or its agents, representing employees of an employer having employees subject to any provisions of this section shall cause or attempt to cause such an employer to discriminate against an employee in violation of paragraph (1) of this subsection.

(3) For purposes of administration and enforcement, any amounts owing to any employee which have been withheld in violation of this subsection shall be deemed to be unpaid minimum wages or unpaid overtime compensation under this chapter.

(4) As used in this subsection, the term "labor organization" means any organization of any kind, or any agency or employee representation committee or plan, in which employees participate and which exists for the purpose, in whole or in part, of dealing with employers concerning grievances, labor disputes, wages, rates of pay, hours of employment, or conditions of work.

Additional Provisions of Equal Pay Act of 1963

AN ACT

To prohibit discrimination on account of sex in the payment of wages by employers engaged in commerce or in the production of goods for commerce. Be it enacted by the Senate and House of Representatives of the United States of America in Congress assembled, That this Act may be cited as the "Equal Pay Act of 1963."

DECLARATION OF PURPOSE

* * *

Not Reprinted in U.S. Code [Section 2]

(a) The Congress hereby finds that the existence in industries engaged in commerce or in the production of goods for commerce of wage differentials based on sex—

(1) depresses wages and living standards for employees necessary for their health and efficiency;

(2) prevents the maximum utilization of the available labor resources;

(3) tends to cause labor disputes, thereby burdening, affecting, and obstructing commerce;

(4) burdens commerce and the free flow of goods in commerce; and

(5) constitutes an unfair method of competition.

(b) It is hereby declared to be the policy of this Act, through exercise by Congress of its power to regulate commerce among the several States and with foreign nations, to correct the conditions above referred to in such industries.

[Section 3 of the Equal Pay Act of 1963 amends section 6 of the Fair Labor Standards Act by adding a new subsection (d). The amendment is incorporated in the revised text of the Fair Labor Standards Act.]

EFFECTIVE DATE

Not Reprinted in U.S. Code *[Section 4]*

The amendments made by this Act shall take effect upon the expiration of one year from the date of its enactment: Provided, That in case of employees covered by a bona fide collective bargaining agreement in effect at least thirty days prior to the date of enactment of this Act, entered into by a labor organization (as defined in section 6(d)(4) of the Fair Labor Standards Act of 1938, as amended), the amendments made by this Act shall take effect upon the termination of such collective bargaining agreement or upon the expiration of two years from the date of enactment of this Act, whichever shall first occur.

Approved June 10, 1963, 12 m.

SIGNIFICANCE

In 1963 the average working woman earned fifty-nine cents for every dollar earned by a man; the primary argument in the Equal Pay Act is the idea of equal pay for equal work. The 1963 Equal Pay Act did not provide employment protections or protection against gender-based employment discrimination; the Civil Rights Act of 1964, coming on the heels of the Equal Pay Act, added to legal protection for females in the labor force.

The Equal Employment Opportunity Commission, created as part of the 1964 Civil Rights Act, gave women legal recourse for violations of the Equal Pay Act and gender-based discrimination, forcing social norms in the workplace to change. From 1964 to 1971 back wages owed to women for gender-based pay inequities totaled more than $26 million dollars for more than 71,000 women. Court cases such as *Schultz v. Wheaton Glass Co.* and *Corning Glass Works v. Brennan* in the early 1970s banned the use of title changes to discriminate against workers; if two jobs have dif-

ferent titles but substantially similar responsibilities, the jobs must pay equal wages. In addition, paying women lower wages because they would accept them as part of the market rate was declared illegal and unacceptable.

The Equal Pay Act gave women legal standing for equal wages but also, in conjunction with the 1964 Civil Rights Act, helped to define and regulate sexual harassment in the workplace. One of the social consequences of legal protection against gender-based discrimination in wages and in treatment in the workplace was use of the courts to address sexual harassment; in 2005 more than 12,000 cases of sexual harassment were filed with the EEOC. Originally used by women workers against male coworkers who use sexual intimidation, language, gestures, or actions in the workplace, by 2005 nearly fifteen percent of all complaints were filed by male workers. Equal pay as well as gender-based discrimination protection has given women in the United States an expanded role in the workplace; from twenty percent of the workforce in 1912, women represented forty-six percent of all workers in 2004. As of 2004 the average working woman earned eighty cents for each dollar earned by men.

FURTHER RESOURCES

Books

Becker, Susan D. *The Origins of the Equal Rights Amendment: American Feminism Between the Wars.* Westport, CT: Greenwood Press, 1981.

Cobble, Dorothy Sue. *The Other Women's Movement: Workplace Justice and Social Rights in Modern America.* Princeton, NJ: Princeton University Press, 2004.

Felder, Deborah G. *A Century of Women: The Most Influential Events in Twentieth-Century Women's History.* Kensington Publishing Corp., 1999.

Friedan, Betty. *The Feminine Mystique.* New York: W.W. Norton, 2001.

Stetson, Dorothy M. *Women's Rights in the U.S.A: Policy Debates and Gender Roles.* New York: Routledge, 2004.

Web sites

Equal Opportunity Employment Commission. <http://www.eeoc.gov> (accessed May 19, 2006).

6 The Great Society

The Great Society

Upon his inauguration in 1961, United States President John F. Kennedy proposed a slate of social programs. Kennedy's New Frontier programs—including proposals for Medicare and social security benefits—stalled in Congress. After the assassination of President Kennedy on November 22, 1963, President Lyndon B. Johnson, formerly Vice-President in the Kennedy administration, sought to reinvigorate interest in Kennedy's social policy agenda. Utilizing an atmosphere of heightened government cooperation in the wake of the Kennedy assassination, Johnson proposed sweeping social reforms in housing, civil rights, education, and healthcare.

On May 22, 1964, President Johnson gave the commencement address at the University of Michigan. In his speech, Johnson introduced his domestic policy agenda. He dubbed the proposed reforms the Great Society. Johnson declared that he would seek the advice of the nation's experts to implement comprehensive social reforms in housing, education, healthcare, and the environment. The elimination of racial injustice was another key element of the social reform plan.

Johnson's Great Society invoked the tradition of the New Frontier and the New Deal. However, unlike the New Deal, which was proposed to relieve the Great Depression, the Great Society was proposed at a time of great economic prosperity. Johnson invoked this prosperity when introducing one of the main components of the Great Society, the so-called War on Poverty. Johnson actually proclaimed a "war on poverty" during his 1964 State of the Union address five months before introducing the Great Society. Johnson's War on Poverty was twofold: eliminating factors that increased the gap between rich and poor and providing relief for individuals living in poverty.

The era of the Great Society was also a time of social conflict. The civil rights movement was at its peak. Great Society reforms, such as the Civil Rights Act, codified the demands of the civil rights movement. As U.S. involvement in Vietnam increased, Johnson claimed that Americans should invest in both "guns and butter," funding the war in Vietnam while also continuing Great Society reforms. However, many programs were scaled back or dismantled by succeeding administrations.

The editors here extend discussion of the Great Society to cover the period from 1964 to 1981. Key parts of the Great Society discussed in this chapter, such as the Civil Rights Act and the Robert T. Stafford Student Loan Program, have stood the test of time. Other programs, such as Medicare, are routinely reformed. In 1981, the first federal budget of President Ronald Reagan scaled-back or curtailed several Great Society programs. Proponents of the Reagan reforms asserted that many Great Society programs exacerbated the social ills they were conceived to reduce. The new conservatives of the 1980s claimed that Great Society programs, especially welfare and housing projects, increased recipient reliance on government benefits. Others contended that the Great Society was fiscally irresponsible and too greatly expanded the size and role of the federal government—the same criticisms once levied by opponents of the New Deal. These controversial assertions are presented in the article on *Losing Ground: American Social Policy 1950–1980*.

The Great Society

Speech

By: Lyndon B. Johnson

Date: May 22, 1964

Source: Johnson, Lyndon B. "The Great Society." Remarks delivered at the University of Michigan commencement exercises, May 22, 1964.

About the Author: Lyndon B. Johnson (1908–1973) served as the thirty-sixth president of the United States from 1963 to 1969. His effort to build a Great Society was significantly hampered by escalating American involvement in the Vietnam War.

INTRODUCTION

President Lyndon B. Johnson envisioned a great society that would unify the United States and inspire the world. Heavily influenced by his admiration for Franklin D. Roosevelt's New Deal, Johnson's Great Society was an ambitious domestic program that aimed to improve the quality of American life by expanding the welfare state.

The sheer amount and scope of Great Society legislation was breathtaking. Johnson, a man with a wealth of political experience and a former majority leader in the U.S. Senate, persuaded the U.S. Congress to act on issues that included racial discrimination, education, medical care, consumer and environmental protections, and housing. Since he had personal experience of poverty as a youth, Johnson had a particular interest in bettering the lives of the poor. His antipoverty programs included a new food stamp program that largely replaced surplus food distribution, giving poor people greater choice in obtaining food. Rent supplements allowed poor people more housing options, enabling them to avoid crime-ridden public housing projects. In addition, with the Model Cities Act, Congress authorized more than $1 billion to improve conditions in the nation's slums.

The federal government's responsibility for health care grew even more under the Great Society. Johnson focused on the elderly, who constituted a large portion of the nation's poor. Congress responded with the Medicare program, providing the elderly with universal compulsory medical insurance financed largely through Social Security taxes. A separate program, Medicaid, authorized federal grants to supplement state-paid medical care for poor people under sixty-five years old. These two programs, in particular, did

President Lyndon B. Johnson at the White House, 1964.
PHOTOGRAPH BY ARNOLD NEWMAN. AP/WIDE WORLD PHOTOS. REPRODUCED BY PERMISSION.

much to better the lives of ordinary Americans and fulfilled the promise that Johnson had made in his speech before the 1964 graduating class of the University of Michigan.

■ PRIMARY SOURCE

President Hatcher, Governor Romney, Senators McNamara and Hart, Congressmen Meader and Staebler, and other members of the fine Michigan delegation, members of the graduating class, my fellow Americans:

It is a great pleasure to be here today. This university has been coeducational since 1870, but I do not believe it was on the basis of your accomplishments that a Detroit high school girl said (and I quote), "In choosing a college, you first have to decide whether you want a coeducational school or an educational school." Well, we can find both here at Michigan, although perhaps at different hours. I came out here today very anxious to meet the Michigan student whose father told a friend of mine that his son's education had been a real value. It stopped his mother from bragging about him.

I have come today from the turmoil of your capital to the tranquility of your campus to speak about the future of your country. The purpose of protecting the life of our Nation and preserving the liberty of our citizens is to pursue the happiness of our people. Our success in that pursuit is the test of our success as a Nation.

For a century we labored to settle and to subdue a continent. For half a century we called upon unbounded invention and untiring industry to create an order of plenty for all of our people. The challenge of the next half century is whether we have the wisdom to use that wealth to enrich and elevate our national life, and to advance the quality of our American civilization.

Your imagination and your initiative and your indignation will determine whether we build a society where progress is the servant of our needs, or a society where old values and new visions are buried under unbridled growth. For in your time we have the opportunity to move not only toward the rich society and the powerful society, but upward to the Great Society.

The Great Society rests on abundance and liberty for all. It demands an end to poverty and racial injustice, to which we are totally committed in our time. But that is just the beginning.

The Great Society is a place where every child can find knowledge to enrich his mind and to enlarge his talents. It is a place where leisure is a welcome chance to build and reflect, not a feared cause of boredom and restlessness. It is a place where the city of man serves not only the needs of the body and the demands of commerce but the desire for beauty and the hunger for community. It is a place where man can renew contact with nature. It is a place which honors creation for its own sake and for what is adds to the understanding of the race. It is a place where men are more concerned with the quality of their goals than the quantity of their goods.

But most of all, the Great Society is not a safe harbor, a resting place, a final objective, a finished work. It is a challenge constantly renewed, beckoning us toward a destiny where the meaning of our lives matches the marvelous products of our labor.

So I want to talk to you today about three places where we begin to build the Great Society—in our cities, in our countryside, and in our classrooms.

Many of you will live to see the day, perhaps 50 years from now, when there will be 400 million Americans—four-fifths of them in urban areas. In the remainder of this century urban population will double, city land will double, and we will have to build homes and highways and facilities equal to all those built since this country was first settled. So in the next 40 years we must re-build the entire urban United States.

Aristotle said: "Men come together in cities in order to live, but they remain together in order to live the good life." It is harder and harder to live the good life in American cities today. The catalog of ills is long: there is the decay of the centers and the despoiling of the suburbs. There is not enough housing for our people or transportation for our traffic. Open land is vanishing and old landmarks are violated. Worst of all expansion is eroding these precious and time honored values of community with neighbors and communion with nature. The loss of these values breeds loneliness and boredom and indifference.

And our society will never be great until our cities are great. Today the frontier of imagination and innovation is inside those cities and not beyond their borders. New experiments are already going on. It will be the task of your generation to make the American city a place where future generations will come, not only to live, but to live the good life. And I understand that if I stayed here tonight I would see that Michigan students are really doing their best to live the good life.

This is the place where the Peace Corps was started.

It is inspiring to see how all of you, while you are in this country, are trying so hard to live at the level of the people.

A second place where we begin to build the Great Society is in our countryside. We have always prided ourselves on being not only America the strong and America the free, but America the beautiful. Today that beauty is in danger. The water we drink, the food we eat, the very air that we breathe, are threatened with pollution. Our parks are overcrowded, our seashores overburdened. Green fields and dense forests are disappearing.

A few years ago we were greatly concerned about the "Ugly American." Today we must act to prevent an ugly America.

For once the battle is lost, once our natural splendor is destroyed, it can never be recaptured. And once man can no longer walk with beauty or wonder at nature his spirit will wither and his sustenance be wasted.

A third place to build the Great Society is in the classrooms of America. There your children's lives will be shaped. Our society will not be great until every young mind is set free to scan the farthest reaches of thought and imagination. We are still far from that goal. Today, 8 million adult Americans, more than the entire population of Michigan, have not finished 5 years of school. Nearly 20 million have not finished 8 years of school. Nearly 54 million—more than one quarter of all America—have not even finished high school.

Each year more than 100,000 high school graduates, with proved ability, do not enter college because they cannot afford it. And if we cannot educate today's youth, what will we do in 1970 when elementary school enrollment will be 5 million greater than 1960? And high school enrollment will rise by 5 million. And college enrollment will increase by more than 3 million.

In many places, classrooms are overcrowded and curricula are outdated. Most of our qualified teachers are underpaid and many of our paid teachers are unqualified. So we must give every child a place to sit and a teacher to learn from. Poverty must not be a bar to learning, and learning must offer an escape from poverty.

But more classrooms and more teachers are not enough. We must seek an educational system which grows in excellence as it grows in size. This means better training for our teachers. It means preparing youth to enjoy their hours of leisure as well as their hours of labor. It means exploring new techniques of teaching, to find new ways to stimulate the love of learning and the capacity for creation.

These are three of the central issues of the Great Society. While our Government has many programs directed at those issues, I do not pretend that we have the full answer to those problems. But I do promise this: We are going to assemble the best thought and the broadest knowledge from all over the world to find those answers for America.

I intend to establish working groups to prepare a series of White House conferences and meetings—on the cities, on natural beauty, on the quality of education, and on other emerging challenges. And from these meetings and from this inspiration and from these studies we will begin to set our course toward the Great Society.

The solution to these problems does not rest on a massive program in Washington, nor can it rely solely on the strained resources of local authority. They require us to create new concepts of cooperation, a creative federalism, between the National Capital and the leaders of local communities.

Woodrow Wilson once wrote: "Every man sent out from his university should be a man of his Nation as well as a man of his time."

Within your lifetime powerful forces, already loosed, will take us toward a way of life beyond the realm of our experience, almost beyond the bounds of our imagination.

For better or for worse, your generation has been appointed by history to deal with those problems and to lead America toward a new age. You have the chance never before afforded to any people in any age. You can help build a society where the demands of morality, and the needs of the spirit, can be realized in the life of the Nation.

So, will you join in the battle to give every citizen the full equality which God enjoins and the law requires, whatever his belief, or race, or the color of his skin?

Will you join in the battle to give every citizen an escape from the crushing weight of poverty?

Will you join in the battle to make it possible for all nations to live in enduring peace—as neighbors and not as mortal enemies?

Will you join in the battle to build the Great Society, to prove that our material progress is only the foundation on which we will build a richer life of mind and spirit?

There are those timid souls that say this battle cannot be won; that we are condemned to a soulless wealth. I do not agree. We have the power to shape the civilization that we want. But we need your will and your labor and your hearts, if we are to build that kind of society.

Those who came to this land sought to build more than just a new country. They sought a new world. So I have come here today to your campus to say that you can make their vision our reality. So let us from this moment begin our work so that in the future men will look back and say: It was then, after a long and weary way, that man turned the exploits of his genius to the full enrichment of his life.

Thank you. Good-bye.

■

SIGNIFICANCE

The winners of the Great Society programs included the poor as well as some unexpected beneficiaries. Most of the funds for economically depressed areas built highways and thus helped the construction industry. Real estate developers, investors, and moderate-income families benefited most from the National Housing Act of 1968. As commercial development and high-income housing often displaced the poor in slum clearance programs, many blacks came to refer to urban renewal as "Negro removal." Physicians' fees and hospital costs soared after the enactment of Medicare and Medicaid.

The 1960s public largely approved of the Great Society, but not all of its measures proved workable over time. The commitment of the federal government to the concept of the welfare state seemed unquestioned. It was this aspect of the Great Society that has aroused the most controversy and backlash in subsequent decades. The expansion of government responsibility for health care has proven particularly worrisome to some political leaders in the twenty-first century who are faced with providing Medicare benefits to the massive baby boom generation. For Johnson, the more immediate problem was how to wage a war on poverty while expanding the war in Vietnam.

FURTHER RESOURCES

Books

Andrew, John A. *Lyndon Johnson and the Great Society.* Chicago: Ivan R. Dee, 1998.

Brown, Michael K. *Race, Money, and the American Welfare State.* Ithaca, N.Y.: Cornell University Press, 1999.

Davies, Gareth. *From Opportunity to Entitlement: The Transformation and Decline of Great Society Liberalism.* Lawrence: University Press of Kansas, 1996.

Gillette, Michael L. *Launching the War on Poverty: An Oral History.* New York: Twayne, 1996.

Title VI of the 1964 Civil Rights Act

Legislation

By: Everett Dirksen

Date: July 2, 1964

Source: *Civil Rights Act of 1964.* Public Law 88–352, Title VI, Sec. 601, 78. *U.S. Statutes at Large* (July 2, 1964).

About the Author: Republican Senator Everett Dirksen (1896–1969) represented the state of Illinois from 1950 until his death in 1969. Elected to the senate minority leader post in 1959, he worked with Lyndon Johnson in the Senate and later with President Johnson in crafting the Civil Rights Act of 1964.

INTRODUCTION

While the issue of civil rights for minorities and women in the United States had been handled through a series of constitutional amendments, court decisions, state laws, and federal laws, by the late 1950s clashes between civil rights activists and anti-civil rights groups—composed largely of white southerners—fueled the need for sweeping federal legislation to address this issue. The Fifteenth Amendment to the Constitution, ratified in 1870, gave African American males the right to vote, and the Nineteenth Amendment, ratified in 1920, broadened voting rights to include all women. By the mid-twentieth century, however, African Americans continued to face numerous obstacles to voting, including poll taxes, literacy tests, harassment, and intimidation. In addition, Supreme Court decisions in 1950 and 1954 requiring integration in public education led to violent standoffs in southern states such as Arkansas and Alabama. Civil rights acts in 1957 and 1960 had helped to flesh out legal protections for minorities, but Lyndon Johnson, a Senate Democrat from Texas and future president of the United States, found these laws lacking in substance and difficult to enforce.

By 1963, civil rights leaders such as Martin Luther King Jr. (1929–1968) expressed frustration that the legal protection and Supreme Court decisions, while important steps forward in the fight for equality under the law, were not enough. In response, President John F. Kennedy (1917–1963) addressed the nation on June 11, 1963, and called for new civil rights legislation. Five months later, Kennedy was assassinated, and Lyndon Johnson (1908–1973), then vice president of the United States, assumed the presidency.

Johnson's long-held desire for a stronger civil rights law played itself out in his negotiations with Senate and House leaders; in the end the Civil Rights Act of 1964 granted minorities and women legal protections in the areas of federal assistance, housing, employment, education, and voting rights. Title VI specifically prohibits discrimination against recipients of federal assistance or those enrolled in programs or institutions receiving federal funds.

■ PRIMARY SOURCE

TITLE 42 -The Public Health and Welfare

SUBCHAPTER V-FEDERALLY ASSISTED PROGRAMS

Sec. 2000d. Prohibition against exclusion from participation in, denial of benefits of, and discrimination under federally assisted programs on ground of race, color, or national origin

No person in the United States shall, on the ground of race, color, or national origin, be excluded from participation in, be denied the benefits of, or be subjected to discrimination under any program or activity receiving Federal financial assistance.

■

SIGNIFICANCE

Title VI of the Civil Rights Act of 1964 covers educational institutions and any other agency or institution receiving or disbursing federal funds; this section also applies to all public welfare and health programs. The provision gives legal protection to

Hispanic Americans protest federal discrimination in New York City's welfare bureaucracy on July 23, 2003. The demonstrators called for support of Intro 38, the Equal Access to Health and Human Services Act, which would provide language access to city services for people with limited English proficiency. PHOTO BY MARIO TAMA/GETTY IMAGES.

minorities and legal immigrants, and over time, African Americans, Hispanics, women, the disabled, and the elderly used Title VI to broaden their legal rights in terms of federal financial assistance.

Title VI reached into the schools but also into health-care programs such as Medicare and Medicaid, nursing home programs, adoption agencies, hospitals, alcohol and drug addiction treatment programs, day care centers, and mental health clinics. The provisions of this law also include a ban on segregation on the basis of race or national origin among recipients of services.

Passed ten years after the 1954 U.S. Supreme Court decision *Brown v. Board of Education of Topeka, Kansas*, part of the purpose of Title VI was to speed up the process of school desegregation, according to author Stephen C. Halpern. In his 1995 book *On the Limits of the Law: The Ironic Legacy of Title VI of the 1964 Civil Rights Act*, Halpern argues that the purpose of Title VI was to reinforce *Brown* and to use litigation

and federal law to push integration. He notes, however, that while Title VI forbids discrimination, it did not solve the problem. It became the responsibility of the court to "identify the parameters of the legal right blacks had to equal, nondiscriminatory treatment in schools. There are formidable conceptual and political problems associated with defining that right."

In essence, like the *Brown v. Board of Education* case, Title VI provided legal rights and protections, but the underlying causes of discrimination could not be addressed by legal institutions. The 1896 Supreme Court decision *Plessy v. Ferguson*, known for creating the "separate but equal" doctrine, had noted that while law could create conditions protecting individual rights, it could not force society or individuals to change opinions and attitudes about race. While many civil rights leaders hailed the 1964 law as a major leap forward in advancing equality for all Americans, the social conditions leading to racial discrimination remained a substantial obstacle for civil rights leaders and everyday citizens to overcome.

FURTHER RESOURCES

Books

Dudziak, Mary L. *Cold War Civil Rights: Race and the Image of American Democracy.* Princeton, N.J.: Princeton University Press, 2002.

Halpern, Stephen C. *On the Limits of the Law: The Ironic Legacy of Title VI of the 1964 Civil Rights Act.* Baltimore, Md.: Johns Hopkins University Press, 1995.

Klarman, Michael J. *From Jim Crow to Civil Rights: The Supreme Court and the Struggle for Racial Equality.* New York: Oxford University Press, 2004.

Rosenberg, Jonathan and Zachary Karabell. *Kennedy, Johnson, and the Quest for Justice: The Civil Rights Tapes.* New York: W. W. Norton, 2003.

Web sites

John F. Kennedy Library and Museum. "Radio and Television Report to the American People on Civil Rights." <http://www.jfklibrary.net/j061163.htm> (accessed May 29, 2006).

Title VII of the Civil Rights Act of 1964

Unlawful Employment Practices

Legislation

By: Everett Dirksen

Date: July 2, 1964

Source: *Civil Rights Act of 1964.* Public Law 88-352, Title VII, Sec. 703, 78. *U.S. Statutes at Large* (July 2, 1964).

About the Author: Republican Senator Everett Dirksen (1896–1969) represented the state of Illinois from 1950 until his death in 1969. Elected to the Senate Minority Leader post in 1959, he worked with Lyndon Johnson in the Senate and later with President Johnson in crafting the Civil Rights Act of 1964.

INTRODUCTION

Labor history for black Americans stretches back to forced slavery in the 1600s, as colonial powers permitted landowners to import slaves from Africa into new colonies in North America. When the slave system in the United States ended between 1863 and 1865, with President Abraham Lincoln's Emancipation Proclamation and later the Thirteenth Amendment to the U.S. Constitution, which abolished slavery, former slaves found themselves free individuals and no longer legally held commodities. The southern states had relied on slave labor for centuries; shifting from an economy based on slave labor to a paid labor system involved serious economic and social adjustments in the post-Civil War period.

At the same time, women began to emerge as part of the growing industrial workforce in the northern United States. The convergence of former slaves migrating north, immigrants arriving from western Europe, and urbanization bringing more women into the workforce in and near city centers changed the labor market dramatically. Immigrants, women, children, and African Americans faced outright discrimination on the job; they were paid lower wages and were the first to be fired. Unions often excluded women and black workers; the Knights of Labor, formed in 1869, welcomed women (and minorities in 1883), but the American Federation of Labor, which became the dominant force in American society, excluded women and minorities for some time.

World War I (1914–1918) and World War II (1939–1945) temporarily changed labor circumstances for women and minorities as wartime industry required a strong supply of workers to fill the void created as white male soldiers were shipped off to war. Between the wars the Great Depression (1929–1941) created severe unemployment in the United States, with women and minorities losing jobs to white males. The Unemployment Relief Act of 1933 was designed to assist with the grinding poverty and desperation of those out of work, and it prohibited discrimination based on sex, race, and national origin. The federal government lacked enforcement mechanisms, however, and employers ignored the law. The National War Labor Board recommended equal wages for women and minorities during World War II; the voluntary program, like the Unemployment Relief Act, found few adherents among private corporations.

While court cases and laws such as the Civil Rights Acts of 1957 and 1960 and the Equal Pay Act of 1963 offered some workplace rights and equal pay laws for minorities and women, President Lyndon Johnson's (1908–1973) project, the Civil Rights Act of 1964, was the first to provide strong legal protection against workplace discrimination. Title VII of the Civil Rights Act of 1964 words this protection in unambiguous terms, creating government agencies with enforcement powers to attempt an end to racial and gender discrimination in the labor force.

Lawyer Johnny Cochran (front right) sits with lawyer Douglas Wigdor (left) as he speaks at a news conference to discuss a complaint made to the Equal Employment Opportunity Commission (EEOC) against Radianz U.S. Inc, in New York on July 31, 2003. © REUTERS/CORBIS.

PRIMARY SOURCE

(a) It shall be an unlawful employment practice for an employer—

1. to fail or refuse to hire or to discharge any individual, or otherwise to discriminate against any individual with respect to his compensation, terms, conditions, or privileges of employment, because of such individual's race, color, religion, sex, or national origin; or
2. to limit, segregate, or classify his employees or applicants for employment in any way which would deprive or tend to deprive any individual of employment opportunities or otherwise adversely affect his status as an employee, because of such individual's race, color, religion, sex, or national origin.

(b) It shall be an unlawful employment practice for an employment agency to fail or refuse to refer for employment, or otherwise to discriminate against, any individual because of his race, color, religion, sex, or national origin, or to classify or refer for employment any individual on the basis of his race, color, religion, sex, or national origin.

(c) It shall be an unlawful employment practice for a labor organization—

1. to exclude or to expel from its membership, or otherwise to discriminate against, any individual because of his race, color, religion, sex, or national origin;
2. to limit, segregate, or classify its membership or applicants for membership, or to classify or fail or refuse to refer for employment any individual, in any way which would deprive or tend to deprive any individual of employment opportunities, or would limit such employment opportunities or otherwise adversely affect his status as an employee or as an applicant for employment, because of such individual's race, color, religion, sex, or national origin; or
3. to cause or attempt to cause an employer to discriminate against an individual in violation of this section.

(d) It shall be an unlawful employment practice for any employer, labor organization, or joint labor-management committee controlling apprenticeship or other training or retraining, including on-the-job training programs to discriminate against any individual because of his race, color, religion, sex, or national origin in admission to, or employment in, any program established to provide apprenticeship or other training.

(e) Notwithstanding any other provision of this subchapter, (1) it shall not be an unlawful employment practice for an employer to hire and employ employees, for an employment agency to classify, or refer for employment any individual, for a labor organization to classify its membership or to classify or refer for employment any individual, or for an employer, labor organization, or joint labor-management committee controlling apprenticeship or other training or retraining programs to admit or employ any individual in any such program, on the basis of his religion, sex, or national origin in those certain instances where religion, sex, or national origin is a bona fide occupational qualification reasonably necessary to the normal operation of that particular business or enterprise, and (2) it shall not be an unlawful employment practice for a school, college, university, or other educational institution or institution of learning to hire and employ employees of a particular religion if such school, college, university, or other educational institution or institution of learning is, in whole or in substantial part, owned, supported, controlled, or managed by a particular religion or by a particular religious corporation, association, or society, or if the curriculum of such school, college, university, or other educational institution or institution of learning is directed toward the propagation of a particular religion.

(f) As used in this subchapter, the phrase "unlawful employment practice" shall not be deemed to include any action or measure taken by an employer, labor organization, joint labor-management committee, or employment agency with respect to an individual who is a member of the Communist Party of the United States or of any other organization required to register as a Communist-action or Communist-front organization by final order of the Subversive Activities Control Board pursuant to the Subversive Activities Control Act of 1950 [50 U.S.C. 781 et seq.]

(g) Notwithstanding any other provision of this subchapter, it shall not be an unlawful employment practice for an employer to fail or refuse to hire and employ any individual for any position, for an employer to discharge any individual from any position, or for an employment agency to fail or refuse to refer any individual for employment in any position, or for a labor organization to fail or refuse to refer any individual for employment in any position, if—

1. the occupancy of such position, or access to the premises in or upon which any part of the duties of such position is performed or is to be performed, is subject to any requirement imposed in the interest of the national security of the United States under any security program in effect pursuant to or administered under any statute of the United States or any Executive order of the President; and
2. such individual has not fulfilled or has ceased to fulfill that requirement.

(h) Notwithstanding any other provision of this subchapter, it shall not be an unlawful employment practice for an employer to apply different standards of compensation, or different terms, conditions, or privileges of employment pursuant to a bona fide seniority or merit system, or a system which measures earnings by quantity or quality of production or to employees who work in different locations, provided that such differences are not the result of an intention to discriminate because of race, color, religion, sex, or national origin, nor shall it be an unlawful employment practice for an employer to give and to act upon the results of any professionally developed ability test provided that such test, its administration or action upon the results is not designed, intended or used to discriminate because of race, color, religion, sex or national origin. It shall not be an unlawful employment practice under this subchapter for any employer to differentiate upon the basis of sex in determining the amount of the wages or compensation paid or to be paid to employees of such employer if such differentiation is authorized by the provisions of section 206(d) of title 29 [section 6(d) of the Fair Labor Standards Act of 1938, as amended]

(i) Nothing contained in this subchapter shall apply to any business or enterprise in or near an Indian reservation with respect to any publicly announced employment practice of such business or enterprise under which a preferential treatment is given to any individual because he is an Indian living on or near a reservation.

(j) Nothing contained in this subchapter shall be interpreted to require any employer, employment agency, labor organization, or joint labor-management committee subject to this subchapter to grant preferential treatment to any individual or to any group because of the race, color, religion, sex, or national origin of such individual or group on account of an imbalance which may exist with respect to the total number or percentage of persons of any race, color, religion, sex, or national origin employed by any employer, referred or classified for employment by any employment agency or labor organization, admitted to membership or classified by any labor organization, or admitted to, or employed in, any apprenticeship or other training program, in comparison with the total number or percentage of persons of such race, color, religion, sex, or national origin in any community, State, section, or other area, or in the available work force in any community, State, section, or other area.

SIGNIFICANCE

Until such legislation as the Equal Pay Act of 1963 and Title VII, "Help Wanted" sections of newspapers contained gender-segregated advertisements for jobs. After the passage of Title VII, employers could no longer legally argue that women were inherently too weak for a particular position or that white clientele would refuse to work with an African American salesperson; such actions constituted discrimination in violation of federal law. At the same time, however, the law could not force social change.

Title VII provided worker protection with the backing of the Equal Employment Opportunity Commission (EEOC). Workers in protected classes could file grievances and lawsuits against companies that violated the new law; women and minorities gained legal standing in the courts. In 1982, the U.S. Supreme Court ruled in favor of Alta Chrapliwy, a worker in a Uniroyal factory, in the 1982 *Chrapliwy v. Uniroyal* case. Uniroyal had a highly gender-segregated workforce in the plant, with women in the footwear division and men in other divisions. The Supreme Court found this division of labor to be in violation of Title VII.

Title VII has been expanded over time; in 1986, the Supreme Court case *Meritor Savings Bank v. Vinson* found that women had a right to protection from a "hostile work environment." The justices broadened the definition of sexual harassment and its application to Title VII in this decision, and later revisions to Title VII included protection against discrimination in the work place for pregnancy, disabilities, and age.

Ironically, this sweeping federal legislation does not apply to federal government employees, nor does it apply to most religious and nonprofit organizations. Small businesses employing fewer than fifteen people are exempt as well. The addition of gender as a protected class came about almost as an afterthought. Howard Smith, a congressman from Virginia and friend of Alice Paul (1885–1977)—the founder of the National Women's Party, author of the Equal Rights Amendment, and longtime suffragist—requested that the word "sex" be added to protect women as well. The addition of "sex" to the act generated some discussion, but the act did pass. The EEOC initially stalled on grievances filed on the basis of gender discrimination, in spite of the fact that more than one-third of all grievances filed in the first year fell into that category. In its infancy, the EEOC was forced to both define issues related to discrimination and to determine enforcement strategies.

The EEOC, the act's primary enforcement mechanism, saw its caseload rise to more than 55,000 complaints related to Title VII violations in the year 2005. The primary agency for discrimination complaints, the EEOC has not only monitored legal cases but also helped usher in the social changes resulting from legal protections for female workers, minorities, and naturalized citizens and other immigrants. Those protected under Title VII's expansion changed American society and the landscape of the workplace.

FURTHER RESOURCES

Books

Dubofsky, Melvyn. *Hard Work: The Making of Labor History.* Champaign: University of Illinois Press, 2000.

Dudziak, Mary L. *Cold War Civil Rights: Race and the Image of American Democracy.* Princeton, N.J.: Princeton University Press, 2002.

Fantasia, Rick and Kim Voss. *Hard Work: Remaking the American Labor Movement.* Berkeley: University of California Press, 2004.

Klarman, Michael J. *From Jim Crow to Civil Rights: The Supreme Court and the Struggle for Racial Equality.* New York: Oxford University Press, 2004.

Rosenberg, Jonathan and Zachary Karabell. *Kennedy, Johnson, and the Quest for Justice: The Civil Rights Tapes.* New York: W.W. Norton, 2003.

Periodicals

"Civil Rights Act of 1964." Public Law 88-352, Title VII, Sec. 703, 78. *U.S. Statutes at Large.* (July 2, 1964).

The Equal Employment Opportunity Commission. "The Equal Pay Act of 1963." <http://www.eeoc.gov/policy/epa.html> (accessed June 27, 2006).

Web sites

FDR Library. "Franklin Roosevelt's Statement on the National Labor Relations Act (The Wagner Act)." <http://www.fdrlibrary.marist.edu/odnlrast.html> (accessed May 29, 2006).

John F. Kennedy Library and Museum. "Radio and Television Report to the American People on Civil Rights." <http://www.jfklibrary.net/j061163.htm> (accessed May 29, 2006).

Maggie Kuhn, founder of the Gray Panthers organization devoted to fighting age discrimination. UPI/BETTMANN. REPRODUCED BY PERMISSION.

Executive Order 11141— Declaring a Public Policy against Discrimination on the Basis of Age

Government record

By: Lyndon B. Johnson

Date: February 12, 1964

Source: Johnson, Lyndon B. "Executive Order 11141— Declaring a Public Policy against Discrimination on the Basis of Age." *Federal Register*, vol. 29. Washington, D.C.: Office of the Federal Register, National Archives and Records Administration, February 12, 1964. p.

About the Author: Lyndon B. Johnson (1908–1973) was the thirty-sixth President of the United States. Vice-President under President John F. Kennedy, Johnson became President after Kennedy's assassination on November 22, 1963. Executive Orders are the form of documentation whereby the President of the United States orders specific directives as the head of the Executive Branch of the government.

INTRODUCTION

Employers in the United States regularly base their decisions as to whom to hire on a wide variety of factors. While it is difficult for the government to affect what motivates someone to hire or not to hire a specific applicant, laws have been set up establishing it as illegal to discriminate against job applicants based on certain factors. Amongst these factors is the issue of age, whereby an employer makes a decision not to hire a person solely based on the applicant's age. Assuming that it can be proven to the satisfaction of the law that an employer failed to hire a specific person only because of their age, the employer would be in violation of current anti-discrimination laws.

The laws protecting job seekers from age discrimination are primarily designed to protect people over the age of forty, who are looking for long-term employment and fear that their ages would lead employers to look elsewhere. The laws stipulate that employers are able to refuse to hire job applicants for other reasons, including if the job requires specific physical involvement that would be difficult to be successfully achieved by an older person. For these reasons, it is often very difficult to prove that an employer was in violation of the law in their hiring practices.

The primary piece of federal anti-discrimination legislation that protects the rights of people over age forty is the Age Discrimination in Employment Act (ADEA) of 1967. The law stipulates that advertisements for jobs cannot mention age restrictions and that—with few exceptions—a person cannot be forced into retirement on account of age.

As life expectancy continues to rise and medical technology improves, individuals are able to work longer. Age discrimination has also been argued to take a toll on the economy whereby workers who are able-bodied are taken out of the workforce and are unable to produce and often become dependent on social security or other welfare programs. Opponents of age discrimination also contend that older workers are often more reliable than new entrants into the workforce and that conceptions of older workers being less productive are often fed by stereotypes, which fuels further discrimination.

PRIMARY SOURCE

Executive Order 11141—Declaring a public policy against discrimination on the basis of age

WHEREAS the principle of equal employment opportunity is now an established policy of our Government and applies equally to all who wish to work and are capable of doing so; and

WHEREAS discrimination in employment because of age, except upon the basis of a bona fide occupational qualification, retirement plan, or statutory requirement, is inconsistent with that principle and with the social and economic objectives of our society; and

WHEREAS older workers are an indispensable source of productivity and experience which our Nation can ill afford to lose; and

WHEREAS President Kennedy, mindful that maximum national growth depends on the utilization of all manpower resources, issued a memorandum on March 14, 1963, 1 reaffirming the policy of the Executive Branch of the Government of hiring and promoting employees on the basis of merit alone and emphasizing the need to assure that older people are not discriminated against because of their age and receive fair and full consideration for employment and advancement in Federal employment; and

WHEREAS, to encourage and hasten the acceptance of the principle of equal employment opportunity for older persons by all sectors of the economy, private and public, the Federal Government can and should provide maximum leadership in this regard by adopting that principle as an express policy of the Federal Government not only with respect to Federal employees but also with respect to persons employed by contractors and subcontractors engaged in the performance of Federal contracts:

NOW, THEREFORE, by virtue of the authority vested in me by the Constitution and statutes of the United States and as President of the United States, I hereby declare that it is the policy of the Executive Branch of the Government that (1) contractors and subcontractors engaged in the performance of Federal contracts shall not, in connection with the employment, advancement, or discharge of employees, or in connection with the terms, conditions, or privileges of their employment, discriminate against persons because of their age except upon the basis of a bona fide occupational qualification, retirement plan, or statutory requirement, and (2) that contractors and subcontractors, or persons acting on their behalf, shall not specify, in solicitations or advertisements for employees to work on Government contracts, a maximum age limit for such employment unless the specified maximum age limit is based upon a bona fide occupational qualification, retirement plan, or statutory requirement. The head of each department and agency shall take appropriate action to enunciate this policy, and to this end the Federal Procurement Regulations and the Armed Services Procurement Regulation shall be amended by the insertion therein of a statement giving continuous notice of the existence of the policy declared by this order.

SIGNIFICANCE

By highlighting the issue of age discrimination, this executive order passed in 1964 by President Lyndon Johnson focused attention on the importance of utilizing all segments of the population as part of the United States labor force. The document would create an important precedent that would be reaffirmed by later legislation aimed at protecting workers from being refused employment simply based on their ages. This order while specifically addressing the issue of age discrimination in the workforce of the federal government, brought the broader issue to the public forefront. Within a short period after this order was issued, the law would be applied to prevent age discrimination in the civilian workforce as well as in other branches and levels of government.

Despite the advent of federal anti-discrimination laws, many states still permit employment "at-will" meaning that an employer can fire employees for any reason not prohibited by federal law. Since an employer can often cite other aspects of employee job performance as the impetus for firing, this makes claims for wrongful termination of employment based on age discrimination somewhat rare and difficult to prove.

While laws aimed at preventing age discrimination have succeeded in some measure to increasing the employment opportunities and employment stability for people over forty, it is often difficult to prove that an employer's decisions to refuse a certain person a job was based on age. For that reason, age discrimination suits are less common than suits claiming other forms of discrimination. Age discrimination laws also prevent employers from choosing between the younger of two elderly applicants. Thus, if one applicant is fifty-five and the other fifty, the law could protect the fifty year old if turned down for a position in a case where it could be proven that age was the deciding factor. By placing these types of laws into the labor environment, legislation designed to prevent age-discrimination has played a significant role in bettering the working conditions of older people in the United States and thus extending many careers.

As a larger number of older individuals remain in the workplace, laws preventing age discrimination become increasingly important. The U.S. Census bureau estimates that in 2015, twenty percent of the U.S. workforce will be age fifty-five or older. Over seventy percent of U.S. workers in 2006 planned to work past the traditional retirement age of sixty-five.

FURTHER RESOURCES

Web sites

American Association of Retired Persons (AARP_. "Age Discrimination at Work." <http://www.aarp.org/money/careers/jobloss/a2004-04-28-agediscrimination.html> (accessed May 22, 2006).

Cornel Law School. "Age Discrimination in Employment." <http://www.law.cornell.edu/uscode/html/uscode29/usc_sup_01_29_10_14.html> (accessed May 22, 2006).

Proposal for a Nationwide War on the Sources of Poverty

Speech

By: Lyndon B. Johnson

Date: March 16, 1964

Source: Johnson, Lyndon. "Proposal for a Nationwide War on the Sources of Poverty." Special Message to Congress, March 16, 1964.

About the Author: Lyndon B. Johnson (1908–1973) served as the 36th president of the United States from 1963 to 1969. His effort to build a "Great Society" by attacking the sources of poverty was significantly hampered by escalating American involvement in the Vietnam War.

President Lyndon Johnson (far left) and his wife Lady Bird meet the family of Tom Fletcher in Inez, Kentucky, on April 24, 1964. Fltecher, a father of eight, has been unemployed for two years. Johnson announced his War on Poverty program from the Fletcher's porch. © BETTMANN/CORBIS. REPRODUCED BY PERMISSION.

INTRODUCTION

In his 1964 State of the Union address, President Lyndon B. Johnson declared war on poverty as part of his goal of creating a "Great Society." Johnson sought to break the cycle of the culture of poverty by attacking its causes in urban ghettos and depressed rural areas. His novel antipoverty efforts, administered through the Office of Economic Opportunity (OEO), did not end poverty but made the issue into one that received continuing national attention long afterward.

Antipoverty activists had long argued that ending poverty required a redistribution of income by such means as raising taxes and using those funds to create jobs, overhaul social welfare systems, and rebuild slums. Great Society programs did invest more heavily in the public sector, but Johnson's antipoverty efforts relied on economic growth rather than new taxes on the rich or middle class to increase revenues. Determined to avoid conflict, he would not take from the advantaged to provide for the disadvantaged.

The Economic Opportunity Act of 1964, which grew out of Johnson's speech, authorized ten programs under the OEO. Many programs targeted impoverished youth, from Headstart, a preschool program, to work-study grants for college students. There were also loans to businesses willing to hire the long-term unemployed, aid to small farmers, and the Volunteers in Service to America (VISTA) program, which paid modest wages to volunteers who worked with the disadvantaged.

■ PRIMARY SOURCE

Because it is right, because it is wise, and because, for the first time in our history, it is possible to conquer poverty, I submit, for the consideration of the Congress and the country, the Economic Opportunity Act of 1964.

The Act does not merely expand old programs or improve what is already being done.

It charts a new course.

It strikes at the causes, not just the consequences of poverty.

It can be a milestone in our one-hundred eighty year search for a better life for our people.

This Act provides five basic opportunities.

It will give almost half a million underprivileged young Americans the opportunity to develop skills, continue education, and find useful work.

It will give every American community the opportunity to develop a comprehensive plan to fight its own poverty—and help them to carry out their plans.

It will give dedicated Americans the opportunity to enlist as volunteers in the war against poverty.

It will give many workers and farmers the opportunity to break through particular barriers which bar their escape from poverty.

It will give the entire nation the opportunity for a concerted attack on poverty through the establishment, tinder my direction, of the Office of Economic Opportunity, a national headquarters for the war against poverty.

This is how we propose to create these opportunities.

First we will give high priority to helping young Americans who lack skills, who have not completed their education or who cannot complete it because they arc too poor...

I therefore recommend the creation of a job Corps, a Work-Training Program, and a Work Study Program.

A new national job Corps will build toward an enlistment of 100,000 young men. They will be drawn from those whose background, health and education make them least fit for useful work...

Half of these young men will work, in the first year, on special conservation projects to give them education, useful work experience and to enrich the natural resources of the country.

Half of these young men will receive, in the first year, a blend of training, basic education and work experience in job Training Centers...

A new national Work-Training Program operated by the Department of Labor will provide work and training for 200,000 American men and women between the ages of 16 and 21. This will be developed through state and local governments and non-profit agencies...

A new national Work-Study Program operated by the Department of Health, Education, and Welfare will provide federal funds for part-time jobs for 140,000 young Americans who do not go to college because they cannot afford it.

There is no more senseless waste than the waste of the brainpower and skill of those who are kept from college by economic circumstance. Under this program they will, in a great American tradition, be able to work their way through school...

Second, through a new Community Action program we intend to strike at poverty at its source—in the streets of our cities and on the farms of our countryside among the very young and the impoverished old.

This program asks men and women throughout the country to prepare long-range plans for the attack on poverty in their own local communities...

Third, I ask for the authority to recruit and train skilled volunteers for the war against poverty.

Thousands of Americans have volunteered to serve the needs of other lands.

Thousands more want the chance to serve the needs of their own land.

They should have that chance.

Among older people who have retired, as well as among the young, among women as well as men, there are many Americans who are ready to enlist in our war against poverty.

They have skills and dedication. They are badly needed...

Fourth, we intend to create new opportunities for certain hard-hit groups to break out of the pattern of poverty.

Through a new program of loans and guarantees we can provide incentives to those who will employ the unemployed.

Through programs of work and retraining for unemployed fathers and mothers we can help them support their families in dignity while preparing themselves for new work.

Through funds to purchase needed land, organize cooperatives, and create new and adequate family farms we can help those whose life on the land has been a struggle without hope.

Fifth, I do not intend that the war against poverty become a series of uncoordinated and unrelated efforts—that it perish for lack of leadership and direction.

Therefore this bill creates, in the Executive Office of the President, a new Office of Economic Opportunity. Its Director will be my personal Chief of Staff for the War against poverty. I intend to appoint Sargent Shriver to this post...

What you are being asked to consider is not a simple or an easy program. But poverty is not a simple or an easy enemy.

It cannot be driven from the land by a single attack on a single front. Were this so we would have conquered poverty long ago.

Nor can it be conquered by government alone...

Today, for the first time in our history, we have the power to strike away the barriers to full participation in our society. Having the power, we have the duty....

We are fully aware that this program will not eliminate all the poverty in America in a few months or a few years. Poverty is deeply rooted and its causes are many.

But this program will show the way to new opportunities for millions of our fellow citizens.

It will provide a lever with which we can begin to open the door to our prosperity for those who have been kept outside.

It will also give us the chance to test our weapons, to try our energy and ideas and imagination for the many battles yet to come. As conditions change, and as experience illuminates our difficulties, we will be prepared to modify our strategy.

And this program is much more than a beginning.

Rather it is a commitment. It is a total commitment by this President, and this Congress, and this nation, to pursue victory over the most ancient of mankind's enemies.

SIGNIFICANCE

The escalation of the Vietnam War undermined the War on Poverty. Johnson now found himself negotiating with his political opponents to limit funding for antipoverty and other Great Society programs in order to maintain congressional support for rapidly rising military expenditures. The administration soon discovered that this strategy was impossible to maintain. The strongest supporters of the antipoverty program, both in mainstream politics and in the activist groups, were also the strongest opponents of the war. In the meantime, the bitterest enemies of the War on Poverty generally were the most loyal supporters of the war. Unlike Franklin D. Roosevelt, who had been able to disappoint radical activists on many issues and still maintain their loyalty and love, Johnson by 1967 was hated by the very activists he needed to mobilize the poor and educate the middle classes of the need to support a program as ambitious as the War on Poverty.

No president before Johnson had made an attack on poverty into a high priority. To a large extent, Johnson succeeded in reducing poverty, although not as much as he had hoped. The number of impoverished Americans fell from forty million in 1959 to twenty-five million in 1968, from over twenty percent of the population to about thirteen percent of the population. Especially through the community action programs, the people most deeply mired in poverty gained more control over their circumstances and a sense of their right to a fairer share of America's bounty.

FURTHER RESOURCES
Books

Andrew, John A. *Lyndon Johnson and the Great Society*. Chicago: Ivan R. Dee, 1998.

Brown, Michael K. *Race, Money, and the American Welfare State*. Ithaca, N.Y.: Cornell University Press, 1999.

Davies, Gareth. *From Opportunity to Entitlement: The Transformation and Decline of Great Society Liberalism.* Lawrence, Kans.: University Press of Kansas, 1996.

Gillette, Michael L. *Launching the War on Poverty: An Oral History.* New York: Twayne, 1996.

Social Security Amendments of 1965

Legislation

By: United States Congress

Date: 1965

Source: *Our Documents.* "Social Security Act Amendments (1965)." <http://ourdocuments.gov/> (accessed May 29, 2006).

About the Author: The United States Congress is the primary law-making branch of the Federal government.

INTRODUCTION

For the first hundred years of the United States' existence, financial security in old age was generally provided by one's children. This model of elder care offered numerous advantages, including simplicity, cost-effectiveness, and an awareness of the quality of care being provided.

As the nineteenth century drew to a close, demographic changes steadily eroded this plan's effectiveness. Industrialization concentrated most of the nation's economic growth in cities; from 1890 to 1940 the proportion of Americans living in urban areas doubled to more than fifty percent. Workers migrating from farms to cities frequently left their parents behind, interrupting the extended family life that predominated in rural areas.

Scientific advances also brought changes. As health care, nutrition, and sanitation improved, life expectancies climbed rapidly, rising by a full decade between 1900 and 1930, thereby increasing the senior population. These changes created a nation with more elderly citizens, along with questions of how to care for them.

While these demographic trends converged, America tumbled into the worst economic collapse of its history, the Great Depression. As the stock market plummeted and thousands of banks failed, the gross national product contracted by more than half. Wages paid to all workers dropped by forty percent and millions of men found themselves jobless. With no safety net to catch them, elderly Americans were particularly susceptible to impoverishment.

As the Depression deepened, Americans began to contemplate previously unthinkable relief measures, including some form of government plan to ensure financial security. In 1934, with economic recovery nowhere in sight, President Franklin D. Roosevelt announced a plan to provide economic security for senior citizens. Noting the demographic changes that had occurred, he framed his proposal simply as a new approach to the traditional values that made America great. The Social Security Act became law the following year.

Social Security's two major provisions targeted senior citizens. Title I provided financial support to state programs for the elderly, while Title II created a system under which workers made contributions throughout their careers, then received a lump sum payment following retirement. Through the years, the Social Security System was amended and expanded to provide additional benefits, including survivor benefits for deceased workers' families and increased benefit amounts for all participants. Beginning in 1940, the system began making monthly payments to retirees, and the first monthly check of $22.54 was issued.

The largest single change to Social Security occurred in 1965 with the creation of the Medicare program. Targeted specifically at health-care costs, Medicare was made available to all senior citizens and became a key element of President Johnson's sweeping War on Poverty and Great Society initiatives.

PRIMARY SOURCE

AN ACT

To provide a hospital insurance program for the aged under the Social Security Act with a supplementary medical benefits program and an extended program of medical assistance, to increase benefits under the Old-Age, Survivors, and Disability Insurance System, to improve the Federal-State public assistance programs, and for other purposes.

Be it enacted by the Senate and House of Representatives of the United States of America in Congress assembled, That this Act, with the following table of contents, may be cited as the "Social Security Amendments of 1965." ...

TITLE I—HEALTH INSURANCE FOR THE AGED AND MEDICAL ASSISTANCE

short title

This title may be cited as the "Health Insurance for the Aged Act."

PART L—HEALTH INSURANCE BENEFITS FOR THE AGED

Entitlement to Hospital Insurance Benefits

SEC. 101. Title II of the Social Security Act is amended by adding at the end thereof the following new section:

"ENTITLEMENT TO HOSPITAL INSURANCE BENEFITS

"SEC. 226. (a) Every individual who—

"(1) has attained the age of 65, and

"(2) is entitled to monthly insurance benefits under section 202 or is a qualified railroad retirement beneficiary, shall be entitled to hospital insurance benefits under part A of title XVIII for each month for which he meets the condition specified in paragraph (2), beginning with the first month after June 1966 for which he meets the conditions specified in paragraphs (1) and (2).

"(b) For purposes of subsection (a)—

"(1) entitlement of an individual to hospital insurance benefits for a month shall consist of entitlement to have payment made under, and subject to the limitations in, part A of title XVIII on his behalf for inpatient hospital services, post-hospital extended care services, post-hospital home health services, and outpatient hospital diagnostic services (as such terms are defined in part C of title XVIII) furnished him in the United States (or outside the United States in the case of inpatient hospital services furnished under the conditions described in section 1814(f)) during such months except that (A) no such payment may be made for post-hospital extended care services furnished before January 1967, and (B) no such payment may be made for post-hospital extended care services or post-hospital home health services unless the discharge from the hospital required to qualify such services for payment under part A of title XVIII occurred after June 30, 1966, or on or after the first day of the month in which he attains age 65, whichever is later; and

"(2) an individual shall be deemed entitled to monthly insurance benefits under section 202, or to be a qualified railroad retirement beneficiary, for the month in which he died if he would have been entitled to such benefits, or would have been a qualified railroad retirement beneficiary, for such month had he died in the next month.

SIGNIFICANCE

The idea of federally funded health insurance did not originate with President Johnson. The concept was first proposed by President Harry Truman, who in 1945 asked Congress to create a national health insurance program. Twenty years of debate followed, as supporters and opponents wrangled over the form such a plan should take.

Today, Medicare, the primary medical insurer for senior citizens, offers multiple benefits. Medicare Part A covers hospitalization and is provided to all Social Security participants. Medicare Part B covers doctor services and some other costs not covered by Part A. Part B is optional, and participants pay both a monthly premium and an annual deductible. In 2006, Medicare added prescription drug coverage, known as Part D, to help seniors pay rising medication costs.

As of 2006, approximately forty million Americans participated in Medicare. Just as demographic trends played a significant role in the birth of the Social Security System, today they threaten to bankrupt it. A 1998 bipartisan report on the programs's future found that the following fifty years would see the number of recipients double, while the number of active workers paying into the system remained roughly constant. The report projected that the Medicare system would be bankrupt by 2010.

Medicare's future appears murky. Despite grim projections pointing to approaching insolvency, however, lawmakers are reluctant to take meaningful action. Changes such as reducing benefits, increasing premiums, restricting coverage of some procedures, or raising the eligibility age are politically unpopular with voters. Some minor changes have been made to shore up Medicare. However, as of 2006, Medicare's insolvency date is projected to be somewhere around 2019.

FURTHER RESOURCES

Books

Cassel, Christine. *Medicare Matters: What Geriatric Medicine Can Teach American Health Care*. Berkeley, California: University of California Press, 2005.

Matthews, Joseph L., and Dorothy Matthews Berman. *Social Security, Medicare & Government Pensions: Get the Most of Your Retirement and Medical Benefits*. Berkeley, California: NOLO Press, 2006.

Oberlander, Jonathan. *The Political Life of Medicare*. Chicago: University of Chicago Press, 2003.

Periodicals

Adams, Rebecca. "Looming Medicare Fixes Make a Bitter Prescription." *CQ Weekly*. 64 (2006):1209–1210.

Gleckman, Howard. "Medicare Surprise." *Business Week.* 3982 (2006): 38.

Marmor, Theodore R., and Gary J. McKissick. "Medicare's Future: Fact, Fiction and Folly." *American Journal of Law & Medicine.* 26 (2000): 225–253.

Web sites

Heritage Foundation. "The Cost of Medicare: What the Future Holds." December 15, 2003 <http://www.heritage.org/Research/HealthCare/HL815.cfm> (accessed May 29, 2006).

Progressive Policy Institute. "An 'ABC' Proposal to Modernize Medicare." February 14, 2003 <http://www.ppionline.org/> (accessed May 29, 2006).

Social Security and Medicare Boards of Trustees. "Status of the Social Security and Medicare Programs." 2006 <http://www.ssa.gov/OACT/TRSUM/trsummary.html> (accessed May 29, 2006).

The Establishment of the Robert T. Stafford Federal Student Loan Program

Legislation

By: Robert T. Stafford

Date: November 8, 1965

Source: Stafford, Robert T. "The Establishment of the Robert T. Stafford Federal Student Loan Program." Title 20, Chapter 28, Subchapter IV. U.S. Code, November 8, 1965.

About the Author: Robert T. Stafford (1913–), a retired Republican politician from Vermont, served as the Governor of Vermont from 1959–1961 and in the United States House of Representatives (1960–1971) and Senate (1971–1989).

INTRODUCTION

Until the 1950s, students enrolled in colleges and universities had few choices for financing their education. Scholarships, small government grants, and parent or student savings were the standard options; student loans were rare and generally administered as personal loans to parents from local banks. The G.I. Bill, which granted educational support to veterans, changed the landscape of higher education after World War II, as tens of thousands of veterans returned home from the war to enroll in universities and colleges, funded by the federal program.

Shortly after WWII, the federal government passed the National Defense Act, which offered low-interest loans to students entering into the sciences or mathematics in college. The program is now called the Federal Perkins Loan program, and the loans are made available to low-income students. In the late 1950s, economists such as University of Chicago professor Milton Friedman advocated providing direct loans for college students to help subsidize education. The Health Education Assistance Act of 1963 established loan programs for students of medicine and those studying public health, while the College Work Study Program, established in 1964, offered jobs to students that were federally subsidized, giving colleges and universities a ready labor force and students an opportunity for on-campus jobs. The 1965 Educational Opportunity Grant Program offered direct grants to lower-income students, and the Guaranteed Student Loan program, later renamed the Stafford Loan, followed.

While some states had loan programs, a federal student loan program gained momentum in the early 1960s and became part of the Higher Education Act of 1965. Championed by Vermont Republican Robert T. Stafford, the program was aimed at the lower and middle classes. Making higher education more accessible for greater numbers of students who were not veterans was viewed as a positive step in developing industry, maintaining scientific progress during the Cold War, and helping universities—which had expanded to meet the needs of veterans after WWII—to maintain high enrollments.

As greater numbers of African Americans and minority students, as well as female students, made their way through high school and on to college, student loan programs could also help these students to gain access to higher education.

■ PRIMARY SOURCE

SEC. 1071. STATEMENT OF PURPOSE; NONDISCRIMINATION; AND APPROPRIATIONS AUTHORIZED

(a) Purpose; discrimination prohibited

(1) Purpose

The purpose of this part is to enable the Secretary—

(A) to encourage States and nonprofit private institutions and organizations to establish adequate loan insurance programs for students

President Bill Clinton announces a lower student loan default rate at a White House ceremony in Washington on October 2, 2000. © REUTERS/CORBIS.

in eligible institutions (as defined in section 1085 of this title),

(B) to provide a Federal program of student loan insurance for students or lenders who do not have reasonable access to a State or private nonprofit program of student loan insurance covered by an agreement under section 1078(b) of this title,

(C) to pay a portion of the interest on loans to qualified students which are insured under this part, and

(D) to guarantee a portion of each loan insured under a program of a State or of a nonprofit private institution or organization which meets the requirements of section 1078(a)(1)(B) of this title.

(2) Discrimination by creditors prohibited

No agency, organization, institution, bank, credit union, corporation, or other lender who regularly extends, renews, or continues credit or provides insurance under this part shall exclude from receipt or deny the benefits of, or discriminate against any borrower or applicant in obtaining, such credit or insurance on the basis of race, national origin, religion, sex, marital status, age, or handicapped status.

(c) Designation

The program established under this part shall be referred to as the "Robert T. Stafford Federal Student Loan Program." Loans made pursuant to sections 1077 and 1078 of this title shall be known as "Federal Stafford Loans."

SIGNIFICANCE

The loan program, informally known as the Guaranteed Student Loan or Stafford Loan program, offered federal government guarantees should students default. In addition, the program, created the year after the landmark Civil Rights Act of 1964, expressly forbids discrimination on the basis of race, sex, national origin, religion, or marital status.

The Stafford Loan program offers subsidized and unsubsidized student loans. For students in lower income brackets, the government pays for the interest, in effect giving the student a zero-interest loan. Such opportunities opened the door to college for many lower-income families, changing the demographics at mostly state-supported schools. At the same time, student loans became available for training in the professions, such as medicine and law, allowing people in lower income brackets access to an education that otherwise might have been out of reach.

While student loans such as the Stafford Loan helped to open doors to colleges and universities for many students who otherwise might never have gained access, critics of the massive student loan culture in American colleges and universities point to the federal government's shift of the cost of higher education from the government to the individual. Student loans rarely can be discharged in a bankruptcy, and for students who assume large loans but drop out of college before receiving a degree, the resulting lack of a degree coupled with massive debt can be life-altering. Private lenders have joined federal programs in making student loans available to a wider audience, providing educational access while designing twenty-year and even thirty-year loan repayment plans.

As a percentage of total aid, student loans have climbed sharply while government grants, such as the Pell Grant, increased by seventy-three percent between 1995 and 2004. During the same time period, college tuition rose five to six percent per year, devaluing the Pell Grant and forcing students to make up the difference with increased earnings from work or, in most cases, student loans. Student loan borrowing reached an average of $17,600 for students graduating from state-sponsored colleges in 2004, and nearly $24,000 for those graduating from private college. In a 2002 survey of student loan holders, thirty-eight percent said that their student loans prevented them from buying a home, and twenty-one percent delayed having children because of their high student loan debts.

FURTHER RESOURCES
Books

Cohen, Arthur M. *The Shaping of American Higher Education: Emergence and Growth of the Contemporary System.* San Francisco: Jossey-Bass, 1998.

Pulliam, John D. and James J. Van Patten. *History of Education in America.* Upper Saddle River, N.J.: Prentice Hall, 2002.

Thelin, John. *A History of American Higher Education.* Baltimore, Md.: The Johns Hopkins University Press, 2004.

Web sites

The Christian Science Monitor. "For Graduates, Student Loans Turn into an Albatross." <http://www.csmonitor.com/2006/0517/p01s02-usec.html> (accessed June 18, 2006).

National Student Loan Data System. <http://www.nslds.ed.gov/nslds_SA> (accessed June 18, 2006).

Remarks with President Truman at the Signing in Independence of the Medicare Bill

Speech

By: Lyndon B. Johnson

Date: July 30, 1965

Source: *Lyndon Baines Johnson Presidential Library.* "Remarks with President Truman at the Signing in Independence of the Medicare Bill." <http://www.lbjlib.utexas.edu/johnson/archives.hom/speeches.hom/650730.asp> (accessed June 18, 2006).

About the Author: Lyndon Baines Johnson (1908–1973) began his tenure as President of the United States on November 23, 1963, when he assumed the presidency upon the assassination of President John F. Kennedy. Johnson remained president until January 1969. The enactment of the Medicare provisions in 1965 was a part of a broader legislative program hailed by Johnson as a part of his vision for America he called "the Great Society."

INTRODUCTION

The passage into law of President Lyndon Johnson's cherished Medicare bill on July 30, 1965 was the culmination of a political and legislative struggle that began in earnest during the Roosevelt Administration with the passage of the Social Security Act in 1935.

Johnson's speech, replete with references to former Presidents Harry Truman and Franklin Roosevelt, pays tribute to the history leading to the

President Lyndon Johnson signs legislation creating the Medicare program at the Truman Library in Independence, Missouri, on July 30, 1965. Vice President Hubert Humphrey (center) and former president Harry Truman note the time. First Lady Claudia "Lady Bird" Johnson and former first lady Elizabeth Truman are standing behind their husbands. © BETTMANN/CORBIS. REPRODUCED BY PERMISSION.

Medicare enactment, a legislative program that provided state-supported health insurance for all American citizens sixty-five years of age or older. The Social Security Act represented the first legislation in the United States to constitute a safety net for a disadvantaged segment of society, and the notion of a similar comprehensive scheme of medical insurance or other assisted health coverage was advanced by Roosevelt at various times in his presidency. In 1943, Roosevelt used the now famous expression "cradle to grave health coverage" to describe his ambitions for an extension of his Social Security structure.

State-sponsored health coverage was attacked during Roosevelt's presidency as a form of socialism that had no place in America. Entrenched and conservative interests such as the American Medical Association were firmly opposed to any form of centralized government health care. When Truman assumed the American presidency in 1945, he also sought a form of universal health coverage and throughout his administration various pitched battles were waged in both Congress and in the forum of public opinion over the issue.

When Johnson assumed the presidency after the Kennedy assassination in November 1963, he and his advisers determined that the government would embark upon a legislative program that was known as the "Great Society." The cornerstones of the Great Society agenda included the passage of both the Civil Rights Act of 1964 and Medicare as an extension of the existing Social Security legislation in 1965.

The passage of the Medicare legislation through both the Congress and the Senate required a concerted effort by the Democratic Party lawmakers to win over more liberal-minded elements of the Republican Party in both Houses, coupled with an intense effort by Johnson to secure the support of the American Medical Association membership. Without the support of the medical profession, it is unlikely that Medicare could have been enacted.

At Independence, Missouri at the Johnson speech, former President Truman became the first American to be enrolled in the Medicare program, a symbolic linkage between the efforts of the Democratic Party since the time of Roosevelt to those of Johnson to secure the establishment of the Medicare provisions.

■ PRIMARY SOURCE

PRESIDENT TRUMAN: Thank you very much. I am glad you like the President. I like him too. He is one of the finest men I ever ran across.

Mr. President, Mrs. Johnson, distinguished guests: You have done me a great honor in coming here today, and you have made me a very, very happy man. This is an important hour for the Nation, for those of our citizens who have completed their tour of duty and have moved to the sidelines. These are the days that we are trying to celebrate for them. These people are our prideful responsibility and they are entitled, among other benefits, to the best medical protection available.

Not one of these, our citizens, should ever be abandoned to the indignity of charity. Charity is indignity when you have to have it. But we don't want these people to have anything to do with charity and we don't want them to have any idea of hopeless despair.

Mr. President, I am glad to have lived this long and to witness today the signing of the Medicare bill which puts this Nation right where it needs to be, to be right. Your inspired leadership and a responsive forward-looking Congress have made it historically possible for this day to come about.

Thank all of you most highly for coming here. It is an honor I haven't had for, well, quite awhile, I'll say that to you, but here it is: Ladies and gentlemen, the President of the United States.

THE PRESIDENT: President and Mrs. Truman, Secretary Celebrezze, Senator Mansfield, Senator Symington, Senator Long, Governor Hearnes, Senator Anderson and Congressman King of the Anderson-King team, CongressmanMills and Senator Long of the Mills-Long team, our beloved Vice President who worked in the vineyard many years to see this day come to pass, and all of my dear friends in the Congress—both Democrats and Republicans:

The people of the United States love and voted for Harry Truman, not because he gave them hell—but because he gave them hope. I believe today that all America shares my joy that he is present now when the hope that he offered becomes a reality for millions of our fellow citizens.

I am so proud that this has come to pass in the Johnson administration. But it was really Harry Truman of Missouri who planted the seeds of compassion and duty which have today flowered into care for the sick, and serenity for the fearful.

Many men can make many proposals. Many men can draft many laws. But few have the piercing and humane eye which can see beyond the words to the people that they touch. Few can see past the speeches and the political battles to the doctor over there that is tending the infirm, and to the hospital that is receiving those in anguish, or feel in their heart painful wrath at the injustice which denies the miracle of healing to the old and to the poor. And fewer still have the courage to stake reputation, and position, and the effort of a lifetime upon such a cause when there are so few that share it.

But it is just such men who illuminate the life and the history of a nation. And so, President Harry Truman, it is in tribute not to you, but to the America that you represent, that we have come here to pay our love and our respects to you today. For a country can be known by the quality of the men it honors. By praising you, and by carrying forward your dreams, we really reaffirm the greatness of America.

It was a generation ago that Harry Truman said, and I quote him: "Millions of our citizens do not now have a full measure of opportunity to achieve and to enjoy good health. Millions do not now have protection or security against the economic effects of sickness. And the time has now arrived for action to help them attain that opportunity and to help them get that protection."

Well, today, Mr. President, and my fellow Americans, we are taking such action—20 years later. And we are doing that under the great leadership of men like John McCormack, our Speaker; Carl Albert, our majority leader; our very able and beloved majority leader of the Senate, Mike Mansfield; and distinguished Members of the Ways and Means and Finance Committees of the House and Senate—of both parties, Democratic and Republican.

Because the need for this action is plain; and it is so clear indeed that we marvel not simply at the passage of this bill, but what we marvel at is that it took so many years to pass it. And I am so glad that Aime Forand is here to see it finally passed and signed—one of the first authors.

There are more than 18 million Americans over the age of 65. Most of them have low incomes. Most of them are threatened by illness and medical expenses that they cannot afford. And through this new law, Mr. President, every citizen will be able, in his productive years when he is earning, to insure himself against the ravages of illness in his old age.

This insurance will help pay for care in hospitals, in skilled nursing homes, or in the home. And under a separate plan it will help meet the fees of the doctors. Now here is how the plan will affect you. During your working years, the people of America—you—will contribute through the social security program a small amount each payday for hospital insurance protection. For example, the average worker in 1966 will contribute about $1.50 per month. The employer will contribute a similar amount. And this will provide the funds to pay up to 90 days of hospital care for each illness, plus diagnostic care, and up to 100 home health visits after you are 65. And beginning in 1967, you will also be covered for up to 100 days of care in a skilled nursing home after a period of hospital care.

And under a separate plan, when you are 65—that the Congress originated itself, in its own good judgment—you may be covered for medical and surgical fees whether you are in or out of the hospital. You will pay $3 per month after you are 65 and your Government will contribute an equal amount. The benefits under the law are as varied and broad as the marvelous modern medicine itself. If it has a few defects—such as the method of payment of certain specialists-then I am confident those can be quickly remedied and I hope they will be.

No longer will older Americans be denied the healing miracle of modern medicine. No longer will illness crush and destroy the savings that they have so carefully put away over a lifetime so that they might enjoy dignity in their later years. No longer will young families see their own incomes, and their own hopes, eaten away simply because they are carrying out their deep moral obligations to their parents, and to their uncles, and their aunts. And no longer will this Nation refuse the hand of justice to those who have given a lifetime of service and wisdom and labor to the progress of this progressive country.

And this bill, Mr. President, is even broader than that. It will increase social security benefits for all of our older Americans. It will improve a wide range of health and medical services for Americans of all ages.

In 1935 when the man that both of us loved so much, Franklin Delano Roosevelt, signed the Social Security Act, he said it was, and I quote him, "a cornerstone in a structure which is being built but it is by no means complete." Well, perhaps no single act in the entire administration of the beloved Franklin D. Roosevelt really

did more to win him the illustrious place in history that he has as did the laying of that cornerstone. And I am so happy that his oldest son Jimmy could be here to share with us the joy that is ours today. And those who share this day will also be remembered for making the most important addition to that structure, and you are making it in this bill, the most important addition that has been made in three decades.

History shapes men, but it is a necessary faith of leadership that men can help shape history. There are many who led us to this historic day. Not out of courtesy or deference, but from the gratitude and remembrance which is our country's debt, if I may be pardoned for taking a moment, I want to call a part of the honor roll: it is the able leadership in both Houses of the Congress.

Congressman Celler, Chairman of the Judiciary Committee, introduced the hospital insurance in 1952. Aime Forand from Rhode Island, then Congressman, introduced it in the House. Senator Clinton Anderson from New Mexico fought for Medicare through the years in the Senate. Congressman Cecil King of California carried on the battle in the House. The legislative genius of the Chairman of the Ways and Means Committee, Congressman Wilbur Mills, and the effective and able work of Senator Russell Long, together transformed this desire into victory.

And those devoted public servants, former Secretary, Senator Ribicoff; present Secretary, Tony Celebrezze; Under Secretary Wilbur Cohen; the Democratic whip of the House, Hale Boggs on the Ways and Means Committee; and really the White House's best legislator, Larry O'Brien, gave not just endless days and months and, yes, years of patience—but they gave their hearts—to passing this bill.

Let us also remember those who sadly cannot share this time for triumph. For it is their triumph too. It is the victory of great Members of Congress that are not with us, like John Dingell, Sr., and Robert Wagner, late a Member of the Senate, and James Murray of Montana.

And there is also John Fitzgerald Kennedy, who fought in the Senate and took his case to the people, and never yielded in pursuit, but was not spared to see the final concourse of the forces that he had helped to loose.

But it all started really with the man from Independence. And so, as it is fitting that we should, we have come back here to his home to complete what he began. President Harry Truman, as any President must, made many decisions of great moment; although he always made them frankly and with a courage and a clarity that few men have ever shared. The immense and the intricate questions of freedom and survival were caught up many times in the web of Harry Truman's judgment. And this is in the tradition of leadership.

But there is another tradition that we share today. It calls upon us never to be indifferent toward despair. It commands us never to turn away from helplessness. It directs us never to ignore or to spurn those who suffer untended in a land that is bursting with abundance. I said to Senator Smathers, the whip of the Democrats in the Senate, who worked with us in the Finance Committee on this legislation—I said, the highest traditions of the medical profession are really directed to the ends that we are trying to serve. And it was only yesterday, at the request of some of my friends, I met with the leaders of the American Medical Association to seek their assistance in advancing the cause of one of the greatest professions of all—the medical profession—in helping us to maintain and to improve the health of all Americans.

And this is not just our tradition—or the tradition of the Democratic Party—or even the tradition of the Nation. It is as old as the day it was first commanded: "Thou shalt open thine hand wide unto thy brother, to thy poor, to thy needy, in thy land."

And just think, Mr. President, because of this document—and the long years of struggle which so many have put into creating it—in this town, and a thousand other towns like it, there are men and women in pain who will now find ease. There are those, alone in suffering who will now hear the sound of some approaching footsteps coming to help.

There are those fearing the terrible darkness of despairing poverty—despite their long years of labor and expectation—who will now look up to see the light of hope and realization. There just can be no satisfaction, nor any act of leadership, that gives greater satisfaction than this.

And perhaps you alone, President Truman, perhaps you alone can fully know just how grateful I am for this day.

SIGNIFICANCE

The escalation of American involvement in the Vietnam War is the most prominent aspect of the presidency of Lyndon Johnson, one that has been most often recalled by both the American public and academic commentators in the relatively short span of history since Johnson left office in early 1969. It is noteworthy that both the Medicare provisions enacted by the Johnson administration in 1965 and the Civil Rights Act of 1964 have each endured. Both laws have become a part of the fabric of American society in the period since their passage.

At the time of the creation of Medicare, Johnson noted that there were eighteen million Americans over the age of sixty-five who would be protected from the potential devastation of large medical costs. It is noteworthy that Medicare is now applicable to over thirty-five million of these senior citizens, or twelve percent of the American population, coupled with a further six million persons under age sixty-five to whom Medicare has been extended since the 1965 enactment. These persons include the seriously disabled and persons who suffer from terminal afflictions, such as Lou Gehrig's disease.

The trends in American population growth as confirmed by current census data suggest that by the year 2050, an estimated twenty-one percent of the population will be sixty-five years of age or older. The growth in this demographic since the 1965 passage of Medicare has bedeviled American administrators of Medicare, who have expressed concerns that the plan may run out of money to fund itself by 2010, if its current resourcing by way of payroll tax and similar revenues is the only funding mechanism.

In the period since 1965, American state governments have enacted supporting legislative schemes that serve the entire population in terms of the provision of medical insurance for the most disadvantaged aspects of society. Medicaid is the name of the state health schemes, with a primary focus on the provision of hospital care for the poor.

The American federal government has been resistant to the "cradle to grave" sentiments first expressed by Roosevelt in 1943 as a government objective in health care. The limitation of Medicare to American senior citizens has rendered the United States something of an anomaly among the Western countries to which it is allied both culturally and politically. Nations such as Australia, Great Britain, and Canada have each had comprehensive universal health care schemes in place for over forty years.

The state of American health care is a frequent source of national political debate. On one side of the health care issue are those who point to the accumulating American national deficit as the key reason why the United States cannot afford a national system of health coverage. On the other side of the issue are those who point to the individual consequences of inadequate medical coverage; the argument is summarized by the assertion that a significant number of American families are one paycheck away from bankruptcy should one of their members sustain a catastrophic illness or injury.

FURTHER RESOURCES

Books

Dallek, Robert. *Flawed Giant: Lyndon Johnson and His Times, 1961–1973*. New York: Oxford University Press, 2000.

Moon, Marilyn. *Medicare: A Policy Primer*. Washington D.C.: Urban Institute Press, 2006.

Web sites

PBS.org. "Now: Science and Health." April 30, 2004. <http://www.pbs.org/now/science/medicare.html> (accessed June 18, 2006).

Social Security Administration. "The History of Medicare." May 1, 2006. <http://www.ssa.gov/history/corning.html> (accessed June 18, 2006).

Guns or Butter

Republicans Pressing the Issue

Newspaper article

By: Tom Wicker

Date: August 15, 1965

Source: *New York Times*

About the Author: Tom Wicker (1926–) is a well regarded American political commentator and author. Wicker's opinion-editorial column "In the Nation" appeared in the *New York Times* for over thirty years. Wicker wrote a number of books concerning contemporary American politics, notably *JFK and LBJ: The Influence of Personality upon Politics*, published in 1968, and his 2004 work, *George Herbert Walker Bush*.

INTRODUCTION

In August 1965, two issues dominated the media coverage of American politics, the Vietnam war and the performance of the U.S. economy. As the level of American military involvement in Southeast Asia had increased since 1964 and appeared poised to increase even further, commentators examined the projected costs of the Johnson administration's social agenda. The initiatives to forge a "Great Society"—legislative programs that included the introduction of Medicare, civil rights initiatives, and various measures designed to eradicate poverty—all appeared to carry significant price tags. The issue was articulated in different ways, but with one central theme. Could an increase in military spending be coupled with the cost of Johnson's

Henry H. Fowler, December 5, 1967. Fowler was Secretary of the Treasury from 1965–1968, and presided over the "guns and butter" economic policy of the Johnson administration. AP IMAGES.

social programs without a negative impact upon the American economy?

The expression "guns or butter" has been used by a number of commentators to characterize the traditional conflict between military spending and social welfare projects. The most famous invocation of the guns or butter comparison was made by German Reich Marshall Hermann Goering (1893–1946), who defended German spending on its military build-up through the 1930s with the observation, "Would you rather have butter or guns?…preparedness makes us powerful. Butter merely makes us fat."

In 1965, the debate as captured in the Wicker article was not whether the expanded role to be played by the United States in Vietnam was appropriate; there is an unstated presumption among all of the political leaders quoted by Wicker that America should be involved in the war effort in Vietnam. The words of House Republican Leader Gerald Ford, the future American President (who was President when the United States left Vietnam), convey a blunt desire for less social spending and more resources for the military.

Wicker employs the phrase the "new economy" throughout his commentary. The economists who took charge of the administration of the nation's finances under President Lyndon Johnson were generally extending the principles of economic management first advanced by the British economist John Maynard Keynes (1883–1946), some aspects of which had been applied in the Roosevelt New Deal legislation in the 1930s. John Kenneth Galbraith (1908–2006) was an advisor to the U.S. government through the introduction of the new economy. Galbraith and others advocated spending on both the military and the social initiatives to create taxable economic activity of the sort that would help the economy grow at a rate greater than the increase in government spending. Inherent in all of the economic approaches adopted by the Johnson administration was the belief that the entire national economy (the macro economy) was capable of being managed by the application of government policy.

PRIMARY SOURCE

Republicans have shifted to the "guns or butter" issue in their creeping barrage against president Johnson's conduct of the war in Vietnam. They picked up important support this week from the influential Georgia Democrat, Richard Russell, who warned in the Senate that there now were "even great dangers" of inflation than at the time of the Korean War.

But Representative Gerald R. Ford of Michigan, the House Republican leader, put the question most directly when he said: "I urge that (the President) take the lead in cutting back new domestic programs to marshal the nation's strength for the military effort."

Representative Melvin Laird pointed to the $8 billion still unappropriated for the education, poverty and other Great Society programs. These, the Wisconsin Republican said, provided "plenty of flexibility…for some serious re-evaluation."

OUTLAYS QUESTIONED

Talking not of increased spending for Vietnam, Mrs. Mary Brooks, assistant chairman of the republican National Committee, asked in a speech at Cooperstown, N.Y.: "Is this the time to appropriate $1.9 billion for an expanded poverty program…is this the time to be undertaking a $935 million housing and urban development

program…which will cost $7 billion over the next four years?"

War abroad and the Great Society at home, Senator Thruston Morton, Republican of Kentucky, said, could only be financed by deficit spending "and the Siamese twin of huge deficit financing is inflation."

This could be a cutting political issue in the months ahead, since it is based solidly on conventional economic wisdom, since inflation is one of the great scare-words of politics and since the Republican arguments have a ringing patriotic theme. But the real Republican challenge is not merely to Mr. Johnson's Vietnamese policy.

It is rather a challenge to the theory and practice of the "new economics" that Presidents Kennedy and Johnson have made official Government policy.

It is also a challenge to the willingness of the American people, if the issue is squarely put in an election campaign, to endorse the "new economics."

That is because the "new economists" in the Administration believe that, the nation not only *can* but *ought* to have both guns and butter in the coming months. They believe it is not merely possible but positively useful to spend money simultaneously for the Vietnamese war and the Great Society. And the President is going along with them.

The main question, therefore, is whether the new economics will work as the Administration expects. Defense spending was $46.2 billion in the fiscal year ended June 30. Spending for the fiscal year now in progress has been estimated at $47.9 billion, but informed sources say additional spending for Vietnam will drive the total to $50–51 billion.

If all Great Society programs also are financed as planned, Federal spending in the current year would reach $102 and perhaps $104 billion. But this leaves out of account the revenue side of the balance sheet.

The theory of the new economics is that more Federal spending or lower taxes, initially increasing the deficit, stimulates more taxable economic activity and hence more Federal revenue. That effect is created only when there is unemployment and idle capacity—and in the American economy, 3.6 million people are without jobs and the industrial plant is running at only 88 to 89 per cent of its potential. If the economy were at full capacity, even the new economists would favor either a tax increase or a cut in spending.

BIGGER DEFICIT?

But the economy is not operating at full capacity and therefore the solid expectation of the new economists is that increased spending on war abroad and the Great

Society at home will further increase this year's revenue growth. This growth will offset some of the increased spending.

The deficit, now estimated at $4.3 billion, probably will be increased by some degree, but that will not displease the new economists, many of whom all along have wanted more spending for stimulative purposes. Vietnamese outlays, for instance, will help to offset the deflationary effect of a $5 billion increase in payroll taxes for Social Security, effective Jan. 1.

Walter Heller, a herald of the new economics, reminded the recent Governors' conference that since the tax cut of 1964, employment had gone up by 2.3 million, industrial production by 10 per cent, and corporate after-tax profits by 20 per cent. At present tax rates, and at a 4 per cent rate of annual economic growth, he said, Federal revenues would increase by $7 billion each year for the rest of the decade. Additional outlays for Vietnam might well increase this bonanza this year or next.

That is the theory the Republicans are challenging, and the question is whether the country has accepted it as the Administration has. After all, only four years ago, with unemployment running at 6 per cent, even President Kennedy came within an eyelash of asking a tax increase to pay for the $3 billion military buildup in the Berlin crisis.

SIGNIFICANCE

The Wicker article is a remarkable encapsulation of the guns or butter debate as it was advanced by the Republican Party on one side and the Johnson Democrats on the other in 1965. The tone adopted by Wicker is measured and dispassionate, in contrast to most analyses of a similarly politically charged issue in the modern American media. Wicker uses budgetary data to illustrate how both sides of the guns or butter issue advance their arguments, as opposed to employing statistics as his centerpiece.

In his State of the Union Address in January 1964, President Johnson made his famous declaration of war on poverty throughout the United States. Then, in August 1964, Johnson sought and obtained approval from the U.S. Congress to take whatever military steps he deemed necessary to pursue American objectives in Southeast Asia. The government had, in essence, declared that it would pursue a more expensive military build-up in Vietnam as well as increase social program spending.

The guns or butter debate takes place against the backdrop of one of the most prosperous periods in American history. The American economic prosper-

ity in 1965 that is inherent in Wicker's review of the guns or butter issue is reflected by the hard economic data from the period. Between 1945 and 1965, the American Consumer Price Index (CPI) rose by a total of seventy-one percent. Between 1965 and 1980, a period characterized by the Vietnam War and the Arab oil crisis of the mid–1970s, the CPI rose 176 percent. The national unemployment rate in the United States remained on average under four percent until 1969; it has been at least six percent in the following years.

Implicit in the Republican position is concern over the size of the budget deficit in 1965. By modern standards, the 4.3 billion dollars is a fraction of the 2006 deficit, estimated at over 400 billion dollars. An even more graphic contrast between the national financial structure of the United States in 1965 and in the present day is the accumulated deficit, currently estimated to be in excess of $8 trillion.

The American government has pursued a guns and butter policy in this modern period of increased budgetary deficits. Military interventions in Iraq, Afghanistan, and increased spending on homeland security have occurred alongside the billions of dollars spent to address social issues such as the Hurricane Katrina relief effort that began in 2005.

It is apparent that in the more than forty years since Wicker commented on the new economy of 1965 in America, huge numbers, such as the accumulated American national debt, do not have a significant impact on the average citizen. Wicker's descriptions of a $4.3 billion deficit and a total federal budget of $102 billion were large numbers that conveyed the immediacy of the financial picture to his readers. The modern American citizen has become so accustomed to media descriptions of ever increasing government expenditures and obligations that they cease to have any real meaning.

FURTHER RESOURCES
Books
Galbraith, John Kenneth. *The Affluent Society*. 40th anniversary edition. New York; Houghton Mifflin, 1998.

Perry, George L., and James Tobin, ed. *Economic Events, Ideas, and Policies: The 1960s and After*. Washington, D.C.: Brookings Institute Press, 2000.

Web sites
Ludwig Von Mises Institute. "The New Economists and the Great Depression of the 1970s." May 7, 2004. <http://www.mises.org/story/1507> (accessed June 1, 2006).

National Public Radio. "Lyndon Johnson's War on Poverty." April 2005. <http://www.npr.org/templates/story/story.php?storyId=1589660> (accessed June 1, 2006).

Loving v. Virginia

Judicial decision

By: U.S. Supreme Court

Date: June 12, 1967

Source: *Loving v. Virginia.* 388 US 1 (1967)

About the Author: The Supreme Court of the United States is the nation's highest court of appeals and final arbiter of the Constitution. The court consists of eight associate justices and one chief justice. The opinion in *Loving v. Virginia* was delivered by Chief Justice Earl Warren.

INTRODUCTION

Segregation did not just involve restaurants and schools. In many states, blacks and whites were prohibited from marrying. Virginia had a ban on black-white interracial marriages that dated to 1691, and violators faced a prison term of one to five years. Nevertheless, Mildred Jeter, a black woman, and Richard Loving, a white man employed as a bricklayer, married in Washington, DC, in 1958. The subsequent events would end with the legalization of interracial marriages across the United States.

Jeter and Loving had grown up together in the small Virginia town of Sparta. They did not know another black-white couple when they married. No one from their families objected to the match, but an anonymous individual later notified authorities about the marriage. On July 15, 1958, three Caroline County, Virginia lawmen entered the Lovings' home at two in the morning and dragged them out of bed and to jail. The couple was convicted of a crime by marrying. In lieu of a prison term, they accepted exile from the state for twenty-five years. In 1965, the Lovings sued to have the law overturned. They lost in the Virginia Supreme Court, but the subsequent 1967 Supreme Court decision in *Loving v. Virginia* overturned Virginia's state prohibition on black-white interracial marriages.

U.S. Supreme Court

Loving v. Commonwealth of Virginia

388 U.S. 1 (1967)

Appeal from the Supreme Court of Appeals of Virginia.

No. 395.

While the state court is no doubt correct in asserting that marriage is a social relation subject to the State's police power, *Maynard v. Hill*, (1888), the State does not contend in its argument before this Court that its powers to regulate marriage are unlimited notwithstanding the commands of the Fourteenth Amendment. Nor could it do so in light of *Meyer v. Nebraska*, (1923), and *Skinner v. Oklahoma*, (1942). Instead, the State argues that the meaning of the Equal Protection Clause, as illuminated by the statements of the Framers, is only that state penal laws containing an interracial element [388 U.S. 1, 8] as part of the definition of the offense must apply equally to whites and Negroes in the sense that members of each race are punished to the same degree. Thus, the State contends that, because its miscegenation statutes punish equally both the white and the Negro participants in an interracial marriage, these statutes, despite their reliance on racial classifications, do not constitute an invidious discrimination based upon race. The second argument advanced by the State assumes the validity of its equal application theory. The argument is that, if the Equal Protection Clause does not outlaw miscegenation statutes because of their reliance on racial classifications, the question of constitutionality would thus become whether there was any rational basis for a State to treat interracial marriages differently from other marriages. On this question, the State argues, the scientific evidence is substantially in doubt and, consequently, this Court should defer to the wisdom of the state legislature in adopting its policy of discouraging interracial marriages.

Because we reject the notion that the mere "equal application" of a statute containing racial classifications is enough to remove the classifications from the Fourteenth Amendment's proscription of all invidious racial discriminations, we do not accept the State's contention that these statutes should be upheld if there is any possible basis for concluding that they serve a rational purpose. The mere fact of equal application does not mean that our analysis of these statutes should follow the approach we have taken in cases involving no racial discrimination where the Equal Protection Clause has been arrayed against a statute discriminating between the kinds of advertising which may be displayed on trucks in *New York City, Railway Express Agency, Inc. v. New York,*

(1949), or an exemption in Ohio's ad valorem tax for merchandise owned by a nonresident in a storage warehouse, *Allied Stores of Ohio, [388 U.S. 1, 9] Inc. v. Bowers*, (1959). In these cases, involving distinctions not drawn according to race, the Court has merely asked whether there is any rational foundation for the discriminations, and has deferred to the wisdom of the state legislatures. In the case at bar, however, we deal with statutes containing racial classifications, and the fact of equal application does not immunize the statute from the very heavy burden of justification which the Fourteenth Amendment has traditionally required of state statutes drawn according to race.

The State argues that statements in the Thirty-ninth Congress about the time of the passage of the Fourteenth Amendment indicate that the Framers did not intend the Amendment to make unconstitutional state miscegenation laws. Many of the statements alluded to by the State concern the debates over the Freedmen's Bureau Bill, which President Johnson vetoed, and the Civil Rights Act of 1866, 14 Stat. 27, enacted over his veto. While these statements have some relevance to the intention of Congress in submitting the Fourteenth Amendment, it must be understood that they pertained to the passage of specific statutes and not to the broader, organic purpose of a constitutional amendment. As for the various statements directly concerning the Fourteenth Amendment, we have said in connection with a related problem, that although these historical sources "cast some light" they are not sufficient to resolve the problem; "[a]t best, they are inconclusive. The most avid proponents of the post-War Amendments undoubtedly intended them to remove all legal distinctions among 'all persons born or naturalized in the United States.' Their opponents, just as certainly, were antagonistic to both the letter and the spirit of the Amendments and wished them to have the most limited effect." *Brown v. Board of Education*, (1954). See also *Strauder v. West Virginia*, [388 U.S. 1, 10] (1880). We have rejected the proposition that the debates in the Thirty-ninth Congress or in the state legislatures which ratified the Fourteenth Amendment supported the theory advanced by the State, that the requirement of equal protection of the laws is satisfied by penal laws defining offenses based on racial classifications so long as white and Negro participants in the offense were similarly punished. *McLaughlin v. Florida*, (1964).

The State finds support for its "equal application" theory in the decision of the Court in *Pace v. Alabama*, (1883). In that case, the Court upheld a conviction under an Alabama statute forbidding adultery or fornication between a white person and a Negro which imposed a greater penalty than that of a statute proscribing similar conduct by members of the same race. The Court rea-

soned that the statute could not be said to discriminate against Negroes because the punishment for each participant in the offense was the same. However, as recently as the 1964 Term, in rejecting the reasoning of that case, we stated "*Pace* represents a limited view of the Equal Protection Clause which has not withstood analysis in the subsequent decisions of this Court." *McLaughlin v. Florida*, supra, at 188. As we there demonstrated, the Equal Protection Clause requires the consideration of whether the classifications drawn by any statute constitute an arbitrary and invidious discrimination. The clear and central purpose of the Fourteenth Amendment was to eliminate all official state sources of invidious racial discrimination in the States. *Slaughter-House Cases*, 16 Wall. 36, 71 (1873); *Strauder v. West Virginia*, (1880); *Ex parte Virginia*, (1880); *Shelley v. Kraemer*, (1948); *Burton v. Wilmington Parking Authority*, (1961). [388 U.S. 1, 11]

There can be no question but that Virginia's miscegenation statutes rest solely upon distinctions drawn according to race. The statutes proscribe generally accepted conduct if engaged in by members of different races. Over the years, this Court has consistently repudiated "[d]istinctions between citizens solely because of their ancestry" as being "odious to a free people whose institutions are founded upon the doctrine of equality." *Hirabayashi v. United States*, (1943). At the very least, the Equal Protection Clause demands that racial classifications, especially suspect in criminal statutes, be subjected to the "most rigid scrutiny," *Korematsu v. United States*, (1944), and, if they are ever to be upheld, they must be shown to be necessary to the accomplishment of some permissible state objective, independent of the racial discrimination which it was the object of the Fourteenth Amendment to eliminate. Indeed, two members of this Court have already stated that they "cannot conceive of a valid legislative purpose...which makes the color of a person's skin the test of whether his conduct is a criminal offense." *McLaughlin v. Florida*, supra, at 198 (STEWART, J., joined by DOUGLAS, J., concurring).

There is patently no legitimate overriding purpose independent of invidious racial discrimination which justifies this classification. The fact that Virginia prohibits only interracial marriages involving white persons demonstrates that the racial classifications must stand on their own justification, as measures designed to maintain White Supremacy. We have consistently denied [388 U.S. 1, 12] the constitutionality of measures which restrict the rights of citizens on account of race. There can be no doubt that restricting the freedom to marry solely because of racial classifications violates the central meaning of the Equal Protection Clause.

Richard P. Loving, and his wife Mildred, challenged Virginia's law against mixed race marriages. In 1967, the Supreme Court ruled Virgina's anti-miscegenation laws unconstitutional in *Loving v. Virginia*. AP IMAGES.

SIGNIFICANCE

In 1960, there were 51,000 black-white couples. By 2000, this number had reached 450,000, still only a fraction of the total in the United States. While American attitudes toward racially mixed marriages have improved over the decades, many Americans continue to oppose a close relative marrying someone of another race. In 2000, eighty-six percent of African Americans surveyed by Harvard University declared that they would welcome a white person into their families, but only fifty-five percent of white families responded in kind.

Increasingly open attitudes toward interracial marriage can be credited in part to *Loving v. Virginia*, which overturned not only the Virginia marriage ban, but also similar laws in fifteen other states. Fourteen other states had already repealed their laws by that

time. A dozen states continued to keep their bans on the books, but such laws were unenforceable in the wake of the court decision. In 2000, Alabama became the last state to remove its antimiscegenation law from the books.

FURTHER RESOURCES

Books

Moran, Rachel F. *Interracial Intimacy: The Regulation of Race & Romance*. Chicago: University of Chicago Press, 2003.

Newbeck, Phyl. *Virginia Hasn't Always Been for Lovers: Interracial Marriage Bans and the Case of Richard and Mildred Loving*. Carbondale, IL: Southern Illinois Press, 2004.

Wallenstein, Peter. *Tell the Court I Love My Wife: Race, Marriage, and Law An American History*. New York: Palgrave, 2004.

Fair Housing Act of 1968

Legislation

By: United States Congress

Date: April 11, 1968

Source: *U.S. Department of Justice.* Fair Housing Act, 1968.

About the Author: The U.S. Congress is the primary law-making branch of the federal government.

INTRODUCTION

Shortly after the assassination of civil rights leader Martin Luther King Jr. (1929–1960), the U.S. Congress passed Title VIII of the Civil Rights Act of 1968. This landmark legislation, known as the Fair Housing Act, codified the principle that access to housing should not be limited or restricted based on an individual's race, gender, religion, or country of origin.

Prior to the passage of this legislation, housing discrimination in the United States was common. Minorities seeking to rent an apartment in a primarily white building were frequently told it had already been rented; those hoping to buy a home in a mostly white neighborhood often found that the seller was not interested in an offer. Advertising for new homes frequently included language suggesting that minorities would not be allowed to purchase a lot in certain neighborhoods. In a segregated nation, housing practices such as these tended to keep housing segregated, which meant that most of the better housing was available only to whites.

Discriminatory practices were frequently employed to maintain housing segregation. *Redlining* is a practice in which banks refuse to offer mortgages or business loans in certain neighborhoods. Specifically, a bank might refuse to make home construction loans in an inner-city neighborhood, making it difficult or impossible for renters to build their own homes in such areas. Real estate agencies also employed redlining by arbitrarily determining that certain areas of town should not be marketed to certain clients.

The Fair Housing Act prohibited all of these practices. Developers could no longer imply that certain races would be excluded, while landlords were required to rent to tenants regardless of race. Further, any consideration of race or gender in potential real estate buying or selling transactions was proscribed,

Philip Maundu, a Kenyan student attending Morehouse College in Atlanta, Georgia, walks past a racially discriminatory real estate sign in Atlanta, 1960. PHOTO BY TED RUSSELL//TIME LIFE PICTURES/GETTY IMAGES.

and public tools of the real estate trade, such as property listing services, were not allowed to discriminate. Ironically, federal legislation dating to 1866 was eventually ruled by the Supreme Court to prohibit most housing discrimination, though this ruling was not handed down until after the Fair Housing Act was in place.

Court challenges to the Fair Housing Act quickly arose. In 1972, the Supreme Court ruled that whites who were denied housing in an area due to action taken under the Fair Housing Act had legal standing to sue. Later decisions stated that the owner of a real estate agency is potentially liable for discrimination practiced by an agent in his employment and that tenant requirements must be applied equally to male and female applicants. Amendments to the Act during the 1970s and 1980s added provisions protecting individuals with physical disabilities, as well as families with children.

PRIMARY SOURCE

Sec. 801. [42 U.S.C. 3601] Declaration of Policy

It is the policy of the United States to provide, within constitutional limitations, for fair housing throughout the United States....

Sec. 804. [42 U.S.C. 3604] Discrimination in sale or rental of housing and other prohibited practices

As made applicable by section 803 of this title and except as exempted by sections 803(b) and 807 of this title, it shall be unlawful—

(a) To refuse to sell or rent after the making of a bona fide offer, or to refuse to negotiate for the sale or rental of, or otherwise make unavailable or deny, a dwelling to any person because of race, color, religion, sex, familial status, or national origin.

(b) To discriminate against any person in the terms, conditions, or privileges of sale or rental of a dwelling, or in the provision of services or facilities in connection therewith, because of race, color, religion, sex, familial status, or national origin.

(c) To make, print, or publish, or cause to be made, printed, or published any notice, statement, or advertisement, with respect to the sale or rental of a dwelling that indicates any preference, limitation, or discrimination based on race, color, religion, sex, handicap, familial status, or national origin, or an intention to make any such preference, limitation, or discrimination.

(d) To represent to any person because of race, color, religion, sex, handicap, familial status, or national origin that any dwelling is not available for inspection, sale, or rental when such dwelling is in fact so available.

(e) For profit, to induce or attempt to induce any person to sell or rent any dwelling by representations regarding the entry or prospective entry into the neighborhood of a person or persons of a particular race, color, religion, sex, handicap, familial status, or national origin....

Sec. 805. [42 U.S.C. 3605] Discrimination in Residential Real Estate-Related Transactions

(a) In General.—It shall be unlawful for any person or other entity whose business includes engaging in residential real estate-related transactions to discriminate against any person in making available such a transaction, or in the terms or conditions of such a transaction,

because of race, color, religion, sex, handicap, familial status, or national origin....

Sec. 806. [42 U.S.C. 3606] Discrimination in provision of brokerage services

After December 31, 1968, it shall be unlawful to deny any person access to or membership or participation in any multiple-listing service, real estate brokers' organization or other service, organization, or facility relating to the business of selling or renting dwellings, or to discriminate against him in the terms or conditions of such access, membership, or participation, on account of race, color, religion, sex, handicap, familial status, or national origin.

Sec. 807. [42 U.S.C. 3607] Religious organization or private club exemption

(a) Nothing in this subchapter shall prohibit a religious organization, association, or society, or any nonprofit institution or organization operated, supervised or controlled by or in conjunction with a religious organization, association, or society, from limiting the sale, rental or occupancy of dwellings which it owns or operates for other than a commercial purpose to persons of the same religion, or from giving preference to such persons, unless membership in such religion is restricted on account of race, color, or national origin. Nor shall anything in this subchapter prohibit a private club not in fact open to the public, which as an incident to its primary purpose or purposes provides lodgings which it owns or operates for other than a commercial purpose, from limiting the rental or occupancy of such lodgings to its members or from giving preference to its members.

(b)(1) Nothing in this title limits the applicability of any reasonable local, State, or Federal restrictions regarding the maximum number of occupants permitted to occupy a dwelling. ...

Sec. 808. [42 U.S.C. 3608] Administration

(a) Authority and responsibility

The authority and responsibility for administering this Act shall be in the Secretary of Housing and Urban Development.

SIGNIFICANCE

In 2000, the U.S. Department of Housing and Urban Development and the Urban Institute conducted a massive study to assess the level of housing discrimination in American cities. The study used paired testing, in which researchers posing as potential home buyers or renters inquire about a property; for each property, both a white and a nonwhite applicant inquired, and then the results were compared. In twenty cities nationwide, researchers conducted 4,600 paired tests to assess the impact of race on housing availability. The results of these tests were then compared to a similar study conducted in 1989.

The project, called the Housing Discrimination Study (HDS2000), found that access to housing in America is more equitable than in 1989, but that inequities still exist. For example, African American renters were shown fewer available units than white renters in approximately twenty percent of cases, while Hispanics received inferior treatment in about twenty-five percent of cases. The study found that discrimination against black home buyers fell substantially, from twenty-nine percent in 1989 to seventeen percent in 2000, though the study also noted an increase in the practice of geographic steering, in which whites and blacks are shown homes in different neighborhoods.

For most Americans, the mythical American Dream begins with home ownership. For many families, home ownership provides freedom from renting, and home appreciation often serves as the cornerstone of long-term financial security. Better homes frequently bring with them faster appreciation, greater security, and higher quality schools. In almost every measurable sense, better housing raises standards of living. For this reason, the objectives of the Fair Housing Act remain valid decades after its enactment.

FURTHER RESOURCES

Books

Schiller, Bradley R. *The Economics of Poverty and Discrimination*. Englewood Cliffs, N.J.: Prentice Hall, 2003.

United States Department of Housing and Urban Development. *Fair Housing Act Design Manual: A Manual to Assist Designers and Builders in Meeting the Accessibility Requirements of the Fair Housing Act*, 2nd ed. Washington, D.C.: Department of Housing and Urban Development, 1998.

Whitley, Bernard E. and Mary E. Kite. *The Psychology of Prejudice and Discrimination*. Belmont, Calif: Wadsworth Publishing, 2006.

Periodicals

Liptak, Adam. "The Ads Discriminate, but Does the Web?" *New York Times* (March 5, 2006): 16.

Newman, Kathe and Elvin K. Wyly. "Geographies of Mortgage Market Segmentation: The Case of Essex County, New Jersey." *Housing Studies* 19 (2004): 53–83.

Nothaft, Frank E. and Vanessa J. Perry. "Do mortgage Rates Vary by Neighborhood? Implications for Loan Pricing

and Redlining." *Journal of Housing Economics* 11 (2002): 244–265.

Web sites

National Fair Housing Council Online, Tennessee Fair Housing Council. "The Fair Housing Act: 35 Years of Evolution." <http://www.fairhousing.com/include/media/pdf/35years.pdf> (accessed May 25, 2006).

Urban Institute. "A Foot in the Door? New Evidence on Housing Discrimination." February 4, 2003. <http://www.urban.org/url.cfm?ID=900587> (accessed May 25, 2006).

U.S. Department of Housing and Urban Development. "Fair Housing Laws and Presidential Executive Orders." <http://www.hud.gov/offices/fheo/FHLaws/> (accessed May 25, 2006).

The National Flood Insurance Program

Legislation

By: United States Congress

Date: 1968

Source: "The National Flood Insurance Program." U.S. Congress, 1968.

About the Author: The Congress of the United States was established by Article 1 of the United States Constitution of 1787. It is the legislative arm of the U.S. Federal Government.

INTRODUCTION

The U.S. Congress established the National Flood Insurance Program (NFIP) with the passage of the National Flood Insurance Act of 1968. The program includes floodplain identification and mapping, floodplain management, and flood insurance. The NFIP enables property owners in participating communities to purchase insurance as a protection against flood losses. In exchange, communities must adopt and enforce floodplain management regulations to reduce future flood damages.

The idea of flood insurance began in the early 1950s with President Harry S. Truman, after massive floods struck his home state of Missouri. Private insurers would not provide flood insurance. They argued that only those most likely to be flooded would buy it and that an avalanche of claims would bring big finan-

A helicopter lifts sandbags used to repair a broken levee on September 4, 2005, in New Orleans, in the aftermath of Hurricane Katrina. AP IMAGES.

cial losses. By 1968, Congress had decided that something needed to be done to address the rising costs of federal disaster relief. Congress also believed that it was important for beneficiaries to help pay the bill.

Under NFIP, the Federal Emergency Management Agency (FEMA) maps areas along coasts, lakes, and rivers with significant flood risk. High flood risk is defined as a one-percent chance of flooding in any year. FEMA then sells NFIP insurance to people in or near flood plains. In 1972, Congress made the insurance mandatory for people in flood zones who have federally regulated mortgages.

PRIMARY SOURCE

§ 4001. CONGRESSIONAL FINDINGS AND DECLARATION OF PURPOSE

(a) Necessity and reasons for flood insurance program

The Congress finds that

1. from time to time flood disasters have created personal hardships and economic distress which have

required unforeseen disaster relief measures and have placed an increasing burden on the Nation's resources;

2. despite the instillation of preventative and protective works and the adoption of other public programs designed to reduce losses caused by flood damage, these methods have not been sufficient to protect adequately against growing exposure to future flood losses;

3. as a matter of national policy, a reasonable method of sharing the risk of flood losses through a program of flood insurance which can compliment and encourage preventative and protective measures; and

4. if such a program is initiated and carried out gradually, it can be expanded as knowledge is gained and experience is appraised, thus eventually making flood insurance coverage available on reasonable terms and conditions to persons who have need for such protection.

(b) Participation of Federal Government in flood insurance program carried out by private insurance industry

The Congress also finds

1. many factors have made it uneconomic for the private insurance industry alone to make flood insurance available to those in need of such protection on reasonable terms and conditions; but

2. a program of flood insurance with large-scale participation of the Federal Government and carried out to the maximum extent practicable by the private industry is feasible and can be initiated.

(c) Unified national program for flood plain management

The Congress further finds that

1. a program of flood insurance can promote the public interest by providing appropriate protection against the perils of flood losses and encouraging sound land use by minimizing exposure of property to flood losses; and

2. the objectives of a flood insurance program should be integrally related to a unified national program for flood plain management and, to this end, it is the sense of Congress that within two year following the effective date of this chapter the President should transmit to the Congress for its consideration any further proposals necessary for such a unified program, including proposals for the allocation of costs among beneficiaries of flood protection.

(d) Authorization of flood insurance program; flexibility in program

It is therefore the purpose of this chapter to

1. authorize a flood insurance program by means of which flood insurance, over a period of time, can be made available on a nationwide basis through the cooperative efforts of the Federal Government and the private insurance industry, and

2. provide flexibility in the program so that such flood insurance may be based on workable methods of pooling risks, minimizing costs, and distributing burdens equitably among those who will be protected by flood insurance and the general public.

(d) Land use adjustments by State and local governments; development of proposed future construction, assistance of lending and credit institutions; relation of Federal assistance to all flood-related programs; continuing studies

It is the further purpose of this chapter to

1. encourage State and local governments to make appropriate land use adjustments to constrict the development of land which is exposed to flood damage and minimize damage caused by flood losses,

2. guide the development of proposed future construction, where practicable, away from locations which are threatened by flood hazards,

3. encourage lending and credit institutions, as a matter of national policy, to assist in furthering the objectives of the flood insurance program,

4. assure that any Federal assistance provided under the program will be related closely to all flood-related programs and activities of the Federal Government, and

5. authorize continuing studies of flood hazards in order to provide for a consistent reappraisal of the flood insurance program and its effects on land use requirements.

§ 4011. AUTHORIZATION TO ESTABLISH AND CARRY OUT PROGRAM

(a) Authorization and establishment

To carry out the purposes of this chapter, the Director of the Federal Emergency Management Agency is authorized to establish and carry out a national flood insurance program which will enable interested persons to purchase insurance against loss resulting from physical damage to or loss of real property or personal property related thereto arising from any flood occurring in the United States.

(b) Additional coverage for compliance with land use and control measures

The national flood insurance program established pursuant to subsection (a) of this section shall enable the purchase of insurance to cover the cost of compliance with land use and control measures established under section 4012 of this title for—

1. properties that are repetitive loss structures,

2. properties that have flood damage in which the cost of repairs equals or exceeds 50 percent of the value of the structure at the time of the flood event; and

3. properties that have sustained flood damage on multiple occasions, if the Director determines that it is cost-effective and in the best interest of the National Flood Insurance Fund to require compliance with the land use and control measures.

SIGNIFICANCE

Most people, with the exception of those in the clearest path of danger, do not believe that they need flood insurance and they do not buy it. As a result, the government has kept flood insurance artificially low since the inception of the NFIP in 1968 to attract participants. Premiums ranged from $300 to $400 per year in 2005 for coverage up to $250,000. At the same time, the government limited the size of the flood zones covered by NFIP, thereby limiting the areas in which people were required to buy insurance.

The problems with NFIP became apparent in 2005. Congress designed NFIP to protect flood victims and to protect taxpayers from spending billions to bail out flood victims. In the wake of Hurricane Katrina in 2005 and the most extensive flooding in decades, the program failed. Nearly half of Katrina victims lacked flood insurance. Claims from the insured homeowners amounted to $25 billion and bankrupted NFIP. The government committed an additional $15 billion for rebuilding in Louisiana and Mississippi in 2006, with this amount expected to rise over subsequent years.

The problems surrounding Katrina coverage led to calls for Congress to overhaul NFIP. However, some lawmakers proposed ending the NFIP. Critics argued that it was unfair to ask taxpayers in areas that rarely flood to rescue people who insist upon building in areas prone to flooding. Real estate interests in particular resisted a radical restructuring. They expressed fears that requiring millions more people to buy flood insurance would stifle development. As a result, the basic flaw in the NFIP remains in 2006: there are not enough policyholders paying enough in premiums to spread out the risk and build a financial cushion against disaster. As of 2006, more than 4.8 million people have NFIP policies, including only half of the households in flood zones.

FURTHER RESOURCES

Books

Federal Emergency Management Agency. *National Flood Insurance Program*. Washington, D.C.: Federal Insurance and Mitigation Administration, 2002.

Miller, E. Willard. *Natural Disasters: Floods, A Reference Handbook*. Santa Barbara, Calif.: ABC-CLIO, 2000.

Web sites

Federal Emergency Management Agency. "Flood." <http://www.fema.gov/hazard/flood/index.shtm> (accessed June 18, 2006).

Executive Order 11521

Authorizing Veterans Readjustment Appointments for Veterans of the Vietnam Era

Government record

By: President Richard Nixon

Date: March 26, 1970

Source: *The National Archives*. "Executive Order 11521—Authorizing veterans readjustment appointments for veterans of the Vietnam era." <http://www.archives.gov/federal-register/codification/executive-order/11521.html> (accessed May 26, 2006).

About the Author: Richard Nixon (1913–1991) was the thirty-seventh president of the United States, serving from 1969–1974. Prior to his presidency he served as a Naval officer and as Dwight Eisenhower's Vice-President. In 1974, he resigned from office.

INTRODUCTION

United States law is created in several distinct ways. Most commonly, a bill is passed by both houses of Congress and signed into law by the president. In some cases, a president may refuse to sign a bill, and if Congress can gather enough votes, the bill becomes law without his signature. At times, federal courts intervene in the law-making process, limiting the scope or impact of a law. This system of checks and balances is intended to limit the power of any single branch of government.

While the president's law-making ability is generally limited by his forced cooperation with Congress, he is able to make some significant policy decisions on his own. Since the earliest days of the United States, presidents have issued executive orders. These procla-

Vietnam Veterans holding an American flag. © LEIF SKOOG-FORS/CORBIS.

mations, which carry the force of law, are generally issued to assist various government agencies in carrying out their assigned missions, such as when the Federal Emergency Management Agency assists disaster victims. However, some executive orders have much more far-reaching effects; President Lincoln's 1862 Emancipation Proclamation, which formally freed all slaves in Confederate territory, took the form of a presidential executive order.

During his presidency, Richard Nixon signed an average of one executive order per month, dealing with topics ranging from the sale of U.S. Savings Bonds to government regulation of industrial pollution levels. As the commander-in-chief of the United States armed forces, President Nixon used executive orders to modify several policies dealing with military affairs. Executive Order 11537 changed federal policy dealing with the military draft; Order 11545 established the Defense Distinguished Service Medal.

As the United States neared the end of the Vietnam conflict, the president turned his attention to returning veterans. Past administrations had also issued orders and passed laws intended to smooth the transition from military to civilian life. Following World War II, veterans were made eligible for a variety of benefits, including cash bonuses, education funding, and mortgage assistance. A 1952 act made Korean War veterans eligible for the same benefits offered under the original G.I. Bill of 1944, and later legislation extended these benefits to Vietnam-era veterans.

Executive Order 11521 was signed in 1970. The act acknowledged that military veterans typically sacrifice career advancement while on overseas assignments and might find it harder to secure work upon returning. It also noted that veterans are often instrumental in recruiting efforts, making their treatment an important element of future recruiting efforts. For these reasons, the act created veterans readjustment appointments, meaning that federal jobs could be preferentially awarded to veterans within one year of their separation from active duty. By allowing such appointments, the act was intended to level the playing field between veterans who had just returned from duty and non-veterans whose recent experience might give them an advantage in securing work. The order extended a previous policy that allowed preferential appointment of veterans, but only on a temporary basis.

PRIMARY SOURCE

Executive Order 11521—Authorizing veterans readjustment appointments for veterans of the Vietnam era

WHEREAS this Nation has an obligation to assist veterans of the armed forces in readjusting to civilian life;

WHEREAS the Federal Government, as an employer, should reflect its recognition of this obligation in its personnel policies and practices;

WHEREAS veterans, by virtue of their military service, have lost opportunities to pursue education and training oriented toward civilian careers;

WHEREAS the Federal Government is continuously concerned with building an effective workforce, and veterans constitute a major recruiting source; and

WHEREAS the development of skills is most effectively achieved through a program combining employment with education or training:

NOW, THEREFORE, by virtue of the authority vested in me by the Constitution of the United States, by sections 3301 and 3302 of title 5, United States Code, and as President of the United States, it is ordered as follows:

Section 1. (a) Subject to paragraph (b) of this section, the head of an agency may make an excepted appointment, to be known as a "veterans readjustment appointment," to any position in the competitive service up to and including GS-5 or the equivalent thereof, of a veteran or disabled veteran as defined in section 2108(1), (2), of title 5, United States Code, who:

(1) served on active duty in the armed forces of the United States during the Vietnam era;

(2) at the time of his appointment has completed not more than fourteen years of education; and

(3) is found qualified to perform the duties of the position.

(b) Employment under paragraph (a) of this section is authorized only under a training or educational program developed by an agency in accordance with guidelines established by the Office of Personnel Management.

(c) An employee given a veterans readjustment appointment under paragraph (a) of this section shall serve subject to:

(1) the satisfactory performance of assigned duties; and

(2) participation in the training or educational program under which he is appointed.

(d) An employee who does not satisfactorily meet the conditions set forth in paragraph (c) of this section shall be removed in accordance with appropriate procedures.

(e) An employee serving under a veterans readjustment appointment may be promoted, reassigned, or transferred.

(f) An employee who completes the training or educational program and who has satisfactorily completed two years of substantially continuous service under a veterans readjustment appointment shall be converted to career-conditional or career employment. An employee converted under this paragraph shall automatically acquire a competitive status.

(g) In selecting an applicant for appointment under this section, an agency shall not discriminate because of race, color, religion, sex, national origin, or political affiliation.

[Sec. 1 amended by Executive Order 12107 of Dec. 28, 1978, 44 FR 1055, 3 CFR, 1978 Comp., p. 264]

Sec. 2. (a) A person eligible for appointment under section 1 of this order may be appointed only within one year after his separation from the armed forces, or one year following his release from hospitalization or treatment immediately following his separation from the armed forces, or one year after involuntary separation without cause from (i) a veterans readjustment appointment or (ii) a transitional appointment, or one year after the effective date of this order if he is serving under a transitional appointment.

(b) The Office of Personnel Management may determine the circumstances under which service under a transitional appointment may be deemed service under a veterans readjustment appointment for the purpose of paragraph (f) of section 1 of this order.

[Sec. 2 amended by Executive Order 12107 of Dec. 28, 1978, 44 FR 1055, 3 CFR, 1978 Comp., p. 264]

Sec. 3. Any law, Executive order, or regulation which would disqualify an applicant for appointment in the competitive service shall also disqualify a person otherwise eligible for appointment under section 1 of this order.

Sec. 4. For the purpose of this order:

(a) "agency" means a military department as defined in section 102 of title 5, United States Code, an executive agency (other than the General Accounting Office) as defined in section 105 of title 5, United States Code, and those portions of the legislative and judicial branches of the Federal Government and of the government of the District of Columbia having positions in the competitive service; and

(b) "Vietnam era" means the period beginning August 5, 1964, and ending on such date thereafter as may be determined by Presidential proclamation or concurrent resolution of the Congress.

Sec. 5. The Office of Personnel Management shall prescribe such regulations as may be necessary to carry out the provisions of this order.

[Sec. 5 amended by Executive Order 12107 of Dec. 28, 1978, 44 FR 1055, 3 CFR, 1978 Comp., p. 264]

Sec. 6. Executive Order No. 11397 of February 9, 1968, is revoked. Such revocation shall not affect the right of an employee to be converted to career-conditional or career employment if he meets the requirements of section 1(d) of Executive Order No. 11397,1 after the effective date of this order.

Sec. 7. This order is effective 14 days after its date.

Editorial note: The provisions of section 1 of Executive Order 11397 of Feb. 9, 1968, 33 FR 2833, 3 CFR, 1966–1970 Comp., p. 712, are as follows:

Section 1 (a) Under such regulations as the Civil Service Commission may prescribe, the head of an agency may make an excepted appointment (to be known as a "transitional appointment") to any position in the competitive service at GS-5 or below, or the equivalent thereof, of a veteran or disabled veteran as defined in section 2108 (1), (2) of title 5, United States Code, who:

(1) served on active duty in the armed forces of the United States during the Vietnam era;

(2) at the time of his appointment has completed less than one year of education beyond graduation from high school, or the equivalent thereof; and

(3) is found qualified to perform the duties of the position.

(b) An employee given a transitional appointment under paragraph (a) of this section serves subject to:

(1) the satisfactory performance of assigned duties; and

(2) the satisfactory completion, within such reasonable time as is prescribed in the regulations of the Civil Service Commission, of not less than one school year of full-time approved education or training, or the equivalent thereof, except that two school years of full-time approved education or training, or the equivalent thereof, shall be required when an employee has not completed high school, or the equivalent thereof, by virtue of that education or training.

(c) An employee who does not satisfactorily meet the conditions set forth in paragraph (b) of this section shall be removed in accordance with appropriate procedures.

(d) An employee who satisfactorily meets the conditions set forth in paragraph (b) of this section and who has completed not less than one year of current continuous employment under a transitional appointment shall, in accordance with the regulations of the Civil Service Commission, be converted to career-conditional or career employment when he furnishes his employing agency proof of the satisfactory completion of the required education or training. An employee converted under this paragraph shall automatically acquire a competitive status.

(e) In selecting an applicant for appointment under this section, an agency head shall not discriminate because of race, color, religion, sex, national origin, or political affiliation.

SIGNIFICANCE

The use of executive orders has been criticized by some legal scholars. Presidents have occasionally used this authority to radically alter U.S. law; President Harry Truman's integration of the armed forces is one example of such an order. Arguably the most extreme use of executive authority was President Franklin Roosevelt's order relocating Japanese American and German American citizens to internment camps during World War II.

Although the court system has the authority to invalidate an executive order, this has occurred only twice in U.S. history. Congress is also empowered to limit executive authority, either by passing legislation that conflicts with the order or by refusing to authorize funds for the order's implementation. A two-thirds majority is necessary to override a presidential veto in such cases.

A recent survey by the Brookings Institution ranked programs to assist veterans in re-entering civilian life among the federal government's fifty most significant achievements in recent history. The Department of Veterans' Affairs currently oversees programs and benefits for more than twenty-four million military veterans at a cost of more than $70 billion per year. In the decades since the first G.I. Bill, more than twenty-one million vets have received federal educational assistance; of these, more than one-third served in the Vietnam era. Additional extensions to veteran benefits have also provided educational assistance for thousands of veterans' spouses and children.

FURTHER RESOURCES

Books

Kimbell, Jefferey P. *Nixon's Vietnam War (Modern War Studies)*. Lawrence: University Press of Kansas, 2002.

Mayer, Kenneth. *With the Stroke of a Pen : Executive Orders and Presidential Power*. Princeton, N.J.: Princeton University Press, 2002.

Mettler, Suzanne. *Soldiers to Citizens : The G.I. Bill and the Making of the Greatest Generation*. New York: Oxford University Press, 2005.

Periodicals

Campbell, Alec. "The Invisible Welfare State: Establishing the Phenomenon of Twentieth Century Veteran's Benefits." *Journal of Political and Military Sociology* 32 (2004): 249ndash;267.

Jaffe, Greg. "As Benefits for Veterans Climb, Military Spending Feels Squeeze." *Wall Street Journal—Eastern Edition* (January 25, 2005): A1–A6.

Ortiz, Stephen R. "The "New Deal" for Veterans: The Economy Act, the Veterans of Foreign Wars, and the Origins of New Deal Dissent." *Journal of Military History* 38 (2006): 27–29.

Web sites

Brookings Institution. "Government's 50 Greatest Endeavors: Support Veteran Readjustment and Training." <http://www.brookings.edu/gs/cps/50ge/endeavors/veterans.htm> (accessed May 26, 2006).

National Archive. "Richard Nixon–1970." <http://www.archives.gov/federal-register/executive-orders/1970.html> (accessed May 27, 2006).

United States Department of Veterans' Affairs. "Fact Sheet: Facts About the Department of Veterans' Affairs." <http://www1.va.gov/opa/fact/vafacts.asp> (accessed May 27, 2006).

Black Students Arrive at South Boston High School in 1974

Photograph

By: Anonymous

Date: September 12, 1974

Source: © Bettmann/Corbis. Reproduced by permission.

About the Photographer: The Corbis Corporation was founded in 1989 and maintains an archive of millions of photographs and moving images.

INTRODUCTION

In 1954, twenty-one states and the District of Columbia either allowed or legally required racially segregated schools. That year, the Supreme Court changed the face of public education with its decision in *Brown v. Board of Education of Topeka, Kansas* in which the court struck down a law allowing racially segregated schools in towns with 15,000 or more residents. Prior to that ruling, school systems had acted under the 1896 ruling *Plessy v. Ferguson* which stipulated that public accommodations including rail cars, water fountains, and public schools could be racially segregated, provided that separate facilities offered equal services and benefits to each racial group. The 1954 ruling bluntly asserted that separate facilities are inherently unequal, and in one broad stroke removed all legal justification for segregated schools.

In the years shortly after the ruling, about half the states with segregated schools voluntarily changed their systems. In some cases, the changes were little more than token adjustments, but they represented initial steps toward racial equality in education. Several states, however, refused to comply with the new ruling at all. When the Little Rock, Arkansas school board made plans to integrate the city's high school, the state's governor mobilized the National Guard to turn black students away. Three weeks later, escorted by federal troops, nine African American students entered the school to begin classes.

■ PRIMARY SOURCE

Black students arrive at South Boston High School in 1974: Police officers stand guard as African American students are bussed to the predominantly white South Boston high school, as part of Boston's school desegregation efforts, September 12, 1974. © BETTMANN/CORBIS. REPRODUCED BY PERMISSION.

In 1958, the state of Virginia elected to close several schools rather than desegregate them; the courts promptly ordered the schools reopened. In 1962, James Meredith, a black student, had to be protected by several hundred U.S. Marshals when he attempted to register for classes at the University of Mississippi. Violence erupted, and two people were killed. The following day, the town was occupied by federal troops, and Meredith began attending classes. In 1963, Alabama governor George Wallace stood in the entrance to the University of Alabama, blocking two black students' entry. After making a prepared speech, Wallace returned to the capital and the students entered the building to register.

A decade later, desegregating the Boston Public Schools proved particularly difficult. A June 1974 court ruling found a consistent pattern of discrimination in city school decisions, and the court ordered mandatory school desegregation by the beginning of school that fall. To comply with the ruling, the Boston Schools developed a court-approved plan to begin mandatory busing of white children to black schools and black children to white schools.

The 1974–1975 school year got off to a rocky start in Boston. Numerous white parents refused to send their children to black schools across town, and the majority of parents at all white South Boston High School kept their children home from school. Police provided protection as black students arrived for their first day of classes, however, protestors threw rocks through the bus windows and several children were injured.

Speaking with reporters and surrounded by protesting whites, four African American students attempt to integrate North Little Rock High School on September 10, 1957. © BETTMANN/CORBIS.

PRIMARY SOURCE

BLACK STUDENTS ARRIVE AT SOUTH BOSTON HIGH SCHOOL IN 1974

See primary source image.

SIGNIFICANCE

The violence in Boston schools continued throughout the school year. Following the stabbing of a white student at Hyde Park High School, the National Guard was dispatched to restore order. A second stabbing several weeks later led to a white mob surrounding another high school, trapping black students inside for several hours. Parents organized marches and continued to protest the forced busing of their children.

In the years following the implementation of busing in Boston, hundreds of white families moved to the suburbs or placed their children in private schools. As a result, by 1980, the Boston Public School system served a majority black student population, while schools in the Boston suburbs were populated primarily with white students.

Through the 1970s and 1980s, court-ordered busing was a common measure for integrating racially segregated schools. Proponents hoped that busing would not only address concerns of facility and resource equality, but would also encourage communities to become more racially integrated. Critics cited the enormous cost of the program (San Francisco, for example, spent more than $200 million on the effort) as well as criticizing the underlying rationale upon which it rested.

By the 1990s, school busing was largely considered a failure. Not only had most of the busing programs failed to integrate neighborhoods or show even modest educational improvements, many had destroyed neighborhood schools and exacerbated a phenomenon known as white flight, in which city dwellers move to the suburbs to escape busing. As a result, many inner city school districts today are more segregated than they were prior to busing. Leaders of both white and black communities have almost unanimously condemned busing as a massive social experiment gone awry. By the year 2000, Boston, along with most other large school systems, was actively dismantling its forced school integration plan, even as new discrimination cases were being filed.

FURTHER RESOURCES
Books

Beals, Melba Patillo. *Warriors Don't Cry: A Searing Memoir of the Battle to Integrate Little Rock's Central High School.* New York: Washington Square Press, 1995.

Formisano, Ronald P. *Boston Against Busing: Race, Class, and Ethnicity in the 1960s and 1970s.* Charlotte, North Carolina: The University of North Carolina Press, 2003.

Rossell, Christine H. *The Carrot or the Stick for School Desegregation Policy: Magnet Schools or Forced Busing.* Philadelphia: Temple University Press, 1992.

Periodicals

Borja, Rhea R. "Legal Group Fights Race-Based Policies in Los Angeles District." *Education Week.* 25 (2005):4.

Trotter, Andrew. "Court Upholds Wisconsin District on Refusal to Bus Charter Students." *Education Week.* 25 (2005): 18.

Wren, Celia. "Stars and Strife." *Smithsonian.* 37 (2006): 21–22.

Web sites

Center for Urban and Regional Policy. "Little Here we go Boston, here we go." < http://www.curp.neu.edu/sitearchive/staffpicks.asp?id=1215> (accessed July 7, 2006).

Harvard University; The Civil Rights Project. "Looking to the Future: Voluntary K–12 School Integration." <http://www.civilrightsproject.harvard.edu/resources/manual/manual.pdf> (accessed June 7, 2006).

National Public Radio. "The Legacy of School Busing." 2006 <http://www.npr.org/templates/story/story.php?storyId=1853532> (accessed June 7, 2006).

Executive Order 12127

Federal Emergency Management Agency (FEMA)

Executive Order

By: President Jimmy Carter

Date: April 1, 1979

Source: *Federation of American Scientists.* "Executive Order 12127—Federal Emergency Management Agency." <http://www.fas.org/irp/offdocs/eo/eo–12127.htm> (accessed May 26, 2006).

About the Author: Jimmy Carter was the thirty-ninth president of the United States, serving from 1977 to 1981. Prior to his presidency, he served as a Naval officer and as governor of Georgia. In 2001, he was awarded the Nobel Peace Prize.

INTRODUCTION

In 1803, fire virtually destroyed the town of Portsmouth, New Hampshire. Local and state officials found themselves with few resources to cope with the disaster. In response, the United States Congress, less than thirty years after its creation, passed the Congressional Act of 1803, providing a variety of forms of assistance to the Portsmouth area. This legislation marked the first time the young federal government had stepped in to financially assist citizens in times of disaster.

As the federal government grew, it began intervening in local disasters more and more frequently. Over the following century, Congress passed an average of one piece of legislation per year intended to help victims of earthquakes, floods, and other natural disasters. Numerous government relief agencies were created, including one responsible for making disaster recovery loans. The Disaster Relief Act of 1974 also gave the president the authority to declare federal disasters.

This collection of disaster relief agencies responded to hurricanes and earthquakes throughout the 1960s and 1970s, but it soon became evident that the more than 100 separate agencies charged with assisting citizens in the wake of disasters were struggling to coordinate their efforts. In 1979, at the request of state governors, President Jimmy Carter issued an executive order merging many of these independent agencies into one new agency, the Federal Emergency Management Agency (FEMA).

FEMA's formation reflected the growing role of the federal government in disaster assistance. While

Displaced New Orleans residents line up on the freeway to board military helicopters that will evacuate them to safety in the aftermath of Hurricane Katrina, September 3, 2005. © MASTER SGT. SCOTT REED/USAF/EPA/CORBIS.

private sector agencies, such as the Red Cross, still provided aid to victims, federal agencies were increasingly seen as the first line of relief. The formation of FEMA served both to streamline the various operations in order to improve relief efforts and to reduce overlap and improve efficiency.

FEMA's abilities were tested in a wide variety of circumstances. In 1979, a nuclear power plant at Three Mile Island near Middletown, Pennsylvania, suffered a loss of coolant and a partial core meltdown, requiring FEMA's assistance for clean-up and public health efforts. When Hurricane Andrew blasted through Florida in 1992, causing $26 billion in damage, FEMA coordinated rescue and recovery efforts.

PRIMARY SOURCE

By the authority vested in me as President by the Constitution and laws of the United States of America, including Section 304 of Reorganization Plan No. 3 of 1978, and in order to provide for the orderly activation of the Federal Emergency Management Agency, it is hereby ordered as follows:

1–101. Reorganization Plan No. 3 of 1978 (43 FR 41943), which establishes the Federal Emergency Management Agency, provides for the transfer of functions, and the transfer and abolition of agencies and offices, is hereby effective.

1–102. The Director of the Office of Management and Budget shall, in accord with Section 302 of the Reorganization Plan, provide for all the appropriate transfers, including those transfers related to all the functions transferred from the Department of Commerce, the Department of Housing and Urban Development, and the President.

1–103.

(a) The functions transferred from the Department of Commerce are those vested in the Secretary of Commerce, the Administrator and Deputy Administrator of the National Fire Prevention and Control Administration (now the United States Fire Administration (Sec. 2(a) of Public Law 95-422)), and the Superintendent of the National Academy for Fire Prevention and Control pursuant to the Federal Fire Prevention and Control Act of 1974, as amended (15 U.S.C. 2201 *et seq.*), but not including any functions vested by the amendments made to other acts by Sections 18 and 23 of that Act (15 U.S.C. 278f and 1511). The functions vested in the Administrator by Sections 24 and 25 of that Act, as added by Sections 3 and 4 of Public Law 95-422 (15 U.S.C. 2220 and 2221), are not transferred to the Director of the Federal Emergency Management Agency. Those functions are transferred with the Administrator and remain vested in him. (Section 201 of the Plan.)

(b) There was also transferred from the Department of Commerce any function concerning the Emergency Broadcast System which was transferred to the Secretary of Commerce by Section 5B of Reorganization Plan No. 1 of 1977 (42 FR 56101; implemented by Executive Order No. 12046 of March 27, 1978). (Section 203 of the Plan.)

1–104. The functions transferred from the Department of Housing and Urban Development are those vested in the Secretary of Housing and Urban Development pursuant to Section 15(e) of the Federal Flood Insurance Act of 1956, as amended (42 U.S.C. 2414(e)), and the National Flood Insurance Act of 1968, as amended, and the Flood Disaster Protection Act of 1973, as amended (42 U.S.C. 4001 *et* seq.), and Section 520(b) of the National Housing Act, as amended (12 U.S.C. 1735d(b)), to the extent necessary to borrow from the Treasury to make payments for reinsured and directly insured losses, and Title XII of the National Housing Act, as amended (12 U.S.C. 1749bbb *et seq.*, and as explained in Section 1 of the National Insurance Development Act of 1975 (Section 1 of Public Law 94–13 at 12 U.S.C. 1749bbb note). (Section 202 of the Plan.)

1–105. The functions transferred from the President are those concerning the Emergency Broadcast System which were transferred to the President by Section 5 of Reorganization Plan No. 1 of 1977 (42 FR 56101; implemented by Executive Order No. 12046 of March 27, 1978). (Section 203 of the Plan.)

1–106. This Order shall be effective Sunday, April 1, 1979.

SIGNIFICANCE

Following the terrorist attacks of 2001, FEMA was merged with more than twenty other offices including the U.S. Customs Service, the Immigration and Naturalization Service, the Office for Domestic Preparedness, and the Nuclear Incident Response Team to form the Department of Homeland Security (DHS). In the same way that FEMA's creation brought together multiple government agencies, the new Homeland Security structure was intended to improve communication and coordination among various government relief agencies. Today, FEMA is one of four branches within DHS.

In the years following the creation of DHS, FEMA lost a significant number of key staffers; some were replaced on an interim basis and others were replaced by employees with little disaster management experience. FEMA director Michael Brown, in particular, had no formal disaster response training and little experience. FEMA's focus also shifted, as many of its resources were directed toward preventing and recovering from a potential terrorist attack. Critics charged that natural disasters remained far more likely than terrorist attacks, and that FEMA's focus was misguided.

In 2005, Hurricane Katrina destroyed much of New Orleans. It caused $40 billion in damage and left hundreds of thousands of people homeless. Television viewers watched as days passed with little visible response from FEMA, creating an impression that the agency was unresponsive and disorganized. Though the debate still rages over who was at fault, FEMA's director Michael Brown resigned two weeks later,

shortly after being removed from his oversight position on the recovery efforts. After his resignation, Brown lashed out at critics, shifting the blame from his agency's 3,000 employees to state and local authorities. Emails released several months later portray Brown as out-of-touch with the scope and seriousness of the disaster as it was occurring.

While Michael Brown had no significant disaster recovery experience, his replacement, David Paulison, brought three decades of firefighting and disaster preparedness experience to the job, including experience with Hurricane Andrew in 1992. Paulison formally accepted the director's position in 2006, at which time he faced the difficult task of rebuilding FEMA even as rumors swirled that the agency might be scaled down or completely reorganized.

FURTHER RESOURCES

Books

Anderson, C. V. *The Federal Emergency Management Agency (FEMA)*. Hauppage, N.Y.: Nova Science Publishing, Inc., 2003.

Binns, Tristan Boyer. *FEMA: Federal Emergency Management Agency*. New York: Heinemann, 2003.

Brinkley, Douglas. *The Great Deluge: Hurricane Katrina, New Orleans, and the Mississippi Gulf Coast*. New York: William Morrow, 2006.

Periodicals

Singer, Paul. "Brown's Flood of Criticism." *National Journal* 38 (2006): 27–29.

Starks, Tim. "Senators Say Scrap FEMA and Start Over." *CQ Weekly* 64 (2006): 1168.

Strohm, Chris. "Collins, Lieberman Suggest FEMA Remain As Part of DHS." *CongressDaily* (March 8, 2006): 7.

Web sites

Center on Congress at Indiana University. "Disaster Relief." <http://congress.indiana.edu/radio_series/disaster_relief.php> (accessed May 25, 2006).

USA Today. "Exposed by Katrina, FEMA's Flaws Were Years in Making." September 7, 2005 <http://www.usatoday.com/news/opinion/editorials/2005-09-07-our-view_x.htm> (accessed May 26, 2006).

Williams, Bob. "Blame Amid the Tragedy." *Wall Street Journal Online*, September 7, 2005. <http://www.opinionjournal.com/extra/?id=110007219> (accessed May 25, 2006).

Executive Order 12138

Executive order

By: Jimmy Carter

Date: May 18, 1979

Source: *The American Presidency Project.* "Jimmy Carter: Women's Business Enterprise Executive Order 12138." May 18, 1979. <http://www.presidency.ucsb. edu/ws/> (accessed June 11, 2006).

About the Author: Jimmy Carter was the thirty-ninth President of the United States of America, and he was in office from 1977 until 1981. Among the highlights of his presidency were an increase of some eight million jobs and a decrease in the nation's budget deficit. Carter was very involved in conserving natural resources and preserving the environment; he significantly increased the number of national parks in the United States and was instrumental in implementing legislation protecting the Alaskan tundra. Carter was deeply committed to human and civil rights issues, both within the United States and worldwide.

INTRODUCTION

The National Women's Business Enterprise Policy was created by then-President Carter's ratification of Executive Order 12138. Essentially, the Policy made some significant changes in the previous Small Business Act so as to enable a variety of means through which there would be development, growth, and expansion of women-owned small businesses and entrepreneurial efforts. It was expanded upon by the Women's Business Ownership Act of 1988 (House Bill 5050), which also served to create the National Women's Business Council (NWBC). The NWBC was created as an advisory council empowered to make policy and recommendations to the federal government. The group advises the Congress, the President, and the United States Small Business Administration on matters considered to be of economic and programmatic significance to female business owners. The NWBC, according to its published data, was specifically designed to "promote bold initiatives, policies, and programs designed to support women's business enterprises at all stages of development in the public and private sector marketplaces—from start-up to success to significance." The current make-up of the NWBC, which was shifted somewhat by the passage of the Small Business Reauthorization Act in 1994, includes representation from both female small

President Jimmy Carter. THE LIBRARY OF CONGRESS.

business owners and larger women's business organizations.

In the creation of the National Women's Business Enterprise Policy, it was necessary to create a specific definition of a woman-owned business organization (in contrast to a small business with a single owner). The legal definition is a business that has a minimum of fifty-one percent ownership, operation, and control by a woman or women. By definition, control refers to the power to make executive and management decisions and to create official policy and procedures. Operation refers to the day-to-day on-site or local management and running of the business. A Women's Business Enterprise is legally defined as consisting of one or more business(es) either currently woman-owned (or women-owned) or in the process of being created, developed, implemented and overseen or managed by a woman or women.

Women have traditionally been significantly under-represented in business ownership and management in the United States (as well as in most of the developed world); among the objectives of then-President Carter was to begin the process of shifting the balance of business power more to the center of the continuum by encouraging the creation, development, implementation, and growth of women-owned businesses and business ventures. It was also among the goals of the Policy to increase the visibility and successful efforts of women in the attainment of federal and state government contracts. In order to provide guidance, monitoring, and oversight for the successful implementation of the Policy, the legislation also created an Interagency Committee on Women's Business Enterprise.

PRIMARY SOURCE

EXECUTIVE ORDER 12138

Creating a National Women's Business Enterprise Policy and Prescribing Arrangements for Developing, Coordinating and Implementing a National Program for Women's Business Enterprise

In response to the findings of the Interagency Task Force on Women Business Owners and congressional findings that recognize:

1. the significant role which small business and women entrepreneurs can play in promoting full employment and balanced growth in our economy;

2. the many obstacles facing women entrepreneurs; and

3. the need to aid and stimulate women's business enterprise;

By the authority vested in me as President of the United States of America, in order to create a National Women's Business Enterprise Policy and to prescribe arrangements for developing, coordinating and implementing a national program for women's business enterprise, it is ordered as follows:

1–1. Responsibilities of the Federal Departments and Agencies.

1–101. Within the constraints of statutory authority and as otherwise permitted by law:

(a) Each department and agency of the Executive Branch shall take appropriate action to facilitate, preserve and strengthen women's business enterprise and to ensure full participation by women in the free enterprise system.

(b) Each department and agency shall take affirmative action in support of women's business enterprise in appropriate programs and activities including but not limited to:

1. management, technical, financial, and procurement assistance,
2. business-related education, training, counselling and information dissemination, and

3. procurement.

(c) Each department or agency empowered to extend Federal financial assistance to any program or activity shall issue regulations requiring the recipient of such assistance to take appropriate affirmative action in support of women's business enterprise and to prohibit actions or policies which discriminate against women's business enterprise on the ground of sex. For purposes of this subsection, Federal financial assistance means assistance extended by way of grant, cooperative agreement, loan or contract other than a contract of insurance of guaranty. These regulations shall prescribe sanctions for noncompliance. Unless otherwise specified by law, no agency sanctions shall be applied until the agency or department concerned has advised the appropriate person or persons of the failure to comply with its regulations and has determined that compliance cannot be secured by voluntary means.

1–102. For purposes of this Order, affirmative action may include, but is not limited to, creating or supporting new programs responsive to the special needs of women's business enterprise, establishing incentives to promote business or business-related opportunities for women's business enterprise, collecting and disseminating information in support of women's business enterprise, and insuring to women's business enterprise knowledge of and ready access to business-related services and resources. If, in implementing this order, an agency undertakes to use or to require compliance with numerical set-asides, or similar measures, it shall state the purpose of such measure, and the measure shall be designed on the basis of pertinent factual findings of discrimination against women's business enterprise and the need for such measure.

1–103. In carrying out their responsibilities under Section 1–1, the departments and agencies shall consult the Department of Justice, and the Department of Justice shall provide legal guidance concerning these responsibilities.

1–2. Establishment of the Interagency Committee on Women's Business Enterprise.

1–201. To help insure that the actions ordered above are carried out in an effective manner, I hereby establish the Interagency Committee on Women's Business Enterprise (hereinafter called the Committee).

1–202. The Chairperson of the Committee (hereinafter called the Chairperson) shall be appointed by the President. The Chairperson shall be the presiding officer of the Committee and shall have such duties as prescribed in this Order or by the Committee in its rules of procedure. The Chairperson may also represent his or her department, agency or office on the Committee.

1–203. The Committee shall be composed of the Chairperson and other members appointed by the heads of departments and agencies from among high level policymaking officials. In making these appointments, the recommendations of the Chairperson shall be taken into consideration. The following departments and agencies and such other departments and agencies as the Chairperson shall select shall be members of the Committee: the Departments of Agriculture; Commerce; Defense; Energy; Health and Human Services; Housing and Urban Development; Interior; Justice; Labor; Transportation; Treasury; the Federal Trade Commission; General Services Administration; National Science Foundation; Office of Federal Procurement Policy; and the Small Business Administration. These members shall have a vote. Nonvoting members shall include the Executive Director of the Committee and at least one but no more than three representatives from the Executive Office of the President appointed by the President.

1–204. The Committee shall meet at least quarterly at the call of the Chairperson, and at such other times as may be determined to be useful according to the rules of procedure adopted by the Committee.

1–205. The Administrator of the Small Business Administration shall provide an Executive Director and adequate staff and administrative support for the Committee. The staff shall be located in the Office of the Chief Counsel for Advocacy of the Small Business Administration, or in such other office as may be established specifically to further the policies expressed herein. Nothing in this Section prohibits the use of other properly available funds and resources in support of the Committee.

1–3. Functions of the Committee. The Committee shall in a manner consistent with law:

1–301. Promote, coordinate and monitor the plans, programs and operations of the departments and agencies of the Executive Branch which may contribute to the establishment, preservation and strengthening of women's business enterprise. It may, as appropriate, develop comprehensive interagency plans and specific program goals for women's business enterprise with the cooperation of the departments and agencies.

1–302. Establish such policies, definitions, procedures and guidelines to govern the implementation, interpretation and application of this order, and generally perform such functions and take such steps as the Committee may deem to be necessary or appropriate to achieve the purposes and carry out the provisions hereof.

1–303. Promote the mobilization of activities and resources of State and local governments, business and trade associations, private industry, colleges and universities, foundations, professional organizations, and volunteer and other groups toward the growth of women's business enterprise, and facilitate the coordination of the efforts of these groups with those of the departments and agencies.

1–304. Make an annual assessment of the progress made in the Federal Government toward assisting women's business enterprise to enter the mainstream of business ownership and to provide recommendations for future actions to the President.

1–305. Convene and consult as necessary with persons inside and outside government to develop and promote new ideas concerning the development of women's business enterprise.

1–306. Consider the findings and recommendations of government and private sector investigations and studies of the problems of women entrepreneurs, and promote further research into such problems.

1–307. Design a comprehensive and innovative plan for a joint Federal and private sector effort to develop increased numbers of new women-owned businesses and larger and more successful women-owned businesses. The plan should set specific reasonable targets which can be achieved at reasonable and identifiable costs and should provide for the measurement of progress towards these targets at the end of two and five years. Related outcomes such as income and tax revenues generated, jobs created, new products and services introduced or new domestic or foreign markets created should also be projected and measured in relation to costs wherever possible. The Committee should submit the plan to the President for approval within six months of the effective date of this Order.

1–4. Other Responsibilities of the Federal Departments and Agencies.

1–401. The head of each department and agency shall designate a high level official to have the responsibility for the participation and cooperation of that department or agency in carrying out this Executive order. This person may be the same person who is the department or agency's representative to the Committee.

1–402. To the extent permitted by law, each department and agency upon request by the Chairperson shall furnish information, assistance and reports and otherwise cooperate with the Chairperson and the Committee in the performance of their functions hereunder. Each department or agency shall ensure that systematic data collection processes are capable of providing the Committee current data helpful in evaluating and promoting the efforts herein described.

1–403. The officials designated under Section 1–401, when so requested, shall review the policies and programs of the women's business enterprise program, and shall keep the Chairperson informed of proposed budget, plans and programs of their departments or agencies affecting women's business enterprise.

1–404. Each Federal department or agency, within constraints of law, shall continue current efforts to foster and promote women's business enterprise and to support the program herein set forth, and shall cooperate with the Chairperson and the Committee in increasing the total Federal effort.

1–5. Reports.

1–501. The Chairperson shall, promptly after the close of the fiscal year, submit to the President a full report of the activities of the Committee hereunder during the previous fiscal year. Further, the Chairperson shall, from time to time, submit to the President the Committee's recommendations for legislation or other action to promote the purposes of this Order.

1–502. Each Federal department and agency shall report to the Chairperson as hereinabove provided on a timely basis so that the Chairperson and the Committee can consider such reports for the Committee report to the President.

1–6. Definitions. For the purposes of this Order, the following definitions shall apply:

1–601. "Women-owned business" means a business that is at least 51 percent owned by a woman or women who also control and operate it. "Control" in this context means exercising the power to make policy decisions. "Operate" in this context means being actively involved in the day-to-day management.

1–602. "Women's business enterprise" means a woman-owned business or businesses or the efforts of a woman or women to establish, maintain or develop such a business or businesses.

1–603. Nothing in subsections 1–601 or 1–602 of this Section (1–6) should be construed to prohibit the use of other definitions of a woman-owned business or women's business enterprise by departments and agencies of the Executive Branch where other definitions are deemed reasonable and useful for any purpose not inconsistent with the purpose of this Order. Wherever feasible, departments and agencies should use the definition of a woman-owned business in subsection 1–601 above for monitoring performance with respect to women's business enterprise in order to assure comparability of data throughout the Federal Government.

1–7. Construction. Nothing in this Order shall be construed as limiting the meaning or effect of any existing Executive order.

SIGNIFICANCE

According to statistics published by women-21.gov, by the end of the twentieth century 9.1 million businesses across the United States were owned by women. Those businesses afforded jobs for 27.5 million employees and were responsible for the infusion of some $3.6 trillion into the American economy. The number of women-owned businesses across America increased by more than one hundred percent between 1987 and 1999. Those new businesses increased employment during that same time period by 320 percent, boosting their sales figures by nearly 450 percent. The Small Business Association data indicated that the burgeoning ranks of women-owned businesses outpaced general business growth nationwide during the last decade of the twentieth century.

Data published by the United States Census Bureau in March of 2006 indicated an enormous upsurge in the number of female business owners during the period from 1997 to 2002, which is the most recent time period for which they had statistical data. The increase was on the order of twenty percent, which is more than twice the national average for the same time period. Of the total number of women in the labor force, which considers both business owners and employees, nearly forty percent were in management or in professional occupations, more than thirty percent worked in sales, one fifth in service fields, six percent reported being employed at materials moving, production, or transportation-related jobs, and the remainder worked in maintenance areas. Two things are important in the interpretation of these statistics: there is a significant working population in the United States that does not appear on any census report because they are not American citizens. Those employees are most likely going to be at the lowest echelons of the world of employment; they are likely to laborers of some sort, whether it is in agriculture, factory or other types of production, or in maintenance, housekeeping, or janitorial types of jobs. The second important piece of information is that there are racial imbalances in the employment hierarchy: the upper employment echelons—management and the professions—are most likely to be occupied by white or Asian females. Hispanic and African-American females are most strongly represented in the sales and office staff positions. In addition, women generally earn less than men for performing the same jobs, even with commensurate (or greater) education, experience, and credentials. Census data indicates that the median salary for all employed women was roughly eighty percent of that earned by a man occupying the same job.

Although there are still some barriers to success in all industries by women business owners (and women-run businesses), enormous positive strides have occurred since Jimmy Carter signed Executive Order 12138. There has been a wellspring of means by which women entrepreneurs and would-be business owners can get training, mentoring, and small business incubation and development assistance. Numerous academic and policy academies have been created that are targeted to helping women-run business organizations flourish. Best practices guidelines have been developed and codified for female entrepreneurs and business owners and have been incorporated into undergraduate, graduate, and professional academic and training programs for women.

The National Foundation for Women Business Owners (NFWBO) reports that the top growth areas for women-owned businesses during the past two decades have been in the areas of construction, wholesale trade, transportation and communications, agriculture and agriculture-related industries, and in manufacturing. Women have moved away from traditionally female-associated occupations to occupy places of importance across the entire business spectrum. There is considerable research underway on the phenomenon of nontraditional women-owned businesses, but the published data suggests that a significant part of the reason that women who are successful management-level employees seek to become business owners concerns what has been termed the "glass ceiling" effect, in which women are only able to rise to a certain finite level in the traditional men's business world—if women wish to rise to the top of a business, it is far more likely to happen if it is owned and run by women as well.

FURTHER RESOURCES

Books

Characteristics of Women Entrepreneurs Worldwide Are Revealed. Washington, D.C.: National Foundation for Women Business Owners, 1999.

Credibility, Creativity, and Independence: The Greatest Challenges and Biggest Rewards of Business Ownership Among Women. Washington, D.C.: National Foundation for Women Business Owners, 1994.

Employment and Earnings: 2005 Averages and the Monthly Labor Review. Washington, D.C.: United States Department of Labor, Bureau of Labor Statistics, 2005.

Entrepreneurial Vision in Action: Exploring Growth Among Women-and Men-Owned Firms. Washington, D.C.: National Foundation for Women Business Owners, 2001.

Entrepreneurship: The Way Ahead, edited by Harold P. Welsch. New York: Routledge, 2003.

Periodicals

Anna, A.L., G.N. Chandler, E. Jansen, and N.P. Mero. "Women Business Owners in Traditional and Nontraditional Industries." *Journal of Business Venturing* 15 (2000): 279–303.

Brush, C. "Women-Owned Businesses: Obstacles and Opportunities." *Journal of Developmental Entrepreneurship* 2, 1 (1997): 1–24.

Davis, S.E.M. and D.D. Long. "Women Entrepreneurs: What Do They Need?" *Business and Economic Review* 45, 4 (1999): 25–26.

Editorial. "Census Report Shows Strong Growth Among Women-Owned Firms." *Small Business Advocate* 25, 3 (March 2006): 1.

Gundry, L.K., M. Ben-Joseph, and M. Posig. "Contemporary Perspectives on Women's Entrepreneurship: A Review and Strategic Recommendations." *Journal of Enterprising Culture* 10, 1 (March 2002): 67–86.

McGeer, B. "Bank Programs Target Women Biz Owners." *American Banker* 166, 87 (2001): 8–10.

Web sites

National Women's Business Council. <http://www.nwbc.gov> (accessed June 11, 2006).

United States Department of Labor. "Women's Bureau: Women in the Labor Force 2005." <http://www.dol.gov/wb/factsheets/Qf-laborforce-05.htm> (accessed June 5, 2006).

Women-21.gov. <http://women-21.gov> (accessed June 11, 2006).

Head Start Act

Legislation

By: U.S. Congress

Date: 1981

Source: *U.S. Department of Health and Human Services. Administration for Children and Families.* "Compilation of the Head Start Act." <http://www.acf.hhs.gov/programs/hsb/budget/headstartact.htm> (accessed June 2, 2006).

About the Author: The U.S. Congress is the legislative branch of the federal government. The U.S. Department of Health and Human Services (HHS) is a Washington, D.C.-based federal agency that is responsible for the health of all of the nation's citizens, through the provision of necessary human services. The Office of Head Start is located within the Administration for Children and Families of HHS.

INTRODUCTION

The Head Start program began in 1964, when the U.S. government, concerned that many of the nation's poorer children were at a disadvantage by the time they began public school, invited a group of experts in child development to devise a program to help these preschool-aged children learn the skills necessary to be prepared for elementary school educations. The initial program ran for eight weeks during the summer of 1965 and covered educational, social, health, nutritional, and psychological needs for children aged three and over who came from low-income families. Because of the positive response from educators, parents, and child development specialists, the program was expanded to cover all fifty states as well as Washington, D.C., Puerto Rico, and the U.S. Territories. It is run by the Administration for Children and Families within the U.S. Department of Health and Human Services (HHS).

▮ PRIMARY SOURCE

QUALITY STANDARDS; MONITORING OF HEAD START AGENCIES AND PROGRAMS

Sec. 641A. [42 U.S.C. 9836A] (a) QUALITY STANDARDS.—

(1) ESTABLISHMENT OF STANDARDS.—The Secretary shall establish by regulation standards, including minimum levels of overall accomplishment, applicable to Head Start agencies, programs, and projects under this subchapter, including—

(A) performance standards with respect to services required to be provided, including health, parental involvement, nutritional, social, transition activities described in section 642(d), and other services;

(B)(i) education performance standards to ensure the school readiness of children participating in a Head Start program, on completion of the Head Start program and prior to entering school; and

(ii) additional education performance standards to ensure that the children participating in the program, at a minimum—

(I) develop phonemic, print, and numeracy awareness;

(II) understand and use language to communicate for various purposes;

(III) understand and use increasingly complex and varied vocabulary;

(IV) develop and demonstrate an appreciation of books; and

(V) in the case of non-English background children, progress toward acquisition of the English language.

(C) administrative and financial management standards;

(D) standards relating to the condition and location of facilities for such agencies, programs, and projects; and

(E) such other standards as the Secretary finds to be appropriate.

(2) CONSIDERATIONS IN DEVELOPING STANDARDS.— In developing the regulations required under paragraph (1), the Secretary shall—

(A) consult with experts in the fields of child development, early childhood education, family services (including linguistically and culturally appropriate services to non-English language background children and their families), administration, and financial management, and with persons with experience in the operation of Head Start programs;

(B) take into consideration—

(i) past experience with use of the standards in effect on the date of enactment of this section;

(ii) changes over the period since the date of enactment of this Act in the circumstances and problems typically facing children and families served by Head Start agencies;

(iii) developments concerning best practices with respect to early childhood education and development, children with disabilities, family services, program administration, and financial management;

(iv) projected needs of an expanding Head Start program;

(v) guidelines and standards currently in effect or under consideration that promote child health services and projected needs of expanding Head Start programs;

(vi) changes in the population of children who are eligible to participate in Head Start programs, including the language background and family structure of such children; and

(vii) the need for, and state-of-the-art developments relating to, local policies and activities designed to ensure that children participating in Head Start programs make a successful transition to public schools; and

(C)(i) review and revise as necessary the performance standards in effect under this subsection; and

(ii) ensure that any such revisions in the performance standards will not result in the elimination of or any reduction in the scope or types of health, education, parental involvement, nutritional, social, or other services required to be provided under such standards as in effect on the date of enactment of the Coats Human Services Reauthorization Act of 1998.

(3) STANDARDS RELATING TO OBLIGATIONS TO DELEGATE AGENCIES.—In developing standards under this subsection, the Secretary shall describe the obligations of a Head Start agency to a delegate agency to which the Head Start agency has delegated responsibility for providing services under this subchapter and determine whether the Head Start agency complies with the standards. The Secretary shall consider such compliance during the review described in subsection (c)(1)(A) and in determining whether to renew financial assistance to the Head Start agency under this subchapter.

(b) RESULTS-BASED PERFORMANCE MEASURES.—

(1) IN GENERAL.—The Secretary, in consultation with representatives of Head Start agencies and with experts in the fields of early childhood education and development, family services, and program management, shall develop methods and procedures for measuring, annually and over longer periods, the quality and effectiveness of programs operated by Head Start agencies, and the impact of services provided through the programs to children and their families (referred to in this subchapter as "results-based performance measures").

(2) CHARACTERISTICS OF MEASURES.—The performance measures developed under this subsection shall—

(A) be used to assess the impact of the various services provided by Head Start programs and, to the extent the Secretary finds appropriate, administrative and financial management practices of such programs;

(B) be adaptable for use in self-assessment, peer review, and program evaluation of individual Head Start agencies and programs, not later than July 1, 1999; and

(C) be developed for other program purposes as determined by the Secretary.

The performance measures shall include the performance standards described in subsection (a)(1)(B)(ii).

(3) USE OF MEASURES.—The Secretary shall use the performance measures developed pursuant to this subsection—

(A) to identify strengths and weaknesses in the operation of Head Start programs nationally, regionally and locally; and

(B) to identify problem areas that may require additional training and technical assistance resources.

(4) EDUCATIONAL PERFORMANCE MEASURES.—Such results-based performance measures shall include educational performance measures that ensure that children participating in Head Start programs—

(A) know that letters of the alphabet are a special category of visual graphics that can be individually named;

(B) recognize a word as a unit of print;

(C) identify at least 10 letters of the alphabet; and

(D) associate sounds with written words.

(5) ADDITIONAL LOCAL RESULTS-BASED PERFORMANCE MEASURES.—

In addition to other applicable results-based performance measures, Head Start agencies may establish local results-based educational performance measures.

SIGNIFICANCE

Child development experts agree that the first few years of a child's life are vital. Skills acquired during these years form the basis for future learning and educational progress throughout childhood and adolescence. Preschool programs help many children gain these skills, but low-income children, whose parents cannot afford the tuition charged by most preschools, are unable to benefit from this early educational environment. As a result, these children miss out on the opportunity to socialize with their peers in a structured environment, to acquire basic early reading and counting skills, and to grow emotionally by following instructions, working with others, and learning how to function independently outside of the home. The Head Start program aims to make certain that these low-income children do not fall behind before they even begin to attend public school by providing them with the skills and experiences necessary for the next step in the learning process.

The Head Start Act provides sponsoring agencies with guidelines for precisely what the children are to learn and how to track their progress and the effectiveness of the program. Minimum accomplishments are expected for every child in the program, including an awareness of their letters and numbers, an appreciation for books, improved vocabulary, problem solving skills, and an improved understanding of English for foreign students. In addition, the Head Start program provides children with supplemental nutrition; instruction in health care and maintenance, such as the importance of washing hands and brushing teeth; and encouragement to socialize successfully with their peers and to form strong relationships with family members.

Strict guidelines are maintained on who may run a Head Start program, and the Head Start Act specifies the required credentials for teachers, parameters for grants and funding, procedures for operation of the programs, eligibility of participants, and how to handle

Mayor Jane Campbell of Cleveland and Mayor Bill Purcell of Nashville visit with a four-year-old boy attending the Tom Joy Head Start Center in Nashville, Tennessee, May 16, 2003. AP IMAGES.

special needs, such as those of disabled children. HHS also tracks the program on a national basis to determine what aspects are working and what require modification. A 2005 HHS report found that the Head Start program was succeeding in preparing low-income students for public school. The study showed that students' pre-reading scores increased by half following a year in the Head Start program, and that general literacy, vocabulary, and pre-writing abilities also improved. Oral skills improved less overall, indicating an area of the program that requires strengthening. The study also followed the Head Start students into kindergarten, where even more significant improvement in reading and writing skills were documented. By the first grade, the report found, the gap between the Head Start students and other students had been nearly eradicated. Earlier exposure to educational activities appears to provide these students with a foundation on which to build future academic success.

Head Start has encountered occasional political challenges, including changes to the quality and accountability guidelines in 1998 and the Head Start Accountability Act of 2005, an amendment designed to make individual agencies participating in the pro-

gram more fiscally accountable. The program also requires regular reauthorization by the U.S. Congress, which is designed to maintain accountability to the federal government as well as high standards. Congress is able to alter the parameters under which the program functions during this reauthorization process, and some proposed changes have included moving the program to the authority of a different federal agency or shifting the responsibility for the program from the federal government to the individual states. At the present, however, the Head Start program has demonstrated its success in its current form, and it continues to receive authorization and funding.

FURTHER RESOURCES
Books

Schorr, Lisbeth B. *The Head Start Debates*. Baltimore, Md.: Brookes Publishing Company, 2004.

Segal, Marilyn, et al. *All About Child Care and Early Education*. Boston: Allyn and Bacon, 2005.

Vinovskis, Maris A. *The Birth of Head Start: Preschool Education Policies in the Kennedy and Johnson Administrations*. Chicago: University of Chicago Press, 2005.

Web sites

U.S. *Department of Health and Human Services. Administration for Children and Families.* "About Head Start." March 3, 2004. <http://www.acf.hhs.gov/programs/hsb/about/index.htm> (accessed June 2, 2006).

U.S. *Department of Health and Human Services. Administration for Children and Families.* "Head Start 101." July 25, 2002. <http://www.headstartinfo.org/infocenter/hs101.htm> (accessed June 2, 2006).

U.S. *House of Representatives. Committee on Education and the Workforce.* "HHS Study Shows Children in Head Start Better Prepared to Succeed in School." June 9, 2005. <http://www.house.gov/apps/list/press/ed31_democrats/rel6905.html> (accessed June 2, 2006).

Losing Ground: American Social Policy 1950–1980

Book excerpt

By: Charles Murray

Date: 1985

Source: Murray, Charles. *Losing Ground: American Social Policy 1950–1980.* New York: Basic Books, 1985.

About the Author: Charles Murray is a resident scholar at the American Enterprise Institute. He holds a doctorate in Political Science from the Massachusetts Institute of Technology and a degree in History from Harvard University. Murray is a co-author of *The Bell Curve* (1994).

INTRODUCTION

On January 1, 1863, President Abraham Lincoln (1809–1865) issued the Emancipation Proclamation, legally freeing all slaves in the Confederate states. While this document marked a fundamental milestone in the fight for racial equality, it served merely as a small first step in what would prove to be a journey of more than a century. The Emancipation Proclamation, while technically freeing the slaves, remained dependent on the political will of the Union to enforce that freedom. Further, despite their status as free men, black Americans remained second-class citizens even in the eyes of the law, a status confirmed by court rulings allowing legally segregated schools.

This inequality would remain, to varying degrees, well into the twentieth century. Beginning with the Franklin Roosevelt (1882–1945) administration in 1933, a series of new laws and executive orders began to chip away at the discriminatory practices that remained pervasive throughout the United States. A progression of civil rights laws methodically outlawed hiring and promotion discrimination and prohibited housing discrimination. In 1954, intentionally segregated schools were declared illegal.

Concurrent with these legal changes, numerous federal programs were implemented in an attempt to help minorities catch up after decades of discrimination. Following his election in 1964, President Lyndon Johnson (1908–1973) announced plans for a massive program of social engineering. Modeled on President Roosevelt's New Deal, Johnson's plans continued the legacy of government efforts to improve the lives of the poorest Americans through federal assistance. Johnson's landslide election victory combined with solid Democratic control of Congress enabled the president to pass eighty of his eighty-three legislative proposals, a number unequaled by any other U.S. president. Johnson's legacy would be a larger and more comprehensive welfare state.

Johnson's programs attacked social problems on numerous fronts, in the hope that a comprehensive assault would finally bring an end to poverty and discrimination in America. Johnson increased funding for education, medical research, and conservation. He launched a massive battle against poverty and crime, funding urban renewal in numerous cities. He passed legislation protecting voting rights and signed the Medicare amendment to Social Security. Johnson's efforts combined federal funding on a previously unseen scale with the best theories about how to correct America's social ills.

Johnson's most ambitious program came to be known as the War on Poverty. Ambitiously intended to end poverty in America, this initiative was launched with the 1964 creation of the Office of Economic Opportunity (OEO). The OEO was charged with overseeing a variety of new federal programs intended to move poor Americans from dependence to self-sufficiency. Funded with $1 billion per year, the OEO oversaw the creation of numerous targeted programs including the VISTA volunteer network, Project Head Start, and Food Stamps as well as much broader efforts to completely reform urban life in the United States.

PRIMARY SOURCE

Black Unemployment Rates: A Peculiarly Localized Problem

Let us first examine unemployment as officially defined among those who were the primary beneficiaries of the jobs-program effort, black youth at the entry point to the labor market....

The picture is a discouraging one. In the early 1950s, black youths had an unemployment rate almost identical to that of whites. In the last half of the 1950s, the rate of unemployment among young blacks increased. John Cogan has recently demonstrated that the increase may be largely blamed on the loss of agricultural jobs for black teenagers, especially in the South. As this dislocating transitional period came to an end, so did the increases in the unemployment rate for black youths. The rate stabilized during the early 1960s. It stabilized, however, at the unacceptably high rate of roughly a quarter of the black labor force in this age group. It appeared to observers during the Kennedy administration that a large segment of black youth was being frozen out of the job market, and this concern was at the heart of the congressional support for the early job programs.

Black unemployment among the older of the job entrants improved somewhat during the Vietnam War years, although the figures remained higher than one would have predicted from the Korean War experience. But in the late 1960s—at the very moment when the jobs programs began their massive expansion—the black youth unemployment rate began to rise again, steeply, and continued to do so throughout the 1970s.

If the 1950s were not good years for young blacks (and they were not), the 1970s were much worse. When the years from 1951 to 1980 are split into two parts, 1951-65 and 1966–80, and the mean unemployment rate is computed for each, one finds that black 20–24 year-olds experienced a 19 percent increase in unemployment. For 18–19-year-olds, the increase was 40 percent. For 16–17-year-olds, the increase was a remarkable 72 percent. If the war years are deleted, the increases in unemployment are higher still. Focusing on the age groups on which the federal jobs programs were focused not only fails to reveal improvement; it points to major losses. Something was happening to depress employment among young blacks.

The "something" becomes more mysterious when we consider that it was not having the same effect on older blacks. Even within the 16–24-year-old age groups, we may note that the relationship between age and deterioration seems to have been the opposite of the one expected. The older the age group, the less the deterioration. What happens if we consider all black age groups,

including the ones that were largely ignored by the jobs and training programs...? The summary statement is that, for whatever reasons, older black males (35 years old and above) did well. Not only did they seem to be immune from the mysterious ailment that affected younger black males, they made significant gains....

During the same fifteen-year period in which every black male age group at or above the age of 25 experienced *decreased* unemployment compared with the preceding fifteen years, every group under the age of 25 showed a major *increase* in unemployment. If it were not for the young, the overall black unemployment profile over 1950–80 would give cause for some satisfaction.

Black Youth versus White Youth: Losing Ground

If young whites had been doing as badly, we could ascribe the trends to macro phenomena that affected everybody, educated or not, rich or poor, discriminated-against or not. But young blacks lost ground to young whites....

The position of black youths *vis-À-vis* white youths worsened for al three groups. For teenagers, the timing was especially odd. From 1961 to 1965, for example, when there were virtually no jobs programs, the black to white ratio for 18–19 year-olds averaged 1.8 to 1. From 1966 to 1969, with a much stronger economy, *plus* the many new jobs programs, the ratio jumped to an average of 2.2 to 1. Without trying at this point to impose an explanation of why black youth unemployment rose so drastically from the late sixties onward, I note in passing that satisfactory explanations do not come easily. The job situation of young blacks deteriorated as the federal efforts to improve their position were most expensive and extensive—efforts not just in employment *per se,* but in education, health, welfare, and civil rights as well. Nor does it help to appeal to competition with women, to automation, to the decay of the position of American heavy industry, or any other change in the job market. These explanations (which may well explain a worsening job situation for unskilled workers) still leave unexplained why blacks lost ground at the height of the boom, and why young blacks lost ground while older black workers (who were hardly in a better position to cope with a changing job market) did *not* lose, and in fact gained, ground. The facile explanation—jobs for young blacks just disappeared, no matter how hard they searched—runs into trouble when it tries to explain the statistics on labor force participation.

The Anomalous Plunge in Black Labor Force Participation

"Labor force participation" is the poor cousin of unemployment in the news media. Each month, the latest unemployment figures are sure to have a spot on the network news broadcasts; if times are hard, the lead.

Labor force participation is less glamorous. It has no immediate impact on our daily lives, and its rise and fall does not decide elections.

Yet the statistics on labor forces participation—"LFP" for convenience—are as informative in their own way as the statistics on unemployment. In the long run, they may be more important. The unemployment rate measures current economic conditions. Participation in the labor force measures a fundamental economic stance: an active intention of working, given the opportunity.

The Great Society reforms were not framed in terms of their effect on LFP, but in reality this was at the center of the planners' concerns. What was commonly called the "unemployment" problem among the disadvantaged was largely a problem of LFP. The hardcore unemployed were not people who were being rebuffed by job interviewers, but people who had given up hope or ambition of becoming part of the labor force. For them, the intended effect of the manpower programs was to be not merely a job, but stable, long-term membership in the labor force.

As in the case of unemployment, my analyses of LFP are based on males. The role of women in the labor market changed drastically during the three decades under consideration, especially during the 1972–80 period. Interpretations of the relationship between LFP and social welfare policy are confounded by this separate revolution. But society's norm for men remained essentially unchanged. In 1050, able-bodied adult men were expected to hold or seek a full-time job, and the same was true in 1980.

Unlike unemployment, LFP historically has been predictable, changing slowly and in accordance with identifiable rules. Therefore the Bureau of Labor Statistics had in the 1050s been able to project LFP into the future with considerable accuracy, and starting in 1057 such projections became part of the basic LFP statistics reported annually in the *Statistical Abstract of the United States*. In the 1967 volume, the *Abstract* for the first time broke down these projections by race, showing anticipated labor force participation to 1980 based on the experience from 1947 to 1964. The trend during those years plus the coming, known demographic shifts in the labor force of the 1970s led to projections of a modest increase in LFP for both black and while males. What actually happened was quite different.

In 1954, 85 percent of black males 16 years and older were participating in the labor force, a rate essentially equal to that of white males; only four-tenths of a percentage point separated the two populations. Nor was this a new phenomenon. Black males had been participating in the labor force at rates as high as or higher than white males back to the turn of the twentieth century.

This equivalence—one of the very few social or economic measures on which black males equaled whites in the 1950s—continued throughout the decade and into the early 1960s. Among members of both groups, LFP began to decline slowly in the mid–1950s, but the difference in rates was extremely small—as late as 1965, barely more than a single percentage point.

Beginning in 1966, black male LFP started to fall substantially faster than white LFP. By 1972, a gap of 5.9 percentage points had opened up between black males and while males. By 1976, the year the slide finally halted, the gap was 7.7 percentage points. To put it another way: from 1954 to 1965, the black reduction on LFP was 17 percent larger than for whites. From 1965 to 1976, it was 217 percent larger.

In the metrics of labor force statistics, a divergence of this size is huge. The change that occurred was not a minor statistical departure from the trendline, but an unanticipated and unprecedented change. America had encountered large-scale *entry* into the labor market before, most recently by women, and had legislated withdrawal from the labor market—of children, in the early part of the century. But we had never witnessed large-scale voluntary withdrawal from (or failure to enlist in) the labor market by able-bodied males.

The decline was most rapid during the exceedingly tight labor market of the last half of the 1960s made the phenomenon especially striking. A contemporary (1967) analysis of LFP published in *The American Economic Review* used data from 1961 to 1965 to reach the confident conclusion that, if unemployment dropped (as in fact was happening), we could expect major reductions in urban poverty among blacks as tight labor market drew wives into the labor force. It was assumed that black male LFP would behave as it had in the past. It was a technically exact extrapolation from recent experience, but it was contradicted by events even as the author was waiting for his manuscript to be published.

Let us take a close look at who was causing the divergence in black and white male LFP.

As in the case of unemployment, age is at the center of the explanation: As before, the young account for most of the divergence with whites. We begin with the three youngest age groups, the "job entrants," aged 16–17, 18–19, and 20-24…

It is the unemployment story replayed. The younger the age group, the greater the decline in black LFP, the greater the divergence with whites, and t he sooner it began. The parallelism with the unemployment age trends is so complete that it is important to note that the two measures are not confounded. The unemployment rate is based only on those who are in the labor force.

The people who were causing the drop in LFP were not affecting the calculation of unemployment.

On the face of things, it would appear that large numbers of young black males stopped engaging in the fundamental process of seeking and holding jobs—at least, visible jobs in the above-ground economy. There are at least two explanations, however, which would render the LFP statistic misleading: (1) that fewer young blacks participated in the labor force because they were going to school instead—a positive development; (2) that fewer young blacks participated in the labor force because the high unemployment rates made "discouraged workers" of them—why bother to look for a job if none are available? Both require examination.

"They Were Going to School Instead"

First, let us consider the merits of the education hypothesis. From 1965 to 1970, LFP among black males dropped by the following amounts (expressed as the percentage of the population in 1970 minus the percentage of the population in 1965).

Age Group	Reduction in LFP
16–17	−4.5
18–19	−4.9
20–24	−6.3

At the same time, school enrollment increased by these amounts, using the same metric:

Age Group	Increase in School Enrollment
16–17	+1.8
18–19	+.5
20–24	+5.2

Even if we make the extreme assumption that *all* of the increased enrollment represented students who would have been in the labor force if they had not gone to school and that *none* of the people who were added to the school population also participated in the labor force, the increases in school enrollment would not cover the decreases in LFP. In fact, of course, those assumptions are incorrect, further shrinking the proportion of the reduction in LFP that could be explained by school enrollment. More than a third of students in those age groups participate in the labor force, and many who are not students do not participate. The white experience indicates that school enrollment may be altogether irrelevant in explaining the change in black LFP. White male LFP in two of the three job-entry age groups increased along with school enrollment:

Age Group	LFP	Changes in School Enrollment
16–17	+4.3	+2.8
18–19	+1.6	+1.6
20–24	+2.0	+2.3

The "school enrollment" hypothesis explains at best a small fraction of the reduction in black LFP; judging from the white experience, we may not be justified in using it to explain any of the reduction.

"They Gave Up Looking For Jobs That Weren't There"

The "discouraged worker" hypothesis sis probably an explanation for part of the reduction in certain age groups in certain years. For rural populations, the disappearance of agricultural jobs meant picking up roots, establishing a new home and a new style of life, and accommodating to the demands of a strange job market. The adjustment was a difficult one, and the reductions in black teenage LFP in the last half of the 1950s can plausibly be read, at least in part, as a reflection of this. Economic bad times also produce discouragement. During recessions—1957-58, for example, or 1974-75—the reductions in LFP among the most vulnerable workers (young black males) are easily seen as discouragement.

But it is not possible to use discouragement as an explanation for the long-term trend. Why should young black males have become "discouraged workers" in greater numbers in the 1060s than they did during the less prosperous 1960s and 1970s? Even within the decade of the 1960s, the "discouraged worker" hypothesis fails. In 1960, young black males (ages 16–24) had an LFP rate of 74.0 percent, 2.7 percentage points higher than the LFP rate of white males of the same age group. By 1970, the gap was 3.6 percentage points in the other direction (whites higher than blacks)....

In the half of the decade when the economy was not only strong but operating at full capacity, the difference between young white and blacks grew fastest—more than two and a half times as fast as during the first half of the decade, with its considerably higher overall unemployment rate.

LFP among older age groups of black males during the same period is given in the appendix. In general, white and black LFP rates changed in tandem. Divergences were perceptible in each of the age groups: The participation rates of blacks and whites in the 1950s were uniformly closer than in 1980. In each case, the major portion of the divergence occurred during the 1970s. But among older workers the absolute changes were quite small.

SIGNIFICANCE

Like his predecessor Harry Truman, Lyndon Johnson found himself stepping in for a deceased, popular liberal president. And like Truman, Johnson soon found himself facing growing opposition to his efforts to expand federal participation in American life. As political resistance to Johnson's growing programs gained momentum, the war in Vietnam became increasingly costly and unpopular, robbing the president of both financial and political capital. Though well funded in its first three years, the War on Poverty simply attempted too much. Given the scope of poverty in America, any short-term attempt to spend it out of existence was probably unrealistic.

As the fiftieth anniversary of Johnson's War on Poverty approaches, poverty remains an ongoing problem in America. In the years since Johnson's initiatives, many of his approaches have been discredited; ill-conceived efforts to build massive high-rise low income housing developments, for example, proved ineffective in reducing poverty. Ironically, seemingly minor initiatives such as Project Head Start have demonstrated a greater net impact than some of the Great Society's headline efforts.

Among the problems that have actually worsened since the 1960s, persistent black unemployment is among the most vexing. Labor Force Participation (LFP), a measure of how many individuals are willing to work, has fallen substantially faster among blacks than among whites. From 1966, when the decline began and many of the Great Society programs were just hitting their stride, to 1976, the difference in white and black LFP broadened to 7.7 percentage points. This change occurred despite low unemployment rates throughout much of the period, which should have kept rates relatively low.

Economists and labor analysts offer little insight into the reason for this increasing black/white disparity. Despite disagreement about the causes, consensus does exist that blacks still face lower rates of employment than whites, and that current trends suggest the problem is worsening. Whether government policies will prove to be the root cause of the problem or its eventual solution remains the topic of a heated political debate.

In 2006, federal spending on entitlement programs including Medicare, Medicaid, and Social Security consumed 8.4 percent of the Gross Domestic Product (GDP); these expenditures were projected to more than double by the year 2050. Like defense and other types of federal spending, high spending in these large programs reduces available funding for other social projects.

FURTHER RESOURCES

Books

Dooley, David, and JoAnn Prause. *The Social Costs of Under-employment: Inadequate Employment as Disguised Unemployment.* Cambridge, U.K., and New York: Cambridge University Press, 2003.

Pissarides, Christopher A. *Equilibrium Unemployment Theory.* Cambridge, Mass.: MIT Press, 2000.

Vedder, Richard, and Lowell Gallaway. *Out of Work: Unemployment and Government in Twentieth-Century America.* Albany: New York University Press, 1997.

Periodicals

Jenkins, J. Craig, et al. "Political Opportunities and African-American Protest, 1948–1997." *American Journal of Sociology* 109 (2003): 277–303.

Malveaux, Julianne. "Despite Education, Black Workers Still Face Challenges." *Black Issues in Higher Education* 15(1998):28.

"The other America." *The Economist* 337 (1995): 19–20.

Web sites

The Heritage Foundation: Policy Research and Analysis. "Federal Budget and Spending." <http://www.heritage.org/Research/features/issues/issuearea/Budget.cfm> (accessed June 6,2006).

National Public Radio. "Examining Causes for High Black Unemployment." <http://www.npr.org/templates/story/story.php?storyId=5062690> (accessed June 6,2006).

U.S. Department of Labor: Bureau of Labor Statistics. "Household Data." <http://www.bls.gov/webapps/legacy/cpsatab2.htm> (accessed June 6,2006).

7

Current Issues in Social Policy: Healthcare, Housing, Welfare, and Social Security

Current Issues in Social Policy: Healthcare, Housing, Welfare, and Social Security

Social issues are long-standing political battlegrounds. Social issues galvanize voters, wedge political opponents, and decide elections, but the fundamental questions of social policy underlie election-time social policy maneuvering. Conservatives traditionally favor individual and private organization remedies for social problems while liberals often advocate for increased and active involvement of the federal government to solve the same problems. The two positions are not mutually exclusive. Few conservatives would argue for the federal government to abandon all social programs, just as few liberals would fail to recognize the necessity and benefit of individual volunteerism and private aid organizations. Current debates over social policy thus still try to answer fundamental questions about what social programs are necessary and beneficial, how best to structure social programs, and who should benefit most from social programs.

Occasionally, the controversy is over whether a specific social problem exists at all, not just how to solve that problem. Most people agree that homelessness, hunger, poverty, unemployment, educational inequality, discrimination, and access to adequate healthcare are all current social concerns in the Untied States. However, some people see morals-related issues such as abortion, euthanasia, and same-sex marriage and adoption rights as key aspects of U.S. social policy. Reasonable minds disagree on whether these represent social ills or are social policy concerns. The melding of political, religious, and moral agendas into social policy is not a new trend. The temperance and abolition movements highlighted in earlier chapters were fueled by religious organizations. However, the editors have chosen to focus their discussion of current social policy issues on the paramount concerns of poverty, housing, healthcare, educational opportunity, employment, anti-discrimination legislation, and established welfare programs.

The following two chapters highlight the development of U.S. social policy since 1980, with emphasis on issues and policies since 2000. This penultimate chapter covers healthcare and housing policies, as well as the on-going debates over welfare and social security reforms. Social policies and issues in education and employment are discussed in the next chapter.

This chapter presents a look at federal welfare programs that combat poverty and offer relief in times of natural disaster, providing the necessities of food, shelter, and healthcare. "Momma Welfare Role" and "'They Think You Ain't Much of Nothing'" look at public perceptions of welfare recipients in the United States. Some issues in social policy presented here stem from the challenges of meeting the needs of an aging population; recent reform proposals for Medicare and Social Security remain controversial.

Two articles—one on the the 2006 South Dakota abortion ban and another on marriage incentives in welfare programs—illustrate recent and divisive trends at the crossroads of religion, morality, politics, and social policy.

Finally, this chapter briefly discusses child welfare systems such as foster care and social services. These social policies and specific programs often vary by state, but may receive substantial federal guidance and funding. A large portion of long-standing child welfare programs, such as after-school care and subsidized meals, are carried out through the public school system.

Emergency Medical Treatment and Active Labor Act

Legislation

By: United States Congress

Date: 1986

Source: United States Congress. "Emergency Medical Treatment and Active Labor Act." *United States Code*, 1986.

About the Author: The United States Congress enacted the Emergency Medical Treatment and Active Labor Act in 1986.

INTRODUCTION

Under the Emergency Medical Treatment and Active Labor Act (EMTALA), hospitals are required to treat patients who are having a medical emergency, including childbirth, regardless of whether or not they have the ability to pay for the services. EMTALA outlines both patient rights and the responsibilities of medical personnel and facilities when such an emergency arises. The act is designed to ensure that hospitals do not dump patients—transfer those who are unable to pay for medical treatment to public hospitals, or to facilities known to serve lower-income patients covered by medical insurance. EMTALA governs when and how patients may be transferred from one hospital to another, and when or how a patient may be refused treatment.

EMTALA is part of the Consolidated Omnibus Budget Reconciliation Act (COBRA), which encompasses several other laws, including the regulations

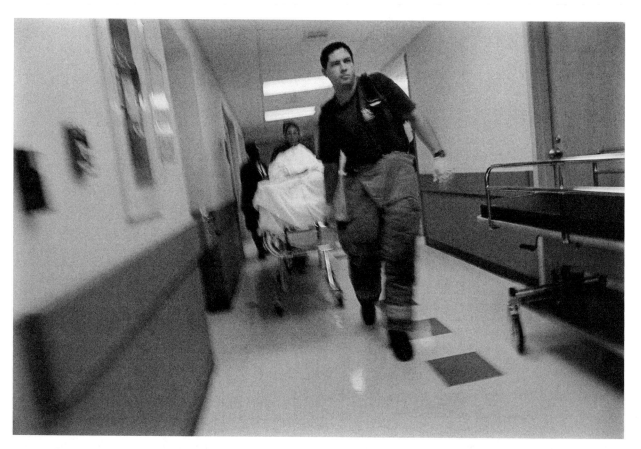

Firefighters bring a patient into a Baltimore trauma center. The Emergency Medical Treatment and Active Labor Act of 1986 requires hospitals to screen and stabilize patients with emergency medical conditions and women in labor, prior to transfer to another facility. © MARC ASNIN/CORBIS SABA.

concerning medical insurance benefits after employment termination. It applies to all hospitals that agree to receive reimbursements for treating Medicare patients (Medicare provides medical insurance for people over age 65, and for others with certain disabilities and conditions). Most hospitals in the United States receive such payments; exceptions include many military hospitals and the Shriners Hospitals for Crippled Children, which run entirely from donations. At qualifying hospitals, EMTALA applies to all patients, not just those covered by the Medicare program.

The Department of Health and Human Services (HHS) regional offices investigate alleged EMTALA violations. If violations are confirmed, the HHS Office of Inspector General (OIG) may issue civil monetary fines without criminal implications. Maximum fines are $25,000 for hospitals with fewer than 100 beds, and up to $50,000 for larger facilities. For severe violations the OIG may also revoke a hospital's Medicare reimbursement agreements—a harsher penalty than a monetary fine, as most hospitals rely heavily on such payments. The OIG has investigated approximately 200 EMTALA violations since the act's passage, but reimbursement agreements are rarely terminated. Citations are typically given for not providing appropriate medical screening exams, not providing stabilizing treatments, not keeping proper patient logs, and inappropriate transfer of patients. Although physicians can be held liable for violating EMTALA regulations, violations are typically settled through a hospital, who may seek reimbursement of penalties from individual doctors who work in the hospital.

▮ PRIMARY SOURCE

§†1395dd. Examination and treatment for emergency medical conditions and women in labor

(a) Medical screening requirement

In the case of a hospital that has a hospital emergency department, if any individual (whether or not eligible for benefits under this subchapter) comes to the emergency department and a request is made on the individual's behalf for examination or treatment for a medical condition, the hospital must provide for an appropriate medical screening examination within the capability of the hospital's emergency department, including ancillary services routinely available to the emergency department, to determine whether or not an emergency medical condition (within the meaning of subsection (e)(1) of this section) exists.

(b) Necessary stabilizing treatment for emergency medical conditions and labor

(1) In general

If any individual (whether or not eligible for benefits under this subchapter) comes to a hospital and the hospital determines that the individual has an emergency medical condition, the hospital must provide either—

(A) within the staff and facilities available at the hospital, for such further medical examination and such treatment as may be required to stabilize the medical condition, or

(B) for transfer of the individual to another medical facility in accordance with subsection (c) of this section.

(2) Refusal to consent to treatment

A hospital is deemed to meet the requirement of paragraph (1)(A) with respect to an individual if the hospital offers the individual the further medical examination and treatment described in that paragraph and informs the individual (or a person acting on the individual's behalf) of the risks and benefits to the individual of such examination and treatment, but the individual (or a person acting on the individual's behalf) refuses to consent to the examination and treatment. The hospital shall take all reasonable steps to secure the individual's (or person's) written informed consent to refuse such examination and treatment.

(3) Refusal to consent to transfer

A hospital is deemed to meet the requirement of paragraph (1) with respect to an individual if the hospital offers to transfer the individual to another medical facility in accordance with subsection (c) of this section and informs the individual (or a person acting on the individual's behalf) of the risks and benefits to the individual of such transfer, but the individual (or a person acting on the individual's behalf) refuses to consent to the transfer. The hospital shall take all reasonable steps to secure the individual's (or person's) written informed consent to refuse such transfer.

(c) Restricting transfers until individual stabilized

(1) Rule

If an individual at a hospital has an emergency medical condition which has not been stabilized (within the meaning of subsection (e)(3)(B) of this section), the hospital may not transfer the individual unless—

(A)

(i) the individual (or a legally responsible person acting on the individual's behalf) after being informed of the hospital's obligations under this section and of the risk of transfer, in writing requests transfer to another medical facility,

(ii) a physician (within the meaning of section 1395x (r)(1) of this title) has signed a certification that†[1] based upon the information available at the time of transfer, the medical benefits reasonably expected from the provision of appropriate medical treatment at another medical facility outweigh the increased risks to the individual and, in the case of labor, to the unborn child from effecting the transfer, or

(iii) if a physician is not physically present in the emergency department at the time an individual is transferred, a qualified medical person (as defined by the Secretary in regulations) has signed a certification described in clause (ii) after a physician (as defined in section 1395x (r)(1) of this title), in consultation with the person, has made the determination described in such clause, and subsequently countersigns the certification; and

(B) the transfer is an appropriate transfer (within the meaning of paragraph (2) to that facility.

A certification described in clause (ii) or (iii) of subparagraph (A) shall include a summary of the risks and benefits upon which the certification is based.

(2) **Appropriate transfer**

An appropriate transfer to a medical facility is a transfer—

(A) in which the transferring hospital provides the medical treatment within its capacity which minimizes the risks to the individual's health and, in the case of a woman in labor, the health of the unborn child;

(B) in which the receiving facility—

(i) has available space and qualified personnel for the treatment of the individual, and

(ii) has agreed to accept transfer of the individual and to provide appropriate medical treatment;

(C) in which the transferring hospital sends to the receiving facility all medical records (or copies thereof), related to the emergency condition for which the individual has presented, available at the time of the transfer, including records related to the individual's emergency medical condition, observations of signs or symptoms, preliminary diagnosis, treatment provided, results of any tests and the informed written consent or certification (or copy thereof) provided under paragraph (1)(A), and the name and address of any on-call physician (described in subsection (d)(1)(C) of this section) who has refused or

failed to appear within a reasonable time to provide necessary stabilizing treatment;

(D) in which the transfer is effected through qualified personnel and transportation equipment, as required including the use of necessary and medically appropriate life support measures during the transfer; and

(E) which meets such other requirements as the Secretary may find necessary in the interest of the health and safety of individuals transferred.

...

[4] (e) **Definitions**

In this section:

(1) The term "emergency medical condition" means—

(A) a medical condition manifesting itself by acute symptoms of sufficient severity (including severe pain) such that the absence of immediate medical attention could reasonably be expected to result in—

(i) placing the health of the individual (or, with respect to a pregnant woman, the health of the woman or her unborn child) in serious jeopardy,

(ii) serious impairment to bodily functions, or

(iii) serious dysfunction of any bodily organ or part; or

(B) with respect to a pregnant woman who is having contractions—

(i) that there is inadequate time to effect a safe transfer to another hospital before delivery, or

(ii) that transfer may pose a threat to the health or safety of the woman or the unborn child.

(2) The term "participating hospital" means a hospital that has entered into a provider agreement under section 1395cc of this title.

(3)

(A) The term "to stabilize" means, with respect to an emergency medical condition described in paragraph (1)(A), to provide such medical treatment of the condition as may be necessary to assure, within reasonable medical probability, that no material deterioration of the condition is likely to result from or occur during the transfer of the individual from a facility, or, with respect to an emergency medical condition described in paragraph (1)(B), to deliver (including the placenta).

(B) The term "stabilized" means, with respect to an emergency medical condition described in paragraph (1)(A), that no material deterioration of the condition is likely, within reasonable medical probability, to result from or occur during the transfer of the individual from a facility, or, with respect to an emergency medical condition described in paragraph (1)(B), that the woman has delivered (including the placenta).

(4) The term "transfer" means the movement (including the discharge) of an individual outside a hospital's facilities at the direction of any person employed by (or affiliated or associated, directly or indirectly, with) the hospital, but does not include such a movement of an individual who

(A) has been declared dead, or
(B) leaves the facility without the permission of any such person.

(5) The term "hospital" includes a critical access hospital (as defined in section 1395x (mm)(1) of this title).

(f) Preemption

The provisions of this section do not preempt any State or local law requirement, except to the extent that the requirement directly conflicts with a requirement of this section.

(g) Nondiscrimination

A participating hospital that has specialized capabilities or facilities (such as burn units, shock–trauma units, neonatal intensive care units, or (with respect to rural areas) regional referral centers as identified by the Secretary in regulation) shall not refuse to accept an appropriate transfer of an individual who requires such specialized capabilities or facilities if the hospital has the capacity to treat the individual.

(h) No delay in examination or treatment

A participating hospital may not delay provision of an appropriate medical screening examination required under subsection (a) of this section or further medical examination and treatment required under subsection (b) of this section in order to inquire about the individual's method of payment or insurance status.

(i) Whistleblower protections

A participating hospital may not penalize or take adverse action against a qualified medical person described in subsection (c)(1)(A)(iii) of this section or a physician because the person or physician refuses to authorize the transfer of an individual with an emergency medical condition that has not been stabilized or against any hospital employee because the employee reports a violation of a requirement of this section.

SIGNIFICANCE

Many in the medical community believe that EMTALA enforcement and implementation increases costs and crowds emergency rooms, decreasing the efficiency of hospitals. To address this concern, the 2001 Consolidated Appropriations Act called for the United States General Accounting Office (GAO) to analyze EMTALA's effect on hospitals and physicians working in emergency units.

The analysis found that demand for nonurgent hospital services had indeed grown, but it was unclear whether this was a result of enforcing EMTALA or the growth of the uninsured population. Some hospitals also claimed that fewer physicians were willing to join their staffs because of the workload required to enforce EMTALA. For their part, the GAO found that technology allowed doctors to perform more procedures in clinics, outside of hospitals, which might explain why fewer specialists worked in hospitals. Hospital and physician representatives said that EMTALA has helped ensure better access to emergency services and less patient dumping; some hospitals, however, said they did not know the full extent of their obligations under EMTALA.

The Medicare Prescription Drug, Improvement, and Modernization Act of 2003 created a technical advisory group to monitor changes in EMTALA implementation. Health and Human Services (HHS) also simplified EMTALA enforcement, including the development of procedures and standards for more effective investigation and resolution of complaints.

FURTHER RESOURCES

Books

Bitterman, Robert A. *Providing Emergency Care under Federal Law: EMTALA*. Dallas, TX: American College of Emergency Physicians, 2000.

Gatewood, Joseph, Loren Johnson, and Ellen Arrington. *A Practical Guide to EMTALA Compliance*. Marblehead, MA: HCPro, Inc., 2004.

Williams, Abigail R. *Outpatient department EMTALA handbook 2002*. Gaithersburg, MD: Aspen Law & Business, 2002.

Periodicals

General Accounting Office. "Emergency Care: EMTALA Implementation and Enforcement Issues: Report to Congressional Committees." *Washington, DC: United States General Accounting Office*. June 2001.

Web sites

United States Department of Human Health and Services. "Centers for Medicare and Medicaid Services: EMTALA." April 17, 2006. <http://www.cms.hhs.gov/EMTALA/01_overview.asp> (accessed May 24, 2006).

Fair Housing Act

Legislation

By: U.S. Department of Justice, Civil Rights Division, Housing and Enforcement Section

Date: 1988

Source: *U.S. Department of Justice.* "Fair Housing Act." 42 U.S.C. 3601–3619, 3631. <http://www.usdoj.gov/crt/housing/title8.htm> (accessed May 18, 2006).

About the Author: The Housing and Enforcement Section is a branch of the Civil Rights Division of the U.S. Department of Justice. The role of the Civil Rights Division is to protect, safeguard, and enforce the federal laws and regulations concerning federal non-discrimination legislation. The division is charged with ascertaining that individuals are not subject to discrimination based on race, national origin, gender, sexual orientation (where applicable), and disability. The Housing and Enforcement Section is specifically tasked with safeguarding the rights of individuals to fair and equal housing opportunities under the statutes of the federal government.

INTRODUCTION

Twenty years after the original Fair Housing Act became law, it was amended to include provisions against discrimination in housing for persons with disabilities or for persons whose child or children have disabilities. The amendments mandate that large scale housing, such as apartments, condominiums, or town homes, be required to have specified accessible units available for rent or purchase by individuals or family members with disabilities, that reasonable accommodations be made for the safe and easy access of common and public areas by persons with disabilities, and that new construction designate a percentage of all units to be handicap accessible.

The Fair Housing Act defines a handicapping condition, or a disability, as a mental or physical impairment that significantly limits one or more major life activities. The mental or physical handicapping condition may include blindness, deafness, significant visual or hearing loss, mental retardation, disorders affecting mobility (including those necessi-

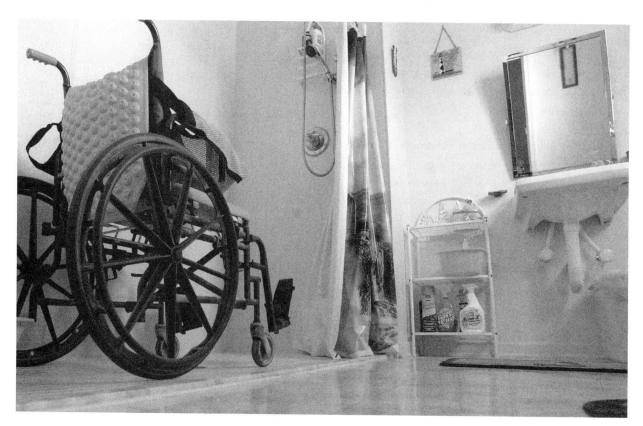

A bathroom specially designed to be accessible to someone in a wheelchair. AP IMAGES.

tating use of a wheelchair, a walker, leg braces, or crutches), HIV infection or AIDS, chronic fatigue syndrome, alcoholism, drug addiction, brain injury, some types of learning disabilities, and mental illness. The impairment may include profound restriction in or loss of sensory ability such as vision or hearing, difficulty ambulating or inability to be mobile without the use of a wheelchair or other assistive device, inability to speak, difficulty breathing, inability to manually or otherwise adequately complete activities of daily living, learning problems, inability to be gainfully employed, and inability to perform manual tasks.

It is illegal to discriminate against an individual or family in a housing situation on the basis of disability status. In fact, it is illegal to even ask questions regarding the existence or extent of disabilities. The property owner must make all reasonable and necessary accommodations in order to ensure that the disabled individual is guaranteed the ability to fully utilize and enjoy the use of the dwelling and attendant common areas. If modifications to the dwelling are required, the landlord, board of directors, or other management entity must implement them within the shortest possible reasonable period of time. The Fair Housing Act places the onus and responsibility for making the modifications on the management, but the financial burden may be shared, absorbed by the facility, or levied upon the occupant.

Typical accommodations or modifications that may be necessary in residential settings include widening doors, placing safety bars in toilet, tub, and shower areas, lowering counter heights and door knobs, installing access ramps, ensuring adequate and appropriate accessible parking, and implementing specific adaptive equipment for persons with significant visual or hearing impairments.

In addition to prohibiting discrimination against persons based on disability status, the Fair Housing Act also makes it illegal to bar service animals from living with their owners, regardless of overall regulations concerning pets.

PRIMARY SOURCE

SEC. 800. [42 U.S.C. 3601 NOTE] SHORT TITLE

This title may be cited as the "Fair Housing Act."

SEC. 801. [42 U.S.C. 3601] DECLARATION OF POLICY

It is the policy of the United States to provide, within constitutional limitations, for fair housing throughout the United States....

SEC. 804. [42 U.S.C. 3604] DISCRIMINATION IN SALE OR RENTAL OF HOUSING AND OTHER PROHIBITED PRACTICES

As made applicable by section 803 of this title and except as exempted by sections 803(b) and 807 of this title, it shall be unlawful—...

(c) To make, print, or publish, or cause to be made, printed, or published any notice, statement, or advertisement, with respect to the sale or rental of a dwelling that indicates any preference, limitation, or discrimination based on race, color, religion, sex, handicap, familial status, or national origin, or an intention to make any such preference, limitation, or discrimination.

(d) To represent to any person because of race, color, religion, sex, handicap, familial status, or national origin that any dwelling is not available for inspection, sale, or rental when such dwelling is in fact so available.

(e) For profit, to induce or attempt to induce any person to sell or rent any dwelling by representations regarding the entry or prospective entry into the neighborhood of a person or persons of a particular race, color, religion, sex, handicap, familial status, or national origin.

(f)

(1) To discriminate in the sale or rental, or to otherwise make unavailable or deny, a dwelling to any buyer or renter because of a handicap of—

(A) that buyer or renter,

(B) a person residing in or intending to reside in that dwelling after it is so sold, rented, or made available; or

(C) any person associated with that buyer or renter.

(2) To discriminate against any person in the terms, conditions, or privileges of sale or rental of a dwelling, or in the provision of services or facilities in connection with such dwelling, because of a handicap of—

(A) that person; or

(B) a person residing in or intending to reside in that dwelling after it is so sold, rented, or made available; or

(C) any person associated with that person.

(3) For purposes of this subsection, discrimination includes—

(A) a refusal to permit, at the expense of the handicapped person, reasonable modifications of existing premises occupied or to be occupied by such person if such modifications may be necessary to afford such person full enjoyment of the premises, except that, in the case of a rental, the landlord may where it is reasonable to do so condition permission for a modification on the renter agreeing to restore the interior of the premises to the condition that existed before the modification, reasonable wear and tear excepted.

(B) a refusal to make reasonable accommodations in rules, policies, practices, or services, when such accommodations may be necessary to afford such person equal opportunity to use and enjoy a dwelling; or

(C) in connection with the design and construction of covered multifamily dwellings for first occupancy after the date that is 30 months after the date of enactment of the Fair Housing Amendments Act of 1988, a failure to design and construct those dwellings in such a manner that—

(i) the public use and common use portions of such dwellings are readily accessible to and usable by handicapped persons;

(ii) all the doors designed to allow passage into and within all premises within such dwellings are sufficiently wide to allow passage by handicapped persons in wheelchairs; and

(iii) all premises within such dwellings contain the following features of adaptive design:

(I) an accessible route into and through the dwelling;
(II) light switches, electrical outlets, thermostats, and other environmental controls in accessible locations;
(III) reinforcements in bathroom walls to allow later installation of grab bars; and
(IV) usable kitchens and bathrooms such that an individual in a wheelchair can maneuver about the space....

SEC. 805. [42 U.S.C. 3605] DISCRIMINATION IN RESIDENTIAL REAL ESTATE-RELATED TRANSACTIONS

(a) In General.—It shall be unlawful for any person or other entity whose business includes engaging in residential real estate-related transactions to discriminate against any person in making available such a transaction, or in the terms or conditions of such a transaction, because of race, color, religion, sex, handicap, familial status, or national origin.

SIGNIFICANCE

One of the central responsibilities of the Civil Rights Division's Housing and Enforcement Section is oversight of zoning and land use regulations in order to ensure that no regulations are implemented that might restrict available housing or dwelling choices for individuals with disabilities. It is important to note, however, that the safety of the community overrides individual preferences—meaning that individuals who might pose a potential threat to other persons or their property by moving into a specific dwelling (based specifically on their behavior) may lawfully be restricted or prevented from doing so. The decision regarding reasonable concern about threat must be made by direct observation and interaction with the specific individual, not based on reports provided by others, regardless of their degree of credibility.

Another of the Housing and Enforcement Section's major responsibilities is the oversight of new construction containing four or more units, in order to ensure that it conforms to the accessibility requirements of the Fair Housing Act, and incorporates necessary accommodations, particularly those allowing ready access for individuals using wheelchairs. Among the regulations for new construction are the placement of thermostats, door and window latches, countertops, electrical outlets, light switches, and other manual or mechanical items (laundry facilities, dishwashers, refrigerator doors, etc.) so that they are easily and comfortably reachable by persons in wheelchairs. Bathrooms must provide grab bars near toilets, in showers, and around tub enclosures, and sinks must be reachable. Public and common areas, including restrooms, must be fully and readily accessible. In addition, entrances to accessible units must themselves be easily accessible, as must their parking areas, sidewalks, and entryways.

Among the less visible disabilities subject to housing discrimination are those that are cognitive, neurological, psychological, or psychiatric. People with learning disabilities, brain injuries, or a history of mental illness regularly face discrimination in many aspects of their lives, particularly employment and housing. The legal rule is that so long as a person meets all of the requirements for acceptance into a particular housing situation, the presence of a mental disability should not be used as a basis for decision-making. The medical or psychiatric history of an individual should have no bearing on ability to meet residential responsibilities, comply with rules and regulations, or meet financial obligations (pay rent, fees, etc.) in a timely or appropriate manner. Only such behavior as is specifically and materially relevant to the individual's ability to perform satisfactorily as a tenant may be considered as a means of evaluating whether he or she will be able to meet residential requirements on an ongoing basis.

The laws against discrimination in housing based on disability status are analogous to those prohibiting discrimination based upon race, culture, gender, ethnicity, and sexual orientation, and the legal ramifications for violation of those rights are equivalent. People with disabilities are legally entitled to equal protection and treatment within the housing realm, and they are equally entitled to self-sufficiency, self-empowerment, actualization, and full access to their living spaces.

FURTHER RESOURCES

Books

Levy, Robert M., and Leonard S. Rubenstein. *The Rights of People with Mental Disabilities: The Authoritative ACLU Guide to the Rights of People with Mental Illness and Mental Retardation.* Carbondale, Ill.: Southern Illinois University Press, 1996.

Percy, Stephen L. *Disability, Civil Rights and Public Policy: The Politics of Implementation.* Tuscaloosa: The University of Alabama Press, 1992.

West, J., ed. *The Americans with Disabilities Act: From Policy to Practice.* New York: Milbank Memorial Fund, 1991.

Periodicals

Colker, R. "ADA Title III: A Fragile Compromise." *Berkeley Journal of Employment and Labor Law* 21 (2000): 377–412.

Colker, R. "Winning and Losing Under the Americans with Disabilities Act." *Ohio State Law Journal* 62 (2001): 239–278.

Health Security for All Americans

Speech

By: William Jefferson Clinton

Date: September 22, 1993

Source: Clinton, William Jefferson. "Health Security for All Americans." September 22, 1993. Available at <http://www.ibiblio.org/nhs/supporting/remarks.html> (accessed June 10, 2006).

About the Author: William Jefferson Clinton (1946–) was the forty-second president of the United States. He held office from 1993 to 2001. Early in his first term as president, he proposed the Health Security Act, which failed.

INTRODUCTION

In 1993, President Bill Clinton proposed a program of sweeping health-care reforms and suggested the creation of a system of universal health-care coverage for all people living in the United States of America. The plan was met with considerable public enthusiasm but little political approval. There was significant buzz in the political and health-care arenas suggesting that the time was right for major changes in the American third-party-payer system, notably making certain that all of the people in the country would have access to free or affordable health care coverage. Numerous public-interest and lobbying groups had suggested plans for health-care reform, and the concept of universal coverage (assuring free or affordable health-care coverage for every person in America) or mandated coverage (requiring that all persons be able to purchase affordable health-care insurance, no matter what their level of employment or degree of personal financial stability) was publicly endorsed by both the Health Insurance Association of America (HIAA) and the American Medical Association (AMA). Many of the country's largest employers and biggest businesses, as well as the U.S. Chamber of Commerce, voiced their support of employer-mandated insurance (all employers would have to provide health coverage to every employee, regardless of degree or level of employment).

During the early 1990s, a number of health-care reforms were suggested, and many bills were proposed, resulting in a level of tumult and confusion within both the political arena and the business world. The first major shake-up came when the U.S. Chamber of Commerce, in recovery from significant internal organizational reform, withdrew its prior support of employer-mandated health-care coverage. This development was followed shortly by a change in the previous stance taken by the American Medical Association, which stated that only larger employers, those with more than one hundred staff members, should be mandated to provide health-care coverage for all workers. Most of the health-care reform bills that were introduced for legislative consideration were withdrawn, and support for the president's massive reform campaign quickly cooled. There was considerable commentary made about the level of government intrusiveness that would be imposed upon private citizens with the advent of universal health-care plans. Within about a year of its official introduction and without ever having been substantially acted upon, the Health Security Act was shelved.

Mr. Speaker, Mr. President, Members of Congress, distinguished guests, my fellow Americans—

Tonight, we come together to write a new chapter in the American story....

It is time for America to fix a health care system that is badly broken.

Despite the dedication of millions of talented health care professionals, our health care is too uncertain and too expensive; too bureaucratic and too wasteful. It has too much fraud and too much greed.

At long last, after decades of false starts, we must make this our most urgent priority: Giving every American health security—health care that's always there—health care that can never be taken away.

On this journey, as on all others of consequence, there will be rough stretches and honest disagreements about how to reach our destination. After all, this is a complicated issue....

So tonight, I want to talk with you about the principles that must guide our reform of America's health care system: Security, simplicity, and savings; choice, quality and responsibility....

Every one of us knows someone who has worked hard and played by the rules but has been hurt by this system that just doesn't work. Let me tell you about just one.

Kerry Kennedy owns a small furniture franchise that employs seven people in Titusville, Florida. Like most small business owners, Kerry has poured his sweat and blood into that company. But over the last few years, the cost of insuring his seven workers has skyrocketed, as did the cost of the coverage for himself, his wife, and his daughter. Last year, however, Kerry could no longer afford to provide coverage for all his workers because the insurance companies had labeled two of them high risk simply because of their age. But, you know what? Those two people are Kerry's Mother and Father who built the family business and now work in the store.

That story speaks for millions of others. And from them, we have learned a powerful truth: we have to preserve and strengthen what is right with our health care system and fix what is wrong with it.

This is what is right: We are blessed with the best health care professionals, the finest health care institutions, the most advanced research, and the most sophisticated medical technology on the face of the earth. My mother is a Nurse, and I grew up around hospitals. The first professional people I ever knew and looked up to were doctors and nurses. They represent what is right with our health care system.

But we cannot ignore what is wrong. Millions of Americans are just a pink slip away from losing their health coverage, and one serious illness away from losing their life savings. Millions more are locked into the wrong jobs, because they'd lose their coverage if they left their companies. And on any given day over 37 million of our fellow citizens, the vast majority of them children or hard working adults, have no health insurance at all. And despite all of this, our medical bills are growing at more than twice the rate of inflation.

Our health care system takes 35% more of our income than any other country, insures fewer people, requires more Americans to pay more and more for less and less, and gives them fewer choices. There is no excuse for that kind of system, and it's time to fix it....

The first principle of health care reform—the most important—must be security. This principle speaks to the human misery and costs that we hear about every day when Americans lack or lose health care coverage.

Security means that those who do not have health care coverage will have it and, for those who have coverage, it will never be taken away. We must achieve that security as soon as possible.

Under our plan, every American will receive a health security card that will guarantee you a comprehensive package of benefits over the course of your lifetime that will equal benefits provided by most Fortune 500 corporations.

This card will guarantee you a comprehensive package of benefits that can never be taken away. And let us pledge tonight: Before this Congress adjourns next year, you will pass, and I will sign a new law to create health security for every American.

With this card, if you lose your job or switch jobs, you're covered.

If you leave your job to start a small business, you're covered.

If you are an early retiree, you're covered.

If you or someone in your family has a preexisting medical condition, you're covered.

If you get sick or a member of your family gets sick, even if it's a life-threatening illness, you're covered.

And if an insurance company tries to drop you for any reason, you'll still be covered—because that will be illegal.

This card will give you comprehensive coverage. You will be covered for hospital care, doctors visits, emergency and laboratory services, diagnostic services like Pap smears and mammograms, substance abuse and mental health treatment.

And our proposal will pay for regular check-ups, well-baby visits and other preventive care. It's just common sense. People will stay healthier and at affordable costs. You know how your mother told you that an ounce of prevention is worth a pound of cure? Well, your mother was right. And we've ignored that lesson for too long.

Security must also apply to older Americans. This is something I feel very strongly about: We will maintain the Medicare program. And for the first time, Medicare will cover the cost of prescription drugs. And over time our proposal will provide assistance in the home for the elderly and disabled who need long term care. As we proceed with health care, we must not break faith with our older Americans.

Simplicity

…Our health care system must be simpler for the patients and simpler for those who actually deliver health care: our physicians, our nurses, and our other medical professionals.…

Under our proposal, there will be one standard insurance form, not hundreds. We will simplify government rules and regulations so that a doctor doesn't have to check with a bureaucrat in an office thousands of miles away before ordering a simple blood test. And you won't have to worry about the fine print, because there won't be any fine print.

Savings

…Reform must produce savings in our health care system.

Today, rampant medical inflation is eating away at our wages, our savings, our investment capital, and our public treasury. It undermines America's economy, competitiveness, confidence, and living standards.…

Unless everyone is covered, we can never put the brakes on health care inflation. Because when people don't have insurance, they wait to see a doctor until their illness is more severe and more costly, and they often seek treatment in the most expensive settings—like emergency rooms. And when they can't pay their bills, because they aren't insured—who do you think picks up the tab?—the rest of us do: through higher hospital bills and higher insurance premiums.

We will also save money by simplifying the system and freeing health care providers from costly and unnecessary paperwork and administrative overload that now costs $100 billion a year. We will crack down on the fraud and abuse that drains billions per year.

This system will work. You don't have to take my word for it. Ask Dr. C. Everett Koop. He says we could spend $200 billion less every year without sacrificing the high quality of American medicine. Ask the public employees in California, who have held their own premiums down by adopting this very same approach. Ask Xerox,

which saved an estimated $1,000 per worker. Ask the staff of the Mayo Clinic, who provide some of the finest care in the world, while holding their cost increases to less than half the national average. Ask the people of Hawaii, the only state that covers virtually all of their citizens, and whose costs are well below the national average.…

Choice

…Americans believe they should be able to choose their own health care plans and their own doctor. And under our plan they will have that right.

But, today, under our broken health care system, that power to choose is slipping away. Now it is usually the employer—and not the employee—who makes the choice of what health care plan will be provided. If your employer only offers one plan, as do nearly three-quarters of small and medium-sized businesses, you're stuck with that plan and the doctors it covers.

We propose to give every American a choice among high quality plans. You can stay with your current doctor, join a network of doctors and hospitals, or join a Health Maintenance Organization. If you don't like your plan, every year you'll have the chance to choose a new one.

The choice will be left to you—not your boss—and not some bureaucrat.

And we also believe that doctors should have a choice as to what plans they practice in. We want to end the discrimination that is now growing against doctors and permit them to practice in several different plans. Choice is important for doctors, and critical for consumers.

Quality

…Quality is something that cannot be left to chance. When you board an airplane, you feel better knowing that plane had to meet standards designed to protect your safety. We must ask no less of our health care system.

We don't propose a government-run health care system. We propose that government sets standards to ensure health care quality.…

Our plan will guarantee that quality health care is available in even the most remote areas of our nation, linking rural doctors and hospitals with high-tech urban medical centers. And our plan will ensure quality by speeding research on effective prevention and treatment measures for cancer, for AIDS, for Alzheimers, for heart disease and for other chronic diseases. Our plan safeguards the finest medical research establishment in the world, and makes it even better.

Responsibility

…We need to restore a sense that we are all in this together, and we all have a responsibility to be a part of the solution.

Responsibility must start with those who have profited from the current health care system. Responsibility means insurance companies will no longer be allowed to cast people aside when they get sick. It must also apply to laboratories that submit fraudulent bills; to lawyers who abuse the malpractice system; to doctors who order unnecessary procedures. It means drug companies will no longer be allowed to charge three times more for prescription drugs here in the United States than they charge overseas. Responsibility must apply to anyone who abuses our system and drives up costs for honest, hardworking citizens and health care providers.

Responsibility also means changing the behavior in this country that drive up our health care costs and cause untold suffering. It's the outrageous costs of violence from far too many handguns, especially among the young. It's high rates of AIDS, smoking and excessive drinking; it's teenage pregnancy, low-birth-weight babies, and not enough vaccinations for the most vulnerable.

But let me also say this. And I hope you will listen, because it is a hard thing to hear. Responsibility in our health care system isn't about "them." It's about you. It's about me. It's about each of us.

Too many Americans have not taken responsibility for their health. Too many Americans use this health care system but don't pay a penny for their health care. I believe those who do not have health insurance should be responsible for paying something. There can be no more something for nothing....

Let us write that new chapter in America's story, and guarantee every American comprehensive health benefits that can never be taken away.

Some people have said that it would be a miracle if we passed health care reform. But, my fellow Americans, I believe we live in a time of great change when miracles do happen....

I believe that forty years from now, our grandchildren will also find it unthinkable that there was a time in our country when hardworking families lost their homes and savings simply because their child fell ill, or lost their health coverage when they changed jobs. Yet, our grandchildren will only find such things unthinkable tomorrow, if we have the courage to change today.

This is our chance. This is our journey. And, when our work is done, we will know that we have answered the call of history and met the challenge of our times.

Thank you. And God bless America.

SIGNIFICANCE

There was much speculation as to what caused the defeat of the Clinton health-care reform bill; many expressed public sentiment that the plan was too involved, too cumbersome, and too government-heavy to appeal to the masses. Essentially, the plan, as it was ultimately structured, advocated what is called a managed competition program. In this type of program, a limited pool of potential health care insurers compete for the individual's or family's business, within a range of acceptable plan options for comprehensive health-care coverage, thereby driving prices for coverage down while frequently increasing the available menu of services and programs available to the consumer. In this way, the consumer is offered significant free choice in plan selection. Significant enhancements were built into the system, in part as a means of seeking buy-in from growing population segments, such as prescription coverage and early retirement benefits for elders. Caps were built into the roll-out of the program, limiting premium cost increase over the first several years of the plan. The health-care reform plan also included such high-cost items as home-based long-term care and services for elders and those with disabilities. A somewhat controversial issue was coverage for abortions, a proposal that had the effect of galvanizing conservative and religious groups to voice their very strong opposition to the plan.

During the period that the Health Security Act was under discussion, there were several health-care reform packages and bills circulating. Generally, the most popular among them contained at least some level of consumer choice and advocated the creation of managed competition among the pool of potential insurers. They also contained a proposal for purchasing cooperatives for health insurance and standard benefit packages—as is the case for most commercial insurance plans, health maintenance organizations, managed care organizations, and federally funded health care coverage providers such as Medicaid. All advocated the establishment of subsidies in order to make the payment of insurance premiums affordable for low-income individuals and families, as well as for those living in poverty.

Critics of the plans, and of the Clinton plan in particular, felt that they were excessively cumbersome (the proposed Health Security Act legislation was well in excess of one thousand pages in length) and overly restrictive. The Clinton plan called for limited choice of health-care providers; many individuals and families feared that they would lose established relationships with health-care professionals. Many others

President Bill Clinton speaks on health care reform.
PHOTO BY CYNTHIA JOHNSON//TIME LIFE PICTURES/GETTY IMAGES.

reported that they were well satisfied with their current type and level of health-care coverage and would object to any mandated changes, despite the reported fact that the health care coverage costs in America are the highest in the world. There was a public perception that everyone who wanted or needed health care coverage could get it, and many believed that few people were either uninsured or underinsured. In a time of economic prosperity, the public seemed to feel that all was universally well and failed to recognize the substantial percentage of the population that earned too much to be eligible for publicly paid health care but not enough to be able to afford private insurers. Also overlooked were those who were too ill or disenfranchised to have the wherewithal to seek federally funded coverage, those who continually resorted to the use of emergency medical services as a means of obtaining health care.

In the end, the ponderousness of the plan, as well as the timing of its launch—when the majority of the voting population expressed comfort with their health-care coverage—led to its demise. Universal health-care coverage would be a boon to the poorer segments of the population, to the underemployed, to the chronically ill, to the homeless and disenfranchised populations, and to those who simply do not have the means or the ability to navigate the administrative systems necessary to obtain federally funded health care. Anything that drives costs down while maintaining or improving the level of health-care provision and stabilizing or broadening the menu of available services benefits everyone, particularly if it can be accomplished universally.

FURTHER RESOURCES
Books

Chapman, Audrey R., ed. *Health Care Reform: A Human Rights Approach*. Washington, D.C.: Georgetown University Press, 1994.

Epstein, Richard A. *Mortal Peril: Our Inalienable Right to Health Care?*. Cambridge, Mass.: Perseus Books, 1999.

Ginzberg, Eli, ed. *Critical Issues in U.S. Health Reform*. Boulder, Colo.: Westview Press, 1994.

Laham, Nicholas. *A Lost Cause: Bill Clinton's Campaign for National Health Insurance*. Westport, Conn.: Praeger, 1996.

Patel, Kant and Mark Rushefsky. *Health Care Politics and Policy in America*. Armonk, N.Y.: M.E. Sharpe, 1995.

Rosenthal, Marilynn and Max Heirich, eds. *Health Policy: Understanding Our Choices from National Reform to Market Choices*. Boulder, Colo.: Westview Press, 1998.

Rushefsky, Mark and Kant Patel. *Politics, Power and Policy-Making: The Case of Health Care Reform in the 1990s*. Armonk, N.Y.: M. E. Sharpe, 1998.

Shelton, Michael W. *Talk of Power, Power of Talk: The 1994 Health Care Reform Debate and Beyond*. Westport, Conn.: Praeger, 2000.

Periodicals

"The Beginning of Health Care Reform: The Clinton Plan." *The New England Journal of Medicine* 329 (21) (November 18, 1993): 1569–1570.

Web sites

The Health Security Act of 1993. "Health Care That's Always There—Executive Summary." <http://www.ibiblio.org/nhs/executive/X-Summary-toc.html> (accessed May 20, 2006).

The White House. "William J. Clinton." <http://www.whitehouse.gov/history/presidents/bc42.html> (accessed May 31, 2006).

The Hidden Side of the American Welfare State

Magazine article excerpt

By: Christopher Howard

Date: 1993

Source: Howard, Christopher. "The Hidden Side of the American Welfare State." *Political Science Quarterly* 108 (1993): 411–416.

About the Author: Christopher Howard (b. 1961) is an Associate Professor of Government at the College of William and Mary. He is the author of *The Hidden Welfare State: Tax Expenditures and Social Policy in the United States* (1997) and *The Welfare State Nobody Knows: Debunking Myths about U.S. Social Policy* (2007).

INTRODUCTION

For the first 150 years of American history, the federal government provided little direct support to American citizens. Throughout most of this period, federal income remained severely limited, relying largely on tariffs and the sale of federally owned real estate. While many Americans felt compassion for the needy, few believed the responsibility for their care lay with the government, and churches and other charitable organizations played the major roles in indigent care.

When the stock market crashed in 1929, the American economy ground to a halt as banks failed, businesses closed, and jobs vanished. The ranks of the unemployed swelled, and poverty ballooned, particularly among the elderly. By the mid–1930s, numerous politicians had concluded that the federal government did have a responsibility to provide income for elderly Americans, as well as other forms of basic assistance for other citizens.

In the two decades before the Depression, several states passed laws providing assistance for single mothers. These programs, known as mothers' pensions, provided monthly cash grants to single mothers and were the first formal welfare programs enacted in the United States. However, these programs were funded and administered locally, meaning that eligibility requirements and benefit levels varied widely across the country.

In 1935, with the United States spending heavily on work programs for the unemployed, President Franklin Roosevelt announced a fundamental change in U.S. government philosophy. In his State of the Union speech, Roosevelt declared that the government should accept responsibility for protecting citizens from the major hazards and uncertainties of life. He hoped to achieve this ambitious goal by instituting federal aid programs for the unemployed, the elderly, and single mothers. Roosevelt's initiative led to the creation of the Social Security system and numerous other agencies collectively known as social welfare programs.

From their inception, the federal government's welfare programs created controversy, as political forces battled over who should be served, how they should be helped, and how much help they should receive. Government social programs grew slowly, then expanded dramatically during the 1960s as part of Lyndon Johnson's War on Poverty. By 2001, the government ran six different departments that distributed benefits including food stamps, housing support payments, assistance for Women, Infants, and Children (WIC), Medicaid, and Head Start. These programs, including both state and federal funds, cost an estimated \$434 billion in 2000, or about \$5,600 per tax-paying household.

While cash payments to single mothers and food stamps clearly qualify as welfare, other government expenditures may also fit that description. For example, some analysts argue that the United States subsidizes home ownership, because homeowners receive government assistance in the form of a mortgage interest deduction. Corporations also receive tax reductions for pensions, insurance, and some other benefits, making them the beneficiaries of an indirect form of government assistance. Though such expenditures are not normally classified as welfare, some analysts argue that they should be.

■ PRIMARY SOURCE

STRUCTURE OF THE HIDDEN WELFARE STATE

Earlier I argued that tax expenditures and other forms of indirect spending belonged in any comprehensive account of modern welfare states, no matter what definition of welfare state was used. The definition does make a difference, however, in determining the overall size of the hidden welfare state. If one defines the welfare sate narrowly as comprising only those programs targeted at the poor, few tax expenditures in the United Sates qualify. On the other hand, such a definition excludes programs like Social Security and Medicare that policy makers, academics, and ordinary citizens routinely include when they discuss U.S. social policy or the American welfare state.

A family receiving welfare in Friars Point, Mississippi, 1995. © SHEPARD SHERBELL/CORBIS SABA.

To most people, a welfare state guarantees a minimum standard of living and protects citizens against losses of income beyond their control, especially those caused by retirement, sickness, disability, or unemployment. This welfare state contains a public assistance component and a social insurance component. It serves both the poor and the middle classes. Tax expenditures loom large under this standard definition of the welfare state....

This simple side-by-side comparison is revealing. Tax expenditures with social welfare objectives cost the national government the equivalent of $175 billion in fiscal year 190. This sum was roughly one-third of what the government spent on traditional social programs. Seen from another angle, the U.S. government paid out an estimated three dollars in tax expenditures with social welfare objectives for every ten dollars it collected in individual and corporate income taxes in 1990.

The relative importance of tax expenditures varies by function. The Untied States spends as much or more on social services and on employment and training through the tax code as it does through direct spending. The key provisions are tax expenditures for charitable contributions and child care. The government spends approxi-

mately one dollar through the tax code on health and on income security for every three dollars of direct spending. Very little is spent on tax expenditures for low-income housing.

In absolute dollars, the most important categories of tax expenditures are income security, especially retirement security, and health care. The tax expenditure for corporate retirement pensions ($60 billion) is the third largest social program in the American welfare state after Social Security and Medicare. Tax expenditures for Social Security benefits and Individual Retirement Accounts (IRAs) add another $28 billion to retirement security. All of these programs benefit the same citizens—workers with long and stable histories of wage-earning—who fare best in the visible welfare state. The tax expenditure for corporate health insurance ($36 billion) is almost as large as Medicaid....

The tax expenditures for corporate pensions, health insurance, and other fringe benefits demonstrate that the line separating public and private is not a rigid barrier...Some medium-size and smaller tax expenditures subsidize public programs: Social Security, Medicare, workers' compensation, and public assistance benefits all enjoy favorable tax treatment. These latter subsidies are comparatively modest. Altogether, tax subsidies for corporate welfare programs are three times those for government programs....

Tax expenditures accentuate the importance of the revenue committees (House Ways and Means, Senate Finance), which already have jurisdiction over Social Security, Medicare, and unemployment insurance. What most distinguishes the visible and hidden welfare states are the agencies responsible for administering their respective programs. Most direct spending programs are administered by the Department of Health and Human Services. Others are administered by the Departments of Labor, Housing and Urban Development, and Agriculture. The Treasury Department, on the other hand, is responsible for all tax expenditures, whether they are classified as income support, health, housing, employment and training, or social services. One could argue that the broad range of tax expenditures makes the Treasury, rather than Health and Human Services, the most comprehensive social welfare agency in the United States. Clearly, the addition of some three dozen tax expenditures and yet another social welfare bureaucracy reinforces the prevailing image of the American welfare state as fragmented and disjointed.

Tax expenditures become even more important if we adopt a broader definition of the welfare state. Some scholars, especially those who use Scandinavian welfare states as their point of reference, believe that welfare states do more than provide assistance to the poor and social insurance to the middle classes. In their view, a third function of welfare sates is "ensuring that all citizens without distinction of status or class are offered the best standards available in relation to a certain agreed range of social services." This range of services varies over time and cross-nationally, but it usually includes education and all housing programs. Laws governing minimum wages, consumer protection, and collective bargaining are sometimes included in this definition, but they are omitted here as borderline cases that are hard to express in terms of dollars spent. Some of these scholars stipulate further that social programs must promote income equality, must redistribute income downward; I do not preserve this restriction.

Using this definition, direct spending for social welfare increases from approximately $540 billion to $590 billion. The change in tax expenditures is more dramatic. They increase from roughly $175 billion to over $300 billion. They now exceed one-half of total direct spending for social welfare and one-half of all income tax receipts. Most of this increase is due to the inclusion of middle-class housing programs such as the home mortgage interest tax deduction....Most housing programs are administered through the tax code rather than appropriations; the U.S. government spends twice as much on housing tax expenditures as on traditional housing programs.

Whether one favors a standard or expansive definition of the welfare state, one crucial fact remains: the middle-and-upper-income classes are the main beneficiaries of the hidden welfare state.

SIGNIFICANCE

Much of the ongoing debate over the scope and focus of federal welfare spending hinges on definitions, specifically concerning which government spending is considered welfare. The U.S. government often directly or indirectly subsidizes activities it feels are beneficial, often by reducing federal taxes for those who participate. Tax breaks for home ownership and charitable contributions are examples of such hidden subsidies, though they are rarely defined as welfare because they do not involve direct cash payments.

Military expenditures frequently provide direct or indirect benefits to corporations; defense contractors for example often receive contracts that virtually guarantee them a profit. U.S. military expenditures in the Middle East directly benefit the gasoline and automotive industries, both of which need steady supplies of petroleum in order to remain profitable. Yet these expenditures, which clearly help maintain profits in both industries, are not generally viewed as welfare spending.

The federal government has occasionally bailed out failing companies or even entire industries. With Chrysler Motors on the verge of bankruptcy in 1979, the federal government guaranteed millions of dollars in loans to keep the floundering carmaker afloat. In mid–2006, Delta Airlines became the latest U.S. airline to announce that it was shutting down its corporate pension plan. Despite the shutdown, the company's pilots will still receive their benefits thanks to the federally funded Pension Benefit Guaranty Corporation, which was expected to shoulder around $6 billion in costs as a result. To the extent that such bailouts help a for-profit corporation remain in business, they amount to corporate welfare, though they are rarely described as such.

The United States government spends more than $2 trillion dollars each year. In many cases, the difference between a worthwhile expenditure and blatant government waste remains entirely a matter of perspective.

FURTHER RESOURCES

Books

Deparle, Jason. *American Dream: Three Women, Ten Kids, and a Nation's Drive to End Welfare*. New York: Penguin Group, 2004.

Nader, Ralph. *Cutting Corporate Welfare*. New York: Seven Stories Press, 2000.

Walker, Robert. *Social Security and Welfare*. New York: Open University Press/McGraw Hill, 2005.

Periodicals

"Corporate Welfare." *Mechanical Engineering*. 125 (2003): 8.

Johnston, David. "Legalities of Corporate Tax Incentives before Court." *New York Times*, March 1, 2006: C1–C4.

"No Pig Left Behind." *Nation* 277 (2003): 3.

Web sites

Congressional Budget Office. "An Overview of the Social Security System." <http://www.cbo.gov/> (accessed June 22, 2006).

Corporate Welfare Information Center. "Corporate Welfare Basics." <http://www.corporations.org/welfare/> (accessed June 22, 2006).

CNN/Money. "Delta to Dump Pension Plans." June 16, 2006. <http://money.cnn.com/2006/06/16/news/companies/delta_pensions/> (accessed June 22, 2006).

The Family and Medical Leave Act of 1993

Legislation

By: United States Congress

Date: February 5, 2003

Source: *United States Department of Labor*. "The Family and Medical Leave Act of 1993." <http://www.dol.gov/esa/regs/statutes/whd/fmla.htm> (accessed May 31, 2006).

About the Author: The Congress of the United States was established by Article 1 of the United States Constitution of 1787. It is the legislative arm of the U.S. Federal Government.

INTRODUCTION

American workers today enjoy a wide range of rights and protections. Many of these rights, largely taken for granted, came into existence during the 1960's. For example, prior to 1963, employers could legally pay a woman lower wages for performing the same work as a man, and employers frequently chose to do this. Following the passage of the Equal Pay Act in June of that year, employers could no longer legally discriminate in compensation practices on the basis of gender.

Other legislation during this period and in the following decades banned other forms of discrimination. The Civil Rights Act of 1964 dealt with a variety of issues; Title VII specifically addressed discrimination in employment practices, prohibiting discrimination in hiring or other work-related practices on the basis of race, religion, sex, or national origin. While few employers today would consider openly discriminating against an applicant based on one of these traits, this practice was both common and legal prior to 1964. These and other pieces of legislation passed during the 1960's laid the groundwork for labor laws and the rights enjoyed by employees today.

Building on this foundation, additional legislation in the following decades expanded worker protections in a variety of situations, including old age and pregnancy. For example, the Americans with Disabilities Act (ADA) was enacted in 1990. ADA requires employers to make reasonable accommodations for workers, such as providing a larger computer monitor for a visually impaired employee. It also requires new public construction to include accessibility for individuals in wheelchairs. The law's goal is to expand workplace opportunities for persons with disabilities.

Many of the work-related laws passed since the 1960's dealt with specific groups of individuals, including the elderly, minorities, and the physically disabled. One of the broadest pieces of employment legislation was passed in 1993, and potentially applies to every employee in America. The Family and Medical Leave Act (FMLA) was created to help employees address pressing family issues without endangering their employment.

FMLA allows an employee to take up to twelve weeks of unpaid leave during any twelve month period without losing his job. Employers are required to grant this request and continue providing group health benefits if offered. Following the leave, the employee is entitled to an equivalent position with pay and benefits equal to the job previously held. FMLA allows leave for family-related health issues, including the birth or adoption of a child, a family member's illness, or personal health problems. In cases where an employer offers benefits, such as maternity leave, workers are allowed to take their FMLA leave in addition to the employer provided leave.

Governor Bill Clinton answers questions about President Bush's veto of the Family Medical Leave Act, while on campaign for the presidency on September 22, 1992. © REUTERS/CORBIS.

■ PRIMARY SOURCE

SEC. 2. FINDINGS AND PURPOSES.

(a) FINDINGS.—Congress finds that—

1. the number of single-parent households and two-parent households in which the single parent or both parents work is increasing significantly;

2. it is important for the development of children and the family unit that fathers and mothers be able to participate in early childrearing and the care of family members who have serious health conditions;

3. the lack of employment policies to accommodate working parents can force individuals to choose between job security and parenting;

4. there is inadequate job security for employees who have serious health conditions that prevent them from working for temporary periods;

5. due to the nature of the roles of men and women in our society, the primary responsibility for family caretaking often falls on women, and such responsibility affects the working lives of women more than it affects the working lives of men; and

6. employment standards that apply to one gender only have serious potential for encouraging employers to discriminate against employees and applicants for employment who are of that gender.

(b) PURPOSES.—It is the purpose of this Act—

1. to balance the demands of the workplace with the needs of families, to promote the stability and economic security of families, and to promote national interests in preserving family integrity;

2. to entitle employees to take reasonable leave for medical reasons, for the birth or adoption of a child, and for the care of a child, spouse, or parent who has a serious health condition;

3. to accomplish the purposes described in paragraphs (1) and (2) in a manner that accommodates the legitimate interests of employers;

4. to accomplish the purposes described in paragraphs (1) and (2) in a manner that, consistent with the Equal

Protection Clause of the Fourteenth Amendment, minimizes the potential for employment discrimination on the basis of sex by ensuring generally that leave is available for eligible medical reasons (including maternity-related disability) and for compelling family reasons, on a gender-neutral basis; and

5. to promote the goal of equal employment opportunity for women and men, pursuant to such clause.

TITLE I—GENERAL REQUIREMENTS FOR LEAVE

SEC. 101. DEFINITIONS.

1. COMMERCE.—The terms "commerce" and "industry or activity affecting commerce" mean any activity, business, or industry in commerce or in which a labor dispute would hinder or obstruct commerce or the free flow of commerce, and include "commerce" and any "industry affecting commerce", as defined in paragraphs (1) and (3) of section 501 of the Labor Management Relations Act, 1947 (29 U.S.C. 142 (1) and (3)).

2. ELIGIBLE EMPLOYEE.—

3. (A) IN GENERAL.—The term "eligible employee" means an employee who has been employed

4. (i) for at least 12 months by the employer with respect to whom leave is requested under section 102; and

5. (ii) for at least 1,250 hours of service with such employer during the previous 12-month period.

6. (B) EXCLUSIONS.—The term "eligible employee" does not include

7. (i) any Federal officer or employee covered under subchapter V of chapter 63 of title 5, United States Code (as added by title II of this Act); or

8. (ii) any employee of an employer who is employed at a worksite at which such employer employs less than 50 employees if the total number of employees employed by that employer within 75 miles of that worksite is less than 50.

9. (C) DETERMINATION.—For purposes of determining whether an employee meets the hours of service requirement specified in subparagraph

10. (A)(ii), the legal standards established under section 7 of the Fair Labor Standards Act of 1938 (29 U.S.C. 207) shall apply.

11. EMPLOY; EMPLOYEE; STATE.—The terms "employ", "employee", and "State" have the same meanings given such terms in subsections (c), (e), and (g) of section 3 of the Fair Labor Standards Act of 1938 (29 U.S.C. 203(c), (e), and (g)).

12. EMPLOYER.—

13. (A) IN GENERAL.—The term "employer"

14. (i) means any person engaged in commerce or in any industry or activity affecting commerce who

employs 50 or more employees for each working day during each of 20 or more calendar workweeks in the current or preceding calendar year;

15. (ii) includes—

16. (I) any person who acts, directly or indirectly, in the interest of an employer to any of the employees of such employer; and

17. (II) any successor in interest of an employer; and

18. (iii) includes any "public agency", as defined in section 3(x) of the Fair Labor Standards Act of 1938 (29 U.S.C. 203(x)).

19. (B) PUBLIC AGENCY.—For purposes of subparagraph (A)(iii), a public agency shall be considered to be a person engaged in commerce or in an industry or activity affecting commerce.

20. EMPLOYMENT BENEFITS.—The term "employment benefits" means all benefits provided or made available to employees by an employer, including group life insurance, health insurance, disability insurance, sick leave, annual leave, educational benefits, and pensions, regardless of whether such benefits are provided by a practice or written policy of an employer or through an "employee benefit plan", as defined in section 3(3) of the Employee Retirement Income Security Act of 1974 (29 U.S.C. 1002(3)).

21. HEALTH CARE PROVIDER.—The term "health care provider" means—

22. (A) a doctor of medicine or osteopathy who is authorized to practice medicine or surgery (as appropriate) by the State in which the doctor practices; or

23. (B) any other person determined by the Secretary to be capable of providing health care services.

24. PARENT.—The term "parent" means the biological parent of an employee or an individual who stood in loco parentis to an employee when the employee was a son or daughter.

25. PERSON.—The term "person" has the same meaning given such term in section 3(a) of the Fair Labor Standards Act of 1938 (29 U.S.C. 203(a)).

26. REDUCED LEAVE SCHEDULE.—The term "reduced leave schedule" means a leave schedule that reduces the usual number of hours per workweek, or hours per workday, of an employee.

27. SECRETARY.—The term "Secretary" means the Secretary of Labor.

28. SERIOUS HEALTH CONDITION. The term "serious health condition" means an illness, injury, impairment, or physical or mental condition that involves

29. (A) inpatient care in a hospital, hospice, or residential medical care facility; or

30. (B) continuing treatment by a health care provider.

31. SON OR DAUGHTER.—The term "son or daughter" means a biological, adopted, or foster child, a

stepchild, a legal ward, or a child of a person standing in loco parentis, who is—

32. (A) under 18 years of age; or

33. (B) 18 years of age or older and incapable of self-care because of a mental or physical disability.

34. SPOUSE.—The term "spouse" means a husband or wife, as the case may be.

SEC. 102. LEAVE REQUIREMENT.

(a) IN GENERAL.—

1. ENTITLEMENT TO LEAVE.—Subject to section 103, an eligible employee shall be entitled to a total of 12 workweeks of leave during any 12-month period for one or more of the following:

2. (A) Because of the birth of a son or daughter of the employee and in order to care for such son or daughter.

3. (B) Because of the placement of a son or daughter with the employee for adoption or foster care.

4. (C) In order to care for the spouse, or a son, daughter, or parent, of the employee, if such spouse, son, daughter, or parent has a serious health condition.

5. (D) Because of a serious health condition that makes the employee unable to perform the functions of the position of such employee.

6. EXPIRATION OF ENTITLEMENT.—The entitlement to leave under subparagraphs (A) and (B) of paragraph (1) for a birth or placement of a son or daughter shall expire at the end of the 12-month period beginning on the date of such birth or placement.

(b) LEAVE TAKEN INTERMITTENTLY OR ON A REDUCED LEAVE SCHEDULE.

IN GENERAL.—Leave under subparagraph (A) or (B) of subsection (a)(1) shall not be taken by an employee intermittently or on a reduced leave schedule unless the employee and the employer of the employee agree otherwise. Subject to paragraph (2), subsection (e)(2), and section 103(b)(5), leave under subparagraph (C) or (D) of subsection (a)(1) may be taken intermittently or on a reduced leave schedule when medically necessary. The taking of leave intermittently or on a reduced leave schedule pursuant to this paragraph shall not result in a reduction in the total amount of leave to which the employee is entitled under subsection (a) beyond the amount of leave actually taken.

ALTERNATIVE POSITION.—If an employee requests intermittent leave, or leave on a reduced leave schedule, under subparagraph (C) or (D) of subsection (a)(1), that is foreseeable based on planned medical treatment, the employer may require such employee to transfer temporarily to an available alternative position offered by the employer for which the employee is qualified and that—

(A) has equivalent pay and benefits; and

(B) better accommodates recurring periods of leave than the regular employment position of the employee.

(c) UNPAID LEAVE PERMITTED. —Except as provided in subsection (d), leave granted under subsection (a) may consist of unpaid leave. Where an employee is otherwise exempt under regulations issued by the Secretary pursuant to section 13(a)(1) of the Fair Labor Standards Act of 1938 (29 U.S.C. 213(a)(1)), the compliance of an employer with this title by providing unpaid leave shall not affect the exempt status of the employee under such section.

(d) RELATIONSHIP TO PAID LEAVE.—

1. UNPAID LEAVE.—If an employer provides paid leave for fewer than 12 workweeks, the additional weeks of leave necessary to attain the 12 workweeks of leave required under this title may be provided without compensation.

2. SUBSTITUTION OF PAID LEAVE.—

3. (A) IN GENERAL.—An eligible employee may elect, or an employer may require the employee, to substitute any of the accrued paid vacation leave, personal leave, or family leave of the employee for leave provided under subparagraph (A), (B), or (C) of subsection (a)(1) for any part of the 12-week period of such leave under such subsection.

4. (B) SERIOUS HEALTH CONDITION.—An eligible employee may elect, or an employer may require the employee, to substitute any of the accrued paid vacation leave, personal leave, or medical or sick leave of the employee for leave provided under subparagraph (C) or (D) of subsection (a)(1) for any part of the 12-week period of such leave under such subsection, except that nothing in this title shall require an employer to provide paid sick leave or paid medical leave in any situation in which such employer would not normally provide any such paid leave.

(e) FORESEEABLE LEAVE.—

1. REQUIREMENT OF NOTICE.—In any case in which the necessity for leave under subparagraph (A) or (B) of subsection (a)(1) is foreseeable based on an expected birth or placement, the employee shall provide the employer with not less than 30 days' notice, before the date the leave is to begin, of the employee's intention to take leave under such subparagraph, except that if the date of the birth or placement requires leave to begin in less than 30

days, the employee shall provide such notice as is practicable.

2. DUTIES OF EMPLOYEE.—In any case in which the necessity for leave under subparagraph (C) or (D) of subsection (a)(1) is foreseeable based on planned medical treatment, the employee—

3. (A) shall make a reasonable effort to schedule the treatment so as not to disrupt unduly the operations of the employer, subject to the approval of the health care provider of the employee or the health care provider of the son, daughter, spouse, or parent of the employee, as appropriate; and

4. (B) shall provide the employer with not less than 30 days' notice, before the date the leave is to begin, of the employee's intention to take leave under such subparagraph, except that if the date of the treatment requires leave to begin in less than 30 days, the employee shall provide such notice as is practicable.

(f) SPOUSES EMPLOYED BY THE SAME EMPLOYER.—In any case in which a husband and wife entitled to leave under subsection (a) are employed by the same employer, the aggregate number of workweeks of leave to which both may be entitled may be limited to 12 workweeks during any 12-month period, if such leave is taken—

under subparagraph (A) or (B) of subsection (a)(1); or

to care for a sick parent under subparagraph (C) of such subsection.

SIGNIFICANCE

As two-income families and single parent homes have become more common, family issues have taken an increasingly central role in quality-of-life discussions. Americans are also marrying later and waiting longer to have children, meaning that more mid-career employees face difficult choices about balancing work and home life. The Family and Medical Leave Act is an attempt to recognize the importance of home life and to honor personal needs such as caring for a dying family member. It attempts to provide options to employees facing difficult situations.

Like all federal legislation, FMLA is in a constant state of re-examination and revision. In some cases, employees have alleged noncompliance by their employers and taken them to court. The U.S. Department of Labor reports that the average cost to defend an FMLA lawsuit is more than $75,000, and employees denied leave have been awarded as much as $19 million in damages. Courts have also penalized individual supervisors up to $500,000 for their actions at work. However, some employee suits have been unsuccessful when courts found that they did not give the required thirty days notice prior to taking leave. Disputes have also arisen over what constitutes a serious medical condition and whether a combination of minor conditions might constitute a single serious one under FMLA's provisions.

The future of FMLA appears bright. Court rulings have repeatedly supported worker rights under FMLA, and some organizations lobby for expanded protections under the bill, including extending its coverage to smaller businesses and including more situations under its definitions of a family emergency. A Department of Labor report issued in 2000 found that a large majority of employers supported the FMLA and that it had no impact on workplace productivity. This finding was despite the fact that thirty-five million American workers took leave under the act in its first seven years of existence. In contrast, approximately this same number of employees remain uncovered by the act's provisions.

FURTHER RESOURCES

Books

Bernstein, Anya. *The Moderation Dilemma: Legislative Coalitions and the Politics of Family and Medical Leave*. Pittsburgh, Penn.: University of Pittsburgh Press, 2001.

Decker, Kurt H. *Family and Medical Leave in a Nutshell*. St. Paul, Minn.: West Publishing, 2000.

Family and Medical Leave Act, edited by Robert M. Hale, Michael J. Ossip, and Gail V. Coleman. Washington, D.C.: BNA Books, 2006.

Periodicals

Armour, Stephanie. "Family, Medical Leave Act at Center of Hot Debate." *USA Today* (May 26, 2005): b1.

Gaspers, Karen. "FMLA Use on the Rise: Costs Employers $21 Billion." *Safety & Health* 171 (2005): 14–16.

Make, Jonathan. "Push to Revamp FMLA Is in Limbo." *Workforce Management* 84 (2005): 24.

Web sites

United States Department of Labor. "Compliance Assistance—Family and Medical Leave Act (FMLA)." <http://www.dol.gov/esa/whd/fmla/> (accessed Maty 24, 2006).

The U.S. Equal Employment Opportunity Commission. "Title VII of the Civil Rights Act of 1964." <http://www.eeoc.gov/policy/vii.html> (accessed May 31, 2006).

The Welfarization of Health Care

Clinton Healthcare Reform

Magazine article

By: Richard K. Armey and Newt Gingrich

Date: February 7, 1994

Source: Armey, Richard K. and Newt Gingrich . "The Welfarization of Health Care: Clinton Healthcare Reform." *The National Review*. February 7, 1994.

About the Author: Richard K. Armey is a former member of the United States House of Representatives. He was the Republican House Majority Leader from 1995 to 2003, beginning his tenure within two years after Newt Gingrich retired from that position. He was among the orchestrators of the so-called Republican Revolution that took place in the early 1990s in the United States Congress. He is the author of several books. Newt Gingrich was the Republican Speaker of the House of Representatives during the Presidency of Bill Clinton (term in office, 1993–2001), between 1995 and 1999. He was among the leaders of what has been called the Republican Revolution in the United States Congress, as he came into political power during a time when there was a shift in power away from the Democratic majority of four decades to a new Republican majority. It was a unique time in American political history as well for the fact that the Republican majority occurred during a democratic Presidency. *Time* magazine named Gingrich its "Man of the Year" for 1995 for his Congressional leadership role during that transitional period. He retired from public life in 1998, at the end of a period in which he was at the center of considerable professional and personal controversy. Since his retirement, he has begun a new career as a consultant and political analyst and has continued to write and publish works of both fiction and nonfiction, primarily in historical genres.

INTRODUCTION

One of the central tenets of President William Jefferson (Bill) Clinton's first administration was a commitment to implement major health care reform initiatives throughout the United States. Among the goals was creation of a system that would provide universal health care coverage. Clinton announced the health policy reforms, called the Health Security Plan, in a public speech delivered from the floor of the United States House of Representatives on the evening of September 23, 1993. The speech, and the plan outlined by the President, met with public approval, based on results of overnight public opinion polls reported to the media by the White House.

Clinton's Health Care Reform Policy was one among several competing health care reform bills and proposals, beginning with the Affordable Health Care Now Act (HR-3-80), sponsored by Senators Bob Michel and Trent Lott, and followed in short order by the Chafee Bill, the Gramm Bill, the Moynihan Bill, the Mitchell Bill, the McDermott Single-Payer Bill, the Cooper Managed Competition Bill, the Grandy Bill, and the Stearns-Nickles Plan. Ultimately, all were defeated, despite concentrated efforts at consensus-building.

It has been said by political pundits that the Clinton Health Care Reform plan was among the most large-scale strategic miscalculations by an American President in recent American history.

Prior to the introduction of the Clinton plan, viewed by many Democrats as a middle of the road approach when viewed in concert with the numerous health care reform propositions being proposed at the time, many politicians, as well as several large corporate interest groups—most notably the Health Insurance Association of America (HIAA) and the American Medical Association (AMA)—had made public statements endorsing universal health care coverage and sweeping health care reforms. Clinton and his cadre of advisors assumed, based upon available data, that the time was right for putting forth a plan that called for substantial health care reform embedded within a framework of consumer choice and within-market competition. Clinton initially planned to construct and launch the health care reform proposal early in his first year in office. Early economy budget battles forced a lengthy delay in the presentation of the plan. Although the plan was formally announced during the September speech, and the bill introduced shortly thereafter, it was assigned a low priority in the face of more pressing national and international concerns. By early 1994, momentum had begun to build among those who were in opposition of the plan, and the AMA had (partially) withdrawn its endorsement of some of the health care reforms proposed by the Administration.

▍PRIMARY SOURCE

Americans have three major concerns about health care: 1) gaining portability, or the ability to retain one's insurance upon changing jobs, 2) controlling the rising costs

A representation of an Anti-Newt Gingrich faction of health reform protesters holding signs and demonstrating against Medicaid and Medicare cuts in 1995. © NAJLAH FEANNY/CORBIS SABA.

that have consistently outstripped inflation over the past decade, and 3) expanding access to the much-discussed 37 million uninsured.

Unfortunately, the Clinton Administration got side-tracked while crafting the health-care package. Rather than using what's right with American health care to fix what's wrong with American health care (to paraphrase President Clinton's inaugural address), the Clinton team opted for a grand experiment that threatens the quality of care for every American.

President Clinton's Health Security Act casts the entangling net of the welfare state ever wider, hauling America's great middle class into dependency. All Americans will have to rely on the government for health care, and the government will tell them what they can get, where they can get it, whom they can get it from, and how much they can spend for it. If you like the way the Federal Government runs public housing and the state government runs the Department of Motor Vehicles, you'll love health care under the Clinton Plan.

The Health Security Act would create 105 new bureaucracies, expand 47 others, make major changes in the tax laws, and promulgate more than 100 new federal regulations. The bills 1,364 pages are teeming with new quasi-governmental agencies, all overseen by a seven-member National Health board whose decisions would not be subject to judicial review. (It is vintage Bill Clinton that at the same time he is proposing the biggest new entitlement program in half a century, he is advocating the creation of a commission to recommend how to reduce federal entitlement spending.)

This plan is being sold with the slogan, "health care that's always there." It would more aptly be called "Government that's always there." The Clinton plan would include an individual health-security ID card that feeds personal medical information into centralized government data tanks; allotments for the number of medical students who may specialize in any given field; regional alliances carved with the precision of gerrymandered congressional districts; and a global budget capping how much can be spent on health care per year.

Two quotes reveal the very essence of the Clinton plan. The first came on September 22, the evening President Clinton unveiled his reform to a joint session of Congress. CBS News anchor Dan Rather lobbed a few soft-balls the Lady's way in an exclusive interview. In explaining why the President's government-run approach is better than market-based Republican approaches, Mrs. Clinton noted, "if individuals were required on their own, we wouldn't know quite how to keep track of all of them...The real bottom line is we want everybody in the system, we want everybody insured, and we want to spread that burden fairly so that every person has responsibility for their health care."

"The system." Without the Clinton plan there is no "system," just millions of people, many of whom never get a law degree (let alone a Rhodes Scholarship), making decisions as to what is best for themselves and their families. This simply cannot go on.

The second quote comes from the original draft plan sent to Capitol Hill: "A single benefit package that covers every eligible American eliminates confusion over coverage." That's right—government must decide for the befuddled masses. What ultimately will bring about the demise of the Clinton health-care plan is the utter arrogance that permeates the thing.

A close reading of the bill suggests it has as much to do with enacting unpopular liberal social policies through the back door as it does with providing health care to all Americans. The New Testament sets forth how people should live in about 180,000 words. The health-care bill does it in 260,000. It is a breathtaking display of social engineering, the scope of which has not been seen since the Great Society on the Sixties.

The Clinton plan is a Trojan horse for federally funded abortion, which was rejected by this congress as recently as June. At the same time, the bill denies funds for extended treatment of congenital conditions such as cystic fibrosis, cerebral palsy, and spina bifida.

Robert Reich told the House Energy and Commerce Committee (October 28, 1993) that the new federal entitlement for early retirees would induce early retirement, "opening up all kinds of job opportunities for younger people."

Rural and suburban areas will be lumped into regional alliances with inner cities so that billions of dollars can be siphoned into urban hospitals for treatment of drug addiction, gunshot wounds, and AIDS.

Productive, innovative, entrepreneurial small businesses will subsidize aging dinosaurs and their union work forces, in essence buying out bad labor-management contracts to the tune of about $14 billion per year, according to the Heritage Foundation.

A Graduate Medical Education Board will allocate the number of students per year who can specialize in cardiology, orthopedic surgery, gynecology, etc., basing its

decisions on the "national need for new physicians in specific specialties." This, along with "physician retraining programs," is designed to increase the percentage of primary-care physicians from the current level of 40 percent to the Administration's preferred 55 percent, thus overruling patient demand.

Such grandiose social schemes cost money, of course, and the Clinton plan is good old-fashioned income redistribution ("We want to spread that burden fairly"). At least 40 percent will pay more, according to HHS Secretary Donna Shalala, which means it's probably more like 60 percent.

As is often the case with government expansion, the Clinton plan is being sold in the name of "security." The Administration tested focus groups, and wrapped its plan in the word that garnered the warmest response. The promise of security is false, however.

The employer mandate on which the plan's financing rests will result in the loss of hundreds and thousands of jobs, mostly in industries with a high percentage of low-wage and part-time employment (which disproportionately hire women and minorities). It's hard to feel secure without a job, but the President's rhetoric ignores this basic fact of life.

Global budgets and other limits on health-care spending, including a government mandate that real per-capita health-care spending be held constant after 1998, will result in diminished returns on research and development. It's hard to feel secure when a possible cure for your daughter's life-threatening ailment stays on the drawing board because of limited funds.

As Harry and Louise (the couple at the kitchen table in the television ad that so infuriates the First Lady) ask: "What happens when our plan runs out of money?" Judging from the experience of two programs that rely on federally prescribed funding levels—the Indian Health Service and the Veterans Administration health-care system—patients will wait in line for services. According to one doctor who worked in VA hospitals, Myra Kleinpeter, when the money Congress had appropriated ran short, elective surgery, including open-heart surgery, had to be delayed.

Most Americans feel secure with their current doctors, but the Clinton plan would limit a family's ability to retain them. When the fee-for-service plans fill up, patients will be allocated to plans via "random selection." Can there be security in "random selection?"

And anyone who tries to circumvent this bureaucratic nightmare—say, by buying a doctor a case of wine for Christmas in exchange for a little fee-for service—can be barred by the Secretary of HHS from "participation in any applicable health plan." Anyone convicted of "health-care-related crimes or patient abuse" would be subject to a "minimum period of exclusion...not less than five years" (p. 940 of the Health Security Act). Are you feeling more secure yet?

The Administration's early polling data also turned up public concern about "choice," and so every Clinton (Hillary or Bill) speech on health care asserts that their plan assures choice.

One of us asked the First Lady at a hearing, "Let's imagine a typical American family. The husband has an internist he likes. The wife has her gynecologist, with whom she is confident and comfortable. Their children have a pediatrician they like. Is there any chance under your plan that this family would have to go to doctors other than the doctors they've known and relied on for years?"

The First lady conceded that "I can't say that in every instance, in every family that it would not happen" that a family would have to go to other doctors. The Clinton plan is the "which doctor" bill, because after it passes you will be forced to choose which doctors to keep and which ones to drop.

The Federal Government imposed price controls on gasoline in the 1970s, and the result was rationing. Drivers waited in lines for hours on "odd/even" days. Health care is a subject to the same laws of supply and demand.

In the same way Jimmy Carter misdiagnosed the "energy crisis" of the 1970s, Bill Clinton has misdiagnosed the "health-care crisis" of the 1990s. As Daniel Casse of the Project for the Republican Future noted in a recent *Wall Street Journal* article, both Carter and Clinton responded with bureaucratic solutions—Carter creating the Department of Energy, Clinton the National Health Board and its teeming offspring—and fit black hats on any who opposed their plans, calling them "naysayers," "profiteers," and "friends of the status quo."

History may not always repeat itself, but Democrats never seem to change their focus from finding new reasons and innovative ways to bring big government further into the lives of the American people. Whether it be the energy "crisis," the environmental "crisis," the homelessness "crisis," the day-care "crisis," or now, the healthcare "crisis," their game plan is fairly constant. By studying history, Republicans can learn from previous mistakes and previous successes.

After defeating President Carter's energy policy, Republicans enacted market-oriented reforms that ended the gasoline lines. Deregulation led, as it inevitably does, to lower prices. By defeating the Clinton plan, Republicans can refocus health-care policy on portability, cost, control, and increased access, and we can do it with market-oriented reform.

President Clinton said in November on *Meet the Press*, "We're the only people who have a plan." Of course, that's not the truth. Quite the contrary. There's the Chafee bill, the Gramm bill, the McDermott single-payer bill, the Cooper managed-competition bill, the Stearns-Nickles plan, and the bill with the largest number of co-sponsors of all, the Affordable Health Care New Act, HR-3060 introduced (more than a month before the Clinton plan was brought to the Hill) by House Republican Leader Bob Michel (R. III) and Senate Republican Conference Secretary Trout Lott (R., Miss.).

The Michel-Lott bill provides a common-sense approach to the three problems that most concern Americans about their health care, without losing sight of the fact that 85 percent of the people have health insurance and 85 percent of them are happy with their own health care.

The GOP bill, shepherded through the House Republican Conference by former high-school wrestling coach Dennis Hastert (R., Ill.) and crafted largely by Tom Bliley (R., Va.), Nancy Johnson (R., Conn.), and Marge Reukema (R., N.J.), begins by looking at the nature of the uninsured.

The figure of 37 million uninsured is the Democrats' rhetorical leverage. But the population of uninsured is constantly in flux; according to a 1990 Urban Institute study more than half of those 37 million will be insured in less than four months, and nearly three-fourths will be insured in less than a year. Other estimates have put the number of the "chronically and involuntarily" uninsured at between 10 and 15 million people, or about 6 percent of the population.

Instead of compelling all Americans to change health-care practices that the vast majority find satisfactory for the benefit of 6 percent of the population, the Michel-Lott bill focuses on expanding access through direct subsidy and market reforms.

It would guarantee continue access to coverage for employees changing jobs. It would establish Medical Savings Accounts so families could serve thousands of dollars per year tax-free, and roll the account over year after year to build. As long as the funds were used for health care, they would remain tax free; otherwise withdrawals would be treated as taxable income and subject to a 10 percent penalty. The bill also changes the tax code to treat long-term-care insurance the same as other health-insurance plans, thus making it easier for older Americans to obtain coverage.

The Michel-Lott bill addresses the underlying causes of rising costs in health care, as opposed to artificially imposing government price controls. Physicians pay nearly $6 billion annually in liability premiums, according to the AMA, and defensive medicine costs the nation between $7 and $12 billion per year. Our Republican bill deals with both these problems by limiting frivolous lawsuits with serious malpractice reforms.

Our bill would cost about $20 billion over five years, most of it to pay for subsidies to families below the poverty line who still do not qualify for Medicaid, for more community health centers targeted for poor women and children, for emergency services for rural communities, and for 100 percent health-insurance deductibility for the self-employed (up from 25 percent). All of it is on the books and paid for, while Clinton's funding is dubious at best, and he seeks to keep the employer/employee payroll taxes—a/k/a the "premiums"—off budget.

According to a new analysis by Morgan Reynolds and Lawrence Hunter, Republican staff economists at the Joint Economic Committee, the shortfall between promised benefits and anticipated revenue in the Clinton plan will be about $425 billion in the year 2000, and will accumulate to more than $1 trillion in the first eight years of implementation.

If the Clinton plan becomes law, therefore, Congress will face some unsavory policy options in the year 2000, specifically: 1) increasing the annual budget deficit by about $425 billion, or 2) raising taxes by the same amount (about $3,500 per household), or 3) diminishing health care by $425 billion (probably through price controls that would result in rationing, as has been the case in other countries), or 4) some combination of the three.

Rarely have Americans been presented with a more stark contrast in policy approaches. The Clinton path leads to a complete government takeover of 14 percent of the U.S. economy. It's a top-down, welfare-state approach that diminishes personal freedom, choice, and quality and would convert a vibrant, innovative industry into a drab, lethargic bureaucracy.

The Republican approach uses what's right with America to fix what's wrong with America, vesting individuals with greater discretion and cutting back on the regulation and litigation that are causing most of the problems Americans face in health care today.

SIGNIFICANCE

At various times during the final decades of the twentieth century, U.S. law and policy makers suggested the creation of a universal health care system to address the issue of adequate and appropriate health care coverage for all of the country's inhabitants. Each time this occurred, opposing factions squashed the efforts. In the early 1990s, Presidential candidate Bill Clinton launched a substantial health care reform effort. The medical superstructure, including the AMA and the HIAA, voiced their support of health care reforms, particularly as the burden of absorbing the cost of health care provision to the uninsured

would be eliminated by a universal coverage system. At the same time, the American public indicated statistically significant endorsement of sweeping health care reforms, as well as support for universal health care coverage. In 1993, when Clinton first announced his plan, momentum was still strong. Had it gone to vote at that time, it might have had a reasonable chance at passage. However, it was several months before any action could be taken.

By early 1994, the economy of the country was improving and unemployment was down, resulting in a larger proportion of the population having health care coverage. Health care costs had decreased as inflation was lessened by the improving economy, so Americans were far less receptive to considering detailed plans centered around the concept of physician assignment and cost controls. Republican politicians strongly opposed the health care reform policies endorsed by the Clinton administration, as they considered them broadening of bureaucracy and insinuating the power of the government into the everyday lives of the American population. Many others criticized the plan as being too cumbersome and difficult to understand.

The proposal was lengthy, spanning almost 1500 pages. One of the central requirements of the plan was that employers would be mandated to provide health care coverage to all employees. The coverage was to be managed and provided by a limited number of tightly monitored health maintenance organizations (HMOs). Virtually the entire health insurance industry opposed the plan. Many of those factions alleged that the plan, in addition to being excessively bureaucratic and potentially intrusive into people's private lives, would sharply restrict personal choice in health care decisions and would likely prevent the general public, the large majority of whom had personal health care practitioners with whom they were satisfied, from being able to exercise free choice among health care providers.

The opponents of the plan launched a successful media campaign featuring a middle class-appearing couple referred to as "Harry and Louise," who lamented over their inability to navigate what they described as a bureaucratic and administrative boondoggle in order to obtain basic health care provision. One of the many apparent strengths of the campaign was the depiction of a middle class that was unable to successfully manage their health care, despite their best efforts—as this subtly suggested that the Clinton administration was denigrating the middle class—which forms the basis of the working, voting, and privately paying (in contrast to those who need to make use of local, state, and federally funded health care options) health-care utilizing public. There was much fragmentation in Congress, as many put forth competing plans, rather than rallying around one or two and negotiating a viable compromise bill. Within just over a year of the plan's initial announcement by Clinton, on September 26, 1994, Senate Majority Leader George Mitchell publicly announced that the bill was defeated and would no longer be considered during that particular Congressional session.

FURTHER RESOURCES

Books

Bowman, Karlyn H. *The 1993–1994 Debate on Health Care reform: Did the Polls Mislead the Policy Makers?*. Washington, D,C,: American Enterprise Institute, 1994.

Chapman, Audrey R., ed. *Health Care Reform: A Human Rights Approach*. Washington, D,C,: Georgetown University Press, 1994.

Flood, Colleen M. *International Health Care Reform: A Legal, Economic and Political Analysis*. London, United Kingdom: Routledge, 2000.

Rushefsky, Mark and Kant Patel. *Politics, Power and Policy-Making: The Case of Welfare Reform in the 1990s*. Armonk, New York: M.E. Sharpe, 1998.

Shelton, Michael W. *Talk of Power, Power of Talk: The 1994 Health Care Debate and Beyond*. Westport, Connecticut: Praeger, 2000.

Periodicals

"The Beginning of Health Care Reform: The Clinton Plan." *The New England Journal of Medicine*. 329(21) (November 18, 1993): 1569–1570.

Web sites

The Health Security Act of 1993. "Health Care That's Always There - Executive Summary." <http://www.ibiblio.org/nhs/executive/X-Summary-toc.html> (accessed May 20, 2006).

Momma Welfare Roll

Poem

By: Maya Angelou

Date: 1994

Source: Angelou, Maya. "Momma Welfare Roll." In *The Complete Collected Poems of Maya Angelou*. New York: Random House, 1994.

Maya Angelou. © MITCHELL GERBER/CORBIS. REPRODUCED BY PERMISSION.

About the Author: Maya Angelou (1928–), perhaps best known as an African-American poet, and the first poet laureate in three decades—also the first female and African-American poet laureate in the nation's history—is also a playwright, actress, author, singer, dancer, political and social activist, teacher, and scholar. She is a prolific writer, and has published nearly three dozen volumes, among which are numerous books of poetry and a six-volume autobiography, as well as two children's books. Among her best known works are *I Know Why the Caged Bird Sings*, *Wouldn't Take Nothing for My Journey Now*, and *All God's Children Need Traveling Shoes*. She also wrote a poem entitled *On the Pulse of Morning*, commissioned by former President Bill Clinton, which was read by her at his 1993 inauguration.

INTRODUCTION

The initial welfare program created in the United States of America was part of then-President Roosevelt's "New Deal" programs, and was implemented in 1935. It was originally entitled "Aid to Dependent

Children" (ADC), and it was part of the Social Security Act. ADC was administrated through the United States Department of Health and Human Services.

In 1960, the program's name was changed to "Aid to Families with Dependent Children," or AFDC. Throughout the course of the program's existence—it was ended by the passage of the "Personal Responsibility and Work Opportunity Act" developed by the Clinton Administration—it was intended to serve as a fail-safe for families in crisis or transition. The program was jointly funded by state and federal government but was administered programmatically by each individual state under the auspices of federal guidelines and program requirements. Each state, based on its unique population mix and demographic characteristics, was responsible for developing, creating, implementing, and administering specific programs based on state and local needs assessments. In addition to developing their own programs, the states each had to set up their own benefit packages, eligibility requirements, and financial need standards. The states generally used an eligibility and benefit determination formula based on the available resources and income of the recipient, as well as the number and type of dependents (ages, disabilities, special medical or behavioral health needs, etc.), and measured those variables against the state's own need standards in order to make determinations.

AFDC required that the household contain at least one dependent child below the age of eighteen years or who has turned eighteen and is still in the process of completing a secondary school education. That dependent child had to be experiencing loss or deprivation of parental care and support as the result of parental absence (death, incarceration, other long-term absence from the home), significant disability, or lack of employment of the head of the household. The dependent child did not need to be living with a parent, but could be in the home of someone acting as a parent and head of household such as a close relative, adult sibling, foster parent, legal guardian, or someone similar.

■ PRIMARY SOURCE

MOMMA WELFARE ROLL

Her arms semaphore fat triangles,

Pudgy hands bunched on layered hips

Where bones idle under years of fatback

And lima beans.

Her jowls shiver in accusation

Of crimes clichéd by

Repetition. Her children, strangers

To childhood's toys, play

Best the games of darkened doorways,

Rooftop tag, and know the slick feel of

Other people's property.

Too fat to whore,

Too mad to work,

Searches her dreams for the

Lucky sign and walks bare-handed

Into a den of bureaucrats for

Her portion.

'they don't give me welfare.

I take it.'

SIGNIFICANCE

The AFDC benefit application was in the name of the dependent child and the eligible parent or legal guardian (to include foster or adoptive parents), as well as any applicable siblings who lived within the household. In essence, one dependent child could generate AFDC benefits for an entire large household. A standardized formula was used for the calculation of each state's need standard, which varied by the size and make-up of the household. The benefit amount was determined based on a comparison against the need standard, and took into consideration minimal assets, income from employment minus work-related expenses, living expenses, and other specific items. Families were paid a monthly stipend and could be eligible for other financial assistance, such as food stamps and government-funded medical care. In the early stages of program development, thee were no specific work requirements.

In 1988, new legislation created the Job Opportunities and Basic Skills Training (JOBS) program, along with new state-overseen welfare-to-work programs. Every state was required to have JOBS programs, providing educational and job-training opportunities, on-the-job training, and work-study experiences. The goal of all of these experiences, academic programs, and work opportunities was to provide a framework for future-oriented employment opportunities—

meaning that they were geared toward gainful employment with potential advancement opportunities aimed at instilling self-sufficiency.

Published research and census data indicate that people who sought government financial assistance in the form of AFDC were typically young and female, were often the teenaged parents of one or more very young children, and were generally poorly educated or undereducated. As a group, their prospects for gainful employment were minimal. Even if they were to obtain jobs, it was likely that they would not earn sufficient income so as to be able to afford childcare, pay for health and medical expenses, and purchase healthy and nourishing food for the family. By providing an avenue to personal empowerment via education and job training, AFDC recipients were offered a realistic opportunity for improving the quality of their lives and attaining the skills necessary for moving out of poverty and into self-sufficiency. JOBS participation was mandatory for all persons who were not exempted for specific conditions, such as parenting an infant below the age of twelve months, chronic and debilitating illness, or disability of such a nature and severity as to render education or job training untenable. Although participation in the JOBS program was mandatory, there were no time limits placed on completion of education or training. As a result, those who engaged in JOBS and were motivated to complete their educational or job training were able to leave the system when they felt fully prepared to do so, rather than at an arbitrary cut-off point.

There were no time limits for AFDC participation; if the stated applicant was an infant, it would ostensibly be possible for the entire household to receive benefits until that child graduated from high school. If there were succeeding younger children, it would be possible to continue until the youngest child turned eighteen. Although there were many successes in which families were able to move beyond poverty into genuine and permanent self-sufficiency as a result of supported opportunities, there were also a large number of families that never left the program. By the late 1980s and early 1990s, it became apparent that the American welfare system, as it was also called, had become an enormous financial burden on the nation's economy. The Personal Responsibility and Work Opportunity Reconciliation Act (PRWORA) ended the AFDC program and completely reorganized the federal cash assistance (welfare) programs throughout the country. A new program, called Temporary Assistance for Needy Families (TANF) was created in its stead. TANF is a strictly time-limited program that includes a lifetime benefit limit of five years or sixty months, with a two-year maximum per eligible benefit period. The rules and requirements for the TANF program are far more stringent than those for AFDC and are enforcing rapid movement from government cash assistance programs. However, the available data have not supported the notion that the new program is more effective than AFDC at moving people out of poverty and into financial self-sufficiency.

FURTHER RESOURCES

Books

Burke, V. *Welfare Reform: TANF Trends and Data*. Washington, D.C.: Congressional Research Service, 2000.

Loprest, P. *How are Families that Left Welfare Doing? A Comparison of Early and Recent Welfare Leavers*. Washington, D.C.: Urban Institute, 2001.

Rodgers, Harrell R., Jr. *American Poverty in a New Era of Reform*. Armonk, N.Y.: M.E. Sharpe, 2000.

Stein, Theodore J. *Social Policy and Policy Making by the Branches of Government and the Public-At-Large*. New York: Columbia University Press, 2001.

The Transition from Welfare to Work: Processes, Challenges, and Outcomes, edited by Sharon Telleen and Judith V. Sayad. New York: The Hayworth Press, 2002.

United States General Accounting Office. *Welfare reform: States Provide TANF-funded Work Support Services to Many Low-income Families Who do Not Receive Cash Assistance*. Washington, D.C.: United States General Accounting Office, 2002.

Welfare Reform, 1996–2000: Is There A Safety Net?, edited by John E. Hansan and Robert Morris. Westport, Connecticut: Auburn House, 1999.

Periodicals

Burn, Timothy. "Welfare-to-Work Forum Touts Successes, Hurdles." *The Washington Times* November 19, 1998: 7.

Cancian, M. and D. R. Meyer. "Work after Welfare: Women's Work Effort, Occupation, and Economic Well-being." *Social Work Research* 24 (2000): 69–96.

Wetzstein, Cheryl. "Welfare-to-Work Gains Strong, Two Studies Find." *The Washington Times* (August 3, 2000): 3.

Web sites

Academy of Achievement. "Biography: Maya Angelou." August 29, 2005. <http://www.achievement.org/autodoc/page/ang0bio-1> (accessed June 11, 2006).

Administration for Children and Families. "ACF Healthy Marriage Mission." <http://www.acf.hhs.gov/healthymarriage/about/mission.html> (accessed June 11, 2006).

Personal Responsibility and Work Opportunity Reconciliation Act of 1996

An HHS Fact Sheet

Pamphlet

By: United States Department of Health and Human Services, Administration for Children and Families

Date: August 22, 1996

Source: *United States Department of Health and Human Services, Administration for Children and Families.* "The Personal Responsibility and Work Opportunity Reconciliation Act of 1996: An HHS Fact Sheet." August 22, 1996. <http://www.acf.dhhs.gov/programs/ofa/prwora96.htm> (accessed June 18, 2006).

About the Author: The Administration for Children and Families is a section of the United States Department of Health and Human Services. Its overall mission is to oversee the safety and welfare of children and their families. Through a variety of federal programs, it aids in assuring that family groups are able to achieve economic independence. It is also engaged in facilitating the growth and empowerment of healthy and productive communities.

INTRODUCTION

President Bill Clinton signed the Personal Responsibility and Work Opportunity Reconciliation Act, also called the PRWORA, or P.L. 104–193, on August 22, 1996. It was designed as a sweeping reform of current welfare policies, with the goal of creating a social service and financial assistance program that was time-limited and required that participants engage in work-related activities, to include education, training, or actual employment. As is typical of federal programs, it was administered on a state and local level, and the individual states were provided incentives for successfully moving welfare recipients off of the rolls

A participant in the New York Work Experience Program (WEP) carries a broom on his shoulder while helping to clean the streets. © NAJLAH FEANNY/CORBIS SABA

and into successful employment. It also required that the states create systems for maintenance of due diligence regarding decreasing the rolls and managing employment and training opportunities, ascertaining that child-support payment systems were overseen and enforced in order to avoid undue hardship for single-parent (typically single-mother) families. The bill also added some additional support mechanisms for single parents and for mothers returning to the workforce: funding assistance of various types for affordable, quality childcare during the workday, and guaranteed federally funded medical coverage (an enormous expense, particularly for low wage earners or part-time employees).

The PRWORA was considered by many to be controversial because of the time-limited nature of the benefits, as well as the requirement that recipients either work or engage in the transition to a gainful employment process. The bill, like its unsuccessful predecessors (unsuccessfully legislated, but successfully defeated), was strongly opposed by civil rights, women's rights, community activist, and religious groups, as well as other human rights advocacy groups. The core of this opposition believed that the changes to the previous program, called Aid to Families with Dependent Children, or AFDC, were so stringent as to minimize positive outcomes for those most in need of the economic and social supports, as well as the life transition safety net, provided by the welfare system as it was then designed.

Among the incentives for the program offered by the Clinton administration were the promise of up to one million newly created jobs by the start of the twenty-first century, financial incentives and tax credits for companies that actively engaged in the process of hiring former welfare recipients, and a program for using monies saved by decreased social-service programming to fund new job opportunities.

■ PRIMARY SOURCE

THE PERSONAL RESPONSIBILITY AND WORK OPPORTUNITY RECONCILIATION ACT OF 1996

MAKING WELFARE A TRANSITION TO WORK

An HHS Fact Sheet

On August 22, President Clinton signed into law "The Personal Responsibility and Work Opportunity Reconciliation Act of 1996," a comprehensive bipartisan welfare reform plan that will dramatically change the nation's welfare system into one that requires work in exchange for time-limited assistance. The bill contains strong work

requirements, a performance bonus to reward states for moving welfare recipients into jobs, state maintenance of effort requirements, comprehensive child support enforcement, and supports for families moving from welfare to work—including increased funding for child care and guaranteed medical coverage.

Highlights of "The Personal Responsibility and Work Opportunity Reconciliation Act of 1996" follow.

Work requirements. Under the new law, recipients must work after two years on assistance, with few exceptions. Twenty-five percent of all families in each state must be engaged in work activities or have left the rolls in fiscal year (FY) 1997, rising to 50 percent in FY 2002. Single parents must participate for at least 20 hours per week the first year, increasing to at least 30 hours per week by FY 2000. Two-parent families must work 35 hours per week by July 1, 1997.

Supports for families transitioning into jobs. The new welfare law provides $14 billion in child care funding—an increase of $3.5 billion over current law—to help more mothers move into jobs. The new law also guarantees that women on welfare continue to receive health coverage for their families, including at least one year of transitional Medicaid when they leave welfare for work.

Work Activities. To count toward state work requirements, recipients will be required to participate in unsubsidized or subsidized employment, on-the-job training, work experience, community service, 12 months of vocational training, or provide child care services to individuals who are participating in community service. Up to 6 weeks of job search (no more than 4 consecutive weeks) would count toward the work requirement. However, no more than 20 percent of each state's caseload may count toward the work requirement solely by participating in vocational training or by being a teen parent in secondary school. Single parents with a child under 6 who cannot find child care cannot be penalized for failure to meet the work requirements. States can exempt from the work requirement single parents with children under age one and disregard these individuals in the calculation of participation rates for up to 12 months.

A five-year time limit. Families who have received assistance for five cumulative years (or less at state option) will be ineligible for cash aid under the new welfare law. States will be permitted to exempt up to 20 percent of their caseload from the time limit, and states will have the option to provide non-cash assistance and vouchers to families that reach the time limit using Social Services Block Grant or state funds.

Personal employability plans. Under the new plan, states are required to make an initial assessment of recipients' skills. States can also develop personal responsibility plans for recipients identifying the education, training, and job placement services needed to move into the workforce.

Job subsidies. The law also allows states to create jobs by taking money now used for welfare checks and using it to create community service jobs or to provide income subsidies or hiring incentives for potential employers.

PROMOTING RESPONSIBILITY

Comprehensive Child Support Enforcement

The new law includes the child support enforcement measures President Clinton proposed in 1994—the most sweeping crackdown on non-paying parents in history. These measures could increase child support collections by $24 billion and reduce federal welfare costs by $4 billion over 10 years. Under the new law, each state must operate a child support enforcement program meeting federal requirements in order to be eligible for Temporary Assistance to Needy Families (TANF) block grants. Provisions include:

Uniform interstate child support laws. The new law provides for uniform rules, procedures, and forms for interstate cases.

Computerized state-wide collections. The new law requires states to establish central registries of child support orders and centralized collection and disbursement units. It also requires expedited state procedures for child support enforcement.

Tough new penalties. Under the new law, states can implement tough child support enforcement techniques. The new law will expand wage garnishment, allow states to seize assets, allows states to require community service in some cases, and enable states to revoke drivers and professional licenses for parents who owe delinquent child support.

"Families First." Under a new "Family First" policy, families no longer receiving assistance will have priority in the distribution of child support arrears. This new policy will bring families who have left welfare for work about $1 billion in support over the first six years.

Access and visitation programs. In an effort to increase noncustodial parents' involvement in their children's lives, the new law includes grants to help states establish programs that support and facilitate noncustodial parents' visitation with and access to their children.

Teen Parent Provisions

Live at home and stay in school requirements. Under the new law, unmarried minor parents will be required to live with a responsible adult or in an adult-supervised setting and participate in educational and training activities in order to receive assistance. States will be responsible for locating or assisting in locating adult-supervised settings for teens.

Teen Pregnancy Prevention. Starting in FY 1998, $50 million a year in mandatory funds would be added to the appropriations of the Maternal and Child Health (MCH) Block Grant for abstinence education. In addition, the Secretary of HHS will establish and implement a strategy to (1) prevent non-marital teen births, and (2) assure that at least 25 percent of communities have teen pregnancy prevention programs. No later than January 1, 1997, the Attorney General will establish a program that studies the linkage between statutory rape and teen pregnancy, and that educates law enforcement officials on the prevention and prosecution of statutory rape.

NECESSARY IMPROVEMENTS

Food Stamps. According to President Clinton, the new law cuts deeper than it should in Food Stamps, mostly for working families who have high shelter costs.

Legal Immigrants. The law includes provisions that would deny most forms of public assistance to most legal immigrants for five years or until they attain citizenship. The President has said that legal immigrants who fall on hard times through no fault of their own and need help should get it, although their sponsors should take additional responsibility for them.

BUILDING ON THE PRESIDENT'S WORK TO END WELFARE AS WE KNOW IT

Even before Congress passed welfare reform legislation acceptable to President Clinton, states were acting to try new approaches. With encouragement, support, and cooperation from the Clinton Administration, 43 states have moved forward with 78 welfare reform experiments. The Clinton Administration has also required teen mothers to stay in school, required federal employees to pay their child support, and cracked down on people who owe child support and cross state lines. As a result of these efforts and President Clinton's efforts to strengthen the economy, child support collections have increased by 40 percent to $11 billion in FY 1995, and there are 1.6 million fewer people on welfare today than when President Clinton took office. "The Personal Responsibility and Work Opportunity Reconciliation Act of 1996" will build on these efforts by allowing states flexibility to reform their welfare systems and to build on demonstrations initiated under the Clinton Administration.

SIGNIFICANCE

One of the cornerstones of the PRWORA is the movement of welfare funding from the federal government to each of the states by means of federal block funding. Because the states had control of the funding, they were then free to structure the programs in the ways that were most efficacious for their demographics and socioeconomics.

One of the central tenets of the welfare reform program was a requirement that the head of every family in the system be gainfully employed within two years. There was also a two-year cap on individual benefits for any particular time period, as well as a five-year lifetime maximum for receipt of welfare assistance. Many states structured their protocols so as to require that all eligible heads of households must be engaged in the employment process within sixty days of commencing benefits, or they would be assigned to perform some type of employment-related community service. However, this was entirely optional and not a mandatory part of the benefit requirements. The individual states were given caps on their maximum welfare benefit funding; generally expenditures had to be kept at not more than seventy-five percent of that spent in 1994 (at the time the bill was legislated in 1996). States that failed to remain within their allotted budgets or meet their employment quotas would be penalized by having their block grant funding cut by five percent in the first year—with the cuts steadily increasing during each year of noncompliance, up to a maximum of twenty-one percent during the ninth year after the legislation was enacted. In contrast, states that met their employment and welfare roll-off rates were eligible to receive financial incentives.

It was anticipated that the welfare-to-work programs could trigger fairly significant increases in the populations labeled the working poor, as many people transitioning from welfare to work were likely to be earning very low wages. Based on the demographics of welfare applicants and recipients, many are very young, most are poorly educated, and many have one or more infants or very young children for whom they are the primary caregivers. There were a disproportionately large number of single mothers and unmarried teenaged parents applying for or receiving social services relative to the percentages found in the general population. In an effort to minimize some of the challenges attendant with a programmatic change of such magnitude, several safety nets were put into place. Food stamp programs were anticipated to be more widely used by the working poor, many states were given special set-aside funds in order to meet unexpected service or funding gaps, and provisions were created in which approximately one-fifth of the families on welfare would be exempted from the five-year cap, as it would constitute an untenable hardship for them. Single custodial parents, or mothers with

children who were below school age would only be required to work half time. Special provisions were made for those who could either find no available childcare or could not find affordable, safe, high-quality childcare providers. Depending upon the state in which they resided, single mothers with infants or with babies who were less than twelve months old could be exempted from the requirement to secure gainful employment for a period of up to twelve months. Finally, special set-aside block grant funds could be utilized by individual states in order to provide various choices for funding or programs used on an emergent basis for families or individuals who have reached the maximum time limits for welfare, and are being rolled off of the programs without having first established viable safety nets (employment, food stamps, and the like) for themselves. Medicaid funding was not cut commensurate with the welfare changes, enabling many of those living at or below poverty to retain health care and prescription benefits. Although the purported intent of the program changes was to increase the size of the available workforce and to decrease the number of individuals and families dependent upon public service programs in order to subsist, there was enormous concern expressed by social service agencies that the programs would have an effect opposite of that which was intended. It was the contention of those groups that the most effective means of increasing financial independence among welfare recipients was to provide incentives for their move into the workforce by providing support for extended education, vocational and technical training, and encouraging them to make individual choices about when the time is most right for them to make major life changes. By allowing people to make major lifestyle changes based on their own needs and decision processes, it was anticipated that they would be far more likely to achieve long-term success: to garner employment that would permit them to earn a living wage (one in which they could safely support self and family), to be able to provide for ancillary services such as childcare, to be able to feed their families in a healthy and adequate way, either with or without the supplemental support provided by food stamps and similar nutrition programs, and to ensure adequate health, dental, and medical care and coverage for the family. Forcing people to leave welfare supports after two or fewer years with no real personal choice often does not allow sufficient time to acquire the skills or training needed to rise permanently out of poverty.

FURTHER RESOURCES

Books

Gooden, Susan. *Washington Works: Sustaining a Vision of Welfare Reform Based on Personal Change, Work Preparation, and Employer Involvement*. New York: Manpower Demonstration Research Corporation, 1998.

Greenberg, Mark. *Welfare-to-Work Grants and Other TANF-Related Provisions in the Balanced Budget Act of 1997*. Washington, D.C.: Center for Law and Social Policy, 1997.

Greenberg, Mark, and Steve Savner. *A Brief Summary of Key Provisions of the Temporary Assistance for Needy Families Block Grant of H.R. 3734*. Washington, D.C.: Center for Law and Social Policy, 1996.

Pavetti, LaDonna. *How Much More Can They Work? Setting Realistic Expectations for Welfare Mothers*. Washington, D.C.: The Urban Institute, 1997.

Pavetti, LaDonna, and Gregory Acs. *Moving Up, Moving Out, or Going Nowhere? A Study of the Employment Patterns of Young Women and the Implications for Welfare Mothers*. Washington, D.C.: The Urban Institute, 1997.

The Transition from Welfare to Work: Processes, Challenges, and Outcomes, edited by Sharon Telleen and Judith V. Sayad. New York: The Haworth Press, 2002.

Welfare Reform, 1996–2000: Is There a Safety Net?, edited by John E. Hansan and Robert Morris. Westport, Conn.: Auburn House, 1999.

Periodicals

Greenwald, J. "Off the Dole and On the Job." *Time* (August 18, 1997): 42–44.

"They Think You Ain't Much of Nothing"

The Social Construction of the Welfare Mother

Journal Article

By: Karen Seccombe, Delores James, and Kimberly Battle-Walters

Date: November, 1998

Source: Seccombe, Karen, Delores James, and Kimberly Battle-Walters. "'They Think You Ain't Much of Nothing': The Social Construction of the Welfare Mother." *Journal of Marriage and the Family*. 60, 4 (1998): 849–865.

About the Author: Karen Seccombe is Professor of Sociology at Portland State University. She has authored three books, including *"So You Think I Drive a Cadillac?": Welfare Recipients' Perspectives on the System and Its Reform* (1999). She recently received a grant from the National Institutes of Health to research the health insurance needs of families leaving welfare to take up employment and their access to health care services. Delores James is Associate Professor in the Department of Health Sciences Education at the University of Florida. She is the editor-in-chief of the 2003 *World Nutrition and Health Encyclopedia* and has published numerous articles in the field of health and welfare research. James has also been involved with several research projects for the state of Florida's Department of Health. Kimberly Battle-Walters is Associate Professor of Social Work at Azusa Pacific University. She is the author of *Sheila's Shop: Working-Class African American Women Talk About Life, Love, Race and Hair* (2004) and several articles in the areas of African American issues, women, welfare reform, and international relations. In 2002 she was the recipient of a Fulbright scholarship to study in South Africa.

INTRODUCTION

The creation of the welfare system in the United States was the result of continued political struggle from the 1930s to the 1970s. The efforts of the labor movement during the depression, the push to provide support to GIs returning from the Second World War and Vietnam, and the civil rights and feminist movements all contributed to the creation of old-age insurance, unemployment insurance, workers' compensation, and a variety of educational and support benefits for military veterans and their families—all programs designed to combat poverty. Lyndon B. Johnson's "war on poverty" in the 1960s saw the introduction of Medicare and Medicaid, affirmative action programs, and community-based anti-poverty initiatives. Despite these reforms, the American welfare system and political support for it has never been as strong as its European and Canadian counterparts. For example, a system of universal healthcare and subsidies for post-secondary education are only a fraction of what is provided in Canada and many European countries.

Since the 1980s, the welfare system in the United States that was so hard-fought for has been subject to numerous reforms and cutbacks. Critics argue that the American approach to welfare and social benefits has been to make their collection and receipt as difficult to obtain and as punitive as possible, emphasizing individual responsibility for poverty and the moral value of work. Consequently, there is stigma associated with collecting cash benefits from the government and wel-

A resident of the welfare Holland Hotel in Manhattan, New York, in 1984. Angel is Puerto Rican. She ran away from her family, and her boyfriend is in jail for dealing heroin. She is the mother of two children. © SOPHIE ELBAZ/SYGMA/CORBIS.

fare recipients are often viewed in a negative light that appears to be linked to stereotypes about the race, gender, marital status, and character of those who collect welfare.

■ PRIMARY SOURCE

"THEY THINK YOU AIN'T MUCH OF NOTHING": THE SOCIAL CONSTRUCTION OF THE WELFARE MOTHER

> I've had people who didn't know I was receiving assistance, and everything was just fine. But when people find out you're receiving assistance, it's like, why? Why did you get lazy all of the sudden? Leah, a 24-year-old mother

Approximately 39 million people are poor in the U.S., according to recent data from the U.S. Bureau of the Census (1997a). Within this large segment of the population are the approximately 3.5 million families, mostly mothers and their dependent children who receive cash welfare assistance, which until recently was called Aid to

Families with Dependent children (AFDC). President Bill Clinton signed monumental welfare reform legislation, which became federal law on July 1, 1997. P.L. 104–193 abolished the AFDC program and replaced it with a new program called Temporary Assistance to Needy Families (TANF). Turning many of the details of welfare law over to the states, it sets lifetime welfare payments at a maximum of 5 years, and the majority of adult recipients are required to work after 2 years. Twenty-five percent of recipients in each state must be working by the end of 1997. By the year 2002, 50% must be employed. Other changes under this reform include child-care assistance, at least 1 year of transitional Medicaid, the identification of the children's biological fathers, and the requirement that unmarried recipients who are minors must live at home and stay in school in order to receive benefits.

AFDC and TANF are virtually synonymous with the word "welfare" in the minds of most people. In the larger sense of the word, "welfare" could also encompass schools, parks, police and fire protection, as the term, "welfare state," popular in most of Western Europe, implies. However, in the U.S. welfare generally brings to mind the cash assistance programs of AFDC and TANF, and therefore, "welfare," "AFDC," and "TANF" are used interchangeably here for ease of discussion. Although welfare was originally created to serve primarily White widows and their children, welfare's recipient base has shifted over the years to mostly divorced and never-married women with children. Many people think that cast programs provide benefits to a large number of never-married, young, African American women and their children, a stereotype that has undoubtedly contributed to the growing sentiment against welfare (Pivan & Cloward, 1993; Quadagno, 1994). Yet, African Americans constitute only 36% of recipients (U.S. House of Representatives, Committee on Ways and Means, 1996). AFDC is criticized as an extravagant and costly program that is spiraling out of control and is responsible for a sizable component of our federal deficit, but it approximates only 1% of federal spending (Congressional Digest, 1995; U.S. House of Representatives, Committee on Ways and Means, 1996). Although money is often cited as the source of these tensions American values of financial independence and hard work are usually at the heart of the hostility toward welfare (Meyer, 1994).

Numerous stereotypes of able-bodied persons who receive welfare persist. Women who are without husbands to support them and their children are viewed as suspect and potentially undeserving (Abramovitz, 1996; Gordon, 1994; Miller, 1992). They are "manless women," as Dorothy Miller reveals, a stigmatized group that is "reduced in our minds from a whole and usual person to a tainted, discounted one" (Goffman, 1963, pp. 3–4). Women who receive welfare have been accused of being lazy, unmotivated, of cheating the system or having additional children simply to increase the amount of their benefit check. The underlying belief is that these women are looking for a free ride at the expense of the American taxpayer (Davis & Hagen, 1996). They are criticized for their supposedly long-term dependency, despite evidence that the median length of a welfare stay is 23 months (U.S. House of Representatives, committee on Ways and Means, 1996). Although some of these women have intermittent spells of employment (Ellwood, 1986; Harris, 1993, 1996), only 7% of recipients remain continuously on welfare for 8 years or longer (congressional Digest, 1995). Race, class, and gender stereotypes become intertwined. Our society despises poor women, particularly African American poor women, who are seen as rejecting the traditional nuclear family that contains at least one and possibly two breadwinners and, instead, "choosing" to remain dependent on the public dole. This is in sharp contrast to the considerably less-stigmatized images of welfare recipients and public programs in most of Western Europe (Bergmann, 1996; Kamerman & Kahn, 1978).

Awareness of Societal Attitudes Toward Welfare Recipients

We found respondents cognizant of their stigmatized status. When asked if they ever hear negative comments about people on welfare, they overwhelmingly answered, "Yes," and most claimed that criticism has been directed at them personally. Consistent with research that indicates the popularity of individualist explanations of poverty, most welfare recipients interviewed—African American and White, young and old—reported that they hear considerable personal blame and criticism. For example, asked what kinds of thing she had heard about welfare recipients, Rhonda, a 28-year old White woman with a young son, explained:

I've heard one girl was going to quit working because all the taxes come to us. Plus, you know, they downgrade us in every kind of way there is. They say we look like slobs; we keep our houses this way and that way. And our children, depending on the way they're dressed, we're like bad parents and all sorts of things like that.

The theme of laziness, an image embodied in the individualist perspective, emerged with relative consistency. Lonnie, an African American mother of five who has been on and off of welfare several times and has most recently received benefits for 2 years reported:

They say you lazy. They say you lazy and don't want to work. You want people to take care of you. You want to sit home and watch stories all day, which I don't. And they say that it's a handout. I stood in the welfare line, and I heard what they called me. And I've went in the grocery store, and when you get ready to buy your groceries, people have made nasty little remarks about the groceries you're buying. They'll go, "We're paying for that." Once there was some university students, and I guess they felt like that. They had a small amount in their buggy, and I had large amounts. He started talking, so his girlfriend kept trying to get him to be quiet. And he kept talking and talking. And then he said, "That's why the President is trying to cut off welfare, because of people like that!" I turned to him, and I say, I say, "Well, you know something? I have worked in my time, too. And I will work again. It's not like I'm asking you for anything. And I hope you don't come and ask me for anything 'cause with me and my five kids I couldn't give you none anyway!" And he stomped out of there when I told him that. But I was being honest with him. I have worked. I felt real bad that day. I really did.

Racist overtones are evident, as well.

One of the many reasons that welfare is stigmatized is because it is incorrectly associated with primarily African Americans (Quadagno, 1994). Whites tend to deny that our social structure limits the opportunities for African Americans (Bobo & Smith, 1994; Kluegal & Smith,

1982; National Opinion Research Center, 1993). They sometimes feel that they, themselves, are victimized by policies of "reverse discrimination" and that African Americans reap employment and social welfare benefits. For example, fewer than 40% of Whites support increased social spending to help African Americans, according to data from the General Social Survey (Bobo & Smith, 1994). This view was epitomized in the comments made by a 27-year-old White woman named Beth when she was asked what kinds of things she had heard people say about welfare recipients:

> Oh, they say silly stuff, prejudiced stuff: "The Black people are getting it, so we might as well—you might as well go ahead and get it too while you can. They're driving Cadillacs," and this and that.

Dee is an African American woman, aged 24, with three children, 4 years old and younger. She attends school full-time and plans to become an accountant. She told us that the most negative comments she has heard come from White males:

> That's mainly who I hear it from. I mean, I hear a couple of things from Black guys, but a lot of Black guys I know grew up on the system. You know, they are trying to get off that system. So you don't really hear it much from them. They have firsthand experience with it. Those who don't have firsthand experience have friends who have. So, the majority of them have come into contact with it sometime in their lifetime. As for the White males, a lot of them grew up in the upper-middle class, you know, above the poverty line, so they never run across it, unless they had friends who were on the system. But there are as many White people on it as Black people.

The grocery store was one social context where negative comments were reported to occur most often. There, stigma symbols, such as food stamps, are in full view and cannot be hidden (Goffman, 1963). Looking for evidence of fraud, cashiers and others closely scrutinize the food that women purchase. The assumption is made that welfare mothers live high on the hog at taxpayers' expense and must be closely monitored in order to prevent irresponsible behavior and abuse of the system. The public looks for women who buy steak with food stamps and feel vindicated when they find them.

A second context where frequent negative comments were heard was the welfare office itself. Rather than seeing the welfare office as a place for help, recipients view it with suspicion and distrust. They suggest that the people who run it are self-serving and have contempt for their clients. "They think you ain't much of nothing...," "they try to make you feel bad and say little mean things...," "some of them talk to you like dirt..." were frequent comments. Respondents felt that the administrative culture of AFDC is more concerned with enforcement of eligibility and compliance than with actually helping clients. "They act like it's their money they're giving away," one woman told us.

Ten women, African Americans, and Whites, said that neither they nor their children have ever experienced stigma or discrimination because of being on welfare, although several followed up this claim with statements such as, "and I don't listen to it anyhow." Three women suggested that people have been especially kind to them when they revealed that they were on welfare. Several other women said that they had not experienced problems because they do not let other people know that they are on welfare: "I tell people I receive aid from the state." I was told that dressing in name-brand clothing and shoes to appear middle class was an important strategy to keep sons away from drug dealers, who offer young children these items as a way to entice them to sell drugs for them. Other respondents said that they try to buck the stereotype and pass as members of the middle class. One young White mother said:

> I think it's all in how you carry yourself. I don't want my children looking any kind of way. I don't want them to think that they're no less, that everybody is better than them, and they're not. So my kids wear name-brand shoes just like anybody else...So I mean, I try not to make them want for nothing.

In sum, it appears that most welfare recipients in our sample are aware of the popular, individualistic stratifications of beliefs in our society. They know that, as a group, welfare recipients are considered largely responsible for their own economic circumstances and their use of welfare. The majority of the women interviewed said that they, personally, have experienced stigma and discrimination.

SIGNIFICANCE

In a famous speech, former president Ronald Reagan contributed to the stereotype of the "welfare queen ...[who] has eighty names, thirty addresses, twelve social security cards and is collecting veteran's benefits on four nonexistent deceased husbands...her tax free cash income alone is over $150,000." While his description was found to be fabricated, the common perception of welfare recipients as people who take advantage of the system and live off of the hard work of others remained and has persisted in the decades since Reagan's administration. This negative social and political construction of welfare recipients contributes to public discontent with the concept of welfare and justifies more restricted policies around welfare eligibility and benefits.

During the Reagan and Bush (Sr.) administrations, congress approved major budget cuts to such programs as Social Security Insurance, Medicaid, food stamps, school food programs, AFDC, energy assistance grants, community development grants, and subsidized housing programs. From 1970 to 1996, there were drastic reductions in the amounts of welfare grants given out in many states and in the number of individuals who were permitted to collect welfare. Under the 1996 welfare reforms, cash aid from the government became linked to work efforts. No longer were women and their families to be given assistance simply because they were poor. The TANF program was a concerted effort to push "lazy" welfare recipients off of public assistance and into paid employment. By putting welfare recipients to work for their benefits, the belief is that welfare will be viewed as a less desirable lifestyle and individuals will be motivated to find employment. Unfortunately, the reality is that many welfare recipients are not educated and do not have many marketable skills, meaning that menial, minimum-wage service and retail jobs are all that is available to them. Given the added costs of childcare, transportation, and the loss of health insurance benefits that accompany paid employment, many single mothers find that when they calculate the costs and benefits of employment, it is more economically practical and better for their children if they remain on welfare. Many women find that they cannot pay their bills and provide adequately for their children on full-time minimum wage, so they choose to remain on welfare, despite the work regulations, thus calling into question the initial motivation for welfare cuts and restrictions.

Another highly controversial aspect of welfare reform is the emphasis on minimizing out-of-wedlock childbirth. The 1996 legislation placed caps on welfare grants, and limited the amount of time that an individual can collect welfare in a lifetime, ostensibly to discourage women from having more children in order to collect a larger welfare benefit. The federal government also offers cash bonuses to states that can reduce the number of "illegitimate" births without increasing the rate of abortion. This approach endeavors to encourage planned, two-parent, self-sufficient families, which is not, on its own, a negative ideal. However, there is little evidence to suggest that welfare policy has any "real" effect on trends in marriage, cohabitation and family planning, and the impact of the legislation is to stigmatize and negatively effect single mothers and their families.

Under President George W. Bush, there continues to be cuts to federal welfare budgets and a trend toward increasing the involvement of religious organizations in the provision of programs and assistance to low-income families. Through expanded tax cuts for charitable donations and the transfer of federal welfare funding to churches and religious charities, welfare services in the United States are becoming increasingly privatized. While many religious groups have traditionally been involved in charity work, the state download of responsibility to private organizations is potentially problematic. The administration of social services by religious organizations opens up the possibility of discrimination against certain groups, such as gays and lesbians and unwed mothers, on religious and moral grounds, all the while protected by the right of religious freedom.

Stereotypes of gender, race, and morality legitimize the continued reduction of welfare spending and the imposition of severe restrictions on the receipt of cash assistance. Current welfare policies in the United States appear to be based on flawed assumptions of individuals' motivations for collecting welfare. Those who stop collecting welfare—by choice or force— often have difficulty obtaining adequate employment and making ends meet on minimum wage. Critics argue that improved access to job training, education, and adequate child and health care would prove more beneficial than cuts to welfare benefits in motivating single mothers to improve their economic position and get off of social assistance.

FURTHER RESOURCES

Books

Hacker, Jacob S. *The Divided Welfare State: The Battle Over Public and Private Social Benefits in the United States.* New York: Cambridge University Press, 2002.

Riemer, Frances Julia. *Working at the Margins: Moving Off Welfare in America.* Albany, N.Y.: State University of New York Press, 2001.

Periodicals

Christopher, Karen. "Welfare as We [Don't] Know It: A Review and Feminist Critique of Welfare Reform Research in the United States." *Feminist Economics* 10, 2 (2004): 143–171.

Fitzgerald, John M. and David C. Ribar. "Welfare Reform and Female Headship." *Demography* 41, 2 (2004): 189–212.

Lambert, Susan. "The Work Side of Welfare-to-Work: Lessons From Recent Policy Research." *Work and Occupations* 30 4 (2003): 474–478.

McCormack, Karen. "Resisting the Welfare Mother: The Power of Welfare Discourse and Tactics of Resistance." *Critical Sociology* 30 2 (2004): 355–383.

Platt, Tony. "The State of Welfare: United States 2003." *Monthly Review* (October 2003): 13–27.

Wiseman, Michael. "Welfare Reform in the United States: A Background Paper." *Housing Policy Debate* 7 4 (1996): 595–648.

Covering the Uninsured through TennCare: Does It Make a Difference?

Journal article

By: Lorenzo Moreno and Sheila D. Hoag

Date: January–February 2001

Source: Moreno, Lorenzo and Sheila D. Hoag. "Covering the Uninsured through TennCare: Does It Make a Difference?" *Health Affairs* 29, no. 1 (January–February 2001): 231–239.

About the Author: Lorenzo Moreno is a senior researcher and Sheila Hoag is a researcher at Mathematica Policy Research in Princeton, New Jersey.

INTRODUCTION

In every state's health care system, there are several categories of people who receive services. A significant percentage of the population is privately, or commercially, insured by third-party payers—these people participate in a variety of different plans, most of which reflect at least some significant aspects of managed care. In these cases, medical and behavioral health-care coverage is paid, at least in part, by the employer, and the insured employees generally work full time. Such individuals, and their families, are usu-

TennCare advocates stage a rally in Nashville, Tennessee on March 15, 2005, in order to halt reforms to the state's beleaguered $8 billion health care program for the poor and uninsured. AP IMAGES.

ally considered to be adequately insured, though they may choose to obtain supplemental medical care policies. People who are adequately insured typically have a personal health care practitioner, whom they see for routine medical care. They go to specialists as necessary, and only use emergency and urgent care services when the situation warrants such usage.

At the other end of the socioeconomic spectrum are those who are not typically able to be employed and who depend upon public assistance to help them meet their financial and personal-care needs. They may be significantly or fully disabled (either physically, cognitively, or due to behavioral health disorders), in which case they probably receive state and federal government benefits supplementing or providing their income, and they benefit from governmentally sponsored health-care plans. They probably see a specific primary care provider and have a medical and behavioral health care plan in which they receive a menu of services. In addition, they are likely to have the ability to exercise some degree of choice in the planning and execution of their health-care programming.

Within the category of the unemployed or unemployable, there are those who receive temporary governmental financial assistance, such as Temporary Assistance to Needy Families (TANF) or other programs falling under the general heading of what has historically been called welfare. If they are children or youth, welfare recipients may be in state custody and reside in foster care or some type of residential or group care setting. If they are adults, they may be currently unemployed and residing in some type of institutional setting, such as a rehabilitation or treatment center or a correctional facility. If they are elders, they may be living in skilled nursing facilities or in assisted-living settings. They may also reside in their own private dwellings, retired and no longer receiving the more traditional types of services, such as commercial health-care plans. A significant group will simply be unemployed and temporarily unable to provide for the financial and health-care needs of their families. For that significant segment of the population, there are governmentally sponsored financial assistance programs, including various types of physical and behavioral health-care programs.

Finally, there is the subpopulation typically referred to as "the working poor." They are employed, but they do not work enough hours or earn enough money to be able to obtain commercially available health-care coverage. Because they are employed, they are unlikely to receive financial assistance from the state or federal government, or perhaps they would obtain minor benefits, such as food stamps. They are not eligible for assistance or state or federal sponsorship of their medical care, but they cannot afford coverage on their own, so they are generally uninsured. Some may be able to afford a minimal plan that provides for catastrophic care, for example, but leaves them significantly underinsured. For that segment of the population, the options have traditionally been few. In the past, they would have had to rely on emergent-care settings to get basic needs met, or they might have gone to free or sliding-scale clinics. Now, many states have created plans to provide low-cost or supplemental health-care coverage for the marginally employed or the working poor. Prior to that development, states generally had to absorb the costs for the health care of the uninsured, creating considerable financial chaos.

PRIMARY SOURCE

Tennessee created TennCare in 1994 to address the needs of the "hundreds of thousands of poor and uninsured citizens...excluded from the health care system."

Under TennCare, Tennessee implemented managed care in its Medicaid program and used savings anticipated from the switch to managed care to expand insurance coverage to uninsured and uninsurable residents. Many policymakers and the press have criticized TennCare over the years, but it has provided coverage to thousands of persons who otherwise would lack insurance.

We examine whether TennCare's expansion program makes a difference in beneficiaries' access to and satisfaction with care compared with that of their uninsured or uninsurable peers. This is critical to study now, since Tennessee, faced with financial difficulties, is considering revamping TennCare. Alternatives range from closing enrollment to new uninsured and uninsurable persons to carving out the expansion program as a state-funded high-risk insurance pool.

Initially, the TennCare expansion offered health insurance coverage through fully capitated managed care organizations to uninsured and uninsurable Tennesseans, known as the "expansion group." This expansion offered subsidized coverage to all uninsured and uninsurable Tennesseans with annual family incomes below 400 percent of the federal poverty level, while those above 400 percent of poverty could receive unsubsidized coverage. This expansion is considerably more ambitious than those of other states (such as California, Delaware, Hawaii, Massachusetts, Minnesota, Oregon, Vermont, and Washington), which targeted persons with incomes at 100–200 percent of poverty. Enrollment in the expansion group has fluctuated over the years; Tennessee closed enrollment in late 1994 to uninsured persons, mostly adults, because of budget problems. Expansion-group enrollment increased steadily since 1997, peaking at 517,607 persons in October 1999….

Effects of Expanding Coverage

Barriers to care. For the majority of measures of barriers to care we examined, expansion group-members scored significantly better than uninsured persons did (Exhibit 2). For instance, more than 92 percent of expansion-group members had a usual place of care, compared with fewer than 74 percent of uninsured persons. Also, more expansion-group adults and children always visited the same provider at their usual place of care than did their uninsured counterparts, signaling better continuity of care. Compared with uninsured persons, expansion-group members were about 30 percent more likely to have paid nothing out of pocket for care and about half as likely to have spent more than $100 in the past year.

Unmet need and delays in receiving care. These measures are important indicators of the match between people's expectations and the care they actually receive. Expansion-group adults reported significantly lower unmet need and service delays on all six measures we examined (not shown). For example, uninsured adults were nearly twice as likely as expansion-group adults were to not see a doctor when they needed one (63.8 versus 33.6 percent), to delay seeing a doctor when needed (53.2 percent versus 32.4 percent), and to take a needed prescription drug less often than recommended (21.9 percent versus 11.3 percent). Uninsured children scored similarly. Uninsured persons reported that the main reason for their unmet need was unaffordability, while transportation and scheduling topped the list for expansion-group members.

Use of services. TennCare appears to have increased access to care, as measured by intensity of service use, the traditional indicator of access to care. On four of the five measures we examined, expansion-group adults used more services than uninsured adults used, while expansion-group children used more services than their uninsured counterparts did on all five measures examined.

An alternative interpretation of these estimates—that the uninsured are simply healthier and less in need of care—is not consistent with other evidence from our survey. When the need for various services (including hospitalization) was measured by either receipt of the service or reported unmet need for it, the expansion and comparison groups appeared to have quite similar care needs. This finding, together with the uninsured persons' primary reason for not getting needed services (unaffordability), provides strong confirmation that the greater

service use among TennCare enrollees is the result of their greater access to care.

Use of preventive services. Nearly three-quarters of expansion-group women who should have received a Pap smear in the past year reported that they received one, compared with half of those in the uninsured group. Similarly, nearly three-quarters of children in TennCare's expansion program received well-child visits on schedule, compared with 55 percent of uninsured children.

Satisfaction with care. Adults and parents or guardians of children in TennCare's expansion group were more satisfied than their uninsured counterparts were with their access to care and the care they received, but our findings are statistically significant for only five of the twelve aspects of care we measured for each group (Exhibit 3). Expansion-group and uninsured persons were about equally likely to rate as very good or excellent the number of doctors they had to choose from, the time spent waiting for and with the doctor, and the courtesy of their doctors. Since the percentage of expansion-group adults who rated specific aspects of care as very good or excellent rarely exceeded 50 percent, our findings suggest that either the managed care organizations or the providers have room to improve various aspects of care under TennCare.

Discussion and Lessons Learned

Tennessee implemented TennCare with the ambitious goals of controlling costs while increasing access to care, improving quality of care, and encouraging use of preventive care for Medicaid-eligible and uninsured/uninsurable Tennesseans. Our findings suggest that TennCare accomplished those goals. This conclusion is corroborated by two recent studies.

Implications for children. Tennessee's success in expanding coverage to uninsured and uninsurable children is particularly relevant right now, as coverage for children is expanding nationwide through the implementation of the State Children's Health Insurance Program (SCHIP). As a precursor to SCHIP, TennCare demonstrates the feasibility of implementing a coverage expansion for children that is popular and improves access to care. TennCare, as the largest family-based expansion of health insurance coverage for low-income persons in recent history, corroborates the findings from dozens of studies that have addressed whether providing insurance coverage to the uninsured makes a difference. Although our findings are specific to Tennessee, they demonstrate that a Medicaid expansion model, the model that twenty-six states plus the District of Columbia have adopted for their SCHIP programs, can greatly improve children's access to care.

Implications for adults. Our findings also have important policy implications for adults. Since the requirements for gaining or maintaining Medicaid eligibility are so stringent, the consequences of losing health insurance coverage can be devastating for this population. Although Tennessee's expansion of coverage initially included uninsured and uninsurable adults, subsequent enrollment closures made it nearly impossible for uninsured adults to enroll in TennCare unless they qualified as uninsurable. Moreover, because TennCare entered the year 2000 with financial problems, Tennessee is proposing that uninsured and uninsurable adults bear the brunt of the intended reduction in TennCare coverage.

Our findings indicate that although drastic changes such as dropping the adult expansion entirely or severely cutting it back might help TennCare to regain financial health and stability in the short term, the long-term implications for the health of uninsured and uninsurable adults are likely to be considerable. Less drastic alternatives, such as revising the incentives to participating managed care plans to really manage care or revising the cost-sharing policies for uninsured and uninsurable adults, might ensure that TennCare's coverage expansion could be maintained.

SIGNIFICANCE

There are several state and federally funded health-care programs for those who live in poverty and are unemployed, or for those who are temporarily unable to work. The most common among these are Medicaid, for children, youth, adults, and families in temporary need of assistance; and Medicare, for elders and those who are significantly disabled. Those who served in the Armed Forces as a career, or were disabled through the course of their military service, receive or are eligible for veteran-related health care. Members of these subpopulations typically have some form of managed-care coverage, see a regular provider, and generally use urgent or emergent care services on an as-needed basis. This type of coverage for such citizens only became the norm at the end of the twentieth century, when government-sponsored medical-care programs were reorganized into a managed-care model. Prior to that time, physical and behavioral care for those who were not privately insured was quite fragmented. Typically, people in that group did not have primary-care coverage and relied upon the emergency room or urgent-care settings in order to get virtually all of their physical and behavioral health-care needs met. Such practices placed a huge drain on both the medical and financial systems, as such settings are typically far more expensive than

standard medical office settings and clinics. It also resulted in overcrowded emergency settings, particularly on nights and weekends, placing the care of those in truly emergent situations in jeopardy.

The working poor, who do not have commercial health care, but who earn too much to be able to avail themselves of government-sponsored programs, have the fewest options of all. In the past, they often went without health-care coverage and relied on emergency medical systems in times of crisis. Many attempted to locate free or low-cost clinics, resigning themselves to very long waits and the inability to develop a relationship with a regular provider who would be familiar with their health-care histories and needs. Alternatively, some used various state-sponsored free programs such as public health-sponsored immunization and well-care clinics. Sometimes, the working poor were able to find settings in which they could tap into county indigent funds, or they could benefit from special programs created for specific disease or disorder categories, such as publicly paid and grant-funded programs for children needing speech or physical therapy for certain types of disorders, like cerebral palsy or premature birth. Such health care was typically spotty and difficult to locate, often had long wait lists, and was almost always inadequate to meet the broad range of health-care needs for the individual and family.

With the advent of Medicare and Medicaid reform and the broadened use of the managed-care paradigm for those whose health care is paid by the government has come another new form of health-care coverage, designed to ease the burden for the underinsured, uninsured, and uninsurable segments of the population. The State Children's Health Insurance Program, or SCHIP (usually called S-Chip), was created in 1997 as an outgrowth of Title XXI of the Social Security Act. SCHIP is designed as a long-term roll-out program designed to meet the needs of lower-income working families. It is geared for those who earn too much money to be eligible to receive Medicaid coverage, but who do not earn enough to be able to afford commercial coverage. There is considerable flexibility in the ways in which the various states can choose to structure their SCHIP programs—some use them only for children, some for children and families, and some have even opened SCHIP up to working adults without children who meet certain (state-determined) poverty standards. Because there is not yet a general level of awareness about these programs, states create means of public education and consciousness-raising in order to bring them to public attention. One way of doing this is by providing educational materials to employers who commonly use large numbers of itinerant, seasonal, or part-time help, so that they can hand out pamphlets and brochures to such workers. Another is through health fairs or by handing out information in public settings such as grocery stores and shopping malls, or by erecting informational kiosks at such places.

Many states are creating new health-care options for the uninsured, underinsured, and uninsurable through waiver programs that combine the flexibility of Medicaid and SCHIP funds, under legislation allowing the development of Health Insurance Flexibility and Accountability Demonstration Initiatives (commonly called HIFAs) that target health services to the poorer segments of the general population. HIFAs allow the states to exercise considerable creativity in sculpting health-care coverage to meet the needs of their individual demographics, designing programs for serving their poorer citizens. One of the most beneficial aspects of the HIFA programs, from the perspectives of state government, is that they provide a degree of federal funding to supplement the costs of health care for this population, reducing the budget strain on the states and, ultimately, making the coverage and care more affordable for those who need it most—the working poor. In many areas, the government funds are being supplemented by grant funds from philanthropic organizations such as the Robert Wood Johnson Foundation (among many others), providing for greater expansion of programming and the development of community-level health care resources and providers.

FURTHER RESOURCES
Books

Birenbaum, Arnold. *Managed Care: Made in America*. Westport, Conn.: Praeger, 1997.

Bryner, Gary. *Managing Medicaid Take-Up: The Relationship between Medicaid and Welfare Agencies*. Albany, N.Y.: The Nelson A. Rockefeller Institute of Government, Federalism Research Group, 2002.

Dubay, Lisa, Ian Hill, and Genevieve Kinney. *Five Things Everyone Should Know about SCHIP*. Washington, D.C.: The Urban Institute, 2002.

Hackey, Robert B. *Rethinking Health Care Policy: The New Politics of State Regulation*. Washington, D.C.: Georgetown University Press, 1998.

Kerson, Toba Schweber. *Boundary Spanning: An Ecological Reinterpretation of Social Work Practice in Health and Mental Health Systems*. New York: Columbia University Press, 2002.

Mann, Cindy. *Issues Facing Medicaid and SCHIP*. Washington, D.C.: The Kaiser Commission on Medicaid and the Uninsured, 2002.

Peterson, Mark A., ed. *Healthy Markets? The New Competition in Medical Care*. Durham, N.C.: Duke University Press, 1998.

Rodgers, Harrell R., Jr. *American Poverty in a New Era of Reform*. Armonk, N.Y.: M.E. Sharpe, 2000.

Stein, Theodore J. *Social Policy and Policy Making by the Branches of Government and the Public-at-Large*. New York: Columbia University Press, 2001.

Periodicals

Friedman, Thomas L. "President Allows States Flexibility on Medicaid Funds." *New York Times* (February 2, 1993): A1(N), A13.

Grogan, Colleen M. "Federalism and Health Care Reform." *American Behavioral Scientist* 36 (6) (1993): 741–759.

Moore, Iyauta. "The SCHIP Program: Continuing Health Care Coverage in Uncertain Times." *Welfare Information Network: Issue Notes* 7 (6) (April 2003).

Randal, Teri. "Insurance—Private and Public: A Payment Puzzle." *Journal of the American Medical Society* 269 (18) (1993): 2344–2345.

Law Limits Ritalin Recommendations

News article

By: Cable News Network

Date: July 17, 2001

Source: *CNN.com*. "Law Limits Ritalin Recommendations." July 17, 2001.

About the Author: CNN.com is the web portal for the Cable News Network, a twenty-four hour news channel launched by Ted Turner in 1980.

INTRODUCTION

In 1937, medical staffers at Bradley Hospital in Providence, Rhode Island fed hyperactive children stimulants in an effort to control their behavior; the drug, dextroamphetamine, helped to calm the children. In 1954, the drug company Ciba Pharmaceutical Company patented the drug methylphenidate, known as Ritalin, for use with patients experiencing depression, narcolepsy, and chronic fatigue. Ritalin quickly

Christian Domenech, age 9, suffers from attention deficit hyperactivity disorder. His parents, Paula and Steve Johnson, of Lawrence, Kansas, filed a complaint with the U.S. Department of Education that staff at Lawrence schools were pressuring them to keep Christian on Ritalin. AP/WIDE WORLD PHOTOS. REPRODUCED BY PERMISSION.

became the drug of choice to treat hyperactivity in children by the 1960s.

Hyperactivity as a medical condition was first reported in medical journals such as *Lancet* in the early 1900s. Restlessness, fidgeting, poor impulse control, inappropriate physical energy in certain contexts are markers for hyperactivity in children that came to be called minimal brain dysfunction in the 1940s, hyperactive child syndrome in the 1950s, attention deficit disorder in the 1970s, and most recently, attention deficit/hyperactivity disorder, or ADHD. Until recently, the cause of clinical ADHD was unknown, though researchers speculate that a dopamine imbalance in the brain triggers the behaviors associated with hyperactivity.

In the United States, boys experience clinical diagnoses of ADHD at a rate four times higher than girls. By the 1990s, in the United States, ADHD diagnoses had increased so dramatically that a backlash

against the disorder in the form of publications, television shows, and websites led to a standoff between doctors and parents who treat children with ADHD with medications and parents, doctors, and educators who argue that the actual incidence of ADHD in the population is very small, and that the over diagnosis is a result of cultural norms and school practices that do not tolerate normal childhood behaviors.

Peter Breggin, a psychiatrist and director of the International Center for the Study of Psychiatry and Psychology, notes that research shows that the calming effects of Ritalin and other stimulant drugs such as Adderall and Strattera are, in fact, toxic reactions to the drugs themselves. In testimony before Congress, Breggin noted that the United States uses more than ninety percent of Ritalin produced worldwide, and that out of a population of approximately 54 million school children, in the year 2000, more than five million were taking prescription stimulants; nearly ten percent of all schoolchildren, but mostly white boys. By comparison, the stimulant rate for school children in Great Britain and France is dramatically lower; in France, prescriptions for stimulants must be written in hospitals, not by primary care physicians or pediatricians.

As ADHD diagnoses soared in the United States, changes in day care and education settings required children to spend longer amounts of time indoors or in institutional environments, reduced indoor and outdoor recess time for schoolchildren, reduced physical education, increased time devoted to standardized testing; some ADHD critics point also to changing expectations from parents and educators concerning childhood behavior. Hyperactivity, in other words, is subjective, and critics of ADHD rates claim that changing social conditions in the United States are creating the ADHD epidemic itself while ADHD proponents state that better detection, awareness, and treatment drive the increase in diagnoses.

By the late 1990s, some parents of children labeled hyperactive by teachers and administrators found themselves in conferences with school teachers, principals, and psychologists discussing an ADHD diagnosis; in many instances, such meetings ended with the school's requirement that the child receive medication as a condition for attending school. At times, parents, concerned about negative side effects of Ritalin and other stimulants that include loss of height, cardiovascular damage, and sleep disturbances, refused to medicate. The conflict that ensued led to laws such as the Connecticut law discussed below.

▮ PRIMARY SOURCE

HARTFORD, Connecticut (AP)—When Sheila Matthews' son was in first grade, a school psychologist diagnosed him with attention deficit/hyperactivity disorder and gave his parents information on Ritalin.

Matthews refused to put him on the drug. She believed the boy was energetic and outgoing but not disruptive, and she suspected the school system was trying to medicate him just to make it easier for the teachers.

Now the state of Connecticut has weighed in on the side of parents like Matthews with a first-in-the-nation law that reflects a growing backlash against what some see as overuse of Ritalin and other behavioral drugs.

The law—approved unanimously by the Legislature and signed by Gov. John G. Rowland—prohibits teachers, counselors and other school officials from recommending psychiatric drugs for any child.

The measure does not prevent school officials from recommending that a child be evaluated by a medical doctor. But the law is intended to make sure the first mention of drugs for a behavior or learning problem comes from a doctor.

The chief sponsor, state Rep. Lenny Winkler, is an emergency room nurse. "I cannot believe how many young kids are on Prozac, Thorazine, Haldol—you name it," Winkler said. "It blows my mind." While she has no problem with the use of Ritalin under a doctor's care, Winkler said a teacher's recommendation is often enough to persuade parents to seek drug treatment for their child's behavior problems.

"It's easier to give somebody a pill than to get to the bottom of the problem," she said.

Nationally, nearly 20 million prescriptions for Ritalin, Adderall and other stimulants used to treat ADHD were written last year—a thirty-five percent increase over 1996, according to IMS Health, a health care information company. Most of those prescriptions were for boys under twelve, IMS Health said.

In some elementary and middle schools, as many as 6 percent of all students take Ritalin or other psychiatric drugs, according to the federal Drug Enforcement Administration.

Dr. Andres Martin, a child psychiatrist at the Yale University Child Study Center, said schools have no business practicing psychiatry.

"We've all heard these horror stories of parents who are told, 'If you don't medicate your child, he can't be in the classroom,'" he said. "You never hear the school say, 'If you don't take the damn appendix out, this kid has a bad outcome.' You say, 'Your kid has a stomach ache. Take him to the doctor.'."

The Connecticut Association of Boards of Education has taken no position on the bill. Nor has the Connecticut Education Association, the state's largest teachers union. But union President Rosemary Coyle said the she believes the problem is overstated.

"I really believe teachers do not practice medicine," Coyle said. "We don't recommend kids get on drugs."

Concern about Ritalin and other drugs is widespread. The Texas Board of Education adopted a resolution last year recommending that schools consider non-medical solutions to behavior problems. The Colorado school board approved a similar resolution in 1999, and legislation regarding psychiatric drugs in school has been proposed in nearly a dozen states.

In the New Canaan school district, Matthews and her husband took their son, now eight, to a private psychologist, who said the boy has trouble with reasoning. He now receives special education from the school system.

"I was able to get, for $2,000, a different label that has an educational connotation, rather than medical," said Matthews, who did not want her son's name used.

New Canaan district officials did not return repeated calls for comment. But Matthews said she has resolved many of her differences with the school system, which did not threaten to remove her son from class.

"I'm really thrilled" about the new law, she said, "because it gives parents an awareness that there should be a clear difference between education and medication. Our schools are now getting into the field of mental health. That's not what we send our children to school for."

SIGNIFICANCE

In addition to Connecticut, states such as Minnesota and Texas passed similar laws. The Minnesota law gives parents the choice not to submit their child for special education testing, while requiring that nonprescription drug strategies, such as diet change, schedule change, and other accommodations, be explored before considering Ritalin or other stimulants for hyperactive behavior.

While proponents of such "anti-Ritalin" laws state that such laws prevent teachers and administrators from assuming the role of physician and diagnosticians, many professional educators claim that the laws go too far. In Connecticut, for instance, the law prohibits school officials from specifically recommending a particular drug; officials may recommend that a child be evaluated, but the evaluation and diagnosis must come from a doctor. Teachers and administrators cannot mention any drugs by name. At the same time, parents have reported threats from school administrators to report parents to Child Protective Services for failure to medicate a child, even when the child has no formal diagnosis. Such state laws are designed to provide clear guidelines concerning ADHD and other developmental and behavioral diagnoses.

In 2005, the revision of the Individuals with Disabilities Education Act included a provision protecting parents from coercion concerning such controlled substances as Ritalin, Adderall, and Dexedrine. In addition, the 108th Congress was, as of May 2006, considering a bill that would remove federal funds from schools where officials required medication as a condition for attendance. As ADHD diagnoses increase in the United States, and with a 500 percent increase in stimulant drug prescriptions in the United States from 1991–2000, such laws shape the approaches schools take in dealing with the crossroads of school structure, family choices, biology, and medicine.

FURTHER RESOURCES

Books

Richardson, J. *Common, Delinquent, and Special: The institutional Shape of Special Education (Studies in the History of Education)*. London: Routledge Falmer, 1999.

Periodicals

Breggin, Peter M.D. "Psychostimulants in the Treatment of Children Diagnosed with ADHD: Risks and Mechanism of Action." *International Journal of Risk & Safety in Medicine*. 12 (1999): 3–35.

Diller, Lawrence H. "The Run on Ritalin: Attention Deficit Disorder and Stimulant Treatment in the 1990s." *The Hastings Center Report*. 26 (1996).

Web sites

U.S. Department of Education. "Special Education & Rehabilitative Services." <http://www.ed.gov/policy/speced/guid/idea/idea2004.html> (accessed May 28, 2006).

Maximize Self Sufficiency Through Work and Additional Constructive Activities

Press release

By: White House Press Secretary

Date: February 2002

Source: *The White House*. "Maximize Self-Sufficiency Through Work and Additional Constructive Activities." February 2002. <http://www.whitehouse.gov/news/releases/2002/02/welfare-book-04.html> (accessed May 17, 2006).

About the Author: The job of the White House Press Secretary is a challenging and delicate one. This person is a member of the President's executive staff, and ranks just below cabinet secretaries in importance. The press secretary must be extremely discrete, and strives to meet the needs of the media for data concerning matters of national and global interest, while maintaining the informational boundaries required by the president and senior administration staff. It is the job of the White House Press Secretary to manage press briefings and to set the tone for many presidential question-and-answer sessions with the media. Briefings can occur as frequently as several times daily and are generally broadcast on television. There are also frequent "gaggles" with the press, which involve only

In August 1997, a bicyclist in Milwaukee, Wisconsin rides past a sign protesting welfare-to-work reforms. AP IMAGES.

the press secretary and the media, and are generally not broadcast live.

INTRODUCTION

In 1996, the concept of public assistance, or welfare, in the United States changed dramatically with the shift toward work and away from the concept of monthly support stipends. The legislation that created this welfare-to-work policy was entitled the Personal Responsibility and Work Opportunity Reconciliation Act of 1996 (P.L. 104–93), abbreviated as PRWORA. Among its main purposes were to mandate the institution of time limits for public assistance for TANF (Temporary Assistance for Needy Families) recipients, to strongly encourage people to train for meaningful employment, to use gainful employment as a means of transitioning individuals from public assistance to independence, and to place time limits on access to public assistance funds. Overall, the goal was to require that individuals take personal responsibility for acquiring independent means of support, moving away from reliance on public assistance. There is no implication in this legislation that people will be able

to earn salaries sufficient to move them above the poverty level and create complete financial and material independence from government and public assistance programs.

Earlier welfare reform legislation—the Family Support Act and its attendant Job Opportunity and Basic Skills Training Program (the acronym for which was JOBS)—was enacted in 1988. This legislation was deemed by many in the federal government to be too lenient, in that it imposed no maximum time limits for receipt of assistance, and did not mandate participation in job-seeking and job-training activities in many states across the country. It created a number of novel initiatives, such as job development, assistance with job seeking, on the job training, and a system by which low income workers could be given a financial supplement in order to help make ends meet—but failed to impose time limits, to mandate working toward independence, or even to require that recipients pursue employment.

As it is currently constructed, the TANF program imposes significant limits on benefits, in that families can access it as a source of financial assistance for periods not to exceed two years at a time, with a lifetime cap of five years of TANF funding per household. The difficulty with those arbitrary time limits, according to sociological theory, is that people make decisions about major life changes based on a complex system of needs, personal and material resources, ability to fulfill specific goals, and the like. Not all people who receive public assistance are fully or equally employable within two years, or will be able to manage without a public safety net, within the specified time frames.

According to data published in 2000 by the U.S. House of Representatives, the previous welfare programs were criticized for providing long-term support to single mothers living below the poverty level, as they felt that this encouraged the dissolution of traditional models of the nuclear family and encouraged single mothers to have multiple children and to refrain from working outside the home. Among the non-employment related initiatives of the current TANF program is encouraging married, two-parent families, through the Administration for Children and Families' Healthy Marriage Mission.

■ PRIMARY SOURCE

OVERVIEW

Since welfare reform was enacted in 1996, the number of dependent families has been cut in half, and more families than ever are working. Yet evidence suggests that almost 1 million of the 1.6 million adults presently on TANF are not engaged in any activity leading toward self-sufficiency. These families cannot be left behind. The heart of welfare reform is encouraging work and requiring all welfare recipients to do everything they can to end their dependency on welfare and gain a secure foothold in the workforce.

The Administration proposal strengthens work rules to ensure that all welfare families are fully engaged in work and other meaningful activities that will lead to self-sufficiency. Along with new requirements for individuals, states are expected to closely monitor the participation and progress of all TANF families. All parents are to be fully and constructively engaged. States will be required to make certain that, over time, the percentage of TANF recipients engaged in work and additional productive activities continues to grow.

At the same time, the Administration proposal gives states greater flexibility to define activities that will lead toward self-sufficiency and that are consistent with the purposes of TANF. Beyond the hours that parents must be engaged directly in work, states have the flexibility to implement education and training programs to help work-

ers advance in their jobs. Furthermore, states will be able to count individuals who are in treatment for substance abuse or undergoing rehabilitation related to work abilities, toward their participation requirement for a limited period of time.

SUMMARY OF PROPOSALS

Require Welfare Agencies to Engage All Families. The Administration proposes the creation of a new universal engagement requirement. States must engage all families in work and other constructive activities leading to self-sufficiency. TANF agencies will be required to ensure that:

- Within 60 days of opening an ongoing TANF case, each family has an individualized plan for pursuing their maximum degree of self sufficiency;
- All families are participating in constructive activities in accordance with their plan, or in the process of being assessed or assigned to an activity;
- Each family's participation in assigned activities is monitored; and
- Each family's progress toward self sufficiency is monitored and regularly reviewed.

States will have full discretion to define and design appropriate activities, subject to the work requirement outlined below, as well as to develop methods for monitoring and review. The provision in current law related to individual responsibility plans will be eliminated, as will the state-plan requirement that families must begin work no later than two years after coming on assistance.

Increase Minimum Participation Rate Requirements. The Administration proposes that in FY 2003, 50 percent of TANF families with one or more adults must be participating in a combination of work and other activities that lead to self-sufficiency as quickly as possible. The percentage will increase annually by 5 percentage points until it reaches 70 percent in 2007. States will be allowed to count families that have left welfare due to employment as part of their participation rate for up to three months. In contrast, under TANF, the required percentage of families engaged in work-related activities began at 25 percent (in 1997) and rose over time to 50 percent in 2002.

Require Families to Participate 40 Hours a Week. This proposal requires that families be involved in constructive activities averaging 40 hours per week in order to count toward the required participation rate. States will have discretion to define approved activities, which must help achieve a TANF purpose. Similar to current law, states will be able, at their option, to exclude parents with children under 12 months of age from the participation rate calculation. However, states must still require such parents to participate at some level.

TANF requires single and two-parent families to be engaged in work-related activities for 30 and 35 hours a week, respectively. The Administration believes that these families should be engaged in a full workweek of activities. States will continue to have flexibility in establishing sanctioning policies, except that states must, as in current law, continue assistance for single, custodial parents who have a child under age 6 but who cannot obtain childcare.

Increase Work Requirements. This proposal requires that families counted toward participation must also average at least 24 hours per week in work, including:

- unsubsidized employment;
- subsidized private sector employment;
- subsidized public sector employment;
- on-the-job-training;
- supervised work experience; and
- supervised community service.

This 24-hour work requirement is part of the 40-hour full participation requirement. TANF payments to families participating in supervised work experience or supervised community service are not considered compensation for work performed. Thus, these payments do not entitle an individual to a salary or to benefits provided under any other provision of law.

Give Work Credit to Families Engaged in Short-Term Substance Abuse Treatment, Rehabilitation, and Work-Related Training. This proposal allows states to count certain activities as meeting the work requirement for limited periods of time. Individuals participating in substance abuse treatment, rehabilitative services designed to maximize self sufficiency through work, and work-related training enabling the recipient to work, can be deemed to have met the three days a week work requirement. This exception would be available for no more than three consecutive months within any 24 month period.

Improve Calculation of Participation. States will be allowed to count only families that meet both the 24-hour work requirement and the 40-hour full participation requirement toward their participation rate. States will be able to obtain pro-rata credit for families engaged in appropriate activities less than full time as long as they meet their 24-hour direct work requirement. States will have the option of not counting cases for the purpose of determining participation rates for the first month after a case is opened.

Eliminate Separate Two-Parent Family Participation Rates. The Administration's proposal will end the separate participation rate for two-parent families; the same participation rate will apply to both single-and two-parent families. This policy removes a disincentive to equitable treatment of two-parent families. Under current law, two-parent families have a far more rigorous work participation rate requirement than do single-parent families (90 percent compared to 50 percent).

Phase Out the Caseload Reduction Credit. The Administration's proposal will phase out the current credit for caseload reduction because it reduces states' minimum required work participation rates. Currently, states receive credit toward meeting participation rates for caseload declines since 1995. With national caseloads declining by more than half, many states effectively have no work participation standards. In FY 2003 the full caseload reduction credit will apply as under current law; in FY 2004 the credit will be halved; beginning in FY 2005, the credit will be eliminated. During this phase-out period the credit will be based on reductions since 1995, as in current law.

Conform Requirements for Teenage Parents. The Administration proposal will conform current law provisions regarding teenage parents who are heads of household. Teen parents who maintain satisfactory school attendance will satisfy both the 24 hours of direct work and the 40 hours of full participation requirements. Teen parents who are not satisfactorily attending school will have to meet the work and full participation standards in order to be counted toward a state's participation rate.

Provide Technical Assistance for Tribes. The Administration proposes to provide technical assistance to Indian tribes to identify and disseminate promising program models and other research information. This approach will help tribes design and implement more effective TANF programs and family formation activities in tribal lands.

Discontinue Outdated State Program Waivers. The Administration proposes to discontinue the few remaining state welfare reform waivers granted prior to the 1996 welfare reform legislation. Flexibility under current law allows states to accomplish all the purposes of TANF without waivers. Furthermore, the requirements of TANF no longer represent an experiment. Abolishing the remaining waivers will put all states on an equal footing. Broad new state waiver authority for integrating programs is proposed in a separate section of this document.

Conform State Penalty Provision to New Requirement. The penalty structure under current law for states failing to meet work participation rates will now apply when a state fails to meet either or both the universal engagement or full participation rate requirements. Penalties will still be limited to a combined maximum of five percent of a state's TANF grant for a fiscal year.

Retain Five-Year Time Limits and Continue Allowing 20 Percent to be Exempted. The Administration's proposal will retain current law provisions with respect to time limits. These provisions restrict families to 60 cumulative months of Federally-funded assistance (or less at state option). States may exempt up to 20 percent of their caseload from the time limit without penalty. These provisions make it clear that TANF assistance is temporary. At the same time, the policy recognizes that certain hardship cases require more time to achieve self-sufficiency.

SIGNIFICANCE

Among the criticisms leveled at the current TANF and time-limited public assistance policies is that they do not consider individual differences in job skills, employability, and ability to transition to full-time work and achievement of economic sufficiency within the allotted timeframes. Another is that the system does not consider whether the amount of income available to be earned by many TANF recipients upon transition from public assistance is sufficient to meet basic needs, to provide for childcare, or even to acquire the job skills and training that might permit them to achieve a higher degree of employability, or to command better salaries.

Those in support of the revised public assistance programs point out the dramatic reduction in the number of people on the rolls for TANF at any given time today when contrasted with data from a decade ago. However, that data must also be examined in terms of the number of people living above and below the poverty level.

Information published by the federal government suggests that between fifty and sixty-five percent of those who leave TANF have jobs at the time or are soon able to obtain gainful employment, and that those rates hold steady for at least a year following departure from public assistance. Although outcome-based research suggests that the wages earned by those who are employed after receiving public assistance continue to gradually rise, many still live below their state's poverty level. A study that was published by the Urban Institute in 2001 indicated that more than forty percent of former TANF recipients still lived in poverty despite being employed, when the actual cash value of food stamps, the Earned Income Tax Credit, and all required payroll deductions (to include local, state, and federal taxes) were subtracted from earned income. Another widely reported conclusion of the welfare-to-work research has been that those who had few job skills and unstable work histories before receiving public assistance are unlikely to improve significantly in those areas as a result of receiving financial help. Poorly educated (those with less than a completed high school education) or poorly skilled individuals are unlikely to advance steadily in pay, even when they are able to maintain steady employment. As the job market continues to become more technologically demanding, more and more jobs require significant post-secondary, vocational, or technical training. Government data suggest that the preponderance of those who receive TANF and are poorly educated or skilled are not readily employable in the current job market. In fact, among those who were in that category, nearly one-third were earning less money five years after leaving public assistance than they did immediately after they left the rolls. Overall, among single women who were poorly educated and lacking in essential skills for the present job market, more than forty percent still lived in poverty five years after leaving public assistance.

Data comparing those who left AFDC (Aid to Families with Dependent Children) and those who left TANF is highly suggestive that those who left public assistance voluntarily (from the AFDC population) tended to do so after completion of work-related training, acquisition of advanced education, or changes in life circumstances that made it possible to return to work. Those who were required to leave the TANF rolls often did so without having completed any education or training that would increase employability, so they were significantly less likely to improve their circumstances. Overall, the published research data indicate that while TANF is quite successful at moving people away from public assistance within the specified time limits, it is considerably less effective in helping them to rise above the poverty level, or to acquire the skills and abilities that might improve their chances of economic advancement.

FURTHER RESOURCES
Books

Burke, V. *Welfare Reform: TANF Trends and Data.* Washington, D.C.: Congressional Research Service, 2000.

Burke, V. *Welfare Reform: Work Activities and Sanctions in State TANF Programs.* Washington, D.C.: Congressional Research Service, 2000.

Hansan, John E., and Robert Morris, eds. *Welfare Reform, 1996–2000: Is There A Safety Net?.* Westport, Conn.: Auburn House, 1999.

Loprest, P. *How Are Families That Left Welfare Doing? A Comparison of Early and Recent Welfare Leavers.* Washington, D.C.: Urban Institute, 2001.

Rodgers, Harrell R., Jr. *American Poverty in a New Era of Reform.* Armonk, N.Y.: M. E. Sharpe, 2000.

Stein, Theodore J. *Social Policy and Policy Making by the Branches of Government and the Public-At-Large*. New York, N.Y.: Columbia University Press, 2001.

Telleen, Sharon, and Judith V. Sayad, eds. *The Transition from Welfare to Work: Processes, Challenges, and Outcomes*. New York, N.Y.: Hayworth Press, 2002.

Welfare Reform: State Sanction Policies and Number of Families Affected. Washington, D.C.: U.S. General Accounting Office, 2000.

Welfare Reform: States Provide TANF-funded Work Support Services to Many Low-income Families Who Do Not Receive Cash Assistance. Washington, D.C.: U.S. General Accounting Office, 2002.

Periodicals

Anderson, S. G., and B. M. Gryzlak. "Social Work Advocacy in the Post-TANF Environment: Lessons From Early TANF Research Studies." *Social Work* 47 (2002): 301–314.

Burn, Timothy. "Welfare-to-Work Forum Touts Successes, Hurdles." *Washington Times* (November 19, 1998): 7.

Cancian, M., and D. R. Meyer. "Work After Welfare: Women's Work Effort, Occupation, and Economic Well-being." *Social Work Research* 24 (2000): 69–96.

Wetzstein, Cheryl. "Welfare-to-Work Experiment Benefits Children, Study Finds: Milwaukee Youths Improved in School Social Behavior." *Washington Times* (June 10, 2003): A08.

Wetzstein, Cheryl. "Welfare-to-Work Gains Strong, Two Studies Find." *Washington Times* (August 3, 2000): 3.

Web sites

Administration for Children and Families. "ACF Healthy Marriage Mission." <http://www.acf.hhs.gov/healthy marriage/about/mission.html> (accessed May 17, 2006).

Food Stamps Program

Photograph

By: Tim Boyle

Date: June 24, 2004

Source: Photo by Tim Boyle/Getty Images.

About the Photographer: Tim Boyle is a photographer with Getty Images, a Seattle-based creator and distributor of a wide variety of image collections.

INTRODUCTION

The Federal Food Stamp Program is considered by many as one of the most significant, government-assisted food-relief programs in the United States. Under this program, impoverished individuals can obtain free food stamps from the government that can then be used to buy food at authorized stores. Those who have low-paying jobs, are unemployed, work part-time, receive public assistance, or are elderly, disabled, or homeless may be eligible for food stamps. The federal government pays for the amount of the benefit received, while states pay the costs of determining eligibility and distributing the stamps.

The amount of food-stamp benefits that an eligible household can receive depends mainly on the number of people in the household and its monthly income (after deduction of certain expenses). The Food Stamp Program, administered by the U.S. Department of Agriculture, was first implemented in the late 1930s. As many as twenty million people, located in nearly half the counties in the United States, were covered by the first Food Stamp Program (1939–1943).

Although the first program was deemed successful, the second Food Stamp Program was not implemented until eighteen years later, in 1961. After a number of proposals, President John F. Kennedy (1917–1963) initiated the Food Stamp Pilot Program on February 2, 1961. Before the program ended in 1964, it had assisted 380,000 participants from twenty-two states. Soon after, President Lyndon B. Johnson (1908–1973) proposed to make this program permanent. Subsequently, with the aim of providing improved levels of nutrition to low-income households, the U.S. Congress passed the Food Stamp Act on August 31, 1964.

During the early 1970s, participation in the Food Stamp Program (FSP) increased rapidly, increasing from half a million participants in 1965 to fifteen million in 1974. With the increases in participation came an increase in the cost of administering the program. Lawmakers proposed changes to the program to reduce costs and to improve the administration and the accountability of the program.

While rising costs led to several curbs in the Food Stamp Program in the early 1980s, a number of factors combined to further increase expenditures during that decade. The United States faced a severe hunger problem between 1985 and 1990. As a result, additional provisions were incorporated into the Food Stamp Program, including the abolition of sales tax for items purchased with food stamps, an increased resource limit, and eligibility for the homeless.

Electronic Food Stamp "Debit" Cards Replace Paper Coupons: Displayed are older, traditional food stamps from the Illinois Department of Human Services in Skokie, Illinois. On June 24, 2004, Agriculture Secretary Ann M. Veneman announced that all fifty states and the U.S. territories would now provide Food Stamp Program benefits with EBT (electronic benefits transfer) cards instead of these traditional paper coupons. PHOTO BY TIM BOYLE/GETTY IMAGES.

According to the U.S. Department of Agriculture (USDA), the increase in benefits cost the government 2.8 billion dollars.

Up until the early 2000s, the Food Stamp Program issued paper stamps. Transactions with such stamps, however, were extremely cumbersome and time-consuming, and the accounting procedures were also quite complex. Consequently, beginning in the mid–1980s, the USDA began a series of demonstrations to test the technical feasibility, cost, and acceptability of a new method of issuing and redeeming benefits. This method, known as Electronic Benefit Transfer (EBT), aims to simplify food-stamp processes by automating them. The Personal Responsibility and Work Opportunities Reconciliation Act of 1996 (PRWORA) mandated that all states convert paper food stamps to EBT cards by 2002. Similar to a bank debit card, the EBT card tracks the total value of food benefits that can be used. Food purchases from authorized stores can be made by simply swiping the card at the checkout counter.

PRIMARY SOURCE

ELECTRONIC FOOD STAMP "DEBIT" CARDS REPLACE PAPER COUPONS

See primary source image.

SIGNIFICANCE

In the decades since the Food Stamp Program was made permanent in 1964, the number of participants has generally increased, especially after the program was implemented in most states. Participation figures generally fluctuate based on the health of the national economy. For instance, participation increased significantly in the early 1990s, when the United States

A large number of people line up outside of a food stamp distribution office in Minneapolis in April, 1940. © MINNESOTA HISTORICAL SOCIETY/CORBIS.

experienced a mild recession, while the period of economic growth from 1994 to 1999 was marked by a decline in participation.

One of the key aims of the Food Stamp Program is to promote nutritional value and healthy eating habits in low-income households. According to the USDA's Office of Analysis, Nutrition, and Evaluation, more than one hundred research studies evaluating the program's impact on diet quality have been conducted. Although many of these studies conclude that the Food Stamp Program leads participants to increase their expenditure on food, there is no conclusive evidence suggesting that the program has improved diet quality. Nevertheless, it is widely accepted that the program is successful.

Throughout the history of the Food Stamp Program, various concerns have included rising costs to the USDA, weak accountability, complex and time-consuming procedures, and cases of fraud. Accountability and cost issues were resolved to an extent through legislative changes, and the EBT cards have simplified procedures and reduced fraud, making them cost-effective for the USDA.

Paper coupons could easily be misused or sold to other people. The EBT system creates an electronic log for each food stamp transaction, making it easier to identify and document instances of food stamp "trafficking." In the past, food stamps were sometimes sold as a form of currency, with proceeds used to buy narcotics and other illegal substances. EBT card holders are less likely to trade their card with others, as the card has access to the entire month's benefits. In addition, a Personal Identification Number (PIN) is required to use the card. Surveys conducted by the USDA indicate that most participants prefer the EBT card to paper stamps. Reportedly, these cards enhance security and convenience for users. They also simplify accounting procedures and reduce labor costs for retailers.

The Implementation of EBT and expanded eligibility standards since the early 2000s resulted in increased participation in the Food Stamp Program. Thirty-seven million individuals were eligible for benefits in 2003. Of these, 56 percent (approximately twenty-one million) participated in the program—higher participation compared to previous years.

Since the EBT system was implemented in all states in 2004, there have been further technological advancements. A pilot phase of "Tier II EBT", also known as Electronic Services Delivery (ESD), has been initiated. The Tier II system includes automating the distribution of a variety of non-economic,

public health, and education-related benefits. These benefits include Temporary Assistance to Needy Families (TANF), child-care assistance, child support payments, and integration of the Women, Infants, and Children (WIC) program. WIC provides food relief to pregnant women and infants.

FURTHER RESOURCES

Books

Ohls, James C. and Harold Beebout. *The Food Stamp Program: Design Tradeoffs, Policy, and Impacts.* Lanham, Md.: University Press of America, 1993.

Web sites

Federal Reserve Bank of Philadelphia. "Assessing the Impact of Electronic Benefits Transfer." September 21, 2004 <http://www.philadelphiafed.org/pcc/conferences/agenda1204.pdf> (accessed May 18, 2006).

Food & Nutrition Service, USDA. "Design Options for Assessing the Food Security and Diet Quality Impacts of FNS Program Participation." December 2005 <http://www.fns.usda.gov/oane/MENU/Published/FSP/FILES/Other/DietQualitySummary.pdf> (accessed May 18, 2006).

Food & Nutrition Service, USDA. "Explaining Changes in Food Stamp Program Participation Rates." September 2004 <http://www.fns.usda.gov/oane/MENU/Published/FSP/FILES/Participation/TrendsSum99-02.pdf> (accessed May 18, 2006).

Food & Nutrition Service, USDA. "Food Stamp Program Participation Rates: 2003 Summary." July 2005 <http://www.fns.usda.gov/oane/MENU/Published/FSP/FILES/Participation/FSPPart2003-Summary.pdf> (accessed May 18, 2006).

Food Research and Action Center. "Federal Food Programs." September 7, 2001 <http://www.frac.org/html/federal_food_programs/programs/fsp_faq.html> (accessed May 18, 2006).

United States General Accounting Office. "Food Stamp Program." January 2002 <http://www.gao.gov/new.items/d02332.pdf> (accessed May 18, 2006).

Race, Class, and Real Estate

What We'll Get from Mixing It Up

Newspaper article

By: Sheryll D. Cashin

Date: August 1, 2004

Source: Cashin, Sheryll D. "Race, Class, and Real Estate: What We'll Get from Mixing It Up." *Washington Post.* (August 1, 2004): B02.

About the Author: Sheryll D. Cashin is an attorney and professor of law at Georgetown University in Washington, DC. She is also an author whose subjects of interest are inequality (especially racial inequality) in the United States, race relations, and government. In addition to the book from which this piece is excerpted, Ms. Cashin has been widely published in both academic and scholarly journals and newspapers. She advised former president Bill Clinton on urban and economic policy. In addition to her graduate degree in law, she has an undergraduate degree in electrical engineering.

INTRODUCTION

Prior to the civil rights movement and subsequent legislation in the middle and latter portions of the twentieth century, racial segregation, particularly in housing, was both institutionalized and widely accepted in America. Immediate neighborhoods were almost exclusively white or black, with a smattering of other minority group members drifting into one enclave or the other, depending on how likely they were to be accepted as white. While there is still considerable racial, ethnic, and socioeconomic division in many contemporary U.S. housing markets, institutional barriers to integrated neighborhoods have decreased with the passage of fair housing and civil rights legislation.

Between the end of the Civil War and the start of the twentieth century, there was substantial integration in housing, largely due to former slaves settling in (primarily) rural and frontier areas that were either familiar or immediately accessible to them. As the United States became more industrialized, especially after World Wars I and II, African Americans began to move to larger urban areas in search of better jobs and higher pay. Public housing initiatives encouraged low-income individuals to dwell in inner cities, as that is where government-assisted housing projects were largely concentrated.

As manufacturers and other employers moved outside the cities as the result of tax incentives and more affordable real estate, suburban areas developed that drew specialized professionals with them. This, in effect, created a large-scale socioeconomic and often racial divide in many of the more densely populated areas of the country. Economic and racial segregation was reinforced by zoning laws and area covenants, which intentionally divided neighborhoods and hous-

A suburban subdivision in Corona, California, 2002.
AP/WIDE WORLD PHOTOS. REPRODUCED BY PERMISSION.

ing areas by race. This was reinforced by county, city, state, and national policies. Private bank programs designed to encourage homeownership and aid home buyers with financing fostered segregation; banks often refused to aid individuals wishing to purchase homes in districts banks considered troubled or high-risk. Individuals wishing to buy homes in predominantly African American, Hispanic, low-income, or recent immigrant populations were often denied loans or mortgages.

Segregation in housing, per the authors of *American Apartheid,* is pivotal in grasping the relative socioeconomic disparities. Essentially, they stated that the concentration of African Americans in inner cities and urban ghettoes, where there is limited opportunity to obtain high paying jobs, a quality education, and safe housing, leads to a cyclical pattern in which people find it difficult to acquire the skills, training, and financial means to move away from the depressed areas.

PRIMARY SOURCE

After writing a book about the limits of race and class integration in America, I recently had the odd experience of being labeled a "fervent" champion of integration by one reviewer (David Garrow, writing for the *Chicago Tribune*) and an "ambivalent integrationist" suffering from "integration exhaustion" by another (Samuel Freedman, writing for the *New York Times Book Review*). How could two reviewers of the same book come to such diametrically opposed conclusions? I suspect perceptions of my ambivalence stem from my brutal honesty about the challenges at hand, and my view of integration as a means to an end, rather than an end in itself.

Like most African Americans, I am most ardent about equality of opportunity, not integration per se. But after several years of exhaustive research about the costs and consequences of segregation—particularly in urban and suburban neighborhoods—I came to the conclusion that it is impossible to afford broad, let alone equal, opportunity in a system where race and class separation is the accepted norm. I decided to have the courage of my convictions and make the case in my book that we can't complete the civil rights revolution without making the integrationist values of that movement a real part of people's daily lives.

No doubt this is hard work. Most Americans are both integrationists and separatists to some degree. To the extent that we do experience race and class diversity on an everyday basis, it is usually in public spaces or the workplace. Most of us return to largely homogenous neighborhoods at the end of the day. We may accept, even desire, racially and economically integrated workplaces and public spheres. But when it comes to our private lives, more visceral needs of personal comfort or security seem to take precedence—especially for families with children.

Discussions about race and class in America are more commonplace than ever, from Sen. John Edwards's signature speech about "two Americas" to Illinois Senate candidate Barack Obama's ringing pronouncement at last week's Democratic National Convention that "there's not a black America and white America and Latino America and Asian America, there's the United States of America." Obama was speaking, of course, about America the ideal; in my research, I found the neighborhoods of America are still far too segregated to call them united.

My own first foray into homeownership is telling. When I was deciding where to buy a house in the early 1990s, I chose Shepherd Park, an integrated, albeit majority-black, upper-middle-class neighborhood in Northwest Washington, east of Rock Creek Park. As a black woman with a strong racial identity, I found the over-

whelmingly white neighborhoods west of the park inherently unattractive. I wanted to be among more than just a smattering of black people. Still, my ideal was an integrated environment, and Shepherd Park was one of the few neighborhoods in the District where both blacks and whites had lived for decades.

I had no illusions about achieving *economic* integration. As a renter I had lived in the Hillcrest area of Ward 8, the District's poorest ward, and in rapidly gentrifying LeDroit Park near Howard University. But in deciding where to buy, I found that the bourgeois, leafy streets of the "Gold Coast" felt safer and more familiar, closer to my roots as a southerner who had grown up in middle-class neighborhoods of detached houses and big lawns.

My thought process in buying a home was not that different from those of most Americans who have choices. I was willing, even eager, to live in a diverse environment as long as people of my own race were well represented. I was not willing to buy in a neighborhood that might be overwhelmed by poverty—because I feared crime and wanted to protect my investment. But the real estate markets offered me precious few alternatives to racial and economic separation.

The only difference between my thinking and that of homebuyers of other races may be their distaste for predominantly black neighborhoods. In research surveys, all non-black groups consistently display a pronounced antipathy toward integrating with sizable numbers of black people. In the 1990s, rates of residential integration increased impressively in metropolitan areas such as Portland, Ore., and Salt Lake City, where the black population is small. Residential integration also seems to fare better in neighborhoods where a third group, typically Latinos, has been introduced into the historically tortured black–white dynamic of American race relations. Yet something mystical seems to happen when the black population reaches a threshold of about 20 percent of a metropolitan area. In those large urban areas, where the majority of blacks still live, racial segregation patterns remain stark and stubborn, especially in the Midwest and Northeast. America still has a "Negro problem," even as it flocks to summer movie blockbusters featuring African Americans such as Will Smith and Halle Berry as action heroes.

Realistically, when searching for a neighborhood to live in, most black people generally have one of two choices: an almost all-black neighborhood or one where blacks are few. It is hardly surprising that many blacks consider an overwhelmingly black neighborhood more attractive than an overwhelmingly white one; they are frustrated by the failed promises of integration and weary of racial hostility. Consequently, many African Americans seem to have adopted a "post-integrationist" mindset, and now most value living among themselves, even as they exhibit a high tolerance for living among other groups. Constantly carrying the assimilator's burden at work can be offset nicely by the spirit-reviving effect of living in a neighborhood that engenders a happy "we" feeling. Black people seem to want the benefits of integrated workplaces and markets not so they can assimilate into white realms, but to gain economic advancement.

Most whites are no less ambivalent about residential integration. They are simply not free to express their doubts. The risk of being labeled a racist is too great. In my numerous dialogues with predominantly white audiences, I have encountered a range of attitudes: from the rare, ardent integrationist who believes I should be exhorting whites to put an end to residential segregation, to the guilt-ridden commentary about how integrated neighborhoods don't offer quality schools, to a seemingly resigned acceptance of the fact of our separation, to … silence.

I take heart in those individuals who go against our collective, separatist grain. We have a lot to learn from them. A woman I know who lives in Brookland, in Northeast Washington, near Catholic University, is someone I would call a committed integrator. She and her husband, both white, have ensconced their brood of five children in a heavily black area that has an average income of about $41,000. She says she has "found the quality" and the "things that work" in D.C. public schools, including a public Montessori school and an arts magnet school, and is pleased with the results.

It is not lost on me that she can afford to work part-time and devote so much energy to her children's lives precisely because her family has chosen to live in a neighborhood with housing prices that are a fraction of those in majority-white bastions. "I don't want to protect my kids from the world," she says. Lamenting the private school prestige chase that pervades upper-income Washington, she argues that instead of giving kids an "artificial perfection" and an "over-elevated success standard," parents should be giving their kids the tools to negotiate the real world.

Another parent, a well-educated black professional, tells me that she feels she has no choice but to be "ruthless" in seeking out the best possible educational opportunities she can afford for her daughter. That means she may be taking her child out of a neighborhood elementary school that she claims has been attracting too many out-of-boundary poor kids, and placing her in a less diverse but also less impoverished private school.

While many of us may harbor separatist inclinations, our racially and economically segregated real estate markets are not inherently natural. They are the result of a host of intentional public and private interventions that created homogeneity even where the existing tendency was toward race or class inclusion. Beginning in the 1930s, the Federal Housing Administration, which underwrote one-third of all mortgages in its first three decades, instructed all private lenders who offered FHA-backed loans that it was "necessary that properties continue to be occupied by the same social and racial classes." Our neighborhoods still suffer from the consequences of that form of segregation.

Current interventions also steer us apart. From local zoning codes that prevent mixed-income or affordable housing, to private marketing data bases that skew public funding and private development toward affluent, heavily white neighborhoods, to still-pervasive racial steering of black and Latino home buyers to "appropriate" areas, our public and private institutional policy choices result in communities of great abundance and communities of great need.

This separatist system comes with palpable costs, especially for black and Latino schoolchildren who, on average, attend majority–minority, heavily poor schools with many fewer advantages than the majority-white, middle-class schools that most white students attend. But whites also bear the costs of American separatism. In a society that sets up "winner" and "loser" communities and schools based upon race and class, everyone has to work harder to get in the "winner" column. Many whites struggle to afford homes in neighborhoods with schools they consider acceptable or struggle with long commutes and a withering quality of life.

With different policy choices, such as inclusionary zoning that requires a diverse housing mix, we could cultivate more stable, economically and racially mixed neighborhoods and schools that offer more choices and more opportunity for everyone. In a more inclusive society, the willing, privileged integrationist would be able to live in a diverse society without fear and confidently participate in its public institutions, especially schools. The marginalized and excluded, especially the black poor, would have more access to the levers of upward mobility.

So yes, I am a champion of a transformative integration of the races and classes because I have become convinced that it is the only route to closing the egregious gaps of inequality that weaken our nation. I can acknowledge the benefits of a minority enclave and still hope to see the day when there will be less need for such a psychic haven. I dare to believe that America could be a society premised upon brotherly love and inclusion, rather than fear and exclusion.

SIGNIFICANCE

In the early decades of the Federal Housing Administration's (FHA) operation, it continued the practice of redlining, classifying urban neighborhoods by relative risk category, and then awarding home purchase loans in relation to degree of risk. People seeking to build or purchase homes in areas furthest from an identified ghetto were most likely to successfully secure funding; the closer the home location to the inner city, the less likely the mortgage was to be approved.

The FHA financed approximately 60 percent of all homes sold in the United States during the 1930s and 1940s, granting loans almost exclusively to white people seeking to move into middle-class white neighborhoods and helping to institutionalize racial segregation in the American housing market. Only about 2 percent of all loans went to people of color. The 1968 Fair Housing Act prohibited discrimination based on race, ethnicity, national origin, sex, and other criteria. The act intended to end the practice of redlining.

According to census data, residential racial segregation persists throughout America: whites still live in predominantly white areas (80 percent white neighborhoods), and African Americans continue to reside in primarily black areas (60 percent or more black). There remains significant debate regarding causality. Some theoreticians posit that people simply wish to live near others who resemble them on many dimensions, suggesting that racially segregated neighborhoods occur strictly by the result of free choice. Others assert that racial and ethnic divisions in neighborhoods are subsets of larger socioeconomic divisions. Still other theorists (such as Massey, Denton, and Kushner) argue that housing segregation stems from intentional social policies and practices that afford greater opportunities and choices to whites than to African Americans.

FURTHER RESOURCES

Books

Babcock, Richard F. *The Zoning Game: Municipal Practices and Policies*. Madison, Wisc.: University of Wisconsin Press, 1966.

Bocian, Debbie Gruenstein, Keith S. Ernst, and Wei Li. *Unfair Lending: the Effect of Race and Ethnicity on the Price of Subprime Mortgages*. Washington, D.C.: Center for Responsible Lending, 2006.

Cashin, Sheryll D. *The Failures of Integration: How Race and Class are Undermining the American Dream*. New York: Public Affairs, 2004.

Conley, Dalton. *Being Black, Living in the Red Race, Wealth, and Social Policy*. Berkeley, Calif.: University of California Press, 1999.

Fader, Steven. *Density by Design: New Directions in Residential Development*. Washington, D.C.: Urban Land Institute, 2000.

Hartman, Chester, ed. *America's Housing Crisis: What's to Be Done?*. Boston, Mass.: Routledge and Kegan Paul, 1983.

Kushner, James A. *Apartheid in America*. New York: Associated Faculty Press, 1982.

Massey, Douglas S. and Nancy A. Denton *American Apartheid: Segregation and the Making of the Underclass*. Cambridge, Mass.: Harvard University Press, 1998.

Smelser, Neil J., ed., William Julius Wilson, ed., and Faith Mitchell, ed. *American Becoming: Racial Trends and their Consequences, Volume I*. Washington, D.C.: National Academy Press, 2001.

Periodicals

Eig, Jonathan. "Mixed Results: How Fear of Integration Turned White Enclave into a Melting Pot." *The Wall Street Journal*. (August 7, 2000): A1.

Galster, George C. "Housing Discrimination and Urban Poverty of African-Americans." *Journal of Housing Research*. 2(2) (1991): 87–124.

Web sites

Georgetown Law Faculty. "Sheryll D. Cashin, Professor of Law." January 8, 2004 (updated). <http://www.law.georgetown.edu/curriculum/> (accessed May 18, 2006).

Once Woeful, Alabama Is Model in Child Welfare

Newspaper article

By: Erik Eckholm

Date: August 20, 2005

Source: Eckholm, Erik. "Once Woeful, Alabama Is Model in Child Welfare." *New York Times*. (June 16, 2005): A1.

About the Author: Erik Eckholm has been both a reporter and editor with the *New York Times* since 1985, including five years as the Beijing bureau chief. Eckholm holds an MA in international affairs from the Johns Hopkins School of Advanced International Studies in Washington, D.C.

INTRODUCTION

The Family Services Partnership of the Alabama Department of Human Resources (DHR) uses sixty-seven local agencies to carry out the state's child welfare programs—protecting children from neglect and abuse. Intervention may include providing social services to families struggling to pay bills or helping a family find daycare for children while a parent is at work. In other cases, parents and other caregivers are required to attend support meetings or other service programs aimed at building proper disciplinary techniques and other parenting skills. If neglect and abuse is ongoing or an imminent threat, children are removed from the home and placed in state-supervised care.

In 1988, a federal lawsuit was filed against Alabama's DHR on behalf of a child diagnosed with attention deficit hyperactivity disorder who was living in foster care. The claim stated that the child, identified by the initials R.C., was not given the proper medical treatment while in foster care. The case was settled with the R.C. Consent Decree, which required the state system offer individualized services based on family strengths and increase efforts to keep families together. Specifically, DHR was to develop a system that focused on preventing foster care placement through early intervention, the reunification of families, and the involvement of children and parents in planning the services administered. An improved system of quality assurance, training, and rights protection was also required. The deadline to meet the decree's goals was originally set for 1999, but was later pushed back to 2002 to give Alabama more time to locate the necessary funding to train and hire staff members.

Funding for Alabama's child welfare initiatives have come from several state and federal funds, including the Children's Trust Fund administered by the the Alabama Department of Child Abuse and Neglect Prevention. In 1998, a new source of funding, the Children First Trust Fund was established with money from tobacco company settlements. Most of Alabama's portion of the multibillion dollar settlement has gone into the Children First Trust Fund.

■ PRIMARY SOURCE

Once Woeful, Alabama Is Model in Child Welfare

Erik Eckholm

MONTGOMERY, Ala. As a mother, Stephanie Harris seemed hopeless. She was 29 and a determined crack addict back in 1993, when she was sent to prison for neglecting her six children, including infant twins. The authorities had little choice, she now agrees, but to give custody of her children to relatives.

"It didn't bother me," she recalled in a recent interview. "All I wanted to do was get high."

She served eight months, failed a urine test, and went back to prison for a year. If history were the guide, in Alabama or perhaps any other state, Ms. Harris might never have regained her children, child welfare officials here say. More likely, the children would have been shuffled among relatives and foster homes.

But officials here had, under court supervision, begun a wholesale overhaul of the child protection system to make it more pro-family, and they did not give up on Ms. Harris. Today she is off drugs, has a job and has custody of all but one of her children, whom an aunt is fighting to keep. Her case illustrates what experts in child welfare say has been one of the country's most sweeping transformations of the handling of neglected and abused children. What by all accounts had been a dysfunctional system in Alabama, scarring too many children by sending them to foster-care oblivion while ignoring others in danger, has over the last 14 years become a widely studied model. But it has not been cheap, and in some ways Alabama has had to be dragged onto its pedestal because of political and philosophical resistance to the reforms and in spite of the state's endemic poverty.

"Alabama set the pace," said Richard Wexler, director of the National Coalition for Child Protection Reform, a private group in Alexandria, Va. "Though they've had some setbacks, I still view Alabama as a national model."

Forced by a legal settlement to make changes after parents and advocates filed a class-action lawsuit charging that the system failed to aid troubled families or protect children from neglect or abuse, Alabama has more than quadrupled its spending on child welfare since 1990, even as it has trimmed other programs in recent years.

One former governor, Fob James, complained about federal interference and questioned whether so much devotion to helping irresponsible parents was leaving children in harm's way. While Mr. James's successors have accepted the changes, they still resent being monitored; in a court brief this month, Attorney General Troy King said that the continuing court supervision defied the principle of "democratic self-rule through officials answerable to the people."

While Alabama's system is far from perfect, local officials and independent experts say, the system now is more likely than before to keep children with their parents, safely, and tries to provide whatever aid might help that happen.

Typical caseloads for social workers have been trimmed to 18 from 50, allowing far more intensive monitoring of families and help. Where reports of neglect or abuse sometimes lay unchecked for months, investigators are now usually on the scene within a day when danger is imminent, and within five days more than 90% of the time, officials report.

In what many call the best measure of a system's ability to protect children from abuse—the share of children who are mistreated after intervention by social workers—Alabama has steadily improved its record. In recent years, a second abuse incident within 12 months of the first one occurred in roughly 5% of cases, down from about 13% in the early 1990's. Studies indicate that the comparable national average is about 11%.

And in a recent federal survey of child welfare systems, Alabama was one of only six states found to be "substantially in compliance" with norms for protecting children from neglect or abuse.

"When the lawsuit was filed, we didn't have the services that could keep children at home safely," said Carolyn B. Lapsley, the state's deputy commissioner for children and family services and a veteran social worker. "Now we're very proud; we have changed the system in every single county."

Though Alabama says it has made enough progress that it should be released from court supervision, skeptics question whether the new, labor-intensive practices can be maintained in the face of stringent budgets, high poverty and other social ills, including methamphetamine use, which state officials blame for a recent rise in the number of children removed from homes.

"We do not dispute that the agency has made progress," said James Tucker, a children's advocate and a lawyer in the suit that produced court monitoring.

"However, we believe that their recent efforts have focused more on creating a paper trail that looks like reform than producing the real reforms we seek," Mr. Tucker said, adding that some counties were lagging substantially, for example, in provision of vital family services.

Judge Ira DeMent of Federal District Court in Montgomery ruled in May that the state had not proved it could sustain its gains and declined to end the oversight for now. The state has asked him to reconsider.

When the class-action suit was filed, in 1988, "those who looked at the Alabama system invariably judged it as one of the worst in the country," Mr. Tucker said.

The 1991 settlement committed the state to a series of principles: quick investigations to head off danger, family preservation if possible, wide-ranging services for struggling parents and faster adoption for those requiring it, among others.

Ira Burnim, a lawyer with the Bazelon Center for Mental Health Law in Washington who helped draw up the agreement, said parents were often seen more as threats than as potential partners. And, Mr. Burnim said, "there's a traditional tendency to focus on 'saving' the children but also to see them as damaged goods."

Child-welfare spending that totaled $71 million in 1990, including $47 million in federal money, rose to $285 million in 2004, $179 million of it from the federal government. Some of that came from Medicaid money the state had not previously tapped.

The state hired hundreds of new social workers and thinned caseloads. Workers could now spend more than 10 hours a week in some homes.

Cindy Letson, who lives in the small town of Moulton in the corn and poultry country of northern Alabama, has seen firsthand how the system works.

Her face weathered beyond her 48 years, Ms. Letson described a history of family violence and recalled the day in 2001 when the police took her for psychiatric evaluation.

She returned home within a day cleared of any serious disorder, she said, but was sent for counseling and help in breaking an addiction to antiseizure drugs. Her twin boys had already been removed and were sent to foster parents.

She followed the directives and was allowed to visit her boys for one hour a week. After repeated entreaties she regained custody two years ago, and now lives on welfare with her 7-year-old boys, Kyle and Kenley.

"I was ready to give up, but in the end the system worked," Ms. Letson said.

Elements of Alabama's approach have been adopted by other states. "A lot of the ideas we used came from the Alabama example," said Benjamin Wolf of the Illinois ACLU, who has helped design changes to the system in Illinois, which is also operating under court supervision.

Alabama's method of evaluating its own system—choosing individual cases and closely examining how each was handled—has been adopted by the federal government for its assessment of child-welfare systems in each state, said Olivia A. Golden, a former federal welfare official now with the Urban Institute in Washington. New York City has also adopted the method.

But here, as in every state, there remain lapses. [On Wednesday, a state judge criticized the Jefferson County Department of Human Resources for failing to protect 2-year-old Sean Porter, who suffered severe bruising to his groin last December, two weeks after school officials reported suspicious bruises on his sister, The *Birmingham News* reported.]

In a report last November, Ivor D. Groves, a welfare expert from Florida who is Alabama's court-appointed monitor, said the state's progress toward the original reform goals had varied by county.

But without question, Mr. Groves said, "the egregious conditions of impossible caseloads and large numbers of uninvestigated" abuse and neglect reports "have been eliminated."

Some Alabama counties show "the best child-welfare practice in the country," Mr. Groves wrote.

Ms. Harris, in Montgomery, has been a beneficiary of Alabama's progress. As she emerged from work-release and a third drug-treatment program in 1995, she showed that she was serious about going straight. So caseworkers, while requiring regular drug tests, helped Ms. Harris rebuild her life and then regain her children.

They paid for years of counseling and helped with expenses like child care, utility bills and, at one point, Christmas presents and shoes for the children.

Ms. Harris has since borne two more children and lives in a subsidized red-brick house in Montgomery with five of her children.

She works the day shift as a carhop and scrambles to provide for her boisterous clan, supplementing her income with Social Security payments for a child needing special education and a father's child support for two of them.

"My social worker was there for me," she said. "I've learned to pay my bills and manage my life."

In June, the child agency finally closed its books on Ms. Harris, satisfied that she could provide a decent home.

SIGNIFICANCE

In addition to the R.C. Consent Decree, Alabama has strengthened its social services for children and low-income families in accordance with federal welfare reforms that were outlined in the Personal Responsibility and Work Opportunity Reconciliation Act (PRWORA) of 1996. The act called for the creation of the Temporary Assistance for Needy Families Fund (TANF) in 1997, which has been used to fund a wide scope of programs, including assistance to families with children. In 2000, Alabama used TANF funds to expand child care programs, substance abuse screening and treatment, transportation initiatives for low-income residents, and other programs aimed at reducing the incidence of child abuse in families. One such program, the Alabama Fatherhood Initiative, focuses on enabling noncustodial fathers to have more constructive involvement in their children's lives, giving them counseling, education, workforce training, and assistance in finding employment opportunities.

Concern has been raised about the lack of coordination between the agencies that administer general social welfare programs and those that administer child welfare and protection services. The DHR encourages its staff and social workers to collaborate between agencies, and to develop joint plans to address community needs, particularly through the Consolidated Child and Family Services Plan (CCFSP), which coordinates several child services programs that serve the same communities.

The State of Alabama filed a legal motion in late 2005 to dismiss the R.C. Consent Decree, claiming all requirements under the decree had been met. The motion cited the training of social workers in all Alabama counties, an improved child welfare oversight system, development of a quality assurance program that repairs weaknesses in the system when they arise, and the securing of funding needed to pay for welfare reforms.

FURTHER RESOURCES
Books

Everett, Joyce E., Sandra P. Chipungu, and Bogart R. Leashore. *Child Welfare Revisited: An Africentric Prespective.* Piscataway, N.J.: Rutgers University Press, 2004.

Mallon, Gerald P. and Peg M. Hess. *Child Welfare for the 21st Century: A Handbook of Practices, Policies, & Programs.* New York: Columbia University Press, 2005.

Periodicals

Holcomb, Pamela A., et al. "Recent Changes in Alabama Welfare and Work, Child Care, and Child Welfare Systems." *The Urban Institute, State Update.* No. 10 (October 2001).

Usher, Charles L., Judith B. Wildfire, and Deborah A. Gibbs. "Measuring performance in child welfare: secondary effects of success." *Child Welfare.* 78:(Jan./Feb. 1999): 31–51.

Web sites

Alabama Department of Human Resources. "Child Protective Services." 2005 <http://www.dhr.state.al.us/page.asp?pageid=312> (accessed May 25, 2006).

Administration for Children and Families. "National Clearinghouse on Child Abuse and Neglect Information." May 16, 2006 <http://nccanch.acf.hhs.gov/index.cfm> (accessed May 25, 2006).

WIC Approved Food List

Document

By: Missouri Department of Health and Senior Services (DHSS)

Date: September 2005

Source: "WIC Approved Food List." *Missouri WIC Approved Foods List, 2005–2007* (2005).

About the Author: The Missouri Department of Health and Senior Services (DHSS) administers the Women, Infants, and Children (WIC) program for the state of Missouri.

INTRODUCTION

The U.S. Women, Infants, and Children (WIC) nutritional assistance program began in 1972 as a two-year pilot program, part of the 1966 Child Nutrition Act. In 1975, WIC became a permanent government program, providing supplemental foods to low-income pregnant women until six weeks postpartum; breastfeeding mothers through the child's first twelve months; infants; and children up to the age of five. WIC was never intended to provide families with 100 percent of food and nutrition needs, but instead it provides nutrition counseling, health monitoring, and foods that meet basic nutrition needs.

The U.S. Department of Agriculture administers funds and requirements for the WIC program through the Food and Nutrition Service. Federal funding then reaches the states, and each state manages WIC program administration with more than 2,000 agencies throughout the fifty states, Washington, D.C., and U.S. territories such as Puerto Rico, Guam, the Virgin Islands, Northern Mariana, and Samoa. In addition, the WIC program reaches thirty-four Indian Tribal Organizations. In the year 2000, WIC enrollees numbered more than 7.2 million; more

The couple pictured with their children are part of the Women, Infants, and Children (WIC) benefits program, which started in 1974 to help provide food for struggling families. AP IMAGES.

than 45 percent of all infants in the United States receive WIC assistance.

The WIC program receives strong congressional and state support; pregnant women, breastfeeding mothers, and children receive vouchers to use in grocery stores and farmers' markets for targeted foods, while infants who are formula-fed receive an allocated amount of formula per month through the age of twelve months. Because each state administers the program according to state guidelines, there are variations in the program's application; in thirty-seven states, for instance, WIC recipients can receive farmers' market vouchers to purchase fresh produce in lieu of other products from the WIC-approved foods list.

The following example, taken from the Missouri WIC approved foods list, demonstrates the targeted nutrition groups that the WIC program distributes to recipients.

PRIMARY SOURCE

Milk

Allowed

Any brand

Reduce/low fat milk (skim, 1/2%, 1%, 2%)

Whole milk (if printed on WIC check)

Gallon plastic containers only

Cultured buttermilk (quart size)

Evaporated milk, store brand only (12 or 13 oz can)

Non-fat, dry milk, store brand only (3 or 8 quart box)

Specialty milk, type and size will be written on the WIC check

Not Allowed

Sweetened condensed milk

Soy milk

Flavored milk

Organic milk

Filled milk

Substitutions

Eggs

Allowed

Medium, white, grade A or AA (1 dozen package)

Not Allowed

Low cholesterol eggs

Organic eggs

Specialty eggs

Brown eggs

Peanut Butter

Allowed

Smooth, creamy or regular, store brand only (18 oz jar)

Not Allowed

Crunchy peanut butter

Low fat peanut butter

Low salt/sodium peanut butter

Organic peanut butter

Mixtures with jams, jellies or honey

Cheese

Allowed

Natural, domestic, plain cheese, store brand only, American, Cheddar, Colby, Colby Jack, Monterey Jack and Mozzarella cheeses (Block cheese in 8, 16 or 32 oz slices only)

Not Allowed

Sliced cheese, except for store brand American

Cheese additives

Deli cheese

Cheese food

Cheese spread

Cheese product

Shredded cheese

String cheese

Cholesterol-reduced cheese

Individually wrapped slices

Flavored cheese

Grated cheese

Dried Beans & Peas

Allowed

Mixed dried beans and peas, store brand only (1 lb bag)

Not Allowed

Organic products

Additives or flavors

Carrots

Allowed

Fresh, including baby or frozen, any cut, any brand (1 or 2 lb package)

Not Allowed

Organic carrots

Flavors

Tuna

Allowed

Water-packed only, chunk, solid or grated, any brand (6 oz can)

Not Allowed

Albacore or white tuna

Reduced or low salt/sodium

Infant Food

Infant Formula

Allowed

Brand printed on WIC check, type and size printed on WIC check

Infant Juice

Allowed

100% juice (32 oz bottle)

Gerber:
Apple
Apple Banana
Apple Cherry
Apple Grape
Mixed Fruit
Pear
White Grape

Beech-Nut:
Apple
Apple Cherry
Mixed Fruit
Pear
White Grape

Nature's Goodness:
Apple
Apple Cherry
Apple Grape
Pear
White Grape

Infant Cereal

Allowed

Plain, dry only (8 or 16 oz)
Gerber
Beech-Nut
Nature's Goodness

SIGNIFICANCE

The average value of WIC vouchers per recipient is $50 per month. This amount is given to each WIC participant in a household; a family with a breastfeeding mother, a four-month-old infant, and a three-year-old child would include three WIC recipients. While infants receive formula and baby food, women and children receive milk, cheese, juice, tuna, carrots, dry cereal, and peanut butter. In some states, such as Pennsylvania, women and children ages four and five can receive $20 per month for use at farmers' markets. A family of four earning $37,000 per year or less can qualify for the WIC program; federal guidelines permit enrollment for families earning less than 185 percent of the federal poverty line.

WIC recipients must report to one of WIC's 10,000 clinics each month to receive the vouchers; children's height and weight are measured and recorded, parents are encouraged to keep their children on immunization schedules, and breastfeeding mothers receive breast pumps in some states and counseling as needed. Critics of WIC claim that in some instances the program reaches too far into the personal choices of parents; parents who choose not to immunize, for instance, have been threatened with disqualification from the program, though keeping children on an immunization schedule is not a requirement for the program. WIC's immunization services, however, aid those parents who do not have ready access to health-care providers in maintaining up-to-date immunization records for their children. Recipients on special diets or with food allergies criticize the program for its inflexibility in the approved food list, which poses an obstacle for affected participants.

Since its inception in 1972, the WIC program has helped to improve birth outcome and to decrease instances of child malnutrition in lower-income populations. According to research studies, child participants in WIC programs have lower rates of iron-deficiency anemia, higher vitamin levels, and higher intake of key nutrients. A 1997 breastfeeding promotion campaign increased breastfeeding rates among mothers enrolled in WIC by 25 percent; WIC experiences a $478 savings per infant when mothers choose to breastfeed exclusively for the child's first three months.

The WIC program is considered by federal, state, and local officials to be one of the most successful food supplement programs in the nation, reaching nearly 4 percent of the population of the United States in any given year.

FURTHER RESOURCES

Books

Richardson, Joe, Donna Viola Porter, and Jean Yavis Jones. *Child Nutrition and WIC Programs: Background and Funding.* New York: Nova Science, 2003.

Periodicals

Montgomery, D.L. and P. L. Splett. "Economic Benefit of Breast-feeding Infants Enrolled in WIC." *Journal of the American Dietetic Association* 97 (April 1997): 385.

Web sites

USDA Food and Nutrition Service. "WIC Farmers' Market Nutrition Programs." March 20, 2006 <http://www.fns.usda.gov/wic/FMNP/FMNPfaqs.htm> (accessed May 30, 2006).

The Drug Decision

Millions Face a Deadline for Choosing a New Medicare Plan

Newspaper Article

By: Milt Freudenheim

Date: November 24, 2005

Source: Freudenheim, Milt. "The Drug Decision: Millions Face a Deadline for Choosing a New Medicare Plan." *New York Times* (November 24, 2005).

About the Author: Milt Freudenheim is a business and financial reporter for the *New York Times*.

INTRODUCTION

On December 8, 2003, the Medicare Prescription Drug, Improvement, and Modernization Act of 2003 enacted a new law concerning a new voluntary prescription drug benefit program. It was the first time in Medicare's forty-year history that a prescription drug plan for seniors had been offered, and was created in response to rising prescription drug prices. The amount spent on prescription drugs increased by four times between 1990 and 2002. The rising costs were brought about by increased utilization, manufacturer price increases, and newer, more expensive drugs replacing older, less expensive ones. Low-income seniors on limited budgets were the greatest population affected. About eleven million low-income seniors are projected to be assisted by the new Medicare Plan D program. As of 2006, Medicare covers persons aged sixty-five or older, those under sixty-five with a disability, and those with End Stage Renal Disease. Medicare Part A covers hospital charges; most recipients do not pay for this coverage. Medicare Part B covers medical expenses and most recipients pay a monthly fee. The new Part D program enables those entitled or enrolled in Medicare benefits under Part A and Part B to enroll in a new optional prescription drug program. This new program became effective on January 1, 2006, and the deadline for signing up without penalty was May 15, 2006.

◼ PRIMARY SOURCE

Decisions, decisions. The clock is ticking for millions of elderly and disabled people, who must decide whether and when to enroll in one of the new Medicare Part D drug plans that start Jan. 1, 2006.

The Part D program, named for its place within the written Medicare law, for the first time brings drugs under the Medicare tent, which covers 42 million people. It has been widely portrayed as hopelessly confusing.

And bewildering it can seem—in part because Congress set it up to be federally subsidized but run by the commercial insurance industry. Companies are clamoring to compete, and some are adding to the confusion by offering dozens of plans with a welter of wrinkles and widely varying prices. And as if to raise the degree of difficulty, some insurers are continually adjusting their offerings, even as consumers are trying to make a decision.

But before you throw up your hands, there are basic steps you can take to help decide which plan, if any, is right for you or for someone you are trying to assist. And as you proceed, take heart from Hari Peterson, a 69-year-old retired nurse in Warwick, R.I., who has survived the process.

"I found it to be confusing, but we really studied it," said Ms. Peterson, whose husband, Ray, 72, has drug coverage from the Department of Veterans Affairs that he plans to keep for now. She collected information on computer printouts from senior centers and talked with state insurance advisers at a Medicare fair at a nearby mall.

"I gave them my prescriptions and they pinpointed it down to two or three plans," she said. Ms. Peterson also plans to consult her longtime pharmacist before making a final selection.

If you are overwhelmed by the thought of wrestling with all this on the brink of the holiday season, there is a reprieve: You can make a selection by Dec. 31 if you want coverage to start in January, but you can also wait until as late as May 15 to select a plan, without penalty.

You have until Dec. 31 to select a plan that starts in January.

And if you make a decision today, you can still check for a better offer next week. Through Dec. 31, you can change your mind as often as you like. And it may pay to keep checking, because some insurers are continually adjusting their offerings. If you see a better deal, take it.

If you would rather wait, you have until May 15 to enroll, with your chosen plan taking effect the month after you sign up. But after Dec. 31, until May 15, you are permitted to change your mind just once.

After May 15, your next chance to enroll will be during the Nov. 15–Dec. 31 sign-up period. But you may have to pay a penalty. Unless you are already enrolled in a plan that an employer or union certifies is as good or better than Part D, your monthly premium could rise by at least 1 percent for each month of delay.

Emaline Palumbo, a senior citizen, receives an explanation of information about different Medicare plans from educator Karina Guilar duing an education program sponsored by the National Council on Aging Access to Benefits Coalition.
© JERRY MCCREA/STAR LEDGER/CORBIS.

People who are not yet eligible for Medicare will have a seven-month window, starting 90 days before they turn 65, to sign up for Part D, without a penalty.

Beginning next November, and every year thereafter, members will have the option of changing plans during the Nov. 15–Dec. 31 annual enrollment. They can also change plans at any time if they enter a nursing home or move to an area not served by their existing plan.

YOU ALREADY HAVE COVERAGE? If you are already covered through an employer or union drug plan, you would probably want to stay put if that plan is as good as, or better than, the minimum requirements of a Medicare Part D plan.

The sponsor of your current plan was required to notify you by Nov. 15 how your coverage compares with the Part D minimum. (If your current plan provider has not sent you notification, contact the plan administrator, which is required by law to provide you with this information.)

Or maybe you already have drug coverage through a Medigap policy—a type of commercially available supplement to Medicare that has been available for years.

Medigap policies with drug coverage will not be sold to new customers after Jan. 1, but you can keep an existing plan at least temporarily or switch to a Medigap policy without drug coverage, to help cover hospital and doctor fees.

But note that under Medicare rules, Medigap drug coverage is generally not considered equivalent to the Part D minimum. So if you wait until after May 15 to switch to Part D, you could be penalized.

Low-income people who are eligible for both Medicaid and Medicare will be automatically enrolled in a Part D plan chosen for them. If they are dissatisfied with that plan, though, they can switch to another.

STAND-ALONE OR PACKAGE DEAL? If you decide to pursue Medicare drug coverage, you have two options. One is to enroll in a stand-alone Part D drug plan and continue to have the federal Medicare system cover treatment by whatever doctors or hospitals you select.

The alternative is a commercial Medicare Advantage plan, that combines drug coverage and doctor and hospital care in a single insurance program. Medicare officials and insurance companies are promoting this approach, which they say will be more efficient and which insurers expect to be more profitable.

In most stand-alone Part D plans, there is an annual $250 deductible, after which enrollees pay an estimated 25 percent of their drug costs, until the total is $2,250.

At that point, in a Congressionally mandated provision nicknamed the "doughnut hole," the consumer has to pay for the next $2,850 worth of drugs. Beyond that point, the Part D plan will pay about 95 percent of the cost of each prescription. Or at least that is the way things will work in 2006.

Federal Medicare officials say that consumers will save money by joining Medicare Advantage plans. Premiums may vary from plan to plan but co-payments and deductibles may be lower and there may be limits on out-of-pocket costs. But in those managed care plans, enrollees typically have to pay more for drugs, doctors and hospitals that are not on the plan's preferred lists.

CHOOSING A PLAN. Before trying to compare plans, make a list of your drugs, including the dosage of each.

AND KEEP IN MIND...Costs of the free-standing plans can vary widely, depending on the number and types of your drugs. In some cases, you may end up spending less over all by paying a higher monthly premium for one of the handful of stand-alone plans that include drug coverage in the "doughnut hole."

Thousands, but not all, pharmacies offer the discounted prices in Part D plans. Some plans also charge lower co-payments if drugs are ordered by mail in 90-day supplies. Some insurers, though, have arranged to offer the same deal on 90-day supplies purchased at national drugstore chains like Walgreen and Rite-Aid.

If your health takes a turn for the worse after you enroll and you need high-cost medicines not on the plan's preferred list, or not covered at all, your doctor can ask your plan to make an exception. Under the law, the plan has to determine if it will grant the exception within 72 hours. Denials can be appealed, which could be a lengthy process.

One worrisome prospect is a rule that permits a Part D plan to increase the co-payment or even end coverage for a drug on 60 days' notice. If the co-payment is raised, plan members could have no choice but to absorb the increase, because unless they move or enter a nursing home, or are on Medicaid, they would not be allowed to switch to a different plan until the next annual November-to-December enrollment period.

Steve Brueckner, a vice president of Humana, a national sponsor of Part D plans, said dropping a drug was unlikely. With dozens of plans competing for members, he said, "practically speaking, that would be a highly damaging action."

But Mr. Brueckner said some plans might indeed raise the co-payments if the manufacturer of a drug raised prices.

SIGNIFICANCE

For the first time, all Medicare recipients regardless of their situation will have prescription drug coverage. Experts anticipate that the implementation of this new prescription program will create a true market for health care. Some people had been paying thousands of dollars a month for prescriptions. For those on a limited budget, everyday expenses often precluded the cost of expensive medicines. People had to do without necessary prescriptions in order to survive. Under the new plan, the costs of these same prescriptions have been cut significantly. The Bush administration is optimistic that the enrollees in the program will save up to 75 percent on their prescription drug costs.

Democrats are not as optimistic. Sen. Hillary Clinton has called the program a "man made disaster" that could be compared to Hurricane Katrina. A version of the plan introduced by Democratic senators called for an all-encompassing drug program that would include everyone, not just those on Medicare.

About 90 percent of those eligible for the new Part D program have signed up. It has been confusing for some due to the competing companies. Each state has their own list of companies that will cover Medicare Part D recipients. For example, the state of North Carolina has sixteen different companies to choose from. Each of these companies has from one to three different prescription drug programs to choose from. Each of the programs varies in price—not only within each company, but from company to company as well. Each program offers a different formulary for covered medicines. A formulary is a group of medicines chosen for inclusion in a prescription plan for their medical effectiveness and cost efficiency. This can be an overwhelming and daunting task for some seniors and those on disability to be able to choose the best program for their particular needs. Once they pick a company, they are locked in until the next enrollment date in November. Different private insurance companies have lowered prices in order to compete with one another. This in turn benefits the Medicare recipients.

The United States Treasury projects that they will spend over $675 billion in ten years under the new Part D program. The hope is that it will enable those who require assistance to pay for their prescriptions and receive Medicare to be able to afford the drug prescriptions that they need.

The new Medicare prescription program is not without its problems. One that is currently being addressed is slow reimbursement rates. This could force community pharmacists to bow out of the Part D program. In fact, on May 24, 2006, community pharmacists with the support of Reps. Walter B. Jones (R-N.C.) and Marion Berry (D-Ark.), went to Washington to try to pass new legislation that would fix the problems that they were facing. Some of these pharmacists are complaining that they are not being fully reimbursed for prescriptions under the new Part D program.

FURTHER RESOURCES

Periodicals

"Medicare and the Midterms." *Washington Times* (May 16, 2006).

Young, Jeffery. "Pharmacists, PBM's Duke It Out Over Part D." *The Hill* (May 23, 2006).

Web sites

Department of Medical Assistance Services. "The Medicare Prescription Drug Benefit (Part D) Fact Sheet." <http://www.seniornavigator.com/learn/connections/pharm-mma_fact_sheet.pdf> (accessed June 11, 2006).

Health Care Financing and Organization. "Medicare Part D: Can the New Outpatient Prescription Drug Benefit Effectively Manage Costs?" March 2005. <http://www.hcfo.net/topic0305.htm> (accessed June 11, 2006).

Kaiser Family Foundation. "Prescription Drug Trends." October 2004. <http://www.kff.org/rxdrugs/upload/Prescription-Drug-Trends-October–2004-UPDATE.pdf> (accessed June 11, 2006).

U.S. Newswire. "Pharmacists Rally on Capitol Hill to Fix Part D; Medicare Prompt Pay Bill Will Help Ensure Patient Access." May 24, 2006. <http://releases.usnewswire.com/GetRelease.asp?id=66354> (accessed June 11, 2006).

Breastfeeding Promotion in WIC

Current Federal Requirements

Federal policy

By: USDA Food and Nutrition Service

Date: March 9, 2005

Source: *Breastfeeding Promotion in WIC.* USDA Food and Nutrition Service, March 9, 2005.

About the Author: The United States Department of Agriculture's Food and Nutrition Service provides access to food for children and low-income individuals and families in the United States. It administers the Women, Infants, and Children (WIC) supplemental nutrition program.

INTRODUCTION

At the beginning of the twentieth century, the United States experienced a sharp decline in breastfeeding rates for infants and toddlers. Until the invention of artificial baby milk, the only acceptable form of nutrition for young infants was breast milk, either from the biological mother or from a wet nurse. While some infants were able to survive on substitutes such as cow's milk or goat's milk, the human stomach is not designed to easily break down the proteins in the milk of other mammals, and such substitutes often led to illness or death.

The first artificial baby milk, now commonly known as "formula" in the United States, was invented in the 1860s in Germany. The Nestle corporation created a powdered version in the 1870s composed of malt, wheat flour, dry cow's milk, and sugar. By 1897, the Sears Roebuck catalog, the primary catalog for dry goods in the United States, advertised eight formula varieties; compared to cow's milk, the formulas were expensive. Breastfeeding was still the norm by the turn of the century.

By the 1910s and 1920s, physicians began to recommend a homemade version of formula: 13 ounces (0.4 liters) of evaporated, canned milk added to 19 ounces (0.6 liters) of boiled water, with two tablespoons of corn syrup or sugar added. Homemade and commercial formula gained in popularity as the scientific management movement of the early twentieth century promoted the idea that anything involving science was better; a formula designed in a laboratory, approved by experts and physicians and endorsed by

Heidi Goldstein (right) nurses her daughter while talking with Amy Berry Pogrebin in Berkeley, California, July 30, 2002. They are discussing an attempt to set a world record for simultaneous breastfeeding that Sibru is organizing. AP IMAGES.

professionals was viewed as superior to traditional breastfeeding and breast milk. In addition, as women moved into the industrial workforce in growing numbers, formula provided a socially acceptable nutritional substitute for the mother's milk.

Lower-income women breastfed in greater numbers than middle- and upper-income women at this time; when lower-income women used formula, it was more likely to be the homemade version, which over time paled in comparison to commercial brands that added fats, vitamins, and minerals to become a more complete form of nutrition for infants and toddlers. Breastfeeding rates in the 1910s were 70 percent, and gradually dropped to 22 percent in 1972, the lowest point in recorded history for breastfeeding in the United States. The rates gradually increased throughout the 1970s, 1980s, and 1990s to reach a rate of 66 percent in 2003.

Sparked by a trend among well-educated, middle- and upper-income white women, the overall breast-feeding rate includes all attempts at breastfeeding—even those infants breastfed for one day of their life. The breastfeeding rate among lower-income women, such as those women receiving nutritional assistance from the Women, Infants, and Children (WIC) supplemental program, has historically been lower than the national rates. Women and children enrolled in WIC receive vouchers for grocery products such as milk, cereal, juice, and eggs; mothers who choose not to breastfeed receive a full year's supply of infant formula. Critics of the WIC program pointed to the formula provision as a factor in discouraging breastfeeding. In response, WIC created the National WIC Breastfeeding Promotion Project.

PRIMARY SOURCE

The current federal WIC regulations contain provisions to encourage women to breastfeed and to provide appropriate nutritional support for breastfeeding participants.

246.2 **Definitions**.

Breastfeeding means the practice of feeding a mother's breast milk to her infant(s) on the average of at least once a day.

Breastfeeding women means women up to one year postpartum who are breastfeeding their infants.

246.3(e)(4) **State staffing standards**.

Each State agency shall designate a breastfeeding promotion coordinator, to coordinate breastfeeding promotion efforts identified in the State plan in accordance with the requirement of 246.4(a)(9). The person to whom the State agency assigns this responsibility may perform other duties as well.

246.4(a)(9) **State Plan**.

The State Plan must include the State agency's nutrition education goals and action plans, including a description of the methods that will be used to promote breastfeeding.

246.7(e)(1)(iii)†**Certification of Participants**.

Breastfeeding Dyads. A breastfeeding mother and her infant shall be placed in the highest priority level for which either is qualified.

Nutritional risk priority system. Priority I: pregnant women, breastfeeding women and infants at nutritional risk as demonstrated by hematological or anthropometric measurements or other documented nutritionally related medical conditions which demonstrate the need for supplemental foods.

246.7(g)(1)(iii) **Certification Periods**.

Breastfeeding women shall be certified at intervals of approximately six months and ending with the breastfed infant's first birthday.

246.10(c)(7) **Supplemental Foods**.

Food Package VII—Breastfeeding Women (Enhanced) contains additional amounts of juice, cheese and legumes, plus carrots and canned tuna.

246.11(c) **Nutrition Education**.

State agencies shall perform the following activities in carrying out nutrition education responsibilities:

246.11(c)(2) Provide training on the promotion and management of breastfeeding to staff at local agencies who will provide information and assistance on this subject to participants.

246.11(c)(3) Identify or develop resources and educational materials for use in local agencies, including breastfeeding promotion and instruction materials; taking reasonable steps to include materials in languages other than English in areas where a significant number of or proportion of the populations needs the information in a language other than English.

246.11(c)(7) Establish standards for breastfeeding promotion and support which include, at a minimum, the following:

    (i) A policy that creates a positive clinic environment which endorses breastfeeding as the preferred method of infant feeding;

    (ii) A requirement that each local agency designate a staff person to coordinate breastfeeding promotion and support activities;

    (iii) A requirement that each local agency incorporate task-appropriate breastfeeding promotion and support training into orientation programs for new staff involved in direct contact with WIC clients; and

    (iv) A plan to ensure that women have access to breastfeeding promotion and support activities during the prenatal and postpartum periods.

Participant Contacts.

All pregnant participants shall be encouraged to breastfeed unless contraindicated for health reasons.

246.14(b)(1)(iii) **Program Costs**.

The State agency may use food funds to purchase or rent breast pumps.

246.14(c)(1) Specified allowable nutrition services and administration (NSA) costs. Each fiscal year, each state agency must spend, for nutrition education activities and breastfeeding promotion and support activities, an aggregate amount that is not less than the sum of one-sixth of the amount expended by the State agency for costs of NSA and an amount equal to its proportionate share of the national minimum expenditure for breastfeeding promotion and support activities. The national minimum expenditure for breastfeeding promotion and support activities shall be equal to $21 multiplied by the number of pregnant and breastfeeding women in the Program, based on the average of the last three months for which USDA has final data. On October 1, 1996 and each October 1 thereafter, the $21 will be adjusted annually using the same inflation percentage used to determine the national administrative grant per person.

246.14(c)(10) Costs of breastfeeding aids which directly support the initiation and continuation of breastfeeding are allowable.

SIGNIFICANCE

The new guidelines offered women an incentive to breastfeed in the form of additional tuna, cheese, juice, carrots, and legumes. In addition, some states offer electric or manual breast pumps for mothers who work out of the home or attend school to use to express breast milk for later consumption by their child; the breast pump program helps mothers to maintain milk supply while reducing the need for infant formula. A 1997 research study published in the *Journal of the American Dietetic Association*, shortly before WIC began the breastfeeding promotion program, showed that the cost benefits to government agencies for WIC participants who breastfeed exclusively for the infant's first three months of life are substantial; $478 per infant is saved over the course of the infant's first six months. The $21 per woman enrolled in WIC allocated to breastfeeding promotion combined with funds for breast pumps and additional food is part of a cost/benefit analysis that drives social change as well.

Throughout the 1990s, organizations such as La Leche League, a breastfeeding advocacy group started by mothers in the 1950s, helped to sponsor laws that guarantee women and infants the right to breastfeed in public. Employment law in many states now includes provisions for pumping breaks for breastfeeding mothers, and corporations and government agencies such as Kaiser Permanente, Mattel, Inc., and NASA have lactation rooms on site for nursing mothers as part of a family-friendly approach.

The WIC breastfeeding promotion campaign showed success in follow-up studies. In Iowa, the initial breastfeeding rate for WIC enrollees went from 57.8 to 65.1 percent, and the rate at which mothers were still breastfeeding after six months increased from 20.4 to 32.2 percent. As a result of the success of the program, WIC continued to promote breastfeeding as part of the agency's overall mission.

Public health officials point to breastfeeding as an important factor in fighting against obesity, asthma, and childhood illnesses. WIC's counselors and fellow and former breastfeeding mothers are trained to assist mothers with supply-and-demand issues, latch questions, growth spurts, and breast pump questions. As breastfeeding increases in the United States across all income levels and races, the WIC campaign combines social change, public health, and cost savings to taxpayers with a single program that harkens back to the nineteenth century with twenty-first-century acumen.

FURTHER RESOURCES

Books

Baumslag, Naomi M. D. and Dia L. Michels. *Milk, Money and Madness: The Culture and Politics of Breastfeeding.* Westport, Conn.: Bergin & Garvey Trade, 1995.

La Leche League International. *The Womanly Art of Breastfeeding.* New York: Plume, 2004.

Periodicals

Montgomery, D. L., and P. L. Splett. "Economic Benefit of Breast-feeding Infants Enrolled in WIC." *Journal of the American Dietetic Association* 97 (April 1997): 385.

Web sites

National Conference of State Legislatures. "50 State Summary of Breastfeeding Laws." <http://www.ncsl.org/programs/health/breast50.htm> (accessed June 15, 2006).

The President's Savings Plans

Editorial

By: Norbert J. Michel

Date: March 29, 2005

Source: *Heritage Foundation.* "The President's Savings Plans: Good for Retirees ... and Everyone Else." 2005 <http://www.heritage.org/Research/Taxes/wm704.cfm> (accessed June 22, 2006).

About the Author: Norbert Michel is a Policy Analyst in the Center for Data Analysis at The Heritage Foundation, a Washington-based public policy research institute.

INTRODUCTION

The concept of retirement, a final phase of life in which seniors leave the workforce to enjoy their accumulated assets, is a relatively modern phenomenon. For much of human history men and women have assumed that work was a necessary part of life, and that those able to work should do so. The idea of quitting work simply to enjoy life while others paid the bills appeared somewhat suspect, possibly implying some form of laziness or lack of morals.

Mortality and retirement statistics give some insight into the recent history of the retirement mindset. In 1930 the average American lived to about age sixty. Despite the fact that many men never reached the current retirement age of sixty-five, among those who did the labor force participation rate (the percentage still working) was surprisingly high: 58 percent. For those who reached old age in the 1930s, work often continued much as before.

With the passage of the Social Security Act of 1935, a financially secure retirement became possible for many more Americans. This guaranteed source of retirement income, coupled with improved healthcare and longer life spans, enabled a growing number of workers to retire and enjoy their "golden years" at home or traveling. By 1970, workforce participation rates for sixty-five-year olds had fallen by almost half to 35.2 percent, and by 2000 fewer than 18 percent of sixty-five-year olds remained in the workforce; as of 2003 approximately one in six Americans was receiving some form of Social Security benefits and the system was paying out almost half a trillion dollars annually.

While the trend toward longer retirement creates more post-work years for Americans to enjoy, it also means that retired workers will receive Social Security benefits for much longer than before. Whereas a typical worker in 1940 might have drawn payments for five years or less, a typical retiree in 2000 will claim benefits for twenty years or more, despite having worked roughly the same length of time. In addition, a 1972 law indexed Social Security payments to inflation, meaning that the dollar value of payments rises automatically each year. This change helps protect retirees from inflation and maintain their buying power, but also increases the financial strain on the system by raising expenditures each year.

By the 1970s, the Social Security System was beginning to show cracks and in 1983 Congress enacted changes to help shore up the program. These changes included raising withholding rates and taxing benefits for some higher income retirees, and were expected to stabilize the system until 2040 or 2050. But within a few years, new projections once again showed the system exhausting its funds earlier than planned. Soon the fate of Social Security became a recurring political topic.

Social Security's problems have spawned numerous suggestions; sure fixes such as cutting benefits or raising the retirement age substantially have been deemed political suicide by most politicians and discarded. However with the Baby Boom generation nearing retirement, the system's structure is mathematically top-heavy: As the number of retirees grows the number of workers supporting them will shrink. Projections in 2006 see the system unable to pay full benefits by approximately 2040.

Beside the attention being paid to Social Security itself, the federal government is also implementing programs that encourage Americans to save more on their own. Individual Retirement Accounts (IRAs), written into law in the 1970s, were one of the first such programs created. In 2004 President Bush proposed two new savings programs that would provide tax breaks to Americans saving for retirement.

PRIMARY SOURCE

THE PRESIDENT'S SAVINGS PLANS: GOOD FOR RETIREES ... AND EVERYONE ELSE

Previous attempts to solve Social Security's problems have relied on a mix of benefit cuts and tax increases, but this approach is not a long-term solution. A more lasting solution to Social Security's problems involves a two-pronged approach that allows workers to invest part of their payroll taxes in their own accounts while also removing barriers to saving outside of the system. Although legislation has not yet been introduced to address the first part of this strategy, bills dealing with the second portion have been introduced in both chambers of Congress.

On March 8, Treasury Secretary John Snow, Senator Craig Thomas (R-WY), and Representative Sam Johnson (R-TX) announced the Save Initiative, a legislative effort that includes three new savings proposals. These savings plans were part of President Bush's 2006 budget proposals and are likely to be included in any tax reform package developed later in the year. The bills would encourage people to save money and would greatly simplify the regulations governing retirement accounts.

Increase Saving, Reduce Complexity

By eliminating multiple layers of taxation, the Save Initiative would give taxpayers added incentives to save money and build their own wealth. Unlike current law, which taxes the money put into regular savings accounts as well as the money earned in those accounts, the new plans would ensure that savings are taxed only once. Just as important, the Save Initiative would consolidate the various types of tax-advantaged savings accounts and simplify their regulations. The proposed savings plans include:

Lifetime Savings Accounts.

LSAs can be used to save for any purpose, not just retirement. There is no tax advantage on the money going into the account (up to $5,000), but the earnings on the money will not be taxed. Unlike typical retirement accounts, there will be no "early withdrawal" penalty, ensuring that savings can be used for whatever purpose individuals choose and that they are taxed only once.

Retirement Savings Accounts.

The RSA is similar to the Roth IRA in that money goes into the account after taxes (up to $5,000) and the account is not taxed again. Investors are allowed to accumulate earnings in the RSA tax-free and then to use the money at retirement without paying additional taxes. Unlike the Roth IRA, there are no income limits preventing people with higher incomes from contributing. Like the Roth IRA, there are no additional age requirements mandating withdrawals after retirement.

Employer Retirement Savings Accounts.

ERSAs would consolidate the plethora of employer-based saving plans, such as 401(k), Simple 401(k), and 403(b) plans, and simplify the qualifying rules. The ERSA rules would be similar to the current-law 401(k) rules, and contributions would be pre-tax. Existing plans could be maintained in their previous form, but new contributions would be disallowed after December 31, 2006.

Help Retirees ... and Everyone Else

Allowing individuals to build their own wealth is an integral part of a market economy, and removing excess layers of taxation on saving can only help to increase private wealth. The Save Initiative would be a boon both to younger workers who currently hold out little hope of receiving their future Social Security benefits and to baby boomers who are on the verge of retiring.

Economists believe that Social Security provides a disincentive to save. As noted in the Economic Report of the President, the current multitude of special-purpose tax advantage accounts encourages people to create several smaller pools of saving that can be used only for specific purposes. There is also evidence that taxing consumption rather than income would be more efficient and would boost economic activity. The Save Initiative would help in all three cases.

The new proposals remove a layer of taxation on saving, thus providing a greater incentive to save for any reason, including retirement. Furthermore, the new savings plans move the income tax system toward a consumption tax because not taxing savings is the equivalent of taxing only consumption. For all individuals, whether young or old, rich or poor, the Save Initiative translates into easier saving through lower costs and less complexity.

Minimal Impact on the Federal Budget

Advocates of tax reform can also take comfort from the fact that the Save Initiative would have a minuscule impact on the federal budget. According to the Joint Committee on Taxation, consolidating the plethora of retirement accounts and creating the new LSA plans would reduce federal revenue by $5.4 billion between 2005 and 2015. This figure represents less than one-fifth of 1 percent of the $3 trillion federal budget.

Conclusion

Allowing individuals to build their own wealth is an integral part of a market economy, and the policies embodied in the Save Initiative can only help to increase private wealth. The Save Initiative should be part of any tax reform package because it provides the proper incentives for individuals to save and reduces complexity in the tax code. These savings plans could also be an important first step toward meaningful Social Security reform because they would encourage people to save for their own retirement. Congress should consider going even further than the current proposals and removing all contribution limits from the new savings plans.

SIGNIFICANCE

Although many members of Congress recognize the need to improve Americans' retirement security, they are divided on how to accomplish this goal. President Bush's proposal attempted to raise non-Social Security savings by offering tax incentives which would allow earners to invest in tax-sheltered savings accounts. Critics of the plan charged that the proposed changes would favor the wealthy, who have income to save, while reducing pressure to shore up Social Security. In place of the president's plan, opponents generally favor higher withholding on wealthy taxpayers.

Despite its popularity with some supporters, the president's savings proposals did not survive the budget process and were eliminated before the final 2004 budget was approved. Similar proposals came from the White House for the 2005 and 2006 budgets, but were again rejected. The proposal was once again recommended for the 2007 federal budget.

FURTHER RESOURCES

Books

Altman, Nancy J. *The Battle for Social Security: From FDR's Vision to Bush's Gamble*. Hoboken, N.J.: John Wiley & Sons, 2005.

Slesnick, Twila et al. *IRAs, 401(k)s & Other Retirement Plans: Taking Your Money Out*. Berkeley, Calif.: Nolo Press, 2001.

Walker, Robert. *Social Security and Welfare*. New York: Open University Press/McGraw Hilll, 2005.

Periodicals

"Evolution of Social Security." *Congressional Digest* 74 (1995): 227.

Johnston, David. "IRA Swaps Could Cost U.S. Billions in Tax Revenue." *New York Times*, May 15, 2006: C3.

"Social Security: A 50 year review." *U.S. News & World Report*. 99(1985):41–45.

Web sites

Congressional Budget Office. "An Overview of the Social Security System." <http://www.cbo.gov/> (accessed June 22, 2006).

Craig Thomas, United States Senator, Wyoming. "SAVE Initiative: Floor Statement." March 8, 2005 <http://www.senate.gov/~thomas/> (accessed June 22, 2006).

Social Security Administration. "Legislative History: Social Security Act of 1935." <http://www.ssa.gov/history/35actii.html> (accessed June 22, 2006).

Officer Next Door Program

U.S. Department of Housing and Urban Development

Government memorandum

By: U.S. Department of Housing and Urban Development

Date: 2004

Source: *U.S. Department of Housing and Urban Development.* "Officer Next Door." <http://www.hud.gov/offices/hsg/sfh/reo/goodn/ond.cfm> (accessed May 27, 2006).

About the Author: The U.S. Department of Housing and Urban Development (HUD) is a government agency charged with increasing home ownership, promoting affordable housing, improving communities, and ensuring equal access to housing.

INTRODUCTION

The federal government first became involved in housing problems in the late nineteenth century by funding the first formal investigations of inner city slum housing. The scope of government housing efforts broadened considerably in the 1930s with the establishment of the Reconstruction Finance Corporation (RFC), whose purpose was to make loans to private corporations building low-income housing. The RFC would become the first of many government-backed corporations established to expand housing options for Americans.

During the 1930s, difficulties in securing private mortgages created significant barriers to individual home ownership. Banks frequently charged high interest rates and offered loan terms of five years or less, making home ownership unaffordable for most Americans. In response, Congress established the Federal Housing Administration (FHA), which provided mortgage insurance, thereby reducing risk to banks and encouraging them to offer longer-term mortgages. The FHA remains the primary government agency providing mortgage insurance today.

Numerous other agencies sprang up to assist the FHA in its efforts, including the Farmers Home Administration (FmHA), the Federal National Mortgage Association (Fannie Mae), and the National Housing Agency (NHA), which oversaw all non-rural housing efforts. In 1943, the NHA was replaced by the Housing and Home Finance Agency (HHFA). Government efforts through the 1950s and 60s centered on efforts to improve housing quality and to reduce housing discrimination. In 1965, the HHFA was superseded by the new Department of Housing and Urban Development, commonly known as HUD.

Among its first tasks, the new agency was charged with enforcing the recently passed Fair Housing Act. This act, part of the comprehensive Civil Rights Act of 1968, guaranteed equal access to housing regardless of an individual's race, gender, or religion. At the time of the act's passage, housing discrimination was rampant, and minorities frequently found themselves locked out of better apartments and nicer neighborhoods. The Housing Act of 1968 also established the Government National Mortgage Association (Ginnie Mae) to improve middle class access to affordable mortgages.

During the 1970s, HUD promoted laws requiring lenders to reveal their lending practices in order to reduce redlining and other discriminatory lending practices. During that same era, HUD provided monthly rent subsidies to almost one million low-income tenants under the Section Eight program.

By the early 1980s, the long-term costs of Section Eight began to spiral upward, and new project development under this program was halted in order to focus resources on other initiatives. In the 1990s, HUD faced a variety of fiscal and political crises, and found itself in a period of extended reassessment. Ironically, part of HUD's financial crisis stemmed directly from the costs associated with FHA loans, which typically carried higher interest rates than conventional bank loans.

HUD is probably best-known for its efforts to increase home ownership by helping lower income residents qualify for mortgages. But much of HUD's energy is devoted to improving existing neighborhoods, particularly in urban areas. Although houses and apartments form the visible structure of a neighborhood, residents make the decisions which raise or lower standards of living. With this principle in mind, HUD has begun offering incentives to a select group of citizens to entice them back to troubled neighborhoods.

PRIMARY SOURCE

The U.S. Department of Housing and Urban Development (HUD) wants to make American communities stronger and to build a safer nation. Public safety improves when police officers live in a neighborhood. The Officer Next Door (OND) program helps make this goal a reality by encouraging these valuable professional public servants to become homeowners in revitalization areas.

Who Can Participate?

You must be a full-time, sworn law enforcement officer who is "employed full-time by a Federal, state, county or municipal government; or a public or private college or university." You must be "sworn to uphold, and make arrests for violations of, Federal, state, county, or municipal law." Your employer must certify that you are a full-time police officer with the general power of arrest. You don't have to be a first-time homebuyer to participate. However, you cannot own any other home at the time you close on your OND home. You must agree to live in the HUD home as your only residence for three years after you move into it.

How do I participate?

OND property is listed and sold exclusively over the Internet. Properties are single family homes located in Revitalization Areas. Properties available through the program are marked with a special Officer Next Door button. Bids are awarded once each week. Your bid must be the amount of the list price. You may submit your bid directly or utilize the services of a real estate broker. Winning bids are randomly selected by computer. The winning bid is posted each week on the website where you made your bid.

You may also buy a home from a government agency or a nonprofit organization that bought the home from HUD. When an agency or nonprofit buys the house, HUD expects the full discount to be passed on to you.

In all cases, HUD requires that you sign a second mortgage and note for the discount amount. No interest or payments are required on this "silent second" provided that you fulfill the three-year occupancy requirement.

What Are the Benefits for the Officer?

The selected bidder may purchase the property at a fifty percent discount from the list price. For example, if a HUD home is listed for $100,000, an officer can buy it for $50,000. To make a HUD home even more affordable, you may apply for an FHA-insured mortgage with a down payment of only $100 and you may finance all closing costs.

If the home you want to purchase needs repairs, you may use FHA's 203(k) mortgage program. This program allows you to finance both the purchase of the home and the cost of needed repairs. You have the benefit of one loan for both costs and one monthly payment.

Discuss these financing options with your lender.

SIGNIFICANCE

While last season's clothing and day-old bread are frequently discounted by 50 percent or more, houses are rarely so drastically reduced. HUD's willingness to sell homes to police officers for half their market value is startling, but HUD benefits in several ways. First, HUD is able to sell some of the hundreds of thousands of properties it has repossessed when buyers defaulted on their loans. Second, by enticing law enforcement officers into a rebuilding neighborhood, HUD can anticipate that safety will improve, pulling property values up for other owners as well. Finally, by selling to police officers who agree to stay for a minimum of three years, HUD has extended credit to members of a reputable profession, raising the odds of loan repayment. HUD is undoubtedly betting that other potential buyers will also be reassured by the sight of a police cruiser sitting in a neighbor's driveway.

HUD is not limiting its efforts to police officers. Similar programs are available for professional firefighters, emergency medical technicians, and school teachers. In each case, HUD offers buyers a downpayment of only $100 along with a price reduction of 50 percent, provided the buyer lives in the house for at least three years.

FURTHER RESOURCES

Books

Hays, R. Allen. *The Federal Government and Urban Housing: Ideology and Change in Public Policy.* Albany, N.Y.: State University of New York Press, 1995.

Hilfiker, David. *Urban Injustice: How Ghettos Happen.* New York: Seven Stories Press, 2003.

Lewis, Sally. *Front to Back: A Design Agenda for Urban Housing.* Burlington, Mass.: Architectural Press, 2005.

Periodicals

Aronauer, Rebecca. "HUD Programs' Loss Hurts Colleges." *Chronicle of Higher Education.* 52(2005):A25.

Chan, Sewell. "Proposed Cut for HUD Is Criticized by Bloomberg." *New York Times.* 155(2006): B3.

Ives-Halperin, Benton. "Subprime Borrowers Could Gain With HUD Plan." *Wall Street Journal.* 47(2006): D5.

Web sites

Habitat for Humanity. "HUD awards $10.7 million to Habit for Humanity." February 23, 2006 <http://www.habitat.org/newsroom/2006archive/02_23_2006_HUD_award

s_10.7_million_to_Habitat_for_Humanity.aspx>
(accessed May 27, 2006).

Urban Issues Program, University of Texas at Austin. "How
HUD's HOPE VI Program Is Destroying a Historic
Houston Neighborhood." <http://www.utexas.edu/
academic/uip/research/docstuds/coll/mcghee.html>
(accessed May 27, 2006).

U.S. Department of Housing and Urban Development. "Good
Neighbor Next Door Loan Servicing." March 7, 2006
<http://www.hud.gov/offices/hsg/sfh/nsc/gnndserv.cfm>
(accessed May 27, 2006).

Yonkers Moves to Limit Where Sex Offenders Live

Newspaper article

By: Michael Gannon

Date: November 8, 2005

Source: Gannon, Michael. "Yonkers Moves to Limit
Where Sex Offenders Live." *Journal News*, November
8, 2005.

About the Author: Michael Gannon is a reporter for the
Journal News, a daily newspaper based in White
Plains, New York, that has served Westchester, Rockland, and Putnam counties since 1829, with an emphasis on local and regional news coverage.

INTRODUCTION

Since the explosion of media and public concern
about child sexual abuse and sexual predators in the
mid–1980s, public pressure for harsher sentences and
tighter regulation of sex offenders has increased. The
1993 murder of twelve-year-old Polly Klaas by
paroled convict Richard Allen Davis led to the passage
of California's "three strikes" law, which mandates a
life sentence upon a third felony conviction.

The following year, seven-year-old Megan Kanka
was raped and murdered by Jesse K. Timmendequas, a
convicted child molester who had moved into her suburban neighborhood after serving seven years at a sex
offender facility. Within a month of her murder, New
Jersey had introduced legislation known as "Megan's
Law" that required sex offenders to register their
address and contact information with the police for ten
years after their release from prison and mandated a
life sentence for a second sexual offense. Megan's Law
also allowed authorities to publicize the names and
addresses of sex offenders. In 1996 Megan's Law was
signed into federal legislation, requiring that released
sex offenders be registered in a national database and
allowing authorities to notify communities whenever a
released sex offender moved to a new residence.

Criminologists and criminal justice policy experts
debate the effectiveness of community notification
legislation, however, arguing that the stress of notoriety and unwelcoming communities often drives
released sex offenders underground and results in failure to comply with registration requirements. The
public, media, and politicians, however, continue to
argue for more stringent regulation of sex offenders
and to limit their freedom in hopes that they will
choose to live elsewhere.

■ PRIMARY SOURCE

Yonkers Moves to Limit Where Sex Offenders Live

YONKERS—The City Council last night unanimously
gave its preliminary blessing to a law that would restrict
where moderate- and high-risk sex offenders can live, a
concept that has met resistance from civil libertarians in
other New York cities and towns.

Council President Richard Martinelli and Majority
Leader Liam McLaughlin, both Republicans running for reelection today, sponsored the measure, which would bar
Level 2 and 3 sex offenders from living within a quarter-
mile of day-care centers or schools. The state considers
Level 2 and 3 offenders to be of moderate and high risk to
reoffend.

The council voted 7–0 to refer the legislation, which
would amend the city's zoning code, to the Planning
Board for review.

"What this legislation will do is help protect our children by not allowing these Level 2 and 3 sex offenders
from moving near our schools," McLaughlin said.

Former Assemblyman Michael Spano, who was sexually molested as a child, urged the council to approve
the law. He said that when he was in the state Legislature he advocated for tougher restrictions on sex offenders, because of their high rate of recidivism. "They will
commit this crime over and over and over again. There is
no cure," he said.

The upstate city of Binghamton last month rescinded
a similar law it passed in May, after the state passed a
law restricting Level 3 sex offenders from visiting school
grounds. The city also was being sued by a group of
unnamed sex offenders aided by the New York Civil Liberties Union, who argued the law effectively prohibited
them from living anywhere in Binghamton.

Linda Berns, executive director of the Lower Hudson Valley chapter of the New York Civil Liberties Union, said the organization would review the Yonkers proposal. She said a local ordinance cannot go further than a state statute.

"It might be in trouble if it's going further than a state law," Berns said.

City lawyers tinkered with the Yonkers proposal since Martinelli and McLaughlin introduced it last month. They removed a provision that would have prevented sex offenders from even traveling within a quarter-mile of not only day-care centers and schools, but school bus stops and parks. That precept was viewed as too restrictive, Corporation Counsel Frank Rubino said.

The law gives the city the power to levy fines of up to $10,000 and to imprison violators for up to one year.

At least 24 known Level 3 sex offenders live in Yonkers, according to the Sex Offender Registry on the state Department of Criminal Justice Services Web site (http://criminaljustice.state.ny.us/nsor). Currently, there are no restrictions on where sex offenders may live, but they must register with local authorities under Megan's Law.

In each of the past six years, the Republican-controlled state Senate has approved civil confinement legislation, which would allow violent sexual predators to be confined in mental hospitals after their release from prison. Civil libertarians, however, have fought the legislation, and the Democrat-led Assembly has not voted on it.

McLaughlin blamed the state's inaction as part of the reason for the Yonkers proposal.

The debate in Albany over civil confinement heated up in June after a White Plains woman, Concetta Russo-Carriero, was stabbed to death in a parking garage next to the Galleria mall. A homeless sex offender who had served more than 20 years in prison for raping three women has been charged in the slaying.

The suspect, Philip Grant, had been kicked out of Westchester County's airport shelter earlier this year, but he would sleep at the drop-in shelter next door and was bused back to downtown White Plains each day.

SIGNIFICANCE

When restrictions are imposed on sex offenders, protection of the community and the safety of children are most often the primary motivators. However, residents and politicians alike often fail to consider the implications of such policies and the potential problems that they may create. While experts recognize the role of registry systems as a useful managerial and investigative tool, community notification is often problematic. Such revelations have been known to spark vigilantism among residents, and sex offenders have been threatened, hounded out of communities, and even physically harmed.

Ironically, there is some evidence that the stress, stigma, and isolation that accompany community notification may trigger a relapse that might not have occurred otherwise. Registration and notification do facilitate the enforcement of more detailed management strategies, such as residence restrictions, but there is no evidence to suggest they reduce recidivism or increase community safety. Despite this, residents and politicians continue to advocate for increasingly restrictive legislation. Megan's Law survived a constitutional challenge that it violated privacy rights in 2002 when the Supreme Court upheld Connecticut's use of an internet registry system.

As of 2005, fourteen states (Alabama, Arkansas, California, Florida, Georgia, Illinois, Indiana, Iowa, Kentucky, Louisiana, Ohio, Oklahoma, Oregon and Tennessee) have enacted legislation that prohibits sex offenders from residing near schools, day care centers, and parks. Several other states, including New York, have local bylaws in place and are considering state legislation. The least restrictive policy is Illinois's 500-foot rule, but most states require a 1,000- or 2,000-foot radius.

Like community notification, housing restrictions increase the former offender's isolation, separate him from available community support, and create financial and emotional stress that may well increase the risk of reoffense. Due to the distribution of schools and parks, restricted zones often overlap, making it extremely difficult or even impossible for offenders to find housing. Offenders also claim that residence restrictions would have no impact on their risk of reoffense, pointing out that sexual predators often commit offenses away from their place of residence to avoid being recognized.

Residence restrictions are unlikely to protect communities and children from sexual victimization—a determined offender will not be deterred by such restrictions. This approach to sex offender management is based on an emotional and intuitive desire to protect children, but fails to take into account relevant research and understanding about the sex offenders' motivations and risk factors. Blanket prohibitions such as residence restriction laws provide community residents with a false sense of security but do not effectively protect children and communities. In fact, the emphasis on sexual predators and "stranger danger" may detract from the much larger problem of familial abuse, since the vast majority of children who are sexually abused are victimized by a parent, family member, or someone in a position of trust. The successful management of sex offenders must be based on individual assessment of offense patterns and risk factors and combined with appropriate treatment, support, monitoring and rehabilitation.

FURTHER RESOURCES

Books

Brown, Mark, and John Pratt, eds. *Dangerous Offenders: Punishment and Social Order.* New York, N.Y.: Routledge, 2000.

Jenkins, Philip. *Moral Panic: Changing Conceptions of the Child Molester in Modern America.* New Haven, Conn.: Yale University Press, 1998.

Periodicals

Edward, William, and Christopher Hensley. "Contextualizing Sex Offender Management Legislation and Policy: Evaluating the Problem of Latent Consequences in Community Notification Laws." *International Journal of Offender Therapy and Comparative Criminology.* 45, no. 1 (2001): 83–101.

Levenson, Jill S., and Leo P. Cotter. "The Impact of Sex Offender Residence Restrictions: 1,000 Feet from Danger or One Step From Absurd?" *International Journal of Offender Therapy and Comparative Criminology.* 49, no. 2 (2005): 168–178.

———. "The Effect of Megan's Law on Sex Offender Reintegration." *Journal of Contemporary Criminal Justice.* 21, no. 1 (2005): 49–66.

Petrunik, Michael G. "The Hare and the Tortoise: Dangerousness and Sex Offender Policy in the United States and Canada." *Canadian Journal of Criminology and Criminal Justice.* 45, no. 1 (2003): 43–72.

———. "Managing Unacceptable Risk: Sex Offenders, Community Response, and Social Policy in the United States and Canada." *International Journal of Offender Therapy and Comparative Criminology.* 46, no. 4 (2002): 483–511.

Federal Costs Dropping Under New Medicare Drug Plan, Administration Reports

Magazine article

By: Robert Pear

Date: February 3, 2006

Source: Pear, Robert. "Federal Costs Dropping Under New Medicare Drug Plan, Administration Reports." *New York Times.* February 3, 2006: A20.

About the Author: Robert Pear is a political columnist for the *New York Times*.

INTRODUCTION

Health care is one of the fastest-growing segments of the American economy. A 2003 report on the expansion of health care costs noted that medical care, as a percentage of the total U.S. economy, doubled in size from 1970 to 2002, rising from just 7 percent of Gross Domestic Product (GDP) to 14 percent during this period. The report also projected that health care costs would continue to climb as a relative share of the nation's economy, reaching almost 17 percent of GDP by 2011.

Medical costs have risen for a variety of reasons. Improvements in nutrition and medical technology have led to longer life spans, and growing ranks of senior citizens require larger health care expenditures. The development of expensive treatments for previously untreatable conditions has also raised health care costs. Employer-funded and government-funded medical benefits have encouraged Americans to take advantage of health care opportunities, thereby raising average medical spending per person. Finally, as the Baby Boom generation (generally, those born between the years 1946 to 1960) moves from early adulthood to old age, this group is incurring increasing medical costs, which contribute to the continuing rise in national health care outlays.

Spending on prescription drugs in particular has climbed. From 1993 to 2003, national spending on prescriptions rose at an average rate of 13 percent annually. From 2002 to 2003, overall medical care expenditures excluding prescriptions rose at a rate of 7 to 9 percent, while prescription costs rose 11 percent. With more than 60 percent of adults and more than ninety percent of seniors taking prescription drugs on an ongoing basis, these rising costs represented a significant drain on the financial resources of a broad segment of the American population. The rising costs of prescription drugs posed a particular burden for many retirees, who in some cases were forced to choose which of several prescriptions to fill each month.

The federal Medicare program was created by President Lyndon Johnson (1908–1973) as part of his "Great Society" initiative to eradicate poverty and improve standards of living. Johnson's success came on the heels of two decades of political debate over the

Pharmacist Milton Chapman poses at Dougherty's Pharmacy in Dallas on January 11, 2006. Chapman is one of many pharmacists across Texas who were covering the costs of medications to make sure that their patients got the care they needed as glitches were fixed in the new Medicare prescription drug program. AP IMAGES.

merits and dangers of establishing federal medical insurance for Americans; his accomplishments included Medicare coverage for seniors and Medicaid for the poor.

Medicare originally included two major sections. Medicare Part A covered hospitalization and related expenses. For most beneficiaries, Part A was provided at no cost as part of participation in the Social Security system, and participants were responsible for a deductible amount before Medicare began paying; in 2006, the Part A deductible was $952.00. Medicare Part B covered doctor visits and outpatient medical expenses; participation in Part B was optional and those who enrolled paid a monthly premium and a deductible; in 2006, these amounts were $88.50 and $124.00 respectively.

Because Medicare did not cover all expenses, private insurers were also authorized by Medicare to offer standardized insurance policies to make up the difference. These Medicare supplements, sometimes known as Medi-gap policies, paid for many of the charges not covered under Medicare Parts A and B. Seniors on Medicare could choose among several standardized benefits packages for their Medicare Supplement.

Despite the comprehensive nature of Medicare coverage, the program originated in an era before prescription drugs were so common or so expensive. For this reason, Medicare never provided coverage for prescription drugs, meaning that participants in the program were expected to pay for their own prescription drugs. Beginning in 2006, all forty million Medicare participants were able to receive prescription drug coverage under the program's newly established Part D. Retirees could choose among plans offered by several local providers in order to maximize their cost savings. Federal spending on Part D was expected to top $38 billion in the program's first year of operation.

■ PRIMARY SOURCE

WASHINGTON, Feb. 2 — Federal spending on the new Medicare drug benefit will be 20 percent lower than expected this year because beneficiaries are choosing prescription drug plans with lower premiums, the Bush administration said Thursday.

"People are tending to sign up for less expensive plans," said Dr. Mark B. McClellan, administrator of the federal Centers for Medicare and Medicaid Services.

To some experts, the new estimates suggest that the Bush administration's philosophical approach of encouraging private-market competition to hold down costs is working.

John K. Gorman, a former Medicare official who is now a consultant to many insurers, said: "Competitive bidding is working for beneficiaries and for taxpayers. This will force some consolidation of drug plans. Only a few big companies, like Humana and UnitedHealth, can keep up with this kind of aggressive pricing."

Beneficiary premiums are now expected to average $25 a month, down from the $37 projected last year, Dr. McClellan said. The figures came from the office of the Medicare actuary, a career civil servant.

Another factor involves a national trend: Insurers reined in drug costs, and as a result spending on prescription drugs grew less than expected in 2004 and 2005. The government now estimates that drug costs for Medicare in 2006 will be lower, as well.

When Congress debated the Medicare drug bill in 2003, lawmakers feared that some regions might not have even two competing drug plans. Now, in almost every state, more than 40 free-standing drug plans are available. Every state but Alaska has at least one plan with a premium less than $20 a month.

The net cost to the federal government for Medicare drug coverage in 2006 is expected to be $30.5 billion, down from a prior estimate of $38.1 billion—a difference of $7.6 billion, or 20 percent. The estimated cost over 10 years is also lower: $678 billion, down 8 percent from the earlier estimate of $737 billion for the decade from 2006 to 2015.

One reason for the lower cost is the intense competition among private insurers offering drug coverage. But the multiplicity of drug plans has caused confusion among beneficiaries and pharmacists.

Senator Thomas R. Carper, Democrat of Delaware, who voted for the 2003 law that created the drug benefit, said: "The Centers for Medicare and Medicaid Services approved too many plans. For many of our seniors, the system is almost incomprehensible." Mr. Carper made the comment Thursday at a hearing of the Senate Special Committee on Aging.

In August, after reviewing bids from private insurers, the Bush administration lowered its estimate of the average premium to $32 a month, from $37. But it had no firm estimate of savings to the government, and it did not anticipate the behavior of beneficiaries in choosing cheaper plans. Enrollment began on Nov. 15.

Insurers try to save money by negotiating discounts with drug manufacturers and retail pharmacists. Actuaries said the discounts proved to be larger than they had expected.

Under blistering criticism from senators of both parties, the Bush administration announced several steps on Thursday to help beneficiaries who could not get their medications through Medicare. Democrats said they doubted the steps would be sufficient to solve all the problems in the program, which began Jan. 1.

On Thursday, the Senate rejected an effort by Democrats to extend the enrollment deadline for the program from May 15 until Dec. 31.

Insurers had been required to provide a temporary 30-day supply of any drug that a beneficiary was previously taking. Beneficiaries and pharmacists say that many insurers have flouted this requirement.

Anticipating more problems, the Bush administration said that insurers must provide an additional 60-day supply of medicine, guaranteeing 90 days of transitional coverage.

At Thursday's hearing, Senator Ron Wyden, Democrat of Oregon, told Dr. McClellan he had done "great damage to the cause of private-sector choice" in health care. With so many plans available, he said, "it's bedlam out there."

Mr. Wyden voted for the drug benefit in 2003, but said: "I did not conceive that the rollout of the new program would be bungled this way."

The aging-panel chairman, Senator Gordon H. Smith, Republican of Oregon, said the administration had not done enough to ensure a smooth transition for six million low-income people who lost Medicaid drug coverage on Jan. 1 and were to receive drug coverage under Medicare.

SIGNIFICANCE

Supporters and critics of of Part D coverage frequently found themselves agreeing on what the plan had done but disagreeing over whether the results were positive or negative. For example, critics of the program claim that the large number of plan options created confusion for many seniors, leading some of them to give up on applying for coverage. Supporters responded that the large number of choices allowed seniors to remain in control of their own medical care; they also credited competition among providers with the lower than expected costs experienced during the program's first year.

Proponents of Part D also point out that the program drastically reduced out-of-pocket costs for most seniors who enroll and that these savings occurred immediately; opponents countered that the program glossed over the high prices being charged by pharmaceutical companies, which they claimed was the root cause of the problems. These critics also derided the plan's inability to negotiate with drug makers, an option that the Veteran's Administration regularly used to reduce drug prices. As Medicare prescription coverage completed its first year, it appeared likely that the first decade of the program's life would be a period of intense disagreement over its success or failure.

Although the new prescription drug benefit was good news for retirees, the future of Medicare remained in doubt. The 2006 annual report by the system's trustees projected that Medicare could be unable to pay its promised benefits by 2018, when its trust fund could be depleted.

FURTHER RESOURCES

Books

CCH Health Law Editors. *Medicare Explained, 2006*. New York: CCH, 2006.

Oberlander, Jonathan. *The Political Life of Medicare*. Chicago: University of Chicago Press, 2003.

Poen, Monte M. . *Harry S. Truman Versus the Medical Lobby: The Genesis of Medicare*. Columbia: University of Missouri Press, 1996.

Periodicals

Gleckman, Howard. "Medicare Surprise." *Business Week*. 3982(2006):38.

Marmor, Theodore R. and Gary J. McKissick . "Medicare's Future: Fact, Fiction and Folly." *American Journal of Law & Medicine*. 26(2000):225-253.

Merric, Amy. "Getting an 'A' in Part D." *The Wall Street Journal - Eastern Edition*. 247(June 21, 2006):B1-B2.

Web sites

Milken Institute. "America's Healthcare Economy." 2003 <http://www.maricopa.edu/bwd/pdfs/healthpole003.pdf> (accessed June 29, 2006).

U.S. Government. "Medicare Prescription Drug Coverage." 2006 <http://www.medicare.gov/pdphome.asp> (accessed June 29, 2006).

Washington Post. "Medicare Will Go Broke By 2018, Trustees Report." 2003 <http://www.washingtonpost.com/wp-dyn/content/article/2006/05/01/AR2006050101448.html> (accessed June 29, 2006).

Ban on Most Abortions Advances in South Dakota

News article

By: Monica Davey

Date: February 22, 2006

Source: Davey, Monica. "Ban on Most Abortions Advances in South Dakota." *New York Times*.

About the Author: Monica Davey is a reporter for the *New York Times* specializing in stories related to immigration and law.

INTRODUCTION

In 1973, the Supreme Court ruled in *Roe v. Wade* that all state laws banning abortion were unconstitutional. Specifically, it ruled that "a State may impose virtually no restriction on the performance of abortions during the first trimester of pregnancy," where the first trimester is the first three months of a pregnancy.

The decision has been intensely controversial. In the years since 1973, most Americans have come to identify themselves as either "pro-choice" or "pro-life." Here quotation marks have been used because the terms themselves are often controversial. For example, many who oppose abortion dispute the view that abortion is a "choice," while many who support abortion dispute the view that only foes of abortion are in favor of "life." Most commonly, "pro-choice" means belief that limiting or banning abortion during the first trimester is unconstitutional and immoral, while "pro-life" means the belief that abortion itself is unconstitutional (despite *Roe v. Wade*) and immoral. Pro-choicers support *Roe v. Wade* and pro-lifers oppose it.

Political struggle between the pro-life and pro-choice camps has intensified over time. In 2005 and 2006, pro-lifers in South Dakota sought to pass a state law banning nearly all abortions. The law bans abortion even when the pregnancy is a result of rape or incest; it does allow abortion to save the life of the mother. The law makes performing an abortion in South Dakota a Class 5 felony, meaning a crime punishable by a fine of up to $5,000 and a prison term of up to five years. The law does make performing an abortion a crime, not having one.

The Women's Health and Human Life Protection Act, HB 1215, was passed by the South Dakota state

Pro-choice and pro-life opponents face off in front of the Supreme Court in Washington on January 23, 2006. The rally was held to mark the 33rd anniversary of the *Roe v. Wade* ruling that legalized abortion. AP IMAGES.

legislature in February 2006 (House, 23–12; Senate, 50–18) and was signed into law by Governor Michael Rounds in early March.

PRIMARY SOURCE

PIERRE, S.D., Feb. 22—Setting up South Dakota to become the first state in 14 years to start a direct legal attack on *Roe v. Wade*, lawmakers voted on Wednesday to outlaw nearly all abortions.

Across the country, abortion rights advocates reacted with outrage and dismay. The Planned Parenthood Federation of America, which runs the sole abortion clinic in South Dakota, said it was bracing to fight the move in court immediately, if the governor signs it.

"This represents a monumental step backward for personal privacy for women," Nancy Keenan, president of Naral Pro-Choice America, said.

Some opponents of abortion rights celebrated what they called a bold and brave move and lauded South Dakota for taking the lead in what they said they hoped would become a series of states to challenge Roe, the 1973 decision that made abortion legal.

The shifting makeup of the United States Supreme Court, the opponents said, offered a crucial opportunity, the first since at least 1992.

"It is a calculated risk, to be sure, but I believe it is a fight worth fighting," State Senator Brock L. Greenfield, a Clark Republican who is also director of the South Dakota Right to Life, told his colleagues in a hushed, packed chamber here.

After more than an hour of fierce and emotional debate, the senators rejected pleas to add exceptions for incest or rape or for the health of the pregnant woman and instead voted, 23 to 12, to outlaw all abortions, except those to save the woman's life.

They also rejected an effort to allow South Dakotans to decide the question in a referendum and an effort to prevent state tax dollars from financing what is certain to be a long and expensive court battle.

To be enacted, the bill, the most sweeping ban approved in any state in more than a decade, requires the signature of Gov. Mike Rounds, a Republican, who opposes abortion.

After overwhelmingly approving the measure this month, the House, too, has to vote on it again because the Senate slightly reworded it, although the intent of the bill was unchanged and the vote there seems unlikely to shift.

Mr. Rounds has said he will not comment on whether he will sign the measure until it reaches his desk. It is likely to arrive there by next week. He has 15 days to make a decision.

In an interview this week, Mr. Rounds said he had doubts about whether now was the time to make a "full frontal attack" on *Roe v. Wade*, as opposed to pressing for more laws that restrict abortions—setting limits, for instance, on their timing, methods or the requirements for parental notification.

Those restrictions, he said, have immediate effects on preventing abortions in South Dakota.

Mr. Rounds suggested that the two approaches might be possible simultaneously, particularly as a way to keep opponents of abortion rights from splintering over strategy questions. The key, he said, was in "saving lives while at the same time appeasing a segment that says you won't know unless you try the direct frontal attack."

Lawmakers opposed to abortion rights here—and advocates opposed to abortion rights around the country—have been split over timing questions. Some argue that the arrivals of Chief Justice John G. Roberts Jr. and Justice Samuel A. Alito Jr. on the Supreme Court and speculation that Justice John Paul Stevens might soon retire, made now an ideal time to challenge Roe.

Others, however, have said a challenge should wait, for the arrival of additional justices who might be open to overturning Roe and for a shift in public opinion.

Nancy Northrup, president of the Center for Reproductive Rights, said the South Dakota action—similarly broad bans have recently been proposed in at least five other states—reminded her of a wave of state challenges to Roe in the years just before 1992, when the Supreme Court reaffirmed a core right to abortion in *Planned Parenthood v. Casey*.

"People have this sense that the court is in flux and is shifting so they want to try to test out how far they can go," Ms. Northrup said. "The answer will be in how the new justices vote."

On Wednesday in the Senate chamber, any division about strategy among opponents of abortion rights seemed to have vanished.

"This state has a right and a duty to step up to the plate," Senator William M. Napoli, Republican of Rapid City, told his colleagues before he voted for the ban.

It passed by a margin larger than many on both sides had predicted.

Opponents, meanwhile, questioned the purpose of such a law and the potential costs of the litigation, and they recited harrowing stories of women who had become pregnant, for example, after having been raped.

"What can we as a state possibly gain by passing a bill that is unconstitutional?" asked Senator Clarence Kooistra, Republican of Garretson, who added that he represented the "silent majority" of South Dakotans who would not approve outlawing abortion nearly entirely.

Leaders of a movement against abortion rights in this state said they had raised $1 million in donations to help pay for the legal fight ahead.

"I didn't want money to be the reason people wouldn't vote for this bill," said Leslee J. Unruh, founder and president of the Abstinence Clearinghouse in Sioux Falls, who said she could not disclose the identities of those who had pledged money. "We're concerned with the 800 children aborted here every year."

After the vote, Kate Looby, state director of Planned Parenthood, left the statehouse promising to press Mr. Rounds to veto the bill.

"I'm very hopeful that he will be a voice of reason in this process and will choose the health and safety of the women of South Dakota over the political tool that this bill was designed to be," Ms. Looby said.

Failing that, she said, Planned Parenthood will sue, and it expects that a court will block the law from going into effect, while the case makes its way through the courts, a process that could take years.

"It scares me," Ms. Looby said, "to think that it may in fact be the reality for my daughter's generation."

SIGNIFICANCE

The 2006 South Dakota abortion law was designed to be incompatible with *Roe v. Wade*, forcing a reconsideration of abortion by the Supreme Court. The law will probably be challenged in a federal district court by pro-choice groups; whichever side loses the case would appeal, taking it to a federal appellate (appeals) court, whence it would be appealed again to the Supreme Court. The Supreme Court's decision could be overridden only by a constitutional amendment.

Many pro-lifers hope that with the recent appointment of two conservative, anti-abortion judges by President George W. Bush (John Roberts and Samuel Alito), the Supreme Court would overturn *Roe v. Wade*, allowing state legislatures to ban abortion. If this were to happen, some states would ban abortion and some would not. It is also possible that the Court could rule more broadly, not only allowing states to ban abortion but declaring abortion unconstitutional.

Alternatively, the law might be overturned by a South Dakota court or retracted by referendum before being challenged in federal court. In March 2006, a pro-choice group including doctors, political leaders, and ministers, the South Dakota Campaign for Healthy Families, began collecting signatures to force a referendum on the law. As of 2006, similar measures were being advocated in at least five other states, making reconsideration of *Roe v. Wade* by the Supreme Court likely at some time in the following five to ten years.

Some conservative strategists have been concerned that the head-on South Dakota approach to overturning *Roe v. Wade* could backfire. They pointed out that the South Dakota law's refusal to exempt cases of rape or incest—requiring, for example, a twelve-year-old who becomes pregnant after being raped by her father to carry the pregnancy to term—might appear too extreme to voters. When polled, about twice as many Americans say that they support the basic abortion right defined by *Roe v. Wade*, though also saying they approve of some restrictions, such as notification of parents by minors seeking abortions. (As of 2006, thirty-four U.S. states had laws requiring such notification.) First-trimester abortion is an extremely popular procedure: about half of all U.S. pregnancies are unintended, and about 40 percent of those pregnancies are ended by abortion (about 1.2 million abortions per year). And despite the conservative tilt of the Supreme Court, legal experts agreed that it was probable, based on voting records and public statements, that five of the nine justices would uphold *Roe v. Wade*. In short, some conservative politicians and strategists feared that if the South Dakota law made pro-life forces appear extremist and led to yet another pro-choice precedent at the level of the Supreme Court, it would do the anti-abortion cause more harm than good. Other conservatives disagreed, supporting the law as not only right but timely. Pro-choice organizations were unanimous in opposing the South Dakota bill.

FURTHER RESOURCES

Books

Ball, Howard. *The Supreme Court in the Intimate Lives of Americans: Birth, Sex, Marriage, Childrearing, and Death.* New York: New York University Press, 2002.

Periodicals

Davey, Monica. "Sizing Up the Opposing Armies in the Coming Abortion Battle." *New York Times* (February 26, 2006).

———. "South Dakota Bans Abortion, Setting up a Battle." *New York Times* (March 7, 2006).

Web sites

Guttmacher Institute. "Facts on Induced Abortion in the United States." May 4, 2006. <http://www.guttmacher.org/pubs/fb_induced_abortion.html> (accessed May 31, 2006).

HUD Charges Philadelphia Landlords with Six Violations of Fair Housing Act

Property Manager Steers Prospective Black Renter Away from Predominantly White Neighborhood

Press release

By: Antoinette Banks

Date: February 6, 2006

Source: *U.S. Department of Housing and Urban Development.* "News Release: HUD Charges Philadelphia Landlords with Six Violations of Fair Housing Act." February 6, 2006 <http://www.hud.gov/news/release.cfm?content=pr06-015.cfm> (accessed May 26, 2006).

About the Author: Antoinette Banks is the media contact for the U.S. Department of Housing and Urban Development (HUD), the primary government agency responsible for ensuring equal access to housing and for improving the quality of affordable housing in the United States.

INTRODUCTION

In spite of the passage of constitutional amendments and civil rights laws after the American Civil War (1861–1865), racial discrimination, including segregated housing practices, was widespread in the South. Beginning in the late 1800s, racial segregation became a legal requirement in that region, a situation that was not undone until new laws were passed during the civil rights movement of the 1950s and 1960s. Racial segregation—in housing, schools, employment, and the like—was common in the North as well, though not supported by legislation.

As the country became progressively more industrialized, poorer and less well educated people began to migrate toward the urban areas, particularly in the northern states, in search of better-paying jobs and an easier way of life. In these areas, public housing projects, urban renewal programs, and geographic area rezoning all served as ways of increasing the racial and socioeconomic divide and subtly promoting segregation, while setting the stage for urban ghettos and deeply impoverished housing projects. Housing ordinances were deliberately worded in ways to ensure that the racial divide was developed. Streets and neighborhoods were zoned specifically by race. As businesses moved away from the cities and into newly created suburban areas, inner-city ghettos and housing projects remained primarily populated by African Americans, while white people migrated toward the suburbs. The racial and cultural divide was both intentionally created and long-lasting. Many areas of the United States remained highly segregated into the twenty-first century.

Title VIII of the Civil Rights Act of 1968, a section also called the Fair Housing Act, was designed to prevent any sort of intentional discrimination—based upon "race, color, religion, sex, familial status, or national origin"—in housing sales or rentals, in the issuance of mortgages or other types of dwelling-related financing, or in any other sort of residential dealings or financial arrangements. Important preceding legislation, in the form of Title VI of the Civil Rights Act of 1964, stated that no programs or entities that receive federal funding could intentionally discriminate against persons based on race, color, or national origin. In addition, there are a series of executive orders that bar discrimination in housing or employment via facilities or agencies that are in any way related to the federal government, and such orders place oversight of housing-related issues under the auspices of HUD and the Fair Housing Council.

■ PRIMARY SOURCE

Washington, D.C.—The U.S. Department of Housing and Urban Development announced today that it has charged Daniel, Helene and Ava Waisbord, and Rhawn Street Apartments LLC, owners of more than 150 rental units, with violating the Fair Housing Act for refusing to rent a property to a prospective African-American renter, steering the person away from a predominantly white neighborhood, and quoting her a higher rental price to discourage her from renting the home.

"The right to housing without regard to one's race or color isn't an option, it's the law," said Kim Kendrick, HUD Assistant Secretary for Fair Housing and Equal Opportunity. "We're working hard to educate housing providers and the public about their fair housing rights and responsibilities, but when a landlord illegally prevents someone from obtaining the housing of their choice, we will take swift enforcement action."

HUD's investigation revealed that Karla Baker, who is African American, met Daniel Waisbord on Gillespie Street in Philadelphia to view a vacant house for rent. Baker liked the house and Waisbord told her a deposit was required to hold the home. Waisbord told her the rent was $775 and that she would have to pay the water bill. Baker asked Waisbord if the rent could be reduced to $750 monthly. Waisbord said that he could not reduce the rent on the property they were viewing, but that he had other properties he could reduce the rent on.

Baker insisted on renting the Gillespie St. property and gave Waisbord a deposit to hold the property. Waisbord then allegedly stated, "The neighbors don't like me and I am a white man, and they are Germans. I can decrease $25 off the other place, but I can't rent this place to you, the neighbors won't like it."

Waisbord insisted that Baker see other properties he had on Rhawn St. Baker relented and later viewed the Rhawn St. properties. When Waisbord showed up for the viewing, Baker informed him that she did not like the location and the lack of security, and that she still wanted to rent the Gillespie St. property. Waisbord declined and returned Baker's deposit.

Less than one month later, Waisbord rented the house on Gillespie St. to two white renters for $700 a month, plus $42 a month for water.

Among other things, HUD is charging the owners, Daniel, Helene and Ava Waisbord, and Rhawn Street Apartments LLC with violating the Fair Housing Act for:

Requiring a higher rent for the Gillespie Street house from Baker than from the white tenants who eventually rented it, because of Baker's race and color;

Telling Baker that she could not rent the Gillespie Street property because the neighbors would object to Baker's race and color;

Misrepresenting to Baker that the Gillespie Street house was not available for rent to her, because of her race and color; and

Steering the Complainant from renting the property at Gillespie Street on account of her race and color.

A hearing on the charges will be held by a HUD Administrative Law Judge on April 25, 2006 in the Philadelphia, Pennsylvania, area, unless either the complainant or respondent elects to have the case decided by a federal judge in U.S. District Court. An election to go to district court must be made by Feb. 21, 2006.

Housing discrimination charges heard before an Administrative Law Judge carry a maximum civil penalty of $11,000 for a first offense—more if the respondent has committed prior violations of the Act—plus actual damages for the complainant, injunctive or other equitable relief, and attorney fees.

Should either party elect to go to district court, either party may request a jury trial. A district court may award the damages available in an administrative proceeding, and may also award punitive damages.

If neither party elects to proceed in federal district court, the case is brought on behalf of the complainant by a HUD attorney before a HUD Administrative Law Judge. If either party does elect, the case is brought on behalf of the complainant by an Assistant United States Attorney or an attorney from the U.S. Department of Justice in federal district court. In either forum, each party has the right to be represented by his or her own attorney.

HUD is the nation's housing agency committed to increasing homeownership, particularly among minorities; creating affordable housing opportunities for low-income Americans; and supporting the homeless, elderly, people with disabilities and people living with AIDS. The Department also promotes economic and community development as well as enforces the nation's fair housing laws.

SIGNIFICANCE

Persons involved in any aspect of the business of real estate are legally prohibited from acting in a discriminatory fashion with customers or potential clients. One of the most problematic and most frequently cited issues in consumer complaints against real estate agents is a practice called "steering." Steering is when a Realtor urges buyers or renters to look at housing only in specific areas or types of dwellings based upon the racial composition of the locale. The behavior may be very subtle: the client may simply be taken to specific areas, or certain neighborhoods or streets may be promoted while others are avoided. Often, a way of encouraging people to refrain from considering certain locations is to state that the schools in a particular neighborhood or area are inferior to the schools in other regions.

One way in which steering occurs, particularly in the rental markets, is by quoting African American, Hispanic, or other minority applicants (including those who are openly homosexual, for instance) higher rates than are given to white people. Another practice is to say that no units or homes in particular subdivisions or neighborhoods are available, offering to enter the individual's name on a waiting list, and then never contacting them again. In the home-buying or refinancing realms, discrimination is often evidenced by charging minorities higher interest rates than non-minorities, by placing them in higher-risk rate categories (resulting in higher interest rates and higher monthly payments), or by refusing to approve mortgages or loans for minorities with a higher degree of frequency than is the case for white individuals who have equal qualifications and similar credit profiles.

In a 2005 article in the *Washington Post*, it was suggested that minority home buyers might fall victim to so-called predatory lending practices, in which loans are structured so as to hold higher interest rates, to have built-in pre-payment penalties, or to otherwise put people in risky and oppressive financial situations in order to secure safe housing. According to data published by HUD, African Americans and Hispanics report experiencing some form of racial or ethnic discrimination in roughly 50 percent of all private housing interactions—that is, those based on response to advertisements, driving up to homes for sale, or stopping at model home or apartment sites.

The National Fair Housing Alliance (NFHA) publishes the *Fair Housing Trends Report* in which unethical, unfair, and illegal housing practices are detailed. The NFHA uses a testing program in which people pose as couples—African American, white, and Hispanic—who are equally matched for demographics and socioeconomics. In some cases the minority applicants show slightly superior profiles, including better credit reports and higher incomes. These "couples" pretend to be potential home buyers and visit a variety of Realtors, rental companies, and lending institutions, in order to ascertain the use of discriminatory practices. The NFHA's 2006 report, which covered a dozen metropolitan housing regions across the nation, revealed a surprisingly high percentage of overt discriminatory acts against African Americans and Hispanics. According to the NFHA's testing rates, nearly 90 percent of the time the minority couples were steered away from primarily white areas. They were also shown fewer homes and were often "stood up" by Realtors after making and confirming appointments.

In contrast, white couples were shown a larger number of homes and Realtors were more likely to show up for scheduled appointments. In addition, the white couples were actively steered away from neighborhoods predominantly populated by minorities and from racially diverse areas. As was reported elsewhere, the NFHA couples were frequently discouraged from considering certain housing areas through language disparaging the quality of the neighborhood public schools. The NFHA report estimated that there are close to three million intentional violations of the Fair Housing Act, based simply on the numbers concerned with racial, ethnic, or cultural discrimination, every year throughout the United States. The NFHA also reported that this is likely to be a vast understatement of true occurrences; the organization estimates that more than 90 percent of the violations are never publicly reported.

FURTHER RESOURCES

Books

Fader, Steven. *Density by Design: New Directions in Residential Development*. Washington, D.C.: Urban Land Institute, 2000.

Lowenstein, Allard. *Submission on Racial Segregation and the Right to Housing*. Washington, D.C.: Poverty & Race Research Action Council, 2005.

Rodwin, Lloyd, and Bishwapriya Sanyal, eds. *The Profession of City Planning: Changes, Images, and Challenges, 1950–2000*. New Brunswick, N.J.: Center for Urban Policy Research, 2000.

Yinger, John. *Closed Doors, Opportunities Lost: The Continuing Costs of Housing Discrimination*. New York: Russell Sage, 1995.

Periodicals

Downey, Kirsten. "Segregation Persists in Housing, Study Says." *Washington Post* (April 6, 2005): E02.

Downs, Anthony. "Some Realities about Sprawl and Urban Decline." *Housing Policy Debate* 10 (1999): 955–974.

Eig, Jonathan. "Mixed Results: How Fear of Integration Turned White Enclave into a Melting Pot." *Wall Street Journal* (August 7, 2000): A1.

Web sites

civilrights.org. "National Fair Housing Alliance Releases Housing Discrimination Data and Denounces Crisis of Segregation." April 5, 2006 <http://www.civilrights.org/issues/housing/details.cfm?id=42073> (accessed May 29, 2006).

U.S. Department of Housing and Urban Development. "Fair Housing Laws and Presidential Executive Orders." March 24, 2006 <http://www.hud.gov/offices/fheo/FHLaws/> (accessed May 29, 2006).

HUD Creates New, Expanded Hurricane Disaster Voucher Program

Bush Administration Provides Additional $390 Million to Assist Families with Housing

Press release

By: Donna White

Date: February 14, 2006

Source: *United States Department of Housing and Urban Development*. " HUD Creates New, Expanded Hurricane Disaster Voucher Program." February 14, 2006 <http://www.hud.gov/news/release.cfm?content=pr06-017.cfm> (accessed June 26, 2006).

About the Author: The U.S. Department of Housing and Urban Development (HUD) is the primary government agency responsible for ensuring equal access to housing and for improving the quality of affordable housing in the United States.

INTRODUCTION

In September 2005, after hurricanes Katrina and Rita decimated areas along the U.S. Gulf Coast, federal agencies scrambled to deploy relief programs effectively. Hampered by dated, inefficient bureaucratic structures, the U.S. Department of Housing and Development (HUD), the Federal Emergency Management Agency (FEMA), and their state counterparts had difficulty coping with the housing crisis that resulted from thousands of homes being badly damaged or completely destroyed. HUD and FEMA were suddenly thrust into a situation that required unprecedented levels of cooperation between the two agencies, and the strain on the existing system was immediately apparent. President George W. Bush seemed oddly hesitant about how to react—a hesitation that some observers have attributed to his administration's ideals about limiting the federal government's involvement in state affairs.

The Katrina Disaster Housing Assistance Program (KDHAP), designed to provide up to eighteen months of housing assistance for displaced families, was a joint initiative of FEMA and HUD. KDHAP was unveiled on September 23, 2005. On September 24, 2005, Hurricane Rita hit the Gulf Coast with unanticipated force. KDHAP had to be rewritten to accommodate the victims of Rita, and this, too, took time and bureaucratic reshuffling.

In the months leading up to the February 2006 release of the annual budget, fiscal conservatives within the Republican Party debated about which federal programs should be cut in order to provide more funds for hurricane relief. House Speaker Dennis Hastert endorsed the recommendation of House Budget Committee Chairman Jim Nussle's (R-Iowa) to amend the FY06 Budget Resolution and cut billions of dollars in mandatory and discretionary spending, but there was dissent within the ranks of the party as to where the funds should ultimately come from. The FY07 Budget Message of the President contained no mention of disaster relief, focusing instead on military efforts in Iraq and Afghanistan and calling for reduced spending on programs deemed inessential by the Bush administration.

■ PRIMARY SOURCE

Washington—The U.S. Department of Housing and Urban Development has used the $390 million supplemental appropriation President Bush signed recently to replace and expand its current rental assistance program that aided families who lost their homes to hurricane Katrina.

The Disaster Voucher Program (DVP) extends eligibility for assistance to families who lost their homes to both Hurricanes Katrina and Rita. The Katrina Disaster Housing Assistance Program (KDHAP) only assisted Katrina evacuees.

"There are still families who desperately need housing," said HUD Assistant Secretary Orlando Cabrera, who heads HUD's Office of Public and Indian Housing. "We are confident this funding and the changes to our original

hurricane rental assistance program will help even more families find stable, more long-term housing solutions."

Families who were eligible for KDHAP—former public housing residents, Section 8 voucher holders and multifamily projects—are eligible for DVP through September 30, 2007, to provide housing anywhere in the U.S. Families who were homeless prior to Katrina or Rita are also eligible for this assistance. The more than 15,000 families who are registered under KDHAP have been transferred to DVP, without assistance interruption....

Families who qualify for DVP are no longer required to get a Federal Emergency Management Agency (FEMA) number. Instead local housing authorities will register and verify eligibility using existing HUD criteria. The additional funding allows HUD to waive the requirement for income and tenant contribution for up to 18 months. If a family's original housing becomes available prior to that time, under DVP the family is eligible to reoccupy that housing.

■

SIGNIFICANCE

In a post-hurricane report prepared by the White House entitled "Hurricane Katrina: Lessons Learned," Frances Fragos Townsend, Assistant to the President for Homeland Security and Counterterrorism, notes that disaster relief in the United States has traditionally been considered the responsibility of local and state governments, with the federal government playing a "supporting role." Among the report's recommendations are greater communication between federal agencies and practice scenarios for future combined relief efforts. A bipartisan Senate panel, led by Republican Susan Collins (R-Maine), concluded in April 2006 that FEMA should be dismantled. Homeland Security officials and former FEMA head Michael Brown responded with skepticism, expressing doubt that yet another bureaucratic reshuffling would create more efficiency. Brown pointed out that the proposed new agency would have much the same mandate as FEMA had before its responsibilities were scaled down.

Pursuant to HUD's announcement about the DVP program, a group consisting of the Center on Budget and Policy Priorities, the Greater New Orleans Fair Housing Action Center, Lawyers Committee for Civil Rights Under Law, New Orleans Legal Assistance, New Orleans School of Law/Loyola University, National Housing Law Project, National Policy and Advocacy Council on Homelessness, Poverty & Race Research Action Council, and the National Low Income Housing Coalition drafted a letter, dated March 10, 2006, to Alphonso Jackson, secretary of HUD. The letter raises concerns about how eligible families would learn about their status and why certain families previously eligible for assistance would lose their eligibility under the new program. It questions the new, dual funding pattern that would sustain the program—funding that would only last until September 30, 2007, unless it was renewed. The overarching worry seems to be that hurricane victims that had been eligible for relief under FEMA programs created specifically for them would get lost within HUD and local Public Housing Authority (PHA) bureaucracy. In spite of widespread FEMA-bashing in the media and among the general population, it may be that the victims themselves were grateful for what protection the beleaguered agency afforded.

As of July 2006, FEMA maintained that it had helped hundreds of thousands of households, paying for thousands of hotel and motel rooms, providing apartment search services and rental assistance, and distributing thousands of manufactured homes. Critiques of FEMA's performance often overlook the fact that every state has its own version of FEMA—the Mississippi Emergency Management Agency, for example, or, in Louisiana, the Governor's Office of Homeland Security and Emergency Preparedness—which further complicated the distribution of resources after the 2005 hurricanes and may do so again in the future.

FURTHER RESOURCES

Web sites

Case Western Reserve University. "Office of Government Relations Legislation and Policy Report." October 2005 <http://www.cwru.edu/pubaff/govrel/oct2005. html> (accessed June 1, 2006).

Executive Office of the President of the United States. "The Budget Message of the President." February 6, 2006 <http://www.gpoaccess.gov/usbudget/fy07/pdf/budget/message.pdf> (accessed June 1, 2006).

MSNBC. "Senate Panel Recommends Abolishing FEMA." April 27, 2006 <http://msnbc.msn.com/id/12505146/> (accessed June 1, 2006).

U.S. Department of Homeland Security. "Federal Gulf Coast Response to Hurricanes Katrina and Rita." September 28, 2005 <http://www.dhs.gov/dhspublic/display?content=4867> (accessed May 31, 2006).

U.S. Department of Housing and Security. "HUD Details New Katrina Disaster Housing Assistance Program—Up to 18 Months of Rental Assistance Available for Displaced Families." September 27, 2005 <http://www.hud.gov/news/release.cfm?content=pr05–135.cfm> (accessed June 1, 2006).

The Washington Post. "Coast Guard's Chief of Staff to Assist FEMA Head Brown." September 7, 2005 <http://www.washingtonpost.com/wp-dyn/content/article/2005/09/06/AR2005090601677.html> (accessed May 31, 2006).

The White House. "Chapter 2: National Preparedness—A Primer." <http://www.whitehouse.gov/reports/katrina-lessons-learned/chapter2.html> (accessed May 31, 2006).

HUD Announces Nearly $25 Million in "Sweat Equity" Grants to Help Families Build Their Own American Dream

More Than 1,500 Affordable Homes To Be Built with SHOP Grants

Press release

By: United States Department of Housing and Urban Development

Date: February 23, 2006

Source: *United States Department of Housing and Urban Development.* "HUD Announces Nearly $25 Million in 'Sweat Equity' Grants to Help Families Build Their Own American Dream." February 23, 2006 <http://www.hud.gov/news/release.cfm?content=pr06-021.cfm> (accessed May 28, 2006).

About the Author: The U.S. Department of Housing and Urban Development (HUD) is the primary government agency responsible for ensuring equal access to housing and for improving the quality of affordable housing in the United States.

INTRODUCTION

The practice of creating low-income housing got its start with the U.S. Housing Act of 1937. The need for affordable housing, however, has always far outstripped its availability. Although the commercial housing market has grown exponentially since the 1930s, the price of real estate has kept pace with its growth, making it progressively more difficult for people living on the fringes of poverty to acquire safe and affordable housing. Interest rates for mortgages have waxed and waned through the years, but the guidelines for creditworthiness have become more stringent along with increases in home and property costs, making it progressively harder for people who are marginalized by class, culture, or socioeconomic status to achieve successful homeownership.

Affordable housing is intended to be accessible and financially manageable for people who earn a low or very low income. Although the poverty line for an individual varies somewhat from year to year, it is typically somewhere around ten thousand dollars in annual income. While those in the upper socioeconomic classes experience rising incomes and increasing financial security corresponding to positive changes in the economy, that is not the case for those living in poverty. According to HUD data, the most impoverished one-fifth of the population has not gained substantially in income during the last three decades, despite enormous economic growth in the United States. A concomitant problem for the poorest citizens of the nation is the cost of housing, particularly of rental units. In order to secure dwellings that are comparatively safe and that are located in relatively convenient areas (within possible commuting distance, whether by public or private means of transportation), the very poor often must dedicate a significant portion of their earnings to the cost of rent—sometimes more than 50 percent of take-home pay. This places an enormous financial burden upon those who are already marginalized and who are leading extremely stressful and difficult lives. Often, furniture, proper clothing, food, and medical care are sacrificed in order to meet the cost of rent.

The creation of safe and affordable housing for those with the lowest incomes makes it possible for them to move out of dangerous, high-crime areas, to provide stability for their families, to improve the level of education within the household, and to generally enhance the quality of life. One potential problem with affordable housing is that it is only accessible to those who have the means of securing commercial funding. For those who are not considered creditworthy, "sweat equity" homes can provide a safety net.

■ PRIMARY SOURCE

New Orleans—More than 1,500 families will realize their American Dream with a little elbow grease and $24.8 million in grants announced today by Housing and Urban Development Assistant Secretary Pamela Patenaude. HUD is awarding these so-called "sweat equity grants" to four national and regional organizations through the Department's Self-Help Homeownership Opportunity Program (SHOP).

Patenaude made the announcement as she joined Habitat for Humanity volunteers constructing 15 afford-

able homes in Covington, Louisiana. First constructed in Rockefeller Center in New York, Jackson, Mississippi, and as far away as Los Angeles, these homes are being reassembled throughout the Gulf Coast region and will eventually provide affordable homes for hurricane evacuees.

"This funding not only helps families to purchase their first home, but taps into their own sweat equity to make them feel more invested in their new neighborhood," said Patenaude. "With a little investment and elbow grease, great things can happen and our SHOP program is proof of that."

HUD Assistant Secretary presented a check for $10 million to Mayor of Covington, LA Candace Watkins and Habitat for Humanity Vice President Paul Rodgers to support "sweat equity" programs like Habitat that assist lower income families [to] realize the American Dream of homeownership. The presentation was made at the site of 15 new homes being constructed for hurricane evacuee families.

The following nonprofit organizations were awarded SHOP grants…:

Recipient Amount
ACORN Housing Corporation $572,000
Community Frameworks $4,500,000
Housing Assistance Council $9,000,000
Habitat for Humanity International $10,773,000
Total $24,800,000

SHOP grants are provided to national and regional nonprofit organizations that have experience in providing self-help housing. These funds are used to purchase land and make improvements on infrastructure, which together may not exceed an average investment of $15,000 per dwelling. These non-profit organizations propose to distribute SHOP funds to several hundred local affiliates that will acquire the land, select homebuyers, coordinate the homebuyer and volunteer efforts for sweat equity, and assist in the arrangement of interim and permanent financing for the homebuyers.

Homebuyers contribute a minimum of 100 hours of sweat equity on the construction of their homes and/or the homes of other homebuyers participating in the local self-help housing program. Self-help housing or sweat equity involves the homebuyer's participation in the construction of the housing, which can include, but is not limited to, assisting in the painting, carpentry, trim work, drywall, roofing and siding for the housing.

Labor contributed by volunteers also helps buyers who are unable to perform their sweat equity tasks due to disabilities or other reasons. Frequently persons with disabilities are able to substitute tasks by performing administrative tasks. The sweat equity and labor contributions by the homebuyers and volunteers significantly reduce the cost of the housing....

SIGNIFICANCE

Because affordable housing is, by definition, less expensive than the typical commercial home, it holds significantly less appeal for contractors and real estate agents, as the profit margins are much slimmer. Generally speaking, commercial developers pursue projects with the intention of making a profit, dealing with a relatively safe market, and obtaining funding easily. Many developers look for housing projects with a limited number of models to choose from, with the home buyer able to choose from a number of extras that can be added in order to appreciably increase the cost. In contrast, affordable housing is typically fairly basic, is unlikely to be embellished by the purchaser, and has a low cost-to-profit margin. Similarly, affordable rental units must be priced within a much smaller range than typical commercial rental properties. In order to make the concept of creating affordable housing somewhat more attractive to financers and developers, the federal government has created a number of programs to provide incentives for developing a range of affordable dwellings. In addition, many states have laws mandating that each new housing area contain a minimum percentage of housing that is considered affordable for the region.

A few of the better-known means of creating affordable housing are rental subsidies (often called Section 8 programs), various types of down-payment and credit or debt management assistance programs, and low-income housing tax credits. However, perhaps the best known, at least within the media and popular press, are the sweat-equity grants. A sweat-equity grant is one in which the potential homeowner must devote a minimum number of hours toward direct participation in the actual construction or rehabilitation of the home or housing unit before it can be purchased. For those persons who are physically unable to be involved in the actual construction process, it is often possible to substitute hands-on labor with administrative time on an hour-for-hour basis.

HUD targets a significant amount of its federal funding toward the creation of affordable-ownership housing (low-income home ownership programs) by nonprofit and community-based organizations. Those groups create packages in which they put together land parcels, providers of low-cost but high-quality materials, and developers or contractors to construct the dwellings. They often work with numerous city, county, and state funding sources, as well as private investors and donors, philanthropists, and, of course, federal granting agencies, in order to create a diverse financial framework to allow them to build affordable housing that is intermingled with market-cost dwellings in heterogeneous neighborhoods. Nonprofits are able to hold down their administrative and operating costs, further adding to the affordability of the housing. Two of the largest nationwide nonprofits that act as developers of low-income or affordable housing through the use of sweat equity are the Housing Assistance Council and Habitat for Humanity International (HFHI). The federal funding that is earmarked for sweat-equity grants typically comes from HUD's Self-Help Homeownership Opportunity Program (SHOP). SHOP brings together volunteer workers, artisans and tradespersons, and the future homeowners, in order to construct each dwelling.

Habitat for Humanity International, the most recognized nonprofit name for sweat-equity homeownership programs, is a faith-based community organization. It has built more than a quarter of a million homes around the globe. The cost of an individual home varies with the region, with homes constructed in third-world countries averaging well under one hundred American dollars, and homes in the United States averaging just over fifty thousand dollars. In addition to keeping down the cost of labor by using significant amounts of low-cost or donated materials, HFHI uses volunteer labor, including a minimum of two hundred hours of direct labor or service by the future homeowner. The homes are sold with no profit margins. They are not donated to the new owners, but financing is often accomplished at zero interest rates. The mortgages paid by the new owners are funneled directly back into HFHI for use in international construction projects, further empowering the new homeowner, who is also making a contribution to the betterment of the world community.

Giving people the opportunity to change their circumstances, to move up from impoverished and often crime-ridden areas to diverse neighborhoods, allows people to become empowered, to raise their standard of living and that of future generations, and to create both financial and sweat equity in the ownership of a home.

FURTHER RESOURCES

Books

Chandler, Mittie Olion. *Urban Homesteading: Programs and Policies.* New York: Greenwood Press, 1988.

Dehavenon, Anna Lou, ed. *There's No Place Like Home: Anthropological Perspectives on Housing and Homelessness in the United States.* Westport, Conn.: Bergin & Garvey, 1999.

von Hassell, Malve. *Homesteading in New York City, 1978–1993: The Divided Heart of Loisaida.* Westport, Conn.: Bergin & Garvey, 1996.

Periodicals

Lerner, Michele. "'Sweat Equity' Works People into Houses." *The Washington Times* (March 14, 2003): F01.

Web sites

United States Department of Housing and Urban Development. "HUD's Mission and History." October 3, 2003 <http://www.hud.gov/library/bookshelf12/hudmission.cfm> (accessed May 29, 2006).

Jackson Addresses Indian Leaders' Washington Summit

HUD Loan Guarantee Program Projected to Create 1,000 New Native American Homeowners in 2006

Press release

By: United States Department of Housing and Urban Development

Date: February 27, 2006

Source: *United States Department of Housing and Urban Development.* "Jackson Addresses Indian Leaders' Washington Summit." February 27, 2006 <http://www.hud.gov/news/release.cfm?content=pr06-023.cfm> (accessed May 30, 2006).

About the Author: The U.S. Department of Housing and Urban Development (HUD) is the primary government agency responsible for ensuring equal access to housing and for improving the quality of affordable housing in the United States.

INTRODUCTION

In 1994, the Section 184 Indian Housing Loan Guarantee Program was created by congressional legislation. The program was intended to assist Native American peoples in securing home ownership on designated tribal, pueblo, or trust lands. It was meant to be used for the construction of new dwellings, as well as for the rehabilitation or refurbishing of damaged or gutted sites. Individuals and families could avail themselves of the program's assistance as could Indian Housing Authority facilities.

The federal government under Title VI makes housing available to tribal or pueblo members who are recipients of Indian Housing Block Grant (IHBG) funds. It creates a federal mortgage loan guarantee for individuals or families wanting to build affordable or low-income housing on tribal or trust lands, somewhat analogous to that afforded by Section 184 programs.

Building upon the earlier Section 184 and Title VI programs, the Native American Housing Assistance and Self-Determination Act (NAHASDA) officially became law when President Bill Clinton signed the legislation in October 1996. It was codified and enacted on October 1, 1997. The overarching goal of the act is to empower Native American peoples—who have been considered to be disenfranchised since the early days of European colonization—to design their own tribal housing programs. Essentially, NAHASDA creates an administrative structure for providing grant money to tribes and pueblos, and engages with them, if they so desire, in the process of determining how they want to orchestrate their local tribal housing. It can be used in any number of ways, from low-income and affordable housing sales, to rental or condominium units, to elder housing. The program can also be used to construct buildings for specific programs, such as drug and alcohol treatment and rehabilitation facilities.

Section 184, Title VI, and NAHASDA programs were designed to increase the mortgage possibilities for Native Americans by guaranteeing loans for home ownership on tribal and trust lands. Tribal and trust lands cannot be owned by individuals—they belong to the tribe or pueblo. In order to build, or to own existing dwellings, the land must be leased from the Bureau of Indian Affairs (BIA). Because of the property ownership issues, conventional lenders generally considered those properties to be too high-risk to fund. The offering of federal guarantees lowered the risk. The government also permits Native Americans and Tribal Housing Authorities, under certain conditions, to utilize interest-free loans for home financing, broadening the possibilities of home ownership for low-income individuals or tribal groups.

▮ PRIMARY SOURCE

Washington—U.S. Department Housing and Urban Development Secretary Alphonso Jackson told Native American leaders today the Bush Administration is committed to increasing the number of Native American homeowners.

Jackson addressed attendees of the National Congress of American Indians' (NCAI) Tribal Nations Legislative

Summit being held in Washington. NCAI is the leading advocacy organization for Native Americans with 250 member tribes. Tribal leaders from across the country have gathered in the Nation's Capital for the next three days to meet with members of Congress and Bush Administration officials on issues important to Indian Country.

"HUD has a vital role in helping more Native Americans realize the American Dream of homeownership," said Jackson. "A family's economic independence often begins with homeownership. HUD is here to help provide this foundation by expanding innovative programs that have proven success."

Jackson spoke specifically about two HUD loan guarantee programs—Section 184 and Title VI—that are helping tribes assist members to purchase or rehabilitate homes by guaranteeing loans at 100 percent.

"These two programs coupled with other HUD initiatives will make the President's commitment to create 5.5 million more minority homeowners by the end of this decade a reality that we can all be proud of," said Jackson.

Just in the past three years, the Section 184 program has proven to be an effective tool to increase Native American homeownership. The program was created in 1994 to address the lack of mortgage lending for Native Americans. It was designed to give Native American families the opportunity to purchase their own homes. Since 1995, when HUD guaranteed its first Section 184 loan, there have been more than 2,800 loans guaranteed with a dollar value in excess of $300 million.

This year alone, HUD's Office of Native American Programs is on pace to guarantee another 1,000 loans for $120 million. The President's 2007 proposed budget includes a $2 million increase for the Section 184 program, which is currently funded at $4 million. The President's request also doubles the amount of money HUD makes available under Section 184 to back mortgages—from $116 million to $251 million.

The Section 184 program provides a 100 percent guarantee for mortgages on Indian lands, enabling private sector lenders to make mortgage loans to eligible Native American families, tribes and tribal housing entities that are purchasing homes. The program can also be used to rehabilitate existing homes, build new homes and refinance higher interest rate loans.

Previously, Native Americans participating in the Section 184 program were limited to the purchase of homes on land owned by the tribe, usually known as "trust" or "restricted" lands. As a result, Native American homeownership opportunities remained primarily on reservations. Under new guidelines, established last year, tribes and tribal housing entities can provide Section 184 homeownership opportunities beyond their reservations.

The Title VI program allows tribes to leverage their Indian Housing Block Grants by pledging current and future block grants to finance affordable housing activities within the tribal community such as buying and rehabilitating homes. The flexibility associated with the Title VI program also allows tribes to use the leverage funds as seed money to build facility infrastructure that support the housing, such as community centers, health clinics and public utilities. Significant changes were made to this program last year that will make it more effective. For example, HUD has created a method to shorten the processing time to guarantee loans. In 2006, the Title VI program has had the highest number of applications since its inception.

HUD is the nation's housing agency committed to increasing homeownership, particularly among minorities; creating affordable housing opportunities for low-income Americans; and supporting the homeless, elderly, people with disabilities and people living with AIDS. The Department also promotes economic and community development as well as enforces the nation's fair housing laws. More information about HUD and its programs is available on the Internet at www.hud.gov and espanol.hud.gov.

SIGNIFICANCE

The fact that the land upon which dwellings are going to be built or reconstructed may not be owned by individuals is one of the aspects of Native American housing programs that make them unlike any of the other initiatives sponsored by HUD. The land, whether it is pueblo, reservation, or trust property, is all overseen by the BIA. Often, lands are held in trust for an entire tribe or pueblo, although a land trust may be held for a specific individual or family as well. When a Native American individual, family, or tribe seeks to make use of a specific land parcel for the purpose of constructing dwellings, the BIA must approve the request and grant a land lease for the property, which is known as a leasehold estate. In order for the holder of the lease to construct or rehabilitate a dwelling on the land, the individual, family, or entity must first apply for a mortgage loan with both HUD and the BIA. In the event that the loan is forfeited or defaulted, the land and home must first be offered for purchase to another eligible member of the tribe or pueblo, or to the local Indian Housing Authority. Should the loan go beyond default and end up in foreclosure, it can be liquidated by the mortgage holding company, but only to another eligible tribal or pueblo member, to the tribe or pueblo itself, or to the Indian Housing Authority that works directly with the tribe or pueblo. It may not move outside of the protected and sovereign status of the tribe or pueblo.

Native Americans who live on tribal or pueblo lands are generally located in rural areas. They have quite specific traditional, spiritual, and cultural practices involving the land on which they live, and the dwellings that they inhabit. Housing assistance programs must be designed to address those unique needs. One way of doing so is by empowering the tribes and pueblos themselves to serve as oversight agencies for local housing. Among the intentions of NAHASDA was to create the means by which tribal and pueblo authorities could design and place homes, so as to create living areas that are consistent with local needs. Another goal of the supported housing and block-grant plans is to encourage the tribes and pueblos to create long-range housing and land development plans for their local communities, to enhance the possibilities of self-sufficiency for populations that have historically been at extreme economic disadvantage.

The plans make a very clear distinction between the funding of dwellings that are designated as public housing by the remainder of the United States and Native American/Indian housing located on sovereign lands. The plans align safe and affordable housing needs with recognition of the sovereign nature of Native American lands and peoples, and they respect cultural, traditional, and spiritual concerns by empowering the Native American communities to use the funding in ways that make the most sense for their needs. HUD works in concert with the tribal and pueblo authorities to create and implement funding programs, in order to further ensure cultural sensitivity. Although the programs are very effective, there are still considerable problems with insufficient, decrepit, or inadequate housing availability on tribal lands, and there is a considerable Native American homeless population.

FURTHER RESOURCES

Books

Chandler, Mittie Olion. *Urban Homesteading: Programs and Policies.* New York: Greenwood Press, 1988.

Dehavenon, Anna Lou, ed. *There's No Place Like Home: Anthropological Perspectives on Housing and Homelessness in the United States.* Westport, Conn.: Bergin & Garvey, 1999.

Prucha, Francis Paul, ed. *Documents of United States Indian Policy.* Lincoln: University of Nebraska Press, 2000.

Stein, Theodore J. *Social Policy and Policy-Making by the Branches of Government and the Public-At-Large.* New York: Columbia University Press, 2001.

von Hassell, Malve. *Homesteading in New York City, 1978–1993: The Divided Heart of Loisaida.* Westport, Conn.: Bergin & Garvey, 1996.

Web sites

United States Department of Housing and Urban Development. "HUD's Mission and History." October 3, 2003 <http://www.hud.gov/library/bookshelf12/hudmission.cfm> (accessed May 29, 2006).

United States Department of Housing and Urban Development. "Section 184 Indian Housing Loan Guarantee Program." March 4, 2005 <http://www.hud.gov/offices/pih/ih/homeownership/184/faq.cfm> (accessed May 29, 2006).

Current Issues in Social Policy: Education, Employment, and Family

Focusing on education, employment, and family, this final chapter continues the discussion of current issues in U.S. social policy.

Though public education is largely controlled at the state and local level, national policy affects curriculum content, teaching standards, quality of school facilities, and student educational opportunities. The role of the federal government in education is itself among the most contentious current social policy issues.

All children in the United States have a legal right to a kindergarten through twelfth-grade education. However, social policy affects each student's educational opportunities. Social policies since the 1950s have sought to address the ills of racial and socioeconomic segregation and inequality of school facilities. Bussing, controversial school voucher and charter school programs, affirmative action, and federal education initiatives seek to remedy these lingering problems. Some parents, looking for an alternative solution, lobbied for the opportunity to school children at home. Government regulation of academic standards also reaches homeschooled students. Like corporate-sponsored charter schools and school voucher programs, homeschooling remains a divisive educational issue. Some claim that such programs hurt public schools, taking away needed resources and talented students. Others claim that students and parents have the right to abandon continually failing public schools and secure the best educational opportunities possible.

Also included in this chapter are articles discussing the recent federal education initiative No Child Left Behind and social programs providing college funding through federal student loans and state-sponsored scholarships. An article on abstinence-only education provides a brief foray into the present-day intersection of moral issues and U.S. social policy. This topic was chosen specifically because it potentially affects a substantial portion of U.S. public school students—a case in point of how religion, morality, and politics influence even existing social policy and programs—even if only for a limited time.

This chapter also contains articles on affirmative action and anti-discrimination in the workplace. Highlighted are issues of employee safety and employment security. While unemployment benefits are available to some in the United States, a more comprehensive system of labor regulation and unemployment insurance exists in Canada and much of Europe. Protections on employment are largely a matter of individual state policies in the United States, leaving a diverse legal landscape. From employment "at-will" granting employers broad rights to hire and fire employees, to "just cause termination" that somewhat restricts an employer's ability to fire workers, job security and employment protections vary by location. National social policy has produced some employment protections. Employment discrimination based on race, ethnicity, gender, or physical handicap is broadly prohibited by federal law. Highlighted here are federal laws prohibiting employment discrimination based on disabilities, and preventing retaliatory actions against employees that disclose illegal actions of corporations. While the United States does not provide nationalized healthcare, varying workers' compensation insurance schemes cover on-the-job injuries and promote worker safety.

Executive Order 12432

Minority Business Enterprise Development

Government record

By: Ronald Reagan

Date: July 14, 1983

Source: National archives

About the Author: In 1966, Ronald Reagan was elected the thirty-third Governor of California. He was reelected to the office in 1970. Following that, Ronald Reagan served as the fortieth President of the United States from 1981–1989.

INTRODUCTION

In 1953, the Small Business Act was passed in the Congress, which created the Small Business Administration (SBA). The expressed goal of this entity was to "aid, counsel, and protect, insofar as is possible, the interests of small business concerns." The charter of the SBA provided for a portion of government con-

tracts to be granted to small business. By 1954, the SBA had begun making loans to small businesses, as well as aiding small businesses to win procurement contracts. In 1958, under the Investment Company Act, the Small Business Administration became a permanent federal agency, licensed and regulated. As the political environment changed, the government began to create programs to ensure equality throughout society. One of these programs was established in Executive Order 10925, in which President Kennedy creates the Community on Equal Employment Opportunity. This committee called upon federally funded programs to use "affirmative action" to prevent racial bias in employment.

The 1960s became a time of expanded opportunities for minorities in business as congress passed legislation and presidents signed orders to create business opportunities. Under the Civil Rights Act of 1964, the committee was incorporated into the Equal Employment Opportunity Commission. During this time, the SBA continued its advocacy work for small businesses. In order to encourage the growth of small businesses, the SBA launched the Equal Opportunity Loan Program, which allowed loan applicants who were living

Ronald N. Langston, left, national director of the Minority Business Development Agency of the U.S. Department of Commerce, visits with Herman McKinney, right, vice president for urban affairs of the Greater Seattle Chamber of Commerce on January 26, 2004. AP IMAGES.

below the poverty level relaxed credit and collateral requirement. The purpose of this was to support sound commercial initiatives that would not otherwise be funded due to poor credit. President Johnson continued this work to aid small and disadvantaged businesses by signing Executive Order 11246 which extended affirmative action to government contractors. By 1968, the Minority Small Business and Capital Ownership Development Program was created as a means to increase federal purchases from disadvantaged small business owners. In 1969, Executive Order 11458 created the Office of Minority Business Enterprise within the Department of Commerce.

Strides continued to be made in the 1970s toward enhanced minority business participation within the government. President Nixon signed Executive Order 11518 which tasks the SBA to represent the entire small business community, including those owned by minorities. By 1971, the procurement regulations expressed in title 41, were changed to require that all federal contracts that exceed $500,000 must include a clause encouraging the use of minority subcontractors. President Nixon also signed Executive Order 11625 which calls on federal agencies to construct program goals and broad plans for a national Minority Business Enterprise program for contracting.

On July 14, 1983, President Ronald Reagan signed Executive Order 12432. The executive order requires that each federal agency with grant making capabilities establish an Annual Minority Business Development Plan with the stated goal to increase minority business participation. Agencies are expected to establish programs that assist minority business enterprises to procure contracts and manage those contracts awarded. As a stipulation of the executive order, the progress toward these goals is to be annually reported to the Secretary of Commerce.

PRIMARY SOURCE

By virtue of the authority vested in me as President by the Constitution and laws of the United States of America, including Section 205(a) of the Federal Property and Administrative Services Act of 1949 (40 U.S.C. 486(a)), in order to provide guidance and oversight for programs for the development of minority business enterprise pursuant to my statement of December 17, 1982 concerning Minority Business Development; and to implement the commitment of the Federal government to the goal of encouraging greater economic opportunity for minority entrepreneurs, it is hereby ordered as follows:

Section 1. *Minority Business Development Plans.*

1. (a) Minority business enterprise development plans shall be developed by each Federal agency having substantial procurement or grantmaking authority. Such agencies shall submit these plans to the Cabinet Council on Commerce and Trade on an annual basis.

2. (b) These annual plans shall establish minority enterprise development objectives for the participating agencies and methods for encouraging both prime contractors and grantees to utilize minority business enterprises. The plans shall, to the extent possible, build upon the programs administered by the Minority Business Development Agency and the Small Business Administration, including the goals established pursuant to Public Law 95-507.

3. (c) The Secretary of Commerce and the Administrator of the Small Business Administration, in consultation with the Cabinet Council on Commerce and Trade, shall establish uniform guidelines for all Federal agencies to be utilized in establishing the minority business programs set forth in Section 2 of this Order.

4. (d) The participating agencies shall furnish an annual report regarding the implementation of their programs in such form as the Cabinet Council on Commerce and Trade may request, and at such time as the Secretary of Commerce shall designate.

5. (e) The Secretary of Commerce shall provide an annual report to the President, through the Cabinet Council on Commerce and Trade, on activities under this Order and agency implementation of minority business development programs.

Sec. 2. *Minority Business Development Responsibilities of Federal Agencies.*

1. (a) To the extent permitted by law and consistent with its primary mission, each Federal agency which is required to develop a minority business development plan under Section 1 of this Order shall, to accomplish the objectives set forth in its plan, establish programs concerning provision of direct assistance, procurement assistance, and management and technical assistance to minority business enterprises.

2. (b) Each Federal agency shall, to the extent permitted by law and consistent with its primary mission, establish minority business development programs, consistent with Section 211 of Public Law 95-507, to develop and implement incentive techniques to encourage greater minority business subcontracting by Federal prime contractors.

3. (c) Each Federal agency shall encourage recipients of Federal grants and cooperative agreements to achieve a reasonable minority business participation

in contracts let as a result of its grants and agreements. In cases where State and local governments are the recipients, such encouragement shall be consistent with principles of federalism.

4. (d) Each Federal agency shall provide the Cabinet Council on Commerce and Trade such information as it shall request from time to time concerning the agency's progress in implementing these programs.

SIGNIFICANCE

Executive Order 12432 directs all federal agencies that possess grant-making capabilities to create a plan that develops minority businesses. Agencies employ their own Office of Small Disadvantaged Business Utilization to carry out their goal to encourage minority businesses to compete for federal contracts. In order to qualify as a small disadvantaged business, the business must be at least fifty-one percent owned by one or more individuals deemed economically or socially disadvantaged, such as African Americans, Hispanic Americans, Asian Pacific Americans, and Native Americans. This minority business enterprise development program requires that each agency report their progress toward meeting these goals to the Secretary of Commerce.

FURTHER RESOURCES

Periodicals

"Looking Back: Significant events in the history of affirmative action." *Minority Business Entrepreneur.* September 1, 2004.

Web sites

Policy Link. "Minority Contracting." <http://www.policylink.org/EDTK/MinorityContracting/policy.html> (accessed May 17, 2006).

Small Business Administration. "Overview & History." <http://www.sba.gov/aboutsba/history.html> (accessed May 17, 2006).

Whistleblower Protection Act of 1989

Legislation

By: U.S. Congress

Date: 1989

Source: *Library of Congress.* "Whistleblower Protection Act of 1989." <http://thomas.loc.gov/cgi-bin/> (accessed May 26, 2006).

About the Author: The U.S. Congress is the primary law-making branch of the federal government.

INTRODUCTION

In 2002, *Time* magazine staff were planning the publication's annual Person of the Year issue. This honor had previously gone to a wide array of persons as well as a few non-persons—the 1982 honoree was the personal computer. Rudy Giuliani, the charismatic mayor who led New York City through the 2001 terrorist attacks, and George W. Bush, winner of the strangest election in modern history, were the two previous winners. Since 2002 had been a year of seemingly endless corporate and government scandal, *Time* chose to honor three women who had played an important role in these events; each woman had risked her job to blow the whistle.

The term "whistleblower" has its origins in athletics, where officials frequently use a whistle to point out rule violations by players. In the workplace, the term refers to an employee who publicly reveals his employer's misdeeds. Blowing the whistle on one's employer is frequently a costly decision. Corporate executives rarely enjoy the negative publicity that accompanies whistleblowing, and in some cases the desire to suppress bad news or even criminal prosecution can lead to punitive actions against whistleblowers. Employees have been threatened, disciplined, and even fired for revealing company misdeeds in public, making the decision to blow the whistle extremely difficult.

As the largest bureaucracy in the country, the federal government has its reasonable share of employee misdeeds. While the government as a whole benefits when improper behavior is revealed, individuals within the government often have an incentive to cover up these actions or to punish those who reveal them. While whistleblowing was already protected by federal law such as the Civil Service Reform Act of 1978, no specific statute broadly protected a government employee's ability to report misdeeds without reprisal. The Whistleblower Protection Act of 1989 addressed this deficiency.

The Whistleblower Protection Act included several specific provisions. It began by noting the value of whistleblowing activity in reducing fraud and self-enrichment by government employees. It also stipulates that government employees shall not suffer reprisals for whistleblowing behavior. In addition, the act empowered the Office of Special Counsel to

Noreen Wolfstitch speaks outside the Statehouse in Montpelier, Vermont, on April 8, 2003. Wolfstitch is one of a group of nurses who gathered at the Statehouse to urge legislators to ban mandatory overtime and enhance protections for health care whistleblowers. AP IMAGES.

enforce the law, specifically by investigating complaints of reprisals and determining penalties. A 1994 amendment to the law extended its protections to employees of government corporations and the Veterans' Administration, and later legislation provided similar safeguards for members of the military.

The Whistleblower Protection Act specifies a series of steps to be followed in response to allegations. First, complaints are investigated for merit and those found worthy are referred to the Office of Special Counsel for further action. A 1999 Congressional report found that twenty to thirty percent of complaints are referred to the Special Counsel, while the rest are closed. Of those referred for further action, about one-fourth result in favorable rulings for the complainant.

PRIMARY SOURCE

SECTION 1. SHORT TITLE.

This Act may be cited as the 'Whistleblower Protection Act of 1989'

SEC. 2. FINDINGS AND PURPOSE.

(a) FINDINGS-The Congress finds that—
(1) Federal employees who make disclosures described in section 2302(b)(8) of title 5, United States Code, serve the public interest by assisting in the elimination of fraud, waste, abuse, and unnecessary Government expenditures;
(2) protecting employees who disclose Government illegality, waste, and corruption is a major step toward a more effective civil service; and
(3) in passing the Civil Service Reform Act of 1978, Congress established the Office of Special Counsel to protect whistleblowers (those individuals who make disclosures described in such section 2302(b)(8)) from reprisal.

(b) PURPOSE-The purpose of this Act is to strengthen and improve protection for the rights of Federal employees, to prevent reprisals, and to help eliminate wrongdoing within the Government by—
(1) mandating that employees should not suffer adverse consequences as a result of prohibited personnel practices; and
(2) establishing—

(A) that the primary role of the Office of Special Counsel is to protect employees, especially whistleblowers, from prohibited personnel practices;

(B) that the Office of Special Counsel shall act in the interests of employees who seek assistance from the Office of Special Counsel; and

(C) that while disciplining those who commit prohibited personnel practices may be used as a means by which to help accomplish that goal, the protection of individuals who are the subject of prohibited personnel practices remains the paramount consideration.

SIGNIFICANCE

While the Whistleblower Protection Act clearly defines the rights of federal employees, critics argue that the actual protections it provides are weak. Specifically, they note that the burden of enforcement lies almost entirely on the Office of Special Counsel, which has frequently appeared less aggressive than they would like. Further, these critics complain that the objective of the process is not to investigate the original alleged misdeeds, but to assess and protect the rights of the individual whistleblower, suggesting that the process primarily treats symptoms rather than addressing the underlying disease. A related criticism is that the system is primarily reactive in its perspective, addressing complaints as they are raised, but doing little to prevent future abuses. Compounding these problems, a 1999 report prepared for Congress found that most government employees know little about their legal rights as whistleblowers, making them potentially less likely to report inappropriate or illegal behavior.

Time magazine's 2002 Person of the Year selection brought whistleblowing back into the spotlight. In response to a perceived pattern of executive and accounting abuses at Enron, WorldCom, and other firms, Congress passed the Sarbanes-Oxley Act, which tightened reporting requirements and stiffened penalties for executives of public corporations. In addition to these well-known changes, the law also protects employees at public firms from retaliation for whistleblowing, as well as requiring firms to set up internal procedures that facilitate such reporting.

FURTHER RESOURCES
Books

Alford, C. Fred. *Whistleblowers: Broken Lives and Organizational Power*. Ithaca, N.Y.: Cornell University Press, 2002.

Busse, Richard C. *Employees Rights: Your Practical Handbook to Workplace Law*. Naperville, Ill.: Sourcebooks, 2004.

Swartz, Mimi, and Sherron Watkins. *Power Failure: The Inside Story of the Collapse of Enron*. New York: Currency, 2004.

Periodicals

Edmonds, Sibel, and William Weaver. "To Tell the Truth." *Bulletin of the Atomic Scientists* 12 (2006): 16–18.

"The Next Step: Federal Government and Whistleblowers." *CQ Researcher* 16 (2006): 287.

"Secrecy Hides Accountability." *USA Today* (March 16, 2006): 14A.

Web sites

Occupational Safety and Health Administration. "What Are My Rights as a Whistleblower?" <http://www.osha.gov/oshdoc/data_whistleblowerfacts/whistleblower_protections-general.pdf> (accessed May 25, 2006).

Public Service Commission of Canada. "Three Whistleblower Protection Models: A Comparative Analysis of Whistleblower Legislation in Australia, the United States, and the United Kingdom." October 2001. <http://www.psc-cfp.gc.ca/research/merit/whistleblowing_e.htm> (accessed May 25, 2006).

U.S. Merit Systems Protection Board. "Questions and Answers About Whistleblower Appeals." <http://www.mspb.gov/foia/forms-pubs/qawhistle.html> (accessed May 25, 2006).

Americans with Disabilities Act of 1990

Legislation

By: Tony Coelho

Date: July 26, 1990

Source: *The United States Equal Employment Opportunity Commission*. "The Americans with Disabilities Act of 1990, Titles I and V."

About the Author: Although the Americans with Disabilities Act of 1990 was legislated through Congress, the principal author is cited as former Congressman Tony Coelho (b. 1942), who was the Chairman of the President's Committee for the Employment of People with Disabilities at the time that the legislation was written. Coelho was also the former Chairman of the Presidential Election Campaign of Al Gore. He experienced epilepsy as a youth and reported that he was impacted when his medical disability was used as a means of denying him employment.

Services and Public Transportation; Title III is related to Public Accommodations and Commercial Facilities; Title IV refers to Telecommunications; and Title V covers Miscellaneous Provisions.

The primary objective of the Americans With Disabilities Act of 1990 is to prevent labor unions, employers, employment agencies, and local, city, or state government entities from acting with bias against appropriately qualified disabled individuals in all aspects of employment, from the application process through hiring, job training, and compensation (to name just a few). The ADA defines a person with a disability as one who either has "a physical or mental impairment that substantially limits one or more major life activities; has a record of such impairment; or is regarded as having such an impairment."

A "qualified employee" is an individual who is capable of fulfilling the primary functions of a specific job, either with or without reasonable accommodations. "Reasonable accommodations" may range from modifying existing facilities or structures so as to render them accessible and functional for persons with disabilities; to changing the nature or responsibilities of a position, altering the assigned work hours, or reassigning the individual to a more suitable position; to acquiring assistive devices, modifying furniture or equipment; restructuring testing and examination conditions, curricula, training materials, policies, or procedures, or providing credentialed or fully qualified assistants, interpreters, or readers, according to the text and provisions of the Americans With Disabilities Act of 1990.

So long as making the reasonable accommodation(s) would not pose an undue financial hardship on the running of a business, the employer must make reasonable accommodations for a qualified applicant or current employee.

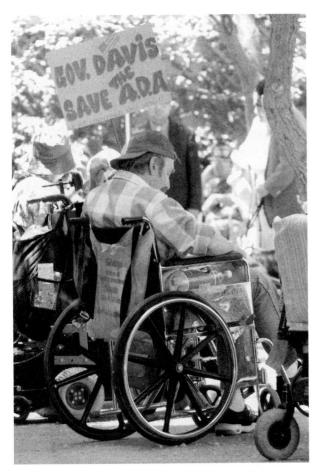

Disabled demonstrators rally on June 13, 2000 in Los Angeles, California, to protest the state's challenge to the Americans with Disabilities Act of 1990. Protesters say the disability community will be denied access to many basic services that enable them to live independently if the ADA is ruled unconstitutional. PHOTO BY DAVID MCNEW/NEWSMAKERS.

INTRODUCTION

The Americans with Disabilities Act (ADA) of 1990, the full title of which is United States Public Law 101-336, 104 Statute 327 (July 26, 1990), codified at 42 U.S.C. § 12101 et seq. was executed into law by former President George H. W. Bush. It broadens the reach of the Civil Rights Act of 1964 by prohibiting discrimination based upon individual disability—in addition to the prohibitions against discrimination based on gender, race, religion, cultural or national origin already imposed by the Civil Rights Act. The ADA consists of three introductory sections: Table of Contents, Findings and Purposes, and Definitions, followed by a main section containing five Titles, each of which applies to a specific area or type of activity: Title I refers to Employment; Title II refers to Public

■ PRIMARY SOURCE

SEC. 2. FINDINGS AND PURPOSES.

(a) Findings.—The Congress finds that—

(1) some 43,000,000 Americans have one or more physical or mental disabilities, and this number is increasing as the population as a whole is growing older;

(2) historically, society has tended to isolate and segregate individuals with disabilities, and, despite some improvements, such forms of discrimination against individuals with disabilities

continue to be a serious and pervasive social problem;

(3) discrimination against individuals with disabilities persists in such critical areas as employment, housing, public accommodations, education, transportation, communication, recreation, institutionalization, health services, voting, and access to public services;

(4) unlike individuals who have experienced discrimination on the basis of race, color, sex, national origin, religion, or age, individuals who have experienced discrimination on the basis of disability have often had no legal recourse to redress such discrimination;

(5) individuals with disabilities continually encounter various forms of discrimination, including outright intentional exclusion, the discriminatory effects of architectural, transportation, and communication barriers, overprotective rules and policies, failure to make modifications to existing facilities and practices, exclusionary qualification standards and criteria, segregation, and relegation to lesser services, programs, activities, benefits, jobs, or other opportunities;

(6) census data, national polls, and other studies have documented that people with disabilities, as a group, occupy an inferior status in our society, and are severely disadvantaged socially, vocationally, economically, and educationally;

(7) individuals with disabilities are a discrete and insular minority who have been faced with restrictions and limitations, subjected to a history of purposeful unequal treatment, and relegated to a position of political powerlessness in our society, based on characteristics that are beyond the control of such individuals and resulting from stereotypic assumptions not truly indicative of the individual ability of such individuals to participate in, and contribute to, society;

(8) the Nation's proper goals regarding individuals with disabilities are to assure equality of opportunity, full participation, independent living, and economic self-sufficiency for such individuals; and

(9) the continuing existence of unfair and unnecessary discrimination and prejudice denies people with disabilities the opportunity to compete on an equal basis and to pursue those opportunities for which our free society is justifiably famous, and costs the United States billions of dollars in unnecessary expenses resulting from dependency and nonproductivity.

(b) Purpose.—It is the purpose of this Act—

(1) to provide a clear and comprehensive national mandate for the elimination of discrimination against individuals with disabilities;

(2) to provide clear, strong, consistent, enforceable standards addressing discrimination against individuals with disabilities;

(3) to ensure that the Federal Government plays a central role in enforcing the standards established in this Act on behalf of individuals with disabilities; and

(4) to invoke the sweep of congressional authority, including the power to enforce the fourteenth amendment and to regulate commerce, in order to address the major areas of discrimination faced day-to-day by people with disabilities.

SEC. 102. DISCRIMINATION.

(a) General Rule.—No covered entity shall discriminate against a qualified individual with a disability because of the disability of such individual in regard to job application procedures, the hiring, advancement, or discharge of employees, employee compensation, job training, and other terms, conditions, and privileges of employment.

(b) Construction.—As used in subsection (a), the term "discriminate" includes—

(1) limiting, segregating, or classifying a job applicant or employee in a way that adversely affects the opportunities or status of such applicant or employee because of the disability of such applicant or employee;

(2) participating in a contractual or other arrangement or relationship that has the effect of subjecting a covered entity's qualified applicant or employee with a disability to the discrimination prohibited by this title (such relationship includes a relationship with an employment or referral agency, labor union, an organization providing fringe benefits to an employee of the covered entity, or an organization providing training and apprenticeship programs);

(3) utilizing standards, criteria, or methods of administration—

(A) that have the effect of discrimination on the basis of disability; or

(B) that perpetuate the discrimination of others who are subject to common administrative control;

(4) excluding or otherwise denying equal jobs or benefits to a qualified individual because of the known disability of an individual with whom the qualified individual is known to have a relationship or association;

(5)(A) not making reasonable accommodations to the known physical or mental limitations of an otherwise qualified individual with a disability who is an applicant or employee, unless such covered entity can demonstrate that the accommodation would impose an undue hardship on the operation of the business of such covered entity; or (B) denying employment opportunities to a job applicant or employee who is an otherwise qualified individual with a disability, if such denial is based on the need of such covered entity to make reasonable accommodation to the physical or mental impairments of the employee or applicant;

(6) using qualification standards, employment tests or other selection criteria that screen out or tend to screen out an individual with a disability or a class of individuals with disabilities unless the standard, test or other selection criteria, as used by the covered entity, is shown to be job-related for the position in question and is consistent with business necessity; and

(7) failing to select and administer tests concerning employment in the most effective manner to ensure that, when such test is administered to a job applicant or employee who has a disability that impairs sensory, manual, or speaking skills, such test results accurately reflect the skills, aptitude, or whatever other factor of such applicant or employee that such test purports to measure, rather than reflecting the impaired sensory, manual, or speaking skills of such employee or applicant (except where such skills are the factors that the test purports to measure).

(c) Medical Examinations and Inquiries.—

(1)In general.—The prohibition against discrimination as referred to in subsection (a) shall include medical examinations and inquiries.

(2) Preemployment—

(A) Prohibited examination or inquiry.—Except as provided in paragraph (3), a covered entity shall not conduct a medical examination or make inquiries of a job applicant as to whether such applicant is an individual with a disability or as to the nature or severity of such disability.

(B) Acceptable inquiry.—A covered entity may make preemployment inquiries into the ability of an applicant to perform job-related functions.

(3) Employment entrance examination.—A covered entity may require a medical examination after an offer of employment has been made to a job applicant and prior to the commencement of the employment duties of such applicant, and may condition an offer of employment on the results of such examination, if—

(A) all entering employees are subjected to such an examination regardless of disability;

(B) information obtained regarding the medical condition or history of the applicant is collected and maintained on separate forms and in separate medical files and is treated as a confidential medical record, except that—

(i) supervisors and managers may be informed regarding necessary restrictions on the work or duties of the employee and necessary accommodations;

(ii) first aid and safety personnel may be informed, when appropriate, if the disability might require emergency treatment; and

(iii) government officials investigating compliance with this Act shall be provided relevant information on request; and

(C) the results of such examination are used only in accordance with this title.

(4) Examination and inquiry.—

(A) Prohibited examinations and inquiries.—A covered entity shall not require a medical examination and shall not make inquiries of an employee as to whether such employee is an individual with a disability or as to the nature or severity of the disability, unless such examination or inquiry is shown to be job-related and consistent with business necessity.

(B) Acceptable examinations and inquiries.—A covered entity may conduct voluntary medical examinations, including voluntary medical histories, which are part of an employee health program available to employees at that work site. A covered entity may make inquiries into the ability of an employee to perform job-related functions.

(C) Requirement.—Information obtained under subparagraph (B) regarding the medical condition or history of any employee are subject to the requirements of subparagraphs (B) and (C) of paragraph (3).

SEC. 103. DEFENSES.

(a) In General.—It may be a defense to a charge of discrimination under this Act that an alleged application of qualification standards, tests, or selection criteria that screen out or tend to screen out or otherwise deny a job or benefit to an individual with a disability has been shown to be job-related and consistent with business necessity, and such performance cannot be accomplished by reasonable accommodation, as required under this title.

(b) Qualification Standards.—The term "qualification standards" may include a requirement that an individual shall not pose a direct threat to the health or safety of other individuals in the workplace.

(c) Religious Entities.—

(1) In general.—This title shall not prohibit a religious corporation, association, educational institution, or society from giving preference in employment to individuals of a particular religion to perform work connected with the carrying on by such corporation, association, educational institution, or society of its activities.

(2) Religious tenets requirement.—Under this title, a religious organization may require that all applicants and employees conform to the religious tenets of such organization.

(d) List of Infectious and Communicable Diseases.—

(1) In general.—The Secretary of Health and Human Services, not later than 6 months after the date of enactment of this Act, shall—

(A) review all infectious and communicable diseases which may be transmitted through handling the food supply;

(B) publish a list of infectious and communicable diseases which are transmitted through handling the food supply;

(C) publish the methods by which such diseases are transmitted; and

(D) widely disseminate such information regarding the list of diseases and their modes of transmissability to the general public. Such list shall be updated annually.

(2) Applications.—In any case in which an individual has an infectious or communicable disease that is transmitted to others through the handling of food, that is included on the list developed by the Secretary of Health and Human Services under paragraph (1), and which cannot be eliminated by reasonable accommodation, a covered entity may refuse to assign or continue to assign such individual to a job involving food handling.

(3) Construction.—Nothing in this Act shall be construed to preempt, modify, or amend any State, county, or local law, ordinance, or regulation applicable to food handling which is designed to protect the public health from individuals who pose a significant risk to the health or safety of others, which cannot be eliminated by reasonable accommodation, pursuant to the list of infectious or communicable diseases and the modes of transmissability published by the Secretary of Health and Human Services.

SEC. 309. EXAMINATIONS AND COURSES.

Any person that offers examinations or courses related to applications, licensing, certification, or credentialing for secondary or postsecondary education, professional, or trade purposes shall offer such examinations or courses in a place and manner accessible to persons with disabilities or offer alternative accessible arrangements for such individuals.

SEC. 502. STATE IMMUNITY.

A State shall not be immune under the eleventh amendment to the Constitution of the United States from an action in Federal or State court of competent jurisdiction for a violation of this Act. In any action against a State for a violation of the requirements of this Act, remedies (including remedies both at law and in equity) are available for such a violation to the same extent as such remedies are available for such a violation in an action against any public or private entity other than a State.

SIGNIFICANCE

Under Title I of the ADA, employers who have fifteen or more employees are prohibited from discriminating against qualified individuals who have disabilities. They are mandated to make reasonable accommodations for qualified disabled employees or job applicants, unless doing so would pose an undue or untenable financial hardship for the employer. Employers retain the right to reject any applicant, or to dismiss any current employee who poses a clear and present danger, or a threat to the safety, health, or well-being of the other employees. The utilization of drug screening, and the right to discharge employees or to reject applicants who are found to use illegal substances, is not in any way waived by the ADA. In addition to prohibiting discrimination against an individual with a known disability, the ADA prohibits discrimination against persons (employees or applicants) who have a close relationship or personal association with an individual who is known to have a disability. Allegations of failure to adhere to the requirements of the ADA are filed with the Equal Employment Opportunity Commission (EEOC).

Public accommodations—which according to the ADA include "restaurants, hotels, theaters, doctor's offices, pharmacies, libraries, retail stores, museums, libraries, parks, private schools, and day care centers"—may not discriminate against an individual based on known disability. Reasonable efforts must be made to ensure accessibility and to avoid discrimination, by offering such auxiliary services as might be necessary to persons who are blind or visually impaired, deaf, or hearing impaired; removing impediments and physical barriers in existing structures, or modifying those that cannot be removed in such a way as to create accessibility or, alternatively, creating equivalent means of providing the same goods or services wherever and whenever it is reasonably possible to do so. All new construction of public facilities must meet accessibility requirements. When a structure or facility is altered, even temporarily, those alterations must contain an accessible pathway whenever and wherever financially or practically possible. When discrimination is experienced in an area of public accommodation and redress is not made readily available, an individual can choose to initiate a private legal action against the discriminatory entity. However, there can be no financial gain from such lawsuits. Alternatively, the individual may exercise the option of filing a formal complaint with the Office of the Attorney General. If a successful lawsuit results from such a complaint, the complainant may receive monetary damages or financial compensation as a result.

Private and public transportation systems such as public buses, public rail and subway systems, and privately owned vans and buses may also not act in a discriminatory fashion toward individuals with known disabilities. All newly built public buses must be accessible; in the case of older buses that are not possible to modify, the bus company must provide an accessible alternate form of transportation covering the same route so long as doing so is not financially prohibitive. Newly constructed bus stations must be accessible, and older stations must be modified or altered so as to make them as fully accessible as is financially feasible. Privately owned van, bus, and other transportation systems must conform to the same requirements for accessibility as those mandated for public systems, stations, and facilities.

New rail vehicles must conform to rules of accessibility, and each existing train must contain at least one accessible car. New train stations must be constructed so as to be accessible, and existing stations must be modified or altered so as to ensure the greatest degree of accessibility that is not cost prohibitive.

State and local government facilities, services, communications, and systems must be made accessible for persons with disabilities.

Communications and telephone service providers must offer telephone relay services to individuals who use TDD's (telecommunications devices for the deaf) or other similar systems.

The ADA is an extremely important piece of legislation and one that has a very broad reach: there is

virtually no aspect of life that is not impacted for people who experience disabilities, and their ability to move comfortably and adequately in society has been severely curtailed by lack of accessibility and reasonable accommodations prior to the passage of the Act. With the ADA, persons who have disabilities are able to be much more a part of mainstream society, and their civil rights are both enforced and protected.

FURTHER RESOURCES
Books

Marshak, Laura E., Milton Seligman, and Fran Prezant. *Disability and the Family Life Cycle*. New York: Basic Books, 1999.

Veres III, John G., ed., and Ronald R. Sims, ed. *Human Resource Management and the Americans with Disabilities Act*. Westport, Conn.: Quorum Books, 1995.

Westerfield, Donald R. *National Health Care: Law, Policy, Strategy*. Westport, Conn.: Praeger, 1993.

Periodicals

Callahan, T. J. "Managers' Beliefs and Attitudes Toward the Americans with Disabilities Act of 1990." *Applied Human Resource Management research* 5 (1994): 28–43.

Hernandez, Brigida, Christopher Keys, and Fabricio Balcazar. "Employer Attitudes Toward Workers with Disabilities and Their ADA Employment Rights: A Literature Review." *Journal of Rehabilitation* 66 (2000): 4–16.

Pierce, P.A. "The Americans with Disabilities Act of 1990: A Symposium." *The Journal of Intergroup Relations* 17 (1991): 17, 34.

Thornburgh, Richard. "The Americans with Disabilities Act: What It Means to All Americans." *The Journal of Intergroup Relations* 17 (1991): 35–41.

Georgia Plan Would Give Top Students Free Tuition

Newspaper article

By: Joye Mercer and Scott Jaschik

Date: September 30, 1992

Source: Mercer, Joye, and Scott Jaschik. "Georgia Plan Would Give Top Students Free Tuition." *Chronicle of Higher Education* (September 30, 1992).

About the Author: Joye Mercer and Scott Jaschik are journalists who have written extensively for the *Chronicle of Higher Education*. Joye Mercer Barksdale (nee Joye Mercer) has also written for the *Washington Post* and served as the Director of Public Relations for the International Council for the Advancement of Education (CASE). Scott Jaschik left the *Chronicle of Higher Education* in 2003, and he subsequently became one of the founding editors of an electronic magazine entitled *Inside Higher Education*. He also writes for the electronic version of *Front Page Magazine*.

INTRODUCTION

Zell Miller, former governor of the state of Georgia, implemented the HOPE (Helping Outstanding Pupils Educationally) initiative both to encourage students to stay in high school through graduation and to inspire them to achieve excellent grades. A lottery-based program was developed to fund the community-college, public, and private four-year college and university scholarships—meaning that a significant portion of lottery proceeds for the entire state would be ear-marked each year for post-secondary scholarship funding as a means of supporting the HOPE programs. The scholarships were intended to be based primarily on the achievement of high grades, rather than strictly by demonstration of financial need. The program was an inclusive one, meaning that students going to vocational or technical schools could get HOPE grants for diploma or certificate programs, and nontraditional or returning students could also be eligible for scholarships or grants even if some time had passed between high school completion and starting college. The HOPE program was also open to students with General Education Diplomas (GEDs), as well as those with traditional high school diplomas.

In order to be considered for a HOPE scholarship in the state of Georgia, a student must have graduated since 1993 if planning to attend a public college or university, and after 1996 if attending a private academic institution. All categories of students must have maintained a "B" or better average in all high school core courses. Those in college preparatory programs are required to achieve a cumulative grade-point average of at least a "B" or 3.0 on a four-point grading scale. For those students engaged in a vocational or technical program while in high school, it is necessary to maintain a "B+" average, or a 3.2 grade-point average on the four-point scale.

HOPE award recipients who enroll at public educational institutions will have their complete tuition bill, as well as HOPE-approved fees paid. They will also receive a stipend toward the purchase of textbooks

Spellman College is the largest African American education center in the U.S. as well as an all-women's school, and which is part of a six school complex known as the Atlanta University Center. © BOB KRIST/CORBIS.

for each academic session. If HOPE award recipients choose to attend private colleges or universities, the scholarship pays $3,000 yearly for full-time students (those registered for a minimum of twelve credit hours per semester) and $1,500 annually for part-time students who register for at least six credit hours per semester. "Eligibility checkpoints" have been instituted as a means of ascertaining that students are maintaining good grades and making satisfactory academic progress. Failure to meet the cutoffs at any checkpoint results in loss of the scholarship or grant award.

PRIMARY SOURCE

Georgia Gov. Zell Miller last week proposed a new student-aid program that would provide two years of free tuition at a public college for any Georgia student with good grades and a family income of less than $66,000.

To be eligible for the grants, high-school graduates must have at least a 3.0-point average in a college preparatory curriculum, or at least a 3.2 in any other curricular track. As freshmen, they would receive grants equal to the annual tuition at any Georgia public college.

As sophomores, the students would qualify to receive "forgivable loans" equal to public-college tuition if they had earned a 3.0 GPA as freshmen. If they maintained the average as sophomores, the loan would be forgiven. Otherwise, it would have to be repaid.

Annual tuition is $1,791 at Georgia's public universities, $1,341 at its four-year colleges, and $1,017 at two-year colleges.

Jerry Davis, who conducts a study of state student-aid programs for the National Association of State Scholarship and Grant Programs, said the Georgia program would be open to a larger segment of the population, based on wealth, than any other state effort. "That would probably take in 90 or 95 per cent of Georgia's college-bound students in terms of the income level alone," he said.

Said Governor Miller: "This new scholarship program is second to none anywhere in this country."

The program, called the Helping Outstanding Pupils Educationally Grant Program, is contingent upon voters' approving a statewide lottery in November. State officials estimated that the program would cost $40-million, an amount that Governor Miller says can be earned through the lottery.

The state projected that as many as 90,000 Georgia students would be eligible for grants.

Private colleges would also benefit under the Governor's proposal. Currently, Georgia provides $1,000 a year for the education of any Georgia resident at a private college in the state. The new proposal would raise that amount to $1,500—without any requirement of students' having a certain grade-point average.

H. Dean Propst, chancellor of the University System of Georgia, called the program "an extraordinary proposal" that would improve Georgia's below-average college-going rate.

Some observers wondered if the grant proposal was an attempt to improve the lottery's chances of passage, but one source said polls consistently had shown that 60 to 65 per cent of Georgia's voters support the lottery, which was a main plank in Mr. Miller's 1990 campaign for Governor.

However, some educators were not optimistic that a lottery would adequately finance college grants.

"If you assume that there will be a lottery, then that use of the proceeds I would wholeheartedly endorse," said Joe Ben Welch, president of Middle Georgia College. "However, I'm not sold on the lottery approach to start with. I'm not sold on the economics of it, because you have to sell millions of dollars in tickets to produce the revenue."

Robert K. Ackerman, president of Wesleyan College, said Governor Miller was to be commended for the scholarship plan. "This man has a real sense of vision. It's remarkable that this is happening at a time when state budgets are in bad shape throughout the country," he said.

Mr. Ackerman said he could not comment on how he would vote on the lottery proposal, which is opposed by many leaders of the Methodist Church, with which Wesleyan is affiliated. He said, however, that he would not join in the leaders' public opposition to the lottery.

Student leaders at Georgia colleges had varying reactions to the plan. Darren M. Strader, editor of *The Technique*, the student newspaper at the Georgia Institute of Technology, said he thought the scholarships would be a "great incentive" for students to work hard in high school and college.

He said he was attracted to the idea because it would place emphasis on raising academic standards. "Let's face it, Georgia high schools aren't the best in the nation," he said.

However, Andrew Vanlandingham, secretary of the Student Government Association at the University of Georgia, said he was troubled by the proposal because the scholarships would be available only to those with good grades. "What about the plain, average student," he said. "When I was in high school, a lot of the above-average students were already getting scholarships."

SIGNIFICANCE

The HOPE programs have become something of a gold standard, as well as a sometimes controversial issue, across the nation. For the academic institutions of Georgia, the program has had significant benefits. Thousands of students have opted to continue their educations in Georgia rather than attending out-of-state colleges and universities. According to data published by the state, some three-quarters of a million students have benefited from HOPE scholarships and grants since 1993. The University of Georgia has experienced a renaissance, transforming itself from a school with an extremely poor nationwide academic reputation to one of reputed excellence. Families are spared extreme financial stresses while being able to assure an in-state college or university education for their children.

In addition to Georgia, more than twelve other states have instituted HOPE, or nearly identical, scholarship and grant programs in which financial awards for in-state college and university studies are based on merit rather than simply on financial need. A federal tuition tax credit, called the HOPE Tax Credit, has been created as another means of making it a bit easier for parents and families to finance post-secondary educations for their children.

Over time, there have been several changes in the HOPE program that have caused some challenges and financial hardship for the state of Georgia. The first challenge arose when the income ceiling for scholarship applicants was removed, opening availability to students from the wealthiest families. Then, stipends were added for books and fees. These three changes greatly widened the pool of potential recipients and exponentially increased the cost to the state of the HOPE programs—outpacing the revenues generated by the state lottery system. A limit on fee and book stipends was proposed, but met with little public or legislative support. One of the ironies involved in using state lottery proceeds to fund merit-and not income-based scholarships is that the lottery is traditionally played by the poorest members of society. In effect, then, the poorest residents of Georgia are also those most likely to be funding (however indirectly) the scholarships that may be going to some of the wealthiest families in the state.

The addition of standardized test scores, such as SAT results, to the algorithm for award determination also has been suggested as a way to limit the HOPE applicant pool. It was hoped that such a requirement might also serve to boost standardized test scores in Georgia, which typically ranks near last place in the nation in that regard. Georgian citizens didn't like this proposal. In addition, it received significant negative public commentary from some Georgia politicians, who expressed concern that such a requirement would negatively impact minority and economically under-privileged students. These students traditionally come from the poorest (financially and academically) school districts and, therefore, also achieve the lowest standardized test scores, based on published statistical and demographic data. Several states that have instituted the SAT score cutoff for scholarship determination have been involved in lawsuits alleging that the arbitrary cutoffs discriminate against minority and impoverished students who traditionally achieve lower test rankings. The use of the cutoffs, it is contended, unfairly limits the educational opportunities for those categories of students.

The people of Georgia, as well as those in other states with HOPE or similar programs, publicly support retaining the programs. Professors at the University of Georgia report that their students have become far more focused on learning and on achieving and maintaining good grades than has ever been reported before. Students are believed to be developing better study habits while in high school, in an effort to achieve a grade-point average that will merit the awards, and they are carrying those behaviors into college in order to retain their funding. All in all, institutions such as the University of Georgia report that they are enrolling students who are better prepared academically for post-secondary studies than they have been in the past. Based on data published in Georgia, the overall grade-point average of in-state students, both while in high school and while attending college or university, has risen significantly—and this is considered by the general public to be sufficient reason to do what is reasonable, necessary, and possible to maintain HOPE.

FURTHER RESOURCES
Books

Borg, Mary O., Paul M. Mason, and Stephen L. Shapiro. *The Economic Consequences of State Lotteries*. New York: Praeger Publishers, 1991.

Herideen, Penelope E. *Policy, Pedagogy, and Social Inequality: Community College Student Realities in Post-Industrial America*. Westport, Conn.: Bergin & Garvey, 1998.

Karabell, Zachary. *What's College For? The Struggle to Define American Higher Education*. New York: Basic Books, 1998.

Townsend, Barbara K., and Susan B. Twombly. *Community Colleges: Policy in the Future Context*. Westport, Conn.: Ablex Publishing, 2001.

Periodicals

Card, David, and A. Abigail Payne. "School Finance Reform, the Distribution of School Spending, and the Distribution of Student Test Scores." *Journal of Public Economics* 83 (2002): 49–82.

Dee, Thomas S. "The Capitalization of Education Finance Reforms." *Journal of Law and Economics* 43 (2000): 185–214.

Healy, Patrick. "HOPE Scholarships Transform the University of Georgia." *Chronicle of Higher Education: Colloquy* (November 9, 1997).

Selingo, Jeffrey. "Hope Wanes for Georgia's Merit-Based Scholarships." *Chronicle of Higher Education* (November 21, 2003).

Spindler, Charles J. "The Lottery and Education: Robbing Peter to Pay Paul?" *Public Budgeting and Finance* 15 (1995): 54–62.

Vela, Susan. "HOPE Scholarships Fuel Young Dreams: Kids' Pledge Paves Way for College Education." *Lansing State Journal* (January 20, 2005).

Web sites

DTAE: Georgia Department of Technical and Adult Education. "HOPE: Helping Outstanding Pupils Educationally." August 30, 2005 <http://www.dtae.org/hope.html#HOPEWORKS> (accessed June 1, 2006).

Georgia Student Finance Commission. "Scholarship and Grant Program Regulations." May 19, 2004 <http://www.gsfc.org/GSFC/grants/dsp_menu.cfm> (accessed June 1, 2006).

The Seven Lesson Schoolteacher

Speech

By: John Taylor Gatto

Date: 1992

Source: Gatto, John Taylor. "The Seven Lesson Schoolteacher." Philadelphia: New Society Publishers, 1992.

About the Author: John Taylor Gatto taught in public schools for more than thirty years and received the New York State Teacher of the Year Award in 1991. "The Seven Lesson Schoolteacher" is a revised version of his acceptance speech for the award. Gatto writes on topics related to the history of compulsory education, homeschooling, and unschooling.

INTRODUCTION

Unlike other industrialized nations such as Great Britain or France, the United States does not have a national curriculum for the fifty-four million children between the ages of five and seventeen who must, according to compulsory education laws, attend school or be homeschooled. State boards of education and local boards of education drive curriculum standards in the United States, creating a variety of schools with different class sizes, course offerings, extracurricular activities, special education services, and wide differences in funding.

In spite of these differences, public schools in the United States follow a remarkably similar pattern: government-funded schools generally have a local school board governing decisions, a superintendent in charge of school policy and personnel, a principal in each school with assorted administrators managing financial and regulatory issues, and teachers and para-professionals performing classroom and special services support. While class sizes, school sizes, bus availability, supplies, and curriculum materials may vary, most children who attend public schools in the United States experience similar social and educational experiences.

Classes are segregated by age, and at the middle- and high-school level students are often tracked within content areas, with higher achievers separated from lower achievers. In high school, college preparatory tracks are distinct from vocational tracks, and some school systems form compacts with others to create a central school for vocational studies such as auto mechanics, culinary arts, or electronics. In the mid–1960s, President Lyndon B. Johnson's "War on Poverty" created funding programs such as Title I, part of the Elementary and Secondary Education Act. Schools qualify for Title I funding when a certain percentage of the population comes from families below the federal poverty line. Title I helped to address funding disparities in education; because most American school districts receive funding from property taxes, schools in affluent neighborhoods can receive twice as much money per pupil than schools in districts with lower property values.

The 1983 report *A Nation at Risk*, published by the National Commission on Excellence in Education, addressed the funding issue, low test scores, low teacher salaries, and an overall decrease in the quality of education in the United States. The report sparked changes in curriculum, as well as teacher literacy exams, graduation exams, smaller class sizes, and increases in teacher pay in some districts. Throughout the late 1980s and early 1990s, the public schools in the United States were considered to be in a crisis state as gang violence, bullying, teenage pregnancy, and higher dropout rates all pointed to a failed system.

John Taylor Gatto taught in public schools from the 1960s through the 1990s. A thirty-year teaching veteran, Gatto won teaching awards in New York City and in 1991 was named New York State Teacher of the Year. Having experienced the "back to basics" movement of the 1970s, the changes brought about by *A Nation at Risk*, increased numbers of students who spoke English as a second or third language, and other systemic, social, and political processes affecting schools, Gatto chose to use his acceptance speech to reflect on the condition of public education as he experienced it.

PRIMARY SOURCE

The first lesson I teach is confusion.

Everything I teach is out of context... I teach the unrelating of everything. I teach disconnections. I teach too much: the orbiting of planets, the law of large numbers, slavery, adjectives, architectural drawing, dance, gymnasium, choral singing, assemblies, surprise guests, fire drills, computer languages, parent's nights, staff-development days, pull-out programs, guidance with strangers you may never see again, standardized tests, age-segregation unlike anything seen in the outside world... what do any of these things have to do with each other?

Even in the best schools a close examination of curriculum and its sequences turns up a lack of coherence, full of internal contradictions.

Fortunately the children have no words to define the panic and anger they feel at constant violations of natural order and sequence fobbed off on them as quality in education. The logic of the school-mind is that it is better to leave school with a tool kit of superficial jargon derived from economics, sociology, natural science and so on than to leave with one genuine enthusiasm. But quality in education entails learning about something in depth. Confusion is thrust upon kids by too many strange adults, each working alone with only the thinnest relationship with each other, pretending for the most part, to an expertise they do not possess.

Meaning, not disconnected facts, is what sane human beings seek, and education is a set of codes for processing raw facts into meaning. Behind the patchwork quilt of school sequences, and the school obsession with facts and theories the age-old human search lies well concealed.

This is harder to see in elementary school where the hierarchy of school experience seems to make better sense because the good-natured simple relationship of "let's do this" and "let's do that now" is just assumed to mean something and the clientele has not yet consciously discerned how little substance is behind the play and pretense.

Think of all the great natural sequences like learning to walk and learning to talk, following the progression of light from sunrise to sunset, witnessing the ancient procedures of a farm, a smithy, or a shoemaker, watching your mother prepare a Thanksgiving feast—all of the parts are in perfect harmony with each other, each action justifies itself and illuminates the past and future. School sequences aren't like that, not inside a single class and not among the total menu of daily classes. School sequences are crazy. There is no particular reason for any

of them, nothing that bears close scrutiny. Few teachers would dare to teach the tools whereby dogmas of a school or a teacher could be criticized since everything must be accepted. School subjects are learned, if they can be learned, like children learn the catechism or memorize the 39 articles of Anglicanism. I teach the un-relating of everything, an infinite fragmentation the opposite of cohesion; what I do is more related to television programming than to making a scheme of order. In a world where home is only a ghost because both parents work or because too many moves or too many job changes or too much ambition or something else has left everybody too confused to stay in a family relation I teach you how to accept confusion as your destiny. That's the first lesson I teach.

The second lesson I teach is your class position. I teach that you must stay in class where you belong. I don't know who decides that my kids belong there but that's not my business. The children are numbered so that if any get away they can be returned to the right class. Over the years the variety of ways children are numbered has increased dramatically, until it is hard to see the human being plainly under the burden of numbers he carries. Numbering children is a big and very profitable business, though what the strategy is designed to accomplish is elusive. I don't even know why parents would allow it to be done to their kid without a fight.

In any case, again, that's not my business. My job is to make them like it, being locked in together with children who bear numbers like their own. Or at the least endure it like good sports. If I do my job well, the kids can't even imagine themselves somewhere else because I've shown how to envy and fear the better classes and how to have contempt for the dumb classes. Under this efficient discipline the class mostly polices itself into good marching order. That's the real lesson of any rigged competition like school. You come to know your place.

In spite of the overall class blueprint which assumes that 99 percent of the kids are in their class to stay, I nevertheless make a public effort to exhort children to higher levels of test success, hinting at eventual transfer from the lower class as a reward. I frequently insinuate that the day will come when an employer will hire them on the basis of test scores and grades, even though my own experience is that employers are rightly indifferent to such things. I never lie outright, but I've come to see that truth and school teaching are, at bottom, incompatible just as Socrates said they were thousands of years ago. The lesson of numbered classes is that everyone has a proper place in the pyramid and that there is no way out of your class except by number magic. Until that happens you must stay where you are put.

The third lesson I teach kids is indifference. I teach children not to care about anything too much, even though they want to make it appear that they do. How I do this is very subtle. I do it by demanding that they become totally involved in my lessons, jumping up and down in their seats with anticipation, competing vigorously with each other for my favor. It's heartwarming when they do that, it impresses everyone, even me. When I'm at my best I plan lessons very carefully in order to produce this show of enthusiasm. But when the bell rings I insist that they stop whatever it is that we've been working on and proceed quickly to the next work station. They must turn on and off like a light switch. Nothing important is ever finished in my class, nor in any other class I know of. Students never have a complete experience except on the installment plan.

Indeed, the lesson of the bells is that no work is worth finishing, so why care too deeply about anything? Years of bells will condition all but the strongest to a world that can no longer offer important work to do. Bells are the secret logic of schooltime; their argument is inexorable. Bells destroy the past and future, converting every interval into a sameness, as an abstract map makes every living mountain and river the same even though they are not. Bells inoculate each undertaking with indifference.

The fourth lesson I teach is emotional dependency. By stars and red checks, smiles and frowns, prizes, honors and disgraces I teach you to surrender your will to the predestined chain of command. Rights may be granted or withheld by any authority, without appeal because rights do not exist inside a school, not even the right of free speech, the Supreme Court has so ruled, unless school authorities say they do. As a schoolteacher I intervene in many personal decisions, issuing a Pass for those I deem legitimate, or initiating a disciplinary confrontation for behavior that threatens my control. Individuality is constantly trying to assert itself among children and teenagers so my judgments come thick and fast. Individuality is a contradiction of class theory, a curse to all systems of classification. Here are some common ways it shows up: children sneak away for a private moment in the toilet on the pretext of moving their bowels; they trick me out of a private instant in the hallway on the grounds that they need water. I know they don't but I allow them to deceive me because this conditions them to depend on my favors. Sometimes free will appears right in front of me in children angry, depressed or happy by things outside my ken; rights in such things cannot be recognized by schoolteachers, only privileges which can be withdrawn, hostages to good behavior.

The fifth lesson I teach is intellectual dependency. Good people wait for a teacher to tell them what to do. It

is the most important lesson, that we must wait for other people, better trained than ourselves, to make the meanings of our lives. The expert makes all the important choices; only I can determine what you must study, or rather, only the people who pay me can make those decisions which I enforce. If I'm told that evolution is fact instead of a theory I transmit that as ordered, punishing deviants who resist what I have been to think.

This power to control what children will think lets me separate successful students from failures very easily. Successful children do the thinking I appoint them with a minimum of resistance and decent show of enthusiasm. Of the millions of things of value to study, I decide what few we have time for, or it is decided by my faceless employer. The choices are his, why should I argue? Curiosity has no important place in my work, only conformity.

Bad kids fight this, of course, even though they lack the concepts to know what they are fighting, struggling to make decisions for themselves about what they will learn and when they will learn it. How can we allow that and survive as schoolteachers? Fortunately there are procedures to break the will of those who resist; it is more difficult, naturally, if the kid has respectable parents who come to his aid, but that happens less and less in spite of the bad reputation of schools. Nobody in the middle class I ever met actually believes that their kid's school is one of the bad ones. Not a single parent in 26 years of teaching. That's amazing and probably the best testimony to what happens to families when mother and father have been well-schooled themselves, learning the seven lessons.

Good people wait for an expert to tell them what to do. It is hardly an exaggeration to say that our entire economy depends upon this lesson being learned. Think of what would fall apart if kids weren't trained to be dependent:

The social-service businesses could hardly survive, they would vanish I think, into the recent historical limbo out of which they arose. Counselors and therapists would look on in horror as the supply of psychic invalids vanished. Commercial entertainment of all sorts, including television, would wither as people learned again how to make their own fun. Restaurants, prepared-food and a whole host of other assorted food services would be drastically down-sized if people returned to making their own meals rather than depending on strangers to plant, pick, chop and cook for them. Much of modern law, medicine, and engineering would go, too, the clothing business and schoolteaching as well, unless a guaranteed supply of helpless people poured out of our schools each year.

The sixth lesson I teach is provisional self-esteem. If you've ever tried to wrestle a kid into line whose parents have convinced him to believe they'll love him in spite of anything, you know how impossible it is to make self-confident spirits conform. Our world wouldn't survive a flood of confident people very long so I teach that your self-respect should depend on expert opinion. My kids are constantly evaluated and judged. A monthly report, impressive in its precision, is sent into students' homes to signal approval or to mark exactly down to a single percentage point how dissatisfied with their children parents should be. The ecology of good schooling depends upon perpetuating dissatisfaction just as much as commercial economy depends on the same fertilizer. Although some people might be surprised how little time or reflection goes into making up these mathematical records, the cumulative weight of the objective-seeming documents establishes a profile of defect which compels a child to arrive at certain decisions about himself and his future based on the casual judgment of strangers.

Self-evaluation, the staple of every major philosophical system that ever appeared on the planet, is never a factor in these things. The lesson of report cards, grades, and tests is that children should not trust themselves or their parents, but need to rely on the evaluation of certified officials. People need to be told what they are worth.

The seventh lesson I teach is that you can't hide. I teach children they are always watched by keeping each student under constant surveillance as do my colleagues. There are no private spaces for children, there is no private time. Class change lasts 300 seconds to keep promiscuous fraternization at low levels. Students are encouraged to tattle on each other, even to tattle on their parents. Of course I encourage parents to file their own child's waywardness, too. A family trained to snitch on each other isn't likely to be able to conceal any dangerous secrets. I assign a type of extended schooling called "homework," too, so that the surveillance travels into private households, where students might otherwise use free time to learn something unauthorized from a father or mother, or by apprenticing to some wise person in the neighborhood. Disloyalty to the idea of schooling is a Devil always ready to find work for idle hands. The meaning of constant surveillance and denial of privacy is that no one can be trusted, that privacy is not legitimate. Surveillance is an ancient urgency among certain influential thinkers, a central prescription set down in Republic, in City of God, in Institutes of the Christian Religion, in New Atlantis, in Leviathan and many other places. All these childless men who wrote these books discovered the same thing: children must be closely watched if you want to keep a society under tight central control. Children will follow a private drummer if you can't get them into a uniformed marching band.

SIGNIFICANCE

Gatto's speech shocked his audience, and later that year he announced that he was quitting teaching because he was "no longer willing to hurt children" by reinforcing the unwritten curriculum that he discussed in his speech. Gatto's analysis of American education was highly influenced by writers such as John Holt and Ivan Illich; Holt's 1964 book *How Children Fail* had detailed the dampening effect of traditional education on a child's intrinsic motivation to learn, while Illich's 1971 book *Deschooling Society* argued that schools are designed to train students to have needs that can be met only through societal institutions and that schools perpetuate social class distinctions.

Gatto's speech came on the heels of the publication of Jonathan Kozol's book *Savage Inequalities*, which examined public schools in the United States through the lens of funding. Kozol shed light on disparities between poor and wealthy public schools—a district on Long Island might spend more than $11,000 per pupil while a nearby district in New York City spends $5,500 per pupil. Local funding created conditions for suburban schools with largely white populations to provide new buildings, up-to-date textbooks, Advanced Placement courses, and new lab equipment, while inner city schools with largely minority populations experienced overcrowding, buildings in disrepair, decades-old textbooks, and underpaid staff. As Kozol, Gatto, and Illich stress, the institutional nature of public education, funding procedures, and compulsory laws enforcing it generated social conditions that perpetuated class inequities, discouraged critical thought, and reinforced Gatto's unspoken curriculum.

Gatto advocates a form of schooling called "unschooling," in which the child's innate interests direct learning. Schools such as Sudbury Valley School and the Albany Free School, called "democratic" or "free" schools because the students—not adults—create and enforce systems of justice, function as unschools. There is no curriculum, though these schools provide resources such as music rooms, libraries, woodshops, sewing rooms, commercial kitchens, art and pottery rooms, and so forth. According to Gatto, when children are neither age-segregated nor subject to forty-five- or fifty-minute divisions in the day, and are free to learn what they wish to learn, when they wish to learn it, applying critical thinking to questions and seeking experts when necessary, the seven lessons in his speech no longer dictate the child's educational experience. Experiential learning via unschooling, Gatto theorizes, allows the child to work within a social community and apply learning to the natural environment, a radically different approach from public institutions of education. Gatto promotes homeschooling as an alternative to sending children to private democratic schools.

As homeschooling increases at a rate of seven to fifteen percent in the United States, Gatto's theories have found fertile ground in the homeschooling movement, particularly among the thirty percent of homeschooling parents who choose to homeschool because of negative social conditions in schools. Gatto's speech hit a nerve among parents, educators, and students alike during his acceptance speech in 1991. As professional educators struggle in the twenty-first century to manage the requirements imposed by the No Child Left Behind Act of 2001 in the United States, which places greater testing requirements on students, Gatto's call for a radically different curriculum—both written and unwritten—challenges educators and parents alike to explore a different vision of education.

FURTHER RESOURCES

Books

Gatto, John Taylor. *Dumbing Us Down: The Hidden Curriculum of Compulsory Schooling*. Philadelphia: New Society Publishers, 2005.

Holt, John C. *How Children Fail*. Cambridge, Mass.: Perseus Publishing, 1995.

——*How Children Learn*. Cambridge, Mass.: Perseus Publishing, 1995.

Web sites

National Center for Education Statistics. "1.1 Million Homeschooled Students in the United States in 2003." July 2004. <http://nces.ed.gov/pubs2004/2004115.pdf> (accessed June 13, 2006).

National Commission on Excellence in Education. "A Nation at Risk." April 1983. <http://www.ed.gov/pubs/NatAtRisk/index.html> (accessed June 13, 2006).

Sudbury Valley School. <http://www.sudval.org> (accessed June 13, 2006).

U.S. Census Bureau. "Home Schooling in the United States: Trends and Characteristics." August 2001. <http://www.census.gov/population/www/documentation/twps0053.html> (accessed June 13, 2006).

Security Is Main Theme of a Spate of New Laws

Newspaper article excerpt

By: Anonymous

Date: December 27, 1993

Source: "Security Is Main Theme of a Spate of New Laws." *New York Times* (December 27, 1993): A13.

About the Author: This article was provided to the *New York Times* by the Associated Press, an international news agency based in New York.

INTRODUCTION

In 2006, the U.S. government spent close to half a trillion dollars on defense, homeland security, and other programs designed to ensure the security of the nation. Despite an ongoing debate about military actions in the Middle East, most Americans believe that providing national security is one of the fundamental duties of representative government. For this reason, direct military spending consistently accounts for fifteen to twenty percent of the U.S. federal budget, and indirect security-related spending substantially increases this figure.

While Americans generally resist government intrusion in their lives, they frequently expect the federal government to protect them from potential danger. In some cases, the desire for protection conflicts with the desire for non-interference. The Food and Drug Administration (FDA), which approves new medications for sale in the United States, is frequently criticized for being too slow in approving new products; conversely, each time an approved drug is found to cause injury, the FDA is generally blamed for lax oversight. Similarly, the Occupational Safety and Health Administration (OSHA) is simultaneously praised for improving safety in the nation's workplaces and for instituting a maze of confusing and seemingly trivial regulations that waste employers' time and money.

A similar situation exists at the state level. In many cases, states pass specific laws intended to protect citizens from harm but are then criticized for limiting citizens' freedom. Some restrictions are passed in response to a tragedy, such as a mass killing or an accident, though such laws are frequently found to be overly restrictive and are later repealed.

PRIMARY SOURCE

"Safety first!" is the nervous theme of many state laws that will take effect in January, doing things like requiring helmets for bike-riding children in California and Tennessee, checking potential teachers for criminal records in Oregon, New Hampshire, and Tennessee, and making barbers train longer in Hawaii.

Whether seeking to protect children from bad apples or consumers from bad haircuts, state legislators strove this year to bolster security in an insecure world.

Florida, stunned by a spate of killings of tourists, banned guns from the hands of anyone under 18, except for hunting, marksmanship practice or competition under adult supervision. The threat of violence inspired a California law to let schools ban gang attire in class.

New Hampshire doctors who test positive for the virus that causes AIDS or for hepatitis B will need special permission to perform invasive surgery.

There is no special reason to enact laws in January, only the symbolism of a fresh start at the top of the calendar. Many states set laws to take effect 60 or 90 days after signing, or after the legislative session ends....

Political scientists were at a loss to explain what, if anything, the lineup of new laws meant.

"We've had a change in the Administration, and maybe the states are waiting for new policy direction," suggested David King, assistant professor of public policy at the John F. Kennedy School of Government at Harvard University.

Some observers forecast a slew of crime bills next year, but for now, safety seems the watchword.

Starting on Jan. 1, riding in the open back of a pickup truck will be illegal in California, where children age 6 and younger will also need life jackets in motorboats and in sailboats less than 26 feet long.

Enforcing Sobriety

New Oklahoma regulations will allow tinted car windows to be only so dark.

Seeking safety against drunken drivers and following the lead of many other states, Florida, New Hampshire and New Mexico lowered the permissible level of alcohol in the blood to 0.08 percent from 0.10 percent. In California, drivers under 21 caught with a blood-alcohol level of just 0.01 will lose their licenses for one year.

Under a yearlong experiment, Illinois joined about 30 states that require repeat drunken drivers to use a device that keeps a car from starting if the driver has alcohol on his breath.

Addressing dangers in the marketplace, Rhode Island required credit agencies to send consumers their credit reports within four days of a request and to inform consumers when credit is denied.

Video stores in New York will be barred from selling their customers' names and rental histories to anyone.

Illinois outlawed unwanted sales pitches by telephone and banned such calls from 9 P.M. to 8 A.M.

Connecticut repealed its two-decade-old no-fault auto insurance law. Motorists should see premiums drop, but they will have to go to court to make accident claims against other drivers.

Car insurance in Illinois and buckling up in Vermont will be mandatory, as they already are in most states.

Some new laws will guard against the inept and the incompetent. Texas acted to regulate the operators of machines that keep blood and oxygen flowing during open heart surgery.

Notably, many of these measures will cost the states nothing, except for enforcement.

Greater expenses may be in the offing, of course, with changes in the national health care and welfare systems. Some states ventured ahead, not waiting for word from Washington.

Universal health care will come to Tennessee with a system called TennCare. And unmarried women in Georgia who are under 18 and pregnant, or are already mothers, must live with a parent or guardian to get welfare. Further, able-bodied recipients must accept job offers to remain eligible for welfare, and benefits will be frozen for two years for mothers on welfare who have another child.

Correction: December 31, 1993, Friday

SIGNIFICANCE

The United States' federal structure frequently results in regulations that differ from state to state; examples include mandatory seat-belt laws, which exist in most but not all states, and definitions of drunk driving, with legal blood-alcohol limits rising and falling within and between states over time. In some cases, the federal government takes a hands-off approach to safety, allowing states and municipalities to handle public safety. In the case of amusement park rides, go-karts, and water slides, no federal safety laws exist, and states and cities are responsible for creating and enforcing safety standards. However, the Consumer Product Safety Commission (CPSC) does analyze accident patterns involving such rides, identifying potential problems with specific types of equipment.

The U.S. government today includes dozens of agencies responsible for specific types of safety regulation. The CPSC tests consumer products for safety, requiring manufacturers to recall products found to be unsafe. In 2006, the agency ordered recalls of products including a child's swing that could break during use and a swimming pool ladder that could be assembled incorrectly, leading to failure. The agency's jurisdiction includes more than 15,000 separate types of products. Some of the agency's actions, such as a recall on window blinds during the 1990s, may seem trivial but in actuality save lives. At the time of the window-blind recall, 160 children accidentally strangled themselves on window blind cords.

The National Transportation Safety Board (NTSB) has responsibility for all forms of public transportation within the United States. NTSB investigators are frequently seen conducting inspections in the wake of an airplane or train accident, though their authority also includes highways, water craft, and hazardous material transportation.

Modern motor vehicles are safer than ever before, and many of the improvements in auto safety came about through the efforts of the National Highway Traffic Safety Administration (NHTSA). This agency is charged with protecting the public against unreasonable risk of crashes due to the design or performance of motor vehicles and with insuring occupants' protection when crashes do occur. NHTSA has issued standards covering seat belts, roof crush resistance, tires, lighting, and occupant crash protection. NHTSA also creates crash-testing standards for all new cars sold in the United States.

The Environmental Protection Agency (EPA) is charged with protecting human health and the environment. The agency is perhaps best known for its ratings of automobile fuel efficiency, however its work extends to numerous aspects of environmental regulation and protection. The EPA also works to promote the use of renewable and other alternative energy sources. In 2006, the agency enacted regulations requiring diesel refiners to reduce the amount of sulfur in diesel fuel by ninety-seven percent. The new low-sulfur fuel allows the use of more advanced pollution-control devices on trucks and buses, reducing their pollution output substantially.

The proper role of government in citizens' lives has been debated since the days of the Founding Fathers. As government rules increasingly encroach on Americans' lives in the name of safety, that debate will likely continue.

FURTHER RESOURCES

Books

Asch, Peter. *Consumer Safety Regulation: Putting a Price on Life and Limb.* New York: Oxford University Press, 1988.

Gad, Shayne C., ed. *Product Safety Evaluation Handbook.* New York: Marcel Dekker, 1999.

Landy, Marc K., Mark Roberts, and Stephen R. Thomas. *The Environmental Protection Agency: Asking the Wrong Questions from Nixon to Clinton.* New York: Oxford University Press, 1994.

Periodicals

"CPSC Approves New Flammability Standard for Mattresses." *Fire Engineering* 159 (2006): 86.

O'donnell, Jayne. "Generator Deaths Spur Feds." *USA Today* (May 24, 2006): 1A.

"Paper Shredders: A Hazard to Toddlers." *Child Health Alert* 24 (2006): 2.

Web sites

National Highway Transportation Safety Administration. "Office of Defects Investigation." <http://www-odi.nhtsa.dot.gov/cars/problems/recalls/> (accessed June 2, 2006).

U.S. Environmental Protection Agency. "35 Years of Protecting Human Health and the Environment." <http://www.epa.gov> (accessed June 2, 2006).

U.S. Food and Drug Administration. "Recalls, Market Withdrawals and Alerts." <http://www.fda.gov/opacom/7alerts.html> (accessed June 2, 2006).

Dealing with Sex Offenders

Newspaper article

By: Anonymous

Date: August 15, 1994

Source: New York Times

About the Author: The *New York Times* is a daily newspaper, published in New York City since September 18, 1851.

INTRODUCTION

On July 29, 1994, seven-year-old Megan Nicole Kanka was sexually assaulted and murdered by Jesse Timmendequas, a convicted sex offender who had previously served seven years for sexual assault against

President Bill Clinton shakes hands with Jeremy Kanka, as his mother Maureen looks on, at a White House ceremony on May 17, 1996. Clinton has just signed legislation known as Megan's Law. It is named after Jeremy's sister, a victim of rape and murder at the hands of a known child molestor. STR/AFP/GETTY IMAGES.

children. Unbeknownst to community members, Timmendequas had taken up residence in the New Jersey suburb where Megan Kanka lived with her family. Megan was lured into Timmendequas's house, across the street from her home, with promises of seeing his puppy, but instead became the victim of a terrible crime.

Community outrage in the wake of Megan's death resulted in efforts to increase community safety and to ensure that this would not happen again, but Megan's murder was certainly not the first of its kind to bring about calls for legislative reform. Five years earlier, a seven-year-old boy in Tacoma, Washington was abducted, sexually assaulted, mutilated, and left for dead by convicted sex offender Earl Shriner. This incident led to the creation of a special task force to create regulations for dangerous sex offenders. The resulting legislation was the Washington Community Protection Act, which included provisions for post-sentence civil commitment of sexually violent predators, a sex offender registry, and a system of tiered notification of criminal justice officials, community groups, and community members upon the release of a sex offender, depending on his risk level. In the case of a very high risk offender, individuals living around the offender's intended place of residence would be notified and provided with his name, address, and other pertinent information.

In 1994 congress passed the *Jacob Wetterling Act*, named in memory of an eleven-year-old boy who was abducted in Minnesota in October 1989 and never seen again. The Jacob Wetterling Act required each state to create a registry system to record and track the whereabouts of released sex offenders. States found to be in noncompliance with this legislation would face a 10 percent reduction in criminal justice funding from the federal government. In the same year, Indiana passed Zachary's Law (named for another child murder victim), creating the first online sex offender registry, with information accessible to the public. In all of these cases, victim advocacy groups and public outcry drove the impetus for legislative change, pushing politicians to react swiftly with sweeping reforms to address public fear and concern.

■ **PRIMARY SOURCE**

DEALING WITH SEX OFFENDERS

August 15, 1994

It was a genuine tragedy when 33-year-old Jesse Timmendequas talked 7-year-old Megan Kanka into entering his house in Hamilton Township, N.J., one day last month. Mr. Timmendequas had been convicted twice for sexually assaulting young girls, and had served six years in a facility for sex offenders. Once Megan was in the house he strangled her to death and raped her.

Small wonder that the angry residents of Megan's town and much of New Jersey's political leadership want to crack down on sex offenders who have served their time in jail and been released back into the community. Proposals range from requiring released sex offenders to register with the police departments of the towns they settle in, to requiring that they report their whereabouts every 30 days, to making them spend the rest of their lives in prison unless they can convince officials that they have been rehabilitated. Under one proposal, the police would be alerted and asked to notify neighborhood residents of a sex offender's presence.

The Speaker of the New York Assembly, Sheldon Silver, also plans to introduce a bill calling for community notification; Gov. Mario Cuomo has said he would press for such a law.

Those who would impose new stringencies on sex offenders are speaking for millions of Americans. But some proposals could do more harm than good—by triggering outbreaks of vigilantism or by destroying the efforts of thousands of law-abiding former sex offenders to rebuild their lives.

Proposals to notify communities of the sex offenders in their midst seem particularly problematic. Why, for instance, should a sex offender be branded when a released drug dealer, armed robber or murderer is not? Some argue that recidivism among sex offenders is so high that "better safe than sorry" should be the rule. But careful studies of sex offenders after release have found that most do not repeat their crimes. Treatment experts claim that recidivism rates are not only exaggerated but depend on a range of factors, including the nature of the crime and whether the offender received treatment. Although several therapies have been shown to lower recidivism rates, the vast majority of jailed sex offenders get no help at all.

Community notification laws do little or nothing to prevent a sex offender from striking again; they simply make it more likely that the offender will be hounded from one town to another. Indeed, sex offenders might actually become more dangerous if driven from communities where family and friends help control their behavior.

The danger of vigilantism is real. A community notification system in the state of Washington, under which the police can, at their discretion, inform anyone from county officials to local newspapers of a released sex offender's presence, has resulted in arson that destroyed a sex offender's house, death threats, assaults, slashed tires and loss of employment and housing.

So how, then, to craft a system that will protect a community from those against whom it must be protected without stigmatizing those from whom it need not be? Carefully, that is how, and without hysteria. Keeping communities safe should be primarily a matter for the police and the criminal justice system, not for a frightened citizenry.

Registration programs that help police keep track of released sex offenders may well have a place in a careful police program, under court supervision that assures procedures meet constitutional safeguards. After all, police professionals already swap information about the whereabouts of many released criminals. But dissemination of the information can only inflame passions.

Penalties for preying on children can be toughened, as they were last week in New Jersey; and juvenile offenders need early counseling and treatment. Those who have spoken for the Megans of this world are speaking from the heart. Now it is time for Americans to use their heads as well.

SIGNIFICANCE

On October 31, 1994, a mere 95 days after the sexual assault and murder of Megan Kanka, the New Jersey state legislature passed Megan's Law. The legislation, based on the earlier, federal Jacob Wetterling Law provided for the registration and tracking of released sexual offenders, but the controversial centerpiece of the new law was a sweeping set of provisions for community notification. Community members, neighbors, and schools were to be informed of the presence of a high-risk offender in their neighborhood. The legislation made intuitive sense to concerned parents and community members who were searching for a means of protecting children from victimization and was vigorously supported by a petition of over 400,000 community members. The pressure to act from Megan Kanka's parents, victim advocacy groups, and the public was instrumental in pushing the bill through the state legislature in record time. Megan's Law was passed so quickly, in fact, that its implications were not carefully considered by policy makers.

While a judiciously used sex offender registry can be a valuable tool for police investigations, criminologists and criminal justice professionals have questioned the wisdom of blanket community notification policies. The use of community notification in communities has led to increased vigilantism, including

harassment and even physical assault against registered sex offenders; occasionally innocent persons have been mistaken for registered sex offenders and harassed or assaulted. The fear, isolation, stigma, and stress that results from the offender's notoriety in the community may, ironically, serve to increase his risk of reoffense and put the community at greater danger than if only the police were aware of his presence. Some offenders have been forced to move away from communities that would not tolerate their presence, and offenders forced out of a community by animosity may choose not to comply with registry requirements to update their addresses, in effect going underground to avoid their identities being revealed once again. As a result, many states who use community notification have high rates of noncompliance with sex offender registries, making the databases significantly less effective and putting the community at greater risk.

In 1996 Congress amended the Jacob Wetterling Act to create a federal Megan's Law statute that requires all states to employ community notification in accordance with a federal standard. At the same time, the Pam Lyncher Act created a national sex offender registry, administered by the FBI, and required the lifetime registration of all offenders who had engaged in coercive, penetrative sex or had victims under the age of twelve. Currently all states utilize some form of sex offender registry and community notification.

About half of the states use a three-tiered approach to notification that takes into account the offender's risk level. The first tier is the lowest risk and registry information on tier one offenders is provided to law enforcement officials only. The second tier presents a moderate level of risk and the names, addresses, photographs, and relevant information are provided to schools, daycare centers, and community groups or agencies that are likely to encounter the individual. The third tier is considered high risk and information about the individual is provided door-to-door throughout the neighborhood of residence; in some states it may be posted on an internet database. The states that do not use a three-tiered approach have a blanket policy on community notification and information about all registered sex offenders is made public through the use of media and internet databases.

Beyond the role stress plays in precipitating a relapse and the potential for vigilante violence, community notification appears to be an attempt at a quick fix to sexual offending. The law promotes the notion that if one knows where sex offenders live then one will be safe. Counterintuitive to this is the fact that the vast majority of sexual assaults are committed by a person known to the victim. Intrafamilial sexual abuse is far more common than the "stranger danger" that sex offender registries and community notification policies target. An overreliance on these types of solutions perpetuates a false sense of security and does nothing to protect and bring awareness to the thousands of children who are abused each day by people that they trust.

Megan's Law continues to draw firm support from politicians and the public, despite general expert agreement on the potential for negative consequences from community notification. As recently as 2002 a constitutional challenge to the legislation on the basis that it violates the offenders' right to privacy failed and the law was subsequently upheld by the United States Supreme Court, suggesting that it is here to stay.

FURTHER RESOURCES

Books

Brown, Mark, and John Pratt, eds. *Dangerous Offenders: Punishment and Social Order*. New York: Routledge, 2000.

Jenkins, Philip. *Moral Panic: Changing Conceptions of the Child Molester in Modern America*. New Haven, CT.: Yale University Press, 1998.

Periodicals

Levenson, Jill S., and Leo P. Cotter. "The Effect of Megan's Law on Sex Offender Reintegration." *Journal of Contemporary Criminal Justice*. 21, no. 1 (2005): 49–66.

Petrunik, Michael G. "The Hare and the Tortoise: Dangerousness and Sex Offender Policy in the United States and Canada." *Canadian Journal of Criminology and Criminal Justice*. 45, no. 1 (2003): 43–72.

———. "Managing Unacceptable Risk: Sex Offenders, Community Response and Social Policy in the United States and Canada." *International Journal of Offender Therapy and Comparative Criminology*. 46, no. 4 (2002): 483–511.

Welchans, Sarah. "Megan's Law: Evaluations of Sexual Offender Registries." *Criminal Justice Policy Review*. 16, no. 2 (2005): 123–140.

Web sites

American Probation and Parole Association. "Revisiting Megan's Law and Sex Offender Registration: Prevention or Problem." 2000. <http://www.appa-net.org/revisitingmegan.pdf> (accessed May 23, 2006).

Jacob Wetterling Foundation. <http://www.jwf.org> (accessed May 23, 2006).

Megan Nicole Kanka Foundation. <http://www.megannicolekankafoundation.org> (accessed May 23, 2006).

Affirmative Action's Long Record

Affirmative Action Special Report

Newspaper article

By: Mann, Judy

Date: November 1, 1995

Source: Mann, Judy. "Affirmative Action's Long Record: Affirmative Action Special Report." *Washington Post*. (November 1, 1995): F12.

About the Author: Judy Mann was a journalist and writer who worked nearly thirty years for the *Washington Post*. She began her career at the newspaper as a city reporter, was quickly promoted to day city editor, and then moved to a slot as a regular columnist. She was particularly well known for her impassioned pieces about the gender gap in employment and education, the women's movement and its politics, issues concerning children, and the concerns of women. She was an outspoken and liberal feminist who won numerous awards for her written work. Ms. Mann died of breast cancer on July 8, 2005, at age 61.

INTRODUCTION

The phrase "affirmative action" was first coined by President Lyndon Baines Johnson in a 1965 speech at Howard University. The country was in a period of social upheaval, sparked in large part by the growing civil rights movement. African-Americans were strongly and vocally seeking equality in a nation in which institutionalized racism and racial oppression had been the norm. Affirmative action was initially a means of making positive changes for African-Americans, but the second wave of the women's movement—following on the heels of the growing civil rights movement—brought the concerns of women as an oppressed group to the forefront of public consciousness as well.

Although the term affirmative action had been in existence for about a decade as a way to redress longstanding inequities in the labor, housing, and educational realms (among others), it was given some measure of political power in 1972, when the Secretary of Labor drafted Revised Order Number 4, a document that created a systematic means of enforcing Executive Order Number 4, written in 1970, which prohibited discrimination by any government contractor. The range of contractors is quite broad, encom-

During a demonstration on October 27, 1995, a crowd of about 150 students protest in favor of affirmative action outside the University of California Irvine campus administration building. They are trying to protect five other students who are on a hunger strike in support of affirmative action. AP IMAGES.

passing everything from airlines to health care facilities to factories to financial institutions.

At first, the concept of affirmative action was poorly understood, and there was much debate as to whether it mandated racial, ethnic, and cultural quotas for hiring, housing, academic admissions, and the like. Ultimately it was adopted to shift the balance toward neutrality in hiring practices, admissions standards, and housing policies, to name just a few. Historically, white males had been at the forefront of each of those areas, and affirmative action was meant to be a positive means of ensuring more adequate representation of statistically underrepresented groups, such as racial, ethnic, cultural, and gender minorities. The underrepresentation was believed to be due primarily to institutionalized discriminatory policies or politics resulting in lack of access for advancement or equality.

In addition to providing minority or underrepresented groups access to economic, demographic, and political equality, affirmative action was also viewed as a means of re-shaping the appearance of the work-

force, academic institutions, and the housing market to reflect the realities of the American population percentages more accurately.

PRIMARY SOURCE

I heard an interesting argument against affirmative action the other day. Put briefly, it boiled down to this: Affirmative action isn't necessary anymore, and besides, it hasn't worked well enough to justify the rancor it is generating.

Overwhelmingly, when people talk about affirmative action, they discuss it in terms of race. But some form of affirmative action has helped every group that has been marginalized since Europeans settled this continent, slaughtered Native Americans and sanctified the rule of white men.

After almost 20 years of litigation, the courts have established a workable framework for affirmative action in which quotas are not permitted but goals and timetables are, people cannot be displaced from jobs, unquali-fied people cannot be given preferential treatment and any white man who feels he is the victim of discrimina-tion can sue.

The purpose of affirmative action is to redress past and present discrimination and to promote equal opportu-nities for women, minorities, and people with disabilities. The idea is to create a climate in which merit will prevail. Thus, affirmative action in employment has meant that qualified women are sought and recruited so that they will be in the mix when hiring and promotional decisions are made.

What's been accomplished, and what has not? The elimination of many sex-based barriers in education is one of affirmative action's best success stories. Women now receive about half of all bachelor's and master's degrees. But they receive only a third of the doctorate and "first professional" (medical, law, theology) degrees and continue to lag in math, engineering and the physical sciences. In 1992, for example, women received 15.4 percent of undergraduate engineering degrees and 9.6 percent of doctorate degrees in engineering.

Women make up nearly half the work force today, but they continue to be clustered in lower-paying jobs that have traditionally been held by women. In 1991, one in four women who worked was in administration sup-port jobs. Women make up 99.3 percent of dental hygien-ists but only 10.5 percent of dentists.

The glass ceiling—that invisible barrier that keeps women from breaking through to the top—is every-where. The Federal Glass Ceiling Commission's report issued in March found that 95 to 97 percent of the senior managers in Fortune 1,000 industrial companies and For-tune 500 companies are men. Women are 48 percent of all journalists, but they hold only 6 percent of the top jobs. They are 23 percent of the lawyers but only 11 percent of law firm partners.

Affirmative action has revolutionized higher educa-tion, the best predictor of economic success. A study of the Federal Contract Compliance program, which requires larger federal contractors to make a good-faith effort to meet goals and timetables for hiring and promot-ing minorities and women, found that female employ-ment rose 15.2 percent at those companies and only 2.2 percent elsewhere. Those women were paid better than women at other companies.

In 1983, women made up 9.4 percent of the nation's police force. A decade later, that number rose to 16 per-cent. Having more women on the force hasn't benefited just women; it has made police more responsive to domestic abuse, according to studies.

Affirmative action has had a major effect on the growth of women-owned businesses, which have increased by more than 57 percent since 1982, providing jobs for white men as well as for women and minorities.

The greatest myth about affirmative action is that it provides preferential treatment to disadvantaged groups. In fact, it is a remedy for the preferential treatment white men have traditionally received and continue to enjoy. In 1993, women made, on average, only 71.5 cents for every dollar made by men. One study found that once adjustments were made for education, experience and other factors, the wage gap was approximately 85 per-cent. Better, certainly, than the 60 percent gap we saw through the mid–1970s, but nowhere near equal. The gap has closed partly because of a decline in the earnings of less-skilled white men, a factor that is surely contributing to the backlash against affirmative action.

But let us get one thing straight: One group—white men—still is getting the best jobs and the highest pay even though it represents less than half the work force. As long as that's the case, we will need affirmative action to ensure that all of us enjoy a fair chance to achieve success.

White men may be feeling rancor these days, and I guess the best thing to say to them is: "Welcome to the club." Women and minorities have been shut out of jobs and paid less for as long as they can remember: They have been feeling rancor for a very long time.

SIGNIFICANCE

From a conceptual standpoint, affirmative action was designed to level the sociodemographic and eco-nomic playing fields by giving people who had histor-ically been denied such educational, occupational, and housing opportunities, for example, based either on perceptions of who they are and what their potential inherent limitations were believed to be (typically based on urban mythology rather than on actual data), the means with which to acquire the tools and skills necessary for success in any given arena, and to dra-matically increase the odds of a positive outcome. Simply putting a person who is unskilled, poorly edu-cated, or unprepared into a novel setting or situation without supports and safety nets is more than likely going to result in failure.

Prior to the inception of affirmative action pro-grams and philosophies, employment decisions, post-secondary institution admissions, and home mortgage applications were, in theory, decided based on a concept referred to as "meritocracy"—the practice of making a decision based solely on merit, rather than on political connections, racial, ethnic or cultural affiliations, or family status. When its tenets are adhered to strictly, meritocracy is thought to afford truly equal opportunity or, at least, to base choices strictly on merit (hence the term). However, as originally conceptualized, meritocracy was only deemed appropriate for white males, typically those with at least middle class means—harkening back to the principles of aristocracy.

Although affirmative action was spoken about by Lyndon Johnson in the middle of the 1960s, it was President Richard Nixon's administration that passed legislation requiring all federal contractors and labor union officials to adopt its principles. The practice quickly spread to college campuses, which had already experienced a watershed of protests against discriminatory admissions practices, which were alleged to be excessively favorable to white middle class males and actively biased against the admission of women and members of racial, ethnic, and cultural minority groups, particularly African-Americans.

At its most fundamental level, affirmative action was intended as a means of making restitution and beginning the process of redressing some of the wrongs and active discriminatory practices historically leveled against minority groups. In practice, it was expected that some degree of extra consideration would be given to minority group members and women in hiring and academic admissions decisions, mortgage lending processes and fair housing availability, and competitive access for successful negotiation of the government contracting process. Affirmative action practices were not meant to give any group special status, to impose quotas in any area, or to select unqualified or inappropriate applicants simply because they are members of a statistically underrepresented minority group. They are not meant to engender reverse discrimination.

As specifically regards women in higher education, a program called Title IX, which was packaged with 1972's Educational Amendments, mandated that academic institutions that received federal funding had to recruit females to submit applications for admission. Affirmative action was reflected in hiring practices through active efforts to place job postings in places likely to be read by women and minority applicants; another was to institute on the job training programs designed to foster occupational advancement.

A central goal of all successful affirmative action programs, no matter what the area of original focus, is to achieve a stable subpopulation, whether of students, contractors, homeowners, or employees, that accurately reflects the diversity of the population at large in terms of gender, race, ethnic and cultural affiliations, and disability status.

FURTHER RESOURCES

Books

Beckwith, Francis, and Todd E. Jones. *Affirmative Action: Social Justice or Reverse Discrimination*. Amherst, New York: Prometheus Books, 1997.

Bergmann, Barbara R. *In Defense of Affirmative Action*. New York, New York: Basic Books, 1996.

Cahn, Steven M., ed. *Affirmative Action and the University: A Philosophical Inquiry*. Philadelphia: Temple University Press, 1993.

Cokorinos, Lee. *The Assault on Diversity: An Organized Challenge to Racial and Gender Justice*. Lanham, MD: Rowman & Littlefield, 2003.

Curry, George E., ed. *The Affirmative Action Debate*. Cambridge, MA: Perseus Books, 1996.

Guinier, Lani, and Susan Sturm. *Who's Qualified?* Boston, Massachusetts: Beacon Press, 2001.

Rai, Kul B., and John Critzer. *Affirmative Action and the University: Race, Ethnicity, and Gender in Higher Education Employment*. Lincoln, Nebraska: University of Nebraska Press, 2000.

Periodicals

Beauchamp, Tom. "In Defense of Affirmative Action." *Journal of Ethics*. 2 (1998): 143–158.

Boylan, Michael. "Affirmative Action: Strategies for the Future." *Journal of Social Philosophy*. 33 (Spring 2002): 117–130.

Web sites

National Organization for Women. "Talking About Affirmative Action." <http://www.now.org/issues/affirm/talking.html?printable> (accessed May 20, 2006).

One Nation...Indivisible

Editorial cartoon

By: Herb Block

Date: 1977

Source: From *Herblock on all Fronts*.

About the Artist: Herb Block (1909–2001) was a political and editorial cartoonist whose work was published in the *Washington Post* for more than fifty years. He viewed editorial cartooning as an effective medium for the expression of political opinions and the conveyance of important information to the public in a concise and often rather humorous way.

INTRODUCTION

The featured cartoon lampoons the notion that there is equality in funding and support for education regardless of the location of racial make-up of the student body. Specifically, it referred to the initial budget created by Jimmy Carter, shortly after he was elected President of the United States. In that document, submitted by President Carter to Congress, he attempted to dramatically increase school funding for children who lived in districts that were primarily below the poverty level. He also tried to increase availability of non-loan funding to college students, and to decrease available monies for districts that were significantly wealthier than the national norm. According to Mr. Block, this cartoon was a gentle (or not so very gentle) reminder that there were considerable differences in the funding, location, and programs available between sprawling suburban schools and their urban or inner-city counterparts.

After the conclusion of the Civil War (1861–1865), with the emancipation of slaves and the abolition of the practice of slavery in the United States, there was enormous racial tension, and considerable racial bias, throughout the country. There was little interaction between African Americans and Caucasians and virtually no social interaction between the races in most areas of the country. There was no integration of the races for public education, public transportation, or attendance of church or religious services. In many ways, this was an informal series of social conventions, not made law until the case of *Plessy v. Ferguson* in 1896. In 1890, Louisiana passed a "separate but equal" law in which "whites" and "coloreds" were not permitted to ride in the same railway car, unless there was only one car attached to the train—in which case, a physical barrier must be erected in order to separate the races. Homer Plessy, a man who was one-eighth black (also called by the colloquial term "octoroon"), entered a train car reserved for whites only and sat down. He was told to move to the "colored" car and refused to vacate his seat. He was summarily ejected from the train (presumably at the next stop). He was found guilty of refusal to sit in the place reserved for members of his race. The legal precedent set by this judicial decision was to be felt all across the nation, as it formalized the "separate but equal" doctrine: It was not necessary for the races ever to intermingle so long as separate but equal facilities could be created but maintained. The theory of "separate but equal" was rapidly institutionalized and extended to nearly every aspect of life in America. There were racial divisions for the use of physicians, hospitals, schools, churches, water fountains, bathrooms, hotels, and housing areas. The proverbial elephant in the living room, however, was that while the facilities created were definitely separate, they were virtually never equal.

PRIMARY SOURCE

ONE NATION...INDIVISIBLE
See primary source image.

SIGNIFICANCE

Although there had been de facto segregation before the legal decision in *Plessy v. Ferguson*, it was codified and sanctioned by the courts at that point. In theory, all public facilities, whether they were medical, educational, or social, were supposed to be created so as to be equal, or at least equivalent, for both races. From a legal perspective, anyone who was not 100 percent Caucasian was considered black, whether they were Asian, Native American, Pacific Islander, multi-racial, or African American—all were equal under the law.

In fact, the differences in facilities for each race were widely reported to be significant, with perhaps one of the greatest disparities occurring in the area of education. In 1864, the Fourteenth Amendment to the Constitution of the United States was ratified, and thereby guaranteed 'equal protection under the law' to all citizens, regardless of race. In 1896, *Plessy v. Ferguson* extended that paradigm to incorporate the notion of 'separate but equal', with the emphasis on *separate*. Although numerous attempts were made to nullify the outcome of *Plessy* by individuals and civil rights groups, including the NAACP (National Association for the Advancement of Colored People), none prevailed until *Brown v. Board of Education* was decided on appeal in 1955.

Initially, the legal challenges, spearheaded by the NAACP, focused on mandating that the separated schools be made truly equal and attempted to significantly raise the standards for the black schools. Not only was this met with, at best, minimal success, the same battle had to be fought nearly incessantly, as it was effective only for one district at a time and had no impact on the larger issue of differential treatment of American citizens based solely on race. At the start of the 1950s, the NAACP made a decision to step the issue of inequalities in education up to a national level and consolidated a group of cases in several different states under the rubric of *Brown v. Board of Education*.

Chief Justice of the Supreme Court of the United States at the time of the ruling, Judge Earl Warren wrote the decision, which stated, in part,

PRIMARY SOURCE

One Nation...Indivisible: A 1977 Herblock cartoon contrasts inner city schools and suburban schools with this ironic title: "...One nation...Indivisible." FROM *HERBLOCK ON ALL FRONTS*.

Today, education is perhaps the most important function of state and local governments. Compulsory school attendance laws and the great expenditures for education both demonstrate our recognition of the importance of education to our democratic society. It is required in the performance of our most basic public responsibilities, even service in the armed forces. It is the very foundation of good citizenship. Today it is a principal instrument in awakening the child to cultural values, in preparing him for later professional training, and in helping him to adjust normally to his environment. In these days, it is doubtful that any child may reasonably be expected to succeed in life if he is denied the opportunity of an education. Such an opportunity, where the state has undertaken to provide it, is a right which must be made available to all on equal terms. We come then to the question presented: Does segregation of children in public schools solely on the basis of race, even though the physical facilities and other "tangible" factors may be equal, deprive the children of the minority group of equal educational opportunities? We believe that it does. Segregation of white and colored children in public schools has a detrimental effect upon the colored children. The impact is greater when it has the sanction of the law, for the policy of separating the races is usually interpreted as denoting the inferiority of the negro group. A sense of inferiority affects the motivation of a child to learn. Segregation with the sanction of law, therefore, has a tendency to [retard] the educational and mental development of negro children and to deprive them of some of the benefits they would receive in a racial[ly] integrated school system. We conclude that, in the field of public education, the doctrine of "separate but equal" has no place. Separate educational facilities are inherently unequal. Therefore, we hold that the plaintiffs and others similarly situated for whom the actions have been brought are, by reason of the segregation complained of, deprived of the equal protection of the laws guaranteed by the Fourteenth Amendment."

Desegregation of the public school system in America proceeded neither naturally nor swiftly. Desegregation plans were developed and adopted by school districts, and districts were not infrequently geographically re-drawn in order to avoid integration. In the early 1960s, America entered an era of mandatory busing of schoolchildren in order to racially balance schools in many areas. The Civil Rights movement in America became more and more visible after the *Brown* decision, as black Americans began to actively engage in the process of ensuring that hard-won rights were enforced. Despite peaceful, and sometimes not so peaceful, efforts for nearly two decades after the *Brown* decision, many schools remained extremely segregated, particularly in the Southern states. In an effort to enforce the civil rights guaranteed to African Americans by the Constitution and a series of legal decisions, the Civil Rights Act of 1964 was made law by then-President Lyndon B. Johnson. The legislation was initially proposed by John F. Kennedy, who firmly believed that all citizens should be treated equally, and that this treatment should be legislatively enforced, particularly as concerned the right and ability for all American people to freely vote for the political candidates of their own choosing, to have equal access to jobs and pay, to be able to socialize freely at all public facilities, to be entitled to the same legal protections and benefits, and to have equal access to quality education within the local public school system.

While the legislation was well-intended and resulted in many efforts at desegregation, there remain racial inequalities, based primarily upon the results of institutionalized racism. There remains considerable disparity between black and white citizens in terms of socioeconomic status; many places of employment do not afford equal pay for positions of equal status. This is not confined to racial disparities—the same holds true for females and elders in the American workforce, as well as those citizens who are not deemed to be of white status, particularly those of Hispanic, Latino, or Native American descent, or those for whom English is not a first language.

FURTHER RESOURCES
Books

Anderson, James, ed., and Dara N. Byrne. *The Unfinished Agenda of Brown v. Board of Education*. Hoboken, N.J.: John Wiley & Sons, 2004.

Armor, David J. *Forced Justice: School Desegregation and the Law*. New York: Oxford University Press, 1995.

Bell, Derrick. *Silent Covenants: Brown V. Board of Education and the Unfulfilled Hopes for Racial Reform*. New York: Oxford University Press, 2004.

Frankenberg, Erika, and Chungmei Lee. *Race in American Public Schools: Rapidly Resegregating School Districts*. Cambridge, Mass.: The Civil Rights Project, Harvard University, August 2002.

Kluger, Richard. *Simple Justice: The History of Brown v. Board of Education and Black America's Struggle for Equality*. New York: Vintage Books, 1977.

Tushnet, Mark V. *The NAACP's Legal Strategy against Segregated Education, 1925–1950*. Chapel Hill: The University of North Carolina Press, 1987.

African American students from the Clarendon County school district march for freedom and equality, May 15, 2004.
AP IMAGES.

Periodicals

Holmes, Steven A. "Administration Cuts Affirmative Action While Defending It." *New York Times* (March 16, 1998): A17.

Reynolds, William B. "Affirmative Action and its Negative Repercussions." *The Annals of the American Academy of Political and Social Science* 523 (September 1992): 38, 49.

Tuch, Stephen A., and Michael Hughes. "Whites' Racial Policy Attitudes." *Social Science Quarterly.* 77(4) (1996):723–745.

Verhovek, Sam H. "In Polls, Americans Reject Means but Not Ends of Racial Diversity." *New York Times* (December 14, 1997): 1, 32.

Web sites

Brown v. Board of Education. "Summary and Excerpt of Ruling." <http://www.pbs.org/jefferson/enlight/brown.htm#summary> (accessed May 15, 2006).

Herblock's History. "One nation, indivisible." February 22, 1977 <http://www.loc.gov/rr/print/swann/herblock/one.html> (accessed May 15, 2006).

No. 60. An Act Relating to Equal Educational Opportunity

Legislation

By: State of Vermont Legislature

Date: June 26, 1997

Source: *State of Vermont Legislature.* "No. 60. An Act Relating to Equal Educational Opportunity." June 26, 1997. <http://www.leg.state.vt.us/docs/1998/acts/ACT060.HTM>

About the Author: Act 60 was written and passed by the state of Vermont legislature, a bicameral body serving Vermont since it became a state in 1791. The legislature crafted and passed Act 60 after the state Supreme Court decision, *Brigham v. State of Vermont,* found the state's local property tax funding program for public schools was unconstitutional.

INTRODUCTION

Unlike many western European nations, funding and curriculum for public schools in the United States is controlled by local districts, not by the federal government. There is no single funding standard nationwide for public schools, just as there is no single national curriculum applied equally throughout the U.S. in all districts. In the United States in the mid–1990s federal funding provided just eight percent of all funds for public schools. In countries that are members of the Organization for Economic Cooperation and Development, federal governments provide more than fifty percent of all public school dollars. Overall, most school districts in the U.S. receive funding from local property taxes, with additional funds from state and federal governments.

Property tax values set the basis for school funding; a portion of property taxes in most states goes to the local school district. If the average property value per pupil in a school district is $80,000 vs. $40,000, then the average tax rate must be increased for the lower property value district in order to raise the same amount of money as is raised in the more affluent district. Raising $8,000 per pupil, for example, would take double the tax rate for the less affluent district, placing a greater financial strain on a population least able to afford the extra taxes.

This funding situation in the U.S. has created social tension in school districts with a high percentage of retirees on fixed incomes, who might own homes outright but be unable to afford high property taxes. In states such as Ohio, voters routinely rejected levies for schools and libraries throughout the 1980s—more than seventy percent of all homeowners in certain districts were retirees. The California Supreme Court, in the 1971 case *Serrano v. Priest*, determined that local property tax funding of schools violated the state's equal protection clause. In his 1991 book *Savage Inequalities*, author Jonathan Kozol documented enormous disparities between poor and rich towns in the quality of education and the services offered. The book was an indictment of local funding of public schools, and it inspired some politicians and school administrators to change the system. By 1997, state Supreme Courts had issued similar rulings in nineteen states, and public school funding was radically altered to redistribute funds more equitably.

Vermont's 1997 Equal Educational Opportunity Act sparked outrage in wealthy communities, since the act mandated taking funds from all communities and redistributing the money. Homeowners in high-performing school districts with higher property values argued that the act would strip control of schools from local officials and parents, while towns with lower property tax bases argued that the current system created huge inequalities in education for all students.

■ PRIMARY SOURCE

PART II: FINANCING EDUCATION: BASIC EDUCATION FUNDING

Sec. 18. 16 V.S.A. chapter 133 is added to read:

CHAPTER 133. STATE AND LOCAL FUNDING OF PUBLIC EDUCATION

Subchapter 1. General Provisions

§ 4000. STATEMENT OF POLICY

(a) The intent of this chapter is to make educational opportunity available to each pupil in each town on substantially equal terms, in accordance with the Vermont Constitution and the Vermont supreme court decision of February 5, 1997, Brigham v. State of Vermont.

(b) Substantially equal access to similar revenues per pupil will be provided by a combination of state block grants and local education spending. This local education spending will be substantially equalized so that each school district will have substantially equal capacity to raise and provide the same amount per pupil on the local tax base.

§ 4001. DEFINITIONS

For the purpose of this chapter:

(1) "Average daily membership" of a school district in any year means:

(A) the full-time equivalent enrollment of pupils, as defined by the state board by rule, who are legal residents of the district attending a school owned and operated by the district, attending a public school outside the district under an interdistrict agreement, or for whom the district pays union school assessment or tuition to one or more approved independent schools or public schools outside the district during the annual census period. The census period consists of the first 40 days of the school year in which school is actually in session; and

(B) the full-time equivalent enrollment in the year between the end of the last census period and the end of the current census period, of any state-placed students as defined in subdivision 11(a)(28) of this title. The full-time equivalent enrollment of state-placed students attending a union school shall be divided among the member districts in the same proportions that the members divide assessment. A school district which provides for the education of its students by paying tuition to an approved independent school or public school outside the district shall not count a state-placed student for whom it is paying tuition for purposes of determining average daily membership. A school district which is receiving the full amount, as defined by the state board by rule, of the student's education costs under subsection 2950(a) of this title, shall not count the student for purposes of determining average daily membership. A state-placed student who is counted in average daily membership shall be counted as a student for the purposes of determining weighted student count.

(2) "Equalized grand list" has the same meaning that equalized education property tax grand list has in chapter 135 of Title 32.

(3) "Equalized pupils" means the long-term weighted average daily membership multiplied by the ratio of the statewide long-term average daily membership to the statewide long-term weighted average daily membership.

(4) "Equalized yield amount" means the amount per equalized pupil for local education spending above the general state support grant, per percent applied to the education property tax liability under section 5402 of Title 32.

(5) "General state support grant" means the per pupil aid grant distributed undersection 4011 of this title.

(6) "Local education spending" means the amount of the school budget which is paid for from the general state support grant and from local share property tax revenues. Local education spending does not include any portion of the school budget paid for by any other sources such as endowments, parental fund raising, federal funds, nongovernmental grants or other state funds such as special education funds paid under chapter 101 of this title.

(7) "Long-term membership" of a school district in any school year means the mean average of the district's average daily membership, excluding full-time equivalent enrollment of state-placed students, over two school years, plus full-time equivalent enrollment of state-placed students for the most recent of the two years.

(8) "Poverty ratio" means the number of persons in the school district who are aged six through 17 and who are from economically deprived backgrounds, divided by the long-term membership of the school district. A person

from an economically deprived background means a person who resides with a family unit receiving Food Stamps. A person who does not reside with a family unit receiving Food Stamps but for whom English is not the primary language shall also be counted in the numerator of the ratio. The commissioner shall use a method of measuring the Food Stamp population which produces data reasonably representative of long-term trends. Persons for whom English is not the primary language shall be identified pursuant to subsection 4010(e) of this title.

(9) "Public school" means an elementary school or secondary school for which the governing board is publicly elected. A public school may maintain evening or summer school for its pupils and it shall be considered a public school.

(10) "School district" means a town school district, city school district, incorporated school district, interstate school district, joint contract school district, the member towns of a unified union district or an unorganized town or gore.

(11) "School year" means a year beginning on July 1 and ending on the following June 30.

(12) "Weighted long-term membership" of a school district in any school year means the long-term membership adjusted pursuant to section 4010 of this title.

§ 4002. PAYMENT; ALLOCATION

(a) State and federal funds appropriated for services delivered by the supervisory union and payable through the department of education shall be paid to the order of the supervisory union and administered in accordance with the plan adopted under subdivision 261a(4) of this title. Funding for special education services under section 2969 of this title shall be paid to the districts in accordance with that section.

(b) The commissioner shall notify the superintendent or chief executive officer of each supervisory union in writing of federal or state funds disbursed to member school districts.

§ 4003. CONDITIONS

(a) No school district shall receive any aid under this chapter unless that school district complies with the provisions of law relative to teachers' salaries, appointment of superintendents, detailed financial reports to the state department of education, and any other requirements of law.

(b) Aid to any district shall not be denied unless such district unreasonably refuses to comply with such requirements of law. Any school district denied aid by reason of the provisions of this section shall have the right within 60 days from the date of such denial to appeal to the superior court in the county where such district is situated.

Subchapter 2. General State Support of Public Education

§ 4010. DETERMINATION OF WEIGHTED MEMBERSHIP

(a) On or before the first day of December during each school year, the commissioner shall determine the average daily membership of each school district for the current school year. The determination shall list separately:

1. resident pupils being provided elementary education; and
2. resident pupils being provided secondary education.

(b) The commissioner shall determine the long-term membership for each school district for each student group described in subsection (a) of this section. The commissioner shall use the actual average daily membership over two consecutive years, the latter of which is the current school year.

(c) The commissioner shall determine the weighted long-term membership for each school district using the long-term membership from subsection (b) of this section and the following weights for each class:
Grade Level Weight
Elementary 1.0
Secondary 1.25

(d) The weighted long-term membership calculated under subsection (c) of this section shall be increased for each school district to compensate for additional costs imposed by students from economically deprived backgrounds. The adjustment shall be equal to the total from subsection (c), multiplied by 25 percent, and further multiplied by the poverty ratio of the district.

(e) The weighted long-term membership calculated under subsection (c) of this section shall be further increased by 0.2 for each pupil in average daily membership for whom English is not the pupil's primary language. The state board of education shall adopt rules which will enable clear and consistent identification of pupils to be counted under this subsection.

§ 4011. GENERAL STATE SUPPORT GRANTS

(a) Annually, the general assembly shall appropriate funds to pay for a general state support grant for each equalized pupil.

(b) Annually, each school district shall receive a general state support grant for support of basic education costs. Funds distributed under this section shall be allocated on the basis of the equalized pupils in each school district.

(c) If a school district provides for the education of its students by paying tuition, the district shall receive the lesser of the tuition paid or the general state support grant amount.

(d) Funds received under this section which are attributable to an increase in student count due to the poverty ratio of the district shall be used by the district to provide learning readiness experiences for preschool age children or early reading and math experiences for school age children. These services shall be provided to children who are at risk of not succeeding in the general education environment. School districts are authorized to work collaboratively to share resources or otherwise find ways to maximize use of funds received under this section.

§ 4012. STATE-PLACED STUDENTS

A district which provides for the education of its students by paying tuition to an approved independent school or a public school outside the district, shall receive from the commissioner an amount equal to the calculated net cost per pupil in the receiving school, as defined in section 825 of this title, prorated for the percentage of annual tuition billed for a state-placed student. If the calculated net cost per pupil in a receiving independent school or school located outside Vermont is not available, the commissioner shall pay the tuition charged. A district shall not receive funds under this section if all the student's education costs are fully paid under subsection 2950(a) of this title.

Subchapter 3. Local Funding of Education

§ 4025. EDUCATION FUND

(a) An education fund is established to be comprised of the following:

1. All revenue paid to the state from the education property tax under chapter 135 of Title 32.
2. Local share property tax revenues from those school districts which adopt budgets with local education spending in excess of the general state support grant and which are able to raise more than the equalized yield amount.
3. General funds appropriated by the general assembly.
4. Revenues from state lotteries under chapter 14 of Title 31.

(b) Moneys in the education fund shall be paid to school districts for the support of education in accordance with the provisions of section 4028 of this title, other provisions of this chapter, and the provisions of chapter 135 of Title 32. The state treasurer shall withdraw funds from the education fund upon warrants issued by the commissioner of finance and management based on information supplied by the commissioner of taxes. The commissioner of finance and management may draw warrants for disbursements from the fund in anticipation of receipts. All balances in the fund at the end of any fiscal year shall be carried forward and remain a part of the fund. Interest accruing from the fund shall remain in the fund.

(c) An equalization and reappraisal account is established within the education fund. Moneys from this account are to be used by the division of property valuation and review for staff, equipment, lister training and administration of the equalization studies pursuant to section 5405 of Title 32, and to assist towns with maintenance or reappraisal on a case-by-case basis; and for reappraisal payments pursuant to section 4041a of Title 32, and equalization studies pursuant to section 5405 of Title 32 and for reappraisal payments pursuant to section 4041a of Title 32.

(d) Upon withdrawal of funds from the education fund for any purpose other than those authorized by this section, chapter 135 of Title 32 (education property tax) is repealed.

SIGNIFICANCE

Act 60 generated a bitter response from opponents such as bestselling fiction author and Dorset, Vermont, resident John Irving, who called the act "Marxism" and later stated that he would stop discussing the issue in the media because "I don't want to make my child a target of trailer-park envy." Irving's comments generated publicity and ire as national newspapers such as the *Wall Street Journal* covered what they termed a "class war" in Vermont. Then-Governor Howard Dean supported Act 60, though the final solution—a $1.10 tax on every $1,000 of assessed property value, plus the option to raise more as outlined above—left both sides uneasy.

Act 60 took money from approximately sixty wealthier towns, such as Stowe and Manchester, as well as money from 211 additional towns, and placed the taxes into one pool. Each district received a determined spending threshold ($5,300 in 2003) and towns that wished to spend more than this amount could raise the money by raising property taxes—but were required to set aside sixty to seventy percent of the proceeds to be shared with the 211 "receiver" towns. Families who chose to spend more to live in wealthier districts with higher property values, costs, and taxes disagreed vehemently with Act 60, arguing that it unfairly penalized them for making financial choices based on school quality, while forcing wealthier districts to support families in other towns.

A 2001 report examining the impact of Act 60, issued by The Rural School and Community Trust, found that just three years into Act 60's application,

academic standards were improving for all students—though students in wealthier communities performed better on achievement scores—and that achievement was directly linked to spending per pupil.

FURTHER RESOURCES

Books

Kozol, Jonathan. *Savage Inequalities: Children in America's Schools.* New York: Harper Perennial, 1992.

Mondale, Sarah. *School: The Story of American Public Education.* Boston: Beacon Press, 2002.

Pulliam, John D., and James J. Van Patten. *History of Education in America.* Upper Saddle River, N.J.: Prentice Hall, 2002.

Web sites

The Rural School and Community Trust. "Vermont's 'Act 60' Has Improved Education Equity, New Report Finds." February 20, 2001. <http://files.ruraledu.org/docs/vte-quity/vt_equity_press.html> (accessed May 31, 2006).

Vermont Department of Education. "Laws and Regulations: Act 60-The Equal Educational Opportunity Act." <http://www.state.vt.us/cduc/ncw/html/laws/act60.html> (accessed May 31, 2006).

Homeschooling

Back to the Future?

Report

By: Lyman, Isabel

Date: January 7, 1998

Source: Lyman, Isabel. *Homeschooling: Back to the Future?* Cato Institute, 1998.

About the Author: Isabel Lyman is a homeschooling parent who holds a doctoral degree in the social sciences. A former newspaper columnist, Lyman writes on various issues related to education, and her work has appeared in the *Wall Street Journal* and other national publications.

INTRODUCTION

Compulsory education laws in the United States began in Massachusetts and spread throughout the nation during the latter half of the nineteenth century. By 1929, every state had some form of legislation concerning compulsory education. While many of these

Daniel Pittman, a home school student, reads from a workbook while watching a video on writing skills at his home in Petal, Mississippi, September 23, 2004. AP IMAGES.

laws exempted mentally and/or physically handicapped children from attending school, by the 1930s high school attendance rates in the U.S. had reached sixty percent; by 1940 the rate was closer to eighty percent.

The concept of school at home was familiar to the wealthier classes of most colonial powers; governesses and tutors trained the male children of the wealthy in preparation for university studies. Girls in such families received a different form of tutoring, with lessons in foreign languages (usually French), music, reading, and needlework. In the United States, such "school at home" situations were rare by the 1940s; private schools and college preparatory academies filled the needs of the wealthier classes, while public schools, funded through taxes, provided education for all children. At the same time, the quality of public schools differed widely, especially for non-white children. The 1954 Supreme Court decision *Brown v. Board of Education* ended the former "separate but equal" doctrine

that had permitted race-based schools, changing the social landscape of public education in the U.S.

The modern homeschooling movement did not begin with one particular person or family. In the late 1960s and early 1970s, education reformers such as John Holt, Ivan Illich, and Drs. Raymond and Dorothy Moore published books on child development, the evolution of modern schools, and analyses of the impact of schools as social institutions on children and society at large. John Holt's 1964 book *How Children Fail* stressed the negative effects of forced schooling on children; according to Holt, compulsory curricula strips the natural curiosity and drive to learn from children, forcing them to learn only enough material to please authority figures, and to inhibit intrinsic motivation. The 1971 publication of Ivan Illich's *Deschooling Society* viewed all structured schools as tools for maintaining social class and for training children to stay within their place in such a hierarchy; Holt used Illich's ideas to fight for children's rights, a relatively new legal and social concept in the mid–1970s.

While education reformers debated such concepts, a quiet but steady stream of parents began to homeschool. Some worked as religious missionaries abroad and needed a flexible education method; others addressed their children's special needs through a homeschooling approach. In the early 1980s, changes in federal tax laws forced many small Christian schools to shut down; the parents of the children enrolled turned to homeschooling as a viable opportunity to preserve family culture, keep secular influences to a minimum, and to teach their children a parent-approved curriculum. Curriculum publishing houses such as Calvert and A Beka had met the needs of missionaries or itinerant families needing educational materials, and soon these companies filled a growing demand for at-home work.

In the mid–1980s, David and Micki Colfax gained national attention when three of their four home-schooled sons attended Harvard. The Colfax's story was the subject of an article in *Time* magazine, bringing attention to the emerging homeschooling movement.

By the early 1990s, homeschooling came to be associated with the religious right in the U.S.; Christian homeschoolers seeking an education free from secular influences, sexuality education, or science education that included evolution removed their children from public schools and chose homeschooling over private school education. The Home School Legal Defense Association, founded in 1983, works with all homeschoolers, though nearly eighty percent of the group's membership homeschools for religious reasons. Groups such as HSLDA helped to pass laws that protect the right to homeschool in all fifty states.

▮ PRIMARY SOURCE

HOMESCHOOLING: BACK TO THE FUTURE?

What Homeschooling Is

Homeschooling is defined simply as the "education of school-aged children at home rather than at a school." Homeschools, according to those who have observed or created them, are as diverse as the individuals who choose that educational method.

> They [homeschools] range from the highly structured to the structured to the unstructured, from those which use the approaches of conventional schools to those which are repulsed by conventional practice, and from the homeschool that follows homemade materials and plans to the one that consumes hun-

dreds of dollars worth of commercial curriculum materials per year.

Homeschoolers like to say that the world is their classroom. Or, as John Lyon, writing for the Rockford Institute, has observed,

> Schooling, rather obviously, is what goes on in schools; education takes place wherever and whenever the nature with which we are born is nurtured so as to draw out of those capacities which conduce to true humanity. The home, the church, the neighborhood, the peer group, the media, the shopping mall …are all educational institutions.

Modern learning theories aside, homeschoolers believe that the student who receives his instruction simultaneously from the home and the community at large will be a more culturally sophisticated child than the one the bulk of whose learning experiences is confined to a school. The historical record offers noteworthy examples of the "world is my teacher" model. Woodrow Wilson, Thomas Edison, Andrew Wyeth, Pearl Buck, and the Founding Fathers were all taught at home. Those famous Americans' parents were pioneers.

The Origins of Homeschooling: Raymond Moore

The seeds of what has grown into the modern-day American homeschooling movement were planted by two unrelated individuals about 30 years ago. In 1969 Raymond Moore, a former U.S. Department of Education employee, laid the groundwork that would legitimatize homeschooling as one of the great, populist educational movements of the 20th century.

Moore, who holds an Ed.D. from the University of Southern California, along with his wife, Dorothy, a reading specialist and former Los Angeles County elementary school teacher, initiated an inquiry into previously neglected areas of educational research. Two of the questions the Moores and a team of like-minded colleagues set out to answer were, Is institutionalizing young children a sound, educational trend, and what is the best timing for school entrance?

They sought advice from over 100 family development specialists and researchers, including Urie Bronfenbrenner of Cornell University, John Bowlby of the World Health Organization, and Burton White of Harvard University. Those professionals recommended "a cautious approach to subjecting [the child's] developing nervous system and mind to formal constraints." Psychologist Bronfenbrenner maintained that subjecting children to the daily routine of elementary school can result in excessive dependence on peers.

In the process of analyzing thousands of studies, 20 of which compared early school entrants with late starters, the Moores began to conclude that development problems, such as hyperactivity, nearsightedness, and dyslexia, were often the result of prematurely taxing a child's nervous system and mind with continuous academic tasks, like reading and writing.

The bulk of the research, which overwhelmingly supported distancing young children from daily contact with institutionalized settings, convinced the Moores that formal schooling should be delayed until at least age 8 or 10, or even as late as 12. Raymond Moore explained the upshot of his research, stating, "These findings sparked our concern and convinced us to focus our investigation on two primary areas: formal learning and socializing. Eventually, this work led to an unexpected interest in homeschools."

The Moores went on to write *Home Grown Kids* and *Home-Spun Schools*, which were published in the 1980s. The books, which are written from a Christian perspective but offer a universal message for all interested parties, have sold hundreds of thousands of copies and offer practical advice to parents on how to succeed as home educators. The Moores advocate a firm but gentle approach to home education that balances study, chores, and work outside the home in an atmosphere geared toward a child's particular developmental needs.

The Influence of John Holt

During the 1960s and early 1970s, another voice emerged in the public school debate, a voice for decentralizing schools and returning greater autonomy to teachers and parents. John Holt, an Ivy League graduate and a teacher in alternative schools, was decrying the lack of humanity toward schoolchildren, even in the most compassionate school settings. Holt was also a critic of the compulsory nature of schooling. He wrote,

> To return once more to compulsory school in its barest form, you will surely agree that if the government told you that on one hundred and eighty days of the year, for six or more hours a day, you had to be at a particular place, and there do whatever people told you to do, you would feel that this was a gross violation of your civil liberties.

Holt, who had long advocated the reform of schools, became increasingly frustrated that so few parents were willing to work toward change within the system. Consequently, after his own years as a classroom teacher, he observed that well-meaning but overworked teachers, who program children to recite right answers and discourage self-directed learning, often retard children's natural curiosity. He chronicled his litany of complaints in *How Children Fail*.

Holt came to view schools as places that produce obedient, but bland, citizens. He saw the child's daily grind of attending school as preparation for the future

adult grind of paying confiscatory taxes and subservience to authority figures. Holt even compared the dreariness of the school day to the experience of having a "full-time painful job." Ultimately, Holt concluded that the most humane way to educate a child was to homeschool him.

To disseminate his views, in 1977 Holt founded *Growing without Schooling*, a bimonthly magazine about and for individuals who had removed their children from school. The magazine became a tool that allowed home educators, particularly those who might be described as the "libertarian left," an opportunity to network and exchange "war stories."

In summary, Holt espoused a philosophy that could be considered a laissez faire approach to home-based education or, as he called it, "learning by living." It is a philosophy that Holt's followers have come to describe as "unschooling."

> What is most important and valuable about the home as a base for children's growth into the world is not that it is a better school than the schools but that it isn't school at all. It is not an artificial place, set up to make "learning" happen and in which nothing except "learning" ever happens. It is a natural, organic, central, fundamental human institution, one might easily and rightly say the foundation of all other human institutions.

The constituencies Raymond Moore and Holt individually attracted reflected the backgrounds and lifestyles of the two researchers. Moore, a former Christian missionary, earned a sizable (but hardly an exclusive) following among parents who chose homeschooling primarily to impart traditional religious mores to their children—the Christian right. Holt, a humanist, became a cult figure of sorts to the wing of the homeschooling movement that drew together New Age devotees, ex-hippies, and homesteaders—the countercultural left.

The two men earned national reputations as educational pioneers, working independently of one another, eloquently addressing the angst that a diverse body of Americans felt about the modern-day educational system—a system that seemed to exist to further the careers of educational elites instead of one that served the developmental needs of impressionable children. In the 1970s the countercultural left, who responded more strongly to Holt's cri de coeur, comprised the bulk of homeschooling families. By the mid–1980s, however, the religious right would be the most dominant group to choose homeschooling and would change the nature of homeschooling from a crusade against "the establishment" to a crusade against the secular forces of modern-day society.

Buttressed by their national media appearances, legislative and courtroom testimony, and speeches to sympathetic communities, Holt and Moore worked tirelessly to deliver to an often-skeptical public the message that homeschooling is a good, if not a superior, way to educate American children; that it is, in a sense, a homecoming, a return to a preindustrial era, when American families worked and learned together instead of apart.

Homeschooling Becomes Mainstream

Today, the growing popularity of homeschooling is evidence that the work of Moore, Holt, and other similar-minded reformers snowballed into a grassroots revolution. Brian Ray of the National Home Education Research Institute posits that homeschooling is growing at the rate of 15 percent to 40 percent per year. Conservative estimates were that the number of homeschooled children in 1985 was 50,000. Patricia Lines, a researcher with the U.S. Department of Education (whose data, used for estimating the homeschooling population from the fall of 1990, were updated for the fall of 1995) estimates that the number of homeschooled children is between 500,000 and 750,000.

In a working paper on home education, Lines explains how she gathered those data:

> The 1990 data came from three independent sources—state education agencies that collect data; distribution of complete, year-long graded curricular packages for homeschoolers from large suppliers; and home school associations' memberships. As each represented the tip of an iceberg, each was adjusted based on data from other sources, including surveys of homeschoolers indicating the extent to which families filed papers with the state, used particular curricular packages, or joined associations.

The Home School Market, published in April 1995, estimated that the number of homeschooled children had doubled since 1990 to 800,000 and would double again in the next five years. The Home School Legal Defense Association maintains that the number is already much higher—1.23 million. The estimate is based on HSLDA's analysis of the numbers provided by major curriculum distributors (such as Calvert, A Beka, and Konos), which supply complete, year-long packages to homeschoolers. HSLDA's estimate is larger than the federal government's because they have calculated high numbers of homeschoolers for populous states, like Texas, that do not monitor or regulate homeschoolers and figured in "underground" homeschoolers who have no contact with schooling authorities or homeschool groups.

A more exact count of homeschoolers is expected when the results of federal government household surveys are published. The Census Bureau, working with the National Center on Education Statistics, has begun to include questions on homeschooling.

SIGNIFICANCE

By the early twenty-first century, religion was no longer the main reason that parents chose to homeschool; a 2004 report from the National Institute for Educational Statistics showed that thirty-one percent of families homeschool out of "concern about environment of other schools" while thirty percent homeschool for religious reasons. Secular homeschoolers cite a wide range of reasons for homeschooling: teaching to the test, social conditions that foster bullying and intimidation of students, consolidation of school districts that breeds large schools, and under-funding or poor quality education.

Two growing sectors in homeschooling include parents of gifted children making the choice to homeschool as well as parents of children with special needs, ranging from autism to ADHD to Down Syndrome choosing to educate such children at home. Unlike early twentieth century "homeschooling" of children with physical or developmental difficulties, modern homeschooling typically includes school services such as occupational therapy, speech therapy, and psychologists for such children; in return for taxpayer-funded services, the parents in some states must agree to allow homeschooled children to sit for standardized tests, allowing the school district to access state money for such students.

The racial breakdown of homeschooled children shows that white homeschooled children represent 2.7 percent of all school-aged children; African-Americans 1.3 percent, and Hispanic children seven percent. African-American homeschoolers, however, are the fastest growing group of any race, with more than 110,000 children homeschooled as of 2003.

As homeschoolers opt out of traditional schools, some social critics and educators question how such children will fit into civil society without the social networks and shared educational experience that traditional schooling brings. Homeschooling advocates point to greater participation rates in community service, higher achievement scores, success in such national competitions as spelling bees and geography bees, and homeschoolers' admission into every Ivy League and high-ranked college in the country as proof that homeschoolers do not experience social problems or difficulties assimilating into society without having experienced traditional school.

As of 2003, more than 1.1 million children in the U.S. were homeschooled, and the rate continued to increase by seven to fifteen percent per year. This figure represents approximately 2.2 percent of all children ages five through seventeen.

FURTHER RESOURCES

Books

Gatto, John Taylor. *Dumbing Us Down: The Hidden Curriculum of Compulsory Schooling*. Gabriola Island, B.C.: New Society Publishers, 2005.

Holt, John C. *How Children Fail*. New York: Perseus Publishing, 1995.

———*How Children Learn*. New York: Perseus Publishing, 1995.

Web sites

National Center for Education Statistics. "1.1 Million Homeschooled Students in the United States in 2003." July 2004. <http://nces.ed.gov/pubs2004/2004115.pdf> (accessed June 15, 2006).

U.S. Census Bureau. "Home Schooling in the United States: Trends and Characteristics." August 2001. <http://www.census.gov/population/www/documentation/twps0053.html> (accessed June 15, 2006).

Students from the U.K. participate in a demonstration February 20, 2002, in London calling for the government to abolish student loans and bring back the grant system. PHOTO BY SION TOUHIG/GETTY IMAGES.

Student Loans: A Slippery Lifeline

Newspaper article

By: Burton Bollag

Date: December 7, 2001

Source: *Chronicle of Higher Education*. (December 7, 2001): A34.

About the Author: Burton Bollag is a journalist who works as an international correspondent for the *Chronicle of Higher Education*.

INTRODUCTION

For many college students, particularly those studying in the United States of America, the process of taking out loans is as much a part of the academic experience as is registering for classes or purchasing textbooks. The cost of a post secondary education has risen steadily and has significantly outpaced the ability of most American (and, increasingly, worldwide) families to save or prepare for the expenses involved in the support of their children's educations.

The history of financial aid for college students, particularly that of the academic loan process, began in the state of Indiana in the mid–1930s. In 1935, there was legislation passed in that state that enabled college-level students who performed above a specific range on competitive standardized testing to receive awards that resulted in having a portion of their tuition reduced. Essentially, this was a program involving the creation and implementation of merit-based grants and scholarships. Several years later, in the 1940s, Indiana University opened its first Financial Aid Office, specifically created for the administration of diverse types of financing for college students.

The protocol was both efficient and effective and was used as a model for other academic institutions.

After the end of World War II in 1945, the United States was in an enormous state of economic and technological growth—industry and technology were growing rapidly, and it was necessary to develop a cadre of professional and technologically-savvy personnel to enhance and evolve the new programs. At the same time, there was an enormous number of young people, particularly young men, returning from the War who had limited ability to compete in a progressively more complex job market. The National Defense Education Act (NDEA) was designed as a means of incentivizing colleges and universities to expand and modernize their programming as well as to create means of making post-high school education affordable and appealing to young adult learners.

In the late 1950s, the NDEA was vastly expanded, as the United States engaged not only in the Cold War but actively competed with other countries, particularly with the United Soviet Socialist Republic (Russia, or the USSR), in the development of space technology. The Russian's successful deployment of the Sputnik satellite was another enormous catalyst for the advancement of the technological professions in America. It became critical for the United States to find a way to make higher educational opportunities more universally available to students. College and university education was extremely expensive, relative to the median salaries of most families, so a creative means of funding academic studies had to be found. The NDEA evolved into what is currently known as the Perkins Loan program, and it offers post-secondary students who demonstrate significant financial need low-interest loans that can be paid back over a period of a decade or more, after the completion of the educational process.

The initial paradigm in most countries other than the United States was that post-secondary education should be made available and affordable to all qualified students. That paradigm has shifted with changing world economies, and many other countries have begun to adopt the American model of student-loan financed education. As has been the case in the United States, the system has had a number of problems, not the least of which have been the imbalance between students' debt burden at graduation and their ability to earn sufficient incomes as to be able to repay the loans, and the frequency with which students (this is a global phenomenon, as is the debt imbalance) default on their loans (cease or fail to make the agreed upon payments).

PRIMARY SOURCE

As more countries institute tuition, borrowing has become crucial and more fraught with problems

With tuition costs going up worldwide, a growing number of countries are throwing young people a new financial lifeline: student loans. But those lifelines are proving to be slippery. A rapid increase in enrollments in recent years has put huge strains on the budgets of countries that traditionally have had free or low-cost public higher education. More and more countries are requiring students and their families to share education costs by paying tuition. Loans are supposed to prevent higher education from becoming an exclusive privilege for the children of the affluent.

But student-loan programs, difficult to get right even in the United States where they have been around since 1958, are proving even more prone to failure elsewhere. Three of the world's most populous countries—China, Russia, and India—have tried to start loan programs in the past two years, but the only one that could be called operational, in China, is plagued by problems. In some countries, programs have been run so inefficiently that administrative costs have eaten up as much as a quarter of the money available for loans. Elsewhere, little of the money lent out was recovered, because few graduates bothered to repay their loans, or governments charged students such low interest rates that the loans ended up functioning largely as grants. Loan programs exist today in some 60 countries, but in many nations they reach only a small share of the young people who need them.

Finding the Right Balance

"The trick is to find a balance between providing subsidies to needy students, and making loan programs financially sustainable," says Jamil Salmi, deputy director for educational policy at the World Bank, which is currently helping about a dozen countries establish or strengthen loan systems. Loans may be intended to reduce the pain of rising fees, but that doesn't mean students are always happy about them. "Loans put people in a trap," says Jacob Henricson, chairman of the National Unions of Students in Europe, known as ESIB. "If you don't have a very large salary, you're going to have problems repaying."

In Europe, with the exception of Britain, public higher education systems are still free or very cheap, and many governments provide students with stipends for living expenses and study materials. But as enrollments continue to climb, the stipends are beginning to come as loans, instead of grants. Henricson, a political science student at the University of Stockholm, says that with Scandinavia's high living costs and expensive imported textbooks, it is not uncommon for Swedish students to graduate $25,000 in debt.

Pressure from students and their families to make borrowing for college cheap leads to one of the thorniest problems policymakers face—how much to subsidize interest rates of loans. A high subsidy, with students charged low or zero interest, means that, due to inflation, students end up paying back only part of the value of the money they borrow. Nicholas Barr, a professor of economics at the London School of Economics and Political Science, says that when subsidies exist they unfairly benefit the middle class. Students usually come from the middle or upper middle classes and can afford to pay back loans at close to commercial rates, he argues. Without subsidies, loan programs are cheaper for the taxpayers, and more money can be made available to more students. Special assistance can then be provided to students from poor backgrounds, or graduates who go into low-paying but socially beneficial professions. But the middle class has considerably more political clout than the poor, Barr says, and policymakers often give in to their demands for cheaper loans for all.

That has been the case in Britain for the last decade. Interest on student loans has been kept so low—generally equal to the inflation rate—that the government has gotten back only about half of the value of the money it has lent out. Now there are strong demands to reduce the interest rate subsidy and give more help to those in greatest need.

Sharing the Burden

One method for spreading out students' debt burden that has attracted international attention is Australia's national loan system, the Higher Education Contribution Scheme. Repayment is pegged to a graduate's income; repayment starts when he or she is earning at least $12,000 per year, and is set at 3 to 6 percent of his or her income above that. So low earners pay back smaller amounts, but for a longer time. Another feature of the program is that administrative costs are kept down by piggybacking on the income-tax system. Payments are billed as a surcharge to income taxes and are generally deducted by employers.

Yale University tried another approach to promoting social equity in the 1970s. Some view the program as having been an embarrassing flop, others as a noble but flawed experiment. The World Bank's Salmi says it "illustrates how the implementation of a theoretically sensible and generous concept turned into a nightmarish adventure." Under Yale's Tuition Postponement Option, graduates had to repay yearly 0.4 percent of their salary for each $1,000 they had borrowed. (Tuition was considerably lower then.) Each borrower had to continue paying until the debt of their entire graduating class was repaid. The program unraveled when high-earning graduates realized they would have to repay far more than they had

borrowed, subsidizing not only students in low-paying professions, but the 15 percent of graduates who were deadbeats. Few students realized how many classmates would renege on the loans.

Even where controversial social policy issues have been resolved, collection of debts has often been a problem, especially in developing countries with poorly functioning or nonexistent tax and credit systems. In the 1980s, Brazil, Venezuela, and Kenya each had loan programs with roughly 90 percent default rates. In an even worse case, an official body in Ghana recently reported that out of $27.5 million loaned to more than 400,000 college students since 1988, only $1.1 million has been paid back. "In many cases," says Salmi, "it would have been cheaper to substitute loans with outright grants or scholarships." But, he adds, "many countries have learned from their mistakes."

Lessons Learned

Jamaica's government-sponsored loan system was near collapse three years ago because only about a third of loans were repaid. The biggest deadbeats were not low-income students, but those who became physicians and lawyers. As part of efforts to make the system more financially viable, the Student Loan Bureau began an advertising campaign appealing to students' civic duty, and published "shame lists" with the names and photographs of those with outstanding debts. Within months, repayments improved substantially.

Even the United States and Canada were plagued by high rates of default in the 1980s. At the end of the decade, U.S. officials began to refuse loans for study at institutions with graduates who had very high default rates—generally for-profit colleges with poor programs that did not lead to good jobs. The default rate for most student loans—government guaranteed but provided by commercial lenders—was 21.4 percent in 1989. Now, the rate is 5.6 percent. A strengthening economy contributed to the improvement.

A number of poor-quality, for-profit institutions that lost the right to provide federal loans to their students were forced to close. The loan system thus played an important secondary role as an instrument for quality promotion. Some loan programs in developing countries, such as one in the state of Sonora in Mexico, have used a similar approach to try to steer students to stronger institutions.

The world's first national student loan program, according to Salmi, was established because one graduate wanted to share his good fortune with others. In the late 1940s, Gabriel Betancourt, a young Colombian from a poor family, persuaded the manager of the company he worked for to lend him money to study abroad. He was so grateful for the opportunity that, after graduating, he successfully lobbied the Colombian government to establish a permanent loan mechanism. In 1950, he became founding director of the Colombian Student Loan Institution. The institution continues providing loans today, but only to 6 percent of students—down from a high of 12 percent—due to a lack of government support.

In many poor countries with largely black market economies and no formal income taxes, economists are skeptical about the possibilities of creating viable loan programs. "Without any means of tracing income, loan programs are not going to work, except on a small scale," warns Bruce Johnstone, a professor and director of the Center for Comparative and Global Studies in Education at the State University of New York at Buffalo.

Creating the Infrastructure

Although this means abandoning the pretense of making higher education available to rich and poor alike, Johnstone says very poor countries may have to settle initially for modest loan programs, perhaps providing the money only to those who can provide collateral, or to graduate students, since they would be more likely to obtain gainful employment after graduation. For many poor countries, especially in Africa, only now contemplating the controversial decision of introducing tuition, the question of whether broadly available loans can work remains unanswered. But the World Bank, stung by past criticisms that its policies have hurt the poor, is committed to the idea. "No country should introduce cost sharing," says Salmi, referring to tuition payments, "without a proper mechanism for student loans and student aid."

SIGNIFICANCE

The United States has traditionally been the world leader in terms of the creation, implementation, and administration of student loan programs for college and university education and, progressively more, for graduate and professional education programs. As the cost of education has risen, so has the ceiling for student loans. There have been special loan categories created for graduate students, particularly those in the medical and health professions. The variety of grant and scholarship funds and sources has grown through the decades as well, but has not kept pace with the exponential growth of the student loan industry. Loan programs have been created that are not based so much on financial need as they are on available resources in comparison with educational and ancillary costs, loans for parents who are helping to fund their children's education have been implemented—those are geared to middle class and wealthier families who are willing to pay substantially higher interest rates in order to assure their children's undergraduate educations. There continue to be specific loan programs for the financially neediest students, which generally are offered at lower interest rates than are other types of loans. Guaranteed student loan programs have become popular; they are offered by banks and other financial institutions, but are backed by federal funding.

The financing of higher education has become a vast and complicated machine and the United States remains the world leader of the industry. The National Association of Student Financial Aid Administrators (NASFAA) was created in the late 1960s, and was tasked with oversight of the mechanics of the process—keeping track of the vast amounts of student and financial data, and making certain that all of the educational financing processes occur in as smooth a fashion as possible. Although student loans now have funding originating all over the globe, as students from more and more countries navigate the business of educational financing, the United States Department of Education still stands at the forefront of loan origination. Among the biggest problems with the student loan industry, worldwide, has been the rate at which student loans are defaulted, either because young college graduates are not making enough money with which to survive, run a household (of whatever dimensions), finance the beginning of a career and an independent life and make monthly student loan payments, or because the borrower simply walks away from the obligation after graduation and hopes to successfully avoid repayment. Much of the published research, and this appears to be a universal phenomenon, regardless of the student borrower's country of origin (see references for Boddington and Lea, below), suggests that students habitually underestimate the amount of debt and fees to be repaid, the length of time that it will take to pay back the loans and attendant interest, and the amount of liquid assets they will have to work with—in short, they grossly miscalculate how much they'll make and how big and long-lasting the bite from the loan repayments will be. At the same time, the recent graduates are attempting to create a career trajectory and life path, which typically costs more than anyone expects—for housing, food, work clothing, commuting expenses, and the like, when the individual is often living a wholly independent existence for the first time and is struggling to learn how to be an autonomous adult. Recent graduates are coming into the start of their adult lives already significantly burdened with educational debt.

The world is gradually becoming more and more organized around debt—first at the national and local government levels, and now at the individual level.

With credit debt an exploding worldwide phenomenon, it seems to add an enormous personal challenge and to set a rather dangerous example for the way in which to conduct the business of life, to begin adulthood and professional life already in a financial deficit position. Student loans have, indeed, become a very slippery lifeline.

FURTHER RESOURCES

Books

Ahier, John, John Beck, and Rob Moore. *Graduate Citizens?: Issues of Citizenship and Higher Education.* London: Routledge/Falmer, 2003.

Ashby, A., G. Robertson, and R. Parata, eds. *Student Debt Casebook.* Wellington, New Zealand: New Zealand University Students' Association and Aotearoa Polytechnic Students' Union, 1996.

Barr, Nicholas, and Iain Crawford. *Financing Education: Answers from the UK.* London: Routledge, 2005.

Colclough, Christopher, ed. *Marketizing Education and Health in Developing Countries: Miracle or Mirage?* Oxford: Clarendon Press, 1997.

Cronin, Joseph Marr, and Sylvia Quarles Simmons, eds. *Student Loans: Risks and Realities.* Dover, Mass.: Auburn House, 1987.

Hayton, Annette, ed., and Anna Paczuska. *Access, Participation and Higher Education: Policy and Practice.* London: Kogan Page 2002.

Karabell, Zachary A. *A What's College For? The Struggle to Define American Higher Education.* New York: Basic Books, 1998.

Periodicals

Boddington, L., and S. Kemp. "Student Debt, Attitudes to Debt, Impulsive Buying and Financial Management." *New Zealand Journal of Psychology* 28 (1999): 89–93.

Lea, S.E. G., and P. Webley. "Student Debt: A Psychological Analysis of the UK Experience." *Frontiers in Economics Psychology* 1 (1995): 430–444.

President George W. Bush greets Steven Tingus, the Public Policy Director of Assistive Technology for the California Foundation for Independent Living Centers, in the White House on February 1, 2001. The occasion is the announcement of the New Freedom Initiative. PAUL J. RICHARDS/AFP/GETTY IMAGES.

The New Freedom Initiative

Initiative

By: George W. Bush

Date: February 2001

Source: *The White House.* "The New Freedom Initiative." February 2001. <http://www.whitehouse.gov/

news/freedominitiative/freedominitiative.pdf> (accessed June 10, 2006).

About the Author: George W. Bush was elected forty-third President of the United States on January 20, 2001. Born on July 6, 1946, in New Haven, Connecticut, Bush grew up in Texas.

INTRODUCTION

The Civil Rights era of the 1960s is credited with establishing key legislation for providing Americans with basic civil rights and equal opportunities. One of the more comprehensive laws of this period—the Civil Rights Act of 1964—did not however, define the rights of individuals with disabilities. The United States had no legislation that specifically addressed discrimination against individuals with disabilities till the 1990s. Ensuing an increasing trend in disability activism, the Americans with Disabilities Act of 1990 (ADA) was formulated. This act, signed into law by

President George H. W. Bush, prohibits discrimination on the basis of disability. According to the act, which became effective as of July 26, 1992, private employers, state and local governments, employment agencies, and labor unions are required to provide equal opportunity to qualified individuals with disabilities in job application procedures, hiring, advancement, compensation, job training, and other terms, conditions, and privileges of employment.

The definition of disability in the ADA, however, is deemed controversial. Critics argue that even if an individual is considered disabled (as per the ADA), he or she may still not be entitled to the above-mentioned rights. The ADA does not cover all people with disabilities but encompasses otherwise qualified individuals with disabilities. Advocates of ADA maintain that the act has proved beneficial to those eligible. By 1995, an additional 800,000 individuals with disabilities were hired in comparison to 1991.

Although the act afforded more employment opportunities to the disabled by the late 1990s, these individuals were still confronted with significant lifestyle challenges. Surveys undertaken in 1997 showed that more than thirty-three percent of adults with disabilities lived in a household with an annual income of less than fifteen thousand dollars, compared to only twelve percent of those without disabilities. More than seventy percent of people without disabilities were homeowners, whereas less than ten percent of those with disabilities could afford to buy their own home.

Subsequently, on February 1, 2001, President George W. Bush announced the New Freedom Initiative to enhance the quality of life of disabled individuals. This initiative represents a comprehensive strategy designed to ensure that Americans with disabilities have the opportunity to participate fully in their communities and engage in productive work that would improve their quality of life.

PRIMARY SOURCE

The Policy

The "New Freedom Initiative" is composed of the following key components:

Increasing Access to Assistive and Universally Designed Technologies

(Title I)

Overview

The Administration's commitment to increase access to assistive and universally designed technologies is based upon the principle that every American must have the opportunity to participate fully in society. In the global new economy, America must draw on the talents and creativity of all its citizens.

Assistive and universally designed technologies can be a powerful tool for millions of Americans with disabilities, dramatically improving one's quality of life and ability to engage in productive work. New technologies are opening opportunities for even those with the most severe disabilities. For example, some individuals with quadriplegia can now operate computers by the glance of an eye. As the National Council on Disability (NCD) has stated, "for Americans without disabilities, technology makes things easier. For Americans with disabilities, technology makes things possible."

Unfortunately, assistive and universally designed technologies are often prohibitively expensive. In addition, innovation is being hampered by insufficient Federal funding for and coordination of assistive technology research and development programs. The New Freedom Initiative will help ensure that Americans with disabilities can access the best technologies of today and that even better technologies will be available in the future. At the core of this effort are proposals that reinvigorate the Federal investment in assistive technologies; improve Federal collaboration and promote private-public partnerships; and increase access to this technology for people with disabilities...

Expanding Educational Opportunities for Americans with Disabilities

(Title II)

Overview

Education is the key to independent living and a high quality of life. Unfortunately, one in five adults with disabilities has not graduated from high school, compared to less than one of ten adults without disabilities. The Administration will expand access to quality education for Americans with disabilities.

Originally passed by Congress in 1975, the Individuals with Disabilities Act, or IDEA, ensures that children with disabilities would have a free public education that would meet their unique needs.

The Administration will increase educational opportunity for children with disabilities by working with Congress to give states increased IDEA funds. This will help meet the needs of students with disabilities and free up additional resources for education at the local level...

Promoting Homeownership for Americans with Disabilities

(Title III)

Overview

Homeownership has always been at the heart of the "American dream." This past year, Congress passed the

"American Homeownership and Economic Opportunity Act of 2000," which reforms Federal rental assistance to give individuals who qualify the opportunity to purchase a home.

Rental assistance for low-income Americans, including those with disabilities, is provided by a program known as Section 8 of the Housing Act of 1937, administered by the U.S. Department of Housing and Urban Development (HUD). Residents are provided Section 8 vouchers so that they can afford rental payments for public housing. And many of those Section 8 vouchers go to individuals with disabilities.

In addition to increasing independence, homeownership also promotes savings. Mortgage payments, unlike rental payments, help build net worth because a portion of the payment goes toward building equity. In turn, as one's home equity increases, it becomes easier to finance other purchases such as a computer or further education…

Integrating Americans with Disabilities into the Workforce

Title IV

(Part A: Promoting Telework)

Overview

Americans with disabilities should have every freedom to pursue careers, integrate into the workforce, and participate as full members in the economic marketplace. The New Freedom Initiative will help tear down barriers to the workplace, and help promote full access and integration.

Computer technology and the Internet have tremendous potential to broaden the lives and increase the independence of people with disabilities. Nearly half of people with disabilities say the Internet has significantly improved their quality of life, compared to 27 percent of people without disabilities.

The computer and Internet revolution has not reached as many people with disabilities as the population without disabilities. Only 25% of people with disabilities own a computer, compared with 66% of U.S. adults. And only 20% of people with disabilities have access to the Internet, compared to over 40% of U.S. adults.

The primary barrier to wider access is cost. Computers with adaptive technology can cost as much as $20,000, which is prohibitively expensive for many individuals. And the median income of Americans with disabilities is far below the national average. The New Freedom Initiative will expand the avenue of teleworking, so that individuals with mobility impairments can work from their homes if they choose…

Integrating Americans with Disabilities into the Workforce

(Part B: Ticket-to-Work)

Overview

In 1999, Congress passed the "Ticket-to-Work and Work Incentives Improvement Act," which will give Americans with disabilities both the incentive and the means to seek employment.

As part of the New Freedom Initiative, the Administration will ensure the Act's swift implementation.

Today, there are more than 7.5 million Americans with disabilities receiving benefits under Federal disability programs. According to a recent Harris Survey, conducted by the National Organization of Disability, 72 percent of the Americans with disabilities want to work. However, in part because of disincentives in Federal law, less than 1 percent of those receiving disability benefits fully enter the workforce.

Prior to the "Ticket to Work" law, in order to continue to receive disability payments and health coverage, recipients could not engage in any substantial work. The Ticket to Work law, however, provides incentives for people with disabilities to return to work by:

- Providing Americans with disabilities with a voucher-like "ticket" that allows them to choose their own support services, including vocational education programs and rehabilitation services.
- Extending Medicare coverage for SSDI beneficiaries so they can return to work without the fear of losing health benefits.
- Expanding Medicaid eligibility categories for certain working people with severe disabilities so that they can continue to receive benefits after their income or condition improves…

Integrating Americans with Disabilities into the Workforce

(Part C: Compliance with Americans with Disabilities Act)

Overview

When the Americans with Disabilities Act (ADA) was signed into law on July 26, 1990, it was the most far reaching law advancing access of individuals with disabilities, workforce integration, and independence. The law, signed by President George Bush, gives civil rights protections to individuals with disabilities that are like those provided to individuals on the basis of race, sex, national origin, and religion.

In the eleven years since it was signed, the ADA has worked to guarantee equal opportunity for individuals with disabilities in employment, public accommodations, transportation, State and local government services, and telecommunications. The law has been especially helpful in providing access to jobs, especially in the small business sector, which has created two-thirds of all net new jobs since the early 1970s.

To encourage small businesses to comply with the ADA, legislation was signed into law in 1990 to provide a credit for 50 percent of eligible expenses up to $5,000 a year. Such eligible expenses include assistive technologies. Unfortunately, many small businesses are not aware of this credit.

President George W. Bush believes that the Americans with Disabilities Act has been an integral component of the movement toward full integration of individuals with disabilities but recognizes that there is still much more to be done. He also recognizes that to further integrate individuals with disabilities into the workforce, more needs to be done to promote ADA compliance.

SIGNIFICANCE

The New Freedom Initiative was launched with the aim of providing better community life to every citizen irrespective of any disability. The initiative has been endorsed by several government organizations that have subsequently introduced programs for accomplishing its goals. For instance, the Department of Health and Human Services (HHS) announced a series of grants to promote community living among disabled citizens. The Department of Labor established a Youth Advisory Committee with the purpose of providing quality employment opportunities to youth with disabilities. Moreover, the Department of Transportation and Project Action encourages inputs from transportation industry experts and disabled individuals to enhance accessible transportation. Further, numerous workshops have been set up by the Equal Employment Opportunity Commission (EEOC) to assist small businesses in hiring people with disabilities.

Another key program, launched as a consequence of the New Freedom Initiative, is Ticket to Work. Implemented by the Social Security Administration, in 2001, this program allows Social Security and Supplemental Security Income (SSI) disability beneficiaries to receive a 'ticket' that can be used to obtain free employment-related training and services. As of 2004, almost five million people in thirty-three states and the District of Columbia have such tickets.

Further, in 2002, the government launched DisabilityInfo.gov—a website that provides federal and state resources pertaining to disability. In the same

year, the U.S. Department of Labor announced the New Freedom Initiative Awards recognizing individuals, non-profit organizations, businesses, and corporations that have demonstrated "commendable and pioneering efforts" in promoting the employment objectives of New Freedom Initiative. In 2004, the Department of Transportation launched the 'United We Ride' campaign which is a coordinated effort by various federal programs to make government transportation policies more responsive to the needs of the citizens who rely on them.

The New Freedom Initiative is acknowledged to be a program with a broad vision. Various federal departments and government-funded institutions consider the initiative essential in promoting equality and solidarity in the United States. The initiative, since its inception, is widely supported by individuals with disabilities.

FURTHER RESOURCES

Books

Colker, Ruth. *Disability Pendulum: The First Decade Of The Americans With Disabilities Act.* New York: New York University, 2005.

Periodicals

"U.S. Society & Values." *U.S. Information Agency.* Vol. 4, No. 1, January 1999.

Web sites

The Arc. "The Americans with Disabilities Act of 1990." <http://www.thearc.org/faqs/adaqa.html> (accessed May 26, 2006).

U.S. Census Bureau. "Census Brief." December, 1997. <http://www.census.gov/prod/3/97pubs/cenbr975.pdf> (accessed May 26, 2006).

U.S. Department of Health and Human Services, Press Office. "HHS Programs Serve Americans with Disabilities." May 9, 2002. <http://www.policyalmanac.org/social_welfare/archive/hhs_disability_programs.shtml> (accessed May 26, 2006).

U.S. Department of Transportation, Office of Public Affairs. "Remarks For The Honorable Norman Y. Mineta Secretary Of Transportation: New Freedom Initiative." March 11, 2004. <http://www.dot.gov/affairs/minetasp31104.htm> (accessed May 26, 2006).

White House. "New Freedom Initiative: A Progress Report." March 2004. <http://www.whitehouse.gov/infocus/newfreedom/newfreedom-report–2004.pdf> (accessed May 26, 2006).

Abstinence-Only Initiative Advancing

Newspaper article

By: Sheryl Gay Stolberg

Date: February 28, 2002

Source: Stolberg, Sheryl Gay. "Abstinence-Only Initiative Advancing." *New York Times.* (February 28, 2002).

About the Author: Sheryl Gay Stolberg is a reporter for the *New York Times*, covering issues that range from politics to stem cell research to public health.

INTRODUCTION

Sexuality education in public schools in the United States began in the mid–1950s with the publication of a series of pamphlets from the American Social Health Association, the country's leading sexually transmitted disease public health organization. This curriculum, titled "Family Life Education," was followed in 1955 by the publication of a similar series by the American Medical Association. Strong opposition to such programs came from religious conservative groups such as the Christian Crusade, the John Birch Society, and Phyllis Schlafly's Eagle Forum, which characterized sexuality education programs as a threat to students' morality. By the 1960s, however, such programs were in place in many public schools, though heated debate over the participation of individual students and the content of sexuality education programs persisted.

The primary argument made by opponents was that exposure to sexuality education led to greater rates of sexual activity among teenagers. By the late 1960s and early 1970s, however, researchers had come to the opposite conclusion: Students enrolled in comprehensive sexuality education courses were sexually active at lower rates, and when they did make choices to participate in sexual activities, they did so with greater responsibility to protect themselves from sexually transmitted diseases and pregnancy.

Early sexuality education programs involved teaching the biology of reproduction, the identifica-

A pro-abstinence billboard in Baltimore, Maryland, 1997. AP IMAGES.

tion of the organs and body parts used for reproduction, menstruation, and sperm and semen production; little attention was given to questions of emotional issues surrounding sexual activity. By the 1970s, however, curriculum shifted to emotional development, self-esteem, and sexually transmitted disease prevention. Late 1970s and early 1980s curricula assumed that teenagers were having sex—educators discussed abstinence as a choice, but also taught approaches to sexual activity that stressed emotional health and contraception.

In 1986 then-Surgeon General C. Everett Koop issued new sexuality education guidelines that would reach students as young as eight years of age. Koop believed that third graders should be the starting point for a comprehensive HIV/AIDS prevention program that would cover emotional development, risk factors for the disease, as well as traditional sexuality education topics, all with the goal of preventing HIV/AIDS. Religious conservatives argued that abstinence was the only 100%-effective method for preventing sexually transmitted diseases (including AIDS) and teen pregnancy.

By the early 1990s teen pregnancy had reached an all-time high in the United States, and social and health agencies struggled to manage the growing issue. In 1996 President William J. Clinton signed Public Law 104–193, which allocated more than $350 million over seven years to states for abstinence-only sexuality education in public schools. In 1990, approximately 2% of all sexuality education programs were based on abstinence-only curricula; by 2005 that figure reached 25%.

PRIMARY SOURCE

Like most groups devoted to curbing the spread of AIDS, the AIDS Resource Center of Wisconsin has spent years promoting condoms. So it was with some surprise that the center received a grant from the Bush administration to persuade teenagers to say no to sex, at least until they are married.

"There won't be any conversation or education about condoms" in the program, said Mike Gifford, the group's deputy executive director. "Our message is going to home in, quite substantially, on the fact that the only 100 percent pure way to protect yourself from HIV is to abstain."

That message—that sex outside marriage can be dangerous to your health—is precisely what the White House wants young Americans to hear.

When he ran for office, President Bush promised to spend as much on programs that teach abstinence until marriage as on medical services that provide contraceptives to teenagers. This month, he made good on that promise, proposing a budget for 2003 that would raise federal spending on "abstinence only" education by $33 million, to $135 million.

"Abstinence is the surest way, and the only completely effective way, to prevent unwanted pregnancies and sexually transmitted disease," Mr. Bush said on Tuesday in outlining his welfare reform plan. "When our children face a choice between self-restraint and self-destruction, government should not be neutral."

The line drew hearty applause from the audience of community activists at a church here. But the initiative is controversial—not because anyone opposes teenage chastity, but because the government requires that abstinence programs avoid mentioning contraceptives, except to state their drawbacks.

The scientific literature, including a recent report by former Surgeon General David Satcher, carries quite a different message. With scant research on abstinence-only programs, studies conclude there is insufficient evidence that they delay teenage sex. The only proven method for reducing pregnancy and sexually transmitted disease, the studies say, is to combine the abstinence message with one that teaches young people how to protect themselves against pregnancy and disease.

"There is no scientific evidence that 'abstinence only until marriage' programs work," Representative James C. Greenwood, Republican of Pennsylvania, said in a recent letter to Mr. Bush. The letter, also signed by Representatives Lynn Woolsey and Barbara Lee, Democrats of California, called increasing spending for abstinence education "dangerous and unnecessary."

The administration replies that this is circular reasoning. "Unless we put money there to find out whether it works," said Claude Allen, who as deputy secretary of health and human services is in charge of the government's abstinence initiative, "we will never know."

The issue is likely to come up on Capitol Hill this year. When Congress passed legislation to overhaul welfare in 1996, it adopted a companion bill that set aside $50 million a year for abstinence education. With both measures up for reauthorization, opponents are promoting a bill, introduced by Representatives Greenwood, Woolsey and Lee, that would devote $100 million for programs that teach both abstinence and contraception.

"We believe in abstinence education," said Tamara Kreinin, president of the Sexuality Information and Education Council of the United States, a nonprofit group that supports the bill. "Most Americans do. It's the 'abstinence only until marriage' message that concerns us."

Despite a steady decline in the teenage birthrate over the past decade, pregnancy and sexually transmitted disease remain a huge problem for American teenagers. By the time they graduate from high school, two-thirds of the nation's young people have had sexual intercourse, according to the federal Centers for Disease Control and Prevention; one in four sexually active teenagers contract sexually transmitted diseases each year.

How to turn that trend around has been the subject of intense study and debate. Scientists at the disease control agency have identified eight programs that have been proved to reduce teenage pregnancy and sexually transmitted disease, including one that stresses abstinence, said Dr. Lloyd Kolbe, who directs the agency's division of school and adolescent health. Interestingly, he said, analysis of that particular program showed that in addition to delaying sex, it increased condom use.

But the vast majority of the more than 700 different abstinence education programs in use in the nation have never been thoroughly studied. The report by Dr. Satcher concluded that without more research, "it is too early to draw definite conclusions about this approach."

A rigorous study, financed by the federal government and led by Rebecca Maynard, a professor of education and social policy at the University of Pennsylvania, is under way, but will not be complete until 2005. Preliminary data will be available next year, Dr. Maynard said.

Yet as the experience of AIDS Resource Center of Wisconsin suggests, abstinence education is catching on, if only because there is more federal money available for it.

Mr. Gifford, the center's deputy executive director, said the idea of teaching abstinence until marriage struck him after his government grant writer identified it as "a new funding opportunity." With 40,000 Americans becoming infected with the AIDS virus every year, he said, "we didn't believe we could just keep doing the status quo."

Nationally, a recent survey by the Alan Guttmacher Institute, the nonprofit organization that focuses on sexual and reproductive health, found that 23 percent of secondary-school teachers said they did not discuss any method other than abstinence as a way to avoid pregnancy, up from just 2 percent in 1988. Federal health officials, meanwhile, say competition for abstinence-only education grants is intense. Of 360 recent applications, 173 were approved and 53 received financing.

At the AIDS Resource Center, the decision to apply for the grant generated intense debate among the staff. Federal law explicitly requires abstinence programs to teach that "sexual activity outside the context of marriage is likely to have harmful psychological and physical effects," and that "a mutually faithful monogamous relationship in the context of marriage is the expected standard of human sexual activity."

These were ticklish requirements for an organization that has a large gay constituency. But ultimately, Mr. Gifford said, center officials concluded that there was a market for abstinence education in their state, particularly in rural areas.

They applied for, and received, a $91,000 grant to plan a program aimed at 12-to 18-year-olds. Their plan is to use "peer educators," teenagers who are trained to talk to other teenagers, and to run four-to six-week sessions to provide support to help young people abstain. The issue of what to say about condoms proved tricky. Years ago, proponents of abstinence education cast the issue in moral terms. Today, abstinence education is more often cast in terms of the risk of disease.

"The more sexual partners a person has, the more risk of disease they have," said Dr. Joe S. McIlhaney, founder of the Medical Institute for Sexual Health, a group based in Austin, Tex., that is a leader in abstinence education. "Our goal is to give objective information that we draw from credible scientific sources."

Those sources include the National Institutes of Health, which last year reported that while condoms reduced the spread of AIDS, there was insufficient evidence that they prevented other sexually transmitted diseases, like herpes and chlamydia.

The Wisconsin center has decided to steer clear of condoms and the institutes' study. "That would leave them with a more negative vision of condoms," said Scott Stokes, the agency's prevention expert. "We can't speak positively about them either. We are just going to leave the issue alone."

SIGNIFICANCE

A December 2004 report on abstinence-only education programs, requested by Representative Henry Waxman, a Democrat from California, examined the content of abstinence-only programs and found a wide range of factual errors as well as gender bias and discrimination against homosexuality. The report found materials in the curricula stating that HIV/AIDS can be spread through sweat and tears, that 43-day-old fetuses can think, that condoms have a failure rate of 14%, and that 10% of women who have abortions later commit suicide. Waxman's report examined thirteen of the most popular abstinence-only curricula, used in twenty-five states, and compared the information taught to current textbooks in obstetrics, gynecology, biology, and other sciences related to reproductive health and sexuality.

Researchers at Columbia University found that of those students educated under abstinence-only programs, although students delay sexual activity, 88% do engage in premarital sex. Many abstinence-only programs offer "virginity pledges" for students. Researchers examined differences in behavior between "pledgers" and "nonpledgers." Abstinence-only educated teens also seek treatment for sexually transmitted diseases at lower rates than traditionally educated teens, and are one-third less likely to use contraception when they engage in sexual intercourse. In addition, oral and anal sex rates for abstinence-only educated teens are higher as such teens seek to preserve traditional virginity. Two percent of teens who did not take a virginity pledge engaged in oral or anal, but not vaginal intercourse, while thirteen percent of pledgers engaged in anal or oral sex, rarely while using any form of protection against sexually transmitted disease.

One in four teenagers acquires a sexually transmitted disease, and public health officials and critics of abstinence-only education point to the growing rates of STD transmission among teens as an epidemic that abstinence-only education cannot prevent; while 7% of nonpledgers acquired a sexually transmitted disease, 4.6% of those who took the virginity pledge also acquired STDs. Between 1996 and 2005, nearly $1 billion was devoted to abstinence-only education.

FURTHER RESOURCES

Books

Luker, Kristin. *When Sex Goes to School: Warring Views on Sex—And Sex Education—Since the Sixties*. New York: W.W. Norton, 2006.

United States House of Representatives. *The Content of Federally Funded Abstinence-Only Programs*. United States House of Representatives. Committee on Government Reform—Minority Staff Special Investigations Division, 2004.

Periodicals

Beh, Hazel Glenn, and Milton Diamond. "The Failure of Abstinence-Only Education: Minors Have a Right to Honest Talk about Sex." *Columbia Journal of Gender and Law*. 15 (January 1, 2006).

Santelli, J., M. A. Ott, M. Lyon, J. Rogers, D. Summers, and R. Schleifer. "Abstinence and Abstinence-Only Programs: A Review of U.S Policies and Programs." *Journal of Adolescent Health*. 38, no. 1 (2006): 72–81.

Wilson, Kelly L. "A Review of 21 Curricula for Abstinence-Only-until-Marriage Programs." *Journal of School Health*. 75, no. 3 (March 2005): 90–98.

Web sites

National Public Radio. Justice Talking. "Abstinence-Only Education." <http://www.justicetalking.org/viewprogram.asp?progID=426> (accessed May 19, 2006).

School Set Aside for Hawaiians Ends Exclusion to Cries of Protest

Magazine article

By: Adam Liptak

Date: July 27, 2002

Source: Liptak, Adam. "School Set Aside for Hawaiians Ends Exclusion to Cries of Protest." *New York Times*, July 27, 2002.

About the Author: Adam Liptak is an attorney, an instructor at Columbia University's Graduate School of Journalism, and a regular writer for the *New York Times* on legal issues. He received the 1999 New York Press Club's John Peter Zenger Award for his efforts on behalf of freedom of the press.

INTRODUCTION

Civil Rights litigation in the United States has most commonly involved minority groups or individuals seeking legislative or judicial protection against discrimination by majority whites. The major civil rights legislation of the 1950s and 1960s addressed the rights of minorities in employment and education, prohibiting hiring or admissions discrimination on the basis of race or ethnic background. In the years since their passage, these laws have helped African-Americans, Hispanics, and other minority groups make great strides in overcoming workplace and educational barriers.

While equal opportunity law is intended to address past injustices in hiring and promotion, it generally does so by making changes to present actions. In practice, such laws mean that minority individuals may be hired or admitted in place of majority applicants who have stronger objective qualifications. In the decades since these laws were passed, their constitutionality has been consistently upheld in court decisions. However, some majority job applicants have filed lawsuits of their own, claiming that they are now victims of discrimination on the basis of their race. These cases, in which majority litigants claim unfair treatment, are referred to as reverse discrimination suits.

Students at Kamehameha Prep School in 1955, a school that traditionally takes only children of Hawaiian descent.
PHOTO BY EVANS/THREE LIONS/GETTY IMAGES.

A typical reverse discrimination action might involve a law school with an affirmative action policy under which minority applicants are given preferences in admissions. Such policies take a variety of forms, but typically involve a modification of applicants' admission scores, such as a ten percent upward adjustment to minority test scores. Such a policy will generally increase minority admissions by rejecting majority applicants with higher scores. Reverse discrimination lawsuits are commonly brought by majority applicants who would have been admitted if the adjustment policy were not in place. Reverse discrimination suits claim that such policies are inherently discriminatory because they give preferential treatment to applicants

of a specific race. Such suits have achieved mixed results.

While race-based admission policies are generally considered a violation of federal law, exceptions do exist. The century-old Kamehameha School System in Hawaii is named for an eighteenth century ruler who unified the Hawaiian Islands; the school was endowed by the ruler's last direct descendent. In the intervening years, the school has grown to include three campuses and serve more than 4,000 students, funded by an endowment estimated to be worth $6–7 billion. In accordance with the terms of the original trust, Kamehameha School continues to extend enrollment preferences to Native Hawaiians. As a result, non-

Hawaiian applicants are admitted only if spaces remain after all qualified applicants have been considered. Because more than 70,000 school-aged children qualify as natives, non-Hawaiians are effectively barred from admission, and only a handful have been admitted in the school's history. In 2002, the school broke this long-standing tradition by admitting a single non-native student.

PRIMARY SOURCE

HONOLULU, July 24—The modern history of Hawaii is, in the view of many people here, a series of tragedies and crimes. The native population was decimated by Western diseases, its monarchy was overthrown by Western businessmen, and its culture and language were for generations actively suppressed.

But one shining thing always belonged to native Hawaiians. The Kamehameha Schools, the only beneficiary of the $6 billion legacy of a 19th-century Hawaiian princess, educates native Hawaiian children—and only native Hawaiian children.

It thus came as a wrenching surprise to many here when the schools recently admitted a student not of Hawaiian ancestry. School policy requires students to prove that at least one ancestor lived on the Hawaiian Islands in 1778, when Capt. James Cook arrived. The competition for admission is intense, and few native Hawaiians make the cut.

The decision to accept the student, Kalani Rosell, into the eighth grade on the schools' Maui campus was driven in part by a concern that the admission policy cannot survive legal scrutiny. The move has set off furious protests, rooted in historical grievances, cultural differences and the conviction that the legal categories developed by mainland courts to promote racial equality cannot address the needs of a multiracial society that was a monarchy little more than a century ago.

"An attempt by kings and queens to help their people has not meshed well with American law," said Beadie Kanahele Dawson, a lawyer here.

The schools' main campus occupies about 600 acres in the lush hills above Honolulu's harbor. Some 3,200 students, from kindergarten through 12th grade, use its 70 buildings, Olympic-sized swimming pool and sports stadium. The view from almost anywhere on campus is so stunning that its beauty is not lost even on teenagers.

Another 1,200 students attend the schools' two other campuses on Maui and the Big Island, and the schools sponsor many other programs from preschool through college. All the programs together reach less than 10 percent of all the children who meet the ancestry requirements. High-school tuition for day students, which is heavily subsidized, is about $1,400.

"If you are a kid with Hawaiian blood and pass the test and get into Kamehameha Schools, man, you have just hit the lottery," said Daniel B. Boylan, a history professor at the University of Hawaii.

Haunani-Kay Trask, a professor of Hawaiian studies at the university, said the schools were unprepared for the outcry over the decision to admit Kalani Rosell, a 12-year-old boy described as a straight-A student and a champion swimmer.

"It really hurt people," Ms. Trask said, "and the pain was so palpable you could almost smell people's anger." At a meeting to discuss the matter last week, alumni angrily attacked the schools' trustees.

"They just got it frontally, full blast, both barrels," Ms. Trask said.

John Tehranian, a University of Utah law professor who has written on the schools' tax status, said the trustees were missing the point.

"Forget all the legal arguments," Professor Tehranian said. "There are profound emotions here. This is the last thing that native Hawaiians have."

At the meeting with alumni, J. Douglas Ing, chairman of the trust's board, likened the issue to chess.

"There are those in this country that would like to erode if not eliminate rights for indigenous and native people," Mr. Ing said. "We're attempting to protect the admissions policy. To do that it may be necessary for us to give up a pawn here and a pawn there."

In an interview in the campus library here, the schools' chief executive, Hamilton McCubbin, said that powerful societal and legal forces were challenging the admissions policy. "We're working against the waves," he said.

But the admissions decision appears to have backfired on all fronts. It has drawn attention to the issue at a time when the schools hope to avoid legal scrutiny, and it has alienated the schools' own constituencies.

"I assume," said John Goemans, a lawyer who has been active in challenging preferences for people of Hawaiian ancestry, "that this was a surfeit of would-be cleverness."

Dr. McCubbin acknowledged the unpopularity of the Rosell admission.

"Many, many people thought the decision of the Kamehameha Schools was a betrayal," he said. "The perception is that if there is any entity that can stand up to the anti-affirmative-action, anti-entitlement forces, it's the Kamehameha Schools."

He emphasized, though, that the issue was not race-based. "Ancestral roots have significant meaning for Hawaiian people," he said. "It is that linkage to ancestral roots that defines who you are."

In one sense the school, like the state, is remarkably diverse racially. In a recent school year, 78 percent of the students said they were part Caucasian, 74 percent said they were part Chinese, 28 percent said they were part Japanese, and 24 percent said they were of other ancestries, including African-American, Arab, Brazilian, Indian, Alaska Native and American Indian.

The requirement of one pre–1778 Hawaiian ancestor means that many students are of Hawaiian descent in only a quite attenuated sense.

"My goodness," said Gladys Brandt, a former principal of the Kamehameha Schools, "you're one-twenty-fourth Hawaiian, you're in." Indeed, assuming nine intervening generations, children who are less than one-five-hundredth original Hawaiian may qualify.

When asked about the legal significance of the decision to admit Kalani Rosell, Dr. McCubbin started to answer but was interrupted by Colleen I. Wong, the schools' chief lawyer, who told him not to respond.

Through a representative, Kalani Rosell's mother and father declined a request for an interview.

The schools have recently dropped several federally supported programs to avoid challenges to its admissions policy. Their key remaining fear is that the trust's tax-exempt status will be revoked, which would cost the schools perhaps $80 million a year. They might also be liable, according to their former accountants, for back taxes of $1 billion.

The trust was created by the will of Bernice Pauahi Bishop, the great-granddaughter and last direct descendant of Kamehameha I, the 18th-century king who unified the Hawaiian Islands. The princess, who died in 1884, left some 400,000 acres, including a prime tract on Waikiki Beach, to the schools.

In 1999, an earlier board of trustees was ousted under pressure from the Internal Revenue Service, which threatened to revoke the trust's tax-exempt status during an investigation of financial mismanagement and self-dealing.

The new trustees, who adopted a more transparent management style, disappointed many in their handling of the admissions decision.

"They've been given legal advice that they should be quite cautious," Jon M. Van Dyke, a University of Hawaii law professor, said. "But something is lost if they move away from the exclusive ancestry criteria. The schools are the only forum in which native Hawaiians can get together as native Hawaiians."

Mr. Goemans said he planned a class-action lawsuit against the Kamehameha Schools. "I would hope that by this fall the racially exclusive policy will be dropped by the school," he said. "If they were smart, they would roll over."

In 2000, in a lawsuit litigated by Mr. Goemans, the United States Supreme Court dealt a blow to the cause of preferences for people of Hawaiian descent. The state had limited the right to vote for the trustees of a state agency to people who could prove Hawaiian ancestry; the court ruled that limitation violated the Fifteenth Amendment, which concerns voting rights.

The court also rejected two of the general premises on which the arguments in favor of preferences for people of Hawaiian ancestry were built.

The court first held that native Hawaiians are not historically or legally akin to American Indians on the mainland. The court said that preferences enjoyed by Indians were permissible because they are based on politics, not race. The court reasoned that Indian tribes are political units.

But Hawaiians, the court held, have no similar political status that would insulate such preferences from challenges.

The court also held that the requirement of proof of Hawaiian ancestry was a proxy for race. Racial distinctions, at least when they are made by the government, are almost always forbidden.

In the context of private entities, the Supreme Court has ruled that race discrimination can result in the loss of tax-exempt status. In 1983, the court held that taxpayers should not be made to support the discriminatory policies of Bob Jones University, at least when "there can be no doubt that the activity involved is contrary to fundamental public policy."

Many legal scholars say that the two Supreme Court cases spell trouble for the Kamehameha Schools.

The Rosell decision was said by the schools to have been a product of ordinary admissions criteria. All qualified applicants of Hawaiian descent were admitted, the schools said, leaving one open slot.

"It's not only insulting," Professor Trask said of this explanation, "it's also untrue. I'm sure they accepted a non-Hawaiian because they were afraid of getting sued."

Samuel P. King, a federal judge here, said the schools misplayed this aspect of the decision. "It was a mistake to say you couldn't find a Hawaiian," he said. "That's like putting a red flag in front of a bull."

SIGNIFICANCE

The public response to the school's admission decision was vocal and overwhelmingly negative. Protestors, including parents and numerous graduates, claimed that admitting non-natives would ultimately destroy the unique educational opportunities which native Hawaiians had enjoyed at the school. In response, the school's leadership responded by reaffirming its policy of admitting native islanders first, and school trustees promised to amend admission policies to further clarify the school's admission objectives. Some observers already critical of the school's admission policy charged that the school administration had accepted the student solely to provide legal defense against potential charges of discriminatory admissions.

In 2003, two lawsuits were filed challenging the school's admissions policy. One of these suits dealt with a student who was mistakenly admitted, then later rejected when his Hawaiian ancestry came into question. The school quickly settled the lawsuit by granting the student admission for the remainder of his educational career.

The second case went to the U.S. District Court, which reviewed the arguments and dismissed the case, ruling in favor of the school. The plaintiff then appealed to the Ninth Circuit Court of Appeals, and in 2005 that three-judge panel ruled the school's admission practices unlawful, ordering the school to change its admission policy. In February 2006, following an appeal by the school, the same court granted an *en banc* review, which provides for an additional hearing before a panel of fifteen Ninth Circuit judges. The school's restrictive admissions policy was left intact pending a ruling in the case.

The Kamehameha case raises several important legal questions. Specifically, it asks the court to determine whether a century-old decision to establish a racially segregated school provides grounds for continued discrimination in the school's policies. In broader terms, the case seeks to further define the specific situations in which privately funded institutions are allowed to apply racial preferences in the pursuit of specific philosophical goals. It also examines the issue of whether non-discrimination law apply in situations where majority citizens may benefit.

FURTHER RESOURCES

Books

Goldman, Alan H. *Justice and Reverse Discrimination*. Princeton, N.J.: Princeton University Press, 1979.

Mayo-Jefferies, Deborah. *Equal Educational Opportunity for All Children: A Research Guide to Discrimination in Education, 1950–1992*. Buffalo, N.Y.: William S. Hein & Company, 1994.

Miller, Arthur Selwyn. *Racial discrimination and private education: A legal analysis*. Charlotte: University of North Carolina Press, 1957.

Periodicals

"Civil Rights—Section 198—Ninth Circuit Holds That Private School's Remedial Admissions Policy Violates Section 1981." *Harvard Law Review*. 119 (2006): 661–668.

Rutherglen, George. "The Improbable History of Section 1981: Clio Still Bemused and Confused." *Supreme Court Review*. 303 (2003): 307–337.

Sullivan, Kathleen M. "Sins of Discrimination: Last Term's Affirmative Action Cases." *Harvard Law Review*. 78 (1986): 93–94.

Web sites

Asian Week. "Kamehameha Schools Seek Justice." August 26, 2005. <http://news.asianweek.com/news/view_article.html?%20article_id=b13172d9cc05d1cc759ba8d9ce43cc23> (accessed June 2, 2006).

Humanitarian Demining. "Landmine Threats." <http://www.humanitarian-demining.org/demining/threats/proliferation.asp> (accessed May 28, 2006).

Kamehameha Schools. "Appeals Court to Rehear Admissions Policy Change." <http://www.ksbe.edu/article.php?story=20060222115656371> (accessed June 1, 2006).

College Is Already Affordable, Likely for Most Recipients

Georgia's HOPE Scholarship Goes to Lots of Kids Who Don't Need It

Newspaper article

By: Andrea Jones

Date: November 11, 2003

Source: Jones, Andrea. "College Is Already Affordable, Likely for Most Recipients." *Atlanta Journal-Constitution* (November 11, 2003).

About the Author: Andrea Jones is a journalist and staff writer for the *Atlanta Journal-Constitution*.

On December 29, 2003 in order to promote the Georgia Higher Education Savings Plan, Gov. Sonny Perdue is joined by grandson, Jack Ghioto, at a Capitol press conference in Atlanta, Georgia. AP IMAGES.

INTRODUCTION

The Helping Outstanding Pupils Educationally (HOPE) Scholarship was created by a former governor of the state of Georgia, Zell Miller (1932–). The intent of the program is to motivate students to achieve excellent grades while in high school by offering them financial incentives for college in the form of lottery-based scholarships. The scholarships are based primarily on the attainment of high grades and only secondarily on financial need. They can be used at technical and vocational schools and colleges, as well as at participating private and public colleges and universities throughout the state of Georgia. The program was begun in 1993, and the funds are derived from the state lottery system, called the Georgia Lottery for Education.

One of the unusual characteristics of this scholarship program is that it may be awarded to those attending post-secondary schools other than standard four-year colleges or universities, in the form of a HOPE grant. Students pursuing certificates or diplomas at technical or vocational schools, as well as those pursuing associate's degrees at those types of educational institutions, may be eligible for HOPE grants, as long as they are engaged in the process of pursuing a terminal degree, certificate, or diploma in their chosen field of study. The academic requirements are somewhat less rigorous than for those in the more traditional post-secondary programs, mandating simply that students make (and continue to achieve) satisfactory progress toward the completion of their programs. They need not be full-time enrollees. They also do not need to achieve a specific grade-point average or to attend post-secondary school immediately after completion of high school. Students can apply for the HOPE grant for as many technical or vocational programs as they wish.

HOPE scholarships have significantly different requirements than do HOPE grants. Students wishing to obtain the scholarships must take college preparatory classes in high school and must achieve an overall average of "B" or higher. This translates to a minimum numeric average of eighty percent or a cumulative grade-point average of at least 3.0 on a four-point grade scale. Students who are engaged in the technical studies programs at their high schools must maintain an average of just under a "B+" (a numeric average of eighty-five percent or a cumulative grade-point average of 3.2 on the four-point grade scale).

Another unusual feature of the HOPE scholarship program is that it is open to nontraditional students, including those who do not attend college or a technical or vocational school immediately after completion of high school; those who have taken some college or technical courses without completion of a program; and those who completed a two-year degree or technical or vocational program and wish to resume studies for a more advanced degree or certificate.

■ PRIMARY SOURCE

More than 90 percent of HOPE scholars would go to college even without the award, University of Georgia researchers say. And many who get the money come from families wealthier than the state average, according to a review by the *Atlanta Journal-Constitution*.

But that's not the image that the public has of HOPE.

Nine out of 10 Georgians believe HOPE has been somewhat or very effective in helping people attend college who otherwise couldn't afford to go, according to a recent poll by the *AJC* and Zogby America.

Throughout the University System, three-quarters of HOPE scholars come from families who either have incomes too high to qualify for the federal government's need-based aid program or who don't bother to apply for it, data for the 2000–2001 school year show.

At Georgia Southern University, parents of about 70 percent of the 4,757 HOPE scholars at the school made more than the average Georgia family's income of

$41,707, according to records for 1999–2000, the last time the university required all HOPE students to report income data.

In fact, HOPE went to 46 Georgia Southern students whose parents earned more than $250,000 a year, averaging $453,000.

UGA economics professors Chris Cornwell and David Mustard compared college enrollment rates in Southeastern states and concluded that less than 10 percent of HOPE money goes to students who would otherwise not have gone to college.

The program isn't generating many new collegegoers, said Cornwell, who has authored several studies and papers on HOPE.

Instead, the scholarship has simply persuaded more students to stay in the state for college, Cornwell said.

"HOPE has been about moving kids around," he said.

Cornwell said that's in part because HOPE's B average requirement limits it to students likely to go to college anyway. He said some studies suggest programs that reach students in early childhood have a greater impact on their education. Georgia's lottery-funded pre-kindergarten program for 4-year-olds is ultimately expected to improve the college attendance rate.

HOPE supporters say the scholarship program has had other successes. It is credited with pumping up SAT scores of incoming freshmen and raising admission standards at Georgia's public colleges.

Gary Henry, a Georgia State University researcher who also studies HOPE, said a change made in the program three years ago is likely to increase the percentage of Georgians who go to college. Before 2000, students who qualified for federal Pell Grants—which are based on financial need—couldn't receive HOPE. With that rule removed, it should be easier for low-income students to go to college, Henry said.

Some students do say HOPE has helped them make it to college.

Sly Colquitt, a 27-year-old bouncer at a bar near Georgia Southern, graduated from the university two years ago. His parents never went beyond high school and mostly worked factory jobs. They contributed all they could to his college education: $600 for his five years in school, said Colquitt, who is from Columbus.

"If I didn't have HOPE at least that first year, I wouldn't have been in college," he said.

But dozens of current students interviewed at five public colleges and universities in Georgia said they would have gone to college even without HOPE. They say HOPE has made their lives easier in other ways.

Some said savings from the scholarship have helped them avoid having to work a part-time job or live at home during college. Others said HOPE has limited the college loans they needed.

And some of the money that families save on tuition is going to buy cars, say researchers Cornwell and Mustard, who have tied increases in car registrations to the amount of HOPE money distributed.

For UGA senior Robin Abramson, who transferred from the University of Tennessee last year, the savings her parents got from HOPE and the fact that she's now attending school in the state means she's been able to afford an off-campus apartment and a car.

Jim Chambers, the owner of Dingus MaGee's, a bar across from Georgia Southern, said he knows where the money scholars save ends up.

"It's going in here," Chambers said, pointing to his cash register. "It's going into Wal-Mart. There are lots of SUVs, Tahoes, BMWs and Lexuses."

SIGNIFICANCE

The most controversial characteristic of the HOPE grants and the HOPE scholarships is that they are based on achievement and academic eligibility, rather than determined by financial need. The annual pool of available grant and scholarship funds is determined by the lottery proceeds of the previous fiscal year. Part of the logic for this system has to do with a belief in equal educational opportunity for all high achievers, rewarding academic excellence rather than supplementing parental or family income. The scholarships, for those attending public community colleges, four-year colleges, and universities, cover tuition, those fees and costs approved by the HOPE program, and a stipend to be used for the purchase of textbooks and academic supplies. The scholarships do not cover the entirety of tuition or fees for eligible and participating private colleges and universities, whose costs are typically significantly higher than for equivalent public institutions. For those students, tuition equalization grants are available, to help offset the cost differential.

The HOPE programs have been in effect for well over a decade, and some changes have been made over time. There is a cap on the number of credit hours that students may attempt in order to achieve a bachelor's-level degree, unless they are in specific types of programs requiring more credits, such as combined degree programs. There is a similar cap for students in vocational or technical programs, limiting the number of courses taken prior to the completion of a program

or course of training. All must achieve satisfactory progress toward program completion for grant award students, or maintain a minimum of a "B" average across all coursework undertaken (meaning that the average must consider every course taken, whether or not it was completed). "Checkpoints" have now been introduced, which are benchmarks that must be achieved by students in order to maintain eligibility for the HOPE grants or scholarships. Once students hit the upper limits for attempted hours of coursework, or paid semesters of college, vocational, or technical school, they will lose their eligibility. Students whose academic performance falls below the accepted levels at the various checkpoints will also lose their eligibility. However, the system has also built in the possibility that students who have lost eligibility based on poor academic performance may also shore up their grades, reapply, and be equitably considered for potential scholarship reinstatement. The state of Georgia has also instituted caps on funding, called "triggers," based on the pool of lottery funds remaining at the end of a given fiscal budget year.

The Georgia HOPE programs have achieved national significance, in part because they represent something of a fiscal experiment in widening the available funding streams for higher education. In part, the goal behind the HOPE scholarships and grants has been the broadening of educational possibilities, particularly for students at public colleges and universities, and for those at technical and vocational schools. By offering students incentives for the achievement of good grades, it was theorized that more students would be motivated toward academic excellence and the pursuit of studies beyond high school. While it was recognized that some recipients' families would have ample financial resources to fund their continuing educations, it was believed that such students would represent a relatively small percentage of the overall number of eligible students. Available published research by the state has suggested that the lottery system in Georgia has been effective thus far, despite contentions that the funds benefit those who could have financed their educations by other means, as well as those for whom the grants and scholarships provide the only viable route to the pursuit of higher education. There is significant census and research data indicating that post-secondary enrollment by students from the poorest and least academically enriched school districts has risen considerably. Some controversy has arisen centered on the use of lottery funds, which are disproportionately derived from people in lower income brackets, but there is good evidence that the programs have benefited a number of students who might otherwise have not pursued higher education.

FURTHER RESOURCES

Books

Borg, Mary O., Paul M. Mason, and Stephen L. Shapiro. *The Economic Consequences of State Lotteries*. New York: Praeger Publishers, 1991.

Herideen, Penelope E. *Policy, Pedagogy, and Social Inequality: Community College Student Realities in Post-Industrial America*. Westport, Conn.: Bergin & Garvey, 1998.

Karabell, Zachary. *What's College For? The Struggle to Define American Higher Education*. New York: Basic Books, 1998.

Townsend, Barbara K. and Susan B. Twombly. *Community Colleges: Policy in the Future Context*. Westport, Conn.: Ablex Publishing, 2001.

Periodicals

Card, David and A. Abigail Payne. "School Finance Reform, the Distribution of School Spending, and the Distribution of Student Test Scores." *Journal of Public Economics* 83 (2002): 49–82.

Dee, Thomas S. "The Capitalization of Education Finance Reforms." *Journal of Law and Economics* 43 (2000): 185–214.

Spindler, Charles J. "The Lottery and Education: Robbing Peter to Pay Paul?" *Public Budgeting and Finance* 15 (1995): 54–62.

Web sites

DTAE: Georgia Department of Technical and Adult Education. "HOPE: Helping Outstanding Pupils Educationally." August 30, 2005 <http://www.dtae.org/hope.html#HOPEWORKS> (accessed June 1, 2006).

Georgia Student Finance Commission. "Scholarship and Grant Program Regulations." May 19, 2004 <http://www.gsfc.org/GSFC/grants/dsp_menu.cfm> (accessed June 1, 2006).

Lies, Distortions and School Choice

e-Journal article

By: Neal McCluskey

Date: October 13, 2003

Source: McCluskey, Neil. "Lies, Distortions and School Choice." *CATO Institute*, October 13, 2003. <http:// www.cato.org/dailys/10–13-03.html> (accessed May 26, 2006).

About the Author: Neal McCluskey is a policy analyst with the Cato Institute. He has served in the U.S. Army, taught high school English, and worked as a freelance reporter. He holds a master's degree in political science from Rutger's University and writes on topics related to education.

INTRODUCTION

Public education is a fundamental part of American society. Since the earliest days of the one-room schoolhouse, Americans have believed in the value of education. As communities grew, schools grew as well, and as the nation wrestled with cultural shifts, schools adapted and changed. Primary education today is a massive undertaking, serving more than fifty million children nationwide.

Even before public education became widespread, some observers proposed coupling government funding with parental choice. In the 1700s, Scottish economist Adam Smith (1723–1790) suggested that the state should provide funds with which parents could hire private teachers of their choice. Two centuries later, economist Milton Friedman's *Capitalism and Freedom* expanded on Smith's ideas, proposing the modern voucher system in which local governments provide school funds to be used at any school of the parents' choosing.

Friedman's case for vouchers was simple. Competition, which is so effective in improving business efficiency, would have the same effect on public schools. By giving parents' school choice, Friedman believed that the marketplace would automatically reward better schools with higher enrollment, forcing inferior schools to either improve or close. By allowing parents' to vote with education dollars, Friedman suggested that top schools would be rewarded, while inferior schools would also improve.

The first modern voucher system was tested in California's Alum Rock school district in 1970. While not a pure voucher arrangement, this system created several mini-schools on each existing campus, and parents chose which mini-school their children would attend. This first formal experiment in school vouchers produced mixed educational results and was disbanded several years later. Shortly thereafter, the state of New York offered vouchers for private and religious schools, but a 1973 U.S. Supreme Court ruling struck down the plan, arguing that public funding for religious schools violated the First Amendment.

In the years since that ruling, states have experimented with a variety of school choice systems. In some cases, ballot initiatives have failed, stalling these efforts. In other cases, school choice plans have won at the ballot box but have been struck down or restricted in the court system. Critics of school choice claim that rather than improving public education, school choice will actually erode the quality of public education for many students. In particular, they argue that school choice plans will drain funds from already underfunded public schools.

By the turn of the twenty-first century, school choice battle lines were clearly drawn. Supporting school choice were a variety of groups unhappy with public education, including supporters of Christian education and many Republicans. Opposing choice were the National Education Association, labeling the program elitist, and other stakeholders in the public school system, along with the Democratic Party. While both sides agreed on the objective of improving education for all American children, they sharply disagreed on the best methods to achieve this goal. And while both sides believed school choice would change American education, they vehemently disagreed on whether school choice would ultimately help or hurt.

PRIMARY SOURCE

A proposed school voucher program for Washington, D.C., offering an escape for children in the worst district schools, is on the brink of suffocation in the U.S. Senate, smothered by opponents happier to bring Senate business to a halt than offer choice. Sadly, opponents have justified their actions with misleading arguments and distortions. For the sake of truth in education—and because there's still a glimmer of hope left for D.C.'s kids—it's time to challenge the three most dubious anti-choice arguments.

Let's start with the contention that vouchers drain public school funds. This lie is obvious in the case of the proposed D.C. program, which doesn't draw a single dollar from the public school system. The recently passed House version of the program underwrites "opportunity scholarships" with a $10 million allocation that is separate from the D.C. public schools' budget. The Senate version is even more generous: It provides $13 million for choice and adds a bonus $26 million for charter and traditional public schools.

But what if the D.C. plan didn't offer choice with new, separate funds, and required full per-pupil funding to follow the kids? In real terms, public schools still wouldn't lose a dime because spending is measured per-child.

That means the only money a school district is supposedly "losing" when a family exercises choice is the amount that would have covered that individual child. The same thing occurs anytime a child's family moves out of a district. In most places this "loss" is called "breaking even." Not so in public education.

Next distortion: Choice programs lack accountability. It is true that nothing is perfect—choice programs have their share of bad schools. But is the overall effect worse than the alternative? Consider one comparison: Arguably the biggest choice accountability flap has occurred in Florida. There, the state's Corporate Tax Credit Scholarship Program has come under scrutiny following the disappearance of over $400,000, and revelations that roughly $350,000 had been spent on a school run by a man with possible terrorist ties. Not good.

Worse, though, is recent news from D.C. In March, the city's school system discovered that it had hired 640 employees for which it had no money budgeted, resulting in a loss of $31 million—an amount that dwarfs the missing and misspent cash in Florida. But the scarier part is that the D.C. revelation is only a symptom of a more pervasive problem. As *The Washington Post* reported: "In an interview…Superintendent Paul L. Vance blamed financial systems that have failed for years. 'It's an accumulation of past ills,' Vance said."

Ultimately, for choice programs to create accountable schools depends on parents making wise choices. Even if only some parents make smart decisions, good schools will thrive because parents will choose them. Likewise, bad schools will disappear as they lose students. Unfortunately, choice opponents don't trust parents, preferring instead to rely on the politicians and bureaucrats whose own accountability is so often suspect.

One last lie: There's no evidence choice works. Actually, this is partly true—there is no proof that *large-scale* choice works. But that's because choice opponents won't let such an experiment take place. To prove that choice works, strong programs must exist, which is exactly what choice opponents don't want. Instead, they have allowed only tightly constricted programs to operate, imposing severe enrollment caps, paltry funding, and constant legal threats.

Even in this hostile environment, though, choice programs have helped both scholarship students and entire school systems. Harvard political scientist Paul Peterson, for instance, found that miniscule $1,400 vouchers in New York City helped African American recipients outpace their peers in math. Peterson's colleague, economist Caroline Hoxby, has shown that states offering a minimum of competition realize systemic improvements, with greater competition yielding greater improvements.

Most recently, Jay Greene of the Manhattan Institute determined that the greater the choice threat to public schools in Florida, the greater their gains on state tests.

Choice, it seems, lifts all schools.

There are other red herrings that choice opponents raise *ad nauseum*. But these three—that choice programs lack accountability, suck public schools dry, and just don't work—are the most dishonest, and shouldn't be allowed to come between kids and a good education. With a little life left in the D.C. choice proposal, it's not too late to make sure they don't in the nation's capital.

SIGNIFICANCE

By the early twenty-first century, school choice initiatives had compiled a mixed record of wins and losses. In 2000, school choice referenda were rejected by wide margins in both California and Michigan. At the same time, philanthropic organizations around the country began funding school choice alternatives for low income students. By 2001, more than 100 privately funded voucher programs were providing school choice to more than 75,000 low-income students. Several of these programs were begun by education reformers who, after years of trying to reform existing school systems, finally concluded that the legislative approach to change was futile.

The education landscape today is more diverse than at any other time in history. Public schools now exist alongside numerous private and parochial institutions, and home schooling is a growing phenomenon. By 2003, more than one million students were being taught in their own homes. Charter schools, which provide alternative educational experiences and are frequently funded by foundations or for-profit firms, have created school choice in many large school systems. And online education, both in the form of resources for home school educators and in the form of entire primary curricula, appears poised to attract a growing share of the market.

The earliest arguments for school choice were based on economic models, in which customer wants and needs lead to the creation of new products and services. Even as voucher advocates and critics have battled to a virtual stalemate in the courts and at the ballot box, other options have emerged, as if guided by Adam Smith's invisible hand. Parental choice now appears to be the future of education. All that remains is to decide what form it will take.

FURTHER RESOURCES

Books

Mondale, Sarah. *School: The Story of American Public Education*. Boston: Beacon Press, 2002.

Salisbury, David, and James Tooley, eds. *What America Can Learn From School Choice in Other Countries*. Washington, D.C.: CATO Institute, 2005.

Weil, Danny. *School Vouchers and Privatization: A Reference Handbook*. Santa Barbara, Calif.: ABC-CLIO, 2003.

Periodicals

Paulson, Amanda. "Milwaukee's Lessons on School Vouchers." *Christian Science Monitor* 98 (2006): 1–11.

Rome, Gregory. "Schoolhouse Socialism." *Journal of Instructional Psychology* 33 (2006): 83–88.

Rubelen, Erik W. "Florida Lawmakers Float New Voucher Plans." *Education Week* 25 (2006): 27–31.

Web sites

Amis, Kelly. "Philanthropy Pushes School Choice Forward." *Heartland Institute*, December 1, 2001. <http://www.heartland.org/Article.cfm?artId=1009> (accessed May 26, 2006).

National Center for Education Statistics. "Digest of Education Statistics." <http://nces.ed.gov/programs/digest/> (accessed May 26, 2006).

PBS. "Choosing or Losing: The School Choice Controversy." <http://www.pbs.org/kcet/publicschool/roots_in_history/choice.html> (accessed May 26, 2006).

People for the American Way. "A Brief History of Vouchers." <http://www.pfaw.org/pfaw/dfiles/file_228.pdf> (accessed May 26, 2006).

CWLA Testimony for the Hearing on the Implementation of the Adoption and Safe Families Act

Congressional testimony

By: Child Welfare League of America

Date: April 8, 2003

Source: *Child Welfare League of America*. "The Adoption and Safe Families Act of 1997." April 8, 2003. <http://www.cwla.org/advocacy/asfatestimony-implementation.htm> (accessed May 17, 2006).

President Clinton, surrounded by members of Congress and adopted children, signs the Adoption and Safe Families Act of 1997 in the East Room of the White House, November 19, 1997. AP IMAGES.

About the Author: The Child Welfare League of America (CWLA) has been in existence since 1920. Its overarching goal is to put the welfare, safety, and best interests of children at the forefront of the American public consciousness. The CWLA is particularly focused on eradicating both the actuality and the underlying causes of child abuse and neglect, child poverty, and lack of adequate shelter, nutrition, and health care for children. Its model is one in which individual, neighborhood, local community, provider agency, local, state, and federal government are all engaged in concert for the promotion of the best possible circumstances for the nation's children.

INTRODUCTION

The initial Adoption and Safe Families Act (ASFA) was made a part of federal law on November 19, 1997. The initial purpose of the act was to facilitate a revamping of the overburdened and fragmented foster care system in the United States. The central problem of the foster care system was the long periods of time spent in the system by children who did not have adequate permanency plans in place, involving long-term goals and objectives regarding either return to family or origin, permanent placement with relatives, or termination of parental rights and clearance for adoption. Often children were in the foster care system for many years as a result of what is called foster care drift, in which children are moved from placement to placement without future plans. To address the problem of foster care drift, the ASFA placed a limit on the length of time that a child could be in foster care (out-of-home) placements before parental rights are summarily terminated. That limit is fifteen of twenty-two months (also called the 15/22 provision), meaning that the parents of children who have been in foster care placements for fifteen of the prior twenty-two months are subject to mandatory termination of their parental rights. The ASFA provides for three circumstances in which this provision is not carried out: when the child is placed with relatives (called kinship placement); when the state can show that the termination of parental rights at that time would not be in the best interests of the child; or if the state has failed to make proper and satisfactory efforts (the legal phrase is "reasonable efforts at reunification") to reunite the family by providing necessary supports and services to facilitate safe and appropriate return of the child to the family of origin.

The concept of permanency planning for children in foster care came from a series of books written by Joseph Goldstein, Anna Freud, Joseph Solnit, and Dorothy Burlingham. The first and most influential book was entitled *Beyond the Best Interests of the Child*. The authors expressed their strongly held beliefs that the child welfare system must place the needs of the child above all other legal considerations, and that permanent and stable placement best facilitates healthy intrapsychic, cognitive, and emotional development. They coined the term psychological parent, reflecting their hypothesis that children form early and strong bonds with their most regular, stable, and dependable caregivers. That being the case, frequent movement to new placements would be extremely damaging to the internal well-being of the child. *Beyond the Best Interests of the Child* also stated that a central rule for facilitating placements most likely to have positive long-term outcomes is to honor the child's need for continuity of already established relationships, such as those with siblings and other relatives (including, when possible, parents).

PRIMARY SOURCE

The Child Welfare League of America welcomes this opportunity to submit testimony on behalf of more than 1,100 public and private nonprofit child-serving agencies nationwide on the implementation of the Adoption and Safe Families Act (ASFA) (P.L. 105–89) and the use of adoption incentive payments. This hearing represents an important opportunity to review the impact of the law and to take a look at what still needs to be done to ensure that all children in this country grow up in safe, nurturing families.

Positive Outcomes and Developments Since ASFA

The primary goal of ASFA was to ensure safety and expedite permanency for children in the child welfare system. This goal has been achieved in part. Although the entries in care appear to be static, the number of children in foster care has dropped slightly, as have the number of children waiting for adoption. The most positive outcome appears to be the increase in the number of legalized

adoptions. The annual number of adoptions increased by 57% since ASFA, from 37,000 in 1998 to 50,000 in 2001. These numbers are much larger than projected, however, the role ASFA played in the increase is unclear because some states had already begun renewed adoption efforts prior to ASFA.

There are other important developments related to ASFA. States have taken the ASFA timeframes seriously. They have enacted new legislation and promulgated regulations to expedite permanency, consistent with ASFA. Jurisdictions are holding permanency hearings sooner, often practicing some type of concurrent planning, and establishing a more expedited track for filing petitions to terminate parental rights when reunification is not possible or appropriate. The length of time before deciding on a permanency plan has been reduced. States are looking for tools to assist in expediting permanency, including concurrent planning, guardianship, and kinship support.

In addition to the permanency option of adoption, there appears to be a broadening of the traditional notion of permanency in some states and localities. This includes states increasingly turning to relatives as a permanency option and making relatives a part of the permanency process. States report an increase in the use of temporary and permanent relative placements over the past few years. There are a number of new state initiatives in the areas of guardianship and kinship support. Some states are working to relieve relative burdens by using mediation and financial support to address relatives' needs, including guardianship programs and kinship assistance (subsidized and unsubsidized).

Additional practice improvements have been noted in some jurisdictions. There is an increased use of family-based approaches and interventions including family group conferencing, family mediation, and Family-to-Family and other neighborhood foster care approaches. These approaches stress non-adversarial, collaborative efforts to achieve permanency for children. Similarly, there is greater use of voluntary relinquishment and open adoption, especially in conjunction with concurrent planning and foster parent adoption.

Finally, to achieve timely permanency for children, in many jurisdictions, there has been an increased and continuing focus on collaboration between public and private agencies and across systems to improve permanency for children.

Areas Where Improvement is Needed

While ASFA has had some impact on increasing the number of adoptions from the foster care system, and possibly reducing the number of children in foster care, it is clear that more needs to be done. **While there has been a decrease in number of children in foster care** in the last year or two, there continue to be over 500,000 children in care.

Families continue to come to the attention of the child welfare system because targeted early intervention supports are not available. Without these services, many families will require intensive and extensive interventions. Appropriate services for families whose children are already in care and who must meet the ASFA time frame are also lacking. In many communities, there continue to be insufficient substance abuse, mental health, and other treatment resources for families, as well as sufficient housing and economic supports. All families—whether formed through reunification, adoption, kinship guardianship, or another permanent plan—need follow-up support and assistance if they are to be successful. These services are rarely offered and are greatly needed to preserve permanency and prevent re-entry into the system.

Children of color continue to be over represented in the child welfare system. For all states, the rate of entry of African American children was higher than the rate for Caucasian children, and in 30 states it was more than 3 times higher. Forty percent of the children in foster care are black, non-Hispanic, 38% are white non-Hispanic, 15% are Hispanic, and 2% are Native American.

The lack of preventive and treatment services appears to be also particularly relevant for families of color, whose children are disproportionately represented in the child welfare system. Preventive and treatment services need to be culturally competent and available in the family and child's language. In five states (NM, CA, AZ, CO and TX), over 30% of the children in the child welfare system are Hispanic. In both North and South Dakota, Native American children make up more than 25% of the children in foster care. Further, AFCARS tells us that minority children are primarily adopted by single parents. These parents, often relatives, need ongoing support by the agency, if they request it, so that they can best care for their children.

The age of children in foster care waiting to be adopted has increased dramatically and there has been limited success in moving older children and youth to permanency. The average age for a child to become legally free for adoption has increased, the median age of waiting children has increased, and over half of the waiting children are over 8 years old. Concerted efforts are still needed to assist youth not only with independent living skills, but also with permanent, supportive relationships. For youth who enter the system at an older age, the use of voluntary relinquishment, open adoption, guardianship and other participatory approaches, are needed to assist youth and their families to achieve permanency.

Additionally, although the time from removal to termination of parental rights (TPR) has decreased, **the time from TPR to adoption has increased**, with the total time in care for waiting children remaining constant at 44 months. Adoption work is intense and time consuming if done right. Yet, child welfare caseloads for adoption workers are increasing. Just this week, the Wisconsin Department of Family Services proposed eliminating 12.5 special needs adoption workers and five offices due to a 3.2 billion state budget shortfall.

Workforce issues pose a challenge to ensuring children's safety and care. A major challenge in reducing the number of children entering or remaining in out-of-home care or waiting for an adoptive family lies in the ability of a well-staffed and well-trained child welfare workforce. Caseworkers must assist families that are experiencing difficult and chronic family problems. They must also achieve the goals of safety and permanency and make lifetime decisions for the child within the ASFA timelines. Yet, the safety and permanency of children is hampered due to large caseloads, caseworker turnover and minimal training.

The need for foster and adoptive families continues to grow. In fiscal year 2001, the federal government reported that foster parents adopted 59% of the children from the foster care system. Many states are instituting expedited permanency planning systems that seek to place foster children with "resource families" who will eventually become the adoptive parents. Despite this trend, the need for unrelated adoptive families has not diminished because there continue to be waiting children.

Geographic barriers continue to delay adoptive placement for some children. ASFA mandated that barriers to inter-jurisdictional adoptive placement be eliminated. *Adoption 2002*, a report issued by the U.S. Department of Health and Human Services (HHS), noted the following geographic barriers to adoptive placements: lack of dissemination of information about waiting families and children; reluctance on the part of agencies to conduct home studies to place children who are outside their jurisdictions; reluctance of agencies to accept some studies conducted by agencies in other jurisdictions, difficulties in transferring Medicaid benefits; and issues with the Interstate Compact on the Placement of Children (ICPC). Although there is a national Internet Photolisting service, AdoptUsKids, and many states have Internet registries that feature waiting children and families, workers do not often search these registries for families. Many remain reluctant to list available families, or to utilize families from other jurisdictions. Yet, adoption recruitment has become increasingly national, even global, in scope, and in order to ensure that children are placed in a timely way with waiting families, these barriers need to be addressed.

ASFA also underscored the continued importance of the courts in ensuring timely permanency for children. Greater judicial involvement and oversight is required to provide added protections for foster children. To be effective, everyone must work together to streamline court processes, ensure timely and complete documentation, ensure the participation of all relevant parties, and maintain a sense of urgency for every child. **Courts have been challenged to fully respond to the ASFA requirements, with limited new resources**. Judicial caseloads, inadequate representation, unnecessary delays, and unprepared workers and legal counsel are but a few of the possible difficulties encountered.

For counting purposes, anchoring this measure by children substantiated makes sense, but we would also like to know about cases that were reported, not substantiated, and resulted in child deaths.

Realizing the Goals of ASFA

While some progress has been reached since the passage of ASFA, much more needs to be done to ensure that all children in this country grow up in safe, nurturing families. Several pieces of legislation have already been introduced this year, which would help advance that goal.

SIGNIFICANCE

The Adoption and Safe Families Act stemmed in part from an emphasis on positive outcomes for children during the administration of former President Bill Clinton. The overarching goal of the act was to facilitate adoptions for children who were living for extended periods of time in foster care and who were not going to be reunited with their families of origin for permanent placement.

In 1980, the Adoption Assistance and Child Welfare Act (AACWA) was created to address the disorganized nature of state foster care systems, in which children often drifted for years, sometimes until adulthood, without benefit of permanent placement. By the end of the 1970s, more than 500,000 children were in foster care across the country, with a large percentage of that number drifting from placement to placement with no permanency plan. Central among the goals of the AACWA was decreasing the overall numbers of children in foster care, while shortening the out-of-home placements for those already in the system. The AACWA instituted programs for family oversight, training, and support in an effort to keep families together whenever possible, while creating and implementing some systems for the facilitation of adoption for children and youth for whom family reunification

was not viable. Although those were considered reasonable goals, and the act was widely supported within local, state, and federal governments, it fell far short of achieving its intended goals. In fact, within just over a decade, the number of children in foster care and without permanency plans had vastly increased. From a sociodemographic perspective, a significant contributor to the increase in out-of-home placements was the upsurge in teen pregnancies, HIV and AIDS, substance abuse—specifically heroin and crack cocaine addiction—and sharp increases in the homeless population in America. The abject failure of the AACWA led to an increasingly overburdened and ineffective foster care system, increasing the already acute need for effective solutions. Hence, the need for the Adoption and Safe Families Act of 1997.

One of the ongoing challenges for the foster care system is that children of color are over-represented. This means that, relative to their overall percentage of the general population, there are more non-white children in the foster care system than one would expect based on population estimates. The Multiethnic Placement Act, signed into law in 1994, was designed to eliminate some of the institutionalized racial bias inherent in the child welfare system. It broadened the scope of possibilities for becoming licensed to provide foster care among those who were qualified to do so. Traditionally, there were far fewer foster families of color than white foster families, and children of color often spent long periods of time waiting to be placed in racially matched homes. Many of the barriers to transracial adoption also were eliminated by this act. It broadened the best-interests concept to permit discretion in the decision regarding whether interracial families could adequately provide for diverse ethnic and cultural needs within a single household, and opened the door to alternative placements, such as allowing white families to adopt black children.

Because far fewer older children and youth who are available for permanent placement are actually adopted than are babies and younger children, it was necessary to create a safety net for those who "age-out" of foster care without having obtained permanent homes. In 1986, the Independent Living Initiative was created as a means of meeting the needs of teenagers who were preparing to leave foster care. The goal of the initiative was to ensure that older adolescents in foster care or group home settings obtained adequate educational, vocational, housing, and life skills training, so that they could safely transition into adulthood and independent living. The John H. Chafee Foster Care Independence Program of 1999 broadened existing initiatives and created funding for transitional housing payments for youth aging-out of foster care. It also extended the age limits for Medicaid eligibility for those individuals, further increasing the likelihood of their safe passage to independent living.

FURTHER RESOURCES
Books

Bottoms, Bette L., Margaret Bull Kovera, and Bradley D. McAuliff, eds. *Children, Social Science, and the Law.* Cambridge, U.K.: Cambridge University Press, 2002.

Brittain, Charmaine, and Debra Esquibel Hunt, eds. *Helping in Child Protective Service: A Competency Based Casework Handbook.* Second edition. New York: Oxford University Press, 2004.

Goldstein, Joseph, et al. *Before the Best Interests of the Child.* New York: The Free Press, 1979.

Goldstein, Joseph, et al. *Beyond the Best Interests of the Child.* New York: The Free Press, 1973.

Goldstein, Joseph, et al. *The Best Interests of the Child: The Least Detrimental Alternative.* New York: The Free Press, 1996.

Goldstein, Joseph, et al. *In the Best Interests of the Child.* New York: The Free Press, 1986.

Laws, Rita, and Tim O'Hanlon. *Adoption and Financial Assistance: Tools for Navigating the Bureaucracy.* Westport, Conn.: Bergin & Garvey, 1999.

Maluccio, Anthony N., Barbara A. Pine, and Elizabeth M. Tracy. *Social Work Practice with Families and Children.* New York: Columbia University Press, 2002.

Petr, Christopher G. *Social Work with Children and their Families: A Pragmatic Foundation.* New York: Oxford University Press, 2003.

Roberts, Dorothy. *Shattered Bonds: The Color of Child Welfare.* Reprint edition. New York: Basic Books, 2003.

Web sites

Child Welfare League of America. "About CWLA: Fact Sheet." <http://www.cwla.org/whowhat/more.htm> (accessed May 17, 2006).

California Workers' Compensation System

Government record

By: California Department of Industrial Relations

Date: March 12, 2004

Source: *California State Government.* "Divison of Workers' Compensation." <http://www.dir.ca.gov/dwc/basics.htm> (accessed June 2, 2006).

About the Author: The California Department of Industrial Relations oversees safety and health issues for California's workforce and employers. Its primary mission is to improve working conditions and to broaden employment opportunities in the state.

INTRODUCTION

The rights of workers and the duties of employers frequently conflict. In the early years of the Industrial Revolution, employees were often treated like any other piece of industrial equipment, to be used while needed then discarded. With an overriding emphasis on cost reduction, factory owners had little incentive to protect worker health or provide safety equipment. In the late nineteenth and early twentieth centuries, industrial accidents and deaths in the United States were rampant.

Injured employees were typically given rudimentary medical care and sent home to recover, normally without pay. While this system provided a strong incentive for workers to return to work as soon as possible, it also encouraged workers to continue working while injured, potentially endangering themselves or others. If an employee was permanently disabled while working, he could normally expect a token payment and little more; in cases of workplace deaths, the employee's survivors were similarly compensated.

American labor law in the early twentieth century characterized employer and employee as equals entering into a contract—an unrealistic perspective which generally benefited the company. In the rare cases when employees sought damages from employers for workplace injuries, the unemployed worker rarely had the time or the money to prevail in court. In cases where the suit did come to trial, companies were often able to drag the proceedings out for many years while the plaintiff ran up legal and medical bills.

Companies also frequently avoided paying large settlements by claiming that employees were injured due to their own negligence, although industrial design decisions by the firm were frequently major contributors. Upton Sinclair's 1906 novel *The Jungle* provided a sobering look at how large corporations often abused the virtually powerless workers on their payrolls and was instrumental in mobilizing legislators to improve workplace protections.

During the 1910's and 1920's, a wave of reform swept through the American workplace. Acknowledging for the first time that companies had a duty to pro-

California Insurance Commissioner John Garamendi tours the Science Center Elementary School, February 10, 2004, before a news conference in Los Angeles. Garamendi unveiled a comprehensive legislative package to reform the state's broken worker's compensation system. AP IMAGES.

vide a safe workplace and that employee injuries should be considered a business expense, states began to enact legislation designed to protect workers. Most of these laws provided a set amount of income for injured workers during the time they were unable to work. In addition, they generally required benefits regardless of whether the fault lay with the employee or the employer.

California has the largest workforce in the country, with more than sixteen million civilian employees, and the state's workers' compensation system is typical of those now found in all fifty states.

PRIMARY SOURCE

Medical care

Injured workers are entitled to receive all medical care reasonably required to cure or relieve the effects of the injury, with no deductible or co-payments by the injured worker. For dates of injury on or after Jan. 1, 2004, an injured worker is limited to 24 chiropractic and 24 physical therapy visits.

Generally, the employer controls the medical treatment for the first 30 days after the injury is reported, and the employee is then free to select any treating physician or facility. However, if the employee has notified the employer in writing prior to the injury that he or she has a "personal physician"—a physician or surgeon who has previously treated the employee—the employee may be treated by that physician from the date of injury. Choice of treating physician differs, however, if the employer and employee have opted for a managed care program.

Temporary disability benefits

Those workers unable to return to work within three days are entitled to temporary disability benefits to partially replace wages lost as a result of the injury. The benefits are generally designed to replace two-thirds of the lost wages, up to a maximum of $728 per week.

Temporary disability benefits are payable every two weeks, on a day designated with the first payment, until the employee is able to return to work or until the employee's condition becomes permanent and stationary.

Permanent disability benefits

Injured workers who are permanently disabled—those who have a permanent labor market handicap—are entitled to receive permanent disability benefits. A worker who is determined to have a permanent total disability receives the temporary disability benefit—up to $728 per week—for life. A worker determined to have a permanent partial disability receives weekly benefits for a period which increases with the percentage of disability, from four weeks for a one percent permanent disability up to 694.25 weeks for a 99.75 percent disability. Permanent partial disability benefits are also payable at two-thirds of the injured worker's average weekly wages, but are subject to a much lower maximum. As of Jan. 1, 2004, the rates are $220 per week for disabilities less than 69.75 percent and $270 per week for disabilities rated at 70 to 99.75 percent. Those with a permanent partial disability of 70 percent or more also receive a small life pension—a maximum of $257.69 per week—following the final payment of permanent partial disability benefits.

The percentage of permanent disability is determined by using the Permanent Disability Rating Schedule and an assessment of the injured worker's permanent impairment and limitations.

The Permanent Disability Rating Schedule specifies standard percentage ratings for permanent impairments and limitations, and provides for the modification of these standard ratings based on the injured worker's age and occupation. The standard rating is adjusted for age by lowering the rating for younger workers and increasing it for older workers on the theory that it is easier for younger people to adjust to a permanent handicap. The standard rating is adjusted for occupation by increasing the rating if the permanent impairment or limitation will be more of an impediment in performing the worker's occupation, and lowering the rating if it will have a lesser impact.

The assessment of the injured worker's permanent impairment and limitations is made by either the treating physician or a "Qualified Medical Evaluator" (QME). The Division of Workers' Compensation's Medical Unit appoints and regulates QME's. If there is disagreement with the treating physician's opinion and the worker is not represented by an attorney, he or she chooses a physician from a three member panel obtained from the DWC Medical Unit. If the worker is represented by an attorney, the parties must attempt to agree on a physician to perform the evaluation. If they are unable to agree, each side may obtain evaluations from a QME of their choice. If the eval-

uations are disparate, the amount of permanent disability will be determined by negotiation or, if necessary, litigation.

Vocational rehabilitation services (for injuries before Jan. 1, 2004)

Injured workers who are unable to return to their former type of work are entitled to vocational rehabilitation services if these services can reasonably be expected to return the worker to suitable gainful employment. This includes the development of a suitable plan, the cost of any training, and a maintenance allowance while participating in rehabilitation.

Once an injured worker is determined unable to return to his or her previous type of work, the employer and worker jointly select a rehabilitation counselor who will determine whether vocational rehabilitation is feasible, and if appropriate, develop a suitable rehabilitation plan. The goal of a rehabilitation plan is to return the injured worker to "suitable gainful employment"—employment or self-employment that is reasonably attainable and which offers an opportunity to restore the injured worker as soon as practicable and as near as possible to maximum self-support.

The maintenance allowance payable to an injured worker while in rehabilitation is, like temporary disability benefits, designed to replace two-thirds of lost earnings, but the maximum weekly amount is lower—$246 per week. The worker may, however, supplement the maintenance allowance with advances of permanent disability benefits up to the point where the worker is receiving the same weekly amount as he or she received in temporary disability benefits. Total costs for rehabilitation are now limited to $16,000 for workers injured on or after Jan. 1, 1994.

For dates of injury on or after Jan. 1, 2003, injured workers who have legal representation may settle vocational rehabilitation for a lump sum. Vocational rehabilitation does not apply for dates of injury after Jan. 1, 2004.

Supplemental job displacement benefit (for injuries on or after Jan. 1, 2004)

This is a nontransferable voucher for education-related retraining or skill enhancement, or both, payable to a state approved or accredited school if the worker is injured on or after Jan. 1, 2004. To qualify for this benefit, the injury must result in a permanent disability, the injured employee does not return to work within 60 days after temporary disability ends, and the employer does not offer modified or alternative work. The maxiumum voucher amount is $10,000.

Death benefits

In the event a worker is fatally injured, reasonable burial expenses, up to $5,000, are paid. In addition, the worker's dependents may receive support payments for a period of time. These payments are generally payable in the same manner and amount as temporary disability benefits, but the minimum rate of payment is $224 per week. The total aggregate amount of support payments depends on the number of dependents and the extent of their dependency. Generally, the maximum (where three or more total dependents are eligible) is $160,000, though additional benefits are payable if there continues to be any dependent children after the basic death benefit has been paid.

The benefit delivery system

Unlike most social insurance programs (e.g., social security, unemployment compensation), workers' compensation in California, as well as in most other states, is not administered by a government agency. Workers' compensation benefits are administered primarily by private parties—insurance companies authorized to transact workers' compensation and those employers secure enough to be permitted to self-insure their workers' compensation liability.

When an employer becomes aware of an on-the-job injury, the employer is expected to begin the process of providing the injured worker the benefits to which he or she is entitled under the law. The benefits are paid by either the employer (if the employer is authorized to self-insure) or the employer's insurer.

The state's role in benefit delivery is to oversee the provision of workers' compensation benefits, provide information and assistance to employees, employers, and others involved in the system, and to resolve disputes that arise in the process.

The vast majority of workers' compensation claims are handled expeditiously and are administered without dispute or litigation. These are, for the most part, the smaller claims—those in which only medical care is provided and those in which the injured worker is disabled for only a few days. These smaller claims account for more than three quarters of all workers' compensation claims.

The balance of the claims—those in which there are significant periods of disability or permanent disability—account for the vast majority of costs and litigation. In these more serious cases, litigation is common.

Most workers' compensation cases are litigated initially before workers' compensation referees employed by the Division of Workers' Compensation (DWC). Rehabilitation disputes are first heard by a consultant in the DWC Rehabilitation Unit, and that decision can be appealed to a workers' compensation referee. The decisions of workers' compensation referees are subject to reconsideration by the seven member Workers' Compensation Appeals Board (WCAB). A WCAB decision is reviewable only by the appellate courts.

Most disputed or "litigated" cases are settled without a decision being rendered by a workers' compensation referee. Most case dispositions are compromise and release settlements—settlements in which all future liability is released in return for a stipulated amount.

Applicants attorneys fees must be approved by a workers' compensation referee, and are generally 9 to 15 percent of the settlement amount. Defense attorneys' fees are not regulated.

The benefit financing system

The benefit financing system is the process by which employers finance their liability for workers' compensation benefits. Employers may finance their liability for workers' compensation benefits by one of three methods: (1) self-insurance, (2) private insurance, or (3) state insurance.

- Self-insurance—Most large, stable employers and most government agencies are self-insured for workers' compensation. To become self-insured, employers must obtain a certificate from the Department of Industrial Relations. Private employers must post security as a condition of receiving a certificate of consent to self-insure.
- Private insurance—Employers may purchase insurance from any of the approximately 300 private insurance companies which are licensed by the Department of Insurance to transact workers' compensation insurance in California. Insurance companies are free to price this insurance at a level they deem appropriate for the insurance and services provided.
- State insurance—Employers may also purchase insurance from the State Compensation Insurance Fund, a state operated entity that exists solely to transact workers' compensation insurance on a nonprofit basis. It actively competes with private insurers for business, and it also effectively operates as the assigned risk pool for workers' compensation insurance.

Special funds

In addition, there are two special funds that pay benefits to injured workers under some circumstances: (1) the Uninsured Employers Fund, and (2) the Subsequent Injuries Fund.

Uninsured Employers Fund—When an employee is injured while working for an employer who is unlawfully uninsured, and the employer fails to pay or post a bond to pay the compensation due the employee, the employee's compensation is paid from the Uninsured Employers Fund. An attempt is made to recover the amount paid from the uninsured employer.

About 1,000 to 1,500 new claims are filed with the Uninsured Employers Fund annually, at a cost that has reached about $26 million per year. Most of this cost is paid from the Uninsured Employers Benefit Trust Fund, which is financed by an annual assessment paid by all employers.

Subsequent Injuries Fund—When an employee has a previous permanent disability or impairment and sustains a subsequent injury, the employer is not liable for the combined disability, but only for that caused by the later injury. However, when the combined permanent disability is at least 70 percent and certain other criteria are met, the employee may receive additional compensation from the Subsequent Injuries Fund.

About 500 claims are filed with the Subsequent Injuries Fund per year, at a cost of about $6.5 million. Claims are paid from the Subsequent Injury Benefit Trust Fund account, into which all employers are required to pay an annual assessment.

SIGNIFICANCE

The passage of worker compensation acts such as the California Workers' Compensation System significantly leveled the playing field between companies and employees, placing the burden for insuring a safe workplace largely on the employer's shoulders. The addition of no-fault recovery, which made employers liable for most workplace injuries regardless of cause, created tremendous incentive for employers to improve workplace safety. As a result, companies began investing heavily in safety equipment and training, as well as instituting penalties for workers who did not comply with established safety procedures.

Typical worker compensation systems today include several categories of benefits. In most cases, an employee temporarily unable to work will receive a percentage of his normal salary until he is able to return. For permanently disabled employees, a benefit amount and length of payment is determined based on the degree of disability. Rehabilitation services are also frequently included to assist employees in returning to work. In cases of employee death, compensation typically includes funeral expenses and support payments for a set period of time.

Workplace safety improved markedly throughout the twentieth century, though regulation and enforcement was far tighter in some states than in others. In 1970, the U.S. Congress, finding that workplace injuries and illnesses created a substantial drain on the economy, passed the Occupational Safety and Health Act. This act authorized the Department of Labor to enact federal health and safety standards for all industries involved in interstate commerce and to provide penalties for employers who violated them. It further created the Occupational Safety and Health Administration (OSHA) to administer and enforce workplace safety regulations.

Today, OSHA is the primary agency responsible for workplace safety in the United States. Its inspectors visit workplaces following major accidents and in response to employee complaints. OSHA proactively schedules inspections at facilities that are found to have injury or illness rates above the national average. The agency also targets specific industries for inspection based on their assessed risk level. In 2005, for example, OSHA fined BP Products North America a record $21 million for violations related to an oil refinery explosion which killed fifteen.

FURTHER RESOURCES

Books

Charney, William, and Guy Fragala, eds. *The Epidemic of Health Care Worker Injury: An Epidemiology.* Boca Raton, Florida: CRC Press, 1999.

Herlick, Stanford D. *California Workers' Compensation Handbook.* Lexis Law Publications, 2002.

Sall, Richard D. *Strategies in Workers' Compensation.* Lanham, MD: Hamilton Books, 2004.

Periodicals

Editor. "Easy Stuff, Government." *Economist.* 371 (April 22, 2004): 31.

Kahley, William J., and Edward C. Woodward. "Workers' Compensation in California: Recent Performance and Outlook." *Benefits Quarterly.* 13(1997):34–40.

LaDou, Joseph, Lawrence Mulryan, and Kevin McCarthy. "Cumulative Injury of Disease Claims: An Attempt to Define Employers' Liability for Workers' Compensation." *American Journal of Law & Medicine.* 6(1980):1–28.

Web sites

California State Government. "Divison of Workers' Compensation." <http://www.dir.ca.gov/dwc/dwc_home_page. htm> (accessed June 1,2006).

Rand Corporation. "California's Workers' Compensation Permanent Disability Rating System: A Pre-Reform and Post-Reform Evaluation." 2005 <http://www.rand. org/pubs/research_briefs/RB9163/index1.html> (accessed June 1,2006).

University of California at Berkeley. Labor Occupational Health Program. "Workers' Compensation." <http:// ist-socrates.berkeley.edu/~lohp/Projects/Workers__ Compensation/workers__compensation.html> (accessed June 1, 2006).

Safety and Stability for Foster Children

The Policy Context

Journal Article

By: MaryLee Allen and Mary Bissell

Date: 2004

Source: Allen, MaryLee, and Mary Bissell. "Safety and Stability for Foster Children: The Policy Context." *Future of Children* (2004).

About the Author: MaryLee Allen is director of the Child Welfare and Mental Health division of the Children's Defense Fund. She has played a significant role in child welfare and children's mental health reforms over the last two decades. Mary Bissell is a senior staff attorney in the Children's Defense Fund. She is a policy expert on child welfare and kinship care issues. Bissell has written extensively on the issue of child welfare in the United States.

INTRODUCTION

The child welfare system in the United States involves a collaborative effort between multiple federal, state, and local government agencies; the juvenile and family courts; and community-based, private social services agencies. The primary responsibility to enforce legal and administrative policies related to child welfare lies with the local government of each state. However, the federal government establishes the framework for these policies.

The federal regulatory agency for child welfare programs (including foster care programs) is known as the Department of Health and Human Services (HHS). In addition, there are other federal agencies such as the Department of Justice that also fund related programs.

Foster Care programs were first constituted in the United States in the mid-nineteenth century. In 1868, the Massachusetts Board of State Charities began a movement to place illegitimate, orphaned, or poor children in private homes rather than in institutions. The New York State Charities Aid Association, set up in 1872, was one of the first organizations in the country that formulated a specific child-placement program in 1898. A few years later in 1912, the United States Children's Bureau became the first federal body that addressed child welfare issues. By 1922, over 3,300 despondent children had been provided a safe haven, or in other words—a foster home. The Social Security Act of 1935, considered the foundation of subsequent social welfare programs, was then framed. It included various programs such as child welfare and provisions to aid disabled children, eventually leading to the expansion of foster care.

Federal funds were provided under this Act to children in poverty-stricken families, as well as those who were abused, neglected, and abandoned. Two years later, the Child Welfare League of America, which laid down minimum standards for adoptive and foster placements, was established. In the following years, several foster care programs were initiated across the country. Foster care, though beneficial, was not strictly regulated. Several concerns such as child abuse were also raised. Subsequently, in 1974, the U.S. Congress passed the Child Abuse Protection and Treatment Act that required states to enforce child abuse reporting laws. In order to further strengthen the child welfare system, Congress formulated the Adoption Assistance and Child Welfare Act in 1980 to establish the framework for the modern child welfare system.

The number of children in foster care grew between 1980 and 2000. According to HHS, there were 260,000 children in foster care in the 1980s compared to 550,000 in 2000. Simultaneously, the number of child abuse and neglect cases also increased, and foster care programs that were mainly dependent on charitable donations experienced lack of funding. There were also several reports that not enough measures were taken to ensure that good families adopted children in foster care.

In November 1997, U.S. President Bill Clinton signed into law the Adoption and Safe Families Act (ASFA). This Act focused on three main issues—emphasizing the safety and well-being of children in foster care, the duration of stays in foster care, and increasing adoption opportunities for children who were abused and neglected. In the following years, many have recommended reforms to strengthen the ASFA further.

PRIMARY SOURCE

SAFETY AND STABILITY FOR FOSTER CHILDREN: THE POLICY CONTEXT

The Current Policy Framework

Federal law has had a major influence on the foster care and child welfare policy framework for more than 40 years. But there was no federal foster care program until 1961, when the Aid to Families with Dependent Children (AFDC) Foster Care Program was established to care for children who could not safely remain with their families receiving AFDC. Nearly 20 years then passed before Congress undertook a comprehensive look at the general structure of federal funding for children who were abused and neglected. Congress was responding to both national and state reports documenting the crisis in child welfare systems and the disincentives in federal law to maintain or find new permanent homes for children and to hold states accountable for the care children received. Up until that time, there had been only perfunctory case reviews of children in care and little attention to tracking the progress of children. But in 1980, a new framework for foster care was created with passage of the Adoption Assistance and Child Welfare Act (AACWA). Since then, several pieces of legislation building on this basic framework have been enacted—most notably, the Adoption and Safe Families Act of 1997 (ASFA).

Recommendations for Future Policy Reform

The impetus for the reforms in the foster care and the child welfare policy framework has been consistent over the years, with major policy changes being driven by the same four concerns: children languishing in care, child safety, the adequacy of services, and system accountability. Despite improvements, child welfare systems across the country are still in crisis, and barriers to reform remain. Why are more than 550,000 children currently in foster care? Why has there been so little progress in getting children and families the help they need? What are the barriers to real reform for these children? It is difficult to talk about reform of foster care without addressing reform of the broader child welfare system. Foster care is a key piece, but just one of many pieces, in the continuum of services and supports that must be in place as communities work to find safe and stable families for maltreated children.

Eliminating Child Poverty

Any serious effort to strengthen the policy framework for child welfare and foster care first must acknowledge the overriding importance of eliminating child poverty. Poor children are more likely than higher-income children to be reported as abused and neglected. Because of the enormous stresses on their families, families' difficulties in obtaining appropriate services such as health care and housing, and families' increased interaction with public systems, these children are more likely to come to the attention of the child welfare system. Poor children are also disproportionately children of color, who are overrepresented in the child welfare system and are more likely to stay in the child welfare system for long periods. Advocates, providers, and policymakers must pursue reforms that will eliminate child poverty and provide all children the health care, early childhood experiences, educational opportunities, and safe homes that

they need to grow and thrive. Achieving these goals will have a major impact on the challenges facing the child welfare system and the children and families it serves.

With the elimination of child poverty as an overarching goal, the driving force behind any future policy reforms in child welfare must be to establish a policy framework that will support a child-centered, family-focused, community-based approach to keeping children safe and in permanent families. Within such a framework, several additional policy reforms in the broader child welfare system could have a positive impact on the future of foster care, as discussed below.

Redirecting Funding Incentives and Increasing Funding Levels

Major alterations in current funding patterns are needed to support important reforms such as enhanced safety and permanence for children. Although federal and state dollars are generally available to keep children in foster care, the dollars often are not there to support children safely within their own families and prevent foster care placements, to serve children in foster care and their families, or to move children into permanent placements in a timely fashion. Consequently, as noted by the Urban Institute, which regularly reviews child welfare spending, "The federal system is not in alignment with the goals of protecting children and providing stable, permanent placements." The federal foster care program provides open-ended funding for the room and board of certain eligible children in foster care, but only very limited funding for the development of alternative services for abused and neglected children and their families, both before a child must be placed in foster care or after a child returns home following placement. As a result, out-of-home care is often the easiest option for workers besieged with large caseloads and few other resources… Further efforts are needed to redirect the funding incentives within foster care. The lack of sufficient funding at both the federal and state levels for ongoing services for children at risk of entering foster care, those in foster care, or those preparing to leave foster care makes it impossible for states to fully comply with the expedited timelines required by ASFA. Changes must involve both increased resources for states and Indian tribal organizations and increased flexibility. Any new funding patterns must accomplish at least three goals:

- Expanded services to keep children safely at home, to facilitate more timely decisions about reunification or other permanent placements, and to prevent children from returning to foster care after they are returned to their families, adopted, or placed permanently with kin.
- Expanded permanency options for children in care through federal support for subsidized guardianship programs and enhanced adoption assistance pay-

ments.

- Eligibility for federal foster care funding and related services based on children's risk of abuse or neglect rather than their parents' financial status.

Improving the Quality of Care for Children and Families

In too many states, neither the child welfare agencies nor the courts have the trained staff, skills, or resources necessary to make decisions about the care and treatment that is appropriate to meet the individual needs of children and their families. A recent General Accounting Office report on the implementation of ASFA found that judges and other court staff were in short supply, training was not available, and judges were somewhat reluctant to move forward as quickly as required under the law. In particular, the lack of appropriate substance abuse treatment programs was identified as a barrier to meeting the ASFA timelines for parents. Some of the biggest service gaps are in the areas of treatment and services for the substance abuse, mental health, and domestic violence problems that so often bring children to the attention of the foster care system and keep them there. These gaps exist because of both the lack of funding for specialized services and the lack of coordination among child-serving systems. They are exacerbated by the failure of agencies to engage families and communities as partners in their mission to protect children. In one national survey, about one third of state agency administrators cited the lack of resources as a barrier to meeting ASFA's time frames. The lack of substance abuse treatment for parents and the fact that child welfare agencies were dependent on outside agencies for needed services were noted as particular problems. Often, families are not asked what they need or are not treated as partners in helping to keep their children safe. Caseloads are overwhelming, procedural timelines are tight, and families' needs are complex. "One size fits all" is too frequently the solution, despite a policy framework that encourages more individualized services.

Services and supports needed to find adoptive families for children in foster care and to ensure that adoptions are permanent are also lacking. With ASFA's new emphasis on termination of parental rights, there is serious concern that many more children may end up as "legal orphans." For example, as of September 30, 2000, some 131,000 children in foster care were waiting to be adopted; 75,000 of these children had had their parental rights terminated and had waited an average of almost two years for adoption. Once children are adopted, there is continuing concern that they will bounce back into foster care without adequate postadoption services to ensure that their needs are met.

Increasing Accountability for Children and Families

The child welfare system has had to struggle with the constant tension between state discretion, federal accountability, and the need for enforcement of basic protections for children.

Increased accountability is needed. It should build on the Child and Family Service Reviews and give states incentives to increase protections for children; improve services and supports for children and families, including those children in foster care; and promptly provide permanent families for children through reunification, adoption, or permanent placements with kinship caregivers. Specific changes should include:

- Funding for Program Improvement Grants to states that are committed to achieving the goals in their Program Improvement Plans and are engaging parents; foster and adoptive parents; advocates; and representatives of the courts, multiple service agencies, and other stakeholders in their program improvement efforts.
- A requirement that states document the steps they are taking with increased funds to improve outcomes for children; enhance the recruitment, retention, and training of staff; alter their service-delivery strategies to partner with families and engage communities in new ways; and address the disproportionate placement of children of color in foster care.
- Incentives for states to develop improved administrative data systems to track the movement of children in and out of care. Such systems will help states monitor children in care over time and know more about who the children are, how long they are staying, what help they are getting, and what they really need to move on to permanent settings without returning to foster care.
- External review bodies in the states, such as foster care review boards, child protection review committees, and courts, to report regularly to DHHS about barriers to safety and permanence that they see facing children in foster care and the child welfare system and to recommend solutions for addressing the barriers.

In its efforts to address specific concerns facing children in the child welfare system, Congress has repeatedly failed to fully understand the complexity of the system and the external and internal services and supports needed to fully realize its intended goals for children and families. A policy framework has been established, but significant gaps remain in services and funding levels and in balancing fiscal incentives. As we look forward to improving the quality of life for children and ensuring them safe and stable families, we must constantly assess what we are doing and what we still need to do to overcome the barriers to reform and to implement real change.

SIGNIFICANCE

The Adoption and Safe Families Act of 1997 is widely acknowledged to be a defining legislation that made significant changes to the existing child welfare provisions. Proponents of ASFA viewed it as an Act that would dramatically change the child welfare system by making the children safer and ensuring prompt permanent adoption. However, according to the critics, there are certain fundamental issues with the child welfare system that have been ignored by the Act. Some of these issues are interaction of the ASFA with the judiciary system, other child welfare laws, local and state child welfare authorities, and providing sufficient incentives to children and their families.

Additionally, there are issues such as continuing maltreatment of children in their families and subsequently in foster homes as well. According to the Department of Health and Human Services the cases of malnutrition in families, and in foster homes continues unabated. The ASFA has also been embroiled in another controversy. The Act introduced an incentive system for states—a state would receive four thousand dollars (in federal funds) for every foster care adoption that exceeded the base number of adoptions for a fiscal year. For instance, if the base number of foster care adoptions for a state was one thousand in a year, and if the actual foster care adoptions were 1,002, the state would receive eight thousand dollars as incentive. Subsequently, parents of children sent to foster care have accused state governments of encouraging adoption for monetary gain.

Nevertheless, the ASFA is deemed successful by most. According to the HHS, the overall child abuse and neglect incidence rate had declined to 12.9 per one thousand children, the lowest rate in ten years. U.S. President George Bush pointed out in 2003 that from 1998 to 2002, states placed more than 230,000 children in adoptive homes—about the same number that had been adopted in the previous ten years. Also, since the implementation of the Act, adoptions from foster care had increased nationwide by fifty-seven percent. Advocates of the ASFA state that the above-mentioned statistics indicate that the act has been successful in addressing its key objectives—reducing cases of child abuse and providing more opportunities for children to be adopted from foster care.

Several proposals to restructure child welfare financing have been introduced since the ASFA became law. Lawmakers suggest that the ultimate aim should be to ensure that the child gets a safe and secure permanent home as quickly as possible. To this effect, recommendations have been made to streamline the process of adoption of children in foster care, to maintain their safety and well being, and to ensure their healthy transition into adulthood.

FURTHER RESOURCES

Books

Reitz, Miriam and Kenneth W. Watson. *Adoption and the Family System: Strategies for Treatment.* New York: The Guilford Press, 1992.

Web sites

The Adoption History Project, University of Oregon. "Timeline of Adoption History." June 22, 2005. <http://darkwing.uoregon.edu/~adoption/timeline.html> (accessed June 5, 2006).

Court Appointed Special Advisors for Children. "Adoption and Safe Families Act: Has It Made a Difference?" September 2003. <http://www.casanet.org/library/adoption/asfa-has-made-a-difference.htm> (accessed June 5, 2006).

U.S. Department of Health & Human Services. "Foster Care: Numbers and Trends." 2005. <http://nccanch.acf.hhs.gov/pubs/factsheets/foster.cfm> (accessed June 5, 2006).

Twinkle, Twinkle Little Star

(Resung by Science)

Advertisement

By: Kaplan Thaler Group

Date: April 5, 2004

Source: "Twinkle, Twinkle"—The Kaplan Thaler Group. http://www.adcouncil.org/files/mathgirls_twinkle_nwsp.jpg (accessed May 20, 2006).

About the Artist: Kaplan Thaler Group is an United States-based advertising corporation. Kaplan Thaler Group donates time and resources to create public service announcements in conjunction with non-profit agencies and the Ad Council. The Advertising Council, or Ad Council, founded in 1942, is a private, non-profit organization that coordinates volunteers from the advertising and media organizations to create public service announcements for U.S. audiences. Kaplan Thaler Group, The Ad Council, and the Girl Scouts

PRIMARY SOURCE

"Twinkle, Twinkle, Little Star" **(Resung by Science):** A public service advertisement urging parents to combat gender stereotyping and encourage interest in math and science among girls.   "TWINKLE, TWINKLE" — THE KAPLAN THALER GROUP.

of the United States of America created the public serive announcement that appears here as part of the "Girls Go Tech—Girl Scouts and Math, Science, and Technology," program to raise awareness of the number of jobs that require technical skills. The Girl Scouts program is designed to use hands-on experiences with math, science, and technology to enhance innate abilities in those areas, and to stimulate girls' interests in pursuing nontraditional careers and personal options.

INTRODUCTION

Based on data published by the National Science Foundation, women represent only about one-quarter of the technology workforce. Girls and young women have traditionally been discouraged from pursuing study and employment in the sciences, math, and technology, based on a long-held belief that they are inherently less able in these fields than males, and that they are more capable of achieving success in the liberal, fine, and performing arts, education, or the social ("soft") sciences.

According to the "Twinkle, Twinkle" and similar ads, sponsored jointly by the Ad Council and the Girl Scouts, girls' interest in math and science has begun to wane—either from lack of exposure or because they have been led to believe that they are less able to succeed in those disciplines. The ad campaign hopes to counter those potential pitfalls and to enlist family support in fostering curiosity, inquisitiveness, and a love of learning—in all areas of study.

From the earliest days of Girl Scouting, founder Juliette Low encouraged girls and young women to pursue careers traditionally dominated by men. Some of the earliest Girl Scout badges concerned the professions of economist and businesswoman, both of which ran counter to the social and occupational mores of the day. Modern Girl Scouting builds on that tradition to engage girls with math, science, technology, and engineering concepts. The goal is both to broaden and enlarge the girls' skill bases and to raise their self-confidence and awareness of their innate intelligence, aptitudes, and abilities in the sciences, math, technology, and engineering.

The Girl Scouts have partnered with a variety of different organizations in an effort to raise skill levels and technological awareness. The Intel Foundation is one corporate partner that uses an experiential curriculum that offers girls the opportunity to explore their interests in science, technology, and engineering by participating with female mentors who are professionals in those fields.

"TWINKLE, TWINKLE, LITTLE STAR" (RESUNG BY SCIENCE)
See primary source image.

SIGNIFICANCE

Other program sponsors are the Lucent Technologies Foundation, which offers a home-based study and support program that suggests simple and inexpensive projects made from materials typically found around the house. Another sponsor, the NASDAQ Educational Foundation, funds programs in which girls create, build, and maintain imaginary investment portfolios by engaging in mock stock trades. The Institute of Electrical and Electronics Engineers (IEEE) promotes the emeritbadges program, which study the methods by which girls are best engaged in learning about technology. The next project phase will involve the design and implementation of gender-and age-appropriate tools and study programs with which to increase girls' technological understanding. The overarching goal is to increase the number of girls and young women entering the science, engineering, and technological occupations.

According to the National Science Foundation (NSF) data, women currently make up nearly fifty percent of the overall work force but hold only about one-fourth of the jobs in technology, and make up only about ten percent of the highest echelon technology positions. NSF data suggests that career paths are often set before the end of elementary school, with many girls steered away from scientific, engineering, or technological professions before they even reach adolescence. Girls Go Tech hopes to change those statistics, and to encourage girls and young women to create new career trajectories, and to pursue paths that will set the stage for a future workforce that is both more gender balanced and more diverse in its makeup.

In an effort to circumvent some of the subtle (and not-so-subtle) gender bias that can still be found within the public school system, several independent all-girls schools emphasizing the study of math, science, and technology have sprung up during the past decade. Research suggests that girls perform considerably better, and express significantly keener interests and aptitudes for the sciences when they attend same-gender schools. Although high school girls' national test scores have begun to catch up to boys' in math and science, they still lag far behind in the area of technology.

There is a growing economic need to close the gender gap in technological occupations as well, since single mothers head a significant proportion of Amer-

James Madison Middle School student Blair Ellis, left, turns to watch teacher Dana Ball explain the class's assignment in this all-girl language arts class on Monday, August 23, 2004, in Madisonville, Kentucky. The class is part of a new program where students are separated by gender for some core classes. AP IMAGES.

ican households. At the start of the twenty-first century, women constituted about half of the labor market, but earned only about 18% of the doctorates in computer science, and just over 10% of the doctorates in engineering earned in any given year. Women represent less than one-quarter of all of the scientists and engineers in the current workforce.

Girls whose interest in science, math, and technology is sparked at an early age, and who are encouraged to pursue their curiosity to the point of success, are more likely to continue to explore those areas, and to pursue advanced education in them. Teaching methods that encourage *all* students are the most likely to lead to sustained interest, and can pave the way to narrowing the gender gap in the technological fields.

FURTHER RESOURCES

Books

American Association of University Women. *Tech-Savvy: Educating Girls in the New Computer Age*. Washington, DC: AAUW Educational Foundation, 2000.

Driscoll, Catherine. *Girls: Feminine Adolescence in Popular Culture and Cultural Theory*. New York: Columbia University Press, 2002.

Margolis, Jane, and Allan Fisher. *Unlocking the Clubhouse: Women in Computing*. Cambridge, Mass.: MIT Press, 2002.

National Science Foundation. *Women, Minorities, and Persons with Disabilities in Science and Engineering: 1998*. Arlington, Virginia: National Science Foundation, 1999.

Periodicals

Crombie, Gail, and P.I. Armstrong. "Effects of Classroom Gender Composition on Adolescents' Computer

Related Attitudes and Future Intentions." *Journal of Educational Computing Research.* 20, no. 4 (1999): 317–327.

Denner, Jill, Linda Werner, Steve Bean, and Shannon Campe. "The Girls Creating Games Program: Strategies for Engaging Middle-School Girls in Information Technology." *Frontiers: A Journal of Women's Studies.* 26, no. 1 (2005):90–92.

Hafner, Katie. "Girls Soak up Technology in Schools of Their Own." *New York Times.* September 23, 1999.

Keller, Johannes. "Blatant Stereotype Threat and Women's Math Performance: Self-Handicapping as a Strategic Means to Cope with Obtrusive Negative Performance Expectations." *Sex Roles.* 47(2002): 193–198.

Liu, Min, and Yu-Ping Hsaio. "Middle School Students as Multimedia Designers: A Look at Their Cognitive Skills Development." *Journal of Interactive Learning Research.* 1 (2002): 1139–1144.

Web sites

Girl Scouts—Girls Go Tech. "Girls in Science, Technology, and Math." <http://www.girlsgotech.org/girls_go_tech.html> (accessed May 20, 2006).

Girl Scouts. "About Girl Scouts of the USA." <http://www.girlscouts.org/who_we_are/> (accessed May 20, 2006).

IEEE. "Girls & Technology." <http://www.emeritbadges.org/girls_and_technology.htm> (accessed May 20, 2006).

Whatever It Takes, Don't Let Your Friends Drop Out

Photograph

By: JWT

Date: 2005

Source: "Bus," JWT, New York. <http://staging.adcouncil.org/files/hs_dropout_bus_ooh.jpg> (accessed June 23, 2006).

About the Artist: This advertisement was produced for the Ad Council by JWT. JWT, formerly known as the J. Walter Thompson Company, is the oldest advertising agency in the world and one of the largest, and is responsible for many famous campaigns, slogans, and brands. Since 1942, the Ad Council has been a leading producer of public service announcements for numerous causes. The Council harnesses a variety of creative and professional resources to produce and distribute messages dealing with social issues such as education, healthcare, and communities.

INTRODUCTION

Public schools existed in North America before the United States was founded. The first public school opened in a Boston schoolmaster's home in 1635, and by the dawn of the twenty-first century American public schools served more than fifty million students each year. Education in America has generally been provided as a public service offered free to all children and made mandatory for those of appropriate age.

Early in the nation's history, law enforcement officials observed that truancy, or skipping school, appeared to be well correlated with criminal behavior. One early criminologist, writing in 1915, noted that roughly one-fourth of the young men appearing in court had a history of truancy. A 1942 study in Chicago mapped juvenile delinquency and truancy, comparing the two and finding a high correlation. A 1979 study of repeat criminal offenders found that more than three of four offenders had criminal records that began with truancy charges.

Not surprisingly, successful attempts to reduce truancy frequently reduce juvenile crime as well. A concerted effort in Inglewood, California to reduce truancy was accompanied by a thirty percent drop in daytime burglaries and a sixty percent decrease in vehicle burglaries; a similar push by combined law enforcement agencies from four other California cities produced similar results. Yet despite several decades of data pointing to a relationship between truancy and crime, local law enforcement officials frequently dismiss truancy as a minor problem, devoting few resources to combating it.

Beyond demonstrated reductions in crime, communities also reap other benefits when students attend school. State school funding is frequently tied to attendance, meaning that each student who skips school costs the local school system a set amount of money. School systems facing tight finances have tremendous incentive to ensure that students show up for class, though many systems struggle with how to achieve this objective.

The biggest losers when teens quit school are usually the teens themselves. High school dropouts earn less than their diploma-holding peers, and the difference is growing. From 1980 to 2000, average earnings for high school dropouts doubled, while annual incomes for high school graduates tripled. When inflation is factored in and constant (2002) dollars are

PRIMARY SOURCE

Whatever It Takes, Don't Let Your Friends Drop Out: An advertisement from the Operation Graduation Campaign encourages students to put pressure on their peers to stay in school. "BUS," JWT, NEW YORK.

used, male dropouts experienced a stunning thirty-five percent decline in earnings, from $35,087 in 1971 to just $23,903 in 2002. Female dropouts saw their earnings fall from almost $20,000 per year to just over $17,000 in the same period.

Despite the many problems associated with dropping out of school and the extensive efforts devoted to reducing dropout rates, recent research suggests the problem may actually be growing worse. In 2005, the Education Testing Service (ETS) released a report examining the current state of high school completion in the United States. The report estimated that high school completion rates peaked at 77.1 percent in 1969 and have fallen ever since, dropping below 70 percent in 2000. Most states continued to experience falling completion rates during the 1990s; the District of Columbia had the lowest completion rate, forty-eight percent, while Vermont had the highest at eighty-eight pecent.

The study found that three primary factors predict dropout rates: socioeconomic charactistics such as household income; the number of parents in the home; and the number of times a student has previously changed schools. Though these factors are often beyond the control of social service agencies, the report notes that a variety of alternative programs and intervention efforts have shown promising results in

reducing dropout rates. However, the report also echoes previous studies with its prediction that dropouts will generally face sporadic employment in low-paying jobs and that many will leave the workforce entirely.

PRIMARY SOURCE

WHATEVER IT TAKES, DON'T LET YOUR FRIENDS DROP OUT
See primary source image.

SIGNIFICANCE

Among the critical problems noted in the ETS report is a shortage of counselors who can provide individual guidance for at-risk teens. A campaign called Boost, cosponsored by the U.S. Army and produced by the Ad Council, encourages at-risk teens, along with their friends and family members, to work together toward school completion. By enlisting a teen's friends and family as supporters, the effort hopes to provide at-risk teens with a level of personal attention that formal programs cannot.

While the military has long been viewed as an alternative for non-college bound students, the service's increasingly technical equipment requires a higher basic level of education among soldiers, and the military has found itself providing an increasing volume of remedial education for recruits. For this reason, the military has chosen to become involved in efforts to promote basic education, in the hopes that the quality of its recruiting pool will improve.

FURTHER RESOURCES

Books

Kronick, Robert F., and Charles Harquis. *Droputs: Who Drops Out and Why—And the Recommended Action.* Springfield, Ill.: Charles C. Thomas, 1998.

Orfield, Gary, ed. *Dropouts in America: Confronting the Graduation Rate Crisis.* Cambridge, Mass.: Harvard Education Press, 2004.

Schargel, Franklin, and Jay Smink. *Strategies to Help Solve Our School Dropout Problem.* Larchmont, N.Y: Eye on Education, 2001.

Periodicals

Greene, Jay R., et al. "Missing the Mark on Graduation Rates." *Education Week* 25 (2006): 39–42.

Robertson, Heather-Jane. "Dropouts or Leftouts? School Leavers in Canada." *Phi Delta Kappan* 87 (2006): 715–717.

Simpson, John B. "A lifeline to high school dropouts." *Christian Science Monitor* 98 (2006): 9.

Web sites

Ad Council. "High School Dropout Prevention." <http://www.adcouncil.org/default.aspx?id=34> (accessed June 24, 2006).

Educational Testing Service. "One-Third of a Nation: Rising Dropout Rates and Declining Opportunities." 2005 <http://www.ets.org/Media/Education_Topics/pdf/onethird.pdf> (accessed June 24, 2006).

Federal Bureau of Investigation. "Truancy: Not Just Kids' Stuff Anymore." <http://www.fbi.gov/publications/leb/1997/mar972.htm> (accessed June 24, 2006).

For Parents Seeking a Choice, Charter Schools Prove More Popular Than Vouchers

Newspaper article

By: Sam Dillon

Date: July 13, 2005

Source: Dillon, Sam. "For Parents Seeking a Choice, Charter Schools Prove More Popular Than Vouchers." *New York Times* (13 July 2005): B8.

About the Author: Sam Dillon won the Pulitzer Prize for reporting on the drug trade in Mexico; he currently writes on issues related to education for the *New York Times.*

INTRODUCTION

In 1988, then-president of the union American Federation of Teachers, Albert Shanker, called for massive reform in public education via the establishment of a "charter" school, a school designed by teachers or other educators that involves a contract with local authorities. The charter school movement began in 1991 in Minnesota with the passage of a law permitting such schools to open; the first, City Academy in St. Paul, received a charter exempting the school from local or state regulations, to allow the school to provide an alternative educational experience for students while being supported by taxpayer dollars.

A charter school can be public or private, though in common terms a charter school denotes a publicly funded school that operates outside of standard government regulations. Each charter school must outline its educational goals to justify exemption from standard local and state regulation; failure to meet these goals over an established period of time can lead to the closing of the charter school.

Unlike private schools, public charter schools receive taxpayer dollars. In some states, such as Massachusetts, charter schools are allotted the same per-pupil amount granted to traditional public schools, but typically do not receive additional funds for buildings and capital expenses; therefore, the charter school must operate under a much tighter budget than a traditional public school. From the establishment of the City Academy of St. Paul in 1992 through the year 2006, the charter school movement has grown to include more than 3,600 schools in more than forty U.S. states.

Charter schools can be organized around educational philosophies such as Waldorf, Montessori, or Reggio Emilia; around particular concentrations such as drama and performing arts, math and science, or foreign language; or managed by for-profit institutions such as SABIS, Inc. or The Edison Project.

At the same time that charter schools gained in popularity, the concept of vouchers—a set amount of money per pupil to be used by parents at the school of choice, public or private—became popular as well.

On October 11, 2005, Claudia Prada, left, teaches Spanish to eighth graders at View Park Prep Charter School in South Los Angeles. AP IMAGES.

School choice, which allows parents to send their child to any public school within their state, has been available in some states such as Vermont since the late 1800s. However, the current voucher movement proposes that state and local tax dollars would be portable and could be spent on any school—including religious private schools.

As noted in the primary source, school choice, vouchers, and charter schools provide a wide array of opportunities for parents and students in some areas, a sharp change from the traditional school policies of previous decades.

PRIMARY SOURCE

CLEVELAND—When Ohio enacted a pilot program of school vouchers here a decade ago, David Brennan, an Ohio businessman, quickly founded two schools for voucher students.

Three years later, with voucher programs under attack, Mr. Brennan closed the schools and reopened them as charter schools, another educational experiment gaining momentum at the time.

That decision reflected the fortunes of the two parallel school choice movements that once shared the cutting edge of the nation's school reform efforts. Charter schools, which are publicly financed but privately administered, have proliferated across the nation, with 3,300 such schools now educating nearly one million students in 40 states. In contrast, voucher programs, which use taxpayer funds to pay tuition at private schools, serve only about 36,000 students in Ohio, Florida, Wisconsin and Washington, D.C.

"Vouchers are moving slowly," said Paul T. Hill, a professor who studies school choice as director of the University of Washington's Center on Reinventing Public Education. "The American people don't want a complete free market in education. They want some government oversight of taxpayer-funded schools."

Last month voucher advocates achieved a rare victory when the Republican-dominated Ohio legislature created 14,000 new publicly financed "scholarships" or vouchers to allow students in failing public schools to attend private schools. That will make Ohio's voucher program, which began in 1996 with the Cleveland pilot program, the largest in the country. Earlier this spring the Utah Legislature also created a small voucher program that will allow disabled students to study at private schools at public expense.

But those twin victories were the meager results from the most ambitious legislative campaign yet by voucher advocates. Republicans introduced proposals in more than 30 legislatures for voucher or tuition tax credits, an arrangement under which parents receive a subsidy for children's private schooling through the tax code rather than as a direct grant. Vouchers were defeated in Florida, South Carolina, Texas, Indiana and Missouri.

Still, in the view of voucher proponents, the legislative sessions brought significant advances, and they are celebrating, especially because this is the 50th anniversary of the 1955 essay in which University of Chicago economist Milton Friedman suggested the use of vouchers.

In an interview, Dr. Friedman, now 93, said he believed that vouchers would eventually become more widespread than charter schools. But he acknowledged disappointment with vouchers' modest growth. "My personal belief is that the rapid expansion of charter schools will be a short-lived phenomenon, because they are only a halfway solution," Dr. Friedman said.

Many voucher students attend parochial schools like St. Agatha-St. Aloysius, housed in a crumbling brick hulk of a building on Cleveland's East Side. The neighborhood has changed much, from mostly Irish-American to mostly black, but the school, where Sister Sandra Soho has been a teacher or principal for 35 years, has not. Boys wear white shirts and ties, shelves in the basement library are stocked with trophies won by teams a half-century ago, discipline is strict and daily homework is a given.

Charter schools here and elsewhere encompass a range of curriculums and styles. The several Hope Academies in Cleveland, managed by Mr. Brennan's company, follow a back-to-basics approach. Some charter schools, like the City Day Community School in Dayton, are intimate academies. Others are technology-rich, where students take notes in class on computers.

Legislative debates over voucher programs and charter schools have tended to become fierce political brawls. "The entire educational establishment—the unions, the administrators, the school boards—is opposed to vouchers," said Kent Grusendorf, a Republican Texas state representative who chairs the House Education Committee.

Several Republican lawmakers voted with Democrats to defeat a voucher proposal in Texas last month. "This is one area where management and unions work in perfect unison," Mr. Grusendorf said.

The nation's first voucher program and its first charter schools began at about the same time. In 1990, Wisconsin enacted the first voucher program, in Milwaukee. A year later, Minnesota voted the nation's first charter school law. Many legislatures approved charter schools because they seemed less radical and aroused less opposition than vouchers, said Clint Bolick, president of the Alliance for School Choice, a Phoenix-based group.

"Charters are glasnost and vouchers are perestroika," Mr. Bolick said, referring to Mikhail Gorbachev's twin reform policies in the Soviet Union, the former a halfway measure of openness, the latter a more radical restructuring. "The educational establishment has been willing to allow charters in some states just to forestall vouchers."

As an example, he cited Arizona, where in 1995 lawmakers came within a few votes of enacting a broad voucher program. Instead, the Legislature passed a law that has made it easier to create charter schools there than anywhere else in the nation. Arizona now has 500 charter schools, but no voucher program. This year, the Legislature enacted a tuition tax credit, but Gov. Janet Napolitano, a Democrat, vetoed it.

Voters got a chance to give their opinions on voucher programs in 2000, when proponents succeeded in getting initiatives on the ballot in California and Michigan. That year voucher programs got much positive publicity when George W. Bush spoke in favor of them during his presidential campaign. But voters overwhelmingly rejected the two state proposals that November.

Ohio launched its pilot voucher program in Cleveland in 1996, offering taxpayer-financed "scholarships" to about 2,000 students. By this past school year, the program had grown to about 5,600 students attending 44 private schools.

Also over the past decade, more than 200 charter schools have been started in Ohio. Mr. Brennan, the businessman who opened and then closed the two voucher schools in Cleveland, today runs 34 profit-making charter schools across Ohio.

The Cleveland voucher program has become quite popular, especially with black parents like Andrea Holland. Black children make up about half of the city's voucher school students.

Ms. Holland, who runs an electrical contracting business with her husband, enrolled their son Jonathan, 13, at St. Agatha-St. Aloysius parochial school two years ago, transferring him from a public elementary school where he had faced bullying, she said.

"I'm not otherwise able, like rich folks, to take my kid out and put him into a private school," Ms. Holland said. "But with this program I can afford to."

Kim Metcalf, an education researcher who conducted a nine-year study of the Cleveland voucher program, concluded that average achievement levels of Cleveland's voucher students were in some instances significantly higher, and were never lower, than those of students in the Cleveland public schools. In contrast, achievement levels at most of Cleveland's charter schools were somewhat lower than in Cleveland's traditional public schools with similar student populations, according to a 2003 study by Ohio's Legislative Office of Education Oversight, a nonpartisan agency.

Because voucher programs divert tax dollars from public to private schools that are not subject to the same government accountability measures—standardized tests, for example—both national teachers' unions, the American Federation of Teachers and the National Education Association, oppose them. Officially, at least, the unions support charter schools, as long as they are governed by nonprofit groups, are held accountable for student achievement and meet other criteria. In New York City, the United Federation of Teachers is working to start its own charter schools.

In states like Ohio that permit private companies to govern whole chains of charter schools, the unions have fought them bitterly.

"Charters and vouchers are equal on our agenda," said Tom Mooney, the president of the Ohio Federation of Teachers. "We consider charters more insidious right now, because they've grown larger, but vouchers could grow, too."

SIGNIFICANCE

The Cleveland experiment, initiated in 1996, was hailed by voucher proponents who viewed the program not only as a free market tool but also as an opportunity for parents to have a true choice in education, without the limits of public education. Critics of vouchers, such as the American Federation of Teachers and other teachers' unions, claim that vouchers violate the separation of church and state when applied to religious schools, deprive public schools of needed tax dollars, and send students into schools with less oversight than is present in the public schools.

As charter schools grow in popularity, families with school-age children face intense competition for limited slots. Since the inception of the charter school program in the United States, more than four hundred charter schools have closed as a result of not meeting stated goals. Achievement standards in charter schools are uneven; a National Education Association report found that students in charter schools with licensed teachers scored higher on achievement tests than students in charter schools with unlicensed teachers. The NEA and other teachers' unions conditionally support charter schools but reject vouchers.

The 2001 No Child Left Behind act, which requires standardized testing for all public school children in the United States in grades three through eight, has led to a greater push for charter schools as well. Many parents and educators, concerned about the growing "teach to the test" mentality that is fostered by the NCLB, seek opportunities outside the traditional school structure; charter schools provide a publicly funded method for using public education for innovation while circumventing NCLB. Vouchers offer this same opportunity if parents select private schools that are not required to follow NCLB; the impact of NCLB remains an unknown as the public school system experiences government-driven reform and choice-driven change at the same time.

FURTHER RESOURCES

Books

Mondale, Sarah. *School: The Story of American Public Education*. Boston: Beacon Press, 2002.

No Child Left Behind?: The Politics and Practice of School Accountability, edited by Paul E. Peterson and Martin R. West. Washington, D.C.: Brookings Institution Press, 2003.

Pulliam, John D. and James J. Van Patten. *History of Education in America*. Upper Saddle River, N.J.: Prentice-Hall, 2002.

Web sites

United States Department of Education. "Evaluation of the Public Charter Schools Program: Final Report." <http://www.ed.gov/rschstat/eval/choice/pcsp-final/index.html> (accessed June 11, 2006).

United States Department of Education. "Overview of Education in the United States." <http://www.ed.gov/offices/OUS/PES/int_over_k12.html#finance> (accessed June 11, 2006).

The President's Physical Fitness Challenge

Pamphlet

By: Anonymous

Date: 2005

Source: *The President's Physical Fitness Challenge.* "10 Ideas to Get Active." <http://www.presidentschallenge.org/tools_to_help/ten_ideas.aspx> (accessed June 18, 2006).

About the Author: This pamphlet was written by staff members of The President's Council on Physical Fitness and Sports (PCPFS), a committee of volunteer citizens who promote the importance of fitness to the public and advise the President through the Secretary of Health and Human Services about physical activity, fitness, and sports in America.

INTRODUCTION

The first "Council on Youth Fitness" was created by President Dwight D. Eisenhower. The official start date was July 16, 1956—with the year 2006 being hailed as the Fiftieth Anniversary Year of the Council. Although Eisenhower was an advocate of healthy living and a proponent of physical fitness, it was when he read the unfavorable results of a study comparing American children with a group of European youth on a cadre of measures of physical fitness that he felt a strong need to create a national initiative. The initial goal was the promotion of a more active lifestyle and a higher degree of physical fitness among the children and youth of America. Later, the goal was broadened to suggest family fitness programs.

In 1960, under President John F. Kennedy, the name was changed to "The President's Council on Physical Fitness." Kennedy was a firm believer in the pursuit of fitness goals for the entire age span, and wished to create more emphasis on family activities as well as adult- and elder-oriented fitness programs. It was his goal to create a fitter, more active country, and to engage every citizen of the United States to be involved in voluntary personal activity programs.

President Lyndon Johnson decided to further push the idea that fitness can be fun and rewarding, and created the "Presidential Physical Fitness Award," creating goals and incentives for youth to excel in school fitness programs. President Lyndon B. Johnson was a strong believer in the positive benefits of organized sports, and believed that they could be part of an active lifestyle no matter what age the individual. He changed the name of the President's Council to reflect that, calling it "The President's Council on Physical Fitness and Sports."

Congress designated the month of May as "National Fitness and Sports Month" beginning in 1983. The Surgeon General's Report on Physical Activity and Health" was made public in 1996; the President's Council on Physical Fitness and Sports' treatise on "Physical Activity and Sport in the Lives of Girls" was published in 1997. It has become progressively more apparent that it is necessary to motivate the United States of America to get active, to get healthy, and to engage in voluntary physical fitness programs, from the youngest to the eldest citizens, in order to combat increasing trends of obesity and chronic diseases that afflict the masses.

PRIMARY SOURCE

TEN IDEAS TO GET ACTIVE

Adults

1. Use a push mower to mow the lawn
2. Go for a walk in a nearby park
3. Take the stairs instead of an elevator
4. Bike to work, to run errands, or visit friends
5. Clean out the garage or the attic
6. Walk with a friend over the lunch hour
7. Volunteer to become a coach or referee
8. Sign up for a group exercise class
9. Join a softball league
10. Park at the farthest end of the lot

Kids

1. Take your dog out for a walk
2. Start up a playground kickball game
3. Join a sports team
4. Go to the park with a friend
5. Help your parents with yardwork
6. Play tag with kids in your neighborhood
7. Ride your bike to school
8. Walk to the store for your mom
9. See how many jumping jacks you can do
10. Race a friend to the end of the block

SIGNIFICANCE

It has been several decades since John F. Kennedy published his article in *Sports Illustrated*, in which he said "We do not want in the United States a nation of spectators. We want a nation of participants in the vigorous life. We are under-exercised as a nation; we look instead of play; we ride instead of walk… Physical fitness is the basis for all other forms of excellence."

During that time, Americans have become, as a group, progressively less healthy. It is an overweight nation, and becoming more obese, at younger ages, with each passing year. Children are now developing lifestyle-related diseases, such as Type II Diabetes, high cholesterol, and the precursors for heart and liver dysfunction, the overwhelming majority of which were previously the province of aging and overweight adults.

In previous generations, most daily work involved significant physical labor, or at least quite a bit of exertion. In an effort to swing the societal pendulum back toward the middle, employers have begun to offer incentives to their workers to increase their daily activity levels by building on-site workout centers, by offering discounts at area fitness facilities, or by allowing time in each workday to leave the office and engage in some sort of exercise regimen. Health insurance providers have begun to recognize the importance of preventive care, and have begun offering discounts for gym memberships, weight loss centers, and smoking cessation programs. Still, the unhealthy lifestyle of the average American continues, and worsens.

In 2002, President George W. Bush sought to pique the interest of the American public by creating the President's Challenge Awards Program aimed at significantly raising public consciousness about the benefits of healthy and fit living. By creating the President's Challenge it was his hope that, ultimately, all of the people of the United States would choose to adopt some form of regular physical activity, and incorporate the concept of fitness into their daily lives. The Challenge is designed to be a strong motivator for improving activity and performance levels for individuals in all stages of life, at all activity levels, and at all possible levels of mobility.

The overarching goal of the The President's Council on Physical Fitness and Sports, as well as that of the President's Challenge, has always been the promotion of healthy and fit living for all Americans. It encourages the development of an active lifestyle based on voluntary regular physical fitness and activity programs, participation in sports, engagement in age-related and level of mobility appropriate group activity programs such as dance, water aerobics, wheelchair sports, community sports programs, master's swimming, and the like. Although the initial target for fitness programming was, and remains, children and youth, it stems from a belief that the creation of behavior patterns and activity preferences in childhood and early adolescence can set the stage for a lifetime of healthy choices and commitment to enduring physical fitness. By extension, healthy and fit children who become equally healthy and fit adults will transmit their values and beliefs to their children (and so on), leading to shared and promoted beliefs in the benefits of active, healthy living.

FURTHER RESOURCES

Books

American College of Sports Medicine. *Guidelines for Exercise Testing and Prescription*, 5th ed. Philadelphia: Lea & Febiger, 1995.

Armstrong, L. and S. Jenkins. *It's Not About the Bike: My Journey Back to Life*. New York: Putnam, 2000.

Aron, C. S. *Working at Play*. New York: Oxford University Press, 1999.

Periodicals

Abbott, R. D., B. L. Rodriguez, C. M. Burchfield, and J. D. Curb. "Physical Activity in Older Middle-Aged Men and Reduced Risk of Stroke: The Honolulu Heart Program." *American Journal of Epidemiology* 139 (1994): 881–893.

Kennedy, John Fitzgerald. "The Soft American." *Sports Illustrated*. 13, 26 (December 26, 1960): 15–17.

Web sites

The President's Challenge. "You're It. Get Fit!" 2006 <http://www.presidentschallenge.org> (accessed June 18, 2006).

School Vouchers: The Wrong Choice for Public Education

Editorial

By: Anonymous

Date: 2001

Source: *Anti-Defamation League*. "School Vouchers: The Wrong Choice for Public Education." October 13, 2003 <http://www.adl.org/vouchers/vouchers_main.asp> (accessed June 22, 2006).

About the Author: Founded in 1913 to fight discrimination and bigotry against Jews, the Anti-Defamation League today works for equal treatment of all Americans. The League maintains thirty regional offices in the United States and has additional offices in Israel and Russia.

Some San Antonio parents and teachers wishing to warn Texas Legislators of what they believe are failures in the Edgewood School voucher program are outside the Capitol in Austin, Texas, April 28, 2005. They called on lawmakers to reject legislation that would create publicly-funded vouchers for private schools. AP IMAGES.

INTRODUCTION

Education is an integral part of the American story. The earliest immigrants to North America recognized the need for widespread public education, and the first public school was begun in Boston in 1635. After moving from the schoolmaster's home to School Street, the historic school educated numerous patriots including Benjamin Franklin, John Hancock, and Samuel Adams.

Despite, or perhaps because of this fundamental commitment to public education, America's drive to teach has not been without controversy. Throughout its history, American schools have wrestled with fundamental questions about what form public education should take. Specifically Americans have debated the purpose of public education, who should receive public education (and how), and how government at the state and federal level should ensure the quality and consistency of the educational product being delivered. Numerous education initiatives and reforms throughout American history have addressed one or more of these questions.

Public education in America is funded by a combination of federal and local sources. In most commu-

nities, state income taxes or property taxes on homes provide the bulk of education funding. Under such a system, the majority of state residents fund the public education system whether they currently receive its services or not; in return, all school-age children are granted free access to public education services, and the nation is assured a high rate of basic literacy among its populace. By the end of the twentieth century, public education served more than fifty million children.

Public education in America has not been an unqualified success. While educating many students at a low cost-per-pupil, the system has often succumbed to the inefficiencies inherent in most large bureaucracies, resulting in waste and poor learning outcomes. In response, some parents have chosen to remove their children from public education and place them in private schools. Private schools have long offered an alternative to public education; private academies predated the establishment of public education in most American cities, though they often served only affluent students.

Private schools have generally been created to address perceived shortcomings in public education.

In many cases, religious organizations have started private schools in order to combine academic and religious training. As of 2005, more than 7,700 private Catholic schools enrolled 2.4 million students nationwide, or about half of all students enrolled in private schools. Catholic schools are typically supported by church funds and private tuition payments. Other religious groups also maintain their own schools with their own distinctive traits.

In a return to education's historical roots, the 1980s and 1990s witnessed an increasing number of parents choosing to educate their children in their own homes. By 2001, an estimated 1.5 to 1.9 million students were being home-schooled in America. Home-schooling parents most commonly cited religious beliefs, low quality levels in public education, and a desire to maintain family closeness as primary reasons for this choice.

As alternatives to public education have expanded, private education supporters have argued that these alternative educational institutions should be entitled to receive state funding as well, because they also provide educational services. This objective, commonly referred to as school choice, would allow parents to determine where and how their children are educated while still providing state funding for their chosen venue. The most common approach to this objective is the use of school vouchers. School vouchers are education coupons, paid for by the state, which parents may redeem at any public or private educational institution.

■ PRIMARY SOURCE

Most Americans believe that improving our system of education should be a top priority for government at the local, state and Federal levels. Legislators, school boards, education professionals, parent groups and community organizations are attempting to implement innovative ideas to rescue children from failing school systems, particularly in inner-city neighborhoods. Many such groups champion voucher programs. The standard program proposed in dozens of states across the country would distribute monetary vouchers (typically valued between $2,500–$5,000) to parents of school-age children, usually in troubled inner-city school districts. Parents could then use the vouchers towards the cost of tuition at private schools—including those dedicated to religious indoctrination.

Superficially, school vouchers might seem a relatively benign way to increase the options poor parents have for educating their children. In fact, vouchers pose a serious threat to values that are vital to the health of American democracy. These programs subvert the constitutional principle of separation of church and state and threaten to undermine our system of public education.

Vouchers Are Constitutionally Suspect

Proponents of vouchers are asking Americans to do something contrary to the very ideals upon which this country was founded. Thomas Jefferson, one of the architects of religious freedom in America, said, "To compel a man to furnish contributions of money for the propagation of opinions which he disbelieves is sinful and tyrannical." Yet voucher programs would do just that; they would force citizens—Christians, Jews, Muslims and atheists—to pay for the religious indoctrination of school children at schools with narrow parochial agendas. In many areas, 80 percent of vouchers would be used in schools whose central mission is religious training. In most such schools, religion permeates the classroom, the lunchroom, even the football practice field. Channeling public money to these institutions flies in the face of the constitutional mandate of separation of church and state.

While the Supreme Court has upheld school vouchers in the *Zelman v. Simmons-Harris* case, vouchers have not been given a green light by the Court beyond the narrow facts of this case. Indeed, Cleveland's voucher program was upheld in a close (5-4) ruling that required a voucher program to (among other things):

- be a part of a much wider program of multiple educational options, such as magnet schools and after-school tutorial assistance,
- offer parents a real choice between religious and non-religious education (perhaps even providing incentives for non-religious education),
- not only address private schools, but to ensure that benefits go to schools regardless of whether they are public or private, religious or not.

This decision also does not disturb the bedrock constitutional idea that no government program may be designed to advance religious institutions over non-religious institutions.

Finally, and of critical importance, many state constitutions provide for a higher wall of separation between church and state—and thus voucher programs will likely have a hard time surviving litigation in state courts.

Thus, other states will likely have a very hard time reproducing the very narrow set of circumstances found in the Cleveland program.

VOUCHERS UNDERMINE PUBLIC SCHOOLS

Implementation of voucher programs sends a clear message that we are giving up on public education. Undoubtedly, vouchers would help some students. But the glory of the American system of public education is that it is for all children, regardless of their religion, their academic talents or their ability to pay a fee. This policy of inclusiveness has made public schools the backbone of American democracy.

Private schools are allowed to discriminate on a variety of grounds. These institutions regularly reject applicants because of low achievement, discipline problems, and sometimes for no reason at all. Further, some private schools promote agendas antithetical to the American ideal. Under a system of vouchers, it may be difficult to prevent schools run by extremist groups like the Nation of Islam or the Ku Klux Klan from receiving public funds to subsidize their racist and anti-Semitic agendas. Indeed, the proud legacy of *Brown v. Board of Education* may be tossed away as tax dollars are siphoned off to deliberately segregated schools.

Proponents of vouchers argue that these programs would allow poor students to attend good schools previously only available to the middle class. The facts tell a different story. A $2,500 voucher supplement may make the difference for some families, giving them just enough to cover the tuition at a private school (with some schools charging over $10,000 per year, they would still have to pay several thousand dollars). But voucher programs offer nothing of value to families who cannot come up with the rest of the money to cover tuition costs.

In many cases, voucher programs will offer students the choice between attending their current public school or attending a school run by the local church. Not all students benefit from a religious school atmosphere—even when the religion being taught is their own. For these students, voucher programs offer only one option: to remain in a public school that is likely to deteriorate even further.

As our country becomes increasingly diverse, the public school system stands out as an institution that unifies Americans. Under voucher programs, our educational system—and our country—would become even more Balkanized than it already is. With the help of taxpayers' dollars, private schools would be filled with well-to-do and middle-class students and a handful of the best, most motivated students from inner cities. Some public schools would be left with fewer dollars to teach the poorest of the poor and other students who, for one reason or another, were not private school material. Such a scenario can hardly benefit public education.

Finally, as an empirical matter, reports on the effectiveness of voucher programs have been mixed. Initial reports on Cleveland's voucher program, published by the American Federation of Teachers, suggest that it has been less effective than proponents argue. Milwaukee's program has resulted in a huge budget shortfall, leaving the public schools scrambling for funds. While some studies suggest that vouchers are good for public schools, there is, as yet, little evidence that they ultimately improve the quality of public education for those who need it most.

Vouchers Are Not Universally Popular

When offered the opportunity to vote on voucher-like programs, the public has consistently rejected them; voters in 19 states have rejected such proposals in referendum ballots. In the November 1998 election, for example, Colorado voters rejected a proposed constitutional amendment that would have allowed parochial schools to receive public funds through a complicated tuition tax-credit scheme. Indeed, voters have rejected all but one of the tuition voucher proposals put to the ballot since the first such vote over 30 years ago.

Voucher proposals have also made little progress in legislatures across the country. While 20 states have introduced voucher bills, only two have been put into law. Congress has considered several voucher plans for the District of Columbia, but none has been enacted.

A recent poll conducted by the Joint Center for Political and Economic Studies demonstrates that support for vouchers has declined over the last year. Published in October 1998, the Poll revealed that support for school vouchers declined from 57.3 percent to 48.1 percent among Blacks, and from 47 to 41.3 percent among whites. Overall, 50.2 percent of Americans now oppose voucher programs; only 42 percent support them.

Conclusion

School voucher programs undermine two great American traditions: universal public education and the separation of church and state. Instead of embracing vouchers, communities across the country should dedicate themselves to finding solutions that will be available to every American schoolchild and that take into account the important legacy of the First Amendment.

SIGNIFICANCE

As early as the 1700s, economists argued for a primitive school voucher system, noting that competition should help raise the overall quality of education in America. Under such a system, parents would generally choose to send their children to higher-performing schools, rewarding better schools with higher enrollment and better funding and simultaneously punishing poorly performing schools. By letting consumers choose among educational options in the same way they choose an automobile or a shirt, economists advocated harnessing free market forces to improve education.

Critics of school vouchers make three primary arguments. First, they worry that vouchers will expend public funds on religious education, because the majority of private schools are religiously based. Second, they argue that redistributing public education funds with vouchers would further undermine already underfunded public school systems, leading to a further exodus of students and funds. Finally, they contend that public schools provide a common experience for rich and poor alike, while private schools are overwhelmingly filled with affluent students; they claim that vouchers will allow more affluent students to leave public schools, further reducing the average income level in the public system and further segregating America.

Voucher systems have produced mixed results when tried and in some cases have been struck down by federal courts. Supporters continue to push vouchers as a needed education reform, though several communities given the opportunity to vote for vouchers have instead rejected them.

FURTHER RESOURCES

Books

Altidor, Jonas N. *School Vouchers and Parents in Cleveland, Milwaukee, and Los Angeles*. Pittsburgh, Pennsylvania: Dorrance Publishing, 2005.

Carnoy, Martin. *School Vouchers: Examining the Evidence*. Washington, D. C.: Economic Policy Institute, 2001.

Moe, Terry M. *Schools, Vouchers, and the American Public*. Washington, D.C.: The Brookings Institution, 2001.

Periodicals

Crawford, Chris. "Milwaukee's School Voucher Program Brings Benefits, Too." *Christian Science Monitor* 98 (2006): 8.

Davis, Wendy N. "Vouchers Tested." *ABS Journal* 92 (2006): 39–47.

Dowling-Sendor, Benjamin. "Revisiting the Voucher Debate." *American School Board Journal* 193 (2006):39–47.

Web sites

Denver Public Schools. "History." <http://www.dpsk12.org/aboutdps/history/> (accessed June 22, 2006).

National Home Education Research Council. "Home Education Research Fact Sheet 1c." 2006 <http://www.nheri.org/content/view/177/54/> (accessed June 22, 2006).

United States Conference of Catholic Bishops. "Renewing Our Commitment to Catholic Elementary and Secondary Schools in the Third Millennium." <http://www.dioceseofjoliet.org/cso/docs/ComOnEdSchoolsStatement.pdf> (accessed June 22, 2006).

State Seeks to Block "No Child Left Behind"

News article

By: Anonymous

Date: February 2, 2006

Source: "State Seeks to Block 'No Child Left Behind.'" *CNN.com*. February 2, 2006.

About the Author: This article was written by a contributor to Reuters, a major worldwide news agency based in London. It appeared on CNN.com, the Web portal for the Cable News Network.

INTRODUCTION

Public education in the United States has gone through many reforms in the twentieth and early twenty-first centuries. Child labor laws and compulsory attendance laws in the late 1800s and early 1900s increased school attendance and literacy while decreasing child labor abuses. Desegregation of public schools in the 1940s and 1950s, by court order or by choice, shaped the social atmosphere and racial make-up of schools, driving some southern white parents to choose private schools in the south while increasing the quality of education and opportunity for African Americans, Asians, and Hispanics in the United States. The Russian launch of *Sputnik*, the first satellite, in 1957 sparked a scientific race; school curricula changed to include more intensive science and math courses to allow the U.S. to stay on pace with the Soviet Union's technological achievements.

In the 1960s and 1970s, parents of children with mental and physical disabilities lobbied successfully for federal and state protections of education rights, leading to the Individuals with Disabilities Education Act in the mid–1970s. The 1983 report *A Nation at Risk*, published by the National Commission on Excellence in Education, chronicled overcrowded classrooms, twelfth graders unable to read, and disparities in teacher salaries and spending per pupil, all part

President George W. Bush speaks about his "No Child Left Behind" education policy at the C.T. Kirkpatrick Elementary School, September 8, 2003. © JAON REED/REUTERS/CORBIS.

of a public education system in crisis. With test scores declining, public education reformers worked on a series of measures such as tighter teacher licensure, exit exams for graduation, and earlier reading intervention programs to improve the quality and experience of public education in the United States.

In the 2000 presidential election, Republican candidate and then-Governor of Texas George W. Bush pointed to education reform laws he had signed regarding public education in Texas. Campaigning on the promise of a sweeping education reform bill that would hold school administrators and teachers more accountable, once in the White House President Bush worked to pass the No Child Left Behind (NCLB) Act. NCLB requires states and schools to create accountability procedures, mandates yearly standardized tests for grades three through eight, holds teachers more accountable for performance, and gives

students the option of other public or private schools if the school they currently attend fails to meet basic NCLB standards three years in a row.

Within two years of NCLB's implementation, state education agencies and local schools struggled to meet the act's demands. Teachers began to trim subjects covered to focus on test material to improve scores. Many of NCLB's requirements came with no matching funds from the federal government. These "unfunded mandates" placed schools in a precarious position; unable to follow the law because they lacked the funding, many schools came closer to being labeled a "failed" school. NCLB requires that achievement gaps based on income, race, and other factors be eliminated in twelve years, but does not provide the funding needed; according to critics from Fairtest, an additional $8 billion in federal funds would be needed to meet this particular unfunded mandate.

By 2006, Connecticut determined that meeting the requirements of the No Child Left Behind act was impossible without appropriate funding—the state faced compromising education quality in order to meet the letter of the law.

■ PRIMARY SOURCE

STATE SEEKS TO BLOCK "NO CHILD LEFT BEHIND"

Connecticut rebels against Bush education policy

NEW HAVEN, Connecticut (Reuters)—The Bush administration's "No Child Left Behind" policy will lead to "dumbing down" tests in public schools because Washington has not fully funded the policy, the state of Connecticut said in a court hearing Tuesday to try to block the program.

Attorney General Richard Blumenthal told the U.S. District Court in New Haven that President Bush's signature education policy was "mistaken" and "misguided," as he fought a motion by the federal government to throw out his lawsuit.

The suit, filed in August, makes Connecticut the first state seeking to block the 2002 policy that calls for standardized testing of students.

"If the federal government asks us to undertake the mandate, we would be willing to do it, but they have to provide the money," Blumenthal told the court in New Haven.

Blumenthal said federal funding was not enough for the state to test in a way that maintains its high standards, leaving Connecticut $41.6 million short of what it needs to comply with the law. He said that dynamic would force Connecticut to rely on multiple choice tests rather than costlier written tests which would better challenge students.

"There is always the option of dumbing down the test to the point that would be inadequate, and we are not willing to do that," he said. "We're left with no choice but to either defy the statute or (follow) an interpretation that we believe is mistaken and misguided."

U.S. Justice Department attorney Elizabeth Goitein, representing the U.S. Education Department, said Connecticut was avoiding its obligations and was aware of the law's demands when the state accepted education funding from Washington.

The promise of education reform has bolstered Bush's support among minorities in a country where only two-thirds of teenagers graduate from high school and only 50 percent of black Americans and Hispanics graduate.

Connecticut has taken the strongest legal stand yet against "No Child Left Behind" but other states have also challenged it. A judge in November threw out a similar lawsuit by the National Education Association on behalf of school districts in three states. The state of Utah has rebelled by passing a measure defying the law.

The heart of the law is standardized testing, currently conducted in Connecticut in grades four, six and eight.

The law requires that students also be tested in grades three, five and seven. Scores and other variables like graduation rates can lead to sanctions against poor-performing schools. In some cases, schools can be forced to close.

Tuesday's arguments also focused on whether the federal government would suspend hundreds of millions of dollars in education funding if Connecticut appealed through the Department of Education rather than through the court.

Connecticut has the highest graduation rate in the country. But it also has the nation's worst gap in academic achievement between rich and poor children, with 18 percent of low-income 9-year-olds proficient in reading, against 53 percent of those who are not poor.

Connecticut Education Commissioner Betty Sternberg says that reflects the extreme wealth and poverty in Connecticut, where Greenwich ranks among America's wealthiest cities and other cities such as Hartford are among the nation's poorest.

■ SIGNIFICANCE

As the article notes, Connecticut faced the greatest achievement gap of all U.S. states: a thirty-five percent difference between higher-income and lower-income nine-year-olds on test scores. Like many other states, such as Utah and Texas, Connecticut determined that the law placed educators in an untenable position; the lawsuit filed by the Attorney General of Connecticut was viewed by education officials as a necessary measure.

One of the major complaints by educators and parents is the provision in NCLB requiring that all students—including students with academic and behavioral disabilities—sit for the standardized tests, and that their scores are included in the aggregate data used to determine whether schools are performing on target. In many poorer school districts, a higher-than-average percentage of students have Individual Education Plans (IEPs), used for students with learning disabilities such as dyslexia or auditory processing disorder as well as developmental disabilities such as autism. The variations in performance on standardized tests from such students can have a dramatic impact on overall test scores, and the time taken from other educational goals to prepare such students for rigorous testing can contribute to poor outcome and overall delay in educational progress for students with IEPs. NCLB does not provide flexible options for students with IEPs, leaving special education teachers with the challenge to assist students in meeting goals and adapting to educational environments while preparing them for testing.

Critics of NCLB, such as Princeton History professor Theodore K. Rabb, also point to the shrinking curriculum for subjects other than those on the tests; time devoted to social studies, certain sciences, art, and music have all dropped since 2002, while time spent on reading and math has increased. The crowding out of non-test subjects has created a form of education that is less well-rounded and more focused on the test; "teaching to the test" has become a pejorative term for some parents and educators.

Private schools and homeschoolers in most states are exempt from NCLB standards; NCLB has helped to create an explosion in demand for private tutoring and on-site, after-school tutoring for standardized tests. As schools shave physical education, lunch time, and recess to increase test teaching time, the social experience for students in academic settings diminishes at the same time that childhood obesity rates climb.

Connecticut's challenge to the No Child Left Behind Act, as of mid–2006, was still making its way through the courts. Viewed as a test case by other state Attorneys General considering similar actions, the court's decision will be watched carefully by professional educators and parents alike.

FURTHER RESOURCES
Books

Mondale, Sarah. *School: The Story of American Public Education*. Boston: Beacon Press, 2002.

No Child Left Behind?: The Politics and Practice of School Accountability, edited by Paul E. Peterson and Martin R. West. Washington, D.C.: Brookings Institution Press, 2003.

Pulliam, John D. and James J. Van Patten. *History of Education in America*. Upper Saddle River, N.J.: Prentice Hall, 2002.

Web sites

National Commission on Excellence in Education. "A Nation at Risk." April 1983. <http://www.ed.gov/pubs/NatAtRisk/index.html> (accessed June 15, 2006).

Your Taxes

It Doesn't Pay to Be in the A.M.T. Zone

Newspaper article

By: David Cay Johnston

Date: February 12, 2006

Source: Johnston, David Cay. "Your Taxes: It Doesn't Pay to Be in the A.M.T. Zone." *New York Times* (February 12, 2006).

About the Author: David Cay Johnston writes for the *New York Times* on topics relating to taxes and commerce. He was awarded the Pulitzer Prize in 2001 for his investigative reporting.

INTRODUCTION

While the American Civil War is remembered both for its high human cost and its ultimate benefits, it also marked the creation of one of the most despised aspects of modern life: the federal income tax. In 1861, facing mounting war costs and a deficit which eventually reached $2 million per day, Congress enacted the first tax on regular income, charging citizens a rate of three percent on all earnings above $800. While income tax is today generally viewed as a necessary evil, the United States government did not tax ordinary income for the first eighty-five years of its existence, relying instead on excise taxes levied against sugar, alcohol, and other products. For the forty-four years prior to the Civil War, the government collected no internal taxes whatsoever, subsisting solely on tariffs and the sale of land. Soon after the Civil War, the first income tax was abolished.

In the years that followed, debates raged over the constitutionality of taxing individual income. The income tax system as it exists today came into being in 1913, when thirty-six states ratified the sixteenth amendment to the Constitution, granting Congress the formal right to tax individual incomes. Later that year, an income tax on the top one percent of earners was passed, with rates ranging from one percent to a top value of seven percent. The twentieth century has seen a progression of tax debates in Washington, with the result being a tax system with both higher rates and far more complications.

While income tax policy remains a hotly debated political topic, most Americans agree that the system should be designed so that wealthier citizens pay a higher percentage of their income, a system known as a progressive tax system. Progressive systems are

Chairman of the Federal Reserve Alan Greenspan speaks at the President's Advisory Panel on Federal Tax Reform at George Washington University in Washington, March 3, 2005. © KEVIN LAMARQUE/REUTERS/CORBIS.

based on the belief that both poor and rich individuals need a similar amount of income to pay for essentials such as food and clothing, so those with more income should have more available to pay higher rates.

In 1969, the Secretary of the Treasury testified before Congress that in tax year 1967, 155 Americans had earned $200,000 or more but had paid no income tax at all. $200,000 in 1967 was approximately equivalent to $1.2 million in 2007, and Americans were outraged to learn that some of the highest earners in the nation were paying no taxes. Congress's solution was the Alternative Minimum Tax, or AMT.

The AMT is a separate income tax structure which exists alongside the standard tax structure. Taxpayers calculate their taxes twice, once using each of the two systems, then pay the higher of the two results. Since the AMT does not include some of the deductions allowed by the standard system, it frequently results in higher tax bills. While the AMT dealt with the immediate problem in 1969, its authors failed to index it to inflation, meaning that the cutoff did not increase over time. By the year 2005, many Americans were earning more than $200,000, and three million of them found themselves paying the

Alternative Minimum Tax, a number projected to balloon to eighteen million by 2006.

PRIMARY SOURCE

After President Bush and Congress cut tax rates on dividends and long-term capital gains to a top rate of 15 percent in 2003, many investors bought stocks that make big cash payouts, expecting to benefit from lower taxes.

For many people, it has not worked out that way. That is because your actual tax rate may not be the one that the politicians talked about or that the Internal Revenue Service prints on its tax forms.

The culprit is the alternative minimum tax, which runs parallel to the regular income tax system. The A.M.T. has its own rules, including fewer deductions and just two tax rates, 26 percent and 28 percent. If the alternative tax is higher than the one you would owe under the regular tax system, you pay the higher bill.

Taxpayers subject to the alternative system pay the 15 percent rate on dividends and long-term capital gains unless they fall into a netherworld known as the phase-out zone. In 2005, that zone included married couples with annual incomes of $150,000 to $382,000, and single filers making $112,500 to $273,000.

Taxpayers in the phase-out zone pay even higher rates on wage income than other people trapped by the A.M.T.—as much as 35 percent on each additional dollar of income. For people whose income exceeds the phase-out zone limits, the statutory rates apply and any additional wages are taxed at 28 percent and dividends and long-term gains are taxed at 15 percent.

But those unfortunate enough to dwell in the zone must pay an effective tax rate on dividends and long-term gains of 21.5 percent or 22 percent, instead of 15 percent.

This extra tax is just one of the many painful features of the alternative levy. Under the alternative tax, people cannot deduct property taxes, for example, so their cost of homeownership climbs. But the interaction of the alternative tax and the 2003 Bush tax cuts directly affect the taxation of investments in stocks.

Imposing higher taxes on people at such incomes was not part of the original intent of the alternative tax. Congress created it in 1969 to make sure that those making more than $200,000—the equivalent of more than $1 million in today's dollars—could not live tax free by making unlimited use of exotic tax breaks like the oil depletion allowance.

Over time, Congress has excluded most of these tax breaks from the alternative levy. And in 1986, Congress revised the list of tax deductions that would push a taxpayer into the alternative system to include those routinely taken by most Americans. They include the standard deduction; personal exemptions for the taxpayer, spouse and children; deductions for state income and local property taxes; and even some medical deductions for the severely ill or injured.

The White House has said repeatedly that it will take measures to mitigate the impact of the alternative tax on people of moderate income, and restore at least some of the benefits of the Bush tax cuts that were taken back by the alternative tax.

In his State of the Union address, President Bush again called for making his tax cuts permanent, but he said nothing about overhauling or repealing the alternative minimum tax.

The A.M.T. has become such a money maker that by 2008 its repeal would cost more than repealing the regular income tax, according to the Tax Policy Center, a joint venture of the Urban Institute and the Brookings Institution, two research institutions in Washington.

Over the next decade, the alternative tax will cost Americans $1.1 trillion in additional taxes, of which $739 billion is a result of the Bush tax cuts not being integrated into the levy, according to a report by the Congressional Joint Committee on Taxation. Those hit hardest are couples with two or more children who own their homes, invest and make $75,000 to $500,000 a year, according to the Tax Policy Center computer model.

While the administration has never proposed a specific plan to change the alternative minimum tax or to exempt dividends and long-term gains from the phase-out range, Congress initiated a small adjustment five years ago. It exempted the first $58,000 earned by married couples ($40,250 for singles) from the alternative tax calculation for 2001 through last year. This patch was not renewed for 2006, dropping the exemption to $45,000 for couples ($33,750 for singles) unless a new patch is voted into law.

Investors who have fallen into the phase-out zone face a quandary. Should they buy high-dividend stocks, even though they will not get the full benefit of reduced tax rates? The short answer is this: if it makes sense to buy the shares for other reasons, the extra tax probably should not deter them.

Rich Carreiro is one of those rare taxpayers who knew before he invested that he would not get the 15 percent rate on dividends. Mr. Carreiro, 38, takes a keen interest in the tax code, which is as complex as the code he works with as a software engineer in Arlington, Mass.

"To move out of dividend-bearing stocks just because I am paying 22 percent instead of the promised 15 percent would cause more harm than good," he said. "The idea in investing is not to minimize your tax; it is to maximize your after-tax return. After all, you can pay no tax by living off money you've stuffed in your mattress, but that doesn't make good sense."

One investing change that Mr. Carreiro and his wife did make because of the alternative tax was to avoid money market and bond funds that buy private activity bonds—those whose proceeds are used by private entities. Under the alternative system, income from these bonds is subject to taxes at the higher rates applied to wages.

Ed Grogan, a financial planner in Gig Harbor, Wash., says he tells clients not to let the extra tax deter them from buying stocks that they believe have a good future just because they will not qualify for the 15 percent rate on dividends.

"Stick with your investing fundamentals," he said.

Stephen J. Entin, a proponent in Washington of the supply-side theory of taxation that favors eliminating most taxes on capital, said last year that denying the 15 percent tax rate to some investors "poisons the tax cut."

Mr. Entin, the president of the Institute for Research on the Economics of Taxation, said in an interview last month that "you should be a little more ticked off at the world" if you are in the phase-out range and, like Mr. Carreiro, pay higher tax rates on dividends.

In a report, Mr. Entin wrote that investors are still better off under the 2003 tax rate cuts even if they are in the phase-out range. That is because the phase-out rates are still significantly lower than the tax rates in effect before the 2003 tax cuts.

Investors who are stuck in the phase-out range and avoid dividend-paying stocks may find that they still have a vexing tax problem. That is because the higher tax rates that apply to taxes on dividends also apply to long-term capital gains. If you are in the zone, you must pay the higher tax on capital gains, and you cannot take a federal deduction for state and local income taxes on them.

Of course, if the stocks pay no dividend, no tax is due until they have been sold. By that time, your income could be above or below the phase-out range, so you could qualify for the 15 percent tax rate on their gains.

By then, though, Congress may have made the tax code even more complicated.

SIGNIFICANCE

In the years since the AMT was enacted, several adjustments have been made to the law. Typical of these was a change in 2005, a temporary adjustment of the floor for the tax, which allowed several thousand taxpayers to avoid falling into the AMT range. In 2005, the Congressional Budget office projected that by 2016 the AMT would impact thirty-three million taxpayers, generating more than $81 billion in revenues.

In mid–2006, with several million more taxpayers facing a potential AMT bill, the U.S. Congress passed a $70 billion tax reduction bill. Along with temporary extensions of several tax reductions, the bill also provided a temporary adjustment to the AMT, preventing approximately fifteen million Americans from falling

under its provisions. While a permanent fix for the AMT is clearly needed, Congress may find such a change politically difficult to swallow. Future budget deficit projections are based on the assumption that the AMT will remain in place; without the AMT and the billions of dollars it is projected to generate, future budget deficits will soar even higher than before, putting pressure on lawmakers to cut spending. For this reason, it appears likely that the AMT may continue to be readjusted each year for the foreseeable future.

FURTHER RESOURCES

Books

Peckron, Harold S. *Alternative Minimum Tax: What You Need to Know About the "Other" Tax*. Naperville, Ill.: Sphinx Publishing, 2005.

Tyson, Eric, Margaret Monro, and David Silverman. *What the IRS Doesn't Want You to Know: A CPA Reveals Tricks of the Trade*. New York: John Wiley & Sons, 2003.

Periodicals

Gleckman, Howard and Paul Barrett. "How the AMT Wallops Capital Gains." *Business Week* 3984 (2006): 45.

Jeffrey, Terrence. "The Anti-Family Tax is Coming Your Way." *Human Events* 62 (2006): 5.

"The GOP's Tax Windfall." *U.S. News & World Report*. 140 (2006): 25.

Web sites

The Brookings Institution. "Key Points on the Alternative Minimum Tax." January 21, 2004. <http://www.brookings.edu/views/op-ed/gale/20040121amt.htm> (accessed June 2, 2006).

Congressional Budget Office. "The Alternative Minimum Tax." April 15, 2004. <http://www.cbo.gov/> (accessed June 2, 2006).

United States Department of the Treasury. "History of the U.S. Tax System." <http://www.ustreas.gov/education/factsheets/taxes/ustax.html> (accessed June 2, 2006).

Sources Consulted

BOOKS AND WEBSITES

Adams, Michael C.C. *The Best War Ever: America and World War II.* Baltimore, Md.: Johns Hopkins University Press, 1994.

Addams, Jane. *Twenty Years at Hull-House with Autobiographical Notes.* New York: The MacMillan Co., 1912.

Administration for Children and Families. "National Clearinghouse on Child Abuse and Neglect Information." May 16, 2006 <http://nccanch.acf.hhs.gov/index.cfm> (accessed May 25, 2006).

Adoption History Project, University of Oregon. "Timeline of Adoption History." June 22, 2005. <http://darkwing.uoregon.edu/~adoption/timeline.html> (accessed June 5, 2006).

Agency for Healthcare Research and Quality. "Agency for Healthcare Research and Quality." <http://www.ahrq.gov> (accessed on July 16, 2006).

AIDS Research Institute (ARI). "AIDS Research Institute (ARI)." <http://ari.ucsf.edu> (accessed on July 16, 2006).

Akers, Donna L. *Living in the Land of Death: The Choctaw Nation, 1830–1860.* East Lansing: Michigan State University Press, 2004.

Alabama Department of Human Resources. "Child Protective Services." 2005 <http://www.dhr.state.al.us/page.asp?pageid=312> (accessed May 25, 2006).

Alford, C. Fred. *Whistleblowers: Broken Lives and Organizational Power.* Ithaca, N.Y.: Cornell University Press, 2002.

Alter, Jonathan. *The Defining Moment: FDR's Hundred Days and the Triumph of Hope.* New York: Simon & Schuster, 2006.

Altidor, Jonas N. *School Vouchers and Parents in Cleveland, Milwaukee, and Los Angeles.* Pittsburgh, Pennsylvania: Dorrance Publishing, 2005 .

Altman, Nancy J. *The Battle for Social Security: From FDR's Vision to Bush's Gamble.* Hoboken, New Jersey: John Wiley & Sons, 2005.

American Association for the Advancement of Science. "Science and Public Policy." <http://www.aaas.org/spp/yearbook/chap29.htm> (accessed May 17, 2006).

American Association of Retired Persons. "Age Discrimination at Work." <http://www.aarp.org/money/careers/jobloss/a2004-04-28-agediscrimination.html> (accessed May 22, 2006).

American Association of University Women. *Tech-Savvy: Educating Girls in the New Computer Age.* Washington, DC: AAUW Educational Foundation, 2000.

American Civil War Homepage. "General resources." May 05, 2006. <http://sunsite.utk.edu/civil-war/warweb.html#general> (accessed May 10, 2006).

American College of Sports Medicine. *Guidelines for Exercise Testing and Prescription,* 5th ed. Philadelphia: Lea & Febiger, 1995.

American Memory. "Library of Congress." <http://memory.loc.gov/ammem/index.html> (accessed on July 16, 2006).

American President. "Franklin Delano Roosevelt." <http://www.americanpresident.org/history/franklindelanoroosevelt/> (accessed June 1, 2006).

American Probation and Parole Association. "Revisiting Megan's Law and Sex Offender Registration: Prevention or Problem." 2000. <http://www.appa-net.org/revisitingmegan.pdf> (accessed May 23, 2006).

American Rhetoric. "American Rhetoric." <http://www.americanrhetoric.com/> (accessed on July 16, 2006).

Amnesty International. "Amnesty International." <http://www.amnesty.org/> (accessed on July 16, 2006).

Anbinder, Tyler. *Nativism and Slavery: The Northern Know Nothings and the Politics of the 1850s.* New York: Oxford University Press, 1992.

Anderson, C. V. *The Federal Emergency Management Agency (FEMA).* Hauppage, N.Y.: Nova Science Publishing, Inc., 2003.

Anderson, James D. *The Education of Blacks in the South, 1860–1935.* Chapel Hill: University of North Carolina Press, 1988.

Anderson, James, ed., and Dara N. Byrne. *The Unfinished Agenda of Brown v. Board of Education.* Hoboken, N.J.: John Wiley & Sons, 2004.

Andrew, John A. *Lyndon Johnson and the Great Society.* Chicago: Ivan R. Dee, 1998.

Arc. "The Americans with Disabilities Act of 1990." <http://www.thearc.org/faqs/adaqa.html> (accessed May 26, 2006).

Armor, David J. *Forced Justice: School Desegregation and the Law.* New York: Oxford University Press, 1995.

Armstrong, L. and S. Jenkins. *It's Not About the Bike: My Journey Back to Life.* New York: Putnam, 2000.

Aron, C. S. *Working at Play.* New York: Oxford University Press, 1999.

Asch, Peter. *Consumer Safety Regulation: Putting a Price on Life and Limb.* New York: Oxford University Press, 1988.

Ashby, LeRoy. *Saving the Waif: Reformers and Dependent Children, 1890–1917.* Philadelphia, Penn.: Temple University Press, 1984.

Babcock, Richard F. *The Zoning Game: Municipal Practices and Policies.* Madison, WI: University of Wisconsin Press, 1966.

Badger, Anthony J. *The New Deal: The Depression Years, 1933–1940.* Chicago: Ivan R. Dee, 2002.

Baggett, Jerome P. *Habitat for Humanity: Building Private Homes, Building Public Religion.* Philadelphia: Temple University Press, 2000.

Baldwin, Robert E. *The Decline of U.S. Labor Unions and the Role of Trade.* Washington, D.C.: The Institute for International Economics, 2003.

Ball, Howard. *The Supreme Court in the Intimate Lives of Americans: Birth, Sex, Marriage, Childrearing, and Death.* New York: New York University Press, 2002.

Barr, Nicholas, and Iain Crawford. *Financing Education: Answers from the UK.* London: Routledge, 2005.

Barry, Brian M. *Theories of Justice.* Berkley, Calif.: University of California Press, 1989.

Baumslag, Naomi M. D. and Dia L. Michels. *Milk, Money and Madness: The Culture and Politics of Breastfeeding.* Westport, Conn.: Bergin & Garvey Trade, 1995.

Baxter, Maurice G. *Henry Clay and the American System.* Lexington: University Press of Kentucky, 1995.

Beals, Melba Patillo. *Warriors Don't Cry: A Searing Memoir of the Battle to Integrate Little Rock's Central High School.* New York: Washington Square Press, 1995.

Becker, Susan D. *The Origins of the Equal Rights Amendment: American Feminism Between the Wars.* Westport, CT: Greenwood Press, 1981.

Beckwith, Francis, and Todd E. Jones. *Affirmative Action: Social Justice or Reverse Discrimination.* Amherst, New York: Prometheus Books, 1997.

Bederman, Gail. *Manliness and Civilization: A Cultural History of Gender and Race in the United States, 1880–1917.* Chicago: University of Chicago Press, 1996.

Bell, Derrick. *Silent Covenants: Brown V. Board of Education and the Unfulfilled Hopes for Racial Reform.* New York: Oxford University Press, 2004.

Bellush, Bernard. *The Failure of the NRA.* New York: W. W. Norton, 1975.

Benedict, Michael Les. *The Impeachment and Trial of Andrew Johnson.* New York: W.W. Norton, 1973.

Bennett, Michael J. *When Dreams Came True: The G.I. Bill and the Making of Modern America.* Washington, D.C.: Brassey's, 1996.

Bently, George R. *A History of the Freedmen's Bureau.* Philadelphia: University of Pennsylvania Press, 1955.

Bergmann, Barbara R. *In Defense of Affirmative Action.* New York, New York: Basic Books, 1996.

Berlin, Ira. *Slaves No More.* New York: Cambridge University Press, 1992.

Bernstein, Anya. *The Moderation Dilemma: Legislative Coalitions and the Politics of Family and Medical Leave.* Pittsburgh, Penn.: University of Pittsburgh Press, 2001.

Binns, Tristan Boyer. *FEMA: Federal Emergency Management Agency.* New York: Heinemann, 2003.

Birenbaum, Arnold. *Managed Care: Made in America.* Westport, Conn.: Praeger, 1997.

Bitterman, Robert A. *Providing Emergency Care under Federal Law: EMTALA.* Dallas, TX: American College of Emergency Physicians, 2000.

Black, Amy M., Douglas M. Koopman, and David K. Ryden. *Of Little Faith: The Politics of George W. Bush's Faith-Based Initiative.* Washington, D.C.: Georgetown University Press, 2004.

Black, Conrad. *Franklin Delano Roosevelt: Champion of Freedom.* New York: Public Affairs, 2003.

Bocian, Debbie Gruenstein, Keith S. Ernst, and Wei Li. *Unfair Lending: the Effect of Race and Ethnicity on the Price of Subprime Mortgages.* Washington, DC: Center for Responsible Lending, 2006.

Borg, Mary O., Paul M. Mason, and Stephen L. Shapiro. *The Economic Consequences of State Lotteries*. New York: Praeger Publishers, 1991.

Bottoms, Bette L., Margaret Bull Kovera, and Bradley D. McAuliff, eds. *Children, Social Science, and the Law*. Cambridge, U.K.: Cambridge University Press, 2002.

Bowman, Karlyn H. *The 1993–1994 Debate on Health Care reform: Did the Polls Mislead the Policy Makers?*. Washington, D.C.: American Enterprise Institute, 1994.

Brand, Donald R. *Corporatism and the Rule of Law*. Ithaca, N.Y.: Cornell University Press, 1988.

Breyer, Stephen. *Active Liberty: Interpreting Our Democratic Constitution*. New York: Knopf, 2005.

Brinkley, Alan. *Voices of Protest: Huey Long, Father Coughlin, and the Great Depression*. New York: Knopf, 1982.

Brinkley, Douglas. *The Great Deluge: Hurricane Katrina, New Orleans, and the Mississippi Gulf Coast*. New York: William Morrow, 2006.

Brinkley, Douglas. *The Great Deluge: Hurricane Katrina, New Orleans, and the Mississippi Gulf Coast*. New York: William Morrow, 2006.

British Library. "British Library Images Online." <http://www.imagesonline.bl.uk/britishlibrary/> (accessed on July 16, 2006).

Brittain, Charmaine, and Debra Esquibel Hunt, eds. *Helping in Child Protective Service: A Competency Based Casework Handbook*. Second edition. New York: Oxford University Press, 2004.

Brookings Institution. "Government's 50 Greatest Endeavors: Support Veteran Readjustment and Training." <http://www.brookings.edu/gs/cps/50ge/endeavors/veterans.htm> (accessed May 26, 2006).

Brown v. Board of Education. "Summary and Excerpt of Ruling." <http://www.pbs.org/jefferson/enlight/brown.htm#summary> (accessed May 15, 2006).

Brown, Mark, and John Pratt, eds. *Dangerous Offenders: Punishment and Social Order*. New York: Routledge, 2000.

Brown, Michael K. *Race, Money, and the American Welfare State*. Ithaca, N.Y.: Cornell University Press, 1999.

Bryan, Mary Lynn McCree. *The Selected Papers of Jane Addams: Volume 1, Preparing to Lead, 1860–81*. Champaign, Ill.: University of Illinois Press, 2003.

Bryner, Gary. *Managing Medicaid Take-Up: The Relationship between Medicaid and Welfare Agencies*. Albany, N.Y.: The Nelson A. Rockefeller Institute of Government, Federalism Research Group, 2002.

BUBL LINK Social Sciences. "Centre for Digital Library Research." <http://bubl.ac.uk/link/linkbrowse.cfm?menuid=2822> (accessed on July 16, 2006).

Buhite, Russel D., and David W. Levy, eds. *FDR's Fireside Chats*. New York: Penguin, 1993.

Burke, V. *Welfare Reform: Work Activities and Sanctions in State TANF Programs*. Washington, D.C.: Congressional Research Service, 2000.

Burnes, Brian. *Harry S. Truman: His Life and Times*. Kansas City, Mo.: Kansas City Star Books, 2003.

Busse, Richard C. *Employees Rights: Your Practical Handbook to Workplace Law*. Naperville, Ill.: Sourcebooks, 2004.

Butchart, Ronald V. *Northern Schools, Southern Blacks, and Reconstruction: Freedmen's Education, 1862–1875*. Westport, Conn.: Greenwood Press, 1980.

Cahn, Steven M., ed. *Affirmative Action and the University: A Philosophical Inquiry*. Philadelphia: Temple University Press, 1993.

California State Government. "Divison of Workers' Compensation." <http://www.dir.ca.gov/dwc/basics.htm> (accessed June 2, 2006).

Cambridge University. "Cambridge University, Institute of Public Health." <http://www.iph.cam.ac.uk> (accessed on July 16, 2006).

Carnoy, Martin. *School Vouchers: Examining the Evidence*. Washington, D. C.: Economic Policy Institute, 2001.

Carpenter, Ronald H. *Father Charles E. Coughlin: Surrogate Spokesman for the Disaffected*. Westwood, CT: Greenwood Press, 1998.

Case Western Reserve University. "Office of Government Relations Legislation and Policy Report." October 2005. <http://www.cwru.edu/pubaff/govrel/oct2005.html> (accessed June 1, 2006).

Cashin, Sheryll D. *The Failures of Integration: How Race and Class are Undermining the American Dream*. New York, NY: Public Affairs, 2004.

Cashman, Sean Dennis. *America, Roosevelt, and World War II*. New York: New York University Press, 1989.

Cassel, Christine. *Medicare Matters: What Geriatric Medicine Can Teach American Health Care*. Berkeley, California: University of California Press, 2005.

CCH Health Law Editors. *Medicare Explained, 2006*. New York: CCH, 2006.

CDC (Centers for Disease Control and Prevention). "CDCSite Index A-Z." <http://www.cdc.gov/az.do> (accessed on July 16, 2006).

Census Bureau. "United States Census Bureau." <http://www.census.gov/> (accessed on July 16, 2006).

Center on Congress at Indiana University. "Disaster Relief." <http://congress.indiana.edu/radio_series/disaster_relief.php> (accessed May 25, 2006).

Center on Hunger and Poverty. "The Millennium Declaration to End Hunger in America." <http://www.centeronhunger.org/pdf/millenniumdeclaration.pdf> (accessed July 16, 2006).

Chandler, Mittie Olion. *Urban Homesteading: Programs and Policies*. New York: Greenwood Press, 1988.

Chandler, William U. *The Myth of the TVA: Conservation and Development in the Tennessee Valley, 1933–83.* Cambridge, Mass.: Bellinger Publishing, 1984.

Chapman, Audrey R., ed. *Health Care Reform: A Human Rights Approach.* Washington, D.C.: Georgetown University Press, 1994.

Charney, William, and Guy Fragala, eds. *The Epidemic of Health Care Worker Injury: An Epidemiology.* Boca Raton, Florida: CRC Press, 1999.

Child Welfare League of America. "About CWLA: Fact Sheet." <http://www.cwla.org/whowhat/more.htm> (accessed May 17, 2006).

Child Welfare League of America. "The Adoption and Safe Families Act of 1997." April 8, 2003. <http://www.cwla.org/advocacy/asfatestimony-implementation.htm> (accessed May 17, 2006).

Choike.org. "In Depth: Millennium Development Goals—MDGs." <http://www.choike.org/nuevo_eng/informes/302.html> (accessed June 8, 2006).

Christy, Ralph D. and Lionel Williamson. *A Century of Service: Land-Grant Colleges and Universities, 1890–1990.* New Brunswick, N.J.: Transaction Publishers, 1991.

City of San Francisco. "Virtual Museum of the City of San Francisco." 2005 <http://www.sfmuseum.org/1906.2/invasion.html> (accessed June 11, 2006).

civilrights.org. "National Fair Housing Alliance Releases Housing Discrimination Data and Denounces Crisis of Segregation." April 5, 2006 <http://www.civilrights.org/issues/housing/details.cfm?id=42073> (accessed May 29, 2006).

Cobble, Dorothy Sue. *The Other Women's Movement: Workplace Justice and Social Rights in Modern America.* Princeton, NJ: Princeton University Press, 2004.

Cohen, Arthur M. *The Shaping of American Higher Education: Emergence and Growth of the Contemporary System.* San Francisco: Jossey-Bass, 1998.

Cokorinos, Lee. *The Assault on Diversity: An Organized Challenge to Racial and Gender Justice.* Lanham, MD: Rowman & Littlefield, 2003.

Colclough, Christopher, ed. *Marketizing Education and Health in Developing Countries: Miracle or Mirage?* Oxford: Clarendon Press, 1997.

Colignon, Richard. *Power Plays: Critical Events in the Institutionalization of the TVA.* Albany, N.Y.: State University of New York Press, 1997.

Colker, Ruth. *Disability Pendulum: The First Decade Of The Americans With Disabilities Act.* New York: New York University, 2005.

Congressional Budget Office. "An Overview of the Social Security System." <http://www.cbo.gov/> (accessed June 22, 2006).

Congressional Budget Office. "The Alternative Minimum Tax." April 15, 2004. <http://www.cbo.gov/> (accessed June 2, 2006).

Conley, Dalton. *Being Black, Living in the Red Race, Wealth, and Social Policy.* Berkeley, CA: University of California Press, 1999.

Cordasco, Francesco. *Jaccob Riis Revisited: Poverty and the Slum in Another Era.* Garden City, N.Y.: Doubleday, 1968.

Cornel Law School. "Age Discrimination in Employment." <http://www.law.cornell.edu/uscode/html/uscode29/usc_sup_01_29_10_14.html> (accessed May 22, 2006).

Cornell University Law School. Legal Information Institute. "Pension Law: An Overview." <http://www.law.cornell.edu/wex/index.php/Pension> (accessed May 23, 2006).

Court Appointed Special Advisors for Children. "Adoption and Safe Families Act: Has It Made a Difference?" September 2003. <http://www.casanet.org/library/adoption/asfa-has-made-a-difference.htm> (accessed June 5, 2006).

Cronin, Joseph Marr, and Sylvia Quarles Simmons, eds. *Student Loans: Risks and Realities.* Dover, Mass.: Auburn House, 1987.

Cross, Coy F. *Justin Smith Morrill: Father of Land-Grant Universities.* East Lansing, Mich.: Michigan State University, 1999.

Curry, George E., ed. *The Affirmative Action Debate.* Cambridge, MA: Perseus Books, 1996.

Dallek, Robert. *Flawed Giant: Lyndon Johnson and His Times, 1961–1973.* New York: Oxford University Press, 2000.

Daniels, Norman. *Reading Rawls: Critical Studies on Rawls' "A Theory of Justice."* New York: Basic Books, 1974.

Daniels, Roger. *Guarding the Golden Door; American Immigration Policy and Immigrants since 1882.* New York, N.Y: Hill and Wang, 2004.

Daniels, Roger. *Politics of Prejudice: The Anti-Japanese Movement in California and the Struggle for Japanese Exclusion.* Berkeley, Calif.: University of California Press, 1999.

Davies, Gareth. *From Opportunity to Entitlement: The Transformation and Decline of Great Society Liberalism.* Lawrence, Kans.: University Press of Kansas, 1996.

Davis, Kenneth. *FDR: The New Deal Years, 1933–1937.* New York: Random House, 1986.

Decker, Kurt H. *Family and Medical Leave in a Nutshell.* St. Paul, Minn.: West Publishing, 2000.

Dehavenon, Anna Lou, ed. *There's No Place Like Home: Anthropological Perspectives on Housing and Homelessness in the United States.* Westport, Conn.: Bergin & Garvey, 1999.

Deparle, Jason. *American Dream: Three Women, Ten Kids, and a Nation's Drive to End Welfare.* New York: Penguin Group, 2004.

Department of Medical Assistance Services. "The Medicare Prescription Drug Benefit (Part D) Fact Sheet." <http://www.seniornavigator.com/learn/connections/pharm-mma_fact_sheet.pdf> (accessed June 11, 2006).

Dexter, Walter Friar. Herbert Hoover and American Individualism: A Modern Interpretation of a National Ideal. New York: MacMillan Co., 1932 .

Dickens, Charles. American Notes. Islington, U.K.: Granville Publishing, 1985.

Dilberto, Gioia. A Useful Woman: The Early Life of Jane Adams. New York: Scribner, 1999.

Dippie, Brian W. Catlin and His Contemporaries: The Politics of Patronage. Lincoln, Nebraska: University of Nebraska Press, 1990.

Doctors Without Borders. "Doctors Without Borders." <http://www.doctorswithoutborders.org/> (accessed on July 16, 2006).

Dooley, David, and JoAnn Prause. The Social Costs of Underemployment: Inadequate Employment as Disguised Unemployment. Cambridge, U.K., and New York: Cambridge University Press, 2003.

Driscoll, Catherine. Girls: Feminine Adolescence in Popular Culture and Cultural Theory. New York: Columbia University Press, 2002.

DTAE: Georgia Department of Technical and Adult Education. "HOPE: Helping Outstanding Pupils Educationally." August 30, 2005 <http://www.dtae.org/hope.html#HOPEWORKS> (accessed June 1, 2006).

Dubay, Lisa, Ian Hill, and Genevieve Kinney. Five Things Everyone Should Know about SCHIP. Washington, D.C.: The Urban Institute, 2002.

Dubofsky, Melvyn. Hard Work: The Making of Labor History. Champaign: University of Illinois Press, 2000.

Dudziak, Mary L. Cold War Civil Rights: Race and the Image of American Democracy. Princeton, N.J.: Princeton University Press, 2002.

Economic Research Service/USDA. "Improving Food Security in the United States." February 2003. <http://www.ers.usda.gov/publications/GFA14/GFA14-h.pdf> (accessed May 26, 2006).

Edmond, J. B. The Magnificent Charter: The Origin and Role of the Morrill Land-Grant Colleges and Universities. Hicksville, N.Y.: Exposition Press, 1978.

Educational Testing Service. "One-Third of a Nation: Rising Dropout Rates and Declining Opportunities." 2005 <http://www.ets.org/Media/Education_Topics/pdf/onethird.pdf> (accessed July 16, 2006).

Eleanor Roosevelt National Historic Site. "Fair Employment Practices Committee." <http://www.nps.gov/elro/glossary/fepc.htm> (accessed May 26, 2006).

Eleanor Roosevelt National Historic Site. "Public Works Administration." <http://www.nps.gov/elro/glossary/pwa.htm> (accessed May 20, 2006).

Elshtain, Jean Bethke. Jane Addams and the Dream of American Democracy. New York: Basic Books, 2001.

Environmental Protection Agency. "Indicator: Infant Mortality." <http://www.epa.gov/ncea/ROEIndicators/pdfs/INFANTMORTALITY_FINAL.pdf> (accessed May 27, 2006).

Epstein, Richard A. Mortal Peril: Our Inalienable Right to Health Care? Cambridge, Mass.: Perseus Books, 1999.

Equal Opportunity Employment Commission. <http://www.eeoc.gov> (accessed May 19, 2006).

Everett, Joyce E., Sandra P. Chipungu, and Bogart R. Leashore. Child Welfare Revisited: An Africentric Prespective. Piscataway, NJ: Rutgers University Press, 2004.

Fader, Steven. Density by Design: New Directions in Residential Development. Washington, D.C.: Urban Land Institute, 2000.

Fantasia, Rick and Kim Voss. Hard Work: Remaking the American Labor Movement. Berkeley: University of California Press, 2004.

Federal Emergency Management Agency. National Flood Insurance Program. Washington, D.C.: Federal Insurance and Mitigation Administration, 2002.

Federal Emergency Management Agency. "Flood." <http://www.fema.gov/hazard/flood/index.shtm> (accessed June 18, 2006).

Federal Government Agencies Directory. "Louisiana State University." <http://www.lib.lsu.edu/gov/fedgov.html> (accessed on July 16, 2006).

Federal Reserve Bank of Philadelphia. "Assessing the Impact of Electronic Benefits Transfer." September 21, 2004 <http://www.philadelphiafed.org/pcc/conferences/agenda1204.pdf> (accessed May 18, 2006).

Federation of American Scientists. "Federation of American Scientists, ProMED Initiative." <http://www.fas.org/promed> (accessed on July 16, 2006).

Federation of American Scientists. "Executive Order 12127—Federal Emergency Management Agency." <http://www.fas.org/irp/offdocs/eo/eo–12127.htm> (accessed May 26, 2006).

FedStats. "FedStats." <http://www.fedstats.gov> (accessed on July 16, 2006).

Felder, Deborah G. A Century of Women: The Most Influential Events in Twentieth-Century Women's History. Kensington Publishing Corp., 1999.

Findlaw. "Findlaw/West." <http://public.findlaw.com/library/> (accessed on July 16, 2006).

Finley, Randy. From Slavery to Freedom. Fayetteville: University of Arkansas Press, 1996.

Fireside, Harvey. Separate and Unequal: Homer Plessy and the Supreme Court Decision that Legalized Racism. New York: Carroll & Graf, 2004.

Flood, Colleen M. *International Health Care Reform: A Legal, Economic and Political Analysis.* London, United Kingdom: Routledge, 2000.

Foner, Eric. *A Short History of Reconstruction.* New York: Harper & Row, 1990.

Foner, Eric. *Free Soil, Free Labor, Free Men: The Ideology of the Republican Party Before the Civil War.* New York: Oxford University Press, 1995.

Foner, Eric. *Reconstruction: America's Unfinished Revolution, 1863–1877.* New York: Harper, 2002.

Food & Nutrition Service, USDA. "Design Options for Assessing the Food Security and Diet Quality Impacts of FNS Program Participation." December 2005 <http://www.fns.usda.gov/oane/MENU/Published/FSP/FILES/Other/DietQualitySummary.pdf> (accessed May 18, 2006).

Food and Agriculture Organization of the United Nations. "Committee on World Food Security: International Alliance against Hunger." September 2004. <http://www.fao.org/docrep/meeting/008/J2789e.htm> (accessed May 26, 2006).

Food Research and Action Center (FRAC). "Hunger in America, and its Solutions: Basic Facts." July 2005. <http://www.frac.org/pdf/HungerFacts.pdf> (accessed May 26, 2006).

Food Research and Action Center. "Federal Food Programs." September 7, 2001 <http://www.frac.org/html/federal_food_programs/programs/fsp_faq.html> (accessed May 18, 2006).

Food Research and Action Center. "National School Lunch Program." March 2006 <http://www.frac.org/html/federal_food_programs/programs/nslp.html> (accessed May 22, 2006).

Formisano, Ronald P. *Boston Against Busing: Race, Class, and Ethnicity in the 1960s and 1970s.* Charlotte, North Carolina: The University of North Carolina Press, 2003.

Frankenberg, Erika, and Chungmei Lee. *Race in American Public Schools: Rapidly Resegregating School Districts.* Cambridge, Mass.: The Civil Rights Project, Harvard University, August 2002.

Friedan, Betty. *The Feminine Mystique.* New York: W.W. Norton, 2001.

Friedenberg, Robert V. *Theodore Roosevelt and the Rhetoric of Militant Decency.* New York: Greenwood Press, 1990.

Friedenberg, Robert V. *Theodore Roosevelt and the Rhetoric of Militant Decency.* New York: Greenwood Press, 1990.

Gabaccia, Donna. *Immigration and American Diversity; A Social and Cultural History.* Malden, Mass.: Blackwell, 2002.

Gad, Shayne C., ed. *Product Safety Evaluation Handbook.* New York: Marcel Dekker, 1999.

Galbraith, J.K. *The Great Crash.* Boston: Houghton Mifflin, 1955.

GAO (Government Account Office). "Site Map." <http://www.gao.gov/sitemap.html> (accessed on July 16, 2006).

Gardner, Michael R. *Harry Truman and Civil Rights: Moral Courage and Political Risks.* Carbondale: Southern Illinois University Press, 2002.

Garvin, Alexander. *The American City: What Works, What Doesn't.* Second edition. New York: McGraw-Hill, 2002.

Gates, Paul Wallace. *Agriculture and the Civil War.* New York: Knopf, 1965.

Gatewood, Joseph, Loren Johnson, and Ellen Arrington. *A Practical Guide to EMTALA Compliance.* Marblehead, MA: HCPro, Inc., 2004.

Gatto, John Taylor. *Dumbing Us Down: The Hidden Curriculum of Compulsory Schooling.* Gabriola Island, B.C.: New Society Publishers, 2005.

Gelber, Sidney. *Politics and Public Higher Education in New York State: Stony Brook.* New York: P. Lang, 2001.

Gillette, Michael L. *Launching the War on Poverty: An Oral History.* New York: Twayne, 1996.

Ginzberg, Eli, ed. *Critical Issues in U.S. Health Reform.* Boulder, Colo.: Westview Press, 1994.

Girl Scouts—Girls Go Tech. "Girls in Science, Technology, and Math." <http://www.girlsgotech.org/girls_go_tech.html> (accessed May 20, 2006).

Girl Scouts. "About Girl Scouts of the USA." <http://www.girlscouts.org/who_we_are/> (accessed May 20, 2006).

Global Policy Forum. "The Millennium Summit and Its Follow-Up." <http://www.globalpolicy.org/msummit/millenni/index.htm> (accessed June 8, 2006).

Goldman, Alan H. *Justice and Reverse Discrimination.* Princeton, N.J.: Princeton University Press, 1979.

Goldstein, Joseph, et al. *Before the Best Interests of the Child.* New York: The Free Press, 1979.

Gooden, Susan. *Washington Works: Sustaining a Vision of Welfare Reform Based on Personal Change, Work Preparation, and Employer Involvement.* New York: Manpower Demonstration Research Corporation, 1998.

Goodwyn, Lawrence. *The Populist Movement: A Short History of the Agrarian Revolt in America.* New York: Oxford University Press, 1978.

Gould, Florence C., and Patrician N. Pando. *Claiming Their Land: Women Homesteaders in Texas* El Paso: Texas Western Press, 1991.

Greenberg, Mark, and Steve Savner. *A Brief Summary of Key Provisions of the Temporary Assistance for Needy Families Block Grant of H.R. 3734.* Washington, D.C.: Center for Law and Social Policy, 1996.

Greenberg, Mark. *Welfare-to-Work Grants and Other TANF-Related Provisions in the Balanced Budget Act of 1997.*

Washington, D.C.: Center for Law and Social Policy, 1997.

Greenberg, Milton. *The G.I. Bill: The Law That Changed America*. New York: Lickle, 1997.

Guelzo, Allen C. *Lincoln's Emancipation Proclamation: The End of Slavery in America*. New York: Simon & Schuster, 2004.

Guinier, Lani, and Susan Sturm. *Who's Qualified?* Boston, Massachusetts: Beacon Press, 2001.

Hacker, Jacob S. *The Divided Welfare State: The Battle Over Public and Private Social Benefits in the United States*. New York: Cambridge University Press, 2002.

Hackey, Robert B. *Rethinking Health Care Policy: The New Politics of State Regulation*. Washington, D.C.: Georgetown University Press, 1998.

Hair, William Ivy. *The Kingfish and His Realm: The Life and Times of Huey P. Long*. Baton Rouge: Louisiana State University, 1991.

Halpern, Stephen C. *On the Limits of the Law: The Ironic Legacy of Title VI of the 1964 Civil Rights Act*. Baltimore, Md.: Johns Hopkins University Press, 1995.

Hansan, John E., and Robert Morris, eds. *Welfare Reform, 1996–2000: Is There A Safety Net?* Westport, Conn.: Auburn House, 1999.

Harbaugh, William H. *The Life and Times of Theodore Roosevelt*. New York: Oxford University Press, 1975.

Harper's Weekly. "About Harper's Weekly." 2006 <http://www.harpersweekly.com/> (accessed May 23, 2006).

Hartman, Chester, ed. *America's Housing Crisis: What's to Be Done?* Boston, Massachusetts: Routledge and Kegan Paul, 1983.

Harvard University; The Civil Rights Project. "Looking to the Future: Voluntary K–12 School Integration." <http://www.civilrightsproject.harvard.edu/resources/manual/manual.pdf> (accessed June 7, 2006).

Haug, Hans. *Humanity for All: The International Red Cross and Red Crescent Movement*. Bern, Switzerland: Paul Haupt Publishers, 1993.

Hays, R. Allen. *The Federal Government and Urban Housing: Ideology and Change in Public Policy*. Albany, New York: State University of New York Press, 1995.

Hayton, Annette, ed., and Anna Paczuska. *Access, Participation and Higher Education: Policy and Practice*. London: Kogan Page 2002.

Health Care Financing and Organization. "Medicare Part D: Can the New Outpatient Prescription Drug Benefit Effectively Manage Costs?" March 2005. <http://www.hcfo.net/topic0305.htm> (accessed June 11, 2006).

Health Resources and Services Administration (HRSA). "Health Resources and Services Administration (HRSA)." <http://www.hrsa.gov> (accessed on July 16, 2006).

Herbert Hoover Presidential Library and Museum. "Herbert Hoover Presidential Library and Museum." <http://hoover.archives.gov/> (accessed July 5, 2006).

Herideen, Penelope E. *Policy, Pedagogy, and Social Inequality: Community College Student Realities in Post-Industrial America*. Westport, Conn.: Bergin & Garvey, 1998.

Herms, Dieter, ed. *Upton Sinclair: Literature and Social Reform*. New York: Peter Lang, 1990.

Hiatt, Liisa and Jacob Alex Klerman. *State Monitoring of National School Lunch Program Nutritional Content*. Santa Monica, Calif: Rand, 2002.

Hilfiker, David. *Urban Injustice: How Ghettos Happen*. New York: Seven Stories Press, 2003.

Hillman, William, and Harry Truman. *Mr. President: The First Publication from the Personal Diaries, Private Letters, Papers, and Revealing Interviews of Harry S. Truman*. New York: Farrar, Straus, and Young, 1952.

Himmelberg, Robert F. *The Origins of the National Recovery Administration: Business, Government, and the Trade Association Issue, 1921–33*. New York: Fordham University Press, 1976.

Holt, John C. *How Children Fail*. Cambridge, Mass.: Perseus Publishing, 1995.

Holt, Michael F. *The Rise and Fall of the American Whig Party: Jacksonian Politics and the Onset of the Civil War*. New York: Oxford University Press, 1999.

Holt, William S. *The Bureau of the Census: Its History, Activities, and Organization*. New York: AMS Press, 1929.

Homan, Lynn M. and Thomas Reilly. *Black Knights: The Story of the Tuskegee Airmen*. Gretna, La.: Pelican Publishing, 2001.

Hoskins, Dalmer, Donate Dubbernack, and Christiane Kuptsch, eds. *Social Security at the Dawn of the Twenty-First Century*. New Brunswick, N.J.: Transaction, 2001.

How, Samuel Blanchard. *Slaveholding Not Sinful*. New Brunswick, NJ: J. Terhune's Press, 1856.

Howson, Embrey Bernard. *Jacob Sechler Coxey: A Biography of a Monetary Reformer*. New York: Arno, 1982.

Huggins, Laura E., ed. *Drug War Deadlock: The Policy Battle Continues*. Stanford, Calif.: Hoover Institution Press, Stanford University, 2005.

Human Rights Watch. "Human Rights Watch." <http://www.hrw.org/> (accessed on July 16, 2006).

Ignatieff, M. *A Just Measure of Pain: The Penitentiary in the Industrial Revolution, 1750–1850*. New York: Pantheon Books, 1978.

International Committee to Ban Landmines. "What does the treaty cover?" <http://www.icbl.org/tools/faq/treaty/cover> (accessed June 2, 2006).

International Federation of Red Cross and Red Crescent Societies. <http://www.ifrc.org> (accessed June 11, 2006).

Internet Modern History Sourcebook. "Fordham University." <http://www.fordham.edu/halsall/mod/modsbook.html> (accessed on July 16, 2006).

Issues in Science and Technology. "Rethinking what research government should fund." <http://www.issues.org/16.1/branscomb.htm> (accessed May 15, 2006).

Jacobs, James B. *Mobsters, Unions, and the Feds: The Mafia and the American Labor Movement.* Albany, N.Y.: New York University Press, 2006.

Jeansonne, Glen. *Messiah of the Masses: Huey P. Long and the Great Depression.* New York: HarperCollins, 1993.

Jeffrey, Julie Roy. *Great Silent Army of Abolitionism: Ordinary Women in the Antislavery Movement.* Chapel Hill, N.C.: University of North Carolina Press, 1998.

Jenkins, Philip. *Moral Panic: Changing Conceptions of the Child Molester in Modern America.* New Haven, CT.: Yale University Press, 1998.

Kaiser Family Foundation. "Prescription Drug Trends." October 2004. <http://www.kff.org/rxdrugs/upload/Prescription-Drug-Trends-October–2004-UPDATE.pdf> (accessed June 11, 2006).

Karabell, Zachary A. *What's College For? The Struggle to Define American Higher Education.* New York: Basic Books, 1998.

Kazin, Michael. *The Populist Persuasion: An American History.* New York: Basic Books, 1995.

Keller, Morton. *The Art and Politics of Thomas Nast.* New York: Oxford University Press, 1968.

Kennedy, David M. *Freedom from Fear: The American People in Depression and War.* New York: Oxford University Press, 1999.

Kerson, Toba Schweber. *Boundary Spanning: An Ecological Reinterpretation of Social Work Practice in Health and Mental Health Systems.* New York: Columbia University Press, 2002.

Kimbell, Jefferey P. *Nixon's Vietnam War (Modern War Studies).* Lawrence: University Press of Kansas, 2002.

Kirst, Sean. *Popular Relief: The WPA Years.* City Newspaper, 1985.

Klarman, Michael J. *From Jim Crow to Civil Rights: The Supreme Court and the Struggle for Racial Equality.* New York: Oxford University Press USA, 2004.

Kluger, Richard. *Simple Justice: The History of Brown v. Board of Education and Black America's Struggle for Equality.* New York: Vintage Books, 1977.

Klunder, Carl. *Lewis Cass and the Politics of Moderation.* Kent, Ohio: The Kent State University Press, 1996.

Knight, Edgar W. *A Documentary History of Education in the South before 1860.* Chapel Hill: University of North Carolina Press, 1953.

Kozol, Jonathan. *Savage Inequalities: Children in America's Schools.* New York: Harper Perennial, 1992.

Kronick, Robert F., and Charles Harquis. *Dropus: Who Drops Out and Why—And the Recommended Action.* Springfield, Ill.: Charles C. Thomas, 1998.

Kushner, James A. *Apartheid in America.* New York, New York: Associated Faculty Press, 1982.

La Leche League International. *The Womanly Art of Breastfeeding.* New York: Plume, 2004.

Labor and Labor Movements. "American Sociological Association." <http://www.bgsu.edu/departments/soc/prof/mason/ASA/> (accessed on July 16, 2006).

Ladd-Taylor, Molly. *Mother-Work: Women, Child Welfare, and the State, 1890–1930.* Urbana, Ill.: University of Illinois Press, 1994.

Laham, Nicholas. *A Lost Cause: Bill Clinton's Campaign for National Health Insurance.* Westport, Conn.: Praeger, 1996.

Landau, Elaine. *Land Mines: 100 Million Hidden Killers.* Berkeley Heights, New Jersey: Enslow, 2000.

Landy, Marc K., Mark Roberts, and Stephen R. Thomas. *The Environmental Protection Agency: Asking the Wrong Questions from Nixon to Clinton.* New York: Oxford University Press, 1994.

Lane, James B. *Jacob A. Riis and the American City.* Port Washington, N.Y.: Kennikat Press, 1974.

Laws, Rita, and Tim O'Hanlon. *Adoption and Financial Assistance: Tools for Navigating the Bureaucracy.* Westport, Conn.: Bergin & Garvey, 1999.

Lawson, Bill E., and Howard McGary. *Between Slavery and Freedom.* Bloomington: Indiana University Press, 1992.

Lee, Erika. *At America's Gates: Chinese Immigration During the Exclusion Era, 1882–1943.* Chapel Hill, N.C.: University of North Carolina Press, 2003.

Legal Information Institute, Cornell University. "Code of Federal Regulations." <http://www4.law.cornell.edu/cfr/> (accessed on July 16, 2006).

Leonard, Gerald. *The Invention of Party Politics: Federalism, Popular Sovereignty, and Constitutional Development in Jacksonian Illinois.* Chapel Hill, North Carolina: University of North Carolina Press, 2002.

Lerner, Gerda. *The Grimké Sisters from South Carolina: Pioneers for Women's Rights and Abolition.* Chapel Hill, NC: University of North Carolina Press, 2004.

Levine, Lawrence W., and Cornelia R. Levine. *The People and the President: America's Conversation with FDR.* Boston: Beacon Press, 2002.

Levy, Robert M., and Leonard S. Rubenstein. *The Rights of People with Mental Disabilities: The Authoritative ACLU Guide to the Rights of People with Mental Illness and Mental Retardation.* Carbondale, Ill.: Southern Illinois University Press, 1996.

Lewis, Sally. *Front to Back: A design agenda for Urban Housing.* Burlington, MA: Architectural Press, 2005.

Library of Congress. Primary Documents in American History. "Compromise of 1850." <http://www.ourdocuments.gov/> (accessed June 18, 2006).

Library of Congress. Thomas. "Whistleblower Protection Act of 1989." <http://thomas.loc.gov/cgi-bin/> (accessed May 26, 2006).

Library of Congress. "Library of Congress Online Catalog." <http://catalog.loc.gov/cgi-bin/Pwebrecon.cgi?DB=local&PAGE=First> (accessed on July 16, 2006).

Litwack, Leon F. *Been in the Storm So Long: The Aftermath of Slavery.* New York: Vintage Books, 1980.

Loprest, P. *How are Families that Left Welfare Doing? A Comparison of Early and Recent Welfare Leavers.* Washington, D.C.: Urban Institute, 2001.

Louchheim, Katie. *The Making of the New Deal: The Insiders Speak.* Cambridge, MA: Harvard University Press, 1983.

Lowenstein, Allard. *Submission on Racial Segregation and the Right to Housing.* Washington, D.C.: Poverty & Race Research Action Council, 2005.

Lubove, Roy. *The Struggle for Social Security, 1900–1935.* Cambridge, Mass.: Harvard University Press, 1968.

Lukacs, John. *Democracy and Populism: Fear and Hatred.* London: Yale University Press, 2005.

Luker, Kristin. *When Sex Goes to School: Warring Views on Sex—And Sex Education—Since the Sixties.* New York: W.W. Norton, 2006.

Lyman, Isabel. *Homeschooling: Back to the Future?* Cato Institute, 1998.

Making of America. "Cornell University." <http://cdl.library.cornell.edu/moa/> (accessed on July 16, 2006).

Mallon, Gerald P. and Hess, Peg M. *Child Welfare for the 21st Century: A Handbook of Practices, Policies, & Programs.* New York: Columbia University Press, 2005.

Maluccio, Anthony N., Barbara A. Pine, and Elizabeth M. Tracy. *Social Work Practice with Families and Children.* New York: Columbia University Press, 2002.

Mann, Cindy. *Issues Facing Medicaid and SCHIP.* Washington, D.C.: The Kaiser Commission on Medicaid and the Uninsured, 2002.

Margolis, Jane, and Allan Fisher. *Unlocking the Clubhouse: Women in Computing.* Cambridge, Mass.: MIT Press, 2002.

Marshak, Laura E., Milton Seligman, and Fran Prezant. *Disability and the Family Life Cycle.* New York: Basic Books, 1999.

Martin, R. *Rawls and Rights.* Lawrence, Kans.: University Press of Kansas, 2001.

Massachusetts Department of Education. "Child Nutrition Programs." <http://www.doe.mass.edu/cnp/programs/nslp.html> (accessed May 22, 2006).

Massey, Douglas S. and Nancy A. Denton. *American Apartheid: Segregation and the Making of the Underclass.* Cambridge, Massachusetts: Harvard University Press, 1998.

Matthews, Joseph L., and Dorothy Matthews Berman. *Social Security, Medicare & Government Pensions: Get the Most of Your Retirement and Medical Benefits.* Berkeley, California: NOLO Press, 2006.

Mayer, Henry. *All on Fire: William Lloyd Garrison and the Abolition of Slavery.* New York: St. Martin's Griffin, 2000.

Mayer, Kenneth. *With the Stroke of a Pen: Executive Orders and Presidential Power.* Princeton, N.J.: Princeton University Press, 2002.

Mayo-Jefferies, Deborah. *Equal Educational Opportunity for All Children: A Research Guide to Discrimination in Education, 1950–1992.* Buffalo, N.Y.: William S. Hein & Company, 1994.

McCullough, David C. *Truman.* New York: Touchstone, 1992.

McDonald, William F. *Federal Relief Administration and the Arts.* Columbus: Ohio State University Press, 1969.

McElvaine, Robert S. *The Great Depression: America 1929–1941.* New York: Times Books, 1993.

McGerr, Michael. *A Fierce Discontent: The Rise and Fall of the Progressive Movement in America, 1870–1920.* New York: Oxford University Press, 2005.

McMath, Robert. *American Populism: A Social History, 1877–1898.* New York: Hill and Wang, 1993.

McMurry, Donald L. *Coxey's Army: A Study of the Industrial Army Movement of 1894.* Seattle: University of Washington Press, 1968.

Medley, Keith Weldon. *We As Freemen: Plessy v. Ferguson.* Gretna, La.: Pelican Publishing Company, 2003.

Meltzer, Milton. *Violins and Shovels: The WPA Arts Projects.* New York: Delacorte Press, 1976.

Merrill, Karen R. *Public Lands and Political Meaning: Ranchers, the Government, and the Property between Them.* Berkeley: University of California Press, 2002.

Mettler, Suzanne. *Soldiers to Citizens: The G.I. Bill and the Making of the Greatest Generation.* New York: Oxford University Press, 2005.

Miki, Roy. *Redress: Inside the Japanese Canadian Call for Justice.* Vancouver, Canada: Raincoast Books, 2005.

Miller, Arthur Selwyn. *Racial Discrimination and Private Education: A Legal Analysis.* Charlotte: University of North Carolina Press, 1957.

Miller, E. Willard. *Natural Disasters: Floods, A Reference Handbook.* Santa Barbara, Calif.: ABC-CLIO, 2000.

Miller, Nathan. *Theodore Roosevelt: A Life.* New York: William Morrow and Company, 1992.

Missouri State University. "Documents on the Populist Party." <http://history.missouristate.edu/wrmiller/Populism/texts/Documents/Documents_on_Pops.htm> (accessed May 28, 2006).

Mitchell, Olivia, and Sylvester Schieber, eds. *Living with Defined Contribution Pensions: Remaking Responsibility for Retirement.* Philadelphia: University of Pennsylvania Press, 1998.

Moe, Terry M. *Schools, Vouchers, and the American Public.* Washington, D.C.: The Brookings Institution, 2001.

Mondale, Sarah. *School: The Story of American Public Education.* Boston: Beacon Press, 2002.

Moon, Marilyn. *Medicare: A Policy Primer.* Washington D.C.: Urban Institute Press, 2006.

Moran, Rachel F. *Interracial Intimacy: The Regulation of Race & Romance.* Chicago: University of Chicago Press, 2003.

Morris, N. and D. J. Rothman, eds. *The Oxford History of the Prison: The Practice of Punishment in Western Society.* New York: Oxford University Press, 1995.

Moss, Sidney Phil. *Charles Dickens' Quarrel with America.* Troy, N.Y.: Whitson Publishing, 1984.

Mulkern, John R. *The Know-Nothing Party in Massachusetts: The Rise and Fall of the People's Movement.* Boston: Northeastern University Press, 1990.

Murray, Charles. *Losing Ground: American Social Policy 1950–1980.* New York: Basic Books, 1985.

Myers, William Starr (ed). *The State Papers and Other Public Writings of Herbert Hoover, vol. 2.* Garden City, California: Doubleday, Doran and Co., 1934.

Myles, John. *Old Age in the Welfare State: The Political Economy of Public Pensions.* Boston: Little Brown, 1984.

Nader, Ralph. *Cutting Corporate Welfare.* New York: Seven Stories Press, 2000.

Nash, George H. *Life of Herbert Hoover: The Humanitarian, 1914–1917.* New York: W. W. Norton, 1988.

National Archive. "Richard Nixon–1970." <http://www.archives.gov/federal-register/executive-orders/1970.html> (accessed May 27, 2006).

National Association of Social Workers. <http://www.naswdc.org> (accessed June 11, 2006).

National Center for Education Statistics. "1.1 Million Home-schooled Students in the United States in 2003." July 2004. <http://nces.ed.gov/pubs2004/2004115.pdf> (accessed June 13, 2006).

National Commission on Excellence in Education. "A Nation at Risk." April 1983. <http://www.ed.gov/pubs/NatAtRisk/index.html> (accessed June 13, 2006).

National Conference of State Legislatures. "50 State Summary of Breastfeeding Laws." <http://www.ncsl.org/programs/health/breast50.htm> (accessed June 15, 2006).

National Immigration Forum. <http://www.immigrationforum.org> (accessed May 21, 2006).

National Organization for Women. "Talking About Affirmative Action." <http://www.now.org/issues/affirm/talking.html?printable> (accessed May 20, 2006).

National Science Foundation. *Women, Minorities, and Persons with Disabilities in Science and Engineering: 1998.* Arlington, Virginia: National Science Foundation, 1999.

National Science Foundation. "About the National Science Foundation." <http://www.nsf.gov/about/history/overview-50.jsp> (accessed May 17, 2006).

National Student Loan Data System. <http://www.nslds.ed.gov/nslds_SA> (accessed June 18, 2006).

National Women's Business Council. <http://www.nwbc.gov> (accessed June 11, 2006).

Newbeck, Phyl. *Virginia Hasn't Always Been for Lovers: Interracial Marriage Bans and the Case of Richard and Mildred Loving.* Carbondale, IL: Southern Illinois Press, 2004.

NICHD - National Institute of Child Health and Human Development. "NICHD - National Institute of Child Health and Human Development." <http://www.nichd.nih.gov> (accessed on July 16, 2006).

Nieman, Donald G., ed. *The Freedmen's Bureau and Black Freedom.* New York: Garland, 1994.

O'Brien, Kenneth Paul, and Lynn Hudson Parsons. *The Home-Front War: World War II and American Society.* Westport, Conn.: Greenwood, 1995.

Oberlander, Jonathan. *The Political Life of Medicare.* Chicago: University of Chicago Press , 2003.

Occupational Safety and Health Administration. "What Are My Rights as a Whistleblower?" <http://www.osha.gov/oshdoc/data_whistleblowerfacts/whistleblower_protections-general.pdf> (accessed May 25, 2006).

Office of Global Health Affairs. "Office of Global Health Affairs." <http://www.globalhealth.gov> (accessed on July 16, 2006).

Ohls, James C. and Harold Beebout. *The Food Stamp Program: Design Tradeoffs, Policy, and Impacts.* Lanham, MD: University Press of America, 1993.

Orfield, Gary, ed. *Dropouts in America: Confronting the Graduation Rate Crisis.* Cambridge, Mass.: Harvard Education Press, 2004.

Oubre, Claude F. *Forty Acres and a Mule: The Freedmen's Bureau and Black Land Ownership.* Baton Rouge: Louisiana State University Press, 1978.

Our Documents. "Social Security Act Amendments (1965)." <http://ourdocuments.gov/> (accessed May 29, 2006).

Palmer, Bruce. *The Southern Populist Critique of American Capitalism.* Chapel Hill: University of North Carolina Press, 1980.

Patel, Kant and Mark Rushefsky. *Health Care Politics and Policy in America.* Armonk, N.Y.: M.E. Sharpe, 1995.

Patterson, James T. *Brown v. Board of Education: A Civil Rights Milestone and Its Troubled Legacy*. New York: Oxford University Press USA, 2001.

Pavetti, LaDonna, and Gregory Acs. *Moving Up, Moving Out, or Going Nowhere? A Study of the Employment Patterns of Young Women and the Implications for Welfare Mothers*. Washington, D.C.: The Urban Institute, 1997.

Pavetti, LaDonna. *How Much More Can They Work? Setting Realistic Expectations for Welfare Mothers*. Washington, D.C.: The Urban Institute, 1997.

Peace Corps. "About the Peace Corps." <http://www.peacecorps.gov/index.cfm?shell=learn> (accessed June 15, 2006).

Peckron, Harold S. *Alternative Minimum Tax: What You Need to Know About the "Other" Tax*. Naperville, Ill.: Sphinx Publishing, 2005.

Percy, Stephen L. *Disability, Civil Rights and Public Policy: The Politics of Implementation*. Tuscaloosa: The University of Alabama Press, 1992.

Perry, George L., and James Tobin, ed. *Economic Events, Ideas, and Policies: The 1960s and After*. Washington, D.C.: Brookings Institute Press, 2000.

Perry, Michael J. *We the People: The Fourteenth Amendment and the Supreme Court*. New York: Oxford University Press, 2001.

Peterson, Mark A., ed. *Healthy Markets? The New Competition in Medical Care*. Durham, N.C.: Duke University Press, 1998.

Petr, Christopher G. *Social Work with Children and their Families: A Pragmatic Foundation*. New York: Oxford University Press, 2003.

Pissarides, Christopher A. *Equilibrium Unemployment Theory*. Cambridge, Mass.: MIT Press, 2000.

Poen, Monte M. . *Harry S. Truman Versus the Medical Lobby: The Genesis of Medicare*. Columbia, Missouri: University of Missouri Press, 1996.

Prucha, Francis Paul, ed. *Documents of United States Indian Policy*. Lincoln: University of Nebraska Press, 2000.

Pulliam, John D. and James J. Van Patten. *History of Education in America*. Upper Saddle River, N.J.: Prentice Hall, 2002.

Rai, Kul B., and John Critzer. *Affirmative Action and the University: Race, Ethnicity, and Gender in Higher Education Employment*. Lincoln, Nebraska: University of Nebraska Press, 2000.

Rawls, John. *Justice as Fairness: A Restatement*. Boston: Harvard University Press, 2001.

Reitz, Miriam and Kenneth W. Watson. *Adoption and the Family System: Strategies for Treatment*. New York: The Guilford Press, 1992.

Remini, Robert. *Andrew Jackson and His Indian Wars*. New York: Viking, 2001.

Remini, Robert. *Henry Clay: Statesman for the Union*. New York: W. W. Norton, 1991.

Richardson, J. *Common, Delinquent, and Special: The institutional Shape of Special Education (Studies in the History of Education)*. London: Routledge Falmer, 1999.

Richardson, Joe, Donna Viola Porter, and Jean Yavis Jones. *Child Nutrition and WIC Programs: Background and Funding*. New York: Nova Science, 2003.

Riemer, Frances Julia. *Working at the Margins: Moving Off Welfare in America*. Albany, N.Y.: State University of New York Press, 2001.

Riis, Jacob A. and Luc Sante. *How the Other Half Lives: Studies among the Tenements of New York*. New York: Penguin Group, 1997.

Riis, Jacob, A. *The Battle with the Slum*. New York: MacMillan, 1902.

Riis, Jacob, A. *The Children of the Poor*. New York: Charles Scribner's Sons, 1892.

Roberts, Dorothy. *Shattered Bonds: The Color of Child Welfare*. Reprint edition. New York: Basic Books, 2003.

Rodgers, Harrell R., Jr. *American Poverty in a New Era of Reform*. Armonk, N.Y.: M. E. Sharpe, 2000.

Rodwin, Lloyd and Bishwapriya Sanyal, eds. *The Profession of City Planning: Changes, Images, and Challenges, 1950–2000*. New Brunswick, N.J.: Center for Urban Policy Research, 2000.

Romasco, Albert U. *The Politics of Recovery: Roosevelt's New Deal*. New York: Oxford University Press, 1983.

Roosevelt, Theodore. *American ideals, and other essays, social and political*. New York, London: G.P. Putnam's sons., 1897.

Roosevelt, Theodore. *The Strenuous Life*. New York: Review of Reviews, 1904.

Rosenberg, Jonathan and Zachary Karabell. *Kennedy, Johnson, and the Quest for Justice: The Civil Rights Tapes*. New York: W. W. Norton, 2003.

Rosenthal, Marilynn and Max Heirich, eds. *Health Policy: Understanding Our Choices from National Reform to Market Choices*. Boulder, Colo.: Westview Press, 1998.

Rossell, Christine H. *The Carrot or the Stick for School Desegregation Policy: Magnet Schools or Forced Busing*. Philadelphia: Temple University Press, 1992.

Rozema, Vicki, ed. *Voices from the Trail of Tears*. Winston-Salem, NC: J.F. Blair, 2003.

Rushefsky, Mark and Kant Patel. *Politics, Power and Policy-Making: The Case of Health Care Reform in the 1990s*. Armonk, N.Y.: M. E. Sharpe, 1998.

Ryan, Halford R. *Harry S. Truman: Presidential Rhetoric*. Westport, Conn.: Greenwood Press, 1993.

Salisbury, David, and James Tooley, eds. *What America Can Learn From School Choice in Other Countries*. Washington, D.C.: CATO Institute, 2005.

Sall, Richard D. *Strategies in Workers' Compensation.* Lanham, MD: Hamilton Books, 2004.

Sanchez Korrol, Virginia E. *From Colonia to Community: The History of Puerto Ricans in New York City.* Los Angeles: University of California Press, 1994.

Satz, Ronald N. *American Indian Policy in the Jacksonian Era.* Norman: University of Oklahoma Press, 1975.

Schargel, Franklin, and Jay Smink. *Strategies to Help Solve Our School Dropout Problem.* Larchmont, N.Y: Eye on Education, 2001.

Schiller, Bradley R. *The Economics of Poverty and Discrimination.* Englewood Cliffs, N.J.: Prentice Hall, 2003.

Schlesinger, Arthur M., Jr. *The Coming of the New Deal: 1933–1935, The Age of Roosevelt, Volume II.* New York: Mariner Books, 2003.

Schorr, Lisbeth B. *The Head Start Debates.* Baltimore, Md.: Brookes Publishing Company, 2004.

Schwantes, Carlos A. *Coxey's Army: An American Odyssey.* Lincoln: University of Nebraska Press, 1985.

Schwartz-Nobel, Laura. *Growing Up Empty: The Hunger Epidemic in America.* New York: HarperCollins, 2002.

Scott, Anna H. *Census, USA: Fact Finding for the American People.* Boston: Houghton Mifflin Co., 1968.

Segal, Marilyn, et al. *All About Child Care and Early Education.* Boston: Allyn and Bacon, 2005.

Shelton, Michael W. *Talk of Power, Power of Talk: The 1994 Health Care Debate and Beyond.* Westport, Connecticut: Praeger, 2000 .

Simon Wiesenthal Center. "Simon Wiesenthal Center." <http://www.wiesenthal.com> (accessed on July 16, 2006).

Sinclair, Upton. *The Jungle.* New York: Doubleday, 1906.

Skyrms, Brian. *Evolution of the Social Contract.* Cambridge, UK; New York: Cambridge University Press, 1996.

Slesnick, Twila et al. *IRAs, 401(k)s & Other Retirement Plans: Taking Your Money Out.* Berkeley, California: Nolo Press, 2001.

Small Business Administration. "Overview & History." <http://www.sba.gov/aboutsba/history.html> (accessed May 17, 2006).

Smelser, Neil J., ed., William Julius Wilson, ed., and Faith Mitchell, ed. *American Becoming: Racial Trends and their Consequences, Volume I.* Washington, D.C.: National Academy Press, 2001.

Social Science Information Gateway. "SOSIG." <http://www.sosig.ac.uk/> (accessed on July 16, 2006).

Social Sciences Virtual Library. "Digilogical." <http://www.dialogical.net/socialsciences/index.html> (accessed on July 16, 2006).

Social Security Administration. "Legislative History: Social Security Act of 1935." <http://www.ssa.gov/history/35actii.html> (accessed June 22, 2006).

Social Security Administration. "Social Security History." May 1, 2006. <http://www.ssa.gov/history> (accessed June 5, 2006).

Social Security Administration. "Social Security Online History Pages." May 1, 2006. <http://www.ssa.gov/history/> (accessed May 17, 2006).

Social Security Administration. "The History of Medicare." May 1, 2006. <http://www.ssa.gov/history/corning.html> (accessed June 18, 2006).

Social Security and Medicare Boards of Trustees. "Status of the Social Security and Medicare Programs." 2006 <http://www.ssa.gov/OACT/TRSUM/trsummary.html> (accessed May 29, 2006).

Social Security Online. "Upton Sinclair." <http://www.ssa.gov/history/sinclair.html> (accessed May 27, 2006).

Social Security Online. "Father Charles E. Coughlin." <http://www.ssa.gov/history/coughlinradio.html> (accessed May 28, 2006).

Social Security Online. "Father Coughlin and the Search for "Social Justice."" <http://www.ssa.gov/history/fcspeech.html> (accessed May 28, 2006).

SocioWeb. "Blairworks." <http://www.socioweb.com/> (accessed on July 16, 2006).

Southern Poverty Law Center. "Southern Poverty Law Center." <http://www.splcenter.org/> (accessed on July 16, 2006).

Spalding, Elizabeth Edwards. *The First Cold Warrior: Harry Truman, Containment, and the Remaking of Liberal Internationalism.* Lexington: University Press of Kentucky, 2006.

Stein, Theodore J. *Social Policy and Policy-Making by the Branches of Government and the Public-At-Large.* New York: Columbia University Press, 2001.

Stetson, Dorothy M. *Women's Rights in the U.S.A: Policy Debates and Gender Roles.* New York: Routledge, 2004.

Sudbury Valley School. <http://www.sudval.org> (accessed June 13, 2006).

Swartz, Mimi, and Sherron Watkins. *Power Failure: The Inside Story of the Collapse of Enron.* New York: Currency, 2004.

Swint, Henry L. *The Northern Teacher in the South, 1862–1870.* Nashville, Tenn.: Vanderbilt University Press, 1941.

Telleen, Sharon, and Judith V. Sayad, eds. *The Transition from Welfare to Work: Processes, Challenges, and Outcomes.* New York, N.Y.: Hayworth Press, 2002.

Texas Secretary of State Roger Williams. "Colonia Legislation in Texas." <http://www.sos.state.tx.us/border/colonias/legislation.shtml> (accessed June 1, 2006).

Thelin, John. *A History of American Higher Education.* Baltimore, Md.: The Johns Hopkins University Press, 2004.

Thornton, Mark. *The Economics of Prohibition.* Salt Lake City: University of Utah Press, 1991.

Townsend, Barbara K. and Susan B. Twombly. *Community Colleges: Policy in the Future Context.* Westport, Conn.: Ablex Publishing, 2001.

Truman Presidential Museum and Library. <http://www.trumanlibrary.org/> (accessed June 6, 2006).

Truman, Margaret. *Where the Buck Stops: Personal and Private Writings of Harry S. Truman.* New York: Warner Books, 1989.

Tsesis, Alexander. *The Thirteenth Amendment and American Freedom: A Legal History.* New York: New York University Press, 2004.

Tushnet, Mark V. *The NAACP's Legal Strategy against Segregated Education, 1925–1950.* Chapel Hill: The University of North Carolina Press, 1987.

Tyson, Eric, Margaret Monro, and David Silverman. *What the IRS Doesn't Want You to Know: A CPA Reveals Tricks of the Trade.* New York: John Wiley & Sons, 2003.

U.S. Senate. "The United States Senate." <http://www.senate.gov/> (accessed on July 16, 2006).

U.S. Census Bureau. "United States Census Bureau." <http://www.census.gov> (accessed on July 16, 2006).

U.S. Census Bureau. "History." May 29, 2003. <http://www.census.gov/acsd/www/history.html> (accessed June 18, 2006).

U.S. Census Bureau. "Measuring America: The Decennial Census from 1790 to 2000." February 6, 2006. <http://www.census.gov/prod/www/abs/ma.html> (accessed June 18, 2006).

U.S. Department of Agriculture. "The National School Lunch Program Background and Development." <http://www.fns.usda.gov/cnd/Lunch/AboutLunch/NSLP-Program%20History.pdf> (accessed May 22, 2006).

U.S. Department of Education. "Overview of Education in the United States." <http://www.ed.gov/offices/OUS/PES/int_over_k12.html#finance> (accessed June 11, 2006).

U.S. Department of Education. "Special Education & Rehabilitative Services." <http://www.ed.gov/policy/speced/guid/idea/idea2004.html> (accessed May 28, 2006).

U.S. Department of Health and Human Services, Administration for Children and Families. "The Personal Responsibility and Work Opportunity Reconciliation Act of 1996: An HHS Fact Sheet." August 22, 1996. <http://www.acf.dhhs.gov/programs/ofa/prwora96.htm> (accessed June 18, 2006).

U.S. Department of Health and Human Services. Administration for Children and Families. "About Head Start." March 3, 2004. <http://www.acf.hhs.gov/programs/hsb/about/index.htm> (accessed June 2, 2006).

U.S. Department of Homeland Security. "Federal Gulf Coast Response to Hurricanes Katrina and Rita." September 28, 2005 <http://www.dhs.gov/dhspublic/display?content=4867> (accessed May 31, 2006).

U.S. Department of Housing and Urban Development. *Fair Housing Act Design Manual: A Manual to Assist Designers and Builders in Meeting the Accessibility Requirements of the Fair Housing Act,* 2nd ed. Washington, D.C.: Department of Housing and Urban Development, 1998.

U.S. Department of Housing and Urban Development. "Fair Housing and Equal Opportunity." <http://www.hud.gov/offices/fheo/index.cfm> (accessed June 2,2006).

U.S. Department of Housing and Urban Development. "Section 184 Indian Housing Loan Guarantee Program." March 4, 2005 <http://www.hud.gov/offices/pih/ih/homeownership/184/faq.cfm> (accessed May 29, 2006).

U.S. Department of Human Health and Services. "Centers for Medicare and Medicaid Services: EMTALA." April 17, 2006. <http://www.cms.hhs.gov/EMTALA/01_overview.asp> (accessed May 24, 2006).

U.S. Department of Justice. "Fair Housing Act." 42 U.S.C. 3601–3619, 3631. <http://www.usdoj.gov/crt/housing/title8.htm> (accessed May 18, 2006).

U.S. Department of Labor: Bureau of Labor Statistics. "Household Data." <http://www.bls.gov/webapps/legacy/cpsatab2.htm> (accessed June 6,2006).

U.S. Department of Labor. "Social Workers." <http://www.bls.gov/oco/ocos060.htm> (accessed June 11, 2006).

U.S. Department of Labor. "The Family and Medical Leave Act of 1993." <http://www.dol.gov/esa/regs/statutes/whd/fmla.htm> (accessed May 31, 2006).

U.S. Department of Labor. "Union Members in 2005." January 20, 2006 <http://www.bls.gov/news.release/pdf/union2.pdf> (accessed June 11, 2006).

U.S. Department of Labor. "Women's Bureau: Women in the Labor Force 2005." <http://www.dol.gov/wb/factsheets/Qf-laborforce-05.htm> (accessed June 5, 2006).

U.S. Department of State. "To Walk the Earth in Safety: The United States Commitment to Humanitarian Demining, 4 ed." <http://www.state.gov/t/pm/rls/rpt/walkearth/2002/14868.htm> (accessed March 1,2006).

U.S. Department of the Treasury. "History of the U.S. Tax System." <http://www.ustreas.gov/education/factsheets/taxes/ustax.html> (accessed June 2, 2006).

U.S. Department of Transportation, Office of Public Affairs. "Remarks For The Honorable Norman Y. Mineta Secretary Of Transportation : New Freedom Initiative." March 11, 2004. <http://www.dot.gov/affairs/minetasp31104.htm> (accessed May 26, 2006).

U.S. Department of Veterans' Affairs. "Fact Sheet: Facts About the Department of Veterans' Affairs." <http://www1.va.gov/opa/fact/vafacts.asp> (accessed May 27, 2006).

U.S. Environmental Protection Agency. "35 Years of Protecting Human Health and the Environment." <http://www.epa.gov> (accessed June 2, 2006).

U.S. Equal Employment Opportunity Commission. "Title VII of the Civil Rights Act of 1964." <http://www.eeoc.gov/policy/vii.html> (accessed May 31, 2006).

U.S. Food and Drug Administration. "Recalls, Market Withdrawals and Alerts." <http://www.fda.gov/opacom/7alerts.html> (accessed June 2, 2006).

U.S. General Accounting Office. *Welfare Reform: States Provide TANF-funded Work Support Services to Many Low-income Families Who do Not Receive Cash Assistance.* Washington, D.C.: United States General Accounting Office, 2002.

U.S. General Accounting Office. "Food Stamp Program." January 2002 <http://www.gao.gov/new.items/d02332.pdf> (accessed May 18, 2006).

U.S. Government. "Medicare Prescription Drug Coverage." 2006 <http://www.medicare.gov/pdphome.asp> (accessed June 29, 2006).

U.S. House of Representatives. "The United States House of Representatives." <http://www.house.gov/> (accessed on July 16, 2006).

U.S. Senate. Lugar, Richard G. "Lugar Introduces Hunger Free Communities Act." May 25, 2005. <http://lugar.senate.gov/pressapp/record.cfm?id=238197> (accessed May 26, 2006).

UNAIDS. "UNAIDS Research." <http://www.unaids.org/en/Issues/Research/default.asp> (accessed on July 16, 2006).

Unger, Nancy C. *Fighting Bob La Follette: The Righteous Reformer.* Chapel Hill: University of North Carolina Press, 1999.

UNICEF. <http://www.unicef.org.uk> (accessed June 11, 2006).

United Nations Development Programme. *Human Development Report 1999: Tenth Anniversary Edition.* New York: Oxford University Press, 1999.

United Nations Office of the High Commissioner for Human Rights. "United Nations." <http://www.ohchr.org/english/> (accessed on July 16, 2006).

United Nations Statistics Division. "Progress towards the Millennium Development Goals, 1990–2005." June 13, 2005. <http://unstats.un.org/unsd/mi/mi_coverfinal.htm> (accessed June 8, 2006).

United Nations. "Further Actions and Initiatives to Implement the Beijing Declaration and Platform for Action." <http://www.un.org/womenwatch/daw/followup/ress233e.pdf> (accessed May 10, 2006).

United Nations. "Road Map Towards the Implementation of the United Nations Millennium Declaration: Report of the Secretary-General." September 6, 2001. <http://www.un.org/documents/ga/docs/56/a56326.pdf> (accessed June 8, 2006).

United Way. <http://www.unitedway.org> (accessed June 8, 2006).

University of California at Berkeley. Labor Occupational Health Program. "Workers' Compensation." <http://ist-socrates.berkeley.edu/~lohp/Projects/Workers__Compensation/workers__compensation.html> (accessed June 1, 2006).

Vedder, Richard, and Lowell Gallaway. *Out of Work: Unemployment and Government in Twentieth-Century America.* Albany: New York University Press, 1997.

Veres III, John G., ed., and Ronald R. Sims, ed. *Human Resource Management and the Americans with Disabilities Act.* Westport, Conn.: Quorum Books, 1995.

Veterans of Foreign Wars (VFW). <http://www.vfw.org/> (accessed May 21, 2006).

Vinovskis, Maris A. *The Birth of Head Start: Preschool Education Policies in the Kennedy and Johnson Administrations.* Chicago: University of Chicago Press, 2005.

Virtual Campus of Public Health. "Virtual Campus of Public Health." <http://www.campusvirtualsp.org/eng/index.html> (accessed on July 16, 2006).

Vise, David A. *The Google Story.* New York: Delacorte Press, 2005.

von Hassell, Malve. *Homesteading in New York City, 1978–1993: The Divided Heart of Loisaida.* Westport, Conn.: Bergin & Garvey, 1996.

Voss-Hubbard, Mark. *Beyond Party: Cultures of Antipartisanship in Northern Politics Before the Civil War.* Baltimore, Md.: Johns Hopkins University Press, 2002.

Walker, Robert. *Social Security and Welfare.* New York: Open University Press/McGraw Hill, 2005.

Wallenstein, Peter. *Tell the Court I Love My Wife: Race, Marriage, and Law An American History.* New York: Palgrave, 2004.

Ward, Peter M. *Colonias and Public Policy in Texas and Mexico: Urbanization by Stealth.* Austin: University of Texas Press, 1999.

Warren, David I. *Radio Priest: Charles Coughlin, the Father of Hate Radio.* New York: Free Press, 1996.

Watts, Sarah Lyons. *Rough Rider in the White House: Theodore Roosevelt and the Politics of Desire.* Chicago: University of Chicago Press, 2003.

Waugh, John C. *On the Brink of Civil War: The Compromise of 1850 and How it Changed the Course of American History.* Wilmington, DE: Scholarly Resources, 2003.

Weil, Danny. *School Vouchers and Privatization: A Reference Handbook.* Santa Barbara, Calif.: ABC-CLIO, 2003.

Wellcome Library for the History and Understanding of Medicine. "The guide to history of medicine resources on the Internet." <http://medhist.ac.uk/> (accessed on July 16, 2006).

West, J., ed. *The Americans with Disabilities Act: From Policy to Practice.* New York: Milbank Memorial Fund, 1991.

Westerfield, Donald R. *National Health Care: Law, Policy, Strategy.* Westport, Conn.: Praeger, 1993.

White House. "White House Office of Communications." <http://www.whitehouse.gov/news/> (accessed on July 16, 2006).

White House. "Chapter 2: National Preparedness—A Primer." <http://www.whitehouse.gov/reports/katrina-lessons-learned/chapter2.html> (accessed May 31, 2006).

White House. "William J. Clinton." <http://www.whitehouse.gov/history/presidents/bc42.html> (accessed May 31, 2006).

Whitley, Bernard E. and Mary E. Kite. *The Psychology of Prejudice and Discrimination.* Belmont, Calif: Wadsworth Publishing, 2006.

Williams, Abigail R. *Outpatient department EMTALA handbook 2002.* Gaithersburg, MD: Aspen Law & Business, 2002.

Willie, Charles V., Antoine M. Garibaldi, and Wornie L. Reed, eds. *The Education of African-Americans.* New York: Auburn House, 1991.

Winslow, Philip C. *Sowing the Dragon's Teeth: Landmines and the Global Legacy of War.* New York: Beacon Press, 1998.

Wisconsin Historical Society. "Excerpts from Robert M. LaFollette's speech: 'The Danger Threatening Representative Government.'" <http://www.wisconsinhistory.org/teachers/lessons/lafollette/pdfs/lfspeech.pdf> (accessed May 28, 2006).

Wisconsin Historical Society. "La Follette and the Progressive Era." <http://www.wisconsinhistory.org/teachers/lessons/lafollette/> (accessed May 28, 2006).

Women-21.gov. <http://women-21.gov> (accessed June 11, 2006).

World Health Organization. "World Health Organization." <http://www.who.int/en> (accessed on July 16, 2006).

Yale University Library Government Documents and Information Center. "Guide to Decennial Censuses." 2002. <http://www.library.yale.edu/govdocs/cengdc.html> (accessed June 18, 2006).

Yinger, John. *Closed Doors, Opportunities Lost: The Continuing Costs of Housing Discrimination.* New York: Russell Sage, 1995.

Zieger, Robert H. and Gilbert J. Gall. *American Workers, American Unions: The Twentieth Century.* Baltimore, Md.: Johns Hopkins University Press, 2002.

Zorach, Marguerite. *Marguerite and William Zorach: Harmonies and Contrasts.* Portland, Maine: Portland Museum of Art, 2001.

Index

Boldface indicates a primary source.
Italics indicates an illustration on the page.